THE MIDNIGHT EYE GUIDE TO
NEW
JAPANESE FILM

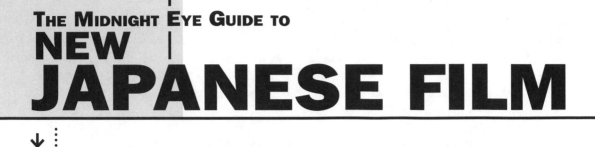

THE MIDNIGHT EYE GUIDE TO
NEW
JAPANESE FILM

Tom Mes and Jasper Sharp

Stone Bridge Press • Berkeley, California

Foreword by
Hideo Nakata

Published by
Stone Bridge Press
P.O. Box 8208, Berkeley, CA 94707
Tel: 510-524-8732 • sbp@stonebridge.com • www.stonebridge.com

We want to hear from you! Updates? Corrections? Comments? Please send all correspondence regarding this book to comments@stonebridge.com

Credits and copyright notices accompany their images throughout. Every attempt has been made to identify and locate rightsholders and obtain permissions for copyrighted images used in this book. Any errors and omissions are inadvertent. Please contact comments@stonebridge.com so that we can make corrections in subsequent printings.

Text © 2005 Tom Mes and Jasper Sharp.

Front cover image from *Dolls*; used by permission of Office Kitano.

Printed in the United States of America.

10 9 8 7 6 5 4 3

LIBRARY OF CONGRESS CATALOGING-IN-PUBLICATION DATA
Mes, Tom, 1974–
  The Midnight Eye guide to new Japanese film / foreword by Hideo Nakata; Tom Mes and Jasper Sharp.
     p. cm.
  Includes bibliographical references.
  ISBN 1-880656-89-2
  1. Motion pictures—Japan—History. I. Sharp, Jasper, 1971– II. Title.
PN1993.5.J3M47 2004
791.43'0952—dc22

2004022653

DEDICATED TO THE MEMORIES OF
Kɪɴᴊɪ Fᴜᴋᴀꜱᴀᴋᴜ & Tᴏᴍɪᴏ Aᴏᴋɪ

TABLE OF CONTENTS

by Hideo Nakata

In 1991, I decided to go to England for a year. I thought it was important for me to get away from Japan for a while and think over my situation within the Japanese film industry. I was an assistant director working for the Nikkatsu film studio, which had at that time ceased producing feature films and was just making TV dramas or straight-to-video films. I couldn't think of any way to get out of the situation other than by taking a break in a distant foreign country.

Thanks to this decision, I experienced a complete change in my career during the 1990s. The Japanese film industry seemed to go through a complete change as well. Nikkatsu went bankrupt in 1993. Shochiku decided to sell all of its production facilities in 1999, closing its lot in Ōfuna in 2000. These were two of the five major studios in Japan, both with long and glorious histories.

Despite this, there were many filmmakers who made their first theatrical features during the decade. Half of the directors introduced in this book made their debuts in the '90s. Many of them were independent filmmakers. I also shot an independent documentary film in England before I directed my first studio feature film. My desperate hunger for making films overcame the financial difficulties. In the meantime, Japanese film studios seemed to be afraid of taking risks in film production. This kind of mentality gradually killed the enthusiasm of the people who worked at the studios. Then, independent filmmakers were spotlighted. They knew how to make good films on low budgets and their enthusiasm never faded.

It was foreign film festival directors who responded to their works very quickly. One of the strongest bridges between the festivals and the independent filmmakers was Takenori Sentō, who produced two of my films. Vigorously and strategically, he sent his films to a large number of foreign film festivals. It was a good opportunity for him to sell the films as well as to receive awards. This may sound quite normal, but surprisingly, most of the Japanese film companies were rather reluctant to enter their own films unless invited. They did not think Japanese films were competitive enough in the market. Sentō is a pioneering figure in this respect.

The '90s was the decade of starting over

for the Japanese film industry. Some film critics like to say, "Japanese filmmaking seems very active now. And the films are received very well at foreign festivals." It may be true in a sense, but I am neither optimistic nor pessimistic, because starting over in the '90s also meant the end of traditional studio filmmaking.

Every Japanese filmmaker has to find his own way to keep going. Curiosity for the new and envy for other good filmmakers are my personal drives. It is obvious that Japanese film production and distribution will become increasingly borderless, not only in East Asia but also universally. Some might say, "Let's make films which are appealing to foreign audiences." I firmly believe a very Japanese film that is different from others can easily cross borders. Although I am now trying to make Hollywood studio movies, it is important for me to make uniquely Japanese films, as well.

INTRODUCTION

This book grew out of four years of watching and writing about Japanese cinema for the website MidnightEye.com. In the course of those four years we've had the great privilege and fortune to meet and speak with some of the leading figures in the Japanese film industry, as well as watch a huge number of brilliant films.

The original idea for this volume was to create something along the lines of "Midnight Eye: The Book," collecting the best reviews, interviews, and essays from the website into a single volume. In the course of developing this concept, however, the idea grew into something much more ambitious. Rather than simply gathering what already existed, we decided to use that material as the starting point for a brand new book, one that would focus on who we felt were the leading filmmakers working in Japan today.

The vast majority of the material in this book is entirely new. Even in the rare cases where we used writing that was previously published on the website, this was extensively rewritten, expanded, updated, and revised. We did this not only because our opinions and knowledge have evolved over these past four years (in a good way, we hope), but also to make the writing fit in with the format of this book. So, not to worry, you have not spent your precious pennies on something that is already available for free on the net.

The choice to focus on contemporary Japanese cinema was inspired above all by the dearth of proper writing on the subject. Aside from Mark Shilling's fine, if somewhat outdated, *Contemporary Japanese Film*, what writing there is largely remains somewhat superficial, usually with one-paragraph, or at most one-page descriptions of contemporary filmmakers and their work. With the amount of talent that has emerged in Japan over the past two decades, the international acclaim many of them have received, and above all the challenging and probing nature of their work, this writing certainly hasn't done justice to its subject.

The existence of this watershed between past and present Japanese cinema is understandable, though. The watershed in question is embodied by the collapse of the Japanese studio system, a gradual process that lasted decades but came to a head in the late 1970s. The six major studios (Toho,

Shochiku, Nikkatsu, Toei, Daiei, and Shintoho) collectively formed the Japanese film industry, and the work of acknowledged masters like Akira Kurosawa, Kenji Mizoguchi, and Yasujirō Ozu were the products of this system. Even as the positions of the studios started to weaken, "New Wave" directors like Nagisa Ōshima and Shōhei Imamura began setting up their own independent production companies to make fascinating, idiosyncratic work. But the New Wave reached its peak in the '60s, becoming less productive in the decade that followed. Once the studios had bitten the dust there seemed little activity at all happening in Japan in the 1980s, certainly from a foreign viewpoint. The year 1983 yielded the Cannes Film Festival selections for Ōshima's *Merry Christmas, Mr. Lawrence* (a British co-production) and Imamura's *The Ballad of Narayama*, the latter being awarded the Palme d'Or. These and two high-profile Akira Kurosawa films (*Kagemusha* and *Ran*, both foreign co-productions) remain the only international accomplishments of note for much of the decade. The 1980s was a period in which even former iconoclasts became conformists, churning out crowd-pleasers for wealthy but cinematically challenged private film producers, simply to be able to keep working. The resulting films were, for the most part, hardly reason for keeping much faith in the future of Japanese cinema.

Yet, at the same time as the studios lost their foothold and just about anything else that wasn't essential for their survival, a renaissance was already under way. The second half of the '70s saw the slow emergence of true independent filmmaking: young enthusiasts with 8mm cameras making their own short films and features on shoestring budgets. This development took over a decade to come to a boil, resulting in a full-blown re-emergence in the 1990s when a new generation of filmmakers appeared, the vast majority coming from roots that lay outside the traditional film industry. They came from 8mm underground experimentalism, from the ranks of film critics, from the erotic "pink film" or porn, from television, and from the straight-to-video filmmaking that had shot up in the late '80s in the wake of the boom in home video player ownership. These were young filmmakers whose attitudes and philosophies of cinema were entirely different from those of the old studio period. They were independent in spirit: artists with nothing to lose, but with everything to gain.

Today, these filmmakers are regulars on the international film festival circuit, critically lauded, and the subject of cult worship by a growing legion of devotees the world over. As more and more of their films are released theatrically and particularly on DVD around the world, some are even courted by Hollywood. The phenomenon of remakes of Japanese hits, kick-started by the American version of Hideo Nakata's *The Ring*, has now advanced to a point where the directors themselves are invited to Tinseltown to helm the remakes of their own films, as with Takashi Shimizu and his tale of ghostly apparitions *The Grudge* (*Juon*).

There is every reason to look at Japanese cinema today with great interest. It's always much more challenging and exciting to venture into uncharted territory rather than walk the well-trodden paths. Therefore this book is an attempt to give contemporary Japanese film its due as well as an attempt to fill a gap, carefully avoiding laments about the good old days. Those days certainly were good. But so are these. And there is no reason why we shouldn't treat them with the same respect, devotion, and enthusiasm as the past.

Certainly, all is not rosy. Japanese filmmakers for the most part still have to work with very low budgets and government support for the industry is minimal, but compared to fifteen or twenty years ago there has been great progress and a huge pool of talent currently occupies the directors' seats. This book attempts to present a selection from that talent pool, presenting twenty of its leading lights and their work, plus a good number more besides. This is not a book that compares figuresj, but one that salutes and makes an effort to understand and value the work of some of the best filmmakers in world cinema today.

Acknowledgments

Firstly, we would like to thank all the filmmakers covered in this book, whose astonishing work has been an inspiration to us for years and will remain so for years to come.

Secondly, we express our appreciation to Peter Goodman, Barry Harris, and all at Stone Bridge Press for making this project a reality, as well as to Beth Cary for her very detailed editorial work.

Thirdly, we are greatly indebted to Martin Mes, the vital link in the ongoing process of making the website Midnight-Eye.com, from which this book originated. He deserves far more recognition for his outstanding design work than he's getting.

A huge round of thanks goes out to the people and the film companies who graciously provided the many gorgeous stills and illustrations in this book: Stephen Alpert of Studio Ghibli, Keiko Araki and the PIA Film Festival, Mari Hashimoto of IMJ Entertainment, Stephan Holl at Rapid Eye Movies, Shōzō Ichiyama of Office Kitano, Tetsuki Ijichi of Tidepoint Pictures, Kiyo Joo of Goldview, Kaijyu Theater, Kana Koido and Tetsu Negami at The Klockworx, Hirofumi Kojima of M3 Entertainment, Helmut Krutsch of Asian Film Network, Yoshihito Kuroki of KSS ME, Keiko Kusakabe of There's Enterprise, Martin Mes, Dai Miyazaki of Omega Micott, Hidehiro Itō and Yuka Morioka of Excellent Film, Asako Nishikawa of TV Man Union, Yasue Nobusawa of Nikkatsu, Takahiro Ohno of Sedic International, Tadayuki Ōkubo of Toei, Martin Rycroft of 100 Meter Films, Yasunari Satake of Bitter's End, Siglo, Yutaka Tsuchiya and Video Act, Hyōe Yamamoto of Kino International, and Yukiko Yamato of TBS.

Furthermore, our thanks go out to:

Tom Mes: Hiromi Aihara, Jonathan Clements, Keiko Funato and Celluloid Dreams, Luk van Haute, the International Film Festival Rotterdam, Herman and Marijke Mes, and Joep Vermaat for being one of the site's co-founders. And of course to Kuriko Satō, without whom no book of mine could ever see the light of day.

Jasper Sharp: Firstly, to Ian and Erica Sharp, for launching me on my path in life and inspiring me with a natural curiosity about the world.

I'd also like to thank Michael Arnold for his vigorous feedback and interesting barroom digressions during the writing of this book, the Barnstaple and Bath crowds for all those years of blithering, Stephen Cremin for being such a mine of information, Roland Domenig, Aaron Gerow, Jason Gray, Shinsuke Nonaka of Studio

Ghibli for the fact checking, Hideo Nakata for his ungrudging assistance, Louise James for her tolerance and friendship over the years, Mark Nornes, Junko Sasaki for her selfless assistance and interpretation, Daniel Sharp and Andy and my new little niece Maddy, Nicholas Rucka, John Williams, Alex Zahlten, the staff of Tokyo Filmex, Tokyo International Film Festival, and Yamagata International Documentary Film Festival, in particular Asako Fujioka. And last, but by no means least, my love and deepest affection to Sharyn Chan, without whose endless patience and support none of this would have been possible.

And to all the readers of MidnightEye.com for their support over the years.

Tom Mes and Jasper Sharp

THE MIDNIGHT EYE GUIDE TO
NEW
JAPANESE FILM

CHAPTER 1
Seijun Suzuki
鈴木清順

"What Suzuki represents to me is anarchy. He's a complete anarchist, and he's the only person in Japanese cinema who could get away with a film like *Story of Sorrow and Sadness*. I was born in 1964 and so I was in my early teens when I experienced punk, and on me Jean-Luc Godard and Seijun Suzuki had the same sort of impact."—Shinji Aoyama

Japanese cinema has been lucky to have such a colorful figure as Seijun Suzuki as one of its ambassadors. Hovering over four decades of filmmaking like a kindly old wizard, with his horn-rimmed specs and scraggly goatee he certainly looks the part of the bohemian artist. Indeed, in 1985 he was even voted "Best Dressed Man" by the Tokyo Fashion Society.

Some have seen him as an iconoclast, a cinematic rebel out to break every rule in the filmmaking book—more likely discarding it entirely—and one whose increasingly mischievous sense of humor was to land him in hot water with his employers at Nikkatsu in the late '60s. Others view him as an aesthetic genius, reconfiguring and reinventing cinema to fit his own uniquely skewed visual perception of the world. The self-effacing Suzuki would probably shrug off both assessments and laugh, wondering what all the fuss is about. The truth is, whichever way you want

to look at it, for more than forty years Suzuki has adorned our screens with some of the most colorful, extraordinary, unpredictable, and downright fun pieces of visual entertainment that are likely to be found anywhere in world cinema.

Suzuki's films are marked out by a style which seems to be devoid of any influence from outside sources. They work to their own peculiar logic, and one which often seems based more on aesthetic than narrative concerns. Why does the nail polish of Reiko, the central character in *Story of Sorrow and Sadness*, dramatically change in hue through yellows and blacks in key scenes? Why is there a sandstorm raging outside the window as a heroin-addicted prostitute receives a whipping from her pimp in *Youth of the Beast*? Why does Tetsuya Watari's renegade gangster in *Tokyo Drifter* continually break into song between his numerous violent scuffles? Suzuki would doubtless answer all of these questions with the same no-nonsense pragmatism as he did in an interview with Kōshi Ueno for his 1986 book, *Suzuki Seijun, Zen Eiga* [trans: Suzuki Seijun, all his films]. When asked why he never followed the standard shot-reverse-shot technique of matching the eyelines when two lovers speak, instead having them seemingly gazing offscreen into space, his reply was:

"Yes, that's right, I never use shot-reverse-shot in those cases. When a man and a woman talk about love in Japan, they don't look each other in the eye. They look at a certain part of the body. In these cases I focus on that part of the body, a woman's hips or legs, for example. In foreign films you hardly ever see two lovers looking into each other's eyes from very close up, whereas in Japanese films, especially historical ones, they do. I think this has to do with the color of the eyes. Because foreigners have light-colored eyes, they only see a reflection of themselves when they look into each other's eyes."

Of course, Seijun Suzuki wasn't always a filmmaker. Born in Nihonbashi, central Tokyo, on May 24, 1923, as Seitarō Suzuki, he was barely out of high school when he was drafted into the army and sent off to fight in the Pacific War. Rescued from a sinking ship en route to Taiwan after it was attacked by the American air force, he returned to a rubble-strewn Japan once the war had ended.

If we are to believe his own account of things, Suzuki's entry into the film industry came because it was the first job he could find in the turmoil that followed in the wake of Japan's defeat. Having failed the entrance exams to Tokyo University, in 1946 he instead enrolled in the film department in Kamakura Academy before he entered Shochiku's nearby studios in Ōfuna as an assistant director in the same year. The studios would become the breeding ground for a generation of new talent such as Nagisa Ōshima, Masahiro Shinoda, and Shōhei Imamura. Like

Filmography

1956
- Harbor Toast: Victory Is in Our Grasp (Minato no Kanpai: Shōri o Wagate ni) (a.k.a. Cheers at the Harbor: Triumph in Our Hands)
- Pure Emotions of the Sea (Hozuna wa Utau: Umi no Junjō)
- Satan's Town (Akuma no Machi)

1957
- Inn of the Floating Weeds (Ukigusa no Yado)
- Eight Hours of Terror (Hachijikan no Kyōfu)
- The Naked Woman and the Gun (Rajo to Kenjū)

1958
- Beauty of the Underworld (Ankokugai no Bijo) (a.k.a. Underworld Beauty)
- The Spring That Didn't Come (Fumihazushita Haru)
- Young Breasts (Aoi Chibusa)
- The Voice without a Shadow (Kagenaki Koe)

1959
- Love Letter (Rabu Retta)
- Passport to Darkness (Ankoku no Ryoken)
- Age of Nudity (Suppadaka no Nenrei)

1960
- Aim at the Police Van (Sono Gosōsha o Nerae)
- Sleep of the Beast (Kemono no Nemuri)
- Clandestine Zero Line (Mikkō Zero Rain)
- Everything Goes Wrong (Subete ga Kurutteru)
- Fighting Delinquents (Kutabare Gurentai)

1961
- Tokyo Knights (Tōkyō Kishitai)
- Reckless Boss (Muteppō Taishō) (a.k.a. The Big Boss Who Needs No Gun)
- The Man With the Hollow-Tip Bullets (Sandanjū no Otoko) (a.k.a. The Man With a Shotgun)
- The Wind-Of-Youth Group Crosses the Mountain Pass (Tōge o Wataru Wakai Kaze) (a.k.a. New Wind over the Mountain)

- Blood Red Water in the Channel (Kaikyō, Chi ni Somete) (a.k.a. Bloody Channel)
- Million Dollar Match (Hyakuman Doru o Tatakidase) (a.k.a. Million Dollar Smash and Grab)

1962
- High-Teen Yakuza (Haitiin Yakuza)
- Those Who Bet on Me (Ore ni Kaketa Yatsura) (a.k.a. The Guys Who Put Money on Me)

1963
- Detective Bureau 2-3: Go to Hell, Bastards (Tantei Jimusho 2-3: Kutabare Akutōdomo)
- Youth of the Beast (Yajū no Seishun) (a.k.a. The Wild Beast of Youth / Wild Youth / The Young Rebel / The Brute)
- Bastard (Akutarō)
- Kanto Wanderer (Kantō Mushuku)

1964
- The Flower and the Angry Waves (Hana to Dotō)

Imamura, Suzuki jumped over to the much better paying Nikkatsu studios when it restarted production in 1954 after a break of over ten years.

At the time, Japanese studios still worked under an apprenticeship system, wherein an assistant could work his way up the hierarchy under the guidance of a mentoring director, from whom he would be instructed in all the tricks and techniques of filmmaking. Suzuki trained under Hiroshi Noguchi, who was to direct Suzuki's first screenwriting effort, co-written with Motomu Ida, *Rakujitsu no Kettō* [trans: Duel at sunset] the year after Suzuki joined Nikkatsu. Noguchi also directed *Chitei no Uta* [trans: Song from the underworld] in 1956, based on the same serial for the Asahi Shinbun newspaper by Taiko Hirabayashi that was later adapted by Suzuki himself as **Kanto Wanderer**. It was not long before

Suzuki had himself progressed to the director's chair with his first batch of films, beginning with *Harbor Toast: Victory is in Our Grasp* (1956) credited to his birth name of Seitarō Suzuki. In 1958, he directed his first film as Seijun Suzuki, *Beauty of the Underworld*.

Throughout the latter half of the '50s and the '60s, Nikkatsu was involved in safe, commercial vehicles starring such celebrated *enka*-singing matinee idols of the era as the immaculately groomed Akira Kobayashi and Yūjirō Ishihara. The latter, who died of liver cancer in 1987, was the brother of the current controversial governor of Tokyo, Shintarō Ishihara, whose highly influential first novel published in 1955, *Taiyō no Kisetsu* [trans: Season of the sun] was adapted by the studios for the screen. A tale of delinquent teenagers and their tearaway exploits, the film

---

- Gate of Flesh (Nikutai no Mon)
- Our Blood Won't Allow It (Ore-tachi no Chi ga Yurusanai)

1965
- Story of a Prostitute (Shunpu-den) (a.k.a. Joy Girls)
- Stories of Bastards: Despite Being Born under a Bad Star (Akutarōden: Warui Hoshi no Shita Demo)
- Life of a Tattooed Man (Ire-zumi Ichidai) (a.k.a. One Generation of Tattoos / Tattooed Life)

1966
- Carmen from Kawachi (Ka-wachi Karumen)
- Tokyo Drifter (Tōkyō Naga-remono)
- Elegy to Violence (Kenka Erejii) (a.k.a. Fighting Elegy / The Born Fighter)

1967
- Branded to Kill (Koroshi no Rakuin)

1968
- Good Evening Dear Husband:

A Duel (Aisaikun Konban Wa: Aru Ketto) [TV]

1969
- There's a Bird inside a Man (Otoko no Naka ni wa Tori ga Iru) [TV]

1970
- A Mummy's Love (Miira no Koi) [TV]

1977
- Story of Sorrow and Sadness (Hishū Monogatari)

1979
- The Fang in the Hole (Ana no Kiba) [TV]

1980
- Zigeunerweisen (Tsigoineru-waizen)
- Chen Wuchen's The Nail of the Holy Beast (Chin Shun-shin no Shinjū no Tsume) [TV]

1981
- Mirage Theater (Kagerōza) (a.k.a. Heat Shimmer Theater)
- Storm of Falling Petals: Banner of a Fireman in the

Flames (Hana Fubuki: Honoo ni Mau Ichiban Matoi) [video]

1983
- Cherry Blossoms in Spring (Haru Sakura: Seijun Sakura Hensō) [TV] (a.k.a. Seijun's Different Stages of Cherry Blossoms)
- The Choice of a Family: I'll Kill Your Husband for You (Kazoku no Sentaku: Anata no Teishu o Koroshite Ageru) [video]

1985
- Capone Cries Hard (Kapone Ōi ni Naku)
- Lupin III: The Golden Legend of Babylon (Rupan Sansei: Babiron no Ōgon Densetsu) [TV, co-directed with Shige-tsugu Yoshida]

1991
- Yumeji

1993
- Marriage (Kekkon) [co-directed with Hideo Onchi and Hiroshi Nagao]

2001
- Pistol Opera (Pisutoru Opera)

© 1964 Nikkatsu Corporation

Seijun Suzuki and the cast of *Gate of Flesh*

not only unleashed a deluge of youth-oriented *taiyōzoku* or "Sun Tribe" pictures from all the majors, but effectively launched the careers of both brothers: Yūjirō Ishihara made his screen debut in Takumi Furukawa's movie adaptation of *Season of the Sun* (1956), with his next role in Kō Nakahira's similarly themed *Crazed Fruit* (*Kurutta Kajitsu*) released months later by Nikkatsu, and Shintarō continued a successful writing career that stretched far beyond the '60s.

Meanwhile, Suzuki was still learning his trade, toiling away on the studio's program pictures, the supporting features on the double bills under which they distributed their output, directing on average three or four pictures a year. These early films are often marked by incredibly short running times—*Pure Emotions of the Sea* was only 48 minutes and *Love Letter* a mere 40 minutes—and shot in black and white, with his first color feature coming with the 1960 release, *Fighting Delinquents*. For the first five years of his directing career, his output remained fairly undistinguished and, even in Japan, none of his films from this period is available on video.

"I was one of the Nikkatsu contract directors, so it was the company that made me direct

films at this pace. It was more about doing a job than getting any kind of enjoyment out of making a film."

Most of Suzuki's period at Nikkatsu saw him saddled with generic formula-bound scripts, either modest literary adaptations, popular action flicks, or *seishun eiga* (youth pictures). In actual fact, there was often little to differentiate these films from the main movies they supported other than a lower budget and a far lower profile, so a B-movie director like Suzuki had to work that much harder to get audiences to sit up and take note. In 1963 he succeeded in this goal, with four features that brought him to the attention of critics and filmgoers alike; *Akutarō*, *Kanto Wanderer* (which played on the bottom half of a double bill with Shōhei Imamura's *Insect Woman*), and two hard-boiled detective thrillers based on stories by Haruhiko Ōyabu, both starring the moon-faced Jō Shishido: the subtly titled *Detective Bureau 2-3: Go to Hell Bastards!* and its companion piece, *Youth of the Beast*.

This latter film is notable for being Suzuki's first work to deviate wildly from the *ninkyō eiga* template, a genre with which he is inaccurately most associated due to the unbalanced sample of his films that have been released in the West. The *ninkyō eiga* was a popular staple amongst blue-collar audiences during the '60s, though during the first half of the decade it had yet to fully solidify into a genre per se—a cluster of motifs, codes, and clichés repeated from film to film using a pool of the same actors, such as Ken Takakura and Kōji Tsuruta. This would come within the next five years as Toei Studios began their work in the field in earnest.

The type of movie Nikkatsu was focusing its energies on at the time was known as *mukokuseki akushon* ("no-nationality action"), typified by such popular star vehicles as the *Wataridori* (*Wandering Bird*) series featuring Akira Kobayashi. Heavily influenced by the American B-movie western and rooted in no particular place or time that would link the setting specifically to Japan, the films were usually little more than a cheap and cheerful series of staged punch-ups and shoot-outs (budgets seldom stretched to convincing car chases), often featuring gangsters, underpinned by straightforward plots in which the goodie pitted his wits against the baddie and ended up coming out of the fray with the girl and the money. It's more useful to look at Suzuki's apparently more genre-bending films in the context of the *mukokuseki akushon* movie than the yakuza film.

Suzuki may not have been able to do much about the scripts, but he could influence what went up on screen. *Youth of the Beast*, for example, features Jō Shishido as a discharged police detective pitting his wits against two rival yakuza gangs in his bid to track down the killer of the friend for whose death he was wrongly sent to jail. Not much to go on, but in Suzuki's hands the material becomes something else entirely. The first thing that bowls you over is the exquisite color cinematography of Kazue Nagatsuka, part of a regular team with which the director surrounded himself during his Nikkatsu years. In the opening scene the initial discovery of the cop and his lover's corpses intertwined in a seedy hotel room is shot in a stark cold monochrome that erupts flamboyantly into blood red as the camera transfixes its gaze on a carnation in a vase on a nearby table. Later on, an exotic dancer ruffles her purple plumes, and an exploding car is enveloped in a gaudy pink fog.

> "Since I was working for a company, I couldn't deviate too much from the company's course. But because my films were in the B category, I had a wider range than an A director. Even if it went off a little bit, it wouldn't be too much of a problem with them. So in that sense I had a little bit of freedom. More than the A directors."

From this point onwards in his career, Suzuki began to experiment wildly within the context of a studio system that ostensibly offered little scope for personal creativity. The most banal of dialogue exchanges or the most minimal of plot turning points are re-staged and shot in such a way as to make them appear as distinct as possible from what has gone before. In his extremes he fills his films with surreal, nonsensical set pieces and frequently uses cinematic techniques that draw attention not only to themselves but also to the entire plasticity of the medium. Suzuki's work at Nikkatsu often bears the hallmarks of a director frantically wrestling to overcome his own boredom. In the otherwise negligible lightweight yakuza melodrama *Our Blood Won't Allow It*, Akira Kobayashi's confession of his involvement with the mob to his younger brother takes place within the confines of their car against an expressionistic backdrop of a stormy sea. The effect has all the heightened artificiality of Hitchcock's car chases, in that the raging waves behind are clearly a back projection. When Suzuki uses exactly the same backdrop after changing the shooting angle ninety degrees so that the two characters are now shown head on, rather than from the side, the effect goes beyond Hitchcock's self-conscious theatricality into the realms of the ludicrous.

It's typical of the Suzuki style of treating the cinema screen as merely a two-dimensional image to be filled with as much color and action as possible, and with only the most tenuous basis in reality. *Youth of the Beast* features a dialogue scene shot entirely from below a glass floor, and there's a stunningly composed shot in **Branded to Kill** where the image of a captive Annu Mari, shot from below as she lies naked and unconscious on a plate of glass, is superimposed over a close-up of Jō Shishido's knitted brow.

Suzuki's approach to editing is similarly nonconformist, abandoning the standard shot-reverse-shot praxis and making heavy use of non-contiguous jump cuts to condense passages of time, reducing his films to a series of striking images. Idiosyncratic it might be, but the end result can sometimes seem more than a little confusing, as individual scenes chop into each other with the beginning and end points not clearly marked out, giving a fragmentary feeling of narrative progression. For his Nikkatsu work at least, this can be in part attributed to the fact that the tight reigns of a B-movie director ensured a minimum of takes during shooting to save film stock. But the fact that such tics persist in his later work suggests that these jarring scene progressions are at least to some measure part of the director's stylistic arsenal.

During his years at Nikkatsu, Suzuki certainly never saw himself as an artist, but rather as a jobbing director, with some of his more bizarre shots more a quick-fix solution to the logistical shackles of time and budget than any personal desire for self-expression. At the same time, however, a traditional Japanese aesthetic is certainly tangible throughout his work, and explicitly so in the series of non-Nikkatsu films he later directed in the '80s, starting with *Zigeunerweisen* and running through to *Yumeji*. Frequently the screen image appears as little more than a flattened projection, filmed in medium to long shot, with the action taking place at ninety degrees to the viewer as if he were directly viewing a stage. Portions of the screen are often masked off or subdivided using walls, windows, sliding doors and solid areas of shadow. In *Pistol Opera*, the main character is introduced in silhouette form performing a balletic pistol practice behind a semi-transparent *shōji* paper screen illuminated to look like a lilac sunset, while *Youth of the Beast* features an exchange in a yakuza's lair containing a one-way mirror acting as a window, a frame within the frame, into a nightclub where a girl is dancing onstage.

Showers of falling cherry blossoms permeate throughout his oeuvre. He even made a straight-to-video feature in 1984 set entirely during the April cherry blossom season, called *Haru Sakura: Seijun Sakura Hensō*, in which a truck driver almost runs over a mysterious parasol-wielding ethereal beauty in a kimono, who appears from out of nowhere in front of his vehicle. With the truck now decked out with cherry flowers, the two travel together through a series of colorful natural outdoor locations against the backdrop of Japan's most beautiful season, though unfortunately the colors are rendered a little drab by the VHS format compared with his more vibrant film work.

Of course, there were more conventional pieces during the Nikkatsu phase of his career. In fact some of the director's more interesting work during this time lies outside the yakuza genre, with the literary adaptations of Tōkō Kon's *Akutarō* and Tajirō Tamura's **Gate of Flesh**, and Kaneto Shindō's meaty script for **Elegy to Violence** going beyond mass audience appeal and proving that Suzuki's talents stretch far beyond the mere formal experimentation that manifested itself in his thematically less ambitious works. One of his most interesting films is *Story of a Prostitute*. Set in 1938 on the Manchurian frontline during the war between China and Japan, the plot, based on a novel by Tamura, had been made once in 1950 by Senkichi Taniguchi for Shintoho as *Akatsuki no Dassō* [trans: Escape at daybreak]. It concerns a love triangle between a military prostitute (or "comfort woman"), her ineffectual soldier boyfriend, and his cruel commanding officer. Shot in black and white CinemaScope on the patched-up sets and costumes of Kon Ichikawa's earlier *Harp of Burma* (*Biruma no Tategoto*, 1956), the film is a potent melodrama set against a pressurized backdrop of violence and impending doom. However, it was not well received either by the critics or the public upon its original release and portended Suzuki's major falling out with the studio three years later.

> "The best thing for a movie is to have a lot of people come to see it when it's released. But back then my films weren't so successful. Now, thirty years later, a lot of young people come to see my films. So either my films were too early or your generation came too late. Either way, the success is coming too late."

More than anything however, Suzuki has come to be appreciated in the West for the retro-

Youth of the Beast

styled, Pop Art-inspired visual excesses of his early work. Bubblegum program potboilers such as *Youth of the Beast* and *Detective Bureau 2-3* are so garish and cartoon-like that it's no real surprise to find that Suzuki made a contribution to the animation field. In 1985, along with Shigetsugu Yoshida, he co-directed *Lupin III: The Golden Legend of Babylon* (1985), based on the series of manga comics drawn by Monkey Punch featuring the snappily dressed simian-looking grandson of French mystery writer Maurice Leblanc's gentleman thief, Arsène Lupin. Suzuki's version sees its protagonist charging across Iraq, battling against a bevy of international beauty contestants in search of hidden treasure. Like the other outside entry in the long running animation series, Hayao Miyazaki's *Castle of Cagliostro* (1979), Suzuki's version fits more comfortably within his own oeuvre than with the series as a whole.

The sensation of kitsch in this early cycle is further enhanced by the frequent casting of Jō Shishido in the lead, whose deadpan hamster-faced demeanor was due to collagen implants he received in his cheeks in order to enhance his box office appeal. Shishido is the star of the best known of Suzuki's films in the West—and undoubtedly the pinnacle of the director's off-the-wall visuals—*Branded to Kill*, as a contract killer aspiring to top dog position in Tokyo's hierarchy of paid assassins, overcoming such obstacles as errant butterflies and a treacherous wife en route. With its stunning monochrome cinematography and highly abstracted approach to both visuals and storytelling, *Branded to Kill* went far beyond anything Suzuki had done before, and deviated so far from the Nikkatsu template that it resulted in his dismissal from the company.

"We don't need directors whose films are unintelligible!" barked company president Kyū-saku Hori. Suzuki's onscreen antics had caused his position within the company to become increasingly tenuous in the years running up to his sacking from the studios in 1968. *Life of a Tattooed Man* and *Tokyo Drifter* had both attracted the attention of the studio head due to their luridly colorful and highly artificial approach to the material, but they had done little to prepare the ground for *Branded to Kill*. Suzuki was on set filming *Aisaikun Konban Wa: Aru Kettō* for the studio's TV division before he was hauled down to Hori's office and given his marching orders. A retrospective of his work was canceled and prints of all his films were withdrawn from circulation.

Within the industry, however, Suzuki's dismissal was widely seen as a scapegoating for the company's flagging fortunes. Always one of the least adventurous of studios, Nikkatsu was the oldest of the majors and yet the last to adapt to sound production. The company's adherence to formula had already more or less killed it off once, when its refusal to move beyond churning out the Edo-period swords and samurai *chanbara* films en masse saw it losing rapid ground to Shochiku, which at the time was specializing in more contemporary family-oriented dramas. Until reopening their studios in 1954 when Suzuki was hired, the company had retreated from production for over ten years, concerning themselves only with distribution and the management of a chain of theaters. During the '60s, failing to adapt to the threat of television, Nikkatsu churned out dozens of interchangeable potboilers aimed squarely at the youth market, few of which are remembered today. When the company set upon a quick-fix solution to the downturn in its fortunes in 1971 after the departure of Kyūsaku Hori by channeling all of its energy into sex films, it pigheadedly refused to budge from the production of steamy Roman Porno dramas for almost twenty years, by which time minimally budgeted AV productions shot on video had stolen the market for big-screen eroticism, forcing Nikkatsu to withdraw from production once more for a brief period in the early '90s.

But Hori's autocratic 1968 decision had annoyed a lot of the staff of Nikkatsu, and indeed the filmmaking world in general. When he decided to take his former employers to court the same year, Suzuki became a cause célèbre for many within the industry. The case dragged on until 1971, ending in a settlement for Suzuki, but by this time the director's name had become so muddied that none of the major studios would touch him. For the next ten years Suzuki was forced to keep himself going mak-ing commercials, a couple of TV dramas, writing newspaper articles and film criticism, and publishing a number of autobiographical works, which include *Hana-Jigoku* [trans: Flower hell, 1972] and *Bōryoku Sagashi ni Machi e Deru* [trans: Going into town looking for violence, 1973]. He was also a defendant in the obscenity case against Nagisa Ōshima surrounding *In the Realm of the Senses* in 1979, in which Ōshima was cleared of all charges. Finally, in 1977, Shochiku studios relented and agreed to distribute his long-awaited comeback feature, though *Story of Sorrow and Sadness*, a melodramatic golfing movie, was a dismal failure at the box office and the '70s remained a decade conspicuous by Suzuki's absence.

With this commercial disaster further conspiring to keep him outside of the industry, some form of vindication arrived when independent producer Genjirō Arato helped finance *Zigeunerweisen*, the first of a trilogy of films produced through the company Cinema Placet set in the Taishō period (1912–25) in which the director was born, one of the most intriguing periods in modern Japanese history. Wedged between the initial opening up to the West and early industrialization of the Meiji period, and the increased nationalism of the early Shōwa period, the era represented a time of relative stability and liberalization under which the arts flourished, with its practitioners hungrily devouring Western influences and melding them to fit into a Japanese cultural environment.

Freed from the shackles of working within the studio context, Suzuki gives full vent to his imagination in these three works in which the image is clearly everything. Both eerie and erotic, *Zigeunerweisen* is a dreamlike tale which shifts from this world to the next and back as it charts the lives of five characters, one of whom dies early on in the film yet whose influence remains very much tangible from beyond the grave. Arato and Suzuki found themselves unable to distribute the film conventionally, so they built a special tent-like exhibition hall with which they toured Japan. The film was a rousing success with critics in Japan, making several "Best of" lists and was awarded a Special Jury Mention when it screened at Berlin in 1981.

His next film in the trilogy, *Mirage Theater*, covers similar territory in a film whose stylistics owe much to the world of kabuki theater, as it details a doomed love affair between a playwright and a mysterious woman who, it turns out, may actually be dead. The final part of the independently produced Taishō trilogy, *Yumeji*, was a fictional biopic about the Okayama-born painter and illustrator Takehisa Yumeji (1884–1934), whose colorful expressionistic portraits of women were heavily influenced by the European Romantic artists. Starring former rock musician Kenji Sawada (a.k.a. "Julie") as the eponymous artist, *Yumeji* is possibly the best-looking of all of Suzuki's films—beginning with a highly stylized shot of a crowd bouncing beachballs over their heads and continuing through a startling succession of images depicting both the confused internal and external worlds of the artist. Hong Kong director Wong Kar-Wai later used the theme music for *In the Mood for Love* (2000).

Between the last two parts of the three films, Suzuki undertook his first work for Shochiku since *Story of Sorrow and Sadness*. *Capone Cries Hard* was about a group of traveling minstrels who bring no less a figure than gangster Al Capone to tears when they tour to the United States to perform a series of musical recitals. Though set in America, the film was in fact shot entirely in Japan.

Suzuki later contributed the third part of the omnibus film *Marriage* along with the directors Hideo Onchi and Hiroshi Nagao, an inconsequential offering that, for a while, looked like it was to be Suzuki's final directorial work. With a number of retrospectives during the '80s and '90s in Italy, the Netherlands, and Canada bringing his name to the international commu-

© 1965 Nikkatsu Corporation

Story of a Prostitute

nity, Suzuki finally began to get noticed outside of Japan. In the meantime, since 1980 the eccentric-looking director had been making a name for himself appearing in a number of television acting roles. After his first feature appearance in a cameo in the Icelandic road movie *Cold Fever* (1994), he began to pop up in a number of films for directors such as Shinji Aoyama (in *Embalming*) and Sabu (*The Blessing Bell*).

"When you become over 60, everything you do is okay with everyone. You can do whatever you want. That's why I started acting. I was invited to be an actor in *Cold Fever*, so I decided to do it."

Branded to Kill may have put Suzuki out of a job, but in the intervening period its showcasing on DVD and video outside of Japan, along with his penultimate film for Nikkatsu, *Tokyo Drifter*, had brought the director's name to a whole new audience. In 2000, over thirty years after the original, producer Satoru Ogura suggested Suzuki make a sequel. In many ways **Pistol Opera** is the zenith of the director's style, a colorful but almost nonsensical plot set against a parade of bizarre and scenic locales.

"The producer, Satoru Ogura, suggested the idea to me of making a sequel to *Branded to Kill*. In the beginning I tried to think of it in

those terms, with a male character, the same as in *Branded to Kill*. That didn't work out so well, so I decided to use a female character in the main role. That worked out better. So it started out as a genuine sequel, but it turned into a very different kind of story."

Pistol Opera was released in Japan in 2001, the same year in which Suzuki was graced with a total of two retrospectives in Tokyo, "Style to Kill" and "Deep Seijun," allowing domestic audiences the rare opportunity to catch the full spectrum of his contribution to Japanese cinema. Wacky, irreverent, occasionally incoherent, but always dazzlingly original and imbued with a playful charm that has become the maverick director's trademark, his work continues to thrill and amuse an entire new generation. Suzuki is a living legend, a man who fought the system and won, and managed to maintain a smile throughout the whole process.

↓ Kanto Wanderer
関東無宿
Kantō Mushuku

1963. **CAST:** Akira Kobayashi, Hiroko Itō, Chieko Matsubara, Keisuke Noro, Daizaburō Hirata, Yūnosuke Itō, 93 minutes. **RELEASES:** DVD, Home Vision Entertainment (U.S., English subtitles), Nikkatsu (Japan, no subtitles).

Suzuki takes on the traditional yakuza and drags him out into the busy post-war streets to show just how old-fashioned he is.

1963 was something of a watershed year for Seijun Suzuki. It was this year that he made his first truly memorable films, the ones in which his audaciousness came to full prominence: *Detective Bureau 2-3: Go to Hell, Bastards!*, *Youth of the Beast*, and *Kanto Wanderer*. These three films developed a stylistic boldness that his previous work had hinted at but not taken to their full potential.

In the case of *Kanto Wanderer*, this audaciousness lies more in Suzuki's attitude toward the basic material than in flamboyant visuals. The film was his first excursion into the *ninkyō eiga*, a traditionalist sub-genre of the yakuza film, enduringly popular throughout the 1960s, which featured honorable gangster heroes faced with a choice between obligation to the gang (*giri*) and friendship to a comrade (*ninjō*). Their decision usually resulted in a spectacular finale that saw the hero going it alone against an entire rival gang.

Always built around this generic scenario, the *ninkyō* films were perfect fodder for the studio production lines, and it's no surprise that Suzuki churned out several of his own while under contract at Nikkatsu. Suzuki being Suzuki, they never were quite as generic as they might have been in lesser hands. In a radical break with the formula, which prescribed a pre-war setting that would convey the traditionalist message, *Kanto Wanderer* was set in the present day, contrasting kimonoed yakuza with giggling high school girls in sailor uniforms.

The effect Suzuki achieved was an emphasis on the outmoded nature of the *ninkyō eiga* subgenre, effectively ridiculing its traditionalist values. Swordfights look particularly out of place when heavy traffic roars through the background. The first scene of the film is a three-way dialogue between chattering schoolgirls shot entirely in close-ups, a scene that couldn't be further removed from the yakuza genre. To demonstrate that it's all a joke, the next shot is of a movie theater showing Nikkatsu program pictures, a discarded flyer exclaiming, "Yakuza movie now showing."

In a further break with traditionalist values, *Kanto Wanderer* is surprisingly frank on the subjects of sex and romance. The conversations of the aforementioned schoolgirls are mainly about whom they'd like to lose their virginity to, with the various members of the two local yakuza

Kanto Wanderer

groups as prime candidates. The girls chase and flirt with their intended paramours shamelessly, and when one of the teens gets sold into prostitution, she ends up enjoying her promiscuous activities even more than her clients do.

Compared to their liberty and energy, the steadfast protagonist Katsuta (Kobayashi) and his pining for the rather homely wife of a professional gambler looks positively dreary. Set against a background of *ryokan* inns, paper screens, and *tatami* mats, this romantic subplot is the film's weakest asset, convolutedly tied in with the main storyline. But then again, perhaps its slow pace and unlikely romance are very intentional parts of Suzuki's game. Even the supposed grand finale is shockingly brief, better remembered for its sudden use of garish red light (tying in with the gangster ethos that a yakuza's path in life leads to either red clothes or white ones, i.e. either prison or death) than for its fight choreography, of which there is little. After the scene is over, there are still 15 minutes of story left to tell, which additionally cushions its impact. In his later *ninkyō* film *Life of a Tattooed Man*, Suzuki would take shock color finales to much more impressive heights.

Effectively a film that undermines itself, *Kanto Wanderer* may not be altogether successful as a viewing experience, but it's all the more interesting as a document of Seijun Suzuki's playfully impertinent approach to studio filmmaking.

↓ Gate of Flesh
肉体の門
Nikutai no Mon

1964. **CAST:** Jō Shishido, Yumiko Nogawa, Kumiko Kawanishi, Kayo Matsuo, Satoko Kasai, Tamiko Ishii, Misako Tominaga, Yōji Wada. 91 minutes. **RELEASES:** DVD. Pagan Films (U.K., English subtitles). HK Video (France, French subtitles, as part of a Seijun Suzuki Vol 1. boxed set, with *Branded to Kill* and *Youth of the Beast*). VHS. Home Vision Entertainment (U.S., English subtitles).

An early masterpiece from Suzuki, in this tale of post-war prostitution amongst the rubble of U.S.-occupied Tokyo.

"After the war, Tokyo was a jungle," laments Maya (Nogawa), the central character of *Gate of Flesh*, as she arrives in the shell-shocked, rubble-strewn wasteland of the nation's capitol in the early stages of the Allied occupation (1945–52). Riddled with poverty and starvation, populated by thieves, looters and black marketeers, and subjected to regular raids by the military police from the nearby U.S. base, Japanese pimps peddle young flesh to the occupying forces and patroling American GIs are a constant feature on the landscape.

Left with no surviving family, Maya seeks shelter with a group of prostitutes who inhabit a bombed-out building in the heart of this confusion. To protect their means of livelihood from exploitation by pimps and competition from rival whores, the group live a close-knit existence, staking out their territory on a regular basis and adhering to a rigid set of codes, the most savagely enforced being "No sex for free." What happens when this last rule is violated is soon demonstrated to Maya on a former member of this makeshift guild, as she is stripped and has her hair shaven off by the other girls, and is left strapped naked on an abandoned rowboat floating in the river, with only a fishing net between her and the burning rays of the sun.

Into this situation wanders ex-serviceman Shintarō (Shishido), wounded and on the run from the military police after having stabbed a soldier. At first the girls agree only to shelter him for one night, but later his petulant manner and far-fetched wartime yarns begin to stir up feelings of affection in the girls' hearts. Sooner or later, as love begins to raise its ugly head, his presence amongst them threatens to tear this fragile solidarity apart.

Youth of the Beast may have been the first time audiences sat up and took note of Suzuki's name, but this next work is nothing short of a minor masterpiece. *Gate of Flesh* is amongst the many films by the director that point to the fact that during his Nikkatsu days Suzuki's skill stretched beyond the mere jazzing up of tawdry scripts. This strong female-oriented drama paints a particularly vivid picture of the period immediately succeeding the war, and resounds with memories of the nation's defeat and the bitterness of those led into it by the strictly enforced ideologies imposed by the militarists and nationalists. With the men debilitated through hunger and stripped of pride, it was up to the women to drag the nation back onto its feet again. "Japanese women are such sluts now!" Shintarō screams at Sen, the gang's feisty ringleader. "So? You men are to blame! You lost the

Gate of Flesh

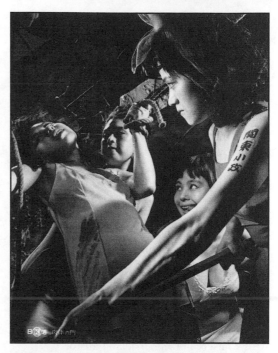

war!" she bawls back. Later, as the girls leave Shintarō hiding out in their lair as they go off to work the streets, one of them makes a passing comment about him playing "housewife."

Suzuki's film is one of four adaptations of *Gate of Flesh* for the big screen, all under the same title. The first was in 1948 by Masahiro Makino, at the time of the novel's publication, and the most recent was by Hideo Gosha in 1988, a big-budget version produced by Toei. Suzuki's essentially shares the most in common with a later version produced by Nikkatsu in 1977, directed by Shōgorō Nishimura as part of their Roman Porno series—Junko Miyashita, the studio's award winning starlet, features as one of the prostitutes. Nishimura is obviously heavily indebted to Suzuki's rendition, seemingly set in the very same shooting locations and negotiating its way through similar plot points, though detailing the scenes of the girls at work with a far greater lip-smacking gusto.

Nishimura's version, however, lacks the heavily stylized melodrama that makes Suzuki's such a work of art: the synergy between the gritty realism of its setting and the concessions to theatricality to communicate the themes and ideas within the original work more expressively. And this goes for the inspirational visual approach as well as the acting. A confrontation between Sen and Shintarō avoids standard eyeline matching techniques in favor of superimposing his face next to a wide shot of her sitting on a bed, picked out in a spotlight. The four main prostitutes are drawn in vibrant hues, as if to express their vitality within the shattered wasteland, each characterized by the color of her dress: the innocence and naiveté of newcomer Maya dressed in dark green, the volatile Sen in red, cheerful and chubby Roku in yellow, and tranquil and compliant Miyo in purple. In one moment, when the girls begin to fall for Shintarō's bullish charm, they are each portrayed individually voicing their internal thoughts to the camera against a theatrical backdrop matching their character. For Maya, he reminds her of her

brother whom she lost in Borneo. Later on she tells him that he reminds her of an angry boy in her class, who wore a paper demon mask in the school play—which explains the rather baffling shot we'd been treated to earlier, of Shishido's face briefly superimposed in the top left corner of the screen with the same paper monster mask perched on his head, fuming after the girls have greeted his tale of battlefield heroics with mocking laughter.

Gate of Flesh was adapted from a best-selling novel about post-war prostitutes (or *pan-pan* girls) written by Taijirō Tamura, a popular writer of the '40s and '50s who specialized in *nikutai bungaku* (literally "flesh literature"), a genre which set its tales within the earthy milieu of the flesh trade to bring its various social, political, or historical points to a wider audience. Owing to its subject matter, *Gate of Flesh* is somewhat of a landmark film regarding the onscreen portrayal of nudity and for the shocking imagery on display—a savage flagellation scene as the punishment for breaking the guild's rules is meted out sadistically by the other girls in lengthy torture sessions, and the slaughter of a bull stolen by Shintarō for sale on the black market appears onscreen in bloody detail.

It was the first of three films Suzuki made about the plight of prostitutes, all set in various points in Japanese history and all featuring the expressive features of Yumiko Nogawa as their plucky protagonist. Suzuki's next film in the series, *Story of a Prostitute*, was also an adaptation of a work by Tamura, who was the first author to focus on the subject of military "comfort women" in stories such as *Inago*, years before it was to become a national source of shame. Suzuki rounded off his trilogy with *Carmen from Kawachi*, based on a novel by Tōkō Kon, a member of the Shinkankaku ("New Perceptionists") school of writers of the 1920s that included Yasunari Kawabata and Riichi Yokomitsu, and who also provided the source material for Suzuki's *Akutarō* the previous year.

↓ Elegy to Violence

けんかえれじい

Kenka Erejii

a.k.a. *Fighting Elegy, The Born Fighter*

1966. CAST: Hideki Takahashi, Junko Asano, Yūsuke Kawatsu, Mitsuo Kataoka, Seijirō Onda. 86 minutes. RELEASES: DVD, Criterion (U.S., English subtitles), Nikkatsu (Japan, no subtitles); VHS, Home Vision Entertainment (U.S., English subtitles).

Acerbic and witty look at violence in the years running up to the war within the microcosm of the schoolyard of Okayama Middle School.

To those familiar with his more populist works, *Elegy to Violence* will no doubt, initially at least, look like a disappointingly conventional piece of low budget '60s cinema, shot in black and white and devoid of much in the way of stylistic flourish or fanfare. However, this film points to the fact that there are actually a lot more strings to the Suzuki bow than many give him credit for. Even within the lower echelons of the studio system there was room for the director to shoehorn in social comment and political satire within his films, factors which are often overlooked in his oeuvre in favor of the more superficial aspects.

Yet that's not to say that any of the director's impish humor has been lost in this fictitious fable set amongst the schoolyard scuffles of Okayama Middle School. In a decade in which questions of national identity, Japan's relationship with the outside world, and its links with its traditional past were being probed by such lofty right-wing thinkers as the ultrapatriotic novelist Yukio Mishima and Tokyo's current governor Shintarō Ishihara, it could only take a wit as razor sharp as Suzuki's to burst the intellectual bubble.

Set in 1935, Kiroku (played by Hideki Takahashi, one of the ranks of Nikkatsu matinee idols of the era and also the star of Suzuki's *Life of a Tattooed Man*) is one of a horde of hot-headed adolescents who partake in a bit of testoster-one-charged rough 'n' tumble after the school bell has sounded, fighting under the aegis of the OSMS (Okayama Second Middle School) gang. "A famous group of young men training their bodies," the OSMS take their brawlings with their local rivals to paramilitary levels of hyperbole, lining their school bags with razor blades and carving *shurikens* out of wood, indulging in lengthy training sessions punching beanbags full of rocks and beating each other with sticks in the nearby forest.

The OSMS live by a number of tenets, including "A man finds rebellion most satisfying" and "No talking to softies." Unfortunately for Kiroku, who's got the hots for Michiko, the daughter of the owner of the Catholic boarding house where he lives, there's also "No chasing after girls." Kiroku, however, is quite willing to have his sentiments educated at the piano by Michiko in the privacy of the house, but when he is caught strolling through the cherry blossoms hand in hand with his sweetheart by Takuan, the leader of the OSMS, it's obvious that he's going to have to try that little bit harder to regain his face in front of his contemporaries.

"My main impression is still that war is ludicrous," the director stated about his own experiences in a 1969 interview for the Japanese publication *Shinema 69*. This viewpoint informs the whole tone of the *Elegy to Violence* as much as it does with any of his films. You can almost imagine Suzuki smirking behind the camera as he pokes fun at the adolescent machismo that equates military discipline with virility. He later goes on in the same interview to recount a story in which during the war he was holed up in a house in Taiwan. "There was a bombing raid and a man was hit while 'doing it.' It would have been better if only the bottom half had been blown off, but that's the only part that was left, his charred bottom half."

As the students of the all-male school environment channel their sexual tensions into acts of aggression, Kiroku's personal diary is peppered with immortal lines such as "Oh Michiko!

Elegy to Violence

I don't masturbate, I fight!" Every time he finds himself hot under the collar at the thought of his virginal love interest at the piano ("My blood throbs at those white hands!"), with an upward glance to the crucifix on the wall of his Catholic boarding house, it's back out for another bout of backstreet brawling.

An adaptation of Takashi Suzuki's novel by renowned scriptwriter Kaneto Shindō, the script was apparently substantially rewritten by the pragmatic director to fit his working methods, allowing him to make use of exterior locations to stage the frantic battle sequences that form the visual high points of the piece. However, more than a broad-edged attack on violence itself, Shindō's script is an absurdist look at the forces that gave rise to fascism in early Shōwa era Japan. When Kiroku's unruly antics get him kicked out of school and he is packed away to study in rural Aizu, he is unimpressed by the "Aizu spirit" of his classmates. Kiroku's outsider status singles him out for attention amongst the local school bullies, but he soon emerges top dog, attracting the shadowy figure of real-life fascist writer and political dissident Ikki Kita in the process.

Kita was a radical nationalist whose writings proved immensely influential with the right wing in the pre-war period. He believed that following the re-establishment of the Imperial system at the beginning of the Meiji period, a whole host of privileged cliques—politicians, bureaucrats, industrialists, military leaders, etc.—had emerged, coming between the Shōwa Emperor Hirohito and the people of Japan, corrupting the concept of *kokutai*—of the nation as one family under the direct rule of a single symbolic patriarch. Kita was executed in 1937 for allegedly influencing the young officers who took place in the failed coup known as the *Niniroku* incident that took place on February 26, 1936, in which 1,400 rebel soldiers occupied a number of crucial government buildings in the center of Tokyo and killed the finance minster and the inspector general of military education. The cel-

ebrated literary figure Yukio Mishima was also to make a 30-minute film inspired by the same event, the somber and highly stylized *Yūkoku* [trans: Patriotism, 1966], and a few years later in 1970, for his ultimate performance, took his own life by ritual *seppuku*, a desperate gesture harking back to the days of pre-war nationalism. Suzuki's film ends during the coup, in which a state of martial law has been declared in Tokyo. With the unattainable Michiko packed off to a nunnery, Kiroku embarks on a lengthy snowbound train journey to Tokyo to join Kita in the revolution.

Elegy to Violence may well be one of Suzuki's meatiest films, both in terms of its political satire and the sheer vigor of the bone-crushing violence on display. The widescreen scope is most impressively used in the lavishly staged fights between the various gangs, armed with swords, rocks, and sticks. But Suzuki doesn't revel in the violence of these scenes. The spectacle of a chaotic mass of writhing schoolboys, rendered all the more ridiculous by the fact that the actors wearing the uniforms are at least 10 years too old for their parts, is, as Suzuki quite rightly suggests, quite ludicrous. He knows as well as we all do, that boys will be boys. It's only when the playful scuffling goes beyond the boundaries of the school playground that we really need to start to worry.

↓ Branded To Kill
殺しの烙印
Koroshi no Rakuin

1966. CAST: Jō Shishido, Mariko Ogawa, Annu Mari, Kōji Nambara, Isao Tamagawa, Hiroshi Minami. 91 minutes. RELEASE: DVD, Criterion Collection (U.S., English subtitles). Second Sight Films (U.K., English subtitles). HK Video (France, French subtitles, as part of a Seijun Suzuki Vol 1. boxed set, with *Gate of Flesh* and *Youth of the Beast*). Nikkatsu (Japan, no subtitles).

Suzuki's landmark film turns the concept of genre cinema on its head, in one of the most stylish, wacky, and gob-smacking pieces of celluloid weirdness ever to hit the screen.

Branded to Kill sees Jō Shishido returning to the Suzuki fold for the first time since **Gate of Flesh**, this time playing Gorō Hanada, a terse assassin in shades and Number Three in the pecking order of hired killers. Turned on by the smell of boiling rice, between killings he indulges in vigorous sexual marathons with his wife, chasing her nakedly around every room of their apartment in order to satisfy his insatiable appetite. He is drawn off course when approached by the beautiful but deadly Misako to undertake a "kill or be killed" contract, and soon finds himself entranced by this mysterious femme fatale, who keeps an apartment full of entomological specimens and an impaled lovebird suspended from the rear view mirror of her car. When he botches the job due to an untimely butterfly landing on his gun-sight, his wife is secretly hired by the mob boss to kill him. From then on it's bullet-riddled mayhem all the way until a head-to-head finale set in a deserted boxing gymnasium with the anonymous phantom Number One.

If Suzuki's previous work in the yakuza genre had demonstrated an ability to rework standard plots and warp them into glorious pieces of comic book flamboyance, then his last for Nikkatsu can surely be said to represent the pinnacle of his vision, the boldest attempt to strip a genre down to its bare atoms and rebuild it into something that can truly be described as pure cinema. Even the director's confinement to monochrome after the garish color palette of *Tokyo Drifter* works in its favor. *Branded to Kill* is almost pure abstraction, one man's rise to the top filtered through the language of Jungian symbolism and perverse dream logic, a series of images and events that have no application to the real world. It was the final nail in the coffin as far as Nikkatsu president Kyūsaku Hori was

concerned. In any measure, one wonders how Suzuki could have topped it if he had been allowed to stay.

Branded to Kill benefits from some stunning high contrast scope shooting doubled with a masterful use of light and shadow, all courtesy of cinematographer Kazue Nagatsuka, a collaborator on some of Suzuki's finest work: *Youth of the Beast*, *The Flower and the Angry Waves*, and *Story of a Prostitute*. Nagatsuka later rejoined the director for the independent productions of *Zigeunerweisen* and *Mirage Theater* in the '80s. Laid down to a sultry '60s jazz accompaniment, Suzuki's film takes place in no recognizable location—a series of austere tenement block apartments, deserted warehouses and smoky lounge bars. Such a topography doesn't tie the film down to any particular country or genre, nor does Suzuki's almost surreal approach to the individual set pieces. For one of Gorō's assassinations, he pokes his pistol up a drainpipe and fires, the bullet ricocheting up and firing out of the plug hole, to find its target as he bends over the basin.

Suzuki melds such cartoon imagery with Shishido's hard-boiled, stone cold sober performance in a film that was to indelibly associate the singular screen presence of the Nikkatsu hardman with Suzuki's equally synthetic aesthetic. Shishido is perfectly matched by the stunning Annu Mari as Misako, who disappears midpoint through the film, leaving Shishido with only a cinematic projection of her left behind by her kidnappers, an illusion to be chased. The exotic actress was born in 1948 to an Indian father and Japanese mother. She made her debut for Toho in 1964 in *Jitensha Dorobō* [trans: The bicycle thief] and later appeared in such fluff for Nikkatsu as *Za Supaidāzu no Daishingeki* [trans: The Spiders' big attack], a vehicle for the then popular beat combo, the Spiders, whose frivolous comedic antics and chirpy croonings recall the Monkees. She later appeared in Shōgorō Nishimura's 1970 pre-Roman Porno pink film *Zankoku Onna Jōshi* [trans: Cruel female love

© 1967 Nikkatsu Corporation

Branded to Kill

suicide]. After an absence from the screen for almost thirty years, Mari recently appeared in the erotic thriller *Reflection* (*Reflection Jubaku no Kizuna*, 1992) by Fujirō Mitsuishi, the director of *Tomie Replay* (2000), and *Ashita ga Arusa THE MOVIE* (Hitoshi Iwamoto, 2002) based on the TV drama from Nippon Television.

The type of film that is virtually impossible to describe to anyone that hasn't seen it, and the type of film where plot takes a severe back seat to the imagery, with the passing of time *Branded to Kill* has become a treasured object of cult film fans with a taste for the truly bizarre all over the world. More recently, it was paid homage by Jim Jarmusch in his *Ghost Dog: Way of the Samurai* (1999), and Suzuki himself almost managed to top it in the sheer weirdness stakes with his be-lated follow-up thirty years later, ***Pistol Opera***.

↓ Story of Sorrow and Sadness
悲愁物語
Hishū Monogatari

1977. **CAST:** Yōko Shiraki, Yoshio Harada, Masu-mi Okada, Kōji Wada, Jō Shishido. 91 minutes. **RELEASES:** DVD, Panorama (Hong Kong, English/ Chinese subtitles).

Golf has never been as fun as when Suzuki wields the 9-iron, in this glossed-over bridging point in the director's career.

If Suzuki's work for Nikkatsu can be typified as free-form experimentations in style within the rigid confines of the clichéd and pedestrian B-movie genre narratives he was handed, this oft-overlooked turning point in the director's oeuvre is of double interest in that here the narrative is even more off-the-wall than the visuals.

During the late '70s, Japan was no different from the rest of the developed world in that increased liberalization regarding onscreen portrayals of sex, violence, and nudity and the increasing prosperity of its citizens seemed to run hand in hand with an increased dearth of imagination in the films being produced. Having now moved on to become exclusively associated with the Roman Porno line of glossy sex films, if anything, Nikkatsu's approach had become even more inflexible in the ten years since Suzuki had shot *Branded to Kill*.

In this context, it might be tempting to look at Suzuki's first film after ten years in the wilderness as something of a two-fingered riposte to his former employers, an attempt to explode back on the scene with a film that was simultaneously refreshing, inventive, and commercially successful. And how did he decide to do this? With a sexy psycho-melodrama based on the popularity of that most bourgeois of sports, golf! *Story of Sorrow and Sadness* was mauled by the critics of the time and flopped at the box office. Suzuki retreated from the filmmaking frontline for a further few years before meeting with a considerably more enthusiastic reception with his next comeback, the self-produced *Zigeunerweisen*.

Glossed over in recent retrospectives of the director and seldom mentioned in discussions of his work, Suzuki's sole work of the '70s is actually one of the most peculiar entries of an oeuvre that is already marked by its peculiarity. From the chintzy '70s decor and cocktail lounge music to the crazy use of zooms interspersed with the usual Suzuki stylistic tropes, not to mention the sheer absurdity of both story and milieu, here is a film that goes far beyond the standard definitions of "cult cinema" that seemed so embodied by the Pop Art kitsch of **Branded to Kill**. "What's so interesting about a game where you hit a ball into a little hole?" asks one of the characters at an early point in the film. Well, watch and learn. . . .

This particular tale of sorrow and sadness concerns professional model Reiko (Shiraki) groomed to the higher ranks of the golf circuit by the editor of a sporting fashion magazine (Harada, a regular in Suzuki's Taishō era-set dramas of the '80s) in order to promote their latest range of sporting wear. Her victory during her first professional competition ("The ball's gonna fly, wherever I will it to go!" she mutters to herself as she wipes the sweat from her furrowed brow) wins her not only the approval of her sideburned, shades-wearing mentor—with whom she immediately dives, newly won trophy in hand, straight beneath the shower after the match—but also with a whole new TV audience, where she makes regular appearances clad in a bikini and wielding a 9-iron. It seems that suddenly everyone wants a piece of Reiko, including neighbor-from-hell Mrs. Semba.

Semba-san's initial attempts to buy into Reiko's fame take the form of a telephoned complaint about the model's garage door. However, the curtain-twitching obsessive soon comes face to face with her idol when asking for autographs on a TV talk show. Things turn a little more sinister when this twisted celebrity stalker is knocked down in a drunken hit-and-run accident by Reiko and her manager. Persuading his protégée that reporting the incident may ruin her newfound fame, the couple leave the injured figure by the road side.

That evening as Reiko practices her putts in the living room, she is confronted by the wounded Semba with a blackmail proposition. With her career seriously threatened, Reiko has no choice but to concur. However, the blackmailer is soon abusing her newly found power, shearing off Reiko's hair and throwing drunken parties with her friends and neighbors in the model's house in which she lives with her adolescent younger brother (who resides up a rope ladder in his attic bedroom for much of the film). After a creepy lesbian kiss, Reiko finds herself succumbing more and more to Semba's violent fantasies.

Coming across like a deranged hybrid of

Clint Eastwood's *Play Misty for Me* (1971) and Robert Aldrich's *What Ever Happened to Baby Jane?* (1962), this sinister social satire of *Stepford Wives* suburban aspiration set against the glamorous world of big budget sports promotion is impossible to pigeonhole as anything other than a Suzuki film (Jō Shishido even crops up in a cameo). Watch the divots fly as Suzuki takes viciously wild swipes at the reciprocally symbiotic relationship between celebrity and fan manifested in both the obligations to the public that put them where they are and the demands of a consumer-driven public who crave the need to worship at their altar.

Periodically interspersed with scenes of the younger brother's innocent flirtations beneath the cherry blossoms with an imaginary girl next door, and riddled with the director's wildly nonconformist use of non-contiguous edits, unhinged shot composition, and violent splashes of color, this crazed and chaotic overlooked work has for too long been buried in the sand bunkers of obscurity and simply cries out for revival.

↓ Pistol Opera
ピストルオペラ
Pisutoru Opera

2001. CAST: Makiko Esumi, Sayoko Yamaguchi, Masatoshi Nagase, Mikijirō Hira, Hanae Kan, Kirin Kiki, Kenji Sawada, Tomio Aoki. 112 minutes. RELEASE: DVD, Tokyo Shock/Media Blasters (U.S., English subtitles). Shochiku Home Video (Japan, no subtitles).

Suzuki's comeback film after almost a decade of absence is a characteristically hyper-stylized, garishly colored sequel to his 1967 hitman delirium *Branded to Kill*.

If ever a sequel could be called belated, Seijun Suzuki's *Pistol Opera* would fit the bill. More than three decades after the fact, the legendary filmmaker returns to what is regarded by many as his masterpiece: **Branded to Kill**. A rush job it certainly wasn't, then, but can the film live up to the towering legacy of its illustrious predecessor, especially with a 78-year-old director who hasn't been at the helm of a film in almost ten years?

Echoing *Branded to Kill*'s plot, *Pistol Opera* revolves around Number Three killer Miyuki Minazuki, nicknamed "Stray Cat," and her attempts at attaining the top rank in the hierarchy of assassins. She is thwarted at every turn by a procession of exotic rivals with names like the Teacher (a wheelchair-bound, tracksuit-wearing killer), Painless Surgeon (a bearded Westerner with a liking for Japanese women, who literally feels no pain) and Dark Horse (Masatoshi Nagase in a blond wig and black cloak).

In spite of rumors abounding that Jō Shishido would return to one of his most memorable roles, the part of Gorō Hanada went to his contemporary Mikijirō Hira, whose more recent roles of note include the sadistic marquis in the two versions of *The Mystery of Rampo*. The exact reason for this bypass remains obscure, with Suzuki himself claiming it to be the decision of producer Satoru Ogura, the project's originator. Laments over a missed opportunity aside, it must be said that Hira acquits himself of the task quite well, giving the aging Hanada the right combination of pathos, anger, and faded glory as he wobbles around in crutches and muses about the good old days.

Suzuki's original intention had been to have the plot revolve around a love affair between Hanada and Miyuki, but in the end he decided against it. Only fleeting moments of reproach between the two remain, which are too halfhearted to work as a romantic subplot, but fit rather well as part of the undetermined professional relationship between the two characters throughout the film. Hanada functions as Miyuki's counselor, turning up at various intervals with cryptic clues and advice. His role as an active assassin is played out, though he's not quite ready to accept it himself. His position in the guild is Number Zero and his nickname is the Champ, representing exactly the ambivalence of his character, who is relegated into a supporting role by his young female colleague.

Suzuki has never been a stranger to putting female characters in the spotlight, his "Flesh" trilogy—**Gate of Flesh**, *Story of a Prostitute*, and *Carmen from Kawachi*—springing most readily to mind. For the most part however, women in his films have been prostitutes, gangsters' molls, and cabaret performers. His 1977 box-office flop **Story of Sorrow and Sadness** broke this cycle by depicting the exploits of a female professional golfer, but with *Pistol Opera* women are finally the men's equals if not more. The cast is made up accordingly. With her tall stature, high-heeled boots and kimono, Makiko Esumi makes a strong physical impression as Miyuki the Stray Cat, moving in a stylized, choreographed, and almost ritualized manner many times removed from her breakthrough performance in Hirokazu Kore-eda's *Maborosi*. She is complemented by the intriguing cross-generational presences of Sayoko Yamaguchi, Kirin Kiki, and the young newcomer Hanae Kan—a quartet that forms the soul of this film.

The director's casting choices fit in rather well with the composed unity of the film. In true Suzuki fashion, the film is driven stylistically rather than narratively. Music, visuals, and even dialogue are parts of a big composition rather than serving to provide narrative verisimilitude. From the opening assassination at Tokyo station, a deserted temple, an *onsen* bath resort, a field of reeds enveloped in yellow smoke, to the final shoot-out amongst a maze of stone columns—all shot in garish colors and angular architectural compositions—*Pistol Opera* takes place in no recognizable world other than Planet Suzuki.

Fittingly, the film is filled with numerous references to *Branded to Kill* and others of the director's earlier works. The shot of an assassin (played by Kenji Sawada, star of Suzuki's 1991 film *Yumeji*) falling from the roof of Tokyo station is framed nearly identically to a fall made by one of Jō Shishido's targets in *Branded to Kill*, while Nagase's black-cloaked figure inevitably brings to mind Tamio Kawachi's Sandeman-esque stalker in *The Flower and the Angry Waves*. Such references are employed rather playfully, but one can't suppress the feeling that they add up to little more than a self-referential in-joke and that the whole thing, running nearly two hours in length, is a tad self-indulgent. Then again, we could also interpret them as a nostalgia-tinted final bow by a director who knows his aging bones won't allow him many more returns to the director's chair. So let him be self-indulgent. Because in doing so, Suzuki also indulges us. And there have been few filmmakers in the history of Japanese cinema whose indulgences have been such a joy to experience.

CHAPTER 2
Shōhei Imamura
今村昌平

Nineteen ninety-seven was a landmark year for the Japanese film industry, long believed to be in a terminal slump as far as the outside world was concerned. Takeshi Kitano won the Golden Lion at Venice for *Fireworks*, Masayuki Suō's **Shall We Dance?** was a sweeping success across North America, Shunji Iwai's *Swallowtail Butterfly* became a cult favorite in Asia, and newcomer Naomi Kawase caused a stir at Cannes with **Suzaku**.

But the year also saw the release of another film that caused the Cannes audiences to sit up and take of note of these new currents in the East, and it came from a director who was then over seventy years old. That year, the celebrated Palme d'Or prize was shared, in a rare joint win, between Iranian director Abbas Kiarostami's *A Taste of Cherry* and Shōhei Imamura's **The Eel**.

Though he has been a vital part of the Japanese film industry since the '50s, Imamura's role in boosting the foreign perception of Japanese cinema has been crucial. Having already picked up the Palme d'Or in 1983 for *The Ballad of Narayama*, Imamura became one of only three directors to win the prestigious prize twice, joining the ranks of Bille August, for *Pelle the Conqueror* in 1987 and *Best Intentions* in 1992, and Emir Kusturica, with *When Father Was Away on Business* in 1985 and *Underground* in 1995. When his *Warm Water Under a Red Bridge* was selected for competition at the Cannes in 2001, there was some speculation as to whether the veteran director would become the first ever to walk away with a third.

At the end of the day *Warm Water* caused a few ripples, but overall received only a lukewarm reception, and Imamura, once described as "the entomologist of modern Japan" by French critic Max Tessier, left empty-handed. More is the pity, as the themes and obsessions that have permeated throughout this fascinating filmmaker's groundbreaking body of work are as pertinent today as they've ever been. Imamura is a director who deserves to be brought to a far wider audience.

With over forty years in the business, Imamura's status as one of Japan's most important cinematic figures is incontestable. Born on September 15, 1926, he started off in the industry in 1951 at Shochiku studios where, among others, he worked as an assistant director on three films by the acclaimed Yasujirō Ozu: *Early Summer* (*Bakushū*, 1951), *The Flavor of Green Tea over Rice* (*Ochazuke no Aji*, 1952), and *Tokyo Story* (*Tōkyō Monogatari*, 1953). Imamura later confessed to not being too taken with Ozu's style of *gendai-geki* (social dramas focused on everyday contemporary life), claiming it too precise and too close to the "official" view of the nation's culture that Japan was eager to promote: that of kabuki, kimonos, and tea ceremonies.

This discrepancy that he saw between how Japan wanted to see itself and the more organic, animalistic side to human society that he had experienced firsthand during the immediate postwar years informs all of Imamura's work. The traditional characteristics of honor, obedience, conformity, and loyalty that are so often associated with the country and that were actively being promoted in the national cinema of the time seemed artificial to him, unrepresentative of the Japanese spirit. Beneath this officially sanctified façade lay an entire underclass which remained unexplored and undepicted: a world of pimps and prostitutes, of drunks and racketeers, of peasants and pornographers, each with their own story to tell. The title alone of his 1970 experimental quasi-documentary *A History of Post-War Japan as Told by a Bar Hostess* sums up this stance.

During the late '50s, other directors were echoing Imamura's dissatisfaction with the golden age of Japanese cinema. Taking heed of this, Shochiku's Ōfuna studios decided to inject new blood into their output by allowing a handful of directors—Nagisa Ōshima, Masahiro Shinoda, and Yoshishige Yoshida—the opportunity to make their directorial debuts whilst still in their late twenties in a move calculated to capitalize on the recent trend of *taiyōzoku* movies. Following the lead set by Jean-Luc Godard and François Truffaut of the French Nouvelle Vague, these directors would be joined by Imamura, as well as Kō Nakahira and Susumu Hani, and would prove instrumental in revitalizing the filmmaking scene during the '60s, in a movement that became known as the *Nūberu Bāgu*, or Japanese New Wave.

Filmography

1958
- Stolen Desire (Nusumareta Yokubō)
- Nishi Ginza Station (Nishi Ginza Eki-Mae)
- Endless Desire (Hateshi naki Yokubō)

1959
- My Second Brother (Nian-chan)

1961
- Pigs and Battleships (Buta to Gunkan)

1963
- The Insect Woman (Nippon Konchūki)

1964
- Intentions of Murder (Akai Satsui) (a.k.a. Unholy Desire)

1966
- The Pornographers (Jin-ruigaku Nyūmon)

1967
- A Man Vanishes (Ningen Jōhatsu)

1968
- The Profound Desire of the Gods (Kamigami no Fukaki Yokubō) (a.k.a. Kuragejima: Tales from a Southern Island)

1970
- A History of Post-War Japan As Told by a Bar Hostess (Nippon Sengoshi: Madamu Onboro no Seikatsu)

1971
- In Search of Unreturned Soldiers (Mikikanhei o Otte, Pts. I and II) [TV]

1972
- The Pirates of Bubuan (Bubuan no Kaizoku) [TV]

1973
- Private Fujita Comes Home (Muhōmatsu Kokyō ni Kaeru) [TV]

1975
- In Search of Unreturned Soldiers (Mikikanhei o Otte, Pt. III) [TV]
- Two Men Named Yoshinobu (Tsuiseki: Futari no Yoshinobu) [TV]

- Karayuki-san, the Making of a Prostitute (Karayuki-San)

1979
- Vengeance Is Mine (Fukushū Suru wa Ware ni Ari)

1981
- Eijanaika (Eejanaika) (a.k.a. Why Not?)

1983
- The Ballad of Narayama (Narayama Bushikō)

1987
- Zegen

1989
- Black Rain (Kuroi Ame)

1997
- The Eel (Unagi)

1998
- Dr. Akagi (Kanzō Sensei)

2001
- Warm Water under a Red Bridge (Akai Hashi no Shita no Nurui Mizu)

2002
- 11'09"01 September 11 [co-director]

In addition to imbuing his work with a degree of humor often absent from the other New Wave directors, Imamura tends to take a bottom-up rather than a top-down approach in his portrayals of Japan. His films are more observational than polemical, and the focus is fixed squarely on the working class or marginal characters that more conventional storytellers might have us ignore. Society is viewed as an instinctive rabble of churning flesh reined in by pressures imposed from above or outside. His 1964 film *Intentions of Murder* features an unlikely heroine in the form of the passive and bovine-looking Sadako, who achieves a transcendence through the events that befall her not through any positive reaction to them, but merely by submitting herself to her own natural instincts. The loose adaptation of Akiyuki Nosaka's novel *The Pornographers*, whose Japanese title translates as "An Introduction to Anthropology," evokes the steamy world of private enterprise surrounding the production of erotic stag films, with whose profits the sleazy Ogata supports his lover and her two children, convinced that the illegal 8mm movies he is surreptitiously making are providing a vital service to his fellow man.

Imamura had already chosen to move on from Shochiku by the time Ōshima et al. were making their debuts there, like Seijun Suzuki, relocating to Nikkatsu studios in 1954. Here he soon found himself working with Yūzō Kawashima, a director under whose apprenticeship he'd already worked at Shochiku, initially in 1951 on the program picture *A Couple Very Much in Love* (*Aibore Tokoton Dōshi*)—Imamura later described the film as "silly." Though the director later claimed that Ozu's influence on him was strong, if only due to the fact that his own style was a rejection of this early mentor's, with Kawashima he found a readymade soul mate.

Though hardly known outside of Japan, Kawashima's brand of populist bawdy comedies and his love of lowlife vulgarity struck a chord with Imamura. The two of them collaborated on a number of films, some successful, some not, though the Imamura-scripted *The Sun Legend of the Tokugawa Era* (*Bakumatsu Taiyōden*, 1957) is now regarded as a classic of the time. Over the five years that they worked together, they became firm friends and riotous drinking partners, until the older director's poor health and hedonistic lifestyle caught up with him. Kawashima died in 1963 whilst still in his midforties. Imamura repaid the debt to the man he often referred to as "my teacher" with the publication of *Sayōnara Dake ga Jinsei Da: Eiga Kantoku Kawashima Yūzō no Shōgai* [trans: *Life is but farewell: the life of Yūzō Kawashima*] in 1969.

Very much active in a screenwriting capacity during the late '50s, Imamura made his own directorial debut in 1958 with *Stolen Desire*, a film that focused on the dynamics within a group of itinerant actors who travel around performing a populist variant of kabuki, a people's theater for lower-class audiences. The film reflects both the director's early love of theater that he developed whilst studying at Waseda University and his interest in grassroots culture. This was followed up with *Nishi Ginza Station*, a rather atypical work that was ostensibly little more than a vehicle for the popular singer Frank Nagai and a film that Imamura didn't even want to make. Then came *Endless Desire*, in which a disparate group of people dig a tunnel to find a stash of morphine buried by the Americans at the end of the war. This was a notable work in that it marked the beginning of a collaboration with cameraman Shinsaku Himeda that lasted until *The Pornographers* in 1966 and whose busy widescreen compositions and high-contrast monochrome cinematography came to typify the director's style. His next film, *My Second Brother*, was a social realist look at the lives of a family of Korean descent in a poor mining town in Kyushu, told through the viewpoint of a diary written by the ten-year-old daughter.

Imamura's first work to find a significant release outside of Japan came in 1961, when *Pigs and Battleships* was distributed in France under the title *Filles et Gangsters* [trans: Girls and gangsters]. The story was heavily influenced by

Imamura's own experiences during the fraught years immediately succeeding the war, and focuses on a gang of small-time racketeers that hang around the naval base of the occupying U.S. forces, foraging food and supplies from the waste bins, whilst working a black market operation in pork meat. With its end coda of a herd of stampeding pigs unleashed into the streets, the film introduced into Imamura's work a unique brand of grotesquery and what was to become one of his dominant themes, that of man's close relation with the animal world.

The man-as-animal metaphor lies at the heart of most of Imamura's films, be it Kōji Yakusho's fishy subconscious in *The Eel*, or the symbolic presence of the carp that floats around in its tank in the family home of the protagonist of *The Pornographers*. Images of the white mouse that futilely spins around on its wheel are juxtaposed with the daily routine of the housewife Sadako in **Intentions of Murder** to represent her status of being trapped in a loveless, dead-end marriage. In the same film, her role is later compared to that of a silkworm, a creature that lives seemingly without goal or purpose, and yet which creates beautiful things as a mere by-product of its existence.

"Insects, animals, and humans are similar in the sense that they are born, they excrete, they reproduce, and die. Nevertheless, I myself am a man. I ask myself what differentiates humans from other animals. What is a human being? I look for the answer by continuing to make films. I don't think I have found the answer."—quoted from *Shohei Imamura: Human, All Too Human*, by Gilles Laprévotte, printed in *Shohei Imamura*, ed. James Quandt

His next, bolder steps towards finding this answer came in 1963 with *The Insect Woman*, a tale of a young country girl lured to the big city to find work as a prostitute. For this film, Imamura's approach was heavily influenced during the scriptwriting stage when the director noticed parallels between an insect circling his ashtray as he was drinking sake and the situation of the main character. *The Insect Woman* also marked a growing preoccupation with reality and its cinematic depiction. For this film, Imamura used a host of documentary techniques, such as live sound recording with hidden microphones and external location shooting, striving for the same kind of synergy between fiction and reality being explored by New Wave contemporaries such as the fascinating Susumu Hani. (Best known for his erotic drama *Inferno of First Love* (*Hatsukoi Jigoku-Hen*, 1968), Hani's previous cinematic explorations into Japanese society resulted in such films as *Bad Boys* (*Furyō Shōnen*, 1960), a docudrama investigating juvenile delinquency; *He and She* (*Kanojo to Kare*, 1963), focusing on the status of women in modern Japan; *Bwana Toshi* (*Bwana Toshi no Uta*, 1965), about a Japanese geologist in Kenya; and *The Bride of the Andes* (*Andesu no Hanayome*, 1966), set in a remote village in South America.)

Imamura's obsession with achieving documentary realism reached its apogee with *A Man Vanishes*, a film unfortunately little known abroad. It was the second of two films (after *The Pornographers*) during the '60s produced independently by the director, after he founded his own company, Imamura Productions, in 1965. Beginning ostensibly as a straightforward investigation into the disappearance of Tadashi Ōshima, who a year and a half prior to filming had evaporated into thin air leaving no trace as to his whereabouts, Imamura's film is a groundbreaking work in highlighting the limitations of rearranging reality within a filmic format in order to present the viewer with an apparently objective "truth." In accordance with Heisenberg's principle that an observed system inevitably reacts with its observer, immediate complications set in when Ōshima's real-life fiancée Yoshie starts falling for the actor. By the end of the film, Imamura has suggested that it is not only the investigation itself that is of interest rather than the solution to the actual mystery, but also that such attempts at investigating reality are compromised from their very offset.

A Man Vanishes is a fascinating investigation into cinematic form and function of the type that seems to have been rife in the '60s, though its production was not without problems. In order for the film to be made, it was necessary for the pivotal figure of Yoshie to take leave from her job for a year, taking an income from the filmmakers themselves and thus adopting a role unavoidably similar to that of an actress. Moreover, Imamura's use of hidden cameras in this instance raised serious ethical questions, and he admits that the film did ultimately end up hurting Yoshie's feelings.

Imamura's subsequent return to fiction with **The Profound Desire of the Gods**, proved problematic in its own right. In his perennial quest to discover the essence of what constitutes "Japaneseness," and following his own personal interest in social anthropology, Imamura relocated to the island of Kurage at the bottom of the Okinawan archipelago (known during the Edo period as Ryūkyū), the southernmost extremity of Japan, to shoot a drama revolving around a fictional community living there in almost Stone Age conditions. In this pre-rational society, ruled by ritual and superstition and where the weaker members of the tribes are ceremonially slaughtered, the deaf, dumb, and primitively sensuous Toriko acts as a shamaness, achieving union with the gods by sleeping indiscriminately with the other tribe members, including her brother. Into the milieu Imamura throws a Tokyo engineer, scouting the island to assess its suitability for the future development of an irrigation scheme.

Beginning with a tribal sacrifice to the gods in which a pig is thrown over the side of a fishing boat to be devoured by sharks, and ending with visions of this former tropical paradise adorned with Coca Cola cans, neon signs, and other such glittering ornaments of modernity as it succumbs to the inevitable forces of material capitalism, Imamura poses the same question as the French post-Impressionist artist Paul Gauguin, whose paintings of Tahitian islanders carried such titles as *Who are we? Where are we going? Where do we come from?* Gauguin's journal, *Noa Noa*, similarly focused on the dichotomy between civilization and barbarism.

Though often described as one of the director's most important works, this epically ambitious project was unfortunately a resounding flop at the box office, almost bankrupting Nikkatsu and making an effective endpoint to the Japanese New Wave of the '60s. The eighteen-month protracted shooting schedule had caused friction with the cast members, and Imamura became disillusioned with making feature films. Frustrated with the limitations of fiction, he retreated into documentary for the next nine years. The new format served the director well. It allowed him to relieve himself of all the baggage that fiction feature making involves by stripping down to a minimal crew of a cameraman, a sound recorder, and himself, thus earning a new flexibility and freedom in getting to the heart of the themes that so fascinated him.

Taking heed of George Orwell's idea in the novel *1984* that "Who controls the past controls the future; who controls the present controls the past," *A History of Post-War Japan as Told by a Bar Hostess* provides an alternate voice to the "official" history writers. Here the film's narrative backbone is provided by Onboro-san (real name Emiko Akaza), the bar hostess of the film's title. No attempt is made to conceal Imamura's editorial presence in this exploration of the relationship between subjective and objective history. Our earthy narrator, with her hair piled up in a makeshift beehive and bosom heaving beneath an open blouse, is seated in front of a projection screen by the director to deliver her own personal life story against a succession of newsreels segments, beginning with the bombing of Hiroshima (which happened when she was fifteen), and going on to detail such major events in the nation's history as the end of World War II, the U.S. Occupation, the repatriation of Japanese prisoners of war from Russia, the Korean War, the Vietnam War, and footage of the student protests that greeted the 1960 revision of the U.S.-Japan Security (Ampo) Treaty: a potted sequence of events of national importance running up to the year that the film was made.

The '70s saw Imamura at the helm of a string of illuminating documentaries, mainly made for television. *In Search of Unreturned Soldiers* is about former Japanese soldiers in Thailand who chose not to come home after the war. Two years later Imamura invited one of these back to Japan, covering his return in *Private Fujita Comes Home*.

Karayuki-san, the Making of a Prostitute focused on the reminiscences of an old woman living in Malaysia who had originally been sent out during Japan's colonial period at the beginning of the century as one of the thousands of girls who worked the brothels, tending to the needs of visiting Japanese merchants and soldiers. Imamura incorporated elements from *Karayuki-san* into his 1987 feature for Toei, *Zegen*, whose title translates as "pimp" or "panderer." The film is based on the autobiography of Iheiji Muraoka, an entrepreneur in the sex-trafficking business and a fervent patriot who set up a string of brothels stretching across Southeast Asia in anticipation of servicing the Emperor's invading forces.

Imamura regular Ken Ogata plays Muraoka, who in 1901 jumps ship and is washed ashore in Hong Kong penniless and destitute. Here he assimilates into the Japanese expatriate community and is soon set up as an apprentice barber. However, the Japanese Consulate there has higher goals for him in mind, and he is sent out to spy on Russian military activity in the Chinese province of Manchuria. His loyalty to the Emperor proven, the mission earns Muraoka enough to invest in his first brothel, and in the

following years he sets up a lucrative string of them running all the way down to Malaysia. Meanwhile his motherland's military activities, starting with the war against the Russians in 1904, begin to impinge seriously on both Muraoka and the girls who work for him, effectively isolating this Japanese community within their adopted homeland. When his long-term love interest begins to stray, Muraoka pitches himself into the task of expanding his own Japanese empire on foreign soil by vigorous attempts at procreating with his harem. By 1941 he has seemingly achieved his goal by setting up his own microcosm of Japanese society, surrounded by hordes of obediently submissive offspring. But the fruitlessness of his loyalty is revealed when the now old man is brushed aside by the Japanese troops that he rushes to greet as they invade Kuala Lumpur.

In 1975, Imamura set up the private film school the Yokohama Academy of Broadcasting and Film, now known as the Japan Academy of Moving Images and based in Shin-Yurigaoka, just south of Tokyo. Its alumni include Takashi Miike and Kazuo Hara, whose *The Emperor's Naked Army Marches On* (*Yuki Yukite Shingun*, 1987) shares similar concerns with Imamura's mid-period work, probably not too surprisingly, as it was produced and conceived by the older director, who is credited as the film's planner. This raw documentary focuses on Kenzō Okuzaki, a seventy-year-old World War II vet leading a one-man crusade against the Shōwa Emperor, asserting that Hirohito should be held accountable for the numerous atrocities committed under his name during the war. First hitting the headlines in 1969 for firing pachinko balls at the Emperor, Okuzaki's reminiscences culminate in revelations of cannibalism, when over the course of a failed expedition through New Guinea, all but 30 of his fellow soldiers were wiped out by malaria and starvation.

Imamura's return to feature making came when he started work in 1976 on *Vengeance Is Mine*, a screen adaptation of the non-fictional account by novelist Ryūzō Saki of a serial murderer who conducted a seventy-eight-day killing spree across the country during the '60s. Thematically one of the director's less typical works, the film does, however, retain certain stylistic traits. Its use of wide long shots with a minimum of edits lends some of the scenes the air of a TV news report, imbuing the depiction of the actual murders with a brutally objective coolness.

The involvement of Shochiku in the production ensured a more widespread distribution for *Vengeance Is Mine* than Imamura's previous films, and its critical and commercial success upon its release in 1979 for the first time brought significant attention to the director's name outside of Japan. Making regular use of leading man Ken Ogata, Imamura became one of the few old-school Japanese directors to keep up a fairly steady output throughout the course of the '80s, a notably troubled decade for the country's industry.

Vengeance Is Mine was followed in 1981 by **Eijanaika**, Imamura's first period piece. Set within the colorful carnival milieu of the slum-dwelling denizens of Edo on the eve of the Meiji Restoration, *Eijanaika* charts the collapse of the Tokugawa period and Japan's 300-year policy of isolationism from the vantage point of a handful of characters from society's lower orders.

If *Vengeance Is Mine* had marked the director's commercial breakthrough outside of Japan, it was his 1983 Cannes-winning adaptation of Shichirō Fukazawa's novel *The Ballad of Narayama* that cemented the director's international reputation. The story details the lives of inhabitants of a remote mountainous village in Nagano Prefecture. Food is scarce, and so tradition dictates that at the age of seventy the elder villagers must make the long journey up to the summit of Mt. Narayama to die, their lives sacrificed in order to ensure the survival of the village's younger inhabitants. Sixty-nine-year-old Orin wishes to see her son married and her family af-

fairs put straight before she agrees to make her final journey.

Originally adapted for the screen by Keisuke Kinoshita in 1958, Imamura's version reworks the rather macabre central concept from a radically different angle, without deviating too far from the central core of the narrative. Kinoshita's version is a heavily stylized kabuki-influenced rendition of the tale, shot in beautiful technicolor widescreen and filled with such hauntingly beautiful moments as the finale when the son carries his mother up to the mountain top, lit in a diffused golden light. In his version, however, Imamura sticks with the documentary-style realism for which he is known, filming on location in an abandoned village in Nagano Prefecture, its wooded environs teeming with wildlife.

Black Rain, not to be confused with Ridley Scott's glossy Osaka-bound thriller of the same name, was a black-and-white adaptation of two books by Masuji Ibuse (*Kuroi Ame* and *Yōhai Taichō*) focusing on the irradiated survivors of the Hiroshima bombing (the title refers to the radioactive fallout). Despite some negative criticism in Asia regarding Japan's wartime involvement, the film picked up a number of awards internationally.

Imamura made only a couple of films during the '90s, with a second Cannes win in 1997 ensuring *The Eel* widespread international distribution. Adopting a sedate approach, owing more to the restrained static framing of his early mentor Ozu than his own cinematic legacy, this tale of an ex-convict, the pet eel he took care of whilst in jail, and his subsequent attempts at redemption is an elliptical, slippery beast of a film that may prove rather difficult to get a hold on for viewers not familiar with the usual themes and concerns intrinsic to Imamura's work. At the time Imamura stated that it was to be his last film, but in the following year came *Dr. Akagi*, set in World War II, about an avuncular doctor whose blanket diagnoses of his patients is always hepatitis.

The Insect Woman

The film did not receive much in the way of distribution outside of Japan, unlike its successor, *Warm Water under a Red Bridge*, which, as its title suggests, is a deeply Freudian tale in which Kōji Yakusho goes in search of deep-sea treasure and instead finds himself involved with a mysterious woman who erupts into geysers of warm water from between her legs during the sexual act.

Like *The Eel*, also scripted by Imamura's son Daisuke Tengan, the results are watchable enough, but one is never quite sure what Imamura is trying to say with this film, or whether, having already mined the rich seam of his imagination in his previous works, he has reached rock bottom.

Even more oblique was the contribution to producer Alan Brigand's omnibus film *11'09"01 September 11* (2002), in which eleven directors from all around the world, including Sean Penn, Ken Loach, and Samira Makhmalbaf delivered an 11-minute 9-seconds and one frame short film based on the New York tragedy. Imamura's film, again scripted by Tengan, was the last in this ill-conceived project, and the only one not to mention 9/11 explicitly, focusing on a shell-shocked soldier who returns home from the trenches, becoming increasingly withdrawn, until he eventually reverts to the form of a snake that slithers into the water and disappears.

Imamura's sporadic output over the past decade has been far more laid-back and introspective than that of the main bulk of his work, increasingly retreating from his barbed observations of society into the realms of pure fantasy. It perhaps marks the final evolution in the director's style, a style which has covered a lot of ground over the past forty years, mapping out unique new territories of thematic expression and continuously pushing the boundaries in his investigation of the key ideas that inform his work.

The themes and obsessions explored throughout Imamura's diverse and ambitious oeuvre not only allow for crucial insights into the nature of Japanese society, but also address broader, more humanistic issues that are just as relevant to any nation and any era: the conflict between instinct and intellect; duty and desire; fiction and reality; objective written history and the fallibility of subjective human memory. These are all themes that are universal in their relevance, and for these reasons and many others, to overlook Imamura's unique vision would be a grave oversight.

↓ Intentions of Murder
赤い殺意
Akai Satsui
a.k.a. *Unholy Desire*

1964. CAST: Masumi Harukawa, Shigeru Tsuyuguchi, Kō Nishimura, Yoshi Katō, Yūko Kusunoki, Haruo Itoga. 150 minutes. RELEASES: VHS, Les Films De Ma Vie (France, French subtitles). Nikkatsu (Japan, no subtitles).

A dull-witted housewife is swept from her tenuous existence when an intruder breaks into the house and rapes her. She soon finds herself caught up in an adventure that leads to betrayal and attempted murder.

Based on a novel by Shinji Fujiwara, this lengthy thriller marks the most complete consolidation of the ideas that inform Imamura's initial cycle of features in the late '50s and early '60s. It also puts forward a strangely subversive view of "modern" Japan. Its tale of a low-caste household drudge who transcends her lowly status, not through any reaction against it, but rather by accepting her place within the order of things, sits at odds with the more traditional image of the family promoted in other films of the time.

Born of peasant stock, Sadako (Harukawa), the dull-witted and lumpen lynchpin of the piece, leads a thankless day-to-day existence tending the tumbledown shanty dwelling in the northern provincial city of Sendai that she inhabits with her unaffectionate common-law husband, Kōichi (Nishimura). Here she plays mother to Kōichi's son, Masaru, a child from a former marriage whom she cares for as if he were her own. Her prostitute grandmother and her lowly café waitress mother now dead (the latter having hung herself), Sadako dutifully and uncomplainingly accepts her thankless position within a society that she is only marginally a part of, as her shrewish mother-in-law regularly reminds her how lucky she is to have been taken into the household.

One day, when her husband is away at a work conference, the house is broken into by a thief, Hiraoka (Tsuyuguchi, the investigator searching for the missing man in the Imamura's *A Man Vanishes*, who later appeared in *Eijanaika*). The intruder rapes her and leaves with the words, "If you tell no one, no one will know." When Hiraoka returns a few days later, she yields once more. Finding herself pregnant by him, she allows herself to be tempted by his offer to leave her cramped and oppressive environment to start a new life in Tokyo with him. But is an uncertain future with a neurotic fugitive with a heart condition really what she desires?

The dim-witted Sadako makes for an unlikely heroine, a typically unrefined Imamura creation running counter to standard depictions of the female role within the Japanese family structure: that of either mothers or wives. Indeed, Imamura's ad hoc unit is the complete antithesis of the middle-class nuclear families being portrayed, for example, in the well-man-

Intentions of Murder

nered and immaculately turned-out works of his early mentor, Yasujirō Ozu.

Yet, despite her pudgy features and her slow and unaffected manner, the director obviously has a lot of respect and affection for his honest and well-meaning lead. Her unsophisticated yet vital presence is at odds with those of the weedy, devious men that surround her: her partner Kōichi is a sickly man often seen wearing a gauze mask, and his son Masaru's ability to continue the family name is later called into question. Kōichi refuses to grant her any official status through marriage, nor any legal claim to Masaru, and is meanwhile conducting an affair with his bookish, bespectacled library assistant.

Sensual and impulsive, Sadako's presence embodies a conflict between desire and duty, underscoring Imamura's recurrent maxim that there is a world of difference between the public face that the Japanese put forward and the individual, more instinctive side. Her giving herself over to pleasure during the initial assault is no male wish-fulfillment fantasy. It is a credible emotional reaction given that the attentions of her assailant represent the first time she has been treated as a sexual being, rather than just for her purely functional role within the makeshift family unit.

This conflict between simple biological urges and societal demands is immediately emphasized when, after being raped the first time, she makes the preliminary suicide preparations, as custom dictates. Then she is distracted by the rumbling of her stomach, and so she gets up to prepare some food. By the time she has fed herself, Masaru has returned from school and it is back to domesticity again, her original intention forgotten.

Typical for the director, our heroine's plight is objectified by way of reference to the animal kingdom, most overtly in Masaru's pet white mouse that futilely spins around in its wheel in the corner of the cluttered apartment symbolizing her inability to escape from the cycle forged by her female predecessors, whilst adding a further dynamism to the already busy shot compositions (Masaru is constantly hyperactive, running or leaping in the background in the domestic scenes in the cramped living room). The silkworm motif is also crucial. After being raped, Sadako has a flashback to her childhood, in which she is angrily scolded by her mother for playing with one that is crawling along her thigh. The meaning of this cryptic image becomes a lot clearer at the film's coda.

Another motif is the encroachment of new technology upon the lives of his characters, running concurrent with Japan's rapid modernization. The frequent crashing past of the express train along the track that borders the bottom of the garden, ominously sounding its horn at key dramatic points in the film, initially suggests that such new developments are to be seen as an oppressive force, hemming Sadako in, and with her the lower-class neighbors in their cramped rows of houses. However, when Sadako flees with Hiraoka by this means of transport, the film opens up considerably into a stunningly shot snowscape, hinting that these same forces can also provide a means of escape. Similarly, in an early scene the heroine is seen failing to cope with the new sewing machine delivered to the house, though by the end of the film, she has mastered it. The pendulum having come full swing, Sadako may have been pitched on her adventure by forces beyond her control, but she is more in control after the rape than she ever was beforehand.

Beautifully photographed in widescreen monochrome and technically polished, still, upon an initial viewing Imamura's film seems a little unwieldy and cluttered, with a plethora of flashbacks, narrative dead ends, and dream sequences permeating its lengthy running time. Approaching *Intentions of Murder* both requires and rewards a good deal of patience on the part of the viewer, but though admittedly long, upon further analysis it is a faultlessly constructed model of sophistication, which uses its messy appearance to suggest that beneath the ordered chaos of modernity with all of its artificial constraints, it is characters such as Sadako that provide the beating heart that enables society to continue.

↓ A Man Vanishes
人間蒸発
Ningen Jōhatsu

1967. CAST: Yoshie Hayakawa, Shigeru Tsuyuguchi, Shōhei Imamura, Sayoko Hayakawa
130 minutes.

In a fascinating exploration of cinema's ability or inability to depict truth, Imamura blurs the lines between fiction and non-fiction in a meticulous and groundbreaking manner that few "mockumentaries" since have been able to equal.

Following his experiments with documentary techniques in his previous film *The Insect Woman*, Shōhei Imamura set out to further explore cinema's grip on reality with this 1967 pseudo-documentary.

The film takes the form of an investigation into the whereabouts of one Tadashi Ōshima, who vanished in 1965 and was never heard from again. His fiancée, Yoshie Hayakawa, is followed by Imamura and crew as she queries Ōshima's friends, family, and colleagues in a search for clues and impressions. Accompanying Hayakawa, and doing most of the actual enquiring, is the actor Shigeru Tsuyuguchi, who functions as the film's anchor, whereas the young woman's role is mostly limited to standing by the side and asking the occasional question.

Several possibilities are given for Ōshima's disappearance. It comes to light that he might have taken part in the embezzlement of 400,000 yen from his employer and that he had been involved with another woman, which comes as news to Yoshie. This woman subsequently dumped him for a more successful rival, and she tells them that this might have been the reason for his disappearance. In the process of uncovering the truth behind her fiancé's evaporation (the literal translation of the word *jōhatsu*), Yoshie also discovers many things about him as a person. When they visit a spiritual medium, the old lady tells them that Ōshima might actually be dead and that Yoshie's elder sister Sayoko might have something to do with his disappearance. Sayoko is a former geisha who has always been much more comfortable around men than Yoshie, a fact that has caused a long-standing conflict between the two sisters.

But just as we start thinking that this might become a document about the nature of relationships, Imamura pulls the rug out from under us. Cracks start to appear in the non-fictional surface. The use of multiple camera angles in some scenes already suggests a certain degree of manipulation on the part of the director, as of course does the presence of Tsuyuguchi. At one point Imamura and the crew confer about Yoshie's role in the making of the documentary, particularly her changing behavior. Suspicions arise that she might be using the camera crew to paint a certain picture of herself and of her vanished fiancé, and that *she* is in fact manipulating the proceedings. Subsequently they realize that Yoshie has in fact fallen in love with her fellow investigator Tsuyuguchi. Soon the question arises: are we still watching a documentary if the role of the supposedly impartial camera becomes more than observer?

Further testament to the fictional nature of the film comes in the guise of a storytelling device Imamura would also employ in his next film: the McGuffin. *A Man Vanishes* is not about the man who vanished or even why he did so.

It's also not about the effects the disappearance has on Yoshie or on Ōshima's family and friends. At the end of the film we still don't know exactly what has happened to him, and this fits in with Imamura's intentions. In a scene that is as pivotal as it is unforgettable, the sisters Yoshie and Sayoko confront each other in what seems like a tea house. At one point in the increasingly heated discussion, in which Sayoko keeps denying the accusations that she might have been more involved with Ōshima beyond simply being his future sister-in-law, Imamura appears in the room and poses the audience the question: "What is truth?" Subsequently, the walls of the tea house are lifted away and it is revealed that the whole scene took place on a soundstage. "Tomorrow they will start filming another work of fiction here," the director declares, voicing the conclusion of his experiment. From the start, *A Man Vanishes* has been an investigation into cinema's inherent inability to depict "truth." The film is a work of fiction about non-fiction, rather than a work of non-fiction, period.

A Man Vanishes predates by eight years Orson Welles' similar *F for Fake*, which is often seen as the first film to overtly draw attention to cinema's inability to depict the truth. But despite its incontestable status as a seminal work, the fact that *A Man Vanishes* remained unseen outside Japan for decades has kept it from receiving the recognition it deserves. It wasn't until a 2001 retrospective of the director's work at the French Cinémathèque in Paris that a subtitled version was projected on a foreign screen (followed by a belated but very welcome limited cinema release in the spring of 2002).

As its subject matter would suggest, *A Man Vanishes* is indeed a fascinating film, as much for its investigation into the relationship between cinema and reality as for its ability to enthrall the viewer as a work of fiction. Precisely because Imamura is not afraid to hide the fact that this is in the end a work of fiction (though all the individuals in it as well as the actual disappearance are, as far as one can tell, real), the film does a rather good job in building up tension and involving the viewer in the goings-on. *A Man Vanishes* works as a documentary, as an experiment, and as narrative fiction, which is a very rare combination indeed.

↓ The Profound Desire of the Gods
神々の深き欲望
Kamigami no Fukaki Yokubō
a.k.a. *Kuragejima: Tales from a Southern Island*

1968. CAST: Kazuo Kitamura, Rentarō Mikuni, Chōichirō Kawarazaki, Hideko Okiyama, Kanjūrō Arashi. 165 minutes.

In this landmark Imamura film, the director continues his exploration of the true identity of the Japanese by showing a primitive island community's reactions to the impending menace of modernization. Impressive, epic, and wholly original.

An engineer from Tokyo arrives on Kuragejima ("Jellyfish Island") with the task of finding a water source to support the construction of a factory. At the center of the island's primitive community is a family led by a gray-haired patriarch who welcomes the engineer with open arms, proclaiming him to be a "god from overseas."

The old man has an iron grip on his kin: His son has been put to the tantalizing task of removing a gigantic boulder from the backyard, which he is forced to do with a chain around his ankle. His daughter takes care of domestic affairs, aided as far as possible by her own mentally challenged daughter, Toriko, whose uninhibited sex drive makes her a target for much of the male island population. The grandson, meanwhile, is spurred on to assist the engineer, with visions of a future career looming on the horizon.

The engineer, who spends much of his time cursing the island, its inhabitants, and its sweltering climate, goes about his business with little regard for local customs and tradition. The boy entrusted in his service by the patriarch is more than once put to the test when he is ordered to perform tasks like cutting down a sacred tree. Inevitably the engineer is confronted with resistance in the form of sabotage, and soon his only allies on the island are the old man and the granddaughter, who has been lusting after him from the beginning, but whose advances he has consistently rebuffed.

When the engineer finally gives in to Toriko's primitive charms (or persistence) and agrees to marry her, this turns out to be one of the picture's most crucial moments. But it's crucial in a rather unexpected way, as from this moment on, the character of the engineer virtually disappears from the story and is only occasionally glimpsed smoking and sweating in the background, not taking part in the action. What for a long time appeared to be our main character turns out to be of only peripheral importance: a classic McGuffin once again. Imamura's aim is not to denounce progress, but to portray the process of change among the islanders themselves. The advent of change, in the shape of the engineer, is a given. What matters here is how the people of Kurage Island deal with it amongst themselves and what their reactions say about them as members of a culture and their community.

The portrayal of this intra-societal process is another example of Imamura's fascination with social anthropology, particularly his search for the 'true' spirit of the Japanese. By setting his story in a more primitive environment, he allows himself to make a seemingly more fundamental statement about this spirit than in a modern-day milieu. Throughout, parallels and comparisons are made between modern civilization and its more primitive roots, with the message that those roots constitute our true selves. The film opens with a series of shots of animals wriggling in shallow water, while that water—the most basic source of life—is what brings the engineer from bustling Tokyo and what will support the industrial progress in his wake. The islanders are

Profound Desire of the Gods

the medium point between these two extremes: human beings who have advanced to the point of living in regulated communities, but who still live side-by-side with lower animal life.

Interestingly enough, however, his comparisons also go the other way. Imamura also puts elements of modern-day life in the primitive environment, most notably in the structure of the family. The head of the family's admiration for a representative of corporate life, how he urges his grandson to make a career (making him a slave in a figurative sense, where the young man's father is one in the literal sense—as signaled by the sounds of clanging chains when the engineer orders the boy to cut down the tree), and how the women are relegated to handling the domestic chores—this hierarchy was far from unusual in post-war Japanese family life. Here it also forms the basis of a family from a far more primitive society. But reversed comparisons or

not, Imamura's intention of revealing the essence of his countrymen remains the same.

The Profound Desire of the Gods is not a film that denounces industrial progress or makes environmentalist statements. In true Imamura fashion, it's not the conflict or the politics that matters, but what goes on underneath: the human behavior they normally tend to obscure.

↓ Eijanaika
ええじゃないか
Eejanaika
a.k.a. *Why Not?*

1981. CAST: Kaori Momoi, Shigeru Izumiya, Ken Ogata, Shigeru Tsuyuguchi, Masao Kusakari 151 minutes. RELEASES: DVD, Platinum (Hong Kong, English/Chinese subtitles).

With an epic sweep and flourish, Imamura portrays the events leading up to the Meiji Restoration from the worm's-eye view of Edo's peasant community.

"I am a country farmer, Ōshima is a samurai," Imamura once told Audie Bock (quoted in *Notes for a Study on Shohei Imamura*, by Donald Richie, printed in *Shohei Imamura*). Though both directors come from well-educated, middle-class backgrounds, the contrast Imamura was actually trying to draw with his fellow leading light from the Japanese New Wave of the '60s was one of approach, rather than a biographical one. In Nagisa Ōshima's films, the characters act as individual agents of change who frequently come head to head against the establishment. Imamura's seem to exist beneath such social strictures and are seldom the engineers of their own fates.

The comparison is best highlighted by the two films the individual directors made surrounding Japan's turbulent transition to a modern nation in the years leading up to the beginning of the Meiji Restoration in 1868. The shift saw the opening up of ports to foreign traders after almost three hundred years of self-imposed isolation during the Tokugawa period (1600–1867); the relocation of the capital from Kyoto to Tokyo (formerly known as Edo); the collapse of the military dictatorship of the Baku-fu shogunate; the restoration of the Meiji Emperor as a single state figurehead; and the shift to an industrial society from an agrarian one, where individual semi-autonomous territories were run along feudal lines by *daimyō* overlords who extracted crippling taxes from the peasants for the right to work their land. The catalysts for this sweeping national change were the slow trickle of foreigners into the country after the arrival of the American Commodore Matthew Calbraith Perry with his "black ships" in 1853, seeking trade between the two nations, and the rise of the anti-Bakufu forces of the Tosa, Satsuma, and Chōshū clans, who sought to revive the direct rule of the imperial line. The cry *sonnō jōi* ("Revere the emperor and repel the barbarians!") was soon ringing throughout the nation.

The drama of Ōshima's *Gohatto* was centered around infighting and pederasty in the upper ranks of the pro-Bakufu forces of the Shinsengumi in Kyoto, symbolizing the inward self-destruction of the old order. Imamura's *Eijanaika* dwells in the ribald arena of the peasant classes swept along by the tides of change. The film, whose title translates loosely as "Why not?" or "What the hell?" takes its influence from the slogan chanted by the processions of rioters from the lower orders who ran wild through the streets of Edo prior to the dawn of the Meiji Restoration. It celebrates the ebullient forces of a society in flux, unleashed by the sudden collapse of tradition and the dawn of an infinite array of new opportunities in its absence.

The location is Edo, 1867. The hero of Imamura's film is Genji. Picked up by an American ship after being shipwrecked and returning to Japanese shores after a six-year sojourn in the United States, he finds himself immediately thrown into jail. Upon his release, he returns home to find that his wife, Ine, has been sold by his family. Genji tracks her down in a carnival sideshow run by the opportunistic merchant Kinzō, where she is performing a lewd stage act entitled "tickle the goddess," hiking up her kimono to a baying crowd who attempt to blow paper streamers between her legs. After buying out Ine's contract, Genji makes plans to move to America, the land of opportunity, with his newly reconciled spouse, but first he has to raise his $50 passage to be paid to the American forces. Ine, however, is teetering on the decision to accompany him.

Meanwhile, inflation is running rampant, with the price of rice escalating insanely on a daily basis. The tension builds, until the rioting unwashed inhabitants of the riverside carnival break over the symbolic Rubicon of the Edo River to the forbidden upper-class area on the other side of the Ryōgoku Bridge, the forces of a sector of the population who no longer have anything to lose exploding in a display of spectacular folly.

Eijanaika is an epic film in every respect. Every shot seems crowded around the margins and teeming with life, the exterior scenes filled with hordes of extras and the action filmed in narrow-angle telephoto shots zeroed in from afar to flatten the perspective. The main forestory, as Ine oscillates between Genji and her former pimp, Kinzō, really only takes up a small proportion of the proceedings, which cover such subsidiary events as a riot at a silk house and the plotting of the downfall of the Tokugawa shogunate by the anti-Bafuku forces as they purchase weapons from the American traders. Incident piles upon incident, with the seemingly random accumulation of peripheral detail giving the impression of a whole broader world off-frame.

But period detail is not so crucial here. Imamura doesn't attempt to recount or reinterpret historical events. He instead gives us a social context, an ethnological snapshot of the mentality of a particular milieu at a particular time. His is a film of color and exuberance, a depiction of a tumultuous society where anything can happen. In the early scenes in the carnival sideshow tent, a woman extends her neck six feet in the air, like a snake, whilst another breathes fire. A couple of turban-wearing Indians roam the streets with a large elephant in tow. Genji croons the lyrics to "Sweet Chariot" whilst Ine accompanies him on the shamisen, as he attempts to seduce her to take this voyage of opportunity across the waves away from her homeland.

Eijanaika in many ways is the culmination of one of Imamura's most consistent ideas, of reinterpreting history through the viewpoint of those most immediately affected by it. He shows the Japanese spirit as he sees it—stubborn, obstinate, but brimming with an unquenchable zest for life. *Eijanaika* is unique in the respect that it was made at a time when Shochiku had enough money to mount such spectacles. Imamura would only attain such a degree of scale again with *Zegen*.

↓ The Eel
うなぎ
Unagi

1997. CAST: Kōji Yakusho, Misa Shimizu, Akira Emoto, Shō Aikawa, Tomorowo Taguchi. 117 minutes. RELEASE: DVD, New Yorker Films (U.S., English subtitles). Ocean Shores (Hong Kong, English and Chinese subtitles), Films Sans Frontières (France, French subtitles).

Absorbingly funny and at times surreal study of an ex-con's attempts to adjust to life outside prison walls. Winner of the Palme d'Or in Cannes, *The Eel* helped usher in a new wave of Western interest in Japanese cinema.

Businessman Yamashita receives an anonymous letter, telling him that a strange man visits his wife whenever he's out at night fishing. After pondering for a long time, he sets out for the seaside one night with the intention of returning early and finding out the truth. Indeed he finds his wife in bed with a stranger, enjoying herself with an abandon Yamashita has never experienced. In a daze, he enters the bedroom with a knife in his hand and kills his wife. Several hours later he walks into the police station, covered in her blood, and turns himself in.

After serving eight years in prison, he is released into the care of his parole officer, an elderly priest who brings him to a deserted barbershop in the priest's hometown. There the former salaryman can ply the new trade he learnt in captivity. Upon his release, Yamashita takes with him only the clothes on his back and the eel he raised in the prison pond. To the institutionalized and alienated Yamashita, the eel serves as a way to avoid communicating with others. But the men of the small, desolate town soon start frequenting his shop, mostly because they have nothing better to do, and a circle of friends quickly forms around the shy, introverted barber.

While out fishing, he saves the life of Keiko, a woman attempting to commit suicide after a disastrous relationship with a scheming boyfriend who used her to get to her mother's money. This act may put Yamashita right in the cosmic scheme of things—he took a life and saved one—but for himself things only become more complicated. It does, however, prove to be a turning point. A few days later, Keiko is assisting him in his barbershop and the possibility of something resembling a normal life is opening up to him. He's not too eager to embrace it, but since both are carrying the weight of a dark past, a bond inevitably forms which grows stronger when both their pasts come back to haunt them. In his case it's a fellow convict who has been put to work as the local garbage man and who threatens to spill the beans on Yamashita's past. In her case, freeloading boyfriend Dōjima is back with several cronies, a lawyer, and a demand for money.

For a study of one man's emotions, *The Eel* seems to make little effort to penetrate its protagonist's mind. As in real life, Yamashita's behavior is our only lead. Occasional voice-overs provide glimpses into his psyche, but Imamura's method of detailing the inner life of his protagonist is done in a rather more indirect fashion, with extensive use of symbolism. The most obvious example is the eel, which in a parallel to Yamashita lives a lonesome and sheltered life in his tank, without the need or the will to communicate with the outside world (the metaphor is somewhat redundantly explained in the final moments of the film). Rather more interestingly executed is the character of local garbage man and fellow convict Tamasaki, who functions as the personification of Yamashita's insecurities and self-doubt. His behavior and actions are irrational and erratic, and when he pops up trouble is never far off.

Based on a novel by Akira Yoshimura and scripted by Imamura and his son Daisuke Tengan (the later screenwriter of Takashi Miike's *Audition*), *The Eel* may lack the social relevance of the director's earlier work, but as a surreal comedy of manners it is quite irresistible.

CHAPTER 3
Kinji Fukasaku
深作欣二

In the beginning there was the bomb. Although he was fifteen years old when it fell, to all intents and purposes the roots of Kinji Fukasaku the artist can be traced back to the dropping of the atomic bombs on Hiroshima and Nagasaki, which signaled Japan's surrender at the end of World War II.

In the work of Kinji Fukasaku, the mushroom cloud, whose image fills the opening shot of his most celebrated film *Battles without Honor and Humanity*, symbolizes not just destruction but liberation. The chaos and anarchy that resulted from the devastation of the old rules and values created the freedom to start anew, releasing an energy that is embodied in the outrageous, riotous, and above all violent actions of his protagonists.

The paradox is that Fukasaku was anything but a supporter of the way Japan set about rebuilding itself in the post-war years. His films were openly critical of the official government policy of reconstruction, the director feeling on the one hand that it left too many people by the roadside and on the other hand that it curbed and eventually destroyed the energy and freedom the bomb had unleashed.

The break with old values was lived very consciously by Kinji Fukasaku himself. In the last years of the war he found himself put to work in a munitions factory to aid the war effort. The factory was a target for American bombing raids, and Fukasaku has said that it was only because he hid beneath the dead bodies of his friends and co-workers that he managed to survive. Clearly, the old system that made him bury his own friends, many of them teenagers like him, had not made a very positive impression on him.

Like many of his countrymen, he found a way to escape the hardships of life in the ruined streets of immediate post-war Japan by going to the cinema. In 1949, inspired by the films of Akira Kurosawa and the spate of foreign films that found their way into Japanese cinemas as a result of the American occupation, he went to study film at Nihon University, where he founded a ciné-club with his friend and later collaborator Koreyoshi Kurahara. He joined Toei studios in 1953 and started an apprenticeship that culminated in his directorial debut in 1961.

To prove his mettle, he first directed two pairs of B-pictures, each of them about an hour in length. Often regarded as little more than preparation for his first real feature, which he would make later the same year, the four films were nevertheless interesting for two reasons. First, their lead actor, then a newcomer who had also made his debut that year, was future action star and frequent Fukasaku collaborator Shinichi "Sonny" Chiba. Second, and more importantly, the films were contemporary action dramas. At the time Toei specialized in *jidai-geki* or period costume dramas, and Fukasaku's choice to make action films in a contemporary setting immediately set him apart from the mainstream.

The setting was no accident. The expression of the chaotic post-war energy was already very much on his mind and there was no other way he could express it but in films with a contemporary storyline. His films became the expression not only of that unbridled energy, translating itself into action, violence, and rebellion, but also of his dissatisfaction with the government's policies for the reconstruction of Japan, which by the early 1960s was in full swing.

> "The most important objective for the government at the time was to really rebuild Japan, so in that sense you may consider the attitude of that government progressive. However, if you put the spotlight on the people, and on the situation I went through, I could not help being very interested in the fact that the people were actually going in the opposite direction, as a result of the government's banner of the reconstruction of Japan. The government was very keen on, and preoccupied with, the reconstruction of Japan and rapid economic growth. But I had doubts. Under that kind of situation where would the government be taking the whole nation? What direction are they taking us? Those were the questions I could never shake off and I even felt resistance to what was going on."

His early films like *Greed in Broad Daylight* (his official debut feature from 1961) and *Wolves, Pigs, and Men* are set largely in slums, where the protagonists battle it out amongst themselves over stolen loot while the dirt poor slum dwellers are reduced to being bystanders or downright ignored, much as they were by the "progressive" government in real life. His 1967 film *The Breakup* made the obvious point of contrasting the shanty towns on one side of the river with the gleaming chemical plant on

© 1978 Toei Company, Ltd.

Shogun's Samurai

the other. As time and economic development went on, Fukasaku started replacing the ruins and slums with heaps of trash and refuse, the by-products of this economic miracle the government was so eager to promote.

His protagonists, too, were outcasts, people ignored by the economic machine. *Greed in Broad Daylight* features a motley crew of foreigners attempting to hold up an armored transport, while a group of displaced young punks were the central characters of 1968's *Call Me Blackmail!*.

Fukasaku's resistance may have been strong, but it was ultimately, and perhaps inherently, futile. In 1964 the rebuilt and reborn Japan delivered its crowning achievements in the shape of the *Shinkansen* bullet train and the Tokyo Olympics, which allowed the world to see exactly how radical the changes and improvements in Japan had been since the war.

The futility also found its way into Fukasaku's films, by way of his characters. By the mid 1960s Toei had started specializing in formulaic yakuza films that came to be known as the *ninkyō eiga* or chivalry films. Set in pre-war Japan, they featured gangster protagonists who were the embodiments of valor and honor (*jingi*).

Although he was known as a specialist in crime and gangster films, the *ninkyō* films were incompatible with Fukasaku's very contemporary concerns. The *ninkyō* films were set in the pre-war period and expressed and celebrated old-time values. Their heroes were traditionally minded men whose enemies were more often than not presented as more modern gangsters. The hero's weapon of choice was the *katana* sword, with which he would invariably defeat an entire gang of men sporting firearms. The *ninkyō* formula pitted tradition versus progress,

and to offer Japanese audiences some respite from their increasingly Westernized surroundings, the former always won.

A clear example of the difference between Fukasaku's work and the *ninkyō* formula can be found in *Wolves, Pigs, and Men*, in which lead actor Ken Takakura plays a vile brute who tortures his own brother to extract information on the whereabouts of a bag of money. After making the film, Takakura starred in his first *ninkyō* picture and promptly became the genre's top star, the embodiment of the honorable, upstanding gangster hero.

Fukasaku's work increasingly moved in the opposite direction. The chaotic energy his characters exuded became only greater, their betrayals and violent reprisals more intense, and their actions had less and less to do with honor. Most

Filmography

1961
- The Drifting Detective (*Fūraibō Tantei: Akai Tani no Sangeki*)
- The Drifting Detective II (*Fūraibō Tantei: Misaki o Wataru Kuroi Kaze*)
- Vigilante in the Funky Hat (*Fankii Hatto no Kaidanji*)
- Vigilante in the Funky Hat: The 200,000-Yen Arm (*Fankii Hatto no Kaidanji: Nisenman En no Ude*)
- Greed in Broad Daylight (*Hakuchū no Buraikan*) (a.k.a. High Noon for Gangsters)

1962
- The Proud Challenge (*Hokori Takaki Chōsen*)
- Gyangu Tai G Men

1963
- Gang Alliance (*Gyangu Dōmei*)

1964
- Jakoman to Tetsu
- Wolves, Pigs and Men (*Ōkami to Buta to Ningen*)

1965

- Odoshi
- Kamikaze Yarō: Mahiru no Kettō
- Hokkai no Abare Ryū

1967
- The Breakup (*Kaisanshiki*)

1968
- Bakuto Kaisanshiki
- Black Lizard (*Kurotokage*)
- Call Me Blackmail! (*Kyōkatsu Koso ga Waga Jinsei*) (a.k.a. Blackmail Is My Life)
- Green Slime (*Ganma 3 Gō: Uchū Daisakusen*)

1969
- Black Rose Mansion (*Kurobara no Yakata*)
- Japan Organized Crime Boss (*Nihon Bōryokudan: Kumichō*)

1970
- Chizome no Daimon
- If You Were Young: Rage (*Kimi ga Wakamono Nara*)
- Tora! Tora! Tora! [co-directed with Richard Fleischer and Toshio Masuda]

1971
- Sympathy for the Underdog

(*Bakuto Gaijin Butai*)

1972
- Under the Flag of the Rising Sun (*Gunki Hatameku Moto Ni*) (a.k.a. Under the Fluttering Military Flag)
- Street Mobster (*Gendai Yakuza: Hitokiri Yota*)
- Hitokiri Yota: Kyōken Sankyōdai

1973
- Battles without Honor and Humanity (*Jingi naki Tatakai*) (a.k.a. Fight without Honor / The Yakuza Papers / Tarnished Code of the Yakuza)
- Battles without Honor and Humanity: Tarnished Loyalty in Hiroshima (*Jingi naki Tatakai: Hiroshima Shitō Hen*)
- Battles without Honor and Humanity: War without Honor (*Jingi naki Tatakai: Dairi Sensō*)

1974
- Battles without Honor and Humanity: Operation Summit (*Jingi naki Tatakai: Chōjō Sakusen*)

of all, they never got what they were after. This latter point is particularly important in light of Fukasaku's acknowledgement of the futility of his own battle. By the early 1970s, Fukasaku's protagonists were doomed to failure, misery, or death. This is as true for his gangster films as for the movies he made outside the genre. His first two independent productions, *If You Were Young: Rage* (1970) and **Under the Flag of the Rising Sun** (1972), were both non-genre films, but their protagonists followed the same path as their gangster colleagues. *If You Were Young: Rage* told the story of a small group of unemployed friends who decide to start their own business, but as the hardships increase, their camaraderie becomes increasingly strained, resulting in friction, fights, and eventually death. *Under the Flag of the Rising Sun*, a powerful anti-war drama, fo-

cuses on a war widow's futile attempts to obtain a military pension from the government. In trying to build a case for her appeal, she comes to learn about the horrors her husband suffered on the front, as well as the true face of the country's contemporary bureaucracy.

But it was in his gangster films of that same period that Fukasaku's themes and concerns found their apogee. *Street Mobster* and *Battles without Honor and Humanity* positively bellowed with rage, energy, vitality, and the frustration of a hopeless fight. By this time, the dark side of the country's economic progress had come to light in the shape of a number of industrial pollution scandals, the most headline grabbing of which was the Minamata mercury poisoning affair. People had started to become aware of the drawbacks and began expressing their dissatisfaction.

- Battles without Honor and Humanity: A Change of the Underworld Supreme Ruler (*Jingi naki Tatakai: Kanketsu Hen*)
- New Battles without Honor and Humanity (*Shin Jingi naki Tatakai*)

1975
- Graveyard of Honor (*Jingi no Hakaba*)
- Cops vs. Thugs (*Kenkei Tai Soshiki Bōryoku*)
- Shikingen Gōdatsu
- New Battles without Honor and Humanity: It's Time to Kill the Boss (*Shin Jingi naki Tatakai: Kumichō no Kubi*)

1976
- Bōsō Panikku: Daigekitotsu
- New Battles without Honor and Humanity: The Boss's Final Day (*Shin Jingi naki Tatakai: Kumichō Saigo no Hi*)
- Yakuza Graveyard (*Yakuza no Hakaba: Kuchinashi no Hana*)

1977
- Hokuriku Proxy War (*Hokuriku Dairi Sensō*)

- The Detective Doberman (*Dōberuman Deka*)

1978
- Shogun's Samurai (*Yagyū Ichizoku no Inbō*) (a.k.a. *The Yagyu Conspiracy*)
- Message from Space (*Uchū Kara no Messēji*)
- The Fall of Ako Castle (*Akō-Jō Danzetsu*)

1980
- Virus (*Fukkatsu no Hi*) (a.k.a. Day of Resurrection)

1981
- Gate of Youth (*Seishun no Mon*) [co-directed with Koreyoshi Kurahara]

1982
- Samurai Reincarnation (*Makai Tensei*)
- Dōtonborigawa
- Fall Guy (*Kamata Kōshin Kyoku*)

1983
- Theater of Life (*Jinsei Gekijō*) [co-directed with Junya Satō and Sadao Nakajima]
- Legend of Eight Samurai

(*Satomi Hakkenden*)

1984
- Shanghai Rhapsody (*Shanghai Bansukingu*)

1986
- House on Fire (*Kataku no Hito*)

1987
- Sure Death 4 (*Hissatsu 4: Urami Harashimasu*)
- The Rage of Love (*Hana no Ran*)

1992
- The Triple Cross (*Itsuka Gira-Gira Suru Hi*)

1994
- Crest of Betrayal (*Chūshingura Gaiden: Yotsuya Kaidan*)

1999
- The Geisha House (*Omocha*)

2000
- Battle Royale

2003
- Battle Royale II—Requiem (*Battoru Rowaiaru II: Chinkonka*) [co-directed with Kenta Fukasaku]

Graveyard of Honor

The student riots of the 1960s had by now made way for more organized urban terrorist groups like the numerous Red Army factions.

In this climate, the *ninkyō* films, which had enjoyed several years of great success, were starting to look very stale indeed. The hugely successful release of Fukasaku's *Battles without Honor and Humanity* in 1973 was their death knell. The false picture the *ninkyō* films painted of organized crime was expressed in the film's title alone. In the film's opening scene, a gangster character carrying a *katana* sword finds himself faced with half a dozen gun-wielding opponents and is unceremoniously shot. Fukasaku was not just lambasting Japan's society, but its cinema as well.

Street Mobster and especially *Battles without Honor and Humanity* are quite rightly seen as the epitome of Fukasaku's oeuvre. They are the most completely realized expressions of all the themes and concerns that characterize his work. The films were symbols, metaphoric entities for what Fukasaku was trying to say. Their protagonists, played in both films by Bunta Sugawara, are the products as well as the embodiments of postwar chaotic energy (the lead character of *Street Mobster* was very significantly born on August 15, 1945, the day of Japan's capitulation). They are gangsters freshly released from jail who acknowledge that their fights are futile and that their world—the world of anarchy, energy, and opportunity—has disappeared, to be replaced by corporate structure and surface respectability. Their old gangs have merged with those who were once their enemies and are deeply intertwined with government affairs. Their reaction to this changed world is one of brutal, almost spastic violence, but against the combined powers of state, corporation, and respectability, a single man is bound to lose. That single man is Fukasaku and that now-respectable gang is Japan. The former spits his venom, in outrage over being betrayed by the country that once expected him to sacrifice his life, but which has now molded itself in the image of the former enemy.

Fukasaku's concerns translated themselves not only into characters and story, but also into the style of his films. Shot in the streets with mostly handheld cameras, this style is reminiscent of the work of the French New Wave directors and of their American followers like William Friedkin and Martin Scorsese, who combined the stylistic traits of the new wave with the B-movie and genre subject matter of American directors like Sam Fuller and Don Siegel. Friedkin's *The French Connection* (1971) is perhaps the closest Western comparison to Fukasaku's films of the same period. But whereas the visual style of the Americans and French was aimed at lending the films a degree of documentary realism, Fukasaku's style originates from a different source. It's the raw, anarchic abandon of the protagonists that is expressed by Fukasaku's extensive use of handheld cameras, lopsided angles, and rapid editing.

Fukasaku has professed to having been influenced by the French New Wave, but the influence lies in the method, not in the intention. In fact, only a few years prior to *Battles without Honor and Humanity*, Fukasaku made a departure into pure style-over-substance with a pair of hyper-stylized films starring female impersonator Akihiro Maruyama. Made while the director was on loan to Shochiku studios (perhaps Toei was unsure what to do with this director who would not fit into their then dominant *ninkyō* film production line), **Black Lizard** and *Black Rose Mansion* are both high camp exercises in style and have very little apparent connection with the crime films he'd made up until then. Garishly colored sets and costumes vie for attention while the glamorous Maruyama takes center stage.

"I was very attached to Mishima's literature. I remember talking with him about making this film with Akihiro Maruyama. He was very happy that this actor was selected to play the role. The play was written about ten years before Maruyama started playing it on stage and the role was played by many other female stars like Yaeko Mizutani and Machiko Kyō, who were not particularly interesting in it. Mishima was very fond of the production in which Akihiro Maruyama performed. Rather than those great actresses, and despite Maruyama not being a veteran stage actor, Mishima seemed very, very happy and felt closest to his play through the performance of Maruyama. I too felt very moved by Maruyama's performance in the stage production of *Black Lizard*. I really enjoyed his performance far more than those of any of the other so-called stars, female stars. I mentioned this to Mishima and I remember we had a really interesting, warm exchange when I talked about that with him."

Interestingly it was uncharacteristic works like *Black Lizard* and a trio of science fiction films that first made Fukasaku's name in the West. Perhaps facilitated by their partly American casts, *The Green Slime* (with Richard Jaeckel), *Message from Space* (co-starring Vic Morrow) and *Virus* (featuring Glenn Ford, Henry Silva, Robert Vaughn, and a theme song by Janis Ian) all found distribution in the United States, albeit in truncated, English-dubbed versions that removed many of the subtleties that marked them as Fukasaku films.

The Green Slime was, like *Black Lizard* and *Black Rose Mansion*, a sidestep made during the period that Toei focused much of its attention on *ninkyō* films. This period also saw the director helming the impressive aerial battle scenes of the Japanese/American co-production *Tora! Tora! Tora!* Showing the events leading up to the Japanese attack on Pearl Harbor from both sides of the conflict, Fukasaku directed the Japanese sequences together with Toshio Masuda (the two of them replacing Akira Kurosawa) while Richard Fleischer took care of the American segments.

Fukasaku's other two science fiction films, however, came about at a time when the director was very intentionally seeking to move away from the yakuza genre. By the late '70s he would in fact leave the yakuza film behind altogether and make a string of commercial projects in a variety of genres.

This turnaround was in large part the result of the commercial success of *Battles without Honor and Humanity*, which spawned no less than seven sequels in the three years that followed the original's release, all of them directed by Fukasaku. Understandably, there was only so far he could go with the material, and much of the vigor had disappeared by the time the series reached its sixth installment. Titled *New Battles without Honor and Humanity* (*Shin Jingi naki Tatakai*, 1974), Fukasaku agreed to direct it only when Toei consented to letting him change story, setting, and characters, resulting in all the series' regulars, including those who had died in previous installments, returning in different guises.

Like his protagonists, Fukasaku finally seemed to surrender to the futility of his battle against post-war Japan. But he was not one to

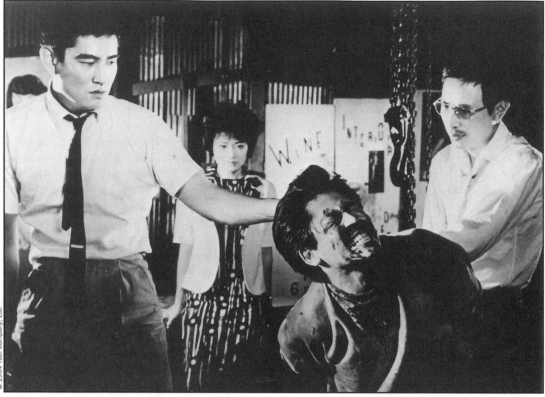

Wolves, Pigs, and Men

give up without a fight. With *Graveyard of Honor*, he attacked his regular targets with one final outburst of savage, destructive rage. The film laid waste to the last vestiges of the gangster-as-hero in its portrayal of a suicidally self-destructive loose cannon yakuza. Having gone from marginal to mainstream thanks to the success of the *Battles* series, Fukasaku used his clout to deliver this intense, furiously violent masterpiece as a studio production, casting one of Japanese cinema's biggest and most beloved stars, Tetsuya Watari, as the reprehensible protagonist.

The aptly titled *Graveyard of Honor* was the director's ultimate statement, its protagonist's determined descent into self-destruction symbolizing Fukasaku's acknowledgement that things had come to a close. From this moment onwards things changed quickly. Not turning

his back on the crime film quite yet, he initially changed his course only slightly and focused on the corruption at the heart of Japan's new power system. With the companion pieces *Cops vs. Thugs* and *Yakuza Graveyard* he laid bare the inextricable links between law enforcement and organized crime, suggesting that to all intents and purposes the two were very much the same.

The big change for Fukasaku came in 1978 when he directed *Shogun's Samurai*, his first venture into period costume drama (at least in terms of feature films, since in 1972 Fukasaku directed three episodes of the TV series *Sure Death*, about a band of paid assassins in the Tokugawa era). The fact that this was the genre he had so consciously avoided in the beginning of his career signaled that the director had turned the page and was starting anew.

The film was as commercial as they came, made to coincide with the first anniversary of Toei's movie theme park Uzumasa Eigamura in Kyoto. Shot on the park's backlots and sound stages, the film was effectively a feature-length commercial for the tourist attraction. Commercial intents of the project notwithstanding, Fukasaku had not entirely denounced his own beliefs. He used the film to gleefully rewrite one of Japan's defining historical moments, the death of Shogun Iemitsu Tokugawa, and his samurai character behaved with as much contempt for honor as his twentieth-century gangsters had done.

Fukasaku's farewell to the gangster film coincided with the collapse of the Japanese studio system. This system had been steadily eroding as economic developments offered people other ways to spend their sparse leisure time, television being one of the most significant. One studio, Shintoho, had already gone bankrupt in 1961 (its name was later resurrected as a distributor for soft-core porn), followed by Daiei ten years later. Nikkatsu had by that time already devoted its entire output to Roman Porno skinflicks in an attempt to save its own hide (which made their top star Tetsuya Watari decide to go freelance, thus landing him *Graveyard of Honor* at Toei). As the '70s drew to a close, production budgets had shrunk drastically and most of the major commercial productions were financed from a variety of sources, with television broadcasters and publishing firms like Kadokawa venturing into film co-production.

Kadokawa in particular made its mark on the period, led by producer Haruki Kadokawa, son of the company's founder. With the capital from dad's successful conglomerate he started Kadokawa Production Company and produced or co-produced some of Fukasaku's biggest hits of the 1980s, including sci-fi and fantasy spectaculars *Virus*, *Samurai Reincarnation* (remade by Hideyuki Hirayama in 2003), and *Legend of Eight Samurai* as well as the melodrama *Fall Guy*, which repeated the success it had known

as a stage play. In the '80s, Kinji Fukasaku had become the commercial mainstream director par excellence, one of the few filmmakers who could be counted on to deliver box office hits in a time of ever-diminishing returns.

But while Fukasaku was making blockbusters, a new generation of filmmakers slowly started emerging. Many of them working independently, they emerged from film schools, 8mm underground filmmaking, or from the circles of film critics. By the time the '90s came around, Japanese cinema was going through something resembling a creative renaissance, and new names came into the limelight: Sōgo Ishii, Shunichi Nagasaki, Kiyoshi Kurosawa, Shinya Tsukamoto, and many others. In the meantime the old studios, with Toei at the head of the pack, had discovered a new market for film productions: video. They started churning out low-budget genre films, made on two-week schedules and aimed for release directly on video. Known as Original Video (OV) or V-cinema (originally the label Toei gave its straight-to-video line), the phenomenon also resurrected the yakuza genre and gave rise to a generation of filmmakers who found ways for self-expression within the low-budget genre confines, including such luminaries as Takashi Ishii, Takashi Miike, Rokurō Mochizuki, Shinji Aoyama, and again Kiyoshi Kurosawa (who had moved from independent filmmaking to OV).

Symbolic for the changing of the guard was the production process of a project Fukasaku was slated to direct, with popular comedian "Beat" Takeshi Kitano playing the lead role. Due to illness, Fukasaku had to step down from the director's chair and the producers, pressed for time with the shooting ready to commence, asked the star to take over directorial duties. *Violent Cop* was Takeshi Kitano's debut as a director and launched him into the vanguard of the new generation of Japanese directors.

Despite his age (he was now in his sixties) and over a decade of directing blockbusters, Fukasaku's fighting spirit had not diminished.

Street Mobster

With 1992's **The Triple Cross** he issued a challenge to the fledgling Young Turks, showing that when it came to intense action-packed filmmaking he could still more than hold his own.

The *Triple Cross* seemed to awaken a renewed vigor in Fukasaku, and the films that followed it once again showed a willingness to go that extra mile. *Crest of Betrayal* was made to mark the centenary of Shochiku studios, but again showed the director's knack for rewriting history to accommodate those it normally leaves in the shadows, in this case by combining two traditional tales: *Chūshingura*, or the loyal 47 ronin, and the ghost story of Yotsuya. In 1999 Fukasaku returned to post-war Japan with *The Geisha House*, the portrait of a group of geisha in the 1950s, whose profession and traditions are threatened by the impending enforcement of a new anti-prostitution act. To the surprise of many, he took a foray into the world of video games two years later, directing sequences for the Capcom game *Clocktower 3*, a gothic tale of ghosts and demons set in Victorian London.

When the new millennium dawned, Kinji Fukasaku finally saw his work recognized and brought to foreign audiences, thanks to the first-ever retrospective of his work at the 2000 Rotterdam Film Festival in Holland. Other countries followed the example and similar retrospectives were held in England, the United States, France, and Germany. While these events were still being held, the director made what would prove to be his international breakthrough. **Battle Royale** emerged from controversy and went on to take Japan and then the world by storm. The story of a group of high school kids who are sent by the government to a desert island with the order to kill each other until only one is left standing, provoked parliamentary debate. Serious attempts were undertaken to ban the film, fearing the effect the film's abundant violence would have on impressionable young minds. In the end, the controversy fizzled out when parliamentarians and concerned parents were finally shown the film they tried to ban and realized that it actually had something to say.

"The fact that adults lost confidence in themselves, that's what is shown in *Battle Royale*. Those adults worked very hard in the '70s in order to rebuild Japan. They went through that period working for the national interest. Of course there was a generation gap between the young and adults, even throughout that period, but consistently adults were in control in terms of political stability and whatever was going on in the nation.

"However, since the burst of the bubble economy, these same adults, many of them salarymen and working class people, were put in a very difficult position with the economic downturn and all of a sudden most of them started to lose confidence in themselves. And the children who have grown up and witnessed what happened to the adults, their anxiety became heightened as well. So I set the film in this context of children versus adults."

Battle Royale brought Fukasaku full circle. With its fifteen-year-old protagonists forced into a life-threatening crisis situation, the director returned to his own youth. He put to film the experience of seeing his friends die in the munitions factory, the event that made him renounce the old values of his country. The experience directly influenced numerous earlier Fukasaku films, particularly in his use of young characters to more dramatically show the full negative effect of Japan's reconstruction: from the young man tortured by his own older broth-

er in *Wolves, Pigs and Men*, via the ruined boys of *If You Were Young: Rage*, to the apprentice geisha who might lose everything she has spent her life preparing for in *The Geisha House*. Fukasaku might have been seventy when he made it, but *Battle Royale* showed how eager he still was to communicate with the young.

"It was just my way of talking to them, saying some words to the children. Young people's existence in the current time presents different issues, to themselves as well as to others, the adults. When I was fifteen I went through certain experiences. For this film I posed myself the question: 'How would it be for these young people to go through those same experiences?' I am fully aware that there is a generation gap between where I stand and where those kids stand."

With its corrupted youth struggling vainly against a society that tries to wipe them out of existence, *Battle Royale* is in all respects a Kinji Fukasaku film. It's appropriate, then, that it was to be his last completed film. In late 2002, at a press conference announcing the start of production on *Battle Royale 2*, Fukasaku declared that he was suffering from cancer in an advanced stage, but that he would forego medical treatment in order to step behind the megaphone one more time. Unfortunately, shortly after shooting began, he collapsed on the set and was rushed off to the hospital, where he passed away soon after. He lost his final battle on January 12, 2003, aged seventy-two.

The validity of Kinji Fukasaku's work for (and as) contemporary Japanese cinema is manifold. The rupture with the *ninkyō* films could be seen as a starting point for contemporary Japanese cinema, trading in traditionalist views for a critical vision of the here and now that marks so much of the work of today's directors. Then there is the influence he's had on the generation that emerged in the '80s and '90s, those upstarts Fukasaku himself challenged with *The Triple*

Cross (which thereby became his own contribution to the early '90s renaissance). For them, born when post-war reconstruction hit its peak, the ferocity and outright social criticism of *Battles without Honor and Humanity* were no less than a counter-cultural statement, much like the non-conformist work of Seijun Suzuki had been several years earlier. Both directors were widely embraced by those who were then in their own rebellious teens, a number of whom would go on to pay tribute to Fukasaku in their own work. Makoto Shinozaki's *Not Forgotten* (2000) deals with a moral soul-searching by veteran soldiers that prompts memories and reinterpretations of their wartime past, a structure influenced by *Under the Flag of the Rising Sun*. Toei resurrected the *Battles* series in the late '90s, assigning Junji Sakamoto to direct *Another Battle* (*Shin Jingi naki Tatakai*, 1999). Aside from its title the middling result had no ties whatsoever with the Fukasaku series, something even its director readily acknowledged. It nevertheless led to a sequel three years later in the shape of Hajime Hashimoto's *Another Battle: Conspiracy* (*Shin Jingi naki Tatakai: Bōsatsu*, 2002), which equally failed to set the world on fire. Takashi Miike's re-adaptation of *Graveyard of Honor* (*Shin Jingi no Hakaba*, 2002), on the other hand, was a stunning revamping. Every inch as brutal as Fukasaku's version and then some, it updated the story to the late '80s bubble economy and its subsequent collapse in the following decade, the protagonist's self-destruction becoming a symbol for Japan's economic free fall.

And finally of course, there is *Battle Royale*, a film that went on to play to local and foreign audiences on a scale few Japanese films have managed in a long, long time. For this reason alone, the film that brought seventy-year-old Kinji Fukasaku full circle with his own childhood is also one of contemporary Japanese cinema's incontestable landmarks.

↓ Black Lizard

黒蜥蜴

Kurotokage

1968. CAST: Isao Kimura, Akihiro Miwa (Akihiro Maruyama), Kikko Matsuoka, Yukio Mishima. 86 minutes. RELEASES: VHS, Cinevista Video (U.S., English subtitles).

Fukasaku's film adaptation of Yukio Mishima's stage adaptation of a novel by Edogawa Rampo is a deliriously flamboyant piece of late '60s excess, as Japan's master detective Kogorō Akechi pits his wits against the cross-dressing presence of fiendish arch-villainess The Black Lizard.

Meet Miss Midorikawa, alias The Black Lizard, out to make off into the night with the priceless gemstone The Star of Egypt from beneath the very nose of its wealthy industrialist owner. To add insult to injury, she also sticks his daughter in a large trunk and drags her off to her island lair with the intention of stuffing the chaste young maiden in order to preserve her beauty and to add her to her collection of similarly preserved human dolls. The fiendish arch-villainess will do anything to be surrounded by beautiful things, and there's only one person who can stop her: Japan's Number One Private Detective, Kogorō Akechi.

In 1968, in a year-long sojourn from Toei, Fukasaku made three films at Shochiku's studios at Ōfuna, allowing him a brief respite from the stream of yakuza movies that his main employer had come to be exclusively associated with. The first of these was the crime drama *Call Me Blackmail!* The other two, *Black Lizard* and its follow-up, *Black Rose Mansion*, released later in 1969, were two rather eccentric projects centered around the camp, sexually ambivalent figure of the cross-dressing Akihiro Maruyama, better known by the stage name of his female alter-ego, Akihiro Miwa.

Miwa was a famous cabaret singer of French-styled *chansons* from the age of 17, with a career track record that leapt with consummate ease from theater, to cinema, to hit records and most recently to providing the voice of Moro in Hayao Miyazaki's animated smash hit, *Princess Mononoke* (*Mononokehime*, 1997). These two films represented his only starring roles, though he did feature prominently in Shūji Terayama's ultra-anarchic *Throw Away Your Books and Go out into the Streets* (*Sho o Suteyo Machi e Deyō*, 1971).

Both of Fukasaku's films are camp, pop art melodramas played out in supersaturated colors that root them firmly as belonging to the latter years of the swinging '60s—think in terms of the extravagant excesses of the *Batman* TV series starring Adam West, or the Euro Spy genre of its day popularized by the early Bond films and typified by such choice offerings as the Italo French *OSS 117* series, Joseph Losey's *Modesty Blaise* (1966), or Jess Franco's *Two Undercover Angels* (1967). In both, Miwa sticks with his transvestite cabaret-singing public persona. In *Black Rose Mansion*, he plays the Black Rose of the film's title, a singer hired by a wealthy businessman to sing in his exclusive men's club mansion—though her presence is soon acting as a magnet for hordes of murderous ghosts from her previous life.

Black Rose, however, is a pale shadow of its precursor. *Black Lizard* has far stronger material to work with. Adapted from the 1929 novel of the same name by Japan's celebrated mystery-horror writer Edogawa Rampo (cf. *The Mystery of Rampo*, 1994), it features Kogorō Akechi as its protagonist, a staple of Rampo's investigative fiction in much the same way Sherlock Holmes was in Conan Doyle's. Described as keen-eyed and debonair, Rampo's kimono-clad creation is a master of disguise, whose winning combination of judo, logic, and reverse psychology led him to the heart of literally dozens of his mystery narratives.

Yukio Mishima's 1956 stage adaptation had already made it onto the screen once in a 1962 production for Daiei by Umetsugu Inoue, a director who found himself working under con-

tract for Shaw Brothers in Hong Kong during the '60s, directing such colorful titles as the 1966 *Hong Kong Nocturne/Xiang Jiang Hua Yue Ye*. This version starred Machiko Kyō in the title role, one of Daiei's top actresses of the '50s in films such as Akira Kurosawa's *Rashomon* (1950) and Teinosuke Kinugasa's *Gate of Hell* (*Jigokumon*, 1954).

However, when it came to the Shochiku remake, adapted for the screen by Masashige Narusawa, a former collaborator with Kenji Mizoguchi in the '50s on such classics as *New Tales of the Taira Clan* (*Shin Heike Monogatari*, 1955), it was decided to stay faithful to the original by casting Akechi's eponymous nemesis with the star of the stage version, Akihiro Miwa, who was reputedly Mishima's homosexual lover at the time. It was a casting coup. From The Black Lizard's very first appearance in the film in a glitzy black sparkling number, sashaying across the stage of her nightclub lair to perform a cabaret number against a luscious Art Nouveau backdrop of Aubrey Beardsley paintings, Maruyama's flamboyant presence dominates the entire exercise. Shamelessly embracing all the gaudy excesses of late '60s pop art culture, Fukasaku's high-camp adaptation boasts enough kitsch and color to make the Austin Powers conceit seem positively dowdy in comparison. Yet these superficial aspects are more than equally matched by the touching repartee of the two foils as they lay out their diametrically opposed philosophies, each skirting around the other in an attempt to gain the upper hand.

Much of this dramatic power can be attributed to the writer of the original stage play. Yukio Mishima (born Kimitake Hiraoka, 1925) remains one of the best-known Japanese novelists of the twentieth century in the West, due to works such as *Confessions of a Mask* (1949) and *The Sound of Waves* (1954). A number of these had been adapted to the big screen before *Black Lizard*, including his 1956 novel *The Temple of the Golden Pavilion*, which was made by Kon

Ichikawa for Daiei under the title *Conflagration* (*Enjō*, 1958). In Japan his work was highly regarded for his fusion of Western and traditional styles, but toward the second half of the '60s this latter aspect of the writer's personality came to predominate. Part of the jetsetter champagne crowd of right-wing intellectuals that included the author of *Taiyō no Kisetsu* ("Season of the Sun") and later governor of Tokyo, Shintarō Ishihara, Mishima's celebrity status was enough to land him a leading role in Yasuzō Masumura's *Afraid to Die* (*Karakkaze Yarō*, 1960), though his performance was not highly regarded by the critics of his day.

His sole stint at filmmaking came with the 28-minute-long adaptation of his short story *Yūkoku* (1966), which was inspired by the *Niniroku* military coup of February 26, 1936 (cf. Seijun Suzuki's **Elegy to Violence**), and details the ritual suicide of a high-ranking naval officer (played by Mishima himself) and his wife (Yoshiko Tsuruoka). Shot in silent black and white, with expository intertitles, in a single, one-room interior with a kanji sign reading "*shisei*" ("fidelity") emblazoned on the wall, *Yūkoku*'s style is carefully made up of static wide shots and lingering close-ups, none of which, incidentally, show Mishima's eyes, which are always just out of frame or obscured by shadow.

Yūkoku remained a chilling premonition of things to come. By the late '60s, Mishima's nationalism had come to predominate. A practicing homosexual and active body builder (he can be seen, fully pumped, as one of the *Black Lizard*'s prized mannequins), in 1968 he founded his own private army, the *Tate no Kai* (Shield Society), consisting of some one hundred followers, and two years after *Black Lizard* was released, on November 25, 1970, in a hollow echo of the *Niniroku* incident, he stormed a military headquarters building in Tokyo. Here, at the age of 45, he took his own life, publicly and perhaps inevitably with that most patriotic form of suicide, *seppuku*. His last words were "Long live the Emperor!"

The event is still treated with a degree of embarrassment by the Japanese, and Mishima's widow ordered all prints of *Yūkoku* to be destroyed (though a number of foreign copies have survived), as well as a national ban on the distribution of Paul Schrader's U.S. made biopic, *Mishima: A Life in Four Chapters* (1985), due to its "misleading" portrayal of Mishima's queer tendencies. *Black Lizard* is also unavailable on video in Japan.

↓ Under the Flag of the Rising Sun
軍旗はためく下に
Gunki Hatameku Moto Ni
a.k.a. *Under the Fluttering Military Flag*

1972. CAST: Sachiko Hidari, Tetsurō Tanba, Shōnosuke Ichikawa, Noboru Mitani, Takeshi Seki. 96 minutes. RELEASE: DVD, Home Vision Entertainment (U.S., English subtitles).

Harrowing and eye-opening account of the madness and the brutal conditions of life among Japanese soldiers in the last days of World War II. Fukasaku's second independent production takes a venomously critical look at both wartime and post-war Japan, unrestrained by genre frameworks.

Despite few of them making their way to Western shores, Japanese films that take a critical look at the country's wartime past are anything but rare. Particularly in the '60s and '70s, films like Seijun Suzuki's *Story of a Prostitute* and Yasuzō Masumura's *Red Angel* (*Akai Tenshi*, 1966) and *Hoodlum Soldier* (*Heitai Yakuza*, 1965) painted a less than glorified portrait of life on the front line. Why these films haven't received proper distribution in the West while similarly humanistic portraits of Germany's battlefield traumas are critically lauded (Wolfgang Petersen's *Das Boot* and Sam Peckinpah's *Cross of Iron* to name two) remains a curiously unjust enigma.

One of these Japanese wartime accounts crying out for international recognition is Kinji Fukasaku's devastating *Under the Flag of the Rising Sun*. Adapted by Kaneto Shindō from the novel by Masaharu Yūki, the film portrays and compares the horrors of the last days on the Pacific frontline and of post-war Japan's bureaucracy. Fukasaku, who had personally acquired the rights to the novel, directed the film for the independent Shinsei Eigasha production company because allegedly no major studio was willing to back him up on such sensitive material. No doubt the studios felt vindicated when the film flopped at the box office, obliging Fukasaku to return to Toei and the gangster genre—in which he simply continued to lay bare the very same social problems.

Under the Flag of the Rising Sun recounts the attempts by soldier's widow Sakie Togashi (Hidari) to be recognized by the state as a war widow and thus be eligible for a pension. She is refused time and time again because according to official records her husband (Tetsurō Tanba) was shot by his own superiors for desertion, mere days after Japan's official surrender, which means he's not an official casualty of war. When she finds out that four of her husband's old comrades in arms never returned their questionnaires about the events that led up to sergeant Togashi's death, she sees an opportunity to discover the truth about her husband and clear his name.

Visiting the four men and questioning them about the events of those fateful days at the end of the war, she meets with varying degrees of resistance, while the accounts she receives from each of the men are more often than not conflicting. The one thing that does become clear is that the conditions the soldiers lived under were beyond barbaric.

Perhaps the biggest problem the mainstream film industry had with the subject matter is not the revelations about wartime atrocities committed by (and to) Japanese soldiers—that soldiers were driven to cannibalism

out of hunger was something Kon Ichikawa already alluded to in *Fires on the Plain* (*Nobi*, 1959, produced by Daiei)—but Fukasaku's implication that the remorseless bureaucracy that denies widows their right to a pension is just another guise of the government responsible for driving its soldiers into acts of barbarism and then executing them for insubordination when they protest. It's in line with the main concern in Fukasaku's work of showing the price the people have to pay for the ideals of their government. This is most strongly felt in the character of one of sergeant Togashi's former comrades, who is now a pig farmer living on a refuse dump in the outskirts of the city. "On the map," he says while overlooking the putrid sty that passes for a farm, "this is officially Tokyo." But not quite the Tokyo of shiny office blocks and Ginza glitz.

Linking Japan's past and present, Fukasaku delivers not only a powerful anti-war film and an eye-opening historical document, but also proof of the historic and social relevance of his own cinematic legacy.

Battles without Honor and Humanity

仁義なき戦い
Jingi naki Tatakai
a.k.a. *Fight without Honor/The Yakuza Papers/Tarnished Code of the Yakuza*

1973. CAST: Bunta Sugawara, Hiroki Matsukata, Kunie Tanaka, Eiko Nakamura, Tsunehiko Watase, Nobuo Kaneko, Tatsuo Umemiya. 99 minutes. RELEASE: DVD, Home Vision Entertainment (U.S., English subtitles), Eureka Video (U.K., English subtitles), Toei Video (Japan, no subtitles).

Fukasaku's quintessential classic. This ferocious account of gang wars in Hiroshima, based on true stories, would prove to be a turning point for the yakuza genre. A huge box office hit, it

Battles Without Honor and Humanity

also propelled the previously rather marginal director Fukasaku into the big league.

Beginning with the atomic bomb and ending with powerboat racing, *Battles without Honor and Humanity* is as much an account of Japan's rise from wartime ashes to economic superpower as it is of the demise of its central characters.

Based on magazine articles recounting the memoirs of a former yakuza, the film chronicles the erratic career path of Shōzo Hirono (Sugawara), one of the millions of Japanese scrounging around the black markets of ruined post-war Japan to make a living. A former soldier, Hirono is a brawler with a set of like-minded friends. When the group gets into trouble with the gangsters who rule the black market, Hirono shoots and kills one of their leaders and ends up in jail.

There he makes the acquaintance of yakuza Wakasugi of the Doi gang, but when he is released, he is welcomed by his old friends who ask him to join them as a member of the Yamamori group, Doi's bitter rivals. A full-scale war breaks out over the two factions' involvement with local politicians, and Hirono is asked to assassinate the leader of the Doi gang. The attempt turns into a messy shooting, in which Hirono runs out of bullets before he can kill off the rival boss. Police begin to crack down on yakuza violence, and as a result of a traitor in his own group, Hirono is almost killed and subsequently arrested. Upon release several years later, he finds out that the fortunes of his group have changed and that it's not the Doi gang that is the biggest threat to his gang's existence, but the treacherous ways of his own boss.

To the uninitiated, *Battles without Honor and Humanity* will probably seem like a flurry of messy assassinations, punch-ups, and chase scenes. Its numerous characters and their ongoing betrayals certainly don't make the film any easier to follow. But such erratic goings-on are part and parcel of Kinji Fukasaku's best work. They express the realities of post-war life and in particular of post-war gang life, where survival was more important than concepts like honor. Such outdated values had died with Japan's defeat, to be replaced by an unrestrained free-for-all.

Honor and heroism are alien notions in this moral wasteland, something Fukasaku emphasizes every chance he gets, giving the image of the valiant yakuza a couple of good smacks upside the head. Guns jam and bullets run out during weasely assassination attempts, hens pick at a freshly chopped-off yakuza pinkie, infighting and betrayal are bigger threats than the rival clan, gang elders break down and cry in front of their subordinates if it will get them what they want, and any means to make money is allowed, including dealing with the American army: a whole host of yakuza genre codes get resolutely shattered.

Fukasaku translates this state of affairs into the way he shoots the proceedings. Extensive use of handheld cameras and fast editing accentuate the chaotic behavior of the characters, while the use of voice-overs, photographs, newspaper clippings, and titles underline the film's attempts at charting history, giving it the feel of a newsreel account. Cramming several decades' worth of material into 99 minutes, Fukasaku attempts to show us an alternative history of post-war Japan, the street-level truth that is covered up by the boastful records of reconstruction and economic growth that form the official reading. (This makes Fukasaku's work closely related to that of Shōhei Imamura, who also focused on the underbelly of society ignored in official readings of history.)

Battles without Honor and Humanity became a huge box-office success; Fukasaku clearly wasn't the only person who harbored these feelings about post-war Japan and how it should be reflected by cinema. Its impact was such that it destroyed the *ninkyō eiga* genre and unleashed a new fashion for more gritty true-life yakuza movies, the so-called *jitsuroku* ('true story') films. But for the director, telling the truth was anything but a fashion; it was the point of the whole exercise.

Fukasaku went on to make seven additional entries in the series in the following three years, thereby contributing to the swift demise of that same *jitsuroku* genre. The last genre the studios could still count on to rake in profits, it went into hibernation with the majors and wouldn't resurface until the rise of V-cinema fifteen years later.

↓ Cops vs. Thugs
県警対組織暴力
Kenkei Tai Soshiki Bōryoku
a.k.a. *State Police vs. Organized Crime*

1975. CAST: Bunta Sugawara, Hiroki Matsukata, Tatsuo Umemiya, Nobuo Kaneko, Shingo Yamashiro, Takuzō Kawatani. 101 minutes. RELEASE: DVD, Eureka Video (U.K., English subtitles), Toei Video (Japan, no subtitles).

Having permanently buried the image of the honorable yakuza, Fukasaku left the post-war gangsters behind him and focused on contemporary issues. Still as defiant as ever, he made *Cops vs. Thugs* as a direct attack on government and police corruption.

Cops vs. Thugs was made at a time when Kinji Fukasaku was at the peak of his powers; a spirited director who made films that were vital and alive. He had perfected his characteristic visual style (freeze frames, handheld cameras, odd angles, the use of text as both a narrative and aesthetic tool), while his stories brimmed with social comment.

With four enormously successful episodes

Cops vs. Thugs

of the *Battles without Honor and Humanity* series behind him, as well as one of the most vicious and relentless cinematic portrayals of yakuza life with *Graveyard of Honor*, Fukasaku had said just about all he could about gangsterdom. With *Cops vs. Thugs* he fixed his sights on the other side of the law: the police.

If the aforementioned films portrayed the yakuza as violence-prone brutes who didn't show the slightest trace of the honorable souls they were traditionally depicted as having, his rendering of the law was hardly more flattering. The word "versus" in the title does not so much refer to opposition, but rather to comparison. *Cops vs. Thugs* examines the differences—or rather the similarities—between gangsters and police, the thin line between good and bad. The message, to no great surprise, is that the two are closer than they ought to be and that the law means little on either side.

This attitude is not only apparent in content (the screenplay, based on true events, was written by Kazuo Kasahara, who also scripted the first four entries in the *Battles* series), but also in form. The confusion that Fukasaku's frenetic visual style can create in a viewer here found its ideal context and the film therefore marks the full maturation of Fukasaku's style, the point at which form and content have become one. The confusion that is central to the subject (i.e., the lack of delineation between police and criminals) is also the defining factor in the mise-en-scène.

The incongruity of a pair of feet in alligator shoes resting on a policeman's desk is illustrative: Gangsters and cops mingle constantly, and frequently find themselves on each other's turfs, as comfortable on one terrain as on the other. Cops are friendlier with gangsters than with their own colleagues and vice versa. Fukasaku's methods reach as far as the casting: Lead actor Bunta Sugawara plays a cop after just having starred in a string of gangster roles. (Sugawara is still typecast in gangster roles today, although he made a refreshing change of pace by providing the voice of the spider-legged Kamajii in Hayao Miyazaki's animated hit *Spirited Away*).

As with much of Fukasaku's mid-'70s work, the frenetic nature of the film's style also results in a film that moves at a brisk pace. Stripped of all extra layers, *Cops vs. Thugs* is still one fast-moving action film. With dashes of humor that often border on the absurd and energetic performances by a bevy of great players, it's hugely entertaining.

↓ Virus
復活の日
Fukkatsu no Hi

1980. **CAST:** Masao Kusakari, Shinichi "Sonny" Chiba, Ken Ogata, Yumi Takigawa, Chuck Connors, Glenn Ford, Olivia Hussey, Edward James Olmos, Robert Vaughn. 156 minutes (export version: 106 minutes). **RELEASE:** DVD, Platinum Disc (U.S., English subtitles). Moonstone (U.K., English subtitles). Kadokawa (Japan, no subtitles).

An apocalyptic vision of a world devastated by a fatal plague. A small international community of survivors cling to existence in an isolated research station in Antarctica, in the most expensive Japanese production of its time.

Doom and gloom abounded in cinema throughout the '70s, as the first waves of pre-millennial tension manifested themselves in a string of extravagant displays of destruction. From straightforward disaster spectacles such as *Hurricane* (Jan Troell, 1974) and *Earthquake* (Mark Robson, 1974) to the apocalyptic social commentary of George Romero's *Dawn of the Dead* (1978), audiences around the world seemed quite happy to shell out their bucks for lavish affirmations of mankind's vulnerability.

Japan—a country which had suffered two nuclear blasts, is constantly besieged by earth tremors and tidal waves, and was then undergoing the preliminary stages of future shock—joined the fray with *Submersion of Japan* (*Nippon Chinbotsu*, a.k.a. *Japan Sinks*, Shirō Moritani, 1973), *Bullet Train* (*Shinkansen Daibakuha*, Junya Satō, 1975) and the Nostradamus-themed *The Last Days of Planet Earth* (*Nosutoradamusu no Daiyogen*, Toshio Masuda, 1974). But by far the best known of these abroad is *Virus*. Like *Submersion of Japan*, it is based upon a best-selling novel by Sakyō Komatsu, and at the time was the most lavishly expensive production in Japanese film history.

Featuring an international all-star cast and an epic vision of a planet devastated by plague, a film the size of *Virus* could never have been made were it not for producer Haruki Kadokawa. During the mid-'70s, the big-thinking mogul had rapidly expanded the publishing company which his father had founded, Kadokawa Shoten. Shrewdly noting the interminable decline of the European and Japanese film industries as they became ever more cowed into submission beneath the big-budget bombast of the Hollywood blockbuster, Kadokawa set out to revolutionize the ailing indigenous production scene by setting up the Kadokawa Haruki Jimusho film production company, pitting his product against the competition with a string of unashamedly populist and cannily publicized seat-fillers.

Veteran director Kon Ichikawa was roped in to helm his first production, *The Inugamis* (*Inugamike no Ichizoku*) which clocked in at No. 2 in the national box office charts in 1976. But it was in 1977 that Kadokawa first cast his net westward, setting the interracial murder mystery *Proof of the Man* (*Ningen no Shōmei*, directed by Junya Satō) in the United States and casting George Kennedy from the successful *Airport* series as the lead. With an eye firmly on the export market, two versions were prepared, with the Japanese- or American-oriented scenes either pruned or added depending upon which side of the Pacific the film was to be released.

In actuality *Proof of the Man* never received a theatrical release in the United States, though the English language print later surfaced on video. Still, the domestic box-office receipts augured well, and the same approach was repeated a couple of years later with *Virus*. Directorial duties were handed over to Kinji Fukasaku, one of the few established directors to weather it through the harsh cinematic climate of the '70s, and who already had some experience in international co-productions due to his involvement with Richard Fleischer in *Tora! Tora! Tora!*.

As with the previous year's *Meteor* (Ronald Neame), *Virus* capitalizes on the conjecture that the one thing that unites the world is our mutual fear of imminent annihilation. The perception that Cold War fever was reaching epidemic proportions is here rendered explicit in the form of the genetically engineered superbug MM-88, which when unleashed from its laboratory in Leipzig, East Germany, takes little time in laying waste the world's population. The handful of survivors are holed up in a number of research stations in Antarctica, where this communist contagion is unable to penetrate due to the severe climate. With only eight women nestling amongst the 858 stationed there, it is clear that the ramifications on what remains of human society are going to be pretty severe. And if that weren't enough, a series of earth tremors in the Washington area look set to fire off the U.S. nuclear arsenal toward the U.S.S.R., triggering an automatic counterattack rendering doomsday imminent within the next fortnight. Well, at least it's not raining.

Distributed by Toho, *Virus* exists in both an international export version and a far longer Japanese version. In its shorter form, with only a few token Japanese faces clamoring for screen time amongst its role call of familiar American stalwarts of the day, you'd be hard pressed to pinpoint the country of origin as Japan. Blink and you'll miss Sonny Chiba and Ken Ogata's almost subliminal appearances in the U.S. release, two actors who should be fairly familiar to Western audiences—Chiba from the *Streetfighter* series (kicking off with *Streetfighter/Gekitotsu! Satsujin Ken* directed by Shigehiro Ozawa in 1974); Ogata from his appearances in Imamura's films of the '80s, the title role in Paul Schrader's *Mishima: A Life in Four Chapters* (1985), and Peter Greenaway's *The Pillow Book* (1996).

The Japanese characters are more fully fleshed out in the longer version, which zeros in more specifically on the effect of the plague on the inhabitants of Tokyo during the first half of its running time. There is also an extended final coda sequence, in which a glimmer of hope, as the Japanese title *Fukkatsu no Hi* ("day of resurrection") suggests, is seen to arise in the southernmost tip of Argentina, though perhaps this detracts from the more pessimistic vision of the shorter version.

Whilst at first glance *Virus* seems to bear little obvious semblance to a Fukasaku film, the situation of an isolated group placed in a high-pressure milieu with no means of escape and forced to make its own rules finds its most obvious parallel with his internationally best-known work, *Battle Royale*.

With the initial half hour devoted to portraying the devastating effects of the virus sweeping across the globe from the steppes of Siberia to the carpeted interiors of the White House by way of Paris, Rome, Tokyo, and London, by the time we are introduced to our Antarctic survivors we're already aware that any future that they might have is a pretty futile one. The bulk of the film details the relationships and tensions which erupt between the various international factions holed up in their sterile rat hole in a manner fascinatingly indicative of the global political system of the time, at a time in which Japan was beginning to see itself as an economic and cultural power on equal footing with its Western counterparts.

Overseen by the patriarchal voice of authority represented by disaster movie veteran George Kennedy, the Russian characters are all bowed heads and apologies, the Japanese beaver away at their seismographic charts, the Chileans throw chairs around, Olivia Hussey plays Norwegian progenitor of the species, one of the handful of women on whom the future of humanity depends, whilst the sole British character maintains a stiff-upper-lipped air of aloof yet efficient authority. It is up to the wholesome forces of Uncle Sam manifested in the form of the towheaded Chuck Connors to leap on the next submarine up to Washington to save the world, but he does at least allow Masao Kusakari to tag along.

Virus fared disappointingly when it was released to the American public, which had by this stage already reached complete saturation point as far as the disaster epic was concerned. But viewed in hindsight as an overblown piece of late '70s dramatic excess, it still has plenty to offer in terms of its sheer entertainment value. The impressive snowscapes of Alaska and Canada which double as the Antarctic exteriors are beautifully shot, and Fukasaku brings an air of professionalism to the entire project which falls well in line with the requirements of the genre.

The end result certainly did no harm to the careers of either director or producer. The Kadokawa company put up the money for Fukasaku's next couple of epics, *Samurai Reincarnation*, *Fall Guy*, and *Legend of Eight Samurai*, and paralleling the "big is better" approach of Hollywood's Jerry Bruckheimer, Kadokawa went on to produce a prolific run of glossy high-concept potboilers, including *Black Magic Wars* (*Iga Ninpōchō*, Mitsumasa Saitō, 1982). He also turned to direction himself, with a number of films including *Cabaret* (*Kyabarē*, 1986), the Spielbergian schmaltz and spectacle of *Heaven and Earth* (*Ten to Chi to*, 1990), and *Rex: A Dinosaur Story* (*Rex: Kyōrū Monogatari*, 1993), before the excess of his own life caught up with him.

In 1993 he was arrested for cocaine smuggling in a very high-profile scandal, and was imprisoned 1996 for a period of four years. Kadokawa Shoten nevertheless survived this blow to the corporate image, and despite the loss of the high-profile producer that had steered the company to success, continued with production. It pumped out popular movies such as *Parasite Eve* (Masayuki Ochiai, 1997) under its own name, as well as buying up distributor Asmik Ace in the late '90s and absorbing Daiei into its corporate structure in 2002.

↓ The Triple Cross
いつかギラギラする日
Itsuka Gira-Gira Suru Hi
a.k.a. *Double Cross*

1991. CAST: Kenichi Hagiwara, Kazuya Kimura, Shinichi "Sonny" Chiba, Keiko Oginome, Renji Ishibashi, Yoshio Harada. 104 minutes. RELEASE: DVD, Tokyo Bullet/MIA; Video, (U.K., English subtitles). Panorama Distributions (Hong Kong, English/Chinese subtitles).

Full-throttle action film that showed the younger generation that Kinji Fukasaku was still a filmmaking force to be reckoned with.

Kinji Fukasaku went through the '70s as perhaps Japan's most revered director, thanks to his revisionist and highly successful takes on the gangster film with **Battles without Honor and Humanity** and its offspring. At the end of the decade however, he seemed to consolidate his bankability by directing an array of big-budget spectaculars that were increasingly slick but also increasingly anonymous, the Kadokawa production *Virus* being a prime example. From a financial point of view it was probably a wise decision, since Fukasaku was one of the few directors who emerged fairly unscathed from the crisis that hit the Japanese film industry full on in the 1980s.

The early '90s saw the emergence of a new generation of Japanese filmmakers, independent artists who challenged conventions (and thus the earlier generations of directors) head on. Who was still going to care for a journeyman director in his sixties who had his best days behind him, when raw energy and spirited zeal oozed from the films of young guns like Sōgo Ishii, Takeshi Kitano, Takashi Ishii and Shinya Tsukamoto?

Watching *The Triple Cross*, one gets the impression that this situation must have bothered Fukasaku himself quite a bit. But rather than quietly disappear into retirement, his reaction was to challenge the new blood head on: by making a film that was as fast, furious, and frenetic as anything on offer at the time.

The Triple Cross certainly is fast, furious, and frenetic. It's a foul-mouthed crime saga in which Fukasaku combines the visual characteristics of his early-'70s action classics with an audaciousness and a willingness to go very far beyond the boundaries of good taste firmly rooted in the '90s: The film features an endless array of violent and exotic shoot-outs and car chases, culminating in a combination of the two, with a school bus full of children thrown in for good measure. The storyline clearly mirrored the director's intentions: A trio of aging bank robbers (including longtime Fukasaku cohort Sonny Chiba) are scammed out of a sizeable amount of loot by their bleached-haired, twenty-something partner (Kazuya Kimura), who kills one, wounds another, and runs off with the young mistress of the third. The only old-timer still standing (Hagiwara) decides to go for revenge and the money, in a fashion that's as relentless as anything this young upstart is capable of.

Leaving no doubt as to which side the director is on, *The Triple Cross* is pervaded by this theme of the generation gap, which manifests itself not just in the storyline, but also in the film's style. Throughout, Fukasaku employs the contrast between young and old, even using musical motifs (jazz versus heavy metal) to emphasize the difference.

Evidence that the three senior characters represent Fukasaku could be found in an additional element: the presence of the young mistress. Although it wasn't widely known at the time, Keiko Oginome, the actress who played the character of the hyperactive paramour, was then romantically involved with her director. The full truth about their affair didn't come to light until more than a decade later, when Oginome wrote *Joyū no Yoru* (trans: Nights of an actress), an account of her affair with Fukasaku. Published in late 2002, three months before the director's death, the book was allegedly written with his consent, and it's not unimaginable that Fukasaku wished to come clean about his past in the knowledge that his health was failing him.

A statement of defiance and a way to redress the balance, *The Triple Cross* remains an essential entry in the development of contemporary Japanese cinema, particularly with regard to Fukasaku's role therein. It showed that the director still had energy to spare despite his advancing years. While many foreign audiences were amazed that a 70-year-old man was capable of delivering a film as fierce and shocking as ***Battle Royale***, those who had seen *The Triple Cross* would probably have taken the carnage and the outrage with a knowing, satisfied smile.

↓ Battle Royale
バトル・ロワイアル
Batoru Rowaiaru

2000. CAST: "Beat" Takeshi Kitano, Tatsuya Fujiwara, Aki Maeda, Tarō Yamamoto, Masanobu Andō, Kō Shibasaki, Chiaki Kuriyama. 113 minutes (special edition: 122 minutes). RELEASES: DVD, Tartan (U.K., English subtitles), Universe (Hong Kong, English/Chinese subtitles).

Forty-two schoolchildren are placed on a remote island, each kitted out with a deadly weapon and told to kill each other within the next few days.

Battle Royale

At the beginning of the twenty-first century Japan is in chaos. The economy has collapsed, the unemployment rate has skyrocketed and the youth are running riot, stabbing teachers and boycotting the classroom. Concerns about juvenile delinquency and disregard for discipline and order have paved the way for extreme measures in the form of the Battle Royale Act: the methodical extermination of teenage children.

Once a year, a group of junior high school students is systematically kidnapped and taken to a deserted island. They are given weapons, enough food and water for several days, and an order: to go out and kill each other. An explosive collar placed around the necks of each of the players imposes a degree of outside control on the proceedings, as well as providing a means of enforcing the game's three-day time limit. Aside from this, there are no other rules, and there can only be one survivor. This time it's the turn of the forty students of Shiroiwa Junior High School Third Year Class B, accompanied by two exchange students, whose reasons for being there are unclear.

Few Japanese films in recent memory have caused as much of a stir as *Battle Royale*, Fukasaku's abrasive adaptation of Kōshun Takami's popular novel of the same name. Playing like a turbo-charged hybrid of *Lord of the Flies*, *Friday the 13th*, and *The Most Dangerous Game*, its content was enough to stir up a government debate at home when, after protesting against the imposition of an R-15 rating from the Japanese censorship board Eirin that effectively barred the audience of the same age as the characters portrayed in the film from seeing it, the director took his struggle all the way to parliament.

Abroad, more than any other film in recent years, it was responsible for bringing in a whole new international audience for Japanese cinema, as perversely, after almost forty years at the di-

Battle Royale II: Requiem

rector's chair, Fukasaku's final film became the one that launched his reputation internationally.

Certainly there had been little in the past twenty years to suggest such a return to form. His previous *The Geisha House*, described by the director as being the first of his films in which no one died, was a lukewarm comedy drama scripted by Kaneto Shindō about the grooming of a young geisha against the backdrop of the government abolition of prostitution in 1958 (itself the focus of Kenji Mizoguchi's *Street of Shame/Akasen Chitai*, 1958). Prior to that, with the exception of *The Triple Cross*, Kinji Fukasaku's career had increasingly become that of a journeyman director of populist domestic productions, albeit highly commercially successful ones.

But *Battle Royale* is something else entirely. The ultimate high-pressure horror scenario of adolescents taking up arms against their classmates at the command of their seniors, where even your best friends can't be trusted, the film packed an undeniable emotional gut punch. Conservative critics lambasted it as a bloodthirsty fantasy that reveled in the deaths of young teenagers, a work with no redeeming social value at all, and indeed, it is very violent.

But the director himself spoke very eloquently about his personal attachment to the project, stressing that first and foremost, it was a fable, an extreme "what if" scenario dealing with the repercussions of a system of violence handed down from generation to generation, a theme very dear to his heart, having grown up in the chaotic aftermath of his own country's defeat in war. Undoubtedly the reason that it struck a chord with so many viewers is simply because it was applicable to any society where the weight of one generation bears heavily down on the next. In the face of seemingly insurmountable odds, do you greet your fate with mock bravado, terror, resignation, or choose to lay down your weapons and die?

Like his finest work, *Battle Royale* deals with conflict between an isolated group of characters under a pressure imposed from outside. In this case, the protagonists are younger, and their emotions are consequently that much more naked and raw. Onscreen text keeps us informed of the immediate death tally, a stylistic trope carried over from his yakuza films, whilst a roll call of the recently deceased is read out over a speaker system at regular points in the proceedings by the game's cold-faced overseer, Kitano, who ends his reports with such trite words of encouragement as, "It's tough when friends die on you, but hang in there!"

Kitano lends not only his familiar star persona but also his name to this character, changed from that of Kimpatsu in the source novel, and whether onscreen or off, his presence is pivotal. "Remember, life is a game," he advises his students shortly before he dispatches them one by one into the night after the initial briefing session. It soon becomes clear, however, that the odds in this particular death match are not evenly stacked, with the weapons ranging from crossbows and pistols to pan lids and binoculars.

As Fukasaku skillfully balances the screen time between the rapidly dwindling numbers of students, much of the power of *Battle Royale* comes from the interplay between the survivors, succinctly flattened down to their school-uniformed archetypes from their more detailed characters in the book. Mistrust reigns amongst a group of girls holed up away from the carnage in a deserted lighthouse. Mitsuko Sōma (Shibasaki, of *GO*), a solitary vixen wielding a scythe, calmly apples her makeup as the list of her dead classmates is read out. As sports jock Shūya Nanahara vows to protect the wounded Noriko Nakagawa, a constant victim of bullying at school due to her position as the classroom favorite of Kitano, Takako Chigusa repels the advances of an unwanted admirer, all the more violently now that there are no rules to govern her social conduct. And what about the two exchange students? What is the hidden past of the practical but secretive Shōgo Kawada (Yamamoto), and just who is Kazuo Kiriyama (a memorable turn by Andō, of Shinobu Yaguchi's Sabu-esque action comedy *Adrenalin Drive*, 1999, and Katsuyuki Motohiro's *Space Travelers*, 2000), an emotionless sociopath rumored to have joined the game just for fun?

Fukasaku had worked closely with his then 28-year-old son, Kenta, on the script of the film, and in bringing the focus from Takami's original story (which the author also adapted as a manga, drawn by Masayuki Taguchi) closer to his own vision, the film avoids some of the frankly more politically naïve aspects of the novel. It also unfortunately rather glosses over some important plot points.

It is never explicitly stated that the film is taking place in an alternate reality in which Japan had won the war. Nor is the reason made clear for why the students of Class 3B seemed oblivious to the existence of the game, when we have seen the victor of the previous year's BR at the film's opening: a blood-spattered young girl clutching a rag doll emerging into a crowd of baying TV journalists, her face cracking into a smile as the cameras are thrust under her nose. Equally confusing, on an initial viewing at least, are the events at the film's denouement, which are more clearly spelled out in the novel.

The original version of *Battle Royale* was released onto screens in Japan in December 2000. Extra scenes were shot immediately after this release, mainly flashback footage of a basketball match adding more weight to the personal dynamics of the class before the game, and a couple of scenes that elucidated the cryptic relationship between Noriko and Kitano. This new version was released the following April, to mark the beginning of the new school year in Japan and to capture a new sector of the audience who would have been just too young to have seen it during the initial release.

Inevitably, the significant commercial success in Japan of *Battle Royale* led to a sequel, based on an original treatment by Kenta. Sadly, Fukasaku collapsed literally days into the shoot of *Battle Royale II: Requiem*, passing away in January 2003. Appropriately the directorial reins were handed over to Kenta, though with the credits quick to stress the involvement of the *Fukasaku Gumi* (Fukasaku Group), the crew of collaborators from the first film, it is clear that Fukasaku Jr. was not left to shoulder the burden single-handedly.

The newer film opens with a spectacular aerial view over Tokyo. Gleaming office buildings dominate the skyline, the image tinged to near sepia by the setting sun. Suddenly an explosion rips through the air, and the phalanx of skyscrapers slowly collapses into rubble. In many ways, *Battle Royale II* retreads the path taken by its predecessor, reprising both the Wagnerian strains of its soundtrack and a number of set pieces and motifs whilst introducing a few new gimmicks, such as a new twist revolving around the explosive collars.

This time however, the premise has been taken further away from Takami's source material (the novelization of the sequel, adapted by Sugie Matsukoi a.k.a. Sugie McCoy, rode high on the Japanese bestseller list at the time of the film's release), as a new class-load of teenagers are abducted by the state, kitted out in camouflage military uniforms and sent out to hunt down and destroy the original survivor of the first film, now mastermind behind a terrorist organization engaged in anti-government activities.

Whereas the intra-personal dynamics of the first film depended on what the individual viewer brought to the table, there's little such room for ambiguity in the sequel. Peppered with such obvious real-world allusions to the post-September 11 world order as that contained in the opening sequence and a TV news-styled sequence of young Afghan children standing surrounded by rubble and waving at the camera, the sequel treads on fairly contentious ground as any metaphor is lost in favor of more obvious allusions to the contemporary state of global affairs.

Regardless of its political dimension, in expanding its vision *Battle Royale II* comes across as far less dramatically cogent than its model, not helped by either the histrionically over-the-top performance by Riki Takeuchi (replacing Kitano as the bullying schoolmaster) or the fact that none of the characters is as richly drawn. Interestingly, the substitution of school uniforms for combat fatigues has an unexpected distancing effect, and we no longer seem to care quite so much about the fates of the individuals. A grueling *Saving Private Ryan*-inspired landing sequence sees the majority of Class 3 wiped out within the first reel. Shot in shaky handheld cameras, this visceral and undeniably exciting section peaks far too soon as the film's dramatic highpoint, and the running time simply cannot maintain the momentum through the subsequent pyrotechnics. The film starts with a bang, then stalls midway.

Though a relative commercial success, the film was poorly received by critics in Japan. Whilst undeniably bigger, bolder, and bloodier than the original, in attempting to be more provocative it lost the potency of the original *Battle Royale*, one of the most genuinely inflammatory films to have emerged from any part of the world in years.

CHAPTER 4
Sōgo Ishii
石井聰亙

Sōgo Ishii was born in the right place at the right time. The man who is often referred to as Japan's punk filmmaker grew up in Hakata on the southernmost of Japan's four main islands, Kyushu. When he was in his teens, he found himself in the middle of the punk rock revolution when northern Kyushu became one of the country's most fertile breeding grounds for new bands.

Ishii himself dabbled in music as a singer and guitarist, but soon found his true calling after moving to Tokyo to study at Nihon University in 1977. In university, nineteen-year-old Sōgo Ishii (then still known by his real name of Toshihiro Ishii) turned to cinema. He founded his own ciné-club, Kyōei-sha ('Crazy Film Group'), and made his first short films on 8mm and 16mm equipment borrowed from the university. The films inevitably carried Ishii's affinity with the punk scene on their sleeves. Shorts like *Panic High School* and *Totsugeki! Hakata Gurentai* [trans: Attack! hooligans of Hakata] featured the struggles of misfits and underdogs against established society.

Even the simple fact that Ishii made these films, that he became a film director by simply grabbing any equipment available and shooting, was an act of punk-spirited rebellion, echoing the do-it-yourself attitude of the movement. This was especially true for an aspiring Japanese filmmaker, since the traditional way to become a director was to get a job at a film studio as an assistant and then make your way up the ranks. Ishii's discovery of cinema, however, coincided with the collapse of the studio system, when assistant directors were no longer being hired.

This collapse could be regarded as the main reason for the rise of independent cinema in Japan in the late '70s, but the spirit of the times was a strong influence as well. After Kinji Fukasaku's *Battles without Honor and Humanity* and Kazuhiko Hasegawa's *The Man Who Stole the Sun* gave a voice to the children of the reconstruction, the generation born in the late '50s and early '60s started taking their first strides on the path of self-expression. Punk became one of those paths. Sōgo Ishii meanwhile wanted to make films. So he picked up a camera and did just that.

> **"At the time it was very difficult for young people to make films in Japan. It still is, in fact. Most directors are over forty, and the normal process is to begin as an assistant director, then gradually move on to directing. I didn't want to be an assistant director and I just started making films by myself."**

Ishii would make his first feature-length film a mere year after first picking up a movie camera.

Nikkatsu, then still up to their necks in Roman Porno, took an interest in the director's short films and offered to produce and distribute a feature-length remake of *Panic High School*. Co-directed with Nikkatsu contract director Yukihiro Sawada, the 94-minute *Panic High School* was released in theaters in the summer of 1978. Ishii was still only a sophomore student, but by graduating from underground 8mm filmmaking to the professional film industry he became one of the most important filmmakers in Japan's cinema history, setting the precedent that would be followed by numerous young directors in the two decades that followed.

Ishii's young age showed through in the film, not because it lacked finesse, but because its subject matter was the pressure students are under when studying for their university entrance exams. Its protagonist is one such student for whom the pressure becomes too great and who commits suicide. When the school's ad-ministration trivializes his death, his classmates revolt and take over the building, leading to a violent clash with authority.

This theme of people cracking under the pressure of society is one that would recur throughout Sōgo Ishii's later work. It also shows how closely related his vision is to that of both Kinji Fukasaku and Kazuhiko Hasegawa, whose work also expressed dissatisfaction with the society that resulted from Japan's post-war economic renaissance. Contemporary Japanese cinema, particularly its sizeable independent segment, was largely born from counterculture and discontent.

For his graduation piece two years later, Ishii upped the ante a bit more. He directed his second feature, the manic biker movie *Crazy Thunder Road*, alone and independently. Shot on 16mm, the film had raw energy to spare, achieved largely through the director's lightning-fast use of camera and editing, and made

Filmography

1977
- Panic High School (*Kōkō Dai Panikku*) [short]

1978
- The Solitude of One Divided by 880,000 (*Hachijū-Hachi-Man Bun no Ichi no Kodoku*) [short]
- Panic High School (*Kōkō Dai Panikku*)
- Totsugeki! Hakata Gurentai [short]

1979
- Hashiru [short]

1980
- Crazy Thunder Road (*Kurui-zaki Sandā Rōdo*)

1981
- Anarchy 80 Ishin [music video]
- Shuffle

1982
- Burst City (*Bakuretsu Toshi*)

- Stop Jap [music video]
- Norikoto: Toriaezu no Taiwa No. 1 [short]

1993
- Asia Strikes Back (*Ajia no Gyakushū*)

1984
- Crazy Family (*Gyaku Funsha Kazoku*)
- Isseifubi Sepia: Genzai ga Suki Desu [video]
- The Roosters: Paranoiac Live [video]
- The Stalin: For Never [video]

1986
- Half Human (½ *Mensch* / *Hanbun Ningen*) [video]

1989
- The Master of Shiatsu (*Shiatsu Ōja*) [short]

1991
- Friction: Dumb Numb Live [video]

1993

- J-Movie Wars: Tokyo Blood [TV]

1994
- Angel Dust (*Enjeru Dasuto*)

1995
- August in the Water (*Mizu no Naka no Hachigatsu*)

1997
- Labyrinth of Dreams (*Yume no Ginga*)

2000
- Gojoe (*Gojō Reisenki*)

2001
- Electric Dragon 80,000 V

2002
- Skirt [music video]
- Kanashimi Johnny [music video]
- Shiritsu Tantei Hama Maiku [TV series, co-director]

2003
- Dead End Run

2004
- Mirrored Mind (*Kyo-shin*)

such a big impression that Toei bought the distribution rights, blew it up to 35mm and released it in theaters. Fresh out of university, Sōgo Ishii had arrived with a bang, and people sat up to take notice of this uncompromising new wunderkind. (In a survey among leading international filmmakers, Takeshi Kitano named *Crazy Thunder Road* one of his ten favorite films of the twentieth century.)

Among those people who took notice was the Tokyo-based punk band Anarchy, who asked the young director to shoot a promotional video. Employing his trusted 16mm format, the 10-minute *Anarchy 80 Ishin* brought Ishii back to his punk roots. The video kick-started a new wave of creativity for the young director, and he followed it up the same year with the 30-minute fiction film *Shuffle*, based on the manga *Run* by Katsuhiro Ōtomo. Very much a forerunner to the work of director Sabu, the film is one long chase scene in which a cop runs after a young, Mohawk-wearing punk who has just killed his own girlfriend.

The two short films were mere warm-ups for what he embarked on next, however. His most ambitious project yet, **Burst City** would become the apotheosis of Ishii's punk cinema and it remains arguably the definitive Sōgo Ishii film. The film combined the biker motif of his previous feature with a cast consisting of a number of famous faces from Japan's punk scene. Many of these musicians took leading roles as well as performing their music in the film. For the production of *Burst City*, bands and musicians from the country's three punk capitals united in the countryside outside Tokyo: The Roosters and the Rockers represented Kyushu, Machizō Machida (better known today as novelist Kō Machida) of the band Inu came from Kansai, while the Stalin served as the Tokyo delegates.

With its apocalyptic sci-fi scenario, the film was an influence on the cyberpunk movement of the second half of the 1980s in Japan. Combining a fascination with technology with a visual style derived from punk, filtered through an

Courtesy of PIA Film Festival

Sōgo Ishii

otaku's obsession with early-'80s science fiction, cyberpunk had particular resonance in urban Japan's technology-obsessed landscape. Its premier exponent, Shinya Tsukamoto, borrowed heavily from Sōgo Ishii's visual style, as the abundant undercranking and rapid-fire editing in the former's early films attest.

The Stalin's involvement in *Burst City* was particularly significant. They had become the country's leading punk exponents, the Japanese equivalent of the Sex Pistols, and their appearance in *Burst City* led to Ishii directing the video for their next single, entitled *Stop Jap*, the same year. Despite their popularity, the band decided to call it quits two years later. Their 1984 farewell tour spawned a final live album plus a concert video directed by Ishii: *The Stalin For Never*. Dark, ominous, and intensely powerful, *The Stalin For Never* captures the boundless energy and soul of the band's live performances, spearheaded by the charismatic yet enigmatic frontman Michirō Endō.

To capture this energy, Ishii used his trademark fast-motion sequences and rapid cutting, culminating in a breathtaking, lightning-speed compilation of images from the band's career. What the concert film showed above all, aside from the spirit and energy of the band, was the affinity of the director with his subject. Sōgo Ishii knew the punk scene, knew the bands, and knew the personalities of the musicians. In fact he was one of them. His instrument just happened to be a movie camera rather than a guitar or drums.

Ishii did pick up a musical instrument on occasion. One of those occasions was in 1983, when he formed Sōgo Ishii and the Bacillus Army. This impromptu band released only one record, a concept album of sorts entitled *Asia Strikes Back*. On side A, the Asia side, the theme was the poverty and struggle of people in Asian countries, while the music on side B, the Japan side, meant to reflect the stress and superficiality of day-to-day life in Japan, a theme closely connected to the subject matter of his films. By contrasting the two situations, the band seemed to say that the salvation for Asia did not lie in striving to copy Japan's advanced economic status. With this concept in mind, Ishii shot a 30-minute film that accompanied the band on tour.

The same year he made the Stalin concert film, the director went to work on his next feature. As its title implies, *Crazy Family* was Ishii's assault on the family unit, in which a father tries to defend his brand-new, ideal suburban home from a termite attack.

"With *Crazy Family* I wanted to show the Japanese family as I saw it."

The film expressed again Ishii's preoccupation with the maddening effects of social pressure on the individual, but here expanded it by having it resonate through the cornerstone of that same society: the family.

The family presented in the film was the picture-perfect image of success: a father suc-cessful in his work, a loving mother, and two children who study hard and don't show a hint of rebellion. The picture of perfection is completed when the family moves into a suburban house, far away from the cramped city. But cracks quickly start to show when grandfather moves in with them and termites are discovered to be nibbling on the woodwork. In no time the entire family spins out of control, with the father at the center trying to protect the image of perfection rather than his wife and children themselves. Dad declares war on the termites, Granddad is unhappy with the fact that he has to live in the basement and declares war on the rest of the family, while the son locks himself in his room to study for his entrance exams, keeping himself awake at nights by stabbing himself with a knife.

Crazy Family would be Ishii's last feature film for quite a while. A look at his filmography of features shows a decade-long gap, in which the director was unable to find financing for any of his projects. As in tune as he was with the punk movement, he was completely out of touch (or rather ahead of) the general audience and the industry at the time.

"*Crazy Family* got a lot of attention abroad, but wasn't very popular in Japan. This was the same situation as before. Everyone in Japan just complained that they didn't understand my films. So it was difficult to work in Japan at that time."

Failing to get any of his projects off the ground, he kept himself busy directing more concert films, music videos, and shorts. His reputation with the music industry was still solid enough, so much so, in fact, that he was asked to work with bands that had little to do with punk. One of those bands was Isseifubi Sepia, who had started out as street performers and dancers but were rapidly becoming national pop idols. The promotional video he made for them, *Genzai ga Suki Desu* [trans: We love the present], is worth a mention for being the acting debut of an Is-

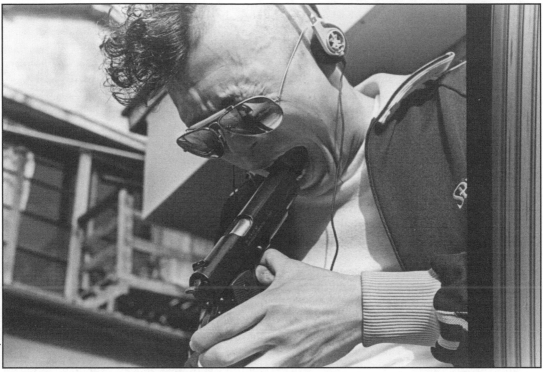

Shuffle

seifubi member who would become one of the biggest stars of V-cinema gangster films in the 1990s: Shō Aikawa.

Ishii followed it up with a concert film for another band that had been featured in *Burst City*, the Roosters. *The Roosters: Paranoiac Live* is something of a watershed in Ishii's career. It forms the transition between his old punk works and the more meditative style he would employ in his films from the '90s. On one hand the concert film was crammed with superimpositions, splitscreen shots, and all manner of delay and distortion effects. On the other hand, he kept intercutting the songs with lingering shots of cloud formations, barren landscapes, and details of ruined, burned-down buildings.

The successful run of *Crazy Family* across international film festivals opened up new opportunities for Ishii. It was at a festival that he came in touch with the German noise band Einstürzende Neubauten. The band was going to tour Japan in 1985 and wanted Ishii to film their concerts. The result, entitled *½Mensch* (a.k.a. *Half Human*), again demonstrated a more conceptual approach to the material. Ishii filmed the band performing for the camera in a ruined warehouse, made complete music videos for three songs, and combined everything with footage from the Japanese tour. The result was an admirable representation of the band's philosophy that all music is noise and that all noise is music. In Neubauten's performance, the human body and all manner of industrial metal objects combine to make music, so Ishii intercut their performances with meditations on the similarity between flesh and metal: zoom in close enough and the truth will reveal itself, Ishii seemed to say. At the level of the atom, everything is equal.

½Mensch is the work of a filmmaker trying

to understand his subject, then expressing that understanding in the shape of conceptual images. This evolution toward a more conceptual and meditative style was partially due to his frustrations over not being able to mount a new feature film project. The style became a way of healing or at least soothing those frustrations, as witnessed by his 1989 short *The Master of Shiatsu*. Starting with a woman undergoing a shiatsu massage at the hands of the titular master, Ishii gradually moves his camera in closer to the points of contact until finally segueing into an abstract visual representation of the sensations shiatsu creates within the human body.

> **"I made it to cure my mental damage. I had so many bad feelings because I couldn't make any other films, so this was a way to cure myself, a kind of therapy."**

In 1991 he made another concert film for one of the last surviving Japanese punk bands, Friction, before another year of inactivity passed. Then in 1993 he was invited to contribute to the ambitious television project of up-and-coming producer Takenori Sentō. J Movie Wars was a series that showcased the work of six directors, each of whom was asked to direct four ten-minute shorts. The four segments that make up Ishii's entry, *Tokyo Blood*, are like a map of the director's evolution as a filmmaker. Starting with a reworking of his favorite theme of people cracking under the pressure of society in a format similar to *Shuffle*, with each segment it moved farther and farther away from narrative, culminating in the entirely conceptual and entirely visual *Heart of Stone*, which heralds some of the ideas he would further explore two years later in **August in the Water**.

Tokyo Blood drew the industry's attention back to Sōgo Ishii, not in the least because it demonstrated how much he had evolved as a person and as a filmmaker. The following year gave him the chance to return to feature filmmaking, albeit as a director-for-hire. *Angel Dust* (1994)

nevertheless offered him ample opportunity to express his newfound style and concerns.

> **"I spent a lot of time reading books in the years before that, especially the work of Philip K. Dick and J. G. Ballard. Reading them, I saw new possibilities of expression and they continue to influence me to this day. By that time, virtual reality was becoming popular in Japan and the meta fiction these writers use in their novels was really similar to what was happening in Japan at the time."**

In a prophetic story of a cult member committing serial killings in the Tokyo subway with a syringe filled with lethal poison (one year before the Aum Shinrikyo cult unleashed its sarin gas attack on that same subway system), Ishii contemplated the human being's displacement from his surroundings, the alienation induced by the cramped metropolis, and the possibility of salvation in nature and mother earth. The film in many ways predates the major work of Kiyoshi Kurosawa, who would develop similar meditations on postmodern man's relation to his surroundings from the basis of genre plotting, in such later films as **Cure**, **Charisma**, and **Pulse**.

He took this approach a few steps further in *August in the Water* (1995), which he made the following year. Rather than using the plot as a stepping stone, he discarded it altogether in favor of creating an abstract audiovisual representation of his themes and concerns. The Sōgo Ishii of *August in the Water* resembled nothing of the young punk who had made such raucous assaults on his own audience as *Crazy Thunder Road*. Those who hadn't kept up with the evolution of his work since *Crazy Family* could be forgiven for thinking that this was a different person working under the same name.

> **"My first four films were made between 1978 and 1983. I call them my punk movies. These films are liked by a lot of people and my public**

image is based on these films, so that's why I'm seen as the 'punk director.' After that I wanted to take up another challenge and also the investors of those later films didn't like the punk style. So those are two reasons why my films changed."

Less thematically abstract than hauntingly atmospheric, *Labyrinth of Dreams* (*Yume no Ginga*, 1997) continued Ishii's preoccupation with the expression of mood over linear plotting. The story of a young bus driver who may or not be a murderer also saw him team up for the first time with actor Tadanobu Asano, the man who would become the actor of choice of the generation of filmmakers that came into prominence in the late '90s. Ishii and Asano continued their collaboration in the director's next two films, *Gojoe* (2000) and *Electric Dragon 80,000 V* (2001).

Gojoe, Ishii's first period piece, was a project the director had been sitting on for over a decade. Based on a half-mythologized part of Japanese history, *Gojoe* plays less like a *jidai geki* costume drama than a true Sōgo Ishii film in period garb. Elements and themes from his films from the '90s—spiritualism, the metaphysical, man being a small but essential part of the greater cosmic scheme—are combined with a resurgence of the boundless energy of his work from the '80s.

"The story is very famous in Japan, though young people hardly know it. But what I did was turn everything into its opposite: the good people became the bad people and the other way around. I didn't set out to make a classical *jidai geki*, so I put elements of science fiction and magic realism into it. I used the story as a kind of set-up. Normally, my films are only seen by young people, but I wanted a lot of people to see it, so this was the first time I could shoot a film on a big budget. It was like five times the amount of money I'm used to working with."

Unfortunately, *Gojoe* was a costly flop at the box office. Meant as the commercial blockbuster that would allow producer Takenori Sentō's Suncent Cinema Works to continue producing its more characteristic arthouse films, it became the company's downfall instead, even more so when all Sentō's efforts to sell it to foreign distributors failed too, leaving only the domestic DVD market as a means to recoup some of the cost.

Electric Dragon 80,000V, which was made back-to-back with Gojoe, did nothing to remedy the situation. At 55 minutes, its format was unsuitable for wide theatrical release, particularly at Japan's inflated ticket prices (which can be as high as U.S. $25). Seen as a fun experiment by both its producer and director, it ended up costing them dearly when the figures for *Gojoe* came in, painfully putting the finger on Sentō's main weakness as a producer: his eagerness to indulge his directors.

For all its failings as a commercial venture, *Electric Dragon 80,000V* is very interesting as a work of art. It marked Ishii's return to the frenzied punk style of his early films, but retained the disregard for plotting that marked his recent films. In fact, the film seemed to have very little in the way of substance, devoid as it was of themes and story. What it presented were actors Tadanobu Asano and Masatoshi Nagase playing high-voltage superheroes who chase one another across rooftops and through back alleys in an attempt to destroy each other, which they try in the most spectacular ways imaginable. In between bouts they recharge themselves using electric chairs, electric beds, wall sockets and entire power stations.

With such a slight premise, *Electric Dragon 80,000V* obviously wasn't meant to tell a story. The film expressed other things, most of all the spirit of the new band Sōgo Ishii had recently formed, an industrial noise/punk group called Mach 1.67, whose fluctuating lineup regularly included his two lead actors Asano and Nagase. Like his early punk films, *Electric Dragon* was an attempt to fuse music with images and to express the equivalent of one in the other. Even though it was a fiction film, *Electric Dragon 80,000V* was closely related to the director's concert films, in which he also tried to express the mood, philosophies, and charisma of individual bands through images.

Although *Electric Dragon* gave the impression that the director had come full circle, Sōgo Ishii continued working, and indeed continued his experimentation with sound and vision, shrugging off the commercial failure of his previous two films. He directed music videos for Tadanobu Asano's pop-star wife, Chara, and for singer UA. The latter he also directed in an episode of the *Shiritsu Tantei Hama Maiku* TV series. Starring and produced by Masatoshi Nagase, the series was a spin-off of Kaizō Hayashi's trilogy of detective films that started with ***The Most Terrible Time in My Life***, which starred Nagase as detective Maiku Hama.

With popular actors like Asano and Nagase all too eager to work with him, it's unlikely that Ishii's desire for uncompromising experimentation will lead him into another dry spell like in the late '80s. Embracing the digital video format, he made *Dead End Run* in 2003, his most audacious audio experiment yet. Starring Asano, Nagase, and increasingly popular actor/model Yūsuke Iseya, the film used an entirely new and specially designed sound system with sixteen audio channels, again making it a work unfit for general release. The fact that he managed to get such a bold project financed in the wake of two box office flops is hopefully a sign that Ishii will be able to continue on his uncompromising path for quite a few years to come.

Sōgo Ishii's influence on contemporary cinema is enormous. Not only did he pave the way for independent filmmakers to have their work shown and recognized, his films, his themes, and his style either preceded or directly influenced many of today's leading directors. Sōgo Ishii's name is, in other words, synonymous with contemporary Japanese cinema

↓ Crazy Thunder Road

狂い咲きサンダーロード

Kuruizaki Sandā Rōdo

1980. CAST: Tatsuo Yamada, Masamitsu Ōike, Toshiji Kobayashi, Kōji Nanjō, Yōsuke Nakajima. 98 minutes.

Raucous, bad-assed biker movie seething with violent inter-gang rivalry and throbbing to a spiky punk soundtrack.

Visions of a bleak, post-apocalyptic urban wasteland strewn with twisted hunks of mechanical wreckage. A rasping electronic buzz on the soundtrack. These impressions kick-start into a jarring, rapid-fire sequence of chrome, neon, and flaming exhaust pipes set against a background of broken tenement blocks and abandoned factories, as boys in black leather with *Be-Bop High School* quiffs ride menacingly out into the night, tearing up the town in the solo theatrical debut from arguably the most important director to emerge from Japan during the '80s. Although it was originally shot on 16mm, Toei was so impressed with the film that the company blew it up to 35mm for theatrical distribution.

This tour de force of automotive auto-eroticism focuses on the conflicts between a gang of bikers and a group of right-wing nationalists, set in motion when gang leader Ken opts out of the front line to settle down for a life of domestic bliss with his girlfriend, Noriko. His departure leaves the rest of the gang floundering with all the direction of a headless chicken, and so into the breach steps Jin. When Jin's hellraising antics begin to incur the ire of rival gangs, erupting into full-blown pitched warfare involving chains, chainsaws, and anything else that is hard-edged and at hand, Ken is soon hauled back into the fray.

Ishii's film has little in the way of stylistic precedent in terms of Japan's previous decade of cinema, though the milieu of the *bōsōzoku* (biker gangs) had been tackled before by Teruo

Crazy Thunder Road

Ishii's *Detonation!* (*Bakuhatsu!*) trio of films during the mid-'70s. Often reminiscent of *Mad Max* (George Miller, 1979), *Crazy Thunder Road* bears more of a relationship with parallel developments in the U.S. underground, namely Sam Raimi's rollercoaster debut, *Evil Dead* (1982). Both films are dazzling showcases of ostentatious film school experimentation coupled with an undeniably accomplished technical proficiency and razor-sharp editing—films which attempt to subdue rather than seduce the viewer.

Ishii and Raimi's films are calling cards to the industry that make a virtue of their minuscule resources to complement the raw-edged aesthetic, demonstrating that when it comes to making fast- paced, abrasive, violent action entertainment, technical innovation stretches one hell of a lot further than big bucks. The story unfolds almost as a series of fragmented image sequences,

its manga-influenced stylistic origins rendered obvious in scenes such as a muted bar room heart-to-heart as the resigned leader communicates to his girlfriend tacitly in a series of speech bubbles in the form of text intertitles. Billowing clouds of dry ice, showering sparks, and strips of neon light keep the screen permanently aflame throughout, whilst the soundtrack throbs to the screams of the brawling bikers, roaring engines, and screeching brakes, interspersed with spiky, energetic punk anthems of the day. Ishii's film is as much about soundscape as it is images.

Loud, brash and in-your-face, what *Crazy Thunder Road* lacks in charm, it more than makes up for in terms of its crude energy and refreshing vitality. This embryonic offering in Ishii's oeuvre proved a sturdy foundation for the director to build his career upon, a career in which the director's explorations, experimentations, and innovations in cinematic technique have continuously marked him out for interest. If you can't hack the pace, then steer well clear.

↓ Burst City
爆裂都市
Bakuretsu Toshi

1982. CAST: Takanori Jinnai, Machizō Machida, Shinya Ohe, Michirō Endō. 117 minutes. RELEASE: DVD, Toei Video (Japan, no subtitles).

The defining film of Japan's punk subculture and the quintessential Sōgo Ishii film is a marvel of stylistic innovation. A true original that remains as impressive for today's audiences as it was in its day.

If Sōgo Ishii can be considered Japan's punk filmmaker, then *Burst City* is his defining statement. It's a film packed to the brim with anger, defiance, and boundless energy, made with a group of like-minded individuals that includes the leading lights of the early-'80s punk movement in starring roles.

There is little in Western cinema that can be properly compared to *Burst City*. Julien Temple's Sex Pistols film *The Great Rock 'n' Roll Swindle* (1980) was a feature-length promo for one band (and its manager). Alex Cox's unjustly maligned *Straight to Hell* (1986) comes closest in terms of concept, featuring punk and rock musicians like Joe Strummer, Elvis Costello, and Courtney Love, if not in terms of quality. Cox's film was made at a moment when punk was all but dead and buried, whereas *Burst City* was shot at the height of the movement's energy, channeling this rage into a raw and raucous explosion of celluloid artistry.

The punk aesthetic permeates the film on all levels, beginning with the story. Loosely structured and episodic rather than actually plotted, *Burst City* features two story lines that converge in the finale. One features a large community of punk rockers and assorted hangers-on chaotically playing and partying in a nighttime wasteland to protest the imminent construction of a nuclear power plant. Drag races, fistfights, feverish mosh pit activity, and clashes with "Battle Police" are accompanied by stage performances by real-life bands the Rockers and the Stalin. The other subplot concerns a pair of *Mad Max*-like bikers in metal get-ups—a young mute and his animalistic protector who roam the land to avenge the murders of the younger man's family. Teaming up with a group of lowlifes working under brutal circumstances on the construction of the power plant, they discover that one of the men they're looking for is the rich industrialist behind the whole scheme. The bikers drag their comrades along in their revenge against the industrialist and his yakuza cohorts, just as riot police start closing in on the punk rockers nearby. An orgiastic cavalcade of violent rebellion ensues.

While obviously a continuation of Ishii's previous film **Crazy Thunder Road**, *Burst City*'s pair of enigmatic bikers are post-apocalyptic equivalents of legendary folk heroes Yoshitsune and Benkei, the scorned young prince and his supernatural protector immortalized in numerous kabuki plays. The director would adapt the tale of these two wandering outcasts again almost twenty years later, its narrative thoroughly spun around, with the spectacular period piece **Gojoe**. The spin he puts on the characters in *Burst City* is to make them agents in a revolution, one fought by workers and punks alike.

In terms of style, Ishii translates the energy of his characters into the pace of the film, most obviously in the editing, changing shots at a pace that was virtually unheard of at the time and which even leaves today's Hollywood fastcutters eating dust. The editing is but one element in his formal approach, however, one that is used in combination with the element of undercranking (a.k.a. fast motion). Ishii's approach is carefully thought out, combining different

© 1982 Toei Company, Ltd.

Burst City

film speeds into a single sequence that mirrors the groundbreaking work with variations of overcranking (a.k.a. slow motion) done by Sam Peckinpah on *The Wild Bunch* (1969).

Ishii's style is not only present in his technique, however. He works with the elements in front of his camera, too, creating an almost carnivalesque atmosphere by filling the frame with numerous extras (all of whom are listed by name as cast members in the closing credits, emphasizing the film's collaborative nature), who like the main cast are dressed in outrageous costumes, hairstyles, and makeup (pasty-faced Takanori Jinnai looks almost goblin-like in his close-ups). The numerous but subtle touches of comedy also add to the creation of this atmosphere, not to mention such spectacles as the Stalin frontman Michirō Endō throwing pigs'

heads at a rioting mob. If it weren't for the deafening punk soundtrack, we would be right in surrealist territory.

But for all its exaggeration and stylization, *Burst City* also employs documentary elements, particularly in capturing the musical performances and the musicians' preparations before taking the stage. This element would become the basis of Ishii's later concert films, in which he in turn employed elements of exaggeration as used in this film. The stylistic similarity between *Burst City* and his concert film *The Stalin For Never*, made two years later, are striking and show how well *Burst City* reflected the Japanese punk scene.

By letting life, rather than cinematic precedents, serve as his main inspiration, Sōgo Ishii created a style that was truly unique in its day.

Some of it has since been appropriated by other filmmakers, but even for today's audiences *Burst City* remains a one-of-a-kind experience.

↓ August in the Water
水の中の八月
Mizu no Naka no Hachigatsu

1995. CAST: Rena Komine, Shinsuke Aoki, Masa-aki Takarai, Reiko Matsuo, Naho Toda, Hideyo Amamoto, Yanosuke Narasaki, Masao Kusakari, Yūji Nakamura. 117 minutes.

A double meteor strike and a plague that turns one's organs to stone. Ishii brings a fresh approach and some stunning images in this uneven grab bag of high school romance and New Age phenomena.

There's a new girl in town, Izumi Hazuki (Komine), whose arrival at Ishido High School in the city of Fukuoka as a high-diving champion creates quite a splash, not least amongst the two best buddies Mao (Aoki) and Ukiya (Takarai). Hot-headed Ukiya heads straight to his childhood friend, Miki (Matsuo), an amateur astrologer, to see what the stars have in store, but is warned away with the message that there will never be any romance between him and the new girl. This leaves the path open for the more reserved and self-conscious Mao, but in the meantime Izumi is having troubles of her own.

Izumi's appearance coincides with a double meteorite strike in the forest outside the town, which inexplicably acts as a catalyst for a drought and a bizarre local epidemic that causes one's inner organs to petrify. Then, on the day of an important diving tournament, a terrible accident occurs in which the water beneath Izumi momentarily turns into stone in mid-dive, leaving her in a coma after belly-flopping on the bare rock. When she awakes, the world seems very different to Izumi, fresh and vibrant, as if she is experiencing it for the first time.

Taking in the whole spectrum of pre-millennial New Age phenomena, the bizarre *August in the Water* is a bit of a mixed bag, an imaginative pseudo-scientific fantasy that stands out fairly uniquely amongst the product of the time. Visually the film is a wonder, full of bright sunlight and lucid blues in its exteriors, and water is, of course, everywhere—in the shimmering hues of the prismatic light dancing on the bottom of the dolphin pool from which Izumi (whose name actually means fountain, or spring) first emerges, quickly drying droplets on the pavements evaporating under the burning August sun, and the slow motion sprays during a lengthy sequence at a Shinto festival held in the city streets.

Like *Angel Dust* before it, it marks rather a change of pace for Ishii from his better-known anarchic fast-paced action films of the early '80s, with their screaming soundtracks and lightning-fast edits. After a break away making music videos, the blip of activity that followed his '90s rediscovery, prompted by *Tokyo Blood*, is marked by a radical shift in cinematic gear. Using a far more studied and sober approach to filmmaking than his frenetic earlier work, the hallucinogenic ambiance of *August in the Water* was hinted at a few years earlier by his mesmeric *The Master of Shiatsu* (1989), an inventive 12-minute short made, according to the director, for "therapeutic reasons."

Here he takes the process of simplification and abstraction one step further. Cinematic technique is almost conspicuous by its absence: the simple aesthetic of the image is the most crucial. To this end Ishii's approach hinges on his masterfully precise editing and strong pictorial composition, for example in the long montage of shots showing Izumi twisting gracefully in mid-air as she practices for the diving competition, or the beautifully composed abstracted close-ups of natural phenomena: the patterns of rock surfaces, the cracking dried bark on trees, fish scales, leaves, insects, etc.

Ishii's almost transcendental approach to a filmmaking in which he claims that the images come from within himself, apparently devoid of any outside cinematic influence, has certainly resulted here in a seductively distinct work. But if *August in the Water* is the least well known of Ishii's second cycle of features, then it is probably due to the fact that it is also the least engaging. Be it conversations with squeaking dolphins or the clumps of mushrooms surrounding the meteor which glow lysergically with an ultraviolet hue, drama takes a firm back seat to the dream logic narrative and the result is a film that is simultaneously hypnotic and beautiful, but maddeningly slow-moving and detached.

Ishii's film is not to be confused with Yoichirō Takahashi's *Fishes in August*. Released in 1998, Takahashi's strong coming of age drama shares not only the same Japanese title as Ishii's film, but also its high school protagonists and the competitive swimming backdrop. Fortunately, it leaves out the magic mushrooms.

↓ Gojoe
五条霊戦記
Gojō Reisenki

2000. CAST: Daisuke Ryū, Tadanobu Asano, Masatoshi Nagase, Ittoku Kishibe, Jun Kunimura 137 minutes. RELEASE: DVD, Media Blasters (U.S., English subtitles), Pioneer (Japan, no subtitles).

Ishii's revisionist period action piece moves the action away from samurai territory and focuses its lens on warrior monks, renegade noblemen, and rebellious bandits. Lavishly shot and lengthy, Gojoe is easily one of the most interesting *jidai geki* in recent years.

A sumptuous and at times super-charged swordplay fantasy, *Gojoe* puts the spin on one of Japan's most popular feudal legends. Warriors of the Heike clan get their heads chopped off by a seemingly invisible force at Kyoto's Gojō Bridge and soon rumors begin to circulate that the clan has incurred the wrath of a supernatural demon. Buddhist monk Benkei (Ryū) is attracted to the evil force that lurks at the bridge on account of the demons of his own past and sets out to confront whatever it is that's causing the Heike blood to flow.

This man of faith encounters and befriends the cynical grave robber Tetsukichi (Nagase), for whom death is only an opportunity for material gain and who collects swords from the bodies of Heike warriors slain by the demon. The pair are witness to a battle between the forces of the Heike clan and the supposed demon, who is in actual fact a young warrior named Shanao (a dashing Tadanobu Asano), a former nobleman from the ranks of Heike's now-vanquished mortal enemy, the Genji clan. Shanao has two equally skillful swordsmen to help him in wreaking his vengeance, one of them an effeminately beautiful young man by the name of Yoshitsune.

The fact that Sōgo Ishii is at the helm should be an indication that this is not your average swords-and-kimonos adventure. *Gojoe* is a radical rethinking of *Kanjinchō*, the kabuki play based on the life of twelfth-century warlord Yoshitsune, most famously brought to the screen in Akira Kurosawa's *The Men Who Tread on the Tiger's Tail* (*Tora no O o Fumu Otokotachi*, 1945). *Gojoe*'s story takes place before the events of Kurosawa's film, which depicted the flight of Yoshitsune and Benkei as they traveled in the guise of monks to escape the wrath of Yoshitsune's brother Yoritomo. According to the play, Benkei had become Yoshitsune's ally and protector after the foolhardy warrior monk had engaged the young lord in a swordfight at Kyoto's Gojō Bridge and lost. Also according to the tradition, Yoshitsune in youth went under the name of Shanao and was taught his impressive martial arts skills by a supernatural demon.

Ishii did some drastic reshuffling with the events, attempting to make what is already one of his country's most enduring and popular myths even more mythical. Allies become mortal enemies, a single character is split into two separate ones, and fantasy is treated as fact. According to the director, the aim was to preserve a part of Japanese history by re-imagining it for a younger generation.

As a result of this approach, the film feels like a breath of fresh air, giving not only much needed new life but also nuance to the overly conformist *jidai geki* genre. The focus here is not on samurai but on rebel guerillas, hermits, thieves, and peasants. It's the lower social strata that form the background to *Gojoe*'s narrative, while the samurai serve mainly as fodder for Shanao's double swords, their battle harnesses so pompously adorned as to become ridiculous.

Whatever else may have changed for him over the years, Ishii clearly hasn't let go of his dissident spirit.

With its nicely defined characters and terrific performances, its impressive battle scenes, and roaring monster of a finale (followed by a denouement that sets up the premise for *The Men Who Tread on the Tiger's Tail*, complete with identical costumes), not to mention Sōgo Ishii's return to powerhouse filmmaking, *Gojoe* should have become at least a minor sensation. Unfortunately it sank mercilessly at the box office, taking producer Takenori Sentō and his Suncent Cinema Works company down with it. Despite the indifference of Japanese audiences, *Gojoe* is a refreshing reinvention of one of the stalwart genres in Japanese cinema, exhilarating and breathtakingly photographed.

CHAPTER 5

Masato Harada
原田眞人

Often referred to as the most American or the most international of today's Japanese filmmakers, Masato Harada currently finds himself at a peculiar crossroads in his career. Born in 1949, Harada was fascinated by cinema from an early age (he remembers witnessing the shooting of Akira Kurosawa's *Seven Samurai* as a child), but found the required studio apprenticeship that would allow him to become a director too bothersome. At age nineteen he left Japan hoping to study filmmaking abroad, first stopping over in London to study English. There he rediscovered American cinema, in particular the work of Howard Hawks, and started writing a column for film magazine *Kinema Jumpo*. After his studies he left for the United States, where he would spend a large part of the '70s working as a foreign correspondent for the Japanese film press in Hollywood. During this time he also got the opportunity to have a five-hour audience with Hawks at the latter's Palm Springs abode, a meeting Harada still recalls with fondness. To this day he considers Hawks a mentor.

"I worked as a film critic one step before filmmaking. I became a film critic and film reporter so that I could cover the actual filmmaking process and interview film directors. Always I thought: "What if I directed this film?" That question became the basis for my film criticism. Maybe for that training it was a good background. I also tried to get information about what goes on behind the camera, what kind of pressure a director was under when he made a certain film. Then you start seeing things. Up to a certain level I think you should ignore the fact of how a movie was made. But I think most film critics should be aware of what kind of budget a film carries and how many shooting days it had. That's a basic element of a reviewer's work. Unfortunately in Japan, 90 percent of film critics just read production notes provided by the production office. They don't double-check anything, because they are paid so little. If you spend too much time on one review, you can't make a living. The level of Japanese film criticism is getting worse every year, because there's no research being done."

His sojourns abroad strongly marked Harada as a human being and as a filmmaker. When he returned to Japan in the late '70s, it was with the perspective of an outsider, someone who had wrested himself loose of the social fabric of his native country. This allowed him to look at Japanese society with a degree of distance and to be less bound by the ruling mores in voicing his dislikes of what he saw.

The basis of Harada's filmmaking is found in these experiences: on the one hand a critical view of Japan and a willingness to lay bare its social problems, and on the other hand a strong attraction to American filmmaking. The balance between these two main foundations would swing back and forth throughout his work, tipping over to one side for the most part, but occasionally (as in 1994's **Kamikaze Taxi**) achieving equilibrium.

With his debut film *Goodbye Flickmania*, made in 1979 after his return to Japan, the scales were, as the title indicated, firmly in favor of Harada's love for American films. Meant as homage to Howard Hawks and to cinema in general, it very autobiographically portrayed a cinephile (Takuzō Kawatani) who can't distinguish between the real world and the world of film.

Following his directorial debut, Harada's knowledge of American film, as well as his fluent English, helped land him the job as writer and director of the Japanese dubbed version of *The Empire Strikes Back* a year later. He would continue working on the dubbing of Hollywood films throughout the decade, directing Japanese voice actors for Joe Dante's *Innerspace*, Barry Levinson's *Good Morning Vietnam*, and Stanley Kubrick's *Full Metal Jacket*. His language proficiency also saw him returning to California to shoot a coffee commercial featuring Kirk Douglas, in addition to being chosen to direct the German/Japanese co-production *Windy* (1984), about a Japanese Grand Prix racer on the international circuit.

During the '80s, Harada remained something of a journeyman director, directing vehicles for singer-turned-actor Ryūdō Uzaki (*Indecent Exposure*, 1985) and the manufactured girl band Onyanko (*Onyanko The Movie: Kiki Ippatsu!*, 1986), a documentary on the Paris–Dakar rally (*Paris–Dakar 15,000*, 1986), a gangster film (*The Heartbreak Yakuza*, 1987) and the cyber sci-fi *Gunhed*. Going on to moderate international success in an English-dubbed version on video, *Gunhed* got Harada temporarily re-installed in Hollywood through the intervention of James Cameron, but his dream of directing a genuine Hollywood film failed to materialize. In an interview with Robin Gatto, Harada stated about *Gunhed*:

Filmography

1979
- *Goodbye Flickmania (Saraba Eiga no Tomoyo: Indian Samā)*

1984
- *Windy (Uindī)*

1985
- *Indecent Exposure (Tōsha: Nihyakugojū Bun no Ichi Byō)*

1986
- *Paris-Dakar 15000 (Paris-Dakar 15000 Eikō e no Chōsen)*
- *Onyanko The Movie: Kiki Ippatsu!*

1987
- *The Heartbreak Yakuza (Saraba Itoshiki Hito Yo)*

1988
- *Gunhed*

1990
- *TUFF Part 1: Tanjō Hen* [video]

1991
- *TUFF Part 3: Bijinesu Satsuriku Hen* [video]
- *TUFF Part 4: Chi no Shūkaku Hen* [video]

1992
- *TUFF Part 5: Kariforunia Koroshi no Ansorojī* [video]

1993
- *Painted Desert*

1994
- *Kamikaze Taxi (Fukushū no Tenshi)*

1995

1988
- *Troubleshooters (Toraburushūtā)* (a.k.a. *Trouble with Nango*)

1996
- *Rowing Through (Eikō to Kyōki)*

1997
- *Bounce KoGals (Baunsu ko GALS)* (a.k.a. *Leaving*)

1999
- *Jubaku: Spellbound (Kinyū Fushoku Rettō: Jubaku)*

2001
- *Inugami*

2002
- *The Choice of Hercules (Totsunyūseyo! Asama Sansō Jiken)*

"It was poorly received in Japan, but it got some sort of a cult following overseas, which included James Cameron. He really liked the film and I was invited to Hollywood at one point to discuss certain projects with him. A buddy from his school days, Randy Frakes, was also very fond of the movie, and we started writing a screenplay together, talking about a lot of things. These were the positive things about *Gunhed*, but nothing happened in Hollywood. At one point, because of *Gunhed*, I was able to get a good agent who represented me and tried to push me into certain areas, but nothing happened. So *Gunhed* quickly became a film of the past."

Although the aspect of social criticism was still virtually absent from his work at that point in his career, the variety of genres he worked in was indicative of the director's love for popular cinema. It's not surprising that Harada would become one of the directors to start working in V-cinema, the newly emerged straight-to-video industry that thrived in the early '90s after film companies discovered video as a second lease on life for their product. Genre films made at budgets that rarely exceed U.S. $500,000 and shot in at most three weeks, V-cinema productions offered their directors many restrictions but at the same time a lot of creative freedom. With the minimal investments made by their producers, profits were almost guaranteed, and directors were largely free to do as they wanted as long as the final film contained enough elements that made it marketable as a commercial genre film.

The yakuza genre was one of the main staples of V-cinema, and Harada found himself helming four of the five parts in the *TUFF* series, shooting them in the space of two years (1990–92), with the fifth and final episode shot partially in Harada's beloved California. Despite his failure to settle in Hollywood after *Gunhed*, America continued to beckon him, and in 1993 he mounted a project co-funded with Japanese and American money that Harada hoped would be his calling

card to Hollywood. But *Painted Desert*, the story of a murderer visiting a roadside diner run by an expatriate Japanese woman in the Nevada desert (a kind of cross between Percy Adlon's film *Bagdad Café* (1988) and Hemingway's short story *The Killers*), would become an experience marked by frustration. In the same interview with Gatto, he summed it up as:

"I made certain wrong choices, particularly when I said no to Samuel Jackson. He wanted to play a cameo in the movie. He was working on *White Sands* at the time, and I was supposed to meet him at one location, and I missed it, and he returned to New York the following day. Still he wanted to do the part, and if my production people had guaranteed his traveling fee, he would have done that for a minimum of money. But I thought: 'Okay, if Samuel Jackson can't do it, I want to work with Vincent Schiavelli.' That was a big mistake, and I should have pursued Samuel Jackson. [...] Once I started shooting that film in Nevada, I realized I had chosen the wrong director of photography. We started arguing constantly. [...] Another problem was, I didn't realize once you start working with team trucks, there are so many trucks and convoys that come by! It's a problem when you want to film improvisational shots on the spot! Normally, with a Japanese crew and cast, there are not so many people, and you can easily change the placement of the camera, and if there is an obstacle in the frame, you can easily remove it. But not ten trucks at the same time! [...] *Painted Desert* could have been my calling card to Hollywood or American filmmaking, and partially because of me, I ruined it. So I decided to go back to Japan so I could concentrate more on the crew and cast and make better Japanese films. And then eventually, if they discovered me, I thought I could come back."

Although *Painted Desert* certainly wouldn't be his last attempt to break into the American

Painted Desert

as a two-part, three-hour film for the video market (but eventually also released in theaters in a single shortened version that was also shown overseas), *Kamikaze Taxi* finally saw the full emergence of Harada's critical stance toward his home country. The story of a young yakuza in trouble with his own superiors and the Peruvian-Japanese taxi driver (played by Kōji Yakusho) who grows into his closest friend and guardian was a scathing attack on the racism that Harada had noticed was still very strongly present in society.

> "Particularly it's about what my son went through, which is reflected in Kōji Yakusho's character. At the climactic point in the film there is a confrontation between Kōji Yakusho's character and the corrupt politician, and the politician hates Yakusho for just one reason: funny Japanese. You speak funny Japanese, so you're a third-rate Japanese person. My son's Japanese was really strange when he went back to Japan after spending his first five or six years in the States. He went to a Japanese elementary school and a lot of people laughed at his Japanese. The way he was treated, I thought that existed twenty or thirty years ago, but it still exists today in the dead center of Tokyo. I put my son into that school because the number of returnee Japanese there was so high. They get used to those foreign-educated kids who speak strange Japanese. But even at that elementary school he was still segregated. I was so frustrated. I made *Kamikaze Taxi* based upon that anger."

Harada mixed several genres in the film, combining the token yakuza film with the rather un-Japanese (read: American) genres of the road movie and the buddy action film, but managed to maintain a balance between the elements of entertainment, characterization, and social criticism. It was a balance he would rarely achieve again: While the element of social critique remained a very noticeable part of his work

film industry, for his next film at least, Harada concentrated firmly on Japan. Originally made from this point onward, more often than not its impact would be diminished by a desire to entertain his audiences with flashy camerawork or too formulaic an approach to storytelling.

This is felt strongly in **Bounce KoGals** (1997), which explored the headline-grabbing phenomenon of teenage prostitution in the form of compensated dating or *enjo kōsai*. Recounting the misadventures of three teenage girls in the big city over a time span of 24 hours, Harada added ample condemnation, but at the same time emphasized the element of adventure in telling his story, thereby downplaying the essentially exploitational and abusive nature of the *enjo kōsai* phenomenon.

> "You need a certain proper entrance, one that people will feel comfortable with. Then once you go in, if you're intelligent enough, then you see other problems behind it. For that reason I picked up on *enjo kōsai*. I thought that by picking up on this phenomenon, I was going to make a good movie about what I wanted to tell about Japanese society and Japanese people today, and not corrupting myself and not compromising the issue. I researched a lot and I explored this *enjo kōsai* story as a sort of interesting anthropological study. I met some of those youngsters and heard a lot of stories. I made the movie as taking place on one night, over 24 hours, but all the episodes represent in chronological order what happened to Japanese girls between 1992 and 1996. So the early episodes happened in 1992 and the later ones in 1996."

In 1999's *Jubaku: Spellbound*, a fictional tale about a bank swindle that certainly had resonance with real-life practices, Harada's entrance was to turn his critical tale into an account of everyman heroism. With Kōji Yakusho again in the lead (who had come to symbolize the Japanese everyman by playing regular Joes in films like **Shall We Dance?**, **Cure**, and Yoshimitsu Morita's *Lost Paradise*),

the story focused on a group of middle managers bravely defying the odds to save their company from bankruptcy after widespread swindling in the upper echelons. Instead of an assault on the country's corrupt financial institutions, *Jubaku: Spellbound* became a life-affirming tale aimed at boosting salaryman morale, something it achieved quite successfully, as the film did excellent business.

The director would use the exact same method on his 2002 film *The Choice of Hercules*, an account of the real-life, ten-day siege on the mountain lair of a group of Red Army revolutionaries by an ever growing and ever more desperate army of cops, which took place in 1972. Focusing entirely on the police procedures and never showing more than a glimpse of the besieged terrorists, Harada again channeled and curbed his critique through brave everyman Kōji Yakusho, whose police captain character struggles persistently against the orders of his stubborn superiors whom he knows to be wrong. Although Harada gave ample space to the infighting among the various police departments and the errors of judgment that resulted from these arguments, in the final scene we are with Yakusho, finally home with his wife, tired but satisfied with a job well done.

> "Ex-left-wingers criticized the fact that I deal with this 1972 hostage situation from the point of view of the police. They say I've become the right-wingers' mouthpiece. But that's totally wrong. It has nothing to do with right or left, it's about Japanese organizations. I chose to use the police force and it's about the struggles within the police force. It's a reflection of Japanese society and Japanese people, who we are today."

This reflection, however, again lost impact as a result of Harada's chosen approach. His account of one of the darker chapters in Japanese post-war history was rendered resolutely inoffensive. Tellingly, the film's premiere screening in Tokyo became a tribute to the bravery of the police officers involved in the siege, with the actual law enforcers taking the stage alongside the actors that portrayed them in the film.

Perhaps the safe approach he took on *The Choice of Hercules* was the result of the disastrous box office results of his previous film, *Inugami*. A supernatural tale of a country family haunted by the spirits of the titular "wild dog gods," Harada intended his film as an allegory for Japan's royal family, provocatively emphasizing the element of incest with an Oedipal story of a young man falling in love with the woman he later realizes is his mother.

> "It's true that most Japanese realize that *Inugami* is about the royal family. But they can't say it. If they say it, they fear they will get hurt by right-wingers. The Oedipal story is present in the history of the royal family, certain types of incest. When the Japanese talk about Oedipus, they immediately make the connection with the royal family."

Harada blamed *Inugami*'s failure at the box office on two factors: bad marketing and a hesitance on the part of the media to broach the film's subject matter.

> "I felt really awkward about the situation. I knew it was going to be less successful at the box office, because of the Kadokawa double bill programming. *Inugami* is not the kind of film for double bills. You need to promote it carefully, sell it as an arty kind of film, a quality film. Kadokawa and Toho didn't listen and just released it as a typical horror movie for youngsters. And the youngsters who want blood and gore and the typical stuff of horror films, they couldn't understand *Inugami* at all. [...] The media just totally ignored it. They didn't even notice. That is the kind of frustration I feel about the film. They don't even want to talk about the taboo-breaking aspect of the film. It was as if they said, 'Let's stay away

> from this film, if I talk about this film it's dangerous for me too.'"

Though intriguing in its subject matter, *Inugami* also made a few too many concessions to entertainment, adding a rather obligatorily villainous patriarch and tons of fancy (though admittedly beautiful) camera set-ups. Like *The Choice of Hercules*, which employed numerous slow and fast motion sequences and fanciful but ultimately pointless moving cameras, its style is too apparent and self-conscious.

There is certainly no denying that, thanks to this and some excellent cinematography, Harada's recent films look great. If any Japanese director can compete with Hollywood cinema in terms of polished, glossy images, it's Harada. But the director is not trying to compete with Hollywood. He is trying to seduce it. As a result, the two foundations of his work are increasingly at odds with one another. As his desire to once again cross the Pacific grows and manifests itself in the way he makes his films, his work's strongest aspect—the social criticism from which he derives his greatest validity as a filmmaker in Japan—is increasingly buried under the weight of his stylistic trickery and narrative maneuvering. His love for American films and filmmaking appears to have become the main motif of his work, with his disillusionment over Japan only fueling his attempts to gain a permanent foothold in California.

> "After *Kamikaze Taxi*, even the business-oriented Japanese investors started to recognize me as a filmmaker who could be bankable. And that was proven with *Jubaku: Spellbound*. Then with *Inugami* they said I went back to my old trade of heavily criticizing Japanese society, so they ignored it. But when I pick *The Choice of Hercules* everybody comes back to me again and I get so many offers now. But the moment I pick up a subject like *Inugami* again I go back to the old system. I'm getting tired of that sort of treatment. Now I have a

new agent in the States and I'll probably start making American movies as of 2003. In the States there's an interesting phenomenon happening. Ever since the success of *Crouching Tiger, Hidden Dragon* they are interested in producing even a Japanese-spoken samurai piece, or a ninja film. It might happen that they will make samurai films with Japanese cast and American money."

Something similar did indeed happen, but Harada was not at the helm. Instead he made a rather remarkable change of career in order to work on the project, showing how strong his desire was to work in American film by appearing as an actor in the Tom Cruise vehicle *The Last Samurai* (Ed Zwick, 2003). Harada's solid performance as the villainous imperial envoy Ōmura turned out to be a pleasant surprise, also for the sizeable part he had in the narrative. Nevertheless, it couldn't be denied that the strange switch of roles indicated a certain amount of desperation on Harada's part. Having tried for over twenty years to succeed as a director in the United States, it must be somewhat bitter for him to see that his filmmaking skills are overlooked just at the moment when Hollywood's interest in Japanese films and filmmakers is reaching its peak.

↓ Kamikaze Taxi
復讐の天使
Fukushū no Tenshi

1995. CAST: Kōji Yakusho, Kazuya Takahashi, Reiko Kataoka, Takashi Naitō, Kenichi Yajima, Tomorowo Taguchi, Mickey Curtis. 134 minutes (Japanese video release: 200 minutes). RELEASE: VHS, Siren Entertainment (Australia, English subtitles), Pony Canyon (Japan, no subtitles—released in two parts); DVD, TLA Releasing (U.S., English subtitles), Media Blasters (U.S., English subtitles).

A young yakuza pursued by his own gang under the command of a corrupt politician makes the acquaintance of a Peruvian-Japanese taxi driver who proves to be more than just an ally. A mixture of road movie, gangster film, and unflinching social critique makes for Masato Harada's best film.

Kamikaze Taxi is a movie of many sides. It's a mixture of genres, which in turn are mixed with strong and frank criticism of the discrimination that lies dormant within Japanese society. In what is without doubt his best film, Harada questions what "being Japanese" constitutes.

Young yakuza Tatsuo is in charge of scouting girls to serve the whims of Dōmon, a corrupt member of parliament who carries his Japaneseness and his history as a kamikaze pilot as a badge of honor. Dōmon turns out to be a first-rate pervert, and a violent one at that. The women usually return bleeding, battered, and bruised. When Tatsuo's girlfriend, also part of the organization, protests, she is beaten to death by the gang's boss. Tatsuo, forced to watch helplessly as his girl is murdered before his eyes, swears revenge on Dōmon and sets out on a plan to rob him of the two million dollars hidden in a safe at his house. Enlisting the help of five buddies, Tatsuo enters the house at night. A panicked, chaotic heist ensues, but the men get hold of the money. The furious Dōmon holds Tatsuo's boss personally responsible and puts the two million debt on his shoulders, plus interest. The following morning, the gangsters have already tracked Tatsuo and his friends down, and from the ensuing shoot-out only Tatsuo escapes unharmed, with the loot.

Fleeing for his life with his former colleagues in hot pursuit, Tatsuo encounters a taxi driver and rather than forcing him at gunpoint, he says he will pay for the ride. It's the start of a very long cab ride indeed, and with it the film's tone switches. The gangster action film becomes a road movie and gains a soul in the process. Trapped together in this situation, the two men increasingly confide in each other. With Tatsuo

© 1995 Pony Canyon

Kamikaze Taxi

we learn that the cab driver, Kantake, was born Japanese, but raised in Peru. Returning to his homeland armed with a rather shaky command of the Japanese language, he has found himself an outcast, unaccepted and discriminated against. He drives a beaten, graffiti-covered station wagon and is a taxi driver not by choice but because he's been unable to get any other kind of job. He is a man with nothing to lose, and when he learns from his passenger about the activities of the corrupt Dōmon, a man who symbolizes the society that has spit him out, he becomes a natural ally and a much more formidable opponent than their pursuers ever imagined.

Kamikaze Taxi is a film built on genuine anger. Its vision of Japan is undiluted in its rage, not shunning to highlight sensitive aspects from both the past and the present. The country's wartime history is dredged up in the shape of the comfort women issue and several painful facts about the military's treatment of its own soldiers. It's Harada's way of debunking a certain image of what "Japaneseness"'means, as personified by the character of Dōmon, the kind of right-leaning conservative stance that continues to hold a strong grip on the official view of things.

The method Harada employs is to take one aspect so dear to the right wing, kamikaze warfare, and scrutinize it microscopically. On the one hand we get the aforementioned debunking of the myth that surrounds the history of kamikaze warfare, while on the other hand the film extols its virtuous, honorable element. Except that this virtue has nothing to do with fascism, conservatism, and nationalism, but is instead about courage and self-sacrifice for one's loved ones. The personification of this is Kantake, Dōmon's polar opposite and the kind of Japanese the politician hates with abandon. Around the figure of Kantake, Harada builds numerous subtle references to the "divine wind": the taxi company he works for is named *Soyokaze* (breeze), and in the final moments of the film, when Kantake volunteers to fight Tatsuo's fight for him and the young yakuza is at the airport waiting for his flight to Peru, an announcement tells us that "due to strong winds, all flights are canceled."

Harada's minorities of choice, those that represent the "other" or the butt of conservative ideology, are the Japanese born or raised in Latin America. The film's opening scene features monologues from mostly real repatriated Brazilian and Peruvian Japanese talking about their experiences upon returning to their native Japanese soil and the problems they encountered. *Kamikaze Taxi* features a Brazilian bar as an expatriate hangout, something Takashi Miike would repeat five years later in the cosmopolitan *The City of Lost Souls* (*Hyōryūgai*, 2000).

More balanced and focused than either his rougher earlier films or his more compromised later work, *Kamikaze Taxi* can be seen as Masato Harada's definitive cinematic statement. And a statement it certainly is.

↓ Bounce KoGals
バウンス　ko GALS
a.k.a. *Leaving*

2000. **CAST:** Hitomi Satō, Yukiko Okamoto, Yasue Satō, Kōji Yakusho, Jun Murakami, Kaori Momoi. 109 minutes. **RELEASE:** DVD, TLA Releasing (U.S., English subtitles).

Twenty-four hours in the lives of three high school girls out to make a quick buck from sex-starved salarymen. Harada ladles on the social commentary in this film about the shocking phenomenon of *enjo kōsai,* or "compensated dating."

In 1997, Ryū Murakami's novel *Love & Pop* was published. Released under the sub-title of *Topāzu 2,* it was a sequel in name and theme only to his earlier work, *Topāzu,* which was a bleak portrait of the mental decline of a call girl specializing in S/M acts against the emotionally sterile backdrop of Tokyo at the peak of its economic boom in the late '80s. Introducing new characters, relocating its milieu and radically altering its dramatic focus but otherwise sticking with the same concerns, *Love & Pop* was a watershed: the first work of fiction to dwell on the world of high school prostitution, or *enjo kōsai,* an expression that literally translates as "paid companionship."

With their loose white socks, pink lipstick, mobile phones, and neatly starched uniforms, these *ko gyaru* (high school girl) call girls offering a quick turn on the karaoke machine to straight-laced, middle-aged salarymen for the price of a Gucci handbag proved a sensational hook. In a country whose economy seemed now set in a terminal downward tailspin, *Love & Pop* portrayed a world in which consumerism had gone mad, where Japan's lost generation roamed the streets of Shibuya in search of sugar daddies, and where love and emotional fulfillment were reduced to a mere economic transaction.

Enjo kōsai became an immediate media talking point, and suddenly everyone began to wonder exactly what their daughters were up to whilst they were away at the office twelve hours a day. Undoubtedly the reality was exaggerated by the media, but at the very least, the furor served the purpose of casting some light on the prevalence of Japan's *rori-kon* (Lolita complex), the fetishization of fresh-faced young girls as validated in literally hundreds of manga comics and *aidoru* (idol) videos of bikini-clad teens. Murakami's novel also opened the way for a number of non-pornographic films vicariously centered around the Japanese sex industry, ranging from the gritty *Scoutman* to the vapid soap opera melodrama of *Platonic Sex* (Masako Matsuura, 2001), a fictionalized biopic reveling in all of the clichés of this new subgenre, based on the life of the AV starlet Ai Iijima.

Murakami himself had directed the film of *Topāzu* (better known to Western viewers as *Tokyo Decadence*), which was released in 1992, but the guiding hand behind the camera for *Love & Pop* seemed an even more bizarre choice. For his first live-action feature, Hideaki Anno, a director better known for his work in the field of animation with the 1990 TV series *The Secret of Blue Water* (*Fushigi no Umi no Nadia*) and the *Neon Genesis Evangelion* (*Shin Seiki Evangelion*) series during the latter half of the '90s, brought a radically unorthodox slant to his material.

Anno's debut—he later made *Ritual* (*Shikijitsu*) starring *Love Letter* director Shunji Iwai in 2000—is a magnificent accomplishment, and one of the great overlooked works of Japanese cinema of the late '90s. Taking the format of a video diary following 24 hours in the life of 17-year-old Hiromi (whose soulless voiceover narration is provided by *Suzaku* director Naomi Kawase) and the exploits of her classmates, and shot entirely on digital camcorder, Anno's film utilizes a frenetic, MTV-inspired style, totally in keeping with the giddy, artificial milieu the girls inhabit. With the majority of shots seldom lasting longer than a second, his dizzying approach treats us to a parade of jagged edits, distorted fisheye lenses, split screens, and a baffling multitude of perspectives—for example, shooting from the bottom of a bowl of soup, gliding at roof level tracking slowly behind the girls as they walk through a tunnel, and such strange POV shots as one taken pointing down from beneath Hiromi's skirt as she pulls on her white school socks in the morning. Yet for all its technical artifice, *Love & Pop* retains a degree of street level rawness and moral ambivalence all but absent from other takes on the subject.

Love & Pop was released in Japan at the beginning of 1998, but it was just beaten to it by Masato Harada's better known, bigger budgeted, and more mainstream-oriented *Bounce KoGals*, released at the tail end of 1997.

As a director, in terms of his approach to addressing social concerns through the cinema screen, Harada can be most readily compared to Oliver Stone. Unfortunately, he also shares many of the same weaknesses as his U.S. counterpart. A perfect example would be his *The Choice of Hercules*, based on the famous Asama Villa incident in 1972, in which a handful of members of the Red Army barricaded themselves inside a mountain chalet with a hostage, and the police spent the next ten days trying to dig them out. In his adaptation of the autobiographical novel by Atsuyuki Sasa, one of the police captains involved, released in 2002 on the thirtieth anniversary of the event, Harada skillfully managed to avoid any political dimension to his film. Instead he concentrated on the infighting between the various police and military factions involved in the rescue attempt, using the incident to critique administrative bungling. Fastidious in its attention to procedural detail at the expense of any background context, it approached its subject matter from a single perspective that gave little scope for viewers to shape their own individual interpretations of the material.

Similarly, *Bounce KoGals* masquerades as an exposé of *enjo kōsai*, but like most of Harada's attempts at transferring Hollywood hyperbole to his homeland, it comes across as uneven and compromised in its concessions to mainstream audience expectations. With the handheld documentary shots of Shibuya street life in the early scenes giving way to more dramatically stylized set pieces and a number of slo-mo musical interludes, the film suffers from uncomfortable shifts in tone between heavy-handed drama, didactic moralizing, and feel-good female bonding sessions between our three unimpeachably attractive guides.

Fresh out of high school in the northern city of Sendai, Lisa (Okamoto) is en route to New York, where she wishes to forge a new life studying at college. Upon arrival in Tokyo, she stops off in Shibuya with the idea of making some fast money before flying off to America the following morning. After trading in her underwear at a *burusera* shop (a fetish shop dealing in schoolgirl uniforms and soiled panties), she is set up by Sap (Murakami), a scout for the sex industry, on a makeshift video shoot in which a number of girls in school uniforms are chased around a bare apartment by a guy with a camcorder. Here she encounters the similarly aged Raku (Yasue Satō) before the shoot is disrupted by a gang of thugs, and in the resulting escape she loses all of the money she had spent the past year saving.

Faced with the task of earning back her lost savings before her departure, she is introduced by Raku to the hard-hearted Jonko (Hitomi Satō), who sets up and agrees to accompany her on a number of lucrative paid dates over the course of the evening, a quick and immediate solution to her predicament. In the meantime, Jonko is being warned away from her own enterprises by yakuza boss Ōshima (the ever-reliable Yakusho), who resents these high school hookers impinging on his own local turf.

With *Bounce KoGals*, Harada points his polemical finger at a society that creates a demand for high school prostitution, and the sexual attitudes and economic realities of male-oriented Japanese society come in for some heavy criticism (in this context it is worth pointing out that the Japanese word for prostitution, *baishun*, is composed of the two Chinese characters meaning "sell youth"). However, for this he needs a sympathetic hook into the drama, here provided by the rather unconvincing narrative conceit of a young innocent's voyage through this purgatory in order to escape from the chauvinistic constraints of her own country en route to the happy dreamland of America, where supposedly a college course is the passport to full sexual emancipation.

In doing so, Harada treads dubious moral water, all but exonerating the three girls. It is the men that are portrayed as pitiable and there to be exploited, sad perverts and lonely old has-beens eager to recapture their youth for a few brief moments. To this end, we are treated to a parade of grotesque caricatures that force us into identifying with the girls. Jonko and Lisa cringe in the corner, as we do, when one twisted pervert licks the layer of filth deposited around the overflow of a urinal during a party of coke-addled young business execs and transsexuals, whilst in an early scene, one of the girls recounts how she was approached in the street and offered 100,000 yen for her shit by a middle-aged businessman. Another character announces that these guys were too busy jerking off and study-ing to have girlfriends when they were in high school.

You can hardly blame the girls for wanting to capitalize on male weakness, but does the end really justify the means? Harada refuses to pass moral judgment on his female subjects, but in order to maintain this moral high ground, he also needs to keep the girls spotless and unsul-lied. Jonko herself swears she never engages in the sexual act with her clients, offering little more than conversation for her steep asking price, and often picking her clients' pockets under the postulation that they will be too em-barrassed to report the incident to the police. The one girl peripheral to the main group who does trade sexual favors for cash ends up in in-tensive care.

For all its weaknesses, *Bounce KoGals* trots along at a brisk pace through a lively succession of set pieces and is generally entertaining and compelling. The semi-documentary style por-trayal of the dynamics between the three main characters and the milieu in which they oper-ate is witty, naturalistically shot with captivating and sympathetic performances from all of the main actresses.

But you never quite get the feeling that Ha-rada is presenting us with the whole picture, nor that he ever really comes to terms with what makes any of these perky young characters tick in the first place. The end result certainly pro-vides enough food for thought, and the drama is never boring, but *Bounce KoGals* is probably best viewed as a piece of fin-de-siècle zeitgeist, an opportunistic morality tale lacking both the skewed insight of *Love & Pop* and the veracity that made *Scoutman* such painful viewing.

CHAPTER 6
Kiyoshi Kurosawa
黒沢清

Virtually unknown outside Japan until his 1997 breakthrough with the haunting *Cure*, Kiyoshi Kurosawa's subsequent rise to fame has been meteoric. In 1999, less than two years after first having one of his films projected on a foreign screen, he pulled the unique stunt of having three different films at each of the world's three major film festivals. In February of that year, his family drama *License to Live* played the Berlin Film Festival. In May, the bizarre eco-allegory *Charisma* was screened in Cannes, and in September the Venice Film Festival showed the equally unclassifiable *Barren Illusion*. That same year, the film festivals of Toronto, Edinburgh, and Hong Kong held mini-retrospectives of his work. Not since Takeshi Kitano had a Japanese director been so quickly and so widely embraced by the international film establishment.

In a way, it was almost a vindication. By the time the West got wind of him through *Cure*, Kurosawa had already been directing feature films for fourteen years and had come to be seen as something of a leading light among the generation of filmmakers that had emerged in the late '70s and early '80s. It's doubtful, however, that Kurosawa would have made as strong an impact overseas if he had emerged with one of his earlier films. Much of his work before *Cure* consisted of genre exercises that occasionally showed a willingness to experiment, but which

on the whole would have been unlikely to entice proclamations of genius.

Born in Kobe in 1955 to an ordinary middle-class family, Kiyoshi Kurosawa left for Tokyo in his teens to study sociology at Rikkyō University. Once there, his already considerable interest in cinema was given a new incentive when he started attending the lectures of Shigehiko Hasumi, one of Japan's leading film theorists. Inspired by Hasumi's vision of cinema and filmmaking, which placed a great deal of emphasis on the American cinema, and in particular genre cinema, of the 1950s, '60s and '70s, Kurosawa began making his own films with a Super 8 camera. To this day, Kurosawa praises Hasumi for the crucial influence the latter had on his life:

"I took his cinema class in university by chance, but it was a very decisive event for me. If I hadn't met him in that period, I wouldn't have become a film director and my view of cinema would be completely different. He was a crucial person for me. It's difficult to sum up what his influence on me has been, but he taught me that cinema, and exploring what cinema is, is worth devoting your life to. Also he insisted and repeated numerous times that, in cinema you can't shoot the things you can't see. It sounds so obvious, but love, peace, hate—such abstract concepts cannot

be shown on film. But that doesn't mean you can't express them. Many directors have tried hard to express them, using their skill, talent, and the support of their crew. You may succeed in expressing them with such effort, but you can never think that you can show them with just your camera. I was really impressed by that."

© 2003 Uplink

Bright Future

Hasumi not only inspired his filmmaking, it also shaped the way he looked at film, as well as his personal cinematic tastes. He adopted Hasumi's predilection for American genre cinema, with a preference for such action-men directors as Robert Aldrich, Don Siegel, Sam Peckinpah, and Richard Fleischer, as well as a liking for horror specialists like Tobe Hooper and John Carpenter. At the same time, European art filmmakers like Jean-Luc Godard, Wim Wenders, and Eric Rohmer, who had themselves been weaned on American cinema, as well as U.S. mavericks like John Cassavetes, formed another considerable strand of influence on Kurosawa.

Kurosawa continued to make 8mm short films throughout his university years. His efforts culminated in a prize for *Vertigo College*, a parody of gangster films set on a university campus, at the 1980 PIA Film Festival, Japan's foremost event for independent film and young filmmakers. The prize allowed Kurosawa to enter the professional film world, where he went to work as an assistant director to such independently minded filmmakers as Kazuhiko Hasegawa, Shinji Sōmai, and Banmei Takahashi.

After three years of apprenticeship, Kurosawa was hired by the Million company, a now defunct player in the erotic *pinku eiga* field. He made his directorial debut with *Kandagawa Wars* (1983), the story of two apartment blocks on opposite sides of the titular river and the erotic encounters of their tenants. The executives were not entirely satisfied with the results, which frequently interrupted the all-important sex scenes with such images as the tribulations involved in crossing the river, the sudden ap-

pearance of a choir on the roof of one of the buildings, and the frequent quoting of film titles. His experimentations on his next film, *Joshi Daisei: Hazukashii Seminar* [trans: College girl: shameful seminar], went so far that Nikkatsu refused to release the film, allegedly because it was not erotic enough.

In an effort to salvage the film, Kurosawa asked the independent Director's Company (formed by several filmmakers including his former employers Kazuhiko Hasegawa and Banmei Takahashi) to buy the film from Nikkatsu. Kurosawa reshot parts of the film and released it in a re-edited version under the title *The Excitement of the Do-Re-Mi-Fa Girl* in 1985. The resulting film had more in common with mid-period Godard than with a Nikkatsu sex romp, featuring its lead actress Yuriko Dōguchi parading in a nightgown carrying an AK-47 machine gun like an Asian Anne Wiazemski. Echoes of Seijun Suzuki's clash with Nikkatsu fifteen years earlier became all the stronger when the studio, having seen themselves overruled by a single young filmmaker, spread the word about Kurosawa's troublesome behavior to the other majors, effectively exiling him to the fringes of the film industry. (The studio later redeemed itself by co-financing *Charisma*, one of Kurosawa's most enigmatic and uncommercial films.)

His banishment was to have a decisive influence on Kurosawa as a filmmaker, but not in an entirely negative way. Although he wouldn't direct a film for the next four years, the course he would take following the clash with Nikkatsu allowed him to explore his fascination for genre cinema and to discover his own relation to genre cinema as a filmmaker.

He also used the time off from directing to return to Rikkyō University to give a series of lectures, following in the footsteps of his mentor Hasumi after the good critical notices his first two films had received in parts of the Japanese film press. His words came to have a similar effect on a new generation of film enthusiasts as Hasumi's had had on him. Several Rikkyō students had come together to form a ciné-club, and it was they who would be the most attentive listeners to Kurosawa's lectures. Among them were people who would later make their own mark on Japanese cinema in the latter part of the '90s, including Shinji Aoyama, Makoto Shinozaki, Akihiko Shiota, Masayuki Suō, and Kunitoshi Manda (director of the Takenori Sentō production *Unloved*, 2001).

Kurosawa's return to filmmaking came in 1989, when Jūzō Itami, who had been enormously successful throughout the decade as both a director and an actor, asked Kurosawa to direct *Sweet Home*, a haunted house thriller in the tradition of Robert Wise's *The Haunting* (1963) and Tobe Hooper's *Poltergeist* (1982). Itami had been an actor in *The Excitement of the Do-Re-Mi-Fa Girl* and he also appeared in *Sweet Home*, giving the lead part to his star actress wife, Nobuko Miyamoto. For the abundant special effects, Kurosawa and Itami flew in Hollywood make-up effects master Dick Smith, best known for his work on *The Exorcist* (1973). The result was a spectacularly entertaining horror film, but Kurosawa again met with interference when Itami, after the film's theatrical run, reshot and re-edited parts of the film for video and TV release. Infuriated, Kurosawa took the unprecedented step of suing his producer, which did nothing to improve his standing in the Japanese film industry.

After directing a segment of the Director's Company omnibus horror film *Dangerous Stories* the same year, Kurosawa's "exile" saw him drifting into made-for-television horror productions like *The Wordholic Prisoner* (1990), *Yorokobi no Uzumaki* (1992) [trans: Vortex of joy], and the Kansai TV horror anthology series *Haunted School* (1994) before being scooped up by the fledgling V-cinema industry.

Filmography

1974
- *Rokkō* [short]

1975
- *Bōryoku Kyōshi: Hakuchū Daisatsuriku* [short]

1976
- *Shingō Chikachika* [short]
- *Fukakutei Ryokōki* [short]

1977
- *Shiroi Hada ni Kuruu Kiba* [short]

1978
- *School Days* [short]

1979
- *Vertigo College (Shigarami Gakuen)*

1982
- *Tōsō Zenya* [short, co-directed with Kunitoshi Manda]

1983
- *Ningensei no Kejime* [short, co-director]
- *Kandagawa Wars (Kandagawa Inran Sensō)*

1985
- *The Excitement of the Do-Re-Mi-Fa Girl (Doremifa Musume no Chi wa Sawagu)*

1988
- *Girl! Girl! Girl! (Fuyuko no Omokage)* [short]

1989
- *Sweet Home (Suīto Hōmu)*
- *Dangerous Stories (Abunai Hanashi)* [co-director]

1990
- *Wordholic Prisoner (Modae Kurushimu Katsuji Chūdoku-sha: Jigoku no Misogura)* [TV]

1992
- *The Guard from Underground (Jigoku no Keibiin)*
- *Yorokobi no Uzumaki* [TV]

1994
- *Haunted School (Gakkō no Kaidan)* [TV, co-directed with Shōji Takano, Kazuya Konaka, and Zenboku Satō]
- *Men of Rage (Jan: Otokotachi no Gekijō)* [video]
- *Yakuza Taxi (893 Takushii)* (video)

1995
- *Suit Yourself or Shoot Yourself! The Heist (Katte ni Shiyagare!! Gōdatsu Keikaku)*
- *Suit Yourself or Shoot Yourself! 2 The Escape (Katte ni*

In that period, however, he did see some of his dignity restored when he became the second Japanese filmmaker invited to Robert Redford's Sundance Institute Screenplay Workshops on the merit of an early draft of the screenplay for *Charisma*, which he would bring with him to Utah and would continue to work on for the next seven years. After his return, he was offered a new chance to direct a film for theatrical release, albeit one with the kind of low budget and tight shooting schedule more commonly associated with V-cinema, as well as getting the opportunity to publish his first book. The film, *The Guard from Underground*, was an interesting variation on the slasher formula that received good notices, while the book *Eizō no Karisuma* [trans: The charisma of the image] allowed him to indulge his own passions as a filmmaker with essays on some of his favorite directors and films.

Although the invitation, the film, and the book went some ways toward restoring his pride, the major studios still wanted little to do with him. His outlaw status put him in a perfect position for the emerging V-cinema industry, which offered opportunities to fringe filmmakers and

© 2000 Nikkatsu Corporation

Kiyoshi Kurosawa

assistant directors where the minimal allocated budgets would not afford production companies to hire seasoned professionals. With the creative freedom given to directors who agreed to stay within budget and on schedule, and its reliance on genre filmmaking, V-cinema would prove to be an important transitional phase in Kurosawa's career.

"It's been very valuable for me to have the experience of making program pictures. Generally

---

Shiyagare Dashutsu Keikaku)

1996
- *Suit Yourself or Shoot Yourself! 3 The Loot (Katte ni Shiyagare!! Ōgon Keikaku)*
- *Suit Yourself or Shoot Yourself! 4 The Gamble (Katte ni Shiyagare!! Gyakuten Keikaku)*
- *Door III*
- *Suit Yourself or Shoot Yourself! 5 The Nouveau Riche (Katte ni Shiyagare!! Narikin Keikaku)*
- *Suit Yourself or Shoot Yourself! 6 The Hero (Katte ni Shiyagare!! Eiyū Keikaku)*

1997
- *The Revenge: A Visit From Fate (Fukushū: Unmei no Hōmonsha)*

- *The Revenge: The Scar that Never Fades (Fukushū: Kienai Shōkon)*
- *Haunted School F (Gakkō no Kaidan F)* [TV, co-directed with Hideo Nakata]
- *Cure (Kyua)*

1998
- *Serpent's Path (Hebi no Michi)*
- *Eyes of the Spider (Kumo no Hitomi)*
- *Haunted School G (Gakkō no Kaidan G)* [TV, co-directed with Tetsu Maeda and Takashi Shimizu]

1999
- *License to Live (Ningen Gōkaku)*
- *Barren Illusion (Ōinaru Genei)*
- *Charisma (Karisuma)*

2000
- *Séance (Kōrei)* [TV]

2001
- *Pulse (Kairo)*
- *Gakkō no Kaidan: Haru no Mononoke Special* [TV, co-directed with Shinobu Yaguchi, Norio Tsuruta, and Akira Ogata]

2002
- *2001 Eiga no Tabi* [short]

2003
- *Cop Festival (Deka Matsuri)* [co-director]
- *Bright Future (Akarui Mirai)*
- *Doppelgänger (Dopperugengā)*

2004
- *Kokoro, Odoru* [short]

Courtesy of PIA Film Festival

Dangerous Stories

in that type of production environment, the subject and the story are already fixed. Also, you recreate the same type of film several times with only a slight difference. When the studio system still existed, many directors went through that experience. Today, there is only V-cinema that can give you a similar experience. For me, compared to before the time I started working in V-cinema, I came to handle the subjects as well as the technical aspects of my films better and with more flexibility.

"Also, I think film is a combination of reality and fiction. Both factors are there. When you start making a movie from scratch, you have to create the fiction. You have to spend a lot of effort and pain creating the story and the screenplay, and only then can you make the film. But the things you actually record on film are real. After spending so much energy creating the fiction you are tired, and you will become careless when making the film

and recording the reality. But in the case of program pictures, the fiction—the story and subject—are already fixed. That means you can concentrate on recording reality. That's a big difference. It's not just true in my case, it's true historically and internationally. Generally you can say that program pictures are often more real than other films. The fact that you can concentrate on reality is the big advantage of program pictures."

Indeed, Kurosawa's films for the video market show an increasing devotion to formal experimentation. Although early works like *Yakuza Taxi*, a comedy about gangsters who find themselves running a taxi service, are still largely dime-a-dozen video productions, the later *Suit Yourself or Shoot Yourself!* series demonstrated a tremendous growth. Six films made in less than two years, they show Kurosawa developing from a cautious experimentalist into a full-blown artist with a signature style, themes, and voice.

Named after the Japanese title of Jean-Luc Godard's *Breathless* (*À Bout de Souffle*, 1957; Japanese title: *Katte ni Shiyagare*), *Suit Yourself or Shoot Yourself!* was also Kurosawa's first encounter with actor Shō Aikawa. Aikawa was, and is, one of the main stars of straight-to-video yakuza films, but his acting abilities and willingness to experiment surprised Kurosawa, and the pair would go on to make over a dozen films together.

His work in V-cinema also saw Kurosawa greatly increasing his productivity, churning out the horror film *Door III* and the two-part cop drama *The Revenge* (also starring Aikawa) in addition to the above-mentioned six films, all between 1995 and 1997. This efficiency is another element that would come to characterize him for the rest of his career.

> **"I'm just a very fast filmmaker. I usually take about two to four weeks to shoot. Also, there's not a lot of money for filmmaking in Japan, so if you only make one film a year, it's very difficult to stay alive."**

The great turnaround for Kurosawa came with 1997's *Cure*. Produced by the recently resurrected former major Daiei, whose own marginal position in relation to the other studios was reflected in their adventurous output and choice of directors, it was Kurosawa's return to the limelight and his biggest hit. Popular with foreign festivals and distributors, it made Kurosawa's name internationally and put him back on the map in his own country, with a best actor award for star Kōji Yakusho (the director's other frequent lead actor) at the Japanese Academy Awards and a nomination for Kurosawa as best director.

Kurosawa had now truly come into his own as a filmmaker. *Cure* was the crowning achievement of a rapid development that started with the final episodes of the *Suit Yourself or Shoot Yourself!* series and ran through *Door III* and *The Revenge*. Combining an openness to genre

cinema, a postmodern willingness to borrow discreetly from his favorite filmmakers, and an eagerness to explore the darker side of our own behavior as individuals and as a society, Kurosawa developed in the course of these films a thematic and stylistic language that he would come to apply and refine in every film that followed.

While their thematic weight and sometimes purely unclassifiable nature at times seem to indicate differently, Kurosawa claims that every film he makes always starts with a genre basis.

> **"Which genre my film ultimately belongs in is up to the audience when it's finished, but certainly as a starting point I always start my next project considering which genre I would like to work in. So in that sense I am a genre director. Actually, I'm often misunderstood. I don't start with a philosophical or thematic approach. Instead I start with a genre that's relatively easy to understand and then explore how I want to work in that genre. And that's how a theme or an approach develops. The genre is first."**

Although often regarded as an art filmmaker rather than a genre filmmaker, his admiration for American genre directors of old makes Kurosawa the last to treat genre cinema with elitist disdain. His own philosophy toward genre is that he works in genres "in order to better distance myself from them," an expression that perfectly sums up his work in V-cinema. Perhaps the best example of his approach is *Charisma*, whose final result at first glance seems to bear no similarity to any genre known to filmdom.

> **"It's a sort of American-style Indiana Jones/ two-teams-vying-for-a-treasure film. That's how I started it. But instead of a box of gold I decided to make the treasure a tree that's in a forest. Then you start to imagine 'what value does the tree have?' and 'what is the condition of the forest it's growing in?' Then you start to realize that you're not making an Indiana Jones movie at all, but that you're making a much**

more complex film. That's the process of my filmmaking. The reason I take this approach to filmmaking is that although film needs a fictional story element, it also is a medium that allows you to record the reality around you. You're filming real forests and real people. I think that film for me is a medium point between a fictional story and reality. You start with the genre, which is fiction, and gradually move toward reality. Somewhere in between you find film. To put it simply: I would like to make a movie like Indy Jones, but there aren't any real people like Indy Jones. That's the beginning of my filmmaking."

Closely related to his openness to genre is Kurosawa's consistent appropriation of elements from other films. Although this postmodernist practice is sometimes referred to as meta-narrative (narrative about narrative), in Kurosawa's case the reference rarely exists for its own sake. Elements are applied discretely and assimilated into the larger whole in a similar way to the distortion of a film's genre roots. His use of existing titles (the aforementioned *Katte ni Shiyagare!!*, but also *Ōinaru Genei*, the original title of *Barren Illusion* as well as the Japanese title of Jean Renoir's *Grande Illusion*) is by far the most overt example of this tendency. Kōji Yakusho's stained overcoat in *Charisma*, Ren Ōsugi's chainsaw in *License to Live*, the solitary lamppost in *Suit Yourself or Shoot Yourself! The Hero*, and the recurring white backgrounds in driving scenes are much more inconspicuous cases of appropriation, which for the most part acquire their own significance within the framework of the film. Kurosawa occasionally even borrows from himself: the two main ghostly encounters in **Pulse** are refined variations on a scene from *Door III*. Perhaps only the habitual close-ups of flashing police sirens are self-acknowledged references, though in this case to a genre cliché rather than to an individual film.

Postmodern or not, Kurosawa's films are undeniably his own. Genre base and occasional references play a decidedly minor role in the overall result of his work compared to themes and style, both of which are uniquely his. Although Kurosawa believes that there is no single motif to his work ("You can never simply grab the motifs and apply them rationally. It's impossible, in cinema at least, because the motif changes with every image."), the overriding theme he explores is that of the individual and in how far that individual lets his identity be defined by his environment.

"I'm interested in the values that the individual has come to embrace: for the individual to reassess those values and understand the way in which those values that he has come to embrace are in fact the forces that have come to oppress him."

His method for letting the individual characters come to that reassessment is by taking him or her out of that environment and away from those values. Usually, a catalyst of some kind (often referred to by Kurosawa as "the monster," demonstrating his acknowledgement of genre roots) compels the protagonist to retreat from the environment into a place where that reassessment can take place. An example of this is the cop played by Kōji Yakusho in *Charisma*, who makes a fatal mistake on the job, resulting in the deaths of two people and his own discharge from the force. Kurosawa then literally places him in a different environment (an opposed environment even, given that he goes from the city to the forest), where all ties with his previous life are severed. In *License to Live*, protagonist Yutaka awakes from a ten-year coma. His last memories are of being fourteen years old and living with his parents and sister on a dude ranch, but when he awakes, he is twenty-four, all the members of his family have lost touch with each other, and the ranch has become a fish farm run by a friend of his father's. In *Cure*, people are forced through hypnotism to look beyond their own conscious definitions

© 1997 KSS ME Inc.

The Revenge: The Scar that Never Fades

of themselves and to face up to, acknowledge, and act on their most basic urges.

What often results from these ruptures with their old lives is that Kurosawa's characters are turned into a *tabula rasa*, a blank page, signifying a new beginning and limitless possibilities. This could go wrong or right, but what interests Kurosawa is the effect an individual's actions can have on the whole of society. The individual can become an active advocate of change through his or her own actions. Kōji Yakusho's cop in *Cure* finds himself wrenched from his life as a result of his meeting with the enigmatic hypnotist, causing murders that wind up self-perpetuating. In *Pulse*, the realization that people are trapped in a cycle of loneliness causes mass suicides that bring about the end of the world. In *Suit Yourself or Shoot Yourself! The Hero*, a young man inspires his neighbors to organize themselves and resist the presence of yakuza in the neighborhood, but

he uses his power to establish a fascistic regime with himself as leader and his former neighbors as deprived homeless.

Although such developments can often turn bad, the overriding sentiment in Kurosawa's films is that negative and positive are irrevocably linked. Death can create life and from evil can come good. In *Charisma*, in which this sentiment is expressed as "accepting life as it is," a young shoot grows inside a dead tree stump. Although a number of his films end with visions of an apocalypse, there is always the sentiment that this is necessary in order to pave the way for new, more positive developments. Society, too, needs to achieve the state of a blank page; only then can the apocalypse make way for a brighter future.

Stylistically, Kurosawa employs numerous tools to underline and facilitate the process outlined above. One of the most impressive is

Excitement of the Do-Re-Mi-Fa Girl

the suggestion of unseen menace, the creation of a world that exists outside the borders of the image, beyond the frame. Kurosawa's thoughts on the creation of this suggestion echo the words of Shigehiko Hasumi:

"I have two points of view about this. Firstly, I believe film can't show everything. It's a frame and you can only show what's in the frame and not what is outside it. You can't see everything, but there definitely is a world outside that frame. The frame is like a window, which means there are things you can't see, but that is the scary part. The audience has to imagine for themselves what is happening outside that frame. Secondly, I live in society. In that society there are also many things I can't

see. Everything looks peaceful on the outside, but elsewhere in the world there are wars and other negative events that we can't see with our own eyes, but which we know are there."

The director makes use of several visual and auditive tools to create this suggestion: keeping the frame's contents sparse, which suggests that there must be more elsewhere; the use of frames within the frame, which isolate and trap his characters in even smaller spaces; introducing elements that were previously off-screen, which suggest that the world of the film doesn't end at the borders of the image; use of background action, which transposes the viewer past the habitual foreground and creates space and depth; and the use of seemingly incongruent sound. The combination of these is enormously effective at suggesting the existence of an off-screen menace, which in turn emphasizes the force of the "monster," as well as the potential impact of the monster's influence on society. *Cure*'s exploration of the aspects of ourselves we keep hidden wouldn't be nearly as effective without it, since these hidden aspects and the unseen menace are one and the same. Neither would *Pulse*'s coming of the apocalypse, of which the unseen menace is a herald.

Kurosawa's skills have not gone unnoticed. The high-concept alarm bells went ringing as soon as Hollywood caught wind of *Pulse*, and the film was promptly snapped up for a remake. Initially there was talk that Kurosawa himself would direct the American version of his own film, but when *Scream* director Wes Craven expressed an interest, Kurosawa was unceremoniously pushed aside. Kurosawa's feelings on the Hollywood interest in remaking Japanese films are understandably mixed:

"Ghosts and monsters that appear in American films have the intention of hurting people, like in *Alien* for example. In my films, and in films like *The Ring*, they don't hurt people but they scare them. I was very surprised that Americans were able to understand that element of fear, but I'm happy that they do. But whether this development with remakes is valuable or dangerous is difficult to judge for now. To actually make a movie in Hollywood is a wonderful thing, but a remake . . . I understand the reason why they would want to do a remake. Making it in English with Western actors is good for selling a film in the international market, but it makes me wonder what the validity of the original is. As a Japanese, there is something unsatisfying about the situation. If you can get the chance to make a brand-new horror movie in Hollywood as a Japanese director, it would be wonderful. But if there is only the occasion of doing a remake, there is something dangerous about it. It's difficult to judge."

The process of the *Pulse* remake, which coincided with the U.S. release of *Cure* and a traveling retrospective of his work in American theaters, nevertheless kept Kurosawa busy for an entire year. The director spent much of 2001 in the States as a result and quite atypically didn't make a single film in that time. It was the first time since 1991 that a year had passed without a new Kiyoshi Kurosawa film. In 2002, once the whole affair was behind him, he went back to Japan and back to the set with an old-fashioned zeal, shooting the films *Bright Future* and *Doppelgänger* almost back-to-back, as well as contributing a ten-minute segment to Makoto Shinozaki's cop comedy omnibus *Cop Festival* (*Deka Matsuri*). The three films appropriately signal a new beginning for Kurosawa himself. *Doppelgänger* and *Cop Festival* are comedies, while the title *Bright Future* itself already announces a change in outlook. Perhaps his year in the United States, away from home and away from a movie set for the longest period in his life, was Kurosawa's personal apocalypse. He saw his old life as a filmmaker come to a destructive close with the *Pulse* remake fiasco, and now it seems he has started anew. By the time *Bright*

Future was selected for the official competition of the 2003 Cannes Film Festival (his third time there), he shed few tears over the missed Hollywood opportunity.

"My films have never been hits. They've never attracted big crowds and they're not really popular films. But even though my audience is relatively small, the people who watch my films are very supportive. Their enthusiasm is what allows me to continue making films."

↓ Sweet Home
スウィートホーム
Suīto Hōmu

1989. CAST: Nobuko Miyamoto, Nokko, Shingo Yamashiro, Jūzō Itami, Fukumi Kuroda. 102 minutes. RELEASES: VHS, Toho Video (Japan, no subtitles).

FX-laden haunted house movie, a million miles removed from Kiyoshi Kurosawa's later cerebral chillers. One of the director's most accessible films.

According to director Kiyoshi Kurosawa, all the films he made before 1997's *Cure* are flawed. In the literal sense, this goes for his very entertaining 1989 haunted house film *Sweet Home* too: After its theatrical run it suffered several alterations at the hands of its producer, the late Jūzō Itami. Though the result is not nearly as disastrous as these kinds of interventions usually tend to be, the film has since then often been described as being more Itami's film than Kurosawa's.

Ironically, this scenario mimicked what happened to Tobe Hooper, a director long admired by Kurosawa, when he made his haunted house film *Poltergeist* (1982) under the auspices of producer Steven Spielberg. Though Hooper has always denied Spielberg's involvement in the creative process aside from some assorted second unit tasks, rumors have consistently abounded that it was actually Spielberg who wielded the megaphone on the set.

A big factor in the regressive disownment debate over *Sweet Home* is the fact that the film looks nothing like the deliberately paced, gloomy, cerebral chillers Kurosawa is known for today. *Sweet Home* takes almost the opposite approach to the genre, resulting in a colorful, action-packed, special effects-laden rollercoaster horror movie.

Starring Itami's wife and frequent star actress Nobuko Miyamoto in the lead role, *Sweet Home* follows the exploits of a group of people venturing to a deserted mansion to restore a priceless mural to its full splendor. Arriving at the site, they find that much of the house is covered in additional murals depicting hellish scenes of a mother losing her child in a blazing fire. When the restorer's daughter uncovers evidence that the mother and child from the paintings had indeed lived in the house, including the discovery of the child's grave in the garden, evil forces are unleashed. Objects start moving seemingly by themselves, and one by one the members of the team start dying gruesome deaths.

As can be judged from the synopsis, *Sweet Home* is hardly a shining example of innovative storytelling. The conventionally structured script echoes Robert Wise's 1963 genre milestone *The Haunting*, albeit with an interesting female-centered narrative revolving around the strength of the mother-daughter bond. Like many of the films Kurosawa made in his pre-*Cure* days (like *The Guard from Underground* and *Door III*), *Sweet Home* is first and foremost an exercise in genre, one with which the cinephile director consciously trod in the footsteps of men like Wise and Hooper.

But while postmodern, the film is never derivative or lacking in imagination. All the elements and, sometimes, clichés of the genre may be firmly in place (with Itami himself appearing as the token hermit with the mysterious past), but the thrills, the chills, and Dick Smith's spe-cial effects come thick and fast. Kurosawa keeps the camera moving, employs fast yet effective editing, and strikes a nice balance between the use of garish colors and ominous shadows, all the while cleverly avoiding the pitfalls of the genre and staying on the right side of the line that recent American effects showcases like *Thirteen Ghosts* and Jan De Bont's remake of *The Haunting* crossed in their misfired attempts to thrill multiplex audiences.

Despite its unsurprising plotting, *Sweet Home* is action-packed, thrill-packed, and effects-packed, resulting in an entertaining, effective, and above all accessible haunted house ride.

↓ Suit Yourself or Shoot Yourself!
勝手にしやがれ！！
Katte ni Shiyagare

1995/96. CAST: Shō Aikawa, Kōyō Maeda, Ren Ōsugi, Yuriko Dōguchi. GUEST CAST: Episode 1: Natsumi Nanase, Shun Sugata, Jun Kunimura, Tarō Suwa. Episode 2: Satoshi Kajiwara, Yumiko Abe, Akira Kuichi, Tarō Suwa. Episode 3: Miki Fujitani, Tarō Suwa. Episode 4: Yūko Nitō, Kenzō. Kawarasaki, Sabu, Tarō Suwa. Episode 5: Sachiko Suzuki, Masayuki Shionoya, Tarō Suwa. Episode 6: Susumu Terajima, Tomoka Kurotani, Hiroshi Shimizu. 484 minutes. RELEASES: VHS, KSS (Japan, no subtitles).

Six-part series of made-for-video gangster comedies, in the course of which Kiyoshi Kurosawa shows an increasing willingness to experiment. The films are hit and miss, but hold great value as transitional works in the director's oeuvre.

Shot in pairs, in the space of less than two years, the six-part *Suit Yourself or Shoot Yourself!* series is a peculiar entry in Kiyoshi Kurosawa's filmography. Essentially formulaic gangster comedies, these six films are firmly rooted in the V-cinema production mill mentality, but allowed Kurosawa to further hone his craft and his style and to arrive at the departure point for his more accomplished and renowned later work.

The standard premise for each narratively unconnected episode is a pair of petty criminal layabouts, Yūji (Aikawa) and Kōsaku (Maeda), who are always willing to take part in any kind of shady business that will make them a bit of cash. They have their hearts in the right place, however, and their convolutedly plotted adventures inadvertently end with them giving up the opportunity for illicit gain in favor of helping out the oppressed underdog. With Yūji and Kōsaku filling the expected roles of older straight man and bumbling young sidekick and with a pair of mysteriously omniscient informants (in the shape of a gay bar owner and his femme fatale regular customer) to guide them, no pretence is made at these films being anything more than run-of-the-mill entertainment.

In terms of story and characters, this is undeniably true. But the interest here lies in the form of these films rather than in their content. The *Suit Yourself or Shoot Yourself!* series is the quintessential example of the role of V-cinema as training ground. In the course of its increasingly interesting six episodes, one filmmaker finds his artistic voice; if the first entry is largely anonymous, the final is unmistakably the work of the Kiyoshi Kurosawa we know of such later films as **Cure**.

Although shot, as mentioned, in pairs, there is a clear division between the first three entries in the series and the last three. The first three fulfill their minimal criteria of providing action-comedy entertainment, with Kurosawa very subtly experimenting with camera set-ups, framing, and the manipulation and creation of space. Episode 1, subtitled *The Heist*, contains one very impressive set-up in which the composition changes from medium close-up to extreme wide shot, while characters move in and out of the frame to change the impact and tone of the sequence. Essentially, the shot is nothing more

Suit Yourself or Shoot Yourself!

than a diagonal dolly, but it packs a remarkable amount of information and movement.

Episodes 2 and 3, *The Escape* and *The Loot*, have few such audacious moments, although Kurosawa's use of space and framing remains consistently interesting and the films contain several effective visual gags that point toward the element of comedy that would continue to be part of the director's work (even his more serious later films like *Cure*, **Charisma**, **Pulse**, and *Bright Future* contain subtle but effective comic moments) and which would come to the fore again in *Doppelgänger* and his segment of *Cop Festival*.

All three films contain almost ridiculously convoluted plots that spring forth from very simple, almost routine premises. *The Heist* is about two men falling in love with the same woman, while *The Escape* is about two women in love with the same man; in both cases the paramour is in trouble with the yakuza, which leads to the aforementioned convolution as Yūji and Kōsaku figure out ways to escape the gangsters' grasp. But where the first three installments are merely artificial in their narrative complexity, episode 4, *The Gamble*, takes this complexity as its very premise and delivers a intriguing meditation on chance as the deciding factor in a human being's life.

Co-written by Akihiko Shiota, *The Gamble* sees Kōsaku winning a trip to Hawaii and Yūji receiving a briefcase full of cash when a gangster seemingly drops dead in front of him. When Yūji tries to woo the girl at the local tobacco stand, their romantic entanglements eventually end up with her debt-ridden father stealing the briefcase of money, just before its original owner returns from the dead to reclaim it, with the yakuza boss he's supposed to hand it over to hot on his heels.

As its title implies, *The Gamble* is all about chance and coincidence. The film has numerous scenes of its characters engaging in gambling and gameplay that serve as a visual metaphor for this principle. The film also contains no real villains, since all the characters are completely aware of the fact that they are mere pawns in this cosmic game of chance, meaning that no one ever resents losing what was easily gained. If you get the opportunity, you take it. If someone takes it from you through the same principle, he is merely doing what you would have done, and did, in the same situation. (Interestingly, this structure based on chance is nearly identical to the main motif in the work of director Sabu, whose debut film **Dangan Runner** was released later the same year and who appears in *The Gamble* as an actor, playing the top yakuza boss.)

Chance plays a major role in episode 5 as well. Entitled *The Nouveau Riche*, it takes the elements of chance and complexity to yet another level, applying a cyclical structure of recurring events. When a young woman named Minako stumbles onto the aftermath of a gangster shoot-out, one of

its blood-drenched participants hands her his stash of heroin before dying of his wounds. Shocked by the experience, she crashes her car into a fence just as Yūji and Kōsaku walk by. When she refuses to go to a hospital to have her face wound taken care of, the two protagonists take her home and discover a bag of heroin in her purse. Not long after the discovery, the entire underworld comes knocking on their door hoping to buy it off them. When they confront Minako with the heroin, she tells Yūji and Kōsaku that there is in fact more and takes them to a locker from which she pulls an entire shopping bag full of drugs. Not long after, the gangsters appear again, but seeing the increased amount, they retreat to their offices to adjust their bids accordingly.

This story structure keeps repeating itself, with the stash of heroin hidden by Minako growing bigger and bigger, and the determination of the gangsters to get hold of it increasing exponentially. Kurosawa emphasizes the cyclical nature of the storyline by also repeating his visual motifs and inserts visual gags that are delightfully absurd, with one yakuza group using a man on a leash as an attack dog and one of their rivals being a kindly independent entrepreneur. In the film's finale, a bag of heroin the protagonists had thrown into the river miraculously reappears at the precise moment when it can save their lives. It's this finely structured and above all very visual comedy that makes *The Nouveau Riche* not only the most satisfying entry in the series, but also one of the more accessible films in Kiyoshi Kurosawa's body of work.

The most typically Kurosawa-esque of all six installments, however, is the final one, *The Hero*. Initially starting out as another unremarkable entry, with Yūji and Kōsaku becoming involved with a young man named Aoyagi (Susumu Terajima) who tries to rally his neighborhood into chasing all yakuza elements from town, it changes tone abruptly after fifty minutes. At this point, the story jumps one year ahead in time to show the kind of dystopian society familiar from such later films as *Charisma* and *Barren Illusion*. Aoyagi's activist movement has turned into a totalitarian regime that tries to rid the city of homeless people and which is not averse to destroying the houses of ideological opponents in order to make them homeless and therefore eligible for arrest.

The Hero's second half starts with an astonishing six-minute, one-take sequence filmed with steadicam that is pure Kurosawa: By way of independent but interacting and overlapping events that take place in a restricted space (in this case a grassy field surrounded by dilapidated houses), it establishes the entire nature of the society in which it is set at the same time as evoking a sense of dread by means of brief visual cues (the irreverent behavior of the characters, a protest march, the omnipresence of campaign posters carrying Aoyagi's portrait). The sequence is a vastly more complex variation on the camera set-up in the first episode and foreshadows a similar intricate scene in the later *License to Live*.

With this rupture in style and narrative, Kurosawa invokes the themes that would come to dominate his later work (the truth that hides behind the everyday façade, the effects of an individual's actions on society as a whole), as well as its stylistic trademarks (evoking an unseen dread by way of framing and use of space, manipulation of the movement of actors, sparing use of close-ups). *The Hero* also contains several postmodern visual nods to other films, including Jean-Pierre Melville's *Le Doulos* (1961) and George Roy Hill's *Butch Cassidy and the Sundance Kid* (1969), the latter inspiring Yūji and Kōsaku's climactic defiance of a hail of bullets from Aoyagi's corrupt police force.

The progression Kurosawa makes in the space of these six films is a remarkable one: from a crafty genre director of modest ambition to a filmmaker who has found his voice and hit his artistic stride. In the end the reasons for this change are the director's own talents, but the role the V-cinema production mentality played in allowing this development to occur is undeniable, underlining the vital role of the straight-to-video industry in the growth of contemporary Japanese cinema.

Although they contain little that is of great appeal to the casual viewer, those with an interest in Kiyoshi Kurosawa's work will find in the *Suit Yourself or Shoot Yourself!* series a significant transitional phase in the career of a very significant director.

↓ Cure

キュア

Kyua

1997. CAST: Kōji Yakusho, Masato Hagiwara, Tsuyoshi Ujiki, Anna Nakagawa, Yuriko Dōguchi, Ren Ōsugi. 111 minutes. RELEASES: DVD, Home Vision Entertainment (U.S., English subtitles), Toshiba (Japan, English subtitles), MK2 Editions (France, French subtitles).

Disturbing, unrelentingly bleak and thought-provoking revision of the serial killer film, which deservedly made Kiyoshi Kurosawa's name internationally.

Cure remains the watershed in Kiyoshi Kurosawa's career, not only in terms of international exposure and recognition but also within the scope of his own work. Whereas *Suit Yourself or Shoot Yourself! The Hero* showed the awakening of Kurosawa's style and themes only in the final thirty minutes and *The Revenge* took him two films to explore their proper application, *Cure* is a single, cohesive, and fully matured unit.

As a result, *Cure* is also Kurosawa's most disturbing film. Later films like *Charisma* and *Pulse* end in visions of death and destruction that are more radical than *Cure*'s, but they differ in their suggestion that after the destruction of the old, new things will emerge. There is no such hope when the credits roll in *Cure*.

Often compared to David Fincher's *Seven*

(1996) for its bleak outlook on mankind's fate and to Jonathan Demme's *The Silence of the Lambs* (1991) for its mind games between killer and cop, *Cure* is, however, intrinsically Kurosawan. More resonant with our everyday lives than either of its American counterparts, it explores how we as human beings hide parts of ourselves in order to live in society and how the repression of those feelings only intensifies them. Without ever denying our individuality, Kurosawa links us all as human beings by way of this habit of repressing "unsocial" emotions. Most serial killer films isolate such hidden urges in a single character, brandishing that character as evil for having those urges and thereby giving the viewer false reassurance that he or she is different. *Cure* instead confronts us with the fact that we all have dark, destructive, and potentially murderous elements to our personalities, and that the harder we try to repress or deny them, the easier they can be coaxed to the surface. *Cure* is the mirror that forces us to look at our naked selves.

The man who holds up that mirror is Mamiya (Hagiwara), a young amnesiac drifter who wanders around Tokyo and its environs doing little more than asking people the same question over and over again: "Who are you?" Invariably, they answer by giving their job titles, an indication of how those individuals define themselves through their roles in society. But this is not what Mamiya is after. He wants them to look deep inside themselves and face up to who they *really* are, to find the part of themselves that they deny. Hypnotizing them through such simple means as the flame from a lighter or water spilled from a cup, he helps them rediscover that part.

At the same time, Tokyo is hit by a wave of seemingly inexplicable murders. All victims carry an identical lethal wound: a big X cut across their throats and chests. All perpetrators are found at or near the crime scene in a state of confusion, with little recollection of why they killed what is in many cases their own partner. None of the murderers seems connected in any way but their

identical MO. The enigmas pile up for police detective Takabe (Yakusho), who is put on the case, aided by psychiatrist Sakuma (Ujiki).

Takabe is already a man under pressure. His wife is mentally ill and gradually deteriorating in her condition. She receives treatment, but regularly goes wandering off on her way from home to the hospital (Kurosawa has acknowledged that this idea was taken from Makoto Shinozaki's **Okaeri**, and repaid the debt by casting his former disciple as an extra). Takabe's progression in the murder cases keeps equal footing with the deterioration of his wife's illness and by the time he discovers the element of hypnosis and finds Mamiya, the burden and frustrations of having to take care of his wife have become so great that the young mesmerist easily taps into them, hoping to make the detective the next in his line of guinea pigs.

What ensues from this is not simply a gripping battle of wills, but a battle over the audience's last vestiges of hope. Takabe has been the viewer's anchor from the beginning of the film, a man of rationality and perceptiveness who is good at his job and cares for his wife. Early in the film there is a scene that not only establishes the film's central theme of what is hidden under the surface, but which also allows the viewer to immediately identify with Takabe: While he is waiting at the dry cleaner's, the customer standing next to him repeatedly mutters a slew of obscenities and murderous intentions to himself. The moment the store clerk appears, the anonymous man's personality switches to that of an everyday, seemingly harmless salaryman. Takabe's fear and confusion will be recognizable to anyone living in a big city, who will have doubtlessly found themselves in a similar situation at least once in their lives.

This scene effectively isolates the element of evil in society in an anonymous "other." We side with Takabe in order to feel safe in the realization that this disturbed individual is not us. By turning Takabe into the audience identification figure, Kurosawa makes his fall later on in the film even more disturbing. When Mamiya grabs hold of his will and forces him to face up to his hidden urges, which he does indeed possess in spades, our own defenses as viewers crumble with him. How can we claim to be immaculate souls when the man in whom we recognized ourselves turns out to be as deeply disturbed as the murderers he arrested?

Cure is the quintessential Kurosawa film. Its success as a genre film depends on its success as a committed exploration of our social fabric, and vice versa. As in the later *Pulse*, not incidentally his other most widely seen film, the two are completely balanced, with the genre framework additionally serving as an entry point for new audiences.

↓ Charisma
カリスマ
Karisuma

1999. CAST: Kōji Yakusho, Hiroyuki Ikeuchi, Jun Fubuki, Ren Ōsugi, Yuriko Dōguchi. 103 minutes. RELEASES: DVD, Home Vision Entertainment (U.S., English subtitles), King Records (Japan, English subtitles), Arte Video (France, French subtitles— two-disc set with *Pulse*).

A burned-out cop wanders into a forest and becomes involved with the various factions waging a battle over a mysterious tree. Kurosawa's most unclassifiable film, this will either have you scratching your head in bewilderment or keep you completely enthralled from beginning to end.

That Kiyoshi Kurosawa's approach to filmmaking can be, to put it somewhat disrespectfully, cerebral, should be a well-known fact to anyone who has seen *Cure* or *Pulse*, his two best-known films. Metaphors and symbolism abound, and telling a neat plot is less important than exploring socially relevant themes. In no film is this more apparent

than in *Charisma*, in which the battle over a rickety tree is fought out in allegorical terms.

After bungling a hostage situation, causing the deaths of both the hostage and the hostage taker, policeman Yabuike (Yakusho, playing what seems like an even more burdened version of his character in *Cure*) is sent on leave. Instead of returning home to his family, he asks a colleague to drop him off at a bus station on the edge of a remote forest. With no bus imminent (the timetable falling off the rusted bus stop sign is the only movement Yabuike sees), he decides to head into the forest, wandering around until night falls, and he finds an abandoned car to sleep in. That night, someone sets fire to the car, but Yabuike is saved from the flames by an unknown figure. His belongings gone, he stumbles into the arms of a group of forest rangers headed by Nakasone (Ōsugi) who give him a dirty old overcoat to wear. The rangers are investigating the gradual deterioration of the forest, whose seemingly healthy trees keep keeling over and dying. One tree in particular has their attention, one which seems nearly dead, but which remains standing despite not bearing so much as a single leaf.

The rangers are not the only ones with an interest in this curious tree, as Yabuike finds out when a young man comes raging at the rangers for approaching it. This young man, Kiriyama (Ikeuchi), has devoted his life to taking care of and protecting the tree, which he has named Charisma, building scaffolding around it to keep it from falling over and even administering it intravenous feeding. Kiriyama is alone in his devotion, however, since he not only has the rangers to contend with, but also a female botanist by the name of Jinbo (Fubuki) who is convinced that Charisma's roots are secreting a poison that is responsible for the gradual decimation of the forest. Not much later, a group of shady businessmen shows up and, claiming to represent a wealthy collector, offers the rangers a big sum of money if they will uproot Charisma and bring it to them.

Yabuike stands amid all this commotion and

Charisma

watches it happen. Moving from one group to another, he gets to know the various factions and their viewpoints without committing to any of them. He is essentially a character without personality, a blank page, an individual who has been removed from his own environment, sent on leave, wandered off, lost his belongings, and is eventually fired from his job altogether. Before he meets Kiriyama, he eats hallucinogenic mushrooms and gets high, signaling his complete liberation from his old self and his old environment. After a while of observing the situation, he seems most drawn to underdog Kiriyama, particularly when Jinbo's loopy younger sister Chizuru (Dōguchi) tells him that the botanist is poisoning the forest herself so as to have an excuse to get rid of Charisma. There is an interesting parallel here with *Suit Yourself or Shoot Yourself! The Hero*, in which Aoyagi shoots himself in the leg with the intent of blaming it on the neighborhood yakuza. In both cases, the characters in question represent reactionary, proto-fascist forces, which gives an insight into the role the various factions in *Charisma*, as well as the tree itself, play. If the botanist represents the reactionary, then Kiriyama is a revolutionary, protecting individualism or the right to individual ideology (the single tree) against those who fear that individual thought will poison the whole of society (the forest). The rangers meanwhile are interested in maintaining the status quo, but are more than willing to modify their interest for a healthy sum.

Increasingly, Yabuike starts to see parallels between his presence amid the warring factions and the hostage situation he was in at the start of the film. His wish to save the lives of both the hostage taker and the hostage ended in death for both of them. Now again, he is faced with the choice of saving either Charisma or the forest, but before he can make a decision, the businessmen and rangers succeed in digging out the prized tree. Yabuike and Kiriyama manage to stop their car, but Jinbo and her sister get to Charisma first and burn it.

When Yabuike finds another seemingly dead tree that he thinks might be a second Charisma, the process seems to start all over again: The businessmen offer money, Jinbo tries to destroy it. But something has changed for Yabuike. With the outcome of the hostage situation in mind, he realizes that his wish to save lives on both sides is futile. To save both means to kill both, since one cannot tolerate the other. Therefore, in a situation where two lives are at stake, if one dies at least the other lives. All this ado about a single tree only blurs the fact that in the end it matters little. The forest does not care about the fuss. Its components will live and die and eventually be replaced by something else.

So, when Jinbo tries to destroy the second Charisma by blowing it up, Yabuike lets her do so and even lends a hand. After the explosion, amid the rubble of the charred tree stump, they discover something that confirms Yabuike's convictions: a young shoot that is growing inside the dead tree. When in the final scene Yabuike leaves the forest to return to the city, he is confronted with a situation that is immediately reminiscent of the one from which he has just emerged: In the distance, the city is in chaos, buildings are on fire, helicopters rush overhead. Here too, there is commotion and destruction. And here too, that destruction will eventually pave the way for a new beginning.

↓ Pulse
回路
Kairo

2001. **CAST:** Haruhiko Katō, Kumiko Asō, Koyuki, Shun Sugata, Kōji Yakusho, Kenji Mizuhashi, Jun Fubuki. 117 minutes. **RELEASES:** DVD, Tokuma (Japan, English subtitles), Universe (Hong Kong, English and Chinese subtitles), Arte Video (France, French subtitles—two-disc set with *Charisma*).

Finely crafted horror that links modern technology with loneliness and loneliness with death. Atmospheric and effective, Pulse takes Kurosawa's vision of apocalypse to its disturbing extreme.

The final shot of *Charisma* showed us a city in flames, a vision of apocalypse as seen by someone who had arrived too late to take part. No explanations were given about what brought it on, but perhaps that explanation can be found in *Pulse*, which makes us eyewitnesses to the coming of the apocalypse and takes us straight into its heart.

Kurosawa's subject is a lot less abstract in *Pulse* than in *Charisma*. Here, the director's concerns are over new technologies, in particular the Internet, and the effect they have on our behavior—as individuals and, as always, by extension as a society. As in his previous works, it's the behavior of individuals that shapes society as a whole, and with these individuals increasingly isolating themselves in what Kurosawa feels is a world of artificial, or illusory, communication, the end result is very dehumanized indeed.

Pulse follows two separate protagonists. One, a young woman named Michi (Asō), sees her computer nerd friend Taguchi (Mizuhashi) commit suicide for motivations she can't fathom. With her friends Junko and Yabe, she tries to find the reason behind his death through the computer disk he'd made for them. On it, they find an image of Taguchi standing alone in his room; on the monitor of his computer is reflected a ghostlike face. Before long, Michi is witness to yet another suicide, as the young woman who lives in her building, whom she had seen closing off the basement door with red duct tape just that morning, jumps off a factory silo and plummets to her death (a powerful, unnerving image, with the jump, fall, and impact all shot in a single take). That same day, Yabe's mobile phone rings. It's the voice of Taguchi, repeating a single word: "Help." Yabe ventures into the sealed-off basement and has an encounter with the ghostly apparition of a young woman.

Pulse's second protagonist is Kawashima (Katō), a student taking his first strides onto the Internet. Clearly not comfortable working with computers, the first thing he sees when he finally manages to log on is a bizarre website that shows him images of young people sitting alone in their rooms at the computer, then a video recording of a young man with a black plastic bag over his head. A text asks him, "Would you like to see a ghost?" Disturbed by what he sees, he turns off the computer and goes searching for help at his university. He makes the acquaintance of Harue (Koyuki), a young woman who teaches computer science. When the images persist and his computer starts logging on to the Internet of its own accord, the two try to investigate further, but soon start to notice bizarre phenomena.

Although dealing with the negative aspects of technology, *Pulse* is not technophobic in the sense of such American films as *Demon Seed* (1976), *War Games* (1983), *The Terminator* (1984), or *The Matrix* (1999). In those films, the machines are out to get us, pure and simple. Technology is inherently and omnipotently evil and the films use their viewer's technophobia to achieve their desired effects. *Pulse* takes a very different approach. It does not feed off the audience's fear, but explores what its director sees as a problematic development, trying to create in its audience an awareness of our behavior in this society. *Pulse* is in this sense very similar to *Cure*, and less abstract than *Charisma* (though the film does contain one moment that echoes *Charisma*'s conclusion of accepting life as it is, when one of the film's very few adult characters chooses to refrain from taking initiative or responsibility, leaving the young to fend for themselves—which in turn also echoes *Barren Illusion*, a film that sees all characters over the age of twenty-five wiped out by a spread of toxic pollen).

Although the plot has its weaker moments ("Let's have a look inside that abandoned factory"), *Pulse* is one of Kurosawa's most successful attempts at conjuring up the existence of a world outside the frame. This is particularly evident in his use of sudden dramatic background action (the woman jumping off the silo is shot as background action), elements moving in and out of the frame, and lighting designs that literally make characters (in particular the ghosts) appear and disappear from the screen. Even the location of Michi's workplace, a greenhouse on a rooftop (with extensive use of the frame-within-a-frame technique by way of the numerous panes of glass), is such an enclosed, isolated place that it creates the impression of being detached from the real world, and therefore of things going on elsewhere.

Unlike in previous films, the sense of dread this evokes receives a true pay-off in *Pulse*, in the film's climactic vision of an empty, dehumanized Tokyo. It's the most literal and confronting vision of apocalypse the director has yet shown in his work and it immediately makes one wonder where he could go next. Apparently Kurosawa himself also felt that he couldn't follow this line of exploration any further and, without a hint of irony, he called his next film *Bright Future*.

CHAPTER 7

Studio Ghibli
(Isao Takahata / Hayao Miyazaki)
↓ 高畑勲 / 宮崎駿

For the Japanese, the output of Studio Ghibli represents something of a national treasure trove. Combining some of the most startling 2D cel animation seen the world over with realistic character design, richly detailed landscapes, sweeping emotional arcs, and a potent whiff of fantasy, the studio has dazzled audiences with its freewheeling, inspirational vision ever since its formation in 1985. Wistfully evoking the faraway, unattainable dreamlands portrayed in the classics of European children's literature, and more recently relocating to imaginary worlds rooted within Japan's mythic past, the work of Ghibli represents escapism in its purest form.

It goes without saying that animation is huge business in Japan. The TV airwaves are jammed with it, video shelves are chock-a-block full of OAV (Original Animation Videos) episodes of a generally more adolescent focus released purely for the home viewing market, and during the school holiday periods, cinemas are crammed with kids flocking to see the latest large-screen escapades of such perennial favorites as the scampish eternal kindergarten brat *Crayon Shin-chan*, or spinoffs from popular manga or video game serials such as *Inuyasha* and *One Piece*.

In 2002, a fairly typical year for the industry, four of the top five highest-grossing domestic productions were animated. Alongside the respective annual theatrical excursions of *Pokémon*

and *Doraemon*—the smiling blue robotic cat who has been making regular appearances in comic books since 1969 (and on TV since 1979)—the second-highest earner for the year was *The Phantom of Baker Street* (*Meitantei Conan: Beikā Sutorīto no Bōrei*), taken from the popular manga and TV series based around the character of a high-schooler detective named Conan. However, by far the top grossing production, its 6.46 billion yen (roughly $55 million) box office take almost double that of its nearest rival's 3.4 billion yen, was Studio Ghibli's double bill of *The Cat Returns* (*Neko no Ongaeshi*, directed by Hiroyuki Morita) and its preceding animated short, *The Ghiblies: Episode 2*, allowing Toho Studios, who distributed all four of these titles, to pretty much clean up that year.

The year's runaway success of *The Cat Returns* is not a new development for Studio Ghibli, and laying its product alongside more typically endemic home-grown animations, usually no more than large-screen cinema outings utilizing simplistic animation techniques based on tried and tested characters and formulas already established on TV, it's easy to see why. Compared with the competition, they are in a different league entirely.

More significantly, from the 1989 release of *Kiki's Delivery Service* onward, they have also successfully fended off competition from bigger budgeted U.S. productions, and not just animated ones. Titles such as **Porco Rosso** and *Whisper of the Heart* have all raked in the cash at the domestic box office. Hayao Miyazaki's *Princess Mononoke*, Ghibli's box-office smash of 1997, was the highest grossing Japanese film of all time, trumped only by the takings of *Titanic* in the year of its release.

Miyazaki's follow-up, *Spirited Away*, went one better. An eclectic mishmash owing much to Lewis Carroll's *Alice in Wonderland*, located within a traditional Japanese bathhouse in a fictional world populated by a colorful variety of ancient gods (some of which are drawn from the traditional Shinto religion but the majority stemming from the imagination of its creator), it had Japanese audiences flocking in droves on its release, outperforming *Titanic* to become the highest earning film ever in Japan. Outside of the country it became the first ever animated film to win the Golden Bear award at the Berlin

Film Festival, and at the 75th Academy Awards romped home with the Oscar for Best Animated Feature, a new category created only the year before, when it was won by DreamWorks' CGI fantasy, *Shrek* (2001).

Miyazaki's Oscar win is symbolic because it not only recognizes almost forty years of top-notch work in the field. Coming in the same year as an Oscar nomination for Kōji Yamamura's bizarre 10-minute *Mt. Head* (*Atama Yama*, 2002), it is also an acknowledgement from the global mainstream that Japanese animation is no longer seen as the reserve of a handful of obsessives, but perhaps the country's main cultural contribution to the world of cinema, with Ghibli firmly leading the way and Miyazaki as its most vocal ambassador.

Nevertheless, the continued guaranteed success of Miyazaki's films at the box office and the plaudits heaped upon the director worldwide have rather drawn attention away from the other

Filmographies

Isao Takahata

1963
- *Ken the Wolf Boy* (*Ōkami Shōnen Ken*) [TV series, 89 episodes, co-director]. Several episodes only.

1965
- *Hustle Punch* (*Hassuru Panchi*) [TV series, 26 episodes, co-director]. Opening sequences only.

1968
- *Adventures of Hols, Prince of the Sun* (*Taiyō no Ōji Horusu no Daibōken*) (a.k.a. *Little Norse Prince Valiant / The Great Adventure of Little Norse Prince Valiant*)

1969
- *Mōretsu Atarō* [TV series, 90 episodes, co-director]. Several episodes only
- *Spooky Kitaro* (*Gegege no Ki-*

tarō) (a.k.a. *Cackling Kitaro*) [TV series, 65 episodes, co-director]. Several episodes only.

1970
- *Apatchi Yakyūgun* [TV series, 26 episodes, co-director]. Several episodes only.

1971
- *Shin Gegege no Kitarō* [TV series, 45 episodes, co-director]. Several episodes only
- *Lupin III* (*Rupan Sansei*) [TV series, 23 episodes, co-director]. Complete series.

1972
- *Akadō Suzunosuke* [TV series, 52 episodes, co-director]. *Several episodes only*
- *Panda! Go Panda!* (*Panda Kopanda*) [short]

1973
- *Panda! Go Panda!—Rainy Day Circus* (*Panda Kopanda—Amefuri Sākasu no*

Maki) [short]

1974
- *Heidi* (*Arupusu no Shōjo Haiji*) [TV series, 52 episodes]

1976
- *3,000 Miles in Search of Mother* (*Haha o Tazunete Sanzenri*) (a.k.a. *From the Alps to the Andes*) [TV series, 52 episodes]

1979
- *Anne of Green Gables* (*Akage no Anne*) [TV series, 52 episodes]

1981
- *Jarinko Chie*

1982
- *Gauche the Cellist* (*Serohiki no Gōshu*)

1987
- *The Story of Yanagawa Canal* (*Yanagawa Horiwari Monogatari*)

talents working at the studio, and more specifically, from the fact that both the history and prehistory of Studio Ghibli is primarily that of two men. Isao Takahata, co-founder of the company and director of the wistfully nostalgic *Only Yesterday* and the tragic wartime tearjerker *Grave of the Fireflies*, has worked alongside Miyazaki since the early '60s; and having directed his first feature, *The Adventures of Hols, Prince of the Sun* in 1968, some ten years before Miyazaki, is by far the more experienced of the two.

It's interesting to note the difference in directorial approach used by the studio's towering twin talents. Miyazaki modestly categorizes himself as merely "a man who draws pictures." He is an illustrator/animator foremost, having spent almost fifteen years as such before adopting the role of director. He has stated that he has little idea of what direction his stories will follow until he starts work on them. Vividly depicting lavish, expansive worlds where teenage girls battle against the forces of environmental devastation, children ride in giant cat-buses, and pigs can fly, his vision is imprinted on every frame of his work, a factor that has made him a far better subject for auteurist-based studies than his more anonymous partner.

But whilst Miyazaki's invigorating freewheeling fantasies may have proven the most successful in straddling the boundaries of both age and nationality at the box office, by reining in the images within the demands of the story, Takahata's more plot-driven narratives more than make up for what they lack in spectacle in terms of their subtlety and pacing. Acting more in the capacity of foreman, Takahata never puts so much as pen or brush to paper during the final animation process. As a result his work looks markedly different from film to film, the story reflected in the design, rather than acting secondarily to it.

In 1999, he directed the superb *My Neigh-*

1988
- *Grave of the Fireflies* (*Hotaru no Haka*) (a.k.a. *Tombstone of the Fireflies*)

1991
- *Only Yesterday* (*Omoide Poroporo*) (a.k.a. *Tearful Thoughts*)

1994
- *Pompoko* (*Heisei Tanuki Gassen Ponpoko*)

1999
- *My Neighbors the Yamadas* (*Hōhokekyo Tonari no Yamada-kun*)

Hayao Miyazaki

1971
- *Lupin III* (*Rupan Sansei*) [TV series, 23 episodes, co-director]. Several episodes only

1978
- *Future Boy Conan* (*Mirai Shōnen Konan*) [TV series, 26 episodes, co-directed with Isao Takahata and Keiji Hayakawa]. All episodes.

1979
- *Lupin III: Castle of Cagliostro* (*Rupan Sansei: Kariosutoro no Shiro*)

1980
- *Lupin III* (*Rupan Sansei*) [TV series, 155 episodes, co-director]

1982
- *Sherlock Hound* (*Meitantei Hōmuzu*) [TV series, 26 episodes, co-director]

1984
- *Nausicäa of the Valley of the Winds* (*Kaze no Tani no Naushika*) (a.k.a. *Warriors of the Wind*)

1986
- *Castle in the Sky* (*Tenkū no Shiro Raputa*) (a.k.a. *Laputa: Castle in the Sky*)

1988
- *My Neighbor Totoro* (*Tonari no Totoro*)

1989
- *Kiki's Delivery Service* (*Majo no Takkyūbin*)

1992
- *Porco Rosso* (*Kurenai no Buta*) (a.k.a. *The Crimson Pig*)
- *Sora Iro no Tane* [TV spot]
- *Nandarō* [TV spots]

1995
- *On Your Mark* [short]

1997
- *Princess Mononoke* (*Mononoke Hime*)

2001
- *Spirited Away* (*Sen to Chihiro no Kamikakushi*)

2004
- *Howl's Moving Castle* (*Hauru no Ugoku Shiro*)

© 1984 Nibariki • Tokuma Shoten • Hakuhodo

Nausicaä of the Valley of the Winds

bors the Yamadas, based on the popular *Asahi Shinbun* newspaper cartoon created by Hisaichi Ishii. An extended comic ode to the Japanese nuclear family told in a series of skits, its flat, sketchy style made up of simple lines and partially water-colored backgrounds, stands unique amongst Ghibli's output.

In marked contrast is Toshitsugu Saida's more solid looking designs for Takahata's pre-Ghibli adaptation of *Sero Hiki no Gōshu*, or *Gauche the Cello Player* in 1981. Based on a tale by Kenji Miyazawa (1896–1933), the most enduringly popular storyteller in Japan, it tells the tale of a left-handed cellist, whose discordant noises see him almost thrown out of the local orchestra yet find favor with the local woodland creatures who come to hear his music as he spends his long nights practicing.

These differences in approach aside, it has to be said that Ghibli is a tightly knit team, using a regular group of the country's finest animators and designers all working closely with one an-

other, a factor which has led to a certain consistency of vision in its output. For years both Miyazaki and Takahata have often acted in the role of producer for one another, a collaboration that can be traced right back to the very roots of Japanese animation when they both started working at Toei Animation (Tōei Dōga) in the early '60s.

Born in 1941, Miyazaki joined Toei in 1963 after graduating from Gakushūin University with a degree in political science and economics. The company had been established in 1956, producing Japan's first color animated feature, *Legend of the White Serpent* (*Hakujaden*) in 1958. The film, based on an ancient Chinese legend and directed by Taiji Yabushita, is largely considered to be the starting point of modern Japanese animation and was released in the U.S. in 1961, having been first showcased abroad in 1959 at the Venice Children's Film Festival. Miyazaki cites it as one of the primary motivating factors in his decision to become an animator.

Miyazaki entered Toei at the very bottom, first working as an "in-betweener," one who draws the intermediary movements that fall between the images designed by the key animator. His first credit was on *Wan Wan Chūshingura* (*Watchdog Bow Wow*, 1963). During the early '60s, the manga artist Osamu Tezuka had just moved into animation after establishing his own company Mushi Productions in 1961, and his adaptation of his own comic book creation *Tetsuwan Atomu*, better known abroad as *Astro Boy*, had become a huge TV hit. In 1963, Toei decided to compete, which is when Miyazaki first made the acquaintance of Takahata, working on one of the episodes of the black-and-white TV series *Ken the Wolf Boy* (*Ōkami Shōnen Ken*).

The two, as with so many working in the artistic field at the time, shared left-wing ideals and formed a close friendship through Toei's labor union. Miyazaki soon moved up to the position of key animator and made valuable creative contributions to all of the projects he worked on, including Yoshio Kuroda's feature length *Gulliver's Space Travels* (*Garibā no Uchū Ryokō*, 1965), inspired by the Jonathan Swift children's classic that would later influence Miyazaki's *Castle in the Sky*.

Though it would be some years before Miyazaki would finally occupy the director's seat, the older Takahata (born in 1935), who had had been with the studio since 1959 after he'd graduated from the prestigious University of Tokyo with a degree in French literature, was rising quickly up the company hierarchy. *Ken the Wolf Boy* marked his directorial debut. After the TV series *Hustle Punch* in 1965, he was given his first chance to direct a feature length animation with *The Adventures of Hols, Prince of the Sun*.

Reflecting the same kind of idealism that would later lead to the formation of Ghibli, the plan was to produce a feature that could take on Disney at its own game whilst at the same time creating something altogether more spectacular, more dramatic, and more cinematic than the simplistic, kids-oriented fare that Toei was increasingly focusing its resources on. Although Toei piled all its energies into the effort, unfortunately *Prince Hols* went way over schedule and way over budget. Nowadays looked upon as a turning point in the history of Japanese animation, ironically when it was completed in 1968, the studio heads were not amused. Toei released it on a tiny two- to three-week run where, predictably enough, it lost the company a lot of money.

Toei's treatment of *Prince Hols* had left a bitter taste, and it became obvious to Takahata that realizing his dream of creating masterfully crafted animation with epic stories that went beyond the basic requirements of mere diversions for children was not going to be fulfilled within such a rigid environment. In 1971, he left the company along with Miyazaki, for the rival A Production where they joined another former Toei animator, Yasuo Ōtsuka, who had proved a powerful guiding influence during Takahata's early years with the company. Whilst Ōtsuka worked on the TV series taken from Finn-

© 1989 Eiko Kadono • Nibariki • Tokuma Shoten

Kiki's Delivery Service

ish writer Tove Jannson's tales of those strange hippo-like creatures *The Moomins* (*Mūmin*), Miyazaki and Takahata put themselves to work on an animated version of the Swedish children's book, *Pippi Longstocking* by Astrid Lindgren, a project that was ultimately aborted.

In 1971, A Production worked alongside Tokyo Movie (which later became Tokyo Movie Shinsha, or TMS) on the first TV series of *Lupin III* (*Rupan Sansei*), bringing what would become, due to this series, one of Japan's most popular manga characters to the screen for the very first time (a 12-minute pilot film was made as a pitch for a theatrical film in 1969 directed by Masaaki Ōsumi, but was rejected and then re-worked later as a pitch for the TV series). Centering around the exploits of the suave swindler who first appeared in *Manga Action Weekly* magazine in 1967, drawn by Kazuhiko Katō under his better known pen name of Monkey Punch, *Lupin*'s mixture of James Bond-style adventure, lewd humor, and the impish charm of its good-

© 1986 Nibariki • Tokuma Shoten

Castle in the Sky

naturedly amoral central character ensured that the series was a massive hit both on the printed page and on screen. Both Takahata and Miyazaki worked on several of the 23 episodes in the first series, which over the next thirty years would spawn a further two TV series and a succession of TV movies and theatrical spin-offs (one of which was directed by Seijun Suzuki). It was through *Lupin III* that Miyazaki would

later get his feature directorial debut, *Castle of Cagliostro*.

Takahata, meanwhile, returned to direction in 1972 with the short animated feature, *Panda! Go Panda!* and its follow-up the next year, *Panda! Go Panda! Rainy Day Circus*, both around thirty minutes in length. These two films are an inversion of the *Goldilocks and the Three Bears* scenario, featuring a young girl named Mimiko left alone in the house by her grandmother, only to find, after returning home from her daily shopping chores, that her abode has been invaded by a family of pandas. They are significant because not only do they represent Miyazaki's first foray into scriptwriting, but they also marked the first collaboration with another newcomer into A Productions, Yoshifumi Kondō, who would later direct *Whisper of the Heart* for Studio Ghibli.

For the rest of the '70s the two directors worked on a number of projects, the most significant of which was bringing Johanna Spyri's *Heidi* to the small screen in 52 episodes of *Arupusu no Shōjo Haiji*, with Takahata directing and Miyazaki working on design. This hugely influential series led Nippon Animation to adapt a number of classics of children's literature for Fuji TV under the title *World Masterpiece Theater* (*Sekai Meisaku Gekijō*), the two of them returning to work in the same capacities on *From the Apennines to the Andes* (*Haha o Tazunete Sanzenri*, 1976), and *Anne of Green Gables* (*Akage no Anne*, 1979) as well as both adding some input on *A Dog of Flanders* (*Furandāsu no Inu*, 1975), all fondly remembered by those who grew up in Japan in the '70s.

Miyazaki had all this time been honing his drawing skills, working on layouts and storyboards and continuing to contribute heavily to the overall artistic conception of the projects he worked on. He had yet to helm his own project, though. This opportunity came with the TV series *Future Boy Conan* (*Mirai Shōnen Konan*), which aired from April to October of 1978. Set in the not too distant future, it is the story of a young boy growing up on a deserted island with only his grandfather for company, believing themselves the sole survivors of the human race after a devastating war, until the arrival of a young girl named Lana on their shores. The series, with which Takahata and Kondō were also involved, was later edited into a theatrical feature released in 1979.

The following year Miyazaki made his theatrical debut with the second *Lupin III* adventure *Castle of Cagliostro* (the first, *Lupin III: The Mystery of Mamo*, was directed by Sōji Yoshikawa in 1978), in which, after an opening heist at a casino, the lovable rogue is pursued all the way to the fictional central European state of Cagliostro. Here he comes head to head against the sole surviving member of the province's ruling family, uncovering a major counterfeiting operation in the process. Cleaning up the nudity and violence of the original manga, and with markedly smoother animation than the first *Lupin* film, Miyazaki's debut is one of the best entries, if not the best, in the series, with its characters and European-based settings more indicative of the director's own body of work than that of the series as a whole.

During the early years of the '80s, Takahata directed two features in rapid succession. The first of these is *Jarinko Chie*, not widely known outside of Japan. Appearing as both a feature and a TV series in the same year, *Chie* is based on a manga about a young girl growing up in Osaka left in charge of the lowly family restaurant with only her pet cat to turn to for companionship after her mother leaves her layabout father. Takahata followed it up with *Gauche the Cello Player*, which was made part-time over a period of four years whilst he was working on other projects. During this time, Miyazaki directed several episodes of the *Sherlock Hound* (*Meitantei Hōmuzu*) TV series, a canine take on Conan Doyle's supersleuth. Co-produced by TMS and the Italian TV station RAI, two of Miyazaki's episodes were later edited together for a theatrical release that found its way onto the lower half of a double bill with his next film, a far more ambitious project.

Miyazaki's manga, *Nausicaä of the Valley of the Winds*, was serialized originally in the magazine *Animage* (it was later translated into English). This original science fiction fantasy, set in a distant, post-apocalyptic future, proved immensely popular, leading *Animage*'s publisher, Tokuma Shoten, to put up the money for a feature-length production. Released in 1984, *Nausicaä* is a landmark opus in the history of Japanese animation, one that would not only put the name of its director firmly on the map, but which would revolutionize the face of the field for years to come, topping magazine fans' and critics' top ten lists for the next two decades and still highly regarded to this day.

Nausicaä is an epic film, and one that would see Miyazaki's reputation rise meteorically from almost nowhere to far outstrip that of his more experienced colleague. Set far into the future, after civilization as we know it has been laid waste by a huge war waged a thousand years previously, the land lies riddled with pollution and toxic spores. In this barren area, the Sea of Corruption, to breathe the air is certain death. One of the few remaining pockets of humanity lies sheltered from the contamination and the encroaching wasteland due to its geographical position in the fertile Valley of the Wind.

Miyazaki opens his story against a desolate backdrop. In a moon-like forest clearing, full of bulbous coral-shaped fungal outgrowths, the air heavy with glowing gas spores and giant snake-like insects buzzing overhead, a solitary figure comes across the discarded shell of an Ohmu, one of the gigantic worm-like crustaceans that occasionally threaten the inhabitants of the valley. Sheltering beneath the prized-off eye-lens of the carapace, a young girl removes her gas mask and lies down on her back, looking up from beneath her glassy shelter at the beautiful display. She is Princess Nausicaä of the Valley and she is undertaking research in the contaminated area to find out what it was that turned the environment against mankind so severely.

Unfortunately, her research is cut short

when a giant aircraft from Tolmekia falls from the sky nearby. Covered in writhing maggots, it contains a princess from the kingdom of Pejite whose people were responsible for unharnessing the devastating power of the Ohmu herds that scour the barren plains surrounding Princess Nausicaä's verdant homeland. In order to guarantee their kingdom's own survival and finally resolve this ancient war, the Tolmekians immediately invade the valley. This time, they are willing to do anything to ensure their victory, even if it means invoking the legendary slumbering God Warriors.

Released in a hideously truncated video version in the United States in the mid-'80s under the title of *Warriors of the Wind*, in its original version *Nausicaä* is a bona-fide classic, a film with all the scope and ambition of its director's later work, and one which firmly establishes a wide variety of themes and motifs that would recur time and again in his films. There's the thinly veiled environmental allegory. There's the anachronistic combination of futuristic and medieval technology: the sleek one-wing flying glider that the princess travels on, whilst her village is powered by ramshackle windmills; the bomber planes and other weapons of warfare taken from the early twentieth century clashing with the Norse-influenced armor and castles of the Tolmekian tribe. And at the core of the drama there's an adolescent girl, the hook of virtually all of Miyazaki's films.

In terms of template, and the explicitness of the environmental message, *Nausicaä*'s closest partner in Miyazaki's oeuvre has to the epic eco-fable *Princess Mononoke*. Even though this later film is located far away from either the futuristic or more European backdrops of its predecessors, set in the Muromachi period (1336–1573) of Japanese history, many parallels are to be found within the similarly episodic and incident heavy plot.

The dramatic opening attack of the Nagonokami, one of the ancient gods of the forest, in the form of a giant wild boar mutated into a slavering beast covered in worm-like tentacles, is similar to the rampaging Ohmu at the beginning of *Nausicaä*. Dashing young warrior Ashitaka is wounded whilst defending his village from the creature, and it is his quest to find a cure that sets the tale in motion, bringing him to the citadel of the Tatara clan, lorded over by the majestic Lady Eboshi, whose bullet initially caused the Nagonokami to run amok. Representing the forces of technological progress, the clan's encroachment upon the neighboring Forest of the Shishigami, or Forest God, is threatening to upset the balance of nature. When the clan declare war on the Shishigami and the rest of the forest denizens, the god's retaliation bears comparison to the fearsome awakening of the God Warrior at the climax of the former film.

But whilst Ashitaka begins as the central focus of the story, the character who draws the closest resemblance with Nausicaä is San, the princess of the title. A young girl raised by wolves, she is fighting alongside her lupine companions to rise up against these human interlopers. Like her counterpart in the earlier film, she stands between the creative forces of nature and the destructive forces of mankind.

Looking at the two films side by side, the most marked difference, of course, is the leap in animation techniques during the 13 years that lie between them. From the initial boar attack to the lavish battle scenes, and the unsparing attention given to such peripheral details as the hordes of chattering apes that slink around the outer walls of the citadel and the mysterious forest sprites, *Princess Mononoke* seldom falls short of breathtaking. Made after a string of hits had swelled the studio's coffers to the extent that the company had the luxury to take as much time and money as required on the project, *Princess Mononoke* was made with resources that simply weren't there for *Nausicaä*. This is not to say that the former film is unimpressive, but in comparison it lacks the intricate background detail and dynamism of its more elaborate successor.

My Neighbor Totoro

Nevertheless, it was the sweeping success of *Nausicaä* that led directly to the formation of Studio Ghibli in 1985, taking its name, which means "hot desert wind," from the nickname for an Italian scout plane that used to fly over the Sahara during the war. Formed under the umbrella of the publishing company Tokuma Shoten that had bankrolled *Nausicaä*, Studio Ghibli's first official film was Miyazaki's *Laputa: Castle in the Sky*, a colorful airborne fantasy drawing its inspiration from the finest tradition of European storytelling.

Miyazaki borrowed both the name and premise of his film from references to a fabulous magnetically guided floating island in the sky, populated by scientists and abstract theoreticians, in the classic tale *Gulliver's Travels* written by Jonathan Swift (1667–1745). The name of this island, Laputa, unfortunately, translates as something a little stronger than "the whore" in Spanish, a pun of which Swift was fully aware, though unfortunately it would seem Miyazaki was not, resulting in the film's later U.S. release

under the title *Castle in the Sky* rather than the original one *Laputa: Castle in the Sky*.

In Miyazaki's film, the action is split between an unspecified rustic European location and this fantastical dreamland laden with riches floating high above. Separating the two worlds is an infinite azure space populated by dirigibles, bombers, blimps, and biplanes. The orphan Pazu dreams of reaching this legendary magical kingdom, which his aviator father had caught a glimpse of years before only to return to find that no one on terra firma believed him. Pazu's wishes look all set to be resolved when a young girl, Sheeta, literally falls out of the sky in front of him. Sheeta is the bearer of a magical jewel that allows one to float in mid-air, something which brings her to the attention not only of the chief of the secret police, Muska, but also of a group of aerial pirates.

Though both *Nausicaä* and *Castle in the Sky* were produced by Takahata, his wholehearted involvement in the latter led him to cede this role to Toshio Suzuki, the former editor of *An-*

Ponpoko

image magazine and one of the driving forces behind the production of *Nausicaä*, in order to concentrate more on his writing and directing work. Suzuki's role in the history of Ghibli cannot be underestimated. Unjustifiably overshadowed by the company's creative forces, he has produced all of Studio Ghibli's theatrical releases from *Kiki's Delivery Service* onward and is currently the president of the company.

Miyazaki's work can be said to fall into two categories, with the grandiose vision of these aforementioned films making way for three more intimate pieces in his mid-career. To many, Miyazaki's films work best when he keeps it simple, and in this respect, *My Neighbor Totoro* is often seen as being amongst his finest. Unlike its two predecessors, this original story by the director takes place in a landscape that is unmistakably Japanese, featuring two young sisters, Satsuki (aged 11) and Mei (aged 4), who move with their father to a tumbledown wooden house in the countryside to be closer to their mother, bedridden with a serious illness in a nearby hospital. Their rickety new abode and its surroundings

are full of intrigues, with nuts showering from the rafters, cupboards scuttling full of tiny black spider-like creatures, and a number of ghosts and strange creatures that are invisible to their father, the most significant being a large woolly monster (described as a "troll" by Mei, mispronounced as "to-to-ro") and his family secreted in a verdant glade in the neighboring forest.

Miyazaki's paean to childhood imagination represents his most universal work in theme, yet at the same time his most personal, containing a semi-autobiographical element in that when he was a child, Miyazaki's mother had spent a long time away from home, bed-bound with spinal tuberculosis. But if it was *Totoro* and the film that accompanied it into the cinemas on the same double bill, Takahata's *Grave of the Fireflies*, that first brought their names to the lips of the general public in Japan, stretching beyond the usual niche market associated with animation, then it was Miyazaki's next film, *Kiki's Delivery Service*, that set off the chain of box-office blockbusters that continued with *Only Yesterday* and beyond to establish Ghibli as a household brand name.

Kiki's is based on a children's book by Eiko Kadono about a young witch forced to leave home when she comes of age on her thirteenth birthday. Moving to a town whose design was based on the Swedish capital Stockholm with her black cat named Jiji, she is initially jeered at by the local brats for her witchlike attire, but has soon triumphed against adversity to set up her own delivery service, by broomstick. And then, she loses her power of flight.

From its background locations and its plucky young heroine, *Kiki's Delivery Service* is unmistakably a Miyazaki film, most specifically in its evocation of flight as a source of untapped power. Whilst, in comparison, Takahata's films are far more firmly rooted on Earth, most of the films Miyazaki is involved in feature their airborne moments, an interest stemming from his father's job working at a factory making airplane parts during the war. To Miyazaki, the sky is an open canvas, an escape route from the confines of being grounded in reality and a mystical gateway that links a variety of exotic locations. *Castle in the Sky*'s levitation stone, *Kiki*'s broomstick, *Spirited Away*'s flying dragon, and the floating angel soaring above a futuristic city in the seven-minute short film screened in movie theaters that Miyazaki directed for the pop duo Chage and Aska entitled *On Your Mark*—airborne adventures all feature heavily in Miyazaki's kingdoms.

This is never more specifically so than in *Porco Rosso*, a more adult-pitched tale in which our porcine protagonist, a once heroic fighter pilot who has now grown old and fat and left his idealistic youth far behind him, patrols the skies against the threat of a fleet of aerial pirates. Pigs are also a recurrent motif in Miyazaki's work: Chihiro's mission in *Spirited Away* is initiated when, after wolfing down a meal at a deserted restaurant, her parents are transformed into mud-swilling, obese swine. Miyazaki once flippantly stated that the reason for this was that pigs are easier to draw—he has also mentioned that these creatures to him represent the mod-

Whisper of the Heart

ern Japanese, a greedy consumer-based culture that devours everything in its path.

During Miyazaki's five-year rest between *Porco Rosso* and the technically groundbreaking *Princess Mononoke* came *Ocean Waves* (a.k.a. *I Can Hear the Sea*), the first film by the studio to be directed by someone other than Ghibli's two main men. Scheduled to be screened during the Golden Week public holiday in May, Tomomi Mochizuki's made-for-TV feature is a blend of romantic melodrama and high school nostalgia, whose appeal was more obviously pitched at an older audience. A chance sighting of former classmate Rikako opens a well of memories for university student Taku. On his return to his hometown of Kōchi in rural Shikoku, where they first came across each other, he meets up with his former best friend Matsuno, reminding him of that crucial year in high school when

© 1997 Nibariki • TNDG

Princess Mononoke

wild creatures with mythical properties that occupy the heart of many a Japanese legend. Battling fruitlessly against bulldozers and bureaucrats to save the Tama Hills, they eventually find a temporary stopgap when they move to Machida (a sprawling dormitory city about an hour south of Tokyo), a place where even if man and nature don't exist completely in harmony, the *tanuki* at least end up as road-kill slightly less often.

The suburban setting of the Tamagawa area was also the backdrop for *Whisper of the Heart*, the first theatrical release by someone other than Miyazaki or Takahata. In its wholehearted embodiment of the in-house style, the Miyazaki influence is very tangible. Perhaps this is not so surprising. First of all, it was scripted by Miyazaki (from an original manga by Aoi Hiiragi), and second, it was directed by Yoshifumi Kondō, whose visual style is clearly noticeable through his design work in a number of the studio's previous films. Kondō's untimely death in 1998 due to an aneurysm unfortunately meant that the touching and inspirational *Whisper of the Heart* remains his sole directorial offering, which is a shame, because it is one of the studio's finest, balancing Miyazaki's elative vision with a stronger attention to character and structure.

Again it features a teenage protagonist, Shizuku, a dreamy 14-year-old schoolgirl who yearns to be a novelist. Whilst indulging her voracious literary appetite in the school library, she notices that the same name continuously crops up in the borrower's list of all of the books she has taken out: Seiji Amasawa. Unfortunately, her initial chance brush with the boy who shares the same tastes in reading crushes any romantic illusions she might have been harboring. Whilst taking the suburban commuter train on an errand for her mother, a fat tomcat wanders across Shizuku's path. Intrigued by the chubby feline's singular sense of purpose, she follows it from the train all the way to the front door of a rickety antique shop. The shop's eccentric aging owner welcomes her into this Aladdin's cave of curios, and Shizuku is overjoyed when an open

the arrival of the pristine but uppity straight "A" transfer student from Tokyo and a school trip to Hawaii threatened to change their relationship for good. Originally intended as a small-scale television showcase for the younger talents in the studio, *Ocean Waves* went over budget and over schedule, and following similar difficulties making the non-Ghibli video series *Here Is Greenwood* (*Koko wa Gurīnuddo*, 1991), the stress of the production, his only for the studio, put its director Mochizuki in hospital.

Ocean Waves was one of the first of Ghibli's works to be relocated away from an anonymous fictional land to a recognizable modern day, real life locale. In this case, the initial scene occurs in Kichijōji station, in the west of Tokyo, a stone's throw away from both Ghibli's current premises in Koganei, where it established a permanent studio space in 1992, and the Ghibli Museum in nearby Mitaka that opened in 2001.

Takahata's *Pompoko* also takes place closer to home, tackling environmental issues through the eyes of a community of *tanuki*, or raccoon dogs, invitation is handed out for her to return any time she wishes. But her glee is short-lived when she discovers that he is the grandfather of none other than Seiji.

Nevertheless, Seiji apologizes for his crassness during their initial meeting, and a budding schoolyard romance begins to develop until Shizuku's beau drops the bombshell that he's shortly to move to Italy to begin an apprenticeship as a violin maker. Initially devastated by this announcement Shizuku rationalizes that if she can't be with Seiji then she should at least attempt to match his ambition. Sacrificing her studies for the end-of-year school examinations, with the encouragement of his grandfather she pours her heart into writing a novel, inspired by a statuette of the Baron, a dandy cat in a top hat with sparkling emerald eyes and the pride of the old man's collection.

Released some seven years later, *The Cat Returns* was a sequel of sorts to Kondō's film, though it owes little to its predecessor other than that it is based on the manga *Baron: Neko no Dunshaku*, by the same artist, Aoi Hiiragi, and brings back a couple of incidental characters, most notably the Baron, whose statue acted as the catalyst for Shizuku's ardent soul-searching in the earlier film, and the tubby tomcat Muta/Moon. It again features a young schoolgirl protagonist, Haru, pitched into a fantastical world after crossing paths with a nonchalant cat which she scoops up from the path of an oncoming truck. She is flabbergasted when the unfazed feline, whom it transpires is none other than an eligible young prince from an alternate world of the Kingdom of the Cats, subsequently gets up, dusts himself off and begins thanking her for saving his life. The local cat community is similarly appreciative of her gesture, leading a ceremonial procession to serenade her on her front doorstep that same evening. However, the cats' final act of gratitude, a decree of marriage offered by none other than the King of Cats to his son, whose life she has just saved, is met with a little less enthusiasm.

© 2001 Nibariki • TGNDDTM

Spirited Away

The Cat Returns is a far safer film than Ghibli's more typical offerings, notably short at only 75 minutes, and more obviously aimed at the younger end of the market, though still retaining the dazzlingly drawn action sequences and touching humanism that has come to be expected from the studio. Whilst completing the pattern of topping the box office charts for the year of its release, in comparison with *Princess Mononoke* and *Spirited Away* it represented a rather modest success. A similar response had greeted Isao Takahata's *My Neighbors the Yamadas*, underscoring the fact that it is Miyazaki's name that is the more powerful draw, rather than that of Studio Ghibli itself. His credit on the publicity material of *The Cat Returns*, responsible for the project concept, all but dwarfed that of its director, Hiroyuki Morita.

Following the vast degree of acclaim awarded to *Spirited Away*, Miyazaki began work on *Howl's Moving Castle*, based on the novel of the same name by British children's writer Diana Wynne Jones. In the event that it should prove his last, then we have nothing to fear. The 25-

minute short *The Ghiblies: Episode 2* (Episode 1 aired on Japanese TV in 2000) that accompanied *The Cat Returns* into cinemas is an impressive testimony to the talent and imagination of the younger creative forces at work in Miyazaki's shadow. A series of skits surrounding the characters of a fictitious animation studio, not all too surprisingly named "Ghibli" (though pronounced "gi bu ri," with a hard "G" to distinguish it from the real Studio, which is pronounced using a soft "J" sound), it is rendered in a variety of styles ranging from the surreal, as in the opening tale of a curry eating competition at a local eatery, through the humorous, to the touching reminiscences of young love forged between two of the characters at an elementary school art exhibition. If nothing else, it is concrete proof that when the time inevitably comes for both Takahata and Miyazaki to hand over the reins, their legacy will be in safe hands.

↓ The Adventures of Hols, Prince of ↓ the Sun
太陽の王子 ホルスの大冒険

Taiyō no Ōji Horusu no Daibōken, a.k.a. *Little Norse Prince Valiant; The Great Adventure of Little Norse Prince Valiant*

1968. **DIRECTOR:** Isao Takahata. **VOICE CAST:** Hisako Ōkata, Mikijirō Hira, Etsuko Ichihara, Masao Mishima. 82 minutes. **RELEASES:** DVD. Toei (Japan, no subtitles), Wild Side (France, French subtitles).

The hallmarks of the Ghibli style can already be seen in this groundbreaking animated feature from Toei Animation (Tōei Dōga), an early collaboration between the studio's twin talents in a tale of a young Norse prince's fight against the forces of darkness.

Made twenty years before his first feature for Ghibli, *Grave of the Fireflies*, and over a full

ten years before Miyazaki would occupy the position of director for the first time with the TV series *Future Boy Conan*, the seeds of what is now recognizable as the Ghibli style can be traced all the way back to this groundbreaking animation from Toei Animation. From the soft, rounded features of the characters, the smooth, effortless animation, and the usage of cinematic techniques to create a world that stretches far beyond the frame of the screen, to the archetypal plot set-up centered around an epic quest that culminates in a Manichean showdown between the forces of light and darkness, the little-seen *The Adventures of Hols* can be justifiably regarded as the Ghibli Studios ur-film.

Turning to a Norse setting, our hero, Hols, is first introduced in the midst of an opening wolf attack, fending off the baying beasties with a only a hand axe for defense. He is saved by a stone giant, Rockor, who, disturbed by the skirmish, rises from the earth and sends the wolves fleeing. Rockor is in obvious discomfort due to a sword thrust deep into his shoulder. Hols repays the giant's assistance in the battle by removing the sword and returns to his village, where his father is lying on his deathbed. With his final dying words, Hols's father tells him of how, many years before, the northerly fishing village where his people come from was laid waste by the evil King of Ice, Grunwald. Claiming the sword drawn from Rockor's shoulder, Hols heads north to regain his ancestral land.

From then on, we follow the doe-eyed Viking boy and his talking pet bear sidekick, Coro, on a lengthy quest to his ancestral village to defeat his demonic nemesis. Battling through snow, ice, avalanches, giant pikes, and plagues of rats, along the way he comes across Hilda, a pure and virginal young maiden blessed with a beautiful singing voice, who may not be all that she at first seems. Meanwhile, Grunwald, clad in a horned helmet and swathed in a black cloak, along with his army of snow wolves, is leaving a wake of destruction in the surrounding area. Hols's presence in the northern village rallies the troops to take up arms against their destructive oppressor.

The Adventures of Hols (retitled *Little Norse Prince Valiant* for its dubbed TV release during the '80s in the United States on TBS) was not only Takahata's first go at directing a feature-length cartoon, but also the first time Miyazaki worked alongside him, in the role of key animator. For his earlier TV outings, *Ken the Wolf Boy* and *Hustle Punch* (though he only directed the opening sequences), Takahata had been guided by a key figure in the world of animation, Yasuo Ōtsuka. Born in 1931, Ōtsuka had been with Toei Animation since its very foundation, working on the first all-color Japanese animated feature *Legend of the White Serpent* as second key animator. It was he, working in the role of production supervisor, who recommended Takahata to helm the project. Starting work in 1965, they were joined by a core team of Toei's finest animators.

During the late '60s, Toei studios dominated the field of commercial Japanese animation, but even then the studio heads dared not compete against the bigger-budgeted product of America, such as that of Disney Studios, preferring to tread water more safely in the domestic arena of TV production. Aimed at children, these series were cheaply produced—filmed in monochrome, and using only the most basic of 2D cel animation techniques—and look primitive in the extreme compared with the high standards that foreign audiences have generally come to associate with Japanese animation since the '80s. Set against simplistic backdrops and predominantly static in nature, character animation was restricted to individual movements within the wider frame, such as mouth motions when characters are talking, or movement of only part of the character, such as an arm moving at any one time (lower-quality Japanese TV animation produced nowadays disguises these deficiencies with a disorienting excess of edits). Though notably superior in technique, even Toei's theatrical excursions were hitherto smaller in scale and ambition compared with that of their American rivals.

For the creative elements working in the studio, *The Adventures of Hols* afforded an ideal opportunity to spread their wings and use the medium to produce something for a wider ranging audience. Unfortunately, this pet project soon got out of hand, in the end taking three years to complete against the originally slotted eight months. Takahata was demoted from future major directing jobs, though amongst other things worked on a couple of episodes of the fondly remembered TV series, *Gegege no Kitarō* (*Spooky Kitaro* a.k.a. *Cackling Kitaro*), a kid's horror cartoon about a young *yōkai*, a one-eyed goblin and his friends (including his father, who nestles in Kitarō's pocket, his body having decomposed to but a single eyeball) based on the 1966 manga by Shigeru Mizuki.

In the meantime, Miyazaki's creative presence made itself felt working as key animator on Toei's feature length *The Flying Ghost Ship* (*Sora Tobu Yūreisen*, 1969), the 55-minute long *Ali Baba and the 40 Thieves* (*Aribaba to Yonjuppiki no Tōzoku*, 1971), and *Animal Treasure Island* (*Dōbutsu Takarajima*, 1971), for which he was also credited as being responsible for the main idea, based on Robert Louis Stevenson's *Treasure Island*.

Ōtsuka left the company for A Productions, and was joined by both Takahata and Miyazaki several years later, along with another member of the original *Adventures of Prince Hols* team, Yōichi Kotabe. Ironically, this third member would later work as an animation supervisor for the Pokémon theatrical features, including *Pikachu: The Movie* (*Pikachū no Natsuyasumi*) and *Pokémon: Mewtwo Strikes Back* (*Poketto Monsutā: Myūtsū no Gyakushū*, 1998), to all intents and purposes the very antithesis of Ghibli's high production value, cross-generational ideal.

↓ Grave of the Fireflies
火垂るの墓

Hotaru no Haka, a.k.a. Tombstone of the Fireflies, Le Tombeau Des Lucioles

1988. DIRECTOR: Isao Takahata. VOICE CAST: Tsutomu Tatsumi, Ayano Shiraishi, Yoshiko Shinohara, Akemi Yamaguchi. 88 minutes. RELEASES: DVD, Warner Home Video (Japan, English subtitles), CPM/US Manga Corps (U.S., English subtitles). Manga Distribution (France, French subtitles).

Heartrending animation of two young innocents whose lives are destroyed in the final days of World War II.

Set in Kobe in 1945, *Grave of the Fireflies*, the first feature Takahata directed within Ghibli, focuses on the plight of teenage Seita and his four-year-old sister Setsuko, and their harrowing descent through homelessness and starvation after the bombing of the city leaves their mother buried beneath the rubble of the family's makeshift air raid shelter. Their father off fighting at sea, the newly orphaned youngsters are initially taken in by their aunt. However, with food shortages and rampant inflation, it's not long before the presence of these two new hungry mouths at their father's sister's table begins to prove a burden on the household.

The situation is brought to a head when their grudging new guardian sells their deceased mother's kimono for the price of a sack of rice. After withdrawing their mother's life savings from the bank, the two decide to go it alone, investing in a stove and relocating to an isolated cave by the lakeside where Seita pledges to look after his sister until the war is over. A forgotten toothbrush is the least of their worries, and it's not long before the money runs out and the two are subsisting on a diet of vegetables stolen from the neighboring farmland and dried frogs (the frog is a commonplace symbol for the home, with the word *kaeru* a homonym for "frog" and the verb "to return home").

A remarkably even-handed affair, Takahata's adaptation of Akiyuki Nosaka's semi-autobiographical novel neatly avoids any mention of the background specifics of the Pacific War, seeking neither to condemn or condone either side in the conflict. Instead it utilizes the broader canvas of Kobe's war-torn backdrop of flaming buildings and falling fire to paint a grueling portrait of two young innocents caught up by forces far beyond their comprehension and control. The futility of Seita's and Setsuko's struggle for survival is never in question, with the inevitable trajectory of their demise through malnutrition signified in the opening moments with the two main characters introduced as ghosts, haloed by the shimmering points of light of fireflies against a plain background. In a cinematic concession deviating from the structure of the original source novel, Takahata then opts to tell his tale from the perspective of these impassive spectral spectators, first seen objectively witnessing Seita's dying moments propped up against the wall of a desolate building surrounded by the corpses of dozens of similarly expired children as one of the city workmen resignedly announces to his colleague: "The Americans are coming. Better get rid of these tramps."

Such macabre background details as the black rain that falls after the bombing, the mass grave into which their mother is unceremoniously dumped, and the pathetic figure spotted running through streets laden with charred corpses screaming "Long live the Emperor!" as death rains down from above, are evenly balanced by the film's many lighter moments, in which it appears as if even the surrounding carnage can't dampen the youthful exuberance of its two protagonists. Seita gulping thirstily from a ruptured water main on his return home from a scavenging mission, and the two romping innocently on the beach as they shirk their work responsibilities open out the picture to show that for civilians unwittingly implicated in the devastation, life must go on.

By abstaining from design duties, Takahata as always manages to vary the visual style of his work to fit in with the tone of the project (his previous film being the completely out of character foray of *The Story of Yanagawa Canal*, a live-action documentary with a few animated sequences about the preservation of the canals in the scenic town of Yanagawa, Kyushu, produced by Miyazaki outside of Ghibli), the pictorial aspects of the film here falling upon the shoulders of Yoshifumi Kondō, a regular collaborator of both Takahata and Miyazaki since long before the foundation of Ghibli, who also contributed his distinctive designs to *Only Yesterday*, and *Kiki's Delivery Service*.

 Grave of the Fireflies was produced and released simultaneously on a double bill with Miyazaki's *My Neighbor Totoro*, an escapist fable more clearly pitched at the family market, thus broadening the original audience of both films. Though occasionally a little grating in its sentimentality, with Setsuko perhaps that little bit too "cute," Takahata's emotive and poignantly humanistic tale is guaranteed to leave an impression on all who see it, as senselessly tragic as the British animated Raymond Briggs adaptation *When the Wind Blows* (Jimmy T. Murakami, 1986), which charted the slow decline of an elderly couple through radiation sickness in the wake of a nuclear strike, or Masaki Mori's not entirely dissimilar *Barefoot Gen* (*Hadashi no Gen*, 1983), adapted from Keiji Nakazawa's 1,400-page manga published in 1973 detailing the aftermath of the bombing of Hiroshima from the viewpoint of a six-year-old boy.

↓ Porco Rosso
紅の豚
Kurenai no Buta, a.k.a. The Crimson Pig

1992. **DIRECTOR:** Hayao Miyazaki. **VOICE CAST:** Shū-ichirō Moriyama, Tokiko Katō, Akio Ōtsuka, Akemi Okamura. 94 minutes. **RELEASES:** DVD, Buena Vista (U.S., English subtitles), IVL (Hong Kong, English/Chinese subtitles), Buena Vista Home Entertainment (Japan, English/French/Japanese subtitles), Fox Pathé (France, French subtitles).

In pre-war Italy, a guilt-plagued aviator has turned himself into a pig, but still patrols the skies to rid the land of a pirate menace. He vies for the attention of a pretty nightclub singer, but finds competition in the form of a brash American pilot. A passionately told tale from Miyazaki, with sweeping aerial scenes.

Set in a typically Miyazaki-esque fantasy image of early twentieth century Europe, in this case the Adriatic coast of pre-war Italy, *Porco Rosso* is the story of a pig who patrols the skies against a menacing, but not too bright, group of pirates. Once, the pig was a man, a World War I fighter pilot named Marco, who saw his friends die in an aerial battle that only he survived. Since then, a mixture of guilt and disillusion has made him retreat from humanity, voluntarily isolating himself on an island with only his red seaplane for company.

 Porco has not entirely given up on mankind, however. Having seen the horrors of war, he is not about to let the innocent be oppressed by sky pirates. When the airborne bandits kidnap a boatload of little girls and a pile of loot, Porco goes into action, trashes the pirate plane, and rescues the children. Swearing revenge, the pirates enlist the help of the brazen American aviator Curtis, who claims to have beaten Italy's best pilots and who's just itching for the challenge of taking on Porco's plane.

 Stated somewhat roughly, the films of Hayao Miyazaki come in two types: cynical and positive. This division reflects the two paradoxical sides of their director's personality: the pessimist who worries about what kind of future we're creating for ourselves and the imaginative artist who dreams up wondrous new and better worlds with only pencil and paper. *Nausicaä of the Valley of the Winds* and *Princess Mononoke* are social allegories in the shape of elaborate, epic scale adventures. For all their sweep, they are driven mainly by frustration over the mess we humans are making of our own planet. They are the works of the pessimist Hayao Miyazaki.

© 1992 Nibariki · TNNG

Porco Rosso

Although most of his films contain at least a hint of that pessimism, with *My Neighbor Totoro*, *Kiki's Delivery Service*, and *Porco Rosso* the animator takes an altogether more positive approach. He shows us what we're doing right rather than what we're doing wrong. Instead of trying to overwhelm us with the full extent of the horrors we've created, he enthralls us with the little details that make life worth living.

Porco Rosso is a special case even among Miyazaki's "positive" works. It's a film he made for himself first and foremost. Covering one of his favorite subjects, airplanes, it's a film that exudes a great sense of passion. Its numerous aerial scenes are dazzling, its airplane designs fanciful and lovingly detailed. The film's hero may be a middle-aged man who feels he doesn't deserve to be human, but he certainly isn't about to give up being a pilot. With its clumsy pirates, its brash protagonists, and its death-defying aerial antics, *Porco Rosso* is also Miyazaki's most mischievous film since *Castle of Cagliostro*. In which other Miyazaki film can we see the

silly sight of two men pelting each other with wrenches and scrap metal in mid-air because the guns on their planes have jammed? It's this combination of positivity, passion, and mischief that makes *Porco Rosso* a standout in the director's body of work.

Watching this film, we sit enthralled, not because we're caught in an exhausting hyperactive roller coaster ride, but because Miyazaki makes us laugh and wonder. *Porco Rosso* is a wholly positive experience, generating an emotional resonance that is sometimes lacking from the director's more epic sagas.

↓ Only Yesterday

おもひでぽろぽろ

Omoide Poroporo, a.k.a. Tearful Thoughts

1991. **DIRECTOR:** Isao Takahata. **VOICE CAST:** Miki Imai, Toshirō Yanagiba, Yoko Honna. 118 minutes. **RELEASES:** DVD, Buena Vista (Japan, English/Japanese subtitles), IVL (Hong Kong, English/Chinese subtitles).

Tender slice of '60s nostalgia seen through the eyes of an '80s office lady.

The term "Family Entertainment" can often set off warning signals in the minds of most viewers, especially when applied to animation, with implications of dumbed down, simplistic fables for the kids peppered with a handful of more topical or risqué gags to keep the parents amused. But Ghibli's output truly does lay claim to such tags.

Take for example, Tomomi Mochizuki's made-for-TV special, *Ocean Waves*, whose "will they, won't they?" tale of high school romance was pitched clearly at older viewers. *Only Yesterday* (whose Japanese title *Omoide Poroporo* translates roughly as Memories Drop By Drop), despite its more grown-up focus, is slightly broader in its appeal and truly features something for everyone, with an emotional arc that can't fail to find resonance with the older generation, yet whose surface details are surely rich enough to engage the youngsters.

Only Yesterday takes a wistful look back at the '60s, more specifically 1966, as filtered through the reminiscences of 27-year-old office lady Taeko Okajima from the vantage point of 1982. First seen asking her boss for time off from work, rather than the standard break to Okinawa or Hawaii, Taeko opts to exchange the gleaming cityscapes of Tokyo and her daily environment of filing cabinets and photocopiers for a ten-day sojourn with relatives in the rural northern prefecture of Yamagata to take part in the annual *benibana* (safflower) harvest.

What prompted the decision is left vague, as Taeko herself grew up in the capital. But then we hark back to a memory in which her ten-year-old self is left abandoned in the suburbs by her classmates at the end of the school year as they all depart to visit their various grandmothers dotted around the Japanese countryside. With her own grandmother living at home, the best on offer is a short break away from the city to an *onsen* hot spring resort in Atami, an exciting enough prospect in its own right until she passes out from heat exhaustion, having overdosed on the hot baths.

Meanwhile, modern-day Taeko is constantly irked by phone calls from her older, married sister, reminding her that she has now passed "Christmas Cake" age (in other words, no good after the 25th) and it's time to find a husband. On the overnight sleeper train to Yamagata, she begins to find herself more and more overwhelmed by the memories of her younger self. These become all the more resonant upon her arrival, where she becomes friendly with her second cousin by marriage, the unsophisticated yet gentle Toshio, who himself has only recently left his office clerk post to get his hands dirty at the family farm. Increasingly the dreamy fifth-grader of her memories seems to be pointing towards a change in direction in her life.

Only Yesterday

Adapted from a manga serialized in *Myōjō* in 1987 written by Hotaru Okamoto and drawn by Yūko Tone, which was set entirely in the '60s, Takahata's script adds this modern-day front-story to form a backbone for the string of nostalgic vignettes that made up the basis of the original comic. Depicted in blanched-out sepia or misted oval frames, these short skits run the gamut of Taeko's more prominent memories, ranging from culturally specific items such as teenage sister Yaeko's crush on a member of the famous cross-dressing, all-female Takarazuka acting troupe and a reference to the manga artist Kazuo Umezu, through to the more global cultural backdrop of the Vietnam War and the influence of the Beatles after their first tour of Japan.

These scenes veer between the humorous and emotive. Oldest sister Nanako studies at art school, and has just bought her first miniskirt. Every time she rides the subway escalator she uses her handbag to cover her backside from the prying eyes of those riding below. Elsewhere there's the family's first encounter with a pineapple, where the initial excitement of the lure of the exotic is soon tempered with the reality. "In one's life one gets to experience many things," the nonplussed granny adds sagely as the two older sisters confirm amongst themselves that "the banana really is the king of fruits," and Taeko is left with a full plate of the nibbled-upon pieces left over from the rest of her family.

Elsewhere the scenes of classroom rites of

passage, hall monitors, school councils, playground romances, and inedible lunches should provide a fascinating counterpart to the similarly themed U.S. TV series, *The Wonder Years* (1988), without the hackneyed "At that moment, I learnt a valuable lesson…" codas one associates with that particular show. As modern-day Taeko muses why this particular time period should prove so evocative, the dreadful specter of puberty is invoked, leading to a wonderful sequence in which the girls are marched off to the school gymnasium, where they are pointed towards the "special pants" available from the infirmary, and the epidemic of skirt peeping which ensues when the boys get wind of the girls' new secret. This scene is treated with a refreshingly matter-of-fact lack of embarrassment, not to mention a fair degree of humor as Taeko recalls the time when she repeatedly refuses to take a sick note into school for the stigma of being excused from the physical education class and being forced to sit on the sidelines with the other girls with periods.

Takahata's addition of the modern-day sequences to these reminiscences does seem to introduce another aspect to the narrative, in the apparently conservative message that women over a certain age in Japan really should be giving up their careers to settle down and get married, though this would appear to be a criticism applied only from outside of Japan and one not even registered by Japanese viewers. It also gives Takahata free rein to indulge in the standard environmental tub-thumping that has run through a fair proportion of Ghibli's

work. Toshio's character often comes across as a mouthpiece for Takahata's own opinions, giving vent to such issues as the death of native traditions in the wake of the massive depopulation of these rural areas for Tokyo and a call to arms for a return to Japan's agricultural roots, before he curtails his rants with a wink and a smile.

This balance between rural and urban seems very much to be a sticking point with Takahata, a theme taken further in his 1994 animation *Pompoko*. One lengthy sequence in which the harvesting of the safflower (a flower cultivated for its deep red dye used in cosmetics) is overlaid with a voiceover detailing the process points out that originally the resulting dye would be tainted with the blood of the rural peasant girls who pricked their hands on the thorns whilst picking the flowers, and who would never get the opportunity to wear the rouge or lipstick manufactured for the wealthy, fashionable ladies of Kyoto. Noble as Takahata's intentions may be, and however well-researched these modern scenes are, they can't help but threaten to detract from the main thrust of the story, which surely belongs to the character of Taeko herself.

For all that, *Only Yesterday* remains a remarkably effective piece of entertainment, and technically well up to the high standards one expects from the team, with the ever-reliable Joe Hisaishi providing a memorably touching score. Too often overlooked in favor of the studio's bigger and bolder efforts, *Only Yesterday* may be an unashamed nostalgia trip, but it stands firmly amongst Ghibli's finest.

CHAPTER 8
Kaizō Hayashi
林海象

The films of Kaizō Hayashi seldom exist far beyond the influential sphere of showbiz. Postmodern and self-referential, first and foremost Hayashi is a movie fan, and his enthusiasm for and love of the medium dominate his every frame. The very model of the pop culture *otaku* (fanboy), his works abound with cat-suited acrobatic jewel thieves, hissing femme fatales, brooding private detectives, ethnic Asian mobsters, performing elephants, and miming white-faced pierrots.

The glare of the bright lights, the smell of the greasepaint, and the roar of the crowd—he celebrates them all. He is our circus ringmaster, with the silver screen acting as his big top, proudly presenting us his latest sensational act. He is a showman with an unrivaled aesthetic sense, a visual stylist without peer, who has worked in tandem with some of the industry's top talents to create a series of works that dazzle and delight. Though any higher message takes a backseat to the sumptuous visuals, it is perhaps on this level of style alone that Hayashi merits mention in any serious discussion of contemporary Japanese cinema.

There never seemed any doubt in the mind of Kaizo Hayashi that his destiny lay within in the film world. Enrolling in Ritsumeikan University in his native Kyoto to study economics, after two years he had dropped out of his course and headed up to Tokyo. Straight away, he became involved in the Tenjōsajiki ("theater viewing gallery"), the renowned theater troupe of the seminal poet/playwright/filmmaker Shūji Terayama. Born in 1935 in Aomori, the most northerly prefecture of Honshu, Terayama was a crucial figure in the avant-garde arts scene of the '60s, and a decisive stylistic influence on the young Hayashi. A graduate of Waseda University, he soon built up a significant reputation for himself through his plays, literary criticism, and most especially his variations on the traditional forms of haiku and tanka poetry. He was also heavily involved in the field of cinema, making a major contribution to the Japanese New Wave movement. Amongst the scripts he wrote were Masahiro Shinoda's *Dry Lake* (*Kawaita Mizu Umi*, 1960) and *My Face Red in the Sunset* (*Yūhi ni Akai Ore no Kao*, 1961), and Susumu Hani's *Inferno of First Love* (*Hatsukoi Jigoku-Hen*, 1968).

But the Tenjōsajiki theatrical group was perhaps Terayama's most legendary contribution to the vibrant counterculture movement of the '60s and '70s. Founded in 1967, it was part of an active experimental theatrical scene known as post-*Shingeki*, which unlike its predecessor *Shingeki* ("modern theater") didn't seek to break completely from traditional forms, but rather to get back to the very aesthetic underpinnings of the now culturally sanctified and conservative theaters of kabuki and Noh. But whilst post-*Shingeki* was concerned with color, form, and movement rather than causative dramatic narrative, like their contemporaries in the cinematic avant-garde of the stormy '60s, those involved were working from a political viewpoint that had become increasingly marginalized from institutionalized politics, either left-wing or right-wing. Their approach to the dramatic portrayal of reality may have been metaphysical, fragmented, and highly artificial, but it used its dreamlike structure to address such real-life concerns as the individual's place within the chaotic, shifting flux of a society rife with student protest and at the mercy of such sweeping political decisions as the renewal of the Japan-U.S. Security Pact, or Ampo Treaty, which allowed the United States to keep its bases on Japanese soil in order to maintain a military presence in Asia.

Given his close association with the cinematic New Wave, it was perhaps inevitable that Terayama's forays into cinema should stretch beyond mere screenwriting. His own film work is as radical and innovative as anything at the time, imposing his cryptically surreal and subversive vision in films such as *Emperor Tomato Ketchup* (*Tomato Kechappu Kōtei*, 1970, best known in a 27-minute shortened version of the longer 75-minute cut that only played at Cannes in 1971), which portrays a totalitarian society under the reign of rifle-toting children, *Throw Away Your Books and Go Out into the Streets* (*Sho o Suteyo Machi e Deyo*, 1970), and *To Die in the Country* (*Denen ni Shisu*, 1974). Unfortunately, little of this has been made available outside of Japan other than the unofficial sequel to *Emmanuelle* director Just Jaeckin's *The Story of O* (*Histoire d'O*, 1975), the glossy piece of porno-chic, *Fruits of Passion* (*Shanhai Ijin Shōkan*, a.k.a. *China Doll*, 1980), starring Klaus Kinski and produced by Anatole Dauman, who was also responsible for the France-Japan co-production of Nagisa Ōshima's controversial *In the Realm of the Senses* (*Ai no Korīda*, 1976).

Hayashi's own involvement with the Tenjōsajiki troupe was short-lived. Terayama died of nephrosis of the kidneys in 1983, and the group disbanded in 1985. Nevertheless, it is not difficult to see the ghost of Terayama lingering throughout much of Hayashi's work, with their fanciful scenarios, grotesque characters, and carnivalesque atmospheres, though radical politics and any reference to the real world order are kept noticeably at bay.

Still, it was through this association that he made the acquaintance of production designer Takeo Kimura and cinematographer Yūichi Nagata, both established figures within the film industry. Kimura's track record stretched back all the way to when he worked as a production design assistant at Daiei in the early '40s, but his most characteristic contributions to the world of film came with his work at Nikkatsu in the '60s. His extravagant, baroque, and vibrantly colored sets and costumes are most prominently show-

Filmography

1986
• To Sleep So As to Dream (Yume Miru Yō ni Nemuritai)

1988
• IDEA

1989
• Circus Boys (Nijū Seiki Shōnen Dokuhon)

1990
• Zipang (Jipangu)

1991
• Figaro Story [co-directed with Claire Denis and Alejandro Agresti]

1992
• Ongyoku no Ran [video]

1994
• The Most Terrible Time in My Life (Waga Jinsei Saiaku no Toki)

1995
• The Stairway to the Distant Past (Haruka na Jidai no Kaidan o)

1996
• The Trap (Wana)
• The Breath (Umi Hōzuki)

1997
• Romance [short]
• Cat's Eye
• Born to Be Baby Chinnane e [short]

1998
• Otome no Inori [short]

2000
• Lost Angeles

cased in the films of Seijun Suzuki, such as *Gate of Flesh* and *Tokyo Drifter*; he also rejoined the veteran director much later for *Pistol Opera*. Nagata had spent the best part of the previous decade lensing pink films for Nikkatsu, Shintoho, and Kokuei, after debuting on Tetsurō Nunokawa's documentary *Bastard on the Border* (*Maboroshi no Konminzoku Kyōwakoku* [trans: The illusion of a mixed race republic]) produced by Yōichi Sai.

Hayashi was lucky to have assistance from such experienced hands. Since moving up to Tokyo, he had been supporting himself with numerous part time jobs whilst he worked on his debut script, but had little experience in working on film outside of his own experimentations as a student back in Kyoto. Nevertheless, he managed to assemble a cast, crew, and 5 million yen budget for his self-produced *To Sleep So As to Dream*.

No one could have hoped for a stronger debut. A stylish homage to the silent screen grounded in the early days of Japan's own cinematic history, the film is a triumph of narrative and technical ingenuity. Aided by Nagata's crisp vintage-style cinematography and Kimura's ornate set design, the film celebrated the illusion of cinema within a Möbius strip plot which sees a private detective engaged to track down a missing actress trapped in an infinite loop of silent film.

The film peaks with a fabulous performance by Japan's then top practitioner of the art of *benshi* film commentary (silent film narration), the late Shunsui Matsuda, set in a reconstruction of the Denkikan theater, the first exhibition hall in Japan given over completely to screening films. In this fairground milieu of carnival barkers, conjurors, card sharps, and circus elephants can be seen Midori Sawato, who took over Matsuda's mantle upon his death and has been responsible for keeping alive the *benshi* tradition, both on television and in live performances at home and abroad throughout the past few decades.

The end results way exceeded both commercial and critical expectations, picking up prizes at festivals left, right, and center domestically, and setting in motion the career of its prolific lead actor, Shirō Sano. It also led to Hayashi contributing the script to Akio Jissōji's live-action/anime hybrid *Tokyo, The Last Megalopolis* (*Teito Monogatari*, 1988), an epic futuristic fantasy starring *Zatoichi* star Shintarō Katsu and based on a novel by Hiroshi Aramata. Set in the early decades of the twentieth century, Katsu plays a visionary city planner who campaigns to reconstruct Tokyo in the form a bold new metropolis, resistant to earthquakes and fitted out with an underground train system. His forward-thinking idealism comes head to head with old school traditionalism in the form of Katō, a right-wing military fanatic. Katō is scheming to unearth the restless spirit of Masakado, the Guardian of Tokyo, a warrior executed a thousand years ago after being branded a traitor for his own plan of building an independent nation in the heart of Japan. A heady brew of demonic horror, period fantasy, magic, and the supernatural, with Swiss artist H.R. Giger contributing to the production design, the film was succeeded by a straight-to-video anime series of the same name in 1991, known as *Doomed Megalopolis* in the West.

After shooting the 16mm *IDEA* in 1988, a film intended for the video market, many of the cast and crew of Hayashi's debut piece were back again for *Circus Boys*—a simple but spellbinding black-and-white work with its basis in wistful nostalgia and carnival fantasy—which increased Hayashi's profile outside of Japan when it won the Charlie Chaplin Award at the Edinburgh International Film Festival in 1989. A shadow puppet display of trapeze artists and tumblers silhouetted by a flickering light against a piece of translucent white paper establishes the circus milieu of the title. This shadow theater is the prize toy of two young boys, Wataru and Jinta, whose home is between the canvas walls of a circus big top set alone on a flat featureless plane whipped by sandstorms. As the camera glides in through the tent flap to reveal a live performance in full swing, the two lads, dressed in

The Most Terrible Time in My Life

sailor suits, stand open-mouthed and entranced by the display, which culminates in an eruption of billowing balloons and showering glitter.

Both boys dream of the day when they can take their place soaring through the air on the flying trapeze, but late one night as they are practicing, with a crack of thunder, Jinta comes tumbling to the ground. The injury robs him of any future hopes of an acrobatic role in the circus, so whilst the years go by and Wataru goes on to become a celebrated trapeze artist, Jinta is relegated to the sidelines to play the clown. Unable to face his frustration, he packs his bags and runs away from the circus, tramping into the dawn on a glistening wooden walkway that stretches far over the horizon, to roam the land selling fake medicinal remedies from his suitcase.

Years go by, and the circus has all but lost its glitter, as audiences fade and the key performers begin to hang up their leotards to retire. Even Wataru's attempt at modernizing his act, by kitting out the circus ring with a spherical iron cage in which he rides around on a motorbike, fails to recapture the magic of the early days. After squashing the ringmaster, Hannibal the Elephant is shot, and one of the circus's final

links with its magical past is lost. Meanwhile, having been roughed up by a bunch of heavies, Jinta is dragged in front of the local yakuza, who are irritated by his incursions on their turf. On the threshold of decapitating him, they soon realize that his guile and his sleight of hand could be put to service, and he is drafted into the gang with a tattoo of a circus tent, clown, and elephant inked onto his back.

Filling the frame with a fairground exuberance, *Circus Boys* is more conventionally plotted and dramatically less tricksy than its predecessor and provided further proof of Hayashi's incredible natural talent at conjuring up images and building atmosphere. By such simple lighting techniques as a selective use of spotlights and masking of parts of the screen in a misty haze, he gives the suggestion of a far bigger world outside of the one in which the film actually plays. Hayashi's later films would look less impressive the more he put in front of the camera.

One of the real stars of *Circus Boys* is of course Hannibal, the wonderful elephantine creation of latex and rubber who had put in a brief appearance in Hayashi's debut film. He was back in a more substantial role in the lavish comic book fantasy *Zipang*, inspired by Marco Polo's tales of a legendary land across the seas to the east of China laden with gold and guarded by mysterious mythical creatures. The Venetian explorer was of course referring to Japan, which he never actually reached in his travels along the Silk Road during the thirteenth century.

Hayashi's film assumes this mythical setting still exists in a parallel dimension. Its gateway is through an ornate seven-pronged sword. When our hero Jigoku-Goku-Raku-Maru stumbles across it with his motley band of treasure hunters (which include a dwarf, a scarecrow-like buffoon with a missing nose, a mad inventor with thick pebble-lensed glasses, and of course the cheery baby elephant of the previous films), he unwittingly unleashes the power of the last person to attempt entering this golden kingdom: a primitive warrior who has lain dormant for over a thousand years, who, wearing little more than a loincloth and a tattoo, looks rather like Herman Melville's description of Queequeg in the novel *Moby Dick*. Meanwhile the attention of the Shogun has been drawn towards Jigoku's discovery of the sword, and with the help of an army of ninjas led by his right-hand man, Hanzō, he sets out to grab a piece of Zipang's wealth all for himself. If this wasn't enough, a bounty has been set on Jigoku's band of merry renegades, and a beautiful kimono-clad assassin named Yuri is on their tail, a lily planted in her Louise Brooks-styled bobbed haircut and a pearl-handled pistol in her grip.

Hayashi's first theatrical feature in color, *Zipang* was shot by one of the most respected cameramen of the '90s, Masaki Tamura (*Suzaku*, *Eureka*). With Kimura again helming production design, the results are a rollercoaster-paced send-up of the pulp *chanbara* favorites of the '60s and '70s, such as the *Zatoichi* films starring Shintarō Katsu, the *Band of Assassins* (*Shinobi no Mono*) ninja films starring Raizō Ichikawa, and the *Lone Wolf and Cub* (*Kozure Ōkami*) series with Tomisaburō Wakayama, as if brought back to life by the idiosyncratic hand of Terry Gilliam. Jigoku and his entourage are virtually unstoppable as they cut their way through the ninja hordes in geyser-like sprays of blood, forge through stone corridors with spears and blades shooting out of every wall à la *Raiders of the Lost Ark* or *Tomb Raider*, before finally entering into the realm of the mummified golden-skinned King of Zipang.

With its amalgam of playful anachronism, such as telephones and auto-focusing binoculars, its rip-roaring momentum, and its colorful costume design, Hayashi lets his imagination run loose, but it is occasionally rather difficult for the viewer to keep up. Unlike the settings of his previous films, whose narratives are at least grounded in their own brand of postmodern reality, *Zipang* is a land where literally anything can happen, and frequently does, leaping from action sequence to action sequence with a minimal of bridging scenes. But nevertheless, the film

earned itself a strong cult following, and scenes such as the Shogun's ninja troops erupting from the ground of a bamboo grove to do battle and the final showdown with the King of Zipang, snow swirling around his icy domain, are filled with an astonishing pictorial beauty. The film's two main characters, Jigoku and Yuri, later found themselves the stars of Konami's cinematic action-adventure video game for the Playstation II, *7 Blades* (2001), which Hayashi worked closely on under the title of direction supervisor.

In 1991 Hayashi expanded his sphere of influence considerably, acting in the capacity of producer alongside *Zipang* producer Kōsuke Kuri on the six-film *Asian Beat* series. It was an ambitious project, with each part starring Masatoshi Nagase as a character named Tokio traveling to a different country somewhere in Asia. The first installment, the Japan-set *I Love Nippon*, was scripted and directed by Shōhei Imamura's son Daisuke Tengan. Other parts were Singapore's *Love from Themasek*, directed by Leow Beng Lee; Thailand's *Powder Road*, from Chatri Chalem Yukol; Malaysia's *Sunrise in Kampon*, from Aziz M. Osman; Taiwan's *Shadow of Nocturne* by Yu Wei Yen; and the final part, *Autumn Moon*, from Hong Kong director Clara Law, which picked up the top prize of the Golden Leopard at the Locarno International Film Festival in 1992.

The series was Hayashi's first collaboration overseas, and indeed one of the first significant collaborations between Japan and mainland Asia. Himself a naturalized Japanese of Korean descent, Hayashi's series was one of a number of films widely regarded as bringing the culture of mainland Asia into vogue in Japan, which would later be reflected in such films as Shunji Iwai's *Swallowtail Butterfly*. It also marked the beginning of Hayashi's fruitful partnership with the Taiwanese Yu Wei Yen, which would last throughout the decade.

Spreading his net even further afield, Hayashi also contributed a section to the three-part omnibus film *Figaro Story*, a co-production between France, Japan, and the United States.

Hayashi directed the second segment, *The Man in the Moon* (*Tsuki no Hito*), bookended between Argentinian director Alejandro Agresti's Paris-bound *Library Love*, in which a budding young novelist becomes infatuated with a woman he spots in the library, and French director Claire Denis's *Keep It for Yourself*, a monochrome portrait of a young French girl lured across to New York by her would-be boyfriend, featuring an early role by Vincent Gallo. An eclectic package, with the unifying theme merely that each of the three films took part in a major cultural capital, Hayashi's story is an extended visual poem in which a wistful young office lady succumbs to visions of a crow-like creature that soars above the cratered surface of the moon.

Coming across like a lush pop promo bathed in a moonlight blue, with Kimura once more contributing to the lavish visuals, it is the most dreamlike and non-narrative addition to the omnibus, a surreal sequence of events unfolding against Tokyo's night time cityscape. Hayashi crams the frame with visual interest—floating balloons, falling feathers, and billowing flocks of flapping birds—and on an aesthetic level the results certainly did little to harm the director's reputation. But a dream sequence coming at mid-point in which the young heroine finds herself in the middle of a hallucinogenic circus sequence of mime artists and ghostly faced pierrots lends the impression that the director was merely ploughing the same furrow as his earlier films.

Still, Hayashi was to invoke this colorful showbiz milieu one more time in *Ongyoku no Ran* [trans: Rebellion of music], a 52-minute promotional video for the band Tokyo Ska Paradise Orchestra, with a script by Daisuke Tengan. This glossy showcase for the musicians opens in the midst of an Edo period street carnival, all shot in garish pinks and reds and swathed in dry ice, complete with unicyclists, plate-spinning clowns, and girls in blue wigs incongruously chatting on mobile phones, before the camera floats into a gaudy house of pleasure, with the lecherous clients ladling handfuls of gold coins at the heaving bevy of foreign beauties. Viewing events in a far-off castle, a *daimyō* sits in front of a TV screen before the story launches into an adventure-driven comic romp set around the foot of the Kamakura Buddha.

It was clear that the time had come for Hayashi to move on to pastures new. This he did, with the aid of Yu Wei Yen, the Taiwanese contributor to the *Asian Beat* project, who acted as co-producer for the first part of the director's celebrated trilogy of detective movies centered around the character of Maiku Hama. Carried along from *Asian Beat*, Nagase took the leading role of the bumbling but well-intentioned private dick loosely modeled on Mickey Spillane's creation, Mike Hammer, in a series of films harking back to the kitsch pop cinema of Nikkatsu's '60s pulp potboilers by way of American film noir.

The first in the series, ***The Most Terrible Time in My Life***, shot in crisp black and white by Nagata, is most definitely the pick of the bunch, with the introduction of color adding precious little extra in the way of novelty to the next two installments, *Stairway to the Distant Past* and *The Trap*. The character was resurrected much later for the Yomiuri TV series *Shiritsu Tantei Hama Maiku* (a.k.a. *The Private Detective Mike Hama*), which aired during the summer of 2002, by which time he had received a complete overhaul from a classic down-on-his-luck detective into an abrasive punk rocker complete with plaid pants and Doc Martens. Each episode of the 12-part series was directed by a different filmmaker, including Sōgo Ishii, Shinobu Yaguchi (*Waterboys*), and Isao Yukisada (***GO***), with the penultimate episode helmed by Liverpudlian iconoclast Alex Cox and featuring a performance from the Tokyo Ska Paradise Orchestra. In addition to the TV versions (running 45–55 minutes in length), each of the contributing filmmakers also delivered a feature-length "director's cut" of his own installment for a DVD release and foreign distribution, though in reality, the only film of the series which made any real impact outside of Japan was Shinji

The Most Terrible Time in My Life

Aoyama's *A Forest with No Name*, which was selected to the Berlin Film Festival earlier in the same year.

There's a feeling that even Hayashi was losing interest in his creation by the third part of the original trilogy, *The Trap*, having just returned to Taiwan to shoot *The Breath* beforehand, again with the assistance of Yu Wei Yen. Whilst there, he also made an appearance in his collaborator's production of director Edward Yang's comedy drama *Mahjong* (1997) starring Virginie Ledoyen of Danny Boyle's *The Beach* (2000) fame. Sticking with a private investigator as his central character, *The Breath* is the very antithesis of the ersatz veneer of the Maiku Hama series. This time Hayashi went back to stylistic basics by filming everything using only available light, resulting in a far grittier-looking film than his usual output. The story is based on a novel and play by Jūrō Kara, a heavyweight of the experimental theater scene from the '60s onward and

a contemporary of Terayama. His previous film work including appearing as himself in Ōshima's *Diary of a Shinjuku Thief* (*Shinjuku Dorobō Nikki*, 1968) and as the rapist/murderer who invades the nurses' dormitory in Kōji Wakamatsu's violent pink film *Violated Angels* (*Okasareta Hakui*, 1967), Kara also plays the lead role here as the private investigator Haida, a washed-up detective with his glory days well and truly behind him. With a balding head and a puffy face that looks like it has lain forgotten for months at the bottom of a laundry basket, he is leagues away from the retro-cool of Nagase's Maiku Hama.

The film opens under the cold light of day, as we find Haida in the midst of a session at a drug rehabilitation center where he has been in therapy for the past ten years. Whilst doing community service, cleaning up the banks of a garbage strewn canal with his fellow members at the center, he tumbles into the water and floats downstream until coming to rest when he bumps into what appears to be a floating corpse. The corpse is actually still alive, and turns out to be a failed suicide attempt called Sagitani (played by a grubby-looking Yoshio Harada, familiar from Seijun Suzuki's films in the '80s). The newly revived Sagitani soon evaporates into the night, but not before informing Haida that their paths will cross once more.

Meanwhile, Haida is approached by a former police associate to search for Mariko, a Japanese student who has gone missing in Taiwan. Upon Haida's arrival in Taipei, he finds himself adrift in a sea of people with whom he can only communicate by scribbling Chinese characters on a portable whiteboard that he carries with him at all times. Help is at hand from a local girl, Ying Hung, who offers herself as an assistant after answering an advertisement placed by Haida. Strangely, this mysterious woman seems to have her own hidden connection with the missing student.

Rather than using the plot as a thread to hang as many gaudy baubles on as the running time allowed, *The Breath* was the first time Hayashi reined in his visual style to the demands of the story. Clocking in at over two hours, it remains among one of his most interesting works, with an ambiguous central character and a low-key cinematic style that enhanced the dreamlike surrealism of its enigmatic plot.

From the sublime to the ridiculous, Hayashi returned the following year with *Cat's Eye*, a kitsch large-screen adaptation of the manga by Tsukasa Hōjō that originally ran from 1981 to 1984. The manga charts the adventures of a trio of slinky feline jewel thieves, whose PVC attire, specifically in this live-action version, invokes memories of Michelle Pfeiffer's Catwoman in *Batman Returns* (Tim Burton, 1992). Unfortunately Hayashi's direction doesn't quite reach the lavish standards of Kimura's set design, and the film, which sees the three cat-burgling sisters, Rui, Hitomi, and Ai, up against a Chinese crime syndicate led by a fiendish villainess straight from the pages of a Sax Rohmer adventure novel, doesn't have much in the way of substance. Despite acting as an obvious precursor to the vapid pap of the Hollywood remakes of *Charlie's Angels* (2000, 2003), this self-consciously camp and knowing film version lacks even the raunchiness of the TV anime series that ran on Nippon TV in the '80s, inspired by the original manga. Nevertheless, it was to prove Hayashi's largest project for quite some time to come.

Around this time Hayashi directed several music videos for MTV, and a number of short films, including the 11-minute comedy, *Romance*, an unreleased 20-minute black-and-white project starring Nagase called *Otome no Inori* [trans: A maiden's prayer], and *Born to Be Baby Chinnane e*, a 43-minute documentary film commissioned by the Museum of Art in Kōchi, which melds a fictional story of a detective (Yoshio Harada) entranced by a mysterious beautiful woman around documentary footage of a butoh dance performance. He also produced Masashi Yamamoto's *Atlanta Boogie*, a multi-ethnic comedy.

Having already proven his ability to mount successful co-productions across Asia, Hayashi's sights were now set on an altogether higher goal: Hollywood. At the end of the '90s, he relocated to Los Angeles with the hope of getting his first English-language production off the ground. The reality was somewhat different, and despite directing a handful of episodes of *Power Rangers* for Fox TV, the only real fruits of this move came with *Lost Angeles*, a *Spinal Tap*–inspired spoof rockumentary in which the three members of real-life Japanese rock band Sunny Cruiser attempt to break into the American market. Unable to scrape together a word of English between them, after being ushered out of the plush villa of top L.A. record producer Rick Handsome disarmed by a deluge of smiles and empty promises, the hapless trio embark on a trip across America that stalls pretty much immediately after they lose all their money on the roulette wheel in Las Vegas. Unable to pay their hotel bill, they attempt a moonlit escape into the night, but their car breaks down in the desert. Here they meet a mysterious beautiful woman, after hunger forces them upon a patch of hallucinogenic mushrooms. Released in Japan as part of a series of five films under the Movie Storm banner by Gaga Communications—which also includes offerings from Shun Nakahara and *Onibi* director Rokurō Mochizuki—shot on video, the amateurish-looking and only sporadically funny *Lost Angeles* makes for a fairly undignified coda to the director's sojourn in America.

Over the years Hayashi has demonstrated a remarkable visual sense, a colorful imagination, and a willingness to experiment. He has spread his talent across cinema screens, television, the stage, and computer games, and has mounted productions across Asia and in America. With the director's two true masterpieces coming so early in his career, however, the diminishing quality of his recent output leaves one wondering if he has anything else left up his sleeve.

Hayashi is still a young director, and one whose oeuvre has developed in a wild and unpredictable fashion. But much like the big top setting from which the two *Circus Boys* traced their common path, over the years Hayashi's tricks of the trade have lost their sheen against his competitors. Maybe it's time to change the act again, or at the very least, bring back the elephant.

↓ To Sleep So As to Dream
夢みるように眠りたい
Yume Miru Yō ni Nemuritai

1986. **CAST:** Shirō Sano, Kōji Ōtake, Yoshio Yoshida, Moe Kamura, Fujiko Fukamizu, Shunsui Matsuda. 80 minutes. **RELEASES:** DVD, Admedia (Japan, no subtitles).

Two private detectives go in search of a silent film actress trapped eternally within the frame of a scratchy old period film from 1915. Hayashi's stunning homage to the early days of cinema is a visual feast.

Tokyo, sometime in the 1950s: When private eye Uotsuka (Sano) and his assistant Kobayashi (Ōtake) are approached by an aging actress to go in search of her kidnapped daughter Bellflower (Kamura), their investigations lead them to the studios of the M. Pathe company. Here they come head to head with a gang of heavies hired by the kidnappers on a deserted sound stage with a decorous peacock backdrop. After being knocked unconscious, the concussed Uotsuka has a strange vision in which he comes face to face with the beautiful Bellflower, who is apparently trapped in a 1915 *chanbara* film that has no ending. From then on, things begin to get a little strange.

Perhaps it's not too surprising that a director who has thus far spent his entire career holding up a mirror to the movie screen should, for his debut feature, begin at the very beginning with this stylish paean to the halcyon days of silent cinema. *To Sleep So As to Dream* takes us all the way back to the dawn of this new magical medium, where prior to developing into the self-contained art form that we know today, the first ghostly dances of light played to enraptured crowds to form the high point of an evening of all-out entertainment that consisted of circus performances, magical tricks, and musical numbers, just in the way that Magic Lantern shows had done before the arrival of the Lumière brothers' Cinématographe on Japanese soil in 1897. In these early days, the film itself was almost subservient to the running narration of the *benshi* silent film commentator, whose relentless patter added a unique dimension to the viewing experience, bringing a level of active audience participation that all but disappeared with the advent of sound.

Hayashi's film is more than an invocation of a bygone era, however, but a cleverly crafted reflection on advances in the media itself, approaching its subject by means of the increased narrative sophistication of the film noir, its two hapless protagonists anticipating the director's later homage to this particular genre with his series of three

Maiku Hama films almost ten years later. In the early days, the use of the *benshi* narrator meant that filmmakers never actually needed to preoccupy themselves with storytelling through means of images alone, and such standards as the use of expository intertitles were pretty much redundant. This led Soviet director Sergei Eisenstein, in his theories of analytical montage published in the 1920s, to be notoriously rude about Japanese films, claiming them to be full of too much unnecessary footage (though obviously he had never witnessed a fully narrated screening of these films). Nevertheless, he saw similarities between his own theories and the ideographical kanji scripts, leading him to state that Japan was "a country that has in its culture an infinite number of cinematographic traits, strewn everywhere with the sole exception of—its cinema."

Hayashi's adoption of the detective narrative in a film which plays for almost the entirety of its running time without dialogue, however, toys with these conventions, making very heavy use of the almost subliminal Japanese text intertitles as if they were part of the image itself, to signal every torturous plot turn in a maze of clues that lead our two investigators through such atmospheric locales as a carnival fairground and a deserted movie set, all the way back to the theater which is playing the scratchy print of the ninja film in which Bellflower is trapped. For this main bulk of the film, the only time any sound other than the occasional musical accompaniment intrudes (alternating between a soft piano riff and a fairground organ) is when certain key points are delivered; for example through the ringing of a telephone (though the actual phone conversation is rendered as onscreen text) or the tape recorded ransom demands that the kidnapper leaves at key points in the investigation.

It is ironically only toward the film's climax during the screening of the fragment of film that acts as Bellflower's prison that any actual dialogue is heard: a *benshi's katsuben* commentary delivered by Shunsui Matsuda, the real-life president of the Friends of Silent Films Association, who up

until his death in 1987 had dedicated his whole life to the preservation of Japanese silent films whilst striving to preserve the art of *benshi* narration with regular public performances accompanying films from his own private collection. This scene takes place in the reconstructed Denkikan theater, built in 1903, the first venue dedicated to film exhibition in Japan (and, indeed the rest of the world), which later closed in 1976.

To Sleep So As to Dream is full of such references to Japan's cinematic history. The M. Pathe company, held responsible in this film for the kidnapping, was in actuality one of the first major importers of foreign films into Japan and a major film producer in its own right. The company's founder, Shokichi Omeya, adopted the monicker without the permission of its original owners Pathé, and the company eventually folded in the late 1910s when it tried to do away with *benshi* narration by use of primitive sound synchronization techniques and use of intertitles. Elsewhere, a *kami shibai* ("paper theater," in which a story is told through use of picture cards) performance of the unfinished silent film is delivered at the fairground to a crowd of wide-eyed children, calling attention to the fairground antecedents of early film screenings in Japan.

Hayashi is fully aware of the games he is playing, and makes us fully aware too, alternating between moments of surreal poetry and a postmodern quirkiness that makes one think of David Lynch directing a Charlie Chaplin comedy. Between mouthing great air bubbles of silent speech like a goldfish, our hard-boiled detective greedily guzzles hard-boiled eggs, and the two investigators motor around the crowded streets of 1910s Tokyo in a cramped tuk-tuk.

A film which runs entirely without dialogue may make for pretty challenging viewing for modern audiences, but Hayashi pulls it off with all the verve of a master storyteller. From the moment the film first flickers into motion with the scratchy old 1915 print screening in a private theater, its single viewer shrouded in darkness, Hayashi conjures up a host of different worlds existing somewhere along the continuum of light and shadow, none existing far away from the point of reference of the cinema screen. Drifting between illusion and allusion, *To Sleep So As to Dream* is one of the most intricately crafted and self-contained Japanese films of the '80s, and great fun to boot.

↓ The Most Terrible Time in My Life
我が人生最悪の時
Waga Jinsei Saiaku no Toki

1994. **CAST:** Masatoshi Nagase, Kiyotaka Nambara, Shirō Sano, Yang Hai-tin, Hou De-jian, Jō Shishido, Kaho Minami, Shinya Tsukamoto, Mika Ōmine, Akaji Maro. 92 minutes. **RELEASES:** DVD, Kino (U.S., English subtitles), For Life (Japan, no subtitles).

Film noir, the Japanese way, as private eye Maiku Hama scours the streets of Yokohama in search of the missing brother of a Taiwanese waiter and finds himself caught between rival groups of Asian gangsters, in the first of Hayashi's hard-boiled Maiku Hama trilogy.

© 1994 For Life Music Entertainment

The Most Terrible Time in My Life

The Most Terrible Time in My Life is the first part of a trilogy conceived and directed by Hayashi, each co-scripted by Daisuke Tengan. A stylish and nostalgic black-and-white reconstruction of '40s American film noir, it fits snugly within the director's long line of postmodern pulp cinema.

The series features an inept private eye who, inspired by Mickey Spillane's fictional creation Mike Hammer, goes by the name of Maiku Hama. He drives a vintage 1954 Nash Metropolitan (owned by the director himself) and operates from a run-down repertory cinema in downtown Yokohama (the real-life location of the Yokohama Nichigeki Theater), where prospective clients need to buy a ticket before being granted an audience in his projection booth office. The very title of the film is an allusion to

Hollywood's Golden Age. As the titles go up, the marquee that adorns the front of Hama's theater is showing William Wyler's *The Best Years of Our Lives* (1946) before the sign spins round to reveal the title of Hayashi's film.

Setting the action in the ethnic melting pot of Yokohama's Kogane-chō district, home to a population of Asian immigrants from China, the Philippines, and Korea, in this first entry we are introduced to the character of Hai Ting, a young Taiwanese waiter first seen being menaced by a bunch of rowdy customers at the local mah jong place for his embryonic grasp of the Japanese language. Fortunately for him, Hama (Nagase, known in the West for his appearances in Jim Jarmusch's *Mystery Train* and Fridrik Thór Fridriksson's *Cold Fever*), a former young tearaway who has turned to detective work in order to put his little sister (Ōmine) through college, is also present with his buddies. Never one to tolerate social injustice, Hama steps into the breach to protect the waiter and promptly loses his pinkie in the resulting fracas. However, the dismembered digit is later grafted back on, and the incident all but forgotten until Hai Ting later tracks Hama down in his office with a request to find his missing brother De Jian, who has become involved in all-out turf warfare between rival gangs of Hong Kong and Taiwanese mobsters.

A Taiwanese co-production assisted by Yu Wei Yen (director of *Moonlight Boy/Yue Guang Shao Nian*, 1993), this initial entry in the series is great fun, with its main lead winking at the camera to let us know that none of this is to be taken too seriously. This is probably just as well, because outside of this role as a wisecracking audience bridging device, he actually seems to do very little detective work, with the events resolving themselves onscreen with very little constructive input from our diligent but otherwise incompetent gumshoe.

Hayashi's piece of retro-kitsch is more concerned with surface appearances than tight plotting. Its high-contrast monochrome photography (from Hayashi's regular cameraman since his debut, Yūichi Nagata) and glitzy pop art sets lend such scenes as a gangland slaying by a masked murderer an exaggerated comic book artifice. There's also some memorable technical tomfoolery in a bare-knuckle fistfight with heads squashing and stretching every time they are punched. Tongue planted firmly in cheek, the appearance of Nikkatsu old boy Shishido in all three films, acting in an expository capacity as Hama's "sensei," is an obvious nod to Seijun Suzuki and golden days of Nikkatsu in the '60s, a comparison rendered inevitable due to the presence of veteran production designer Takeo Kimura on set, who was responsible for the gaudy hues of many a Suzuki film.

Joining Shishido in this potpourri of cinematic references and in-jokes is a cast of familiar faces from the world of Japanese film, including *Tetsuo* director Shinya Tsukamoto and *Angel*

Dust starlet Kaho Minami. Many of these characters turn up throughout the entire series, including his cab driving informant buddy Hoshino (Nambara), the surly, ineffectual Lieutenant Nakayama (Maro), and a sinister scarfaced Korean mobster named Kanno (Sano).

Not many films begin with an endorsement from the Japan Association of Detective Agencies, but then again, director Kaizō Hayashi certainly earned the distinction. Whilst putting in the groundwork for the project he studied for and received his own private detective licence. This perhaps explains why he would stick with Hama for a further two films, whilst resurrecting the character for the new millennium in a twelve-part TV series that aired in 2002.

The first in the series works well as an enjoyable fluffy self-contained work, and received positive reviews both at home and abroad. Arguably Hayashi should have left it there, because the dramatic weaknesses of the first title are far more in evidence in its two throwaway sequels, which don't quite possess the same panache that their subject requires. *The Stairway to the Distant Past* fills in more biographical background to Nagase's main man, whose detective career seems to have hit rather a rough spell as we join him at the film's opening searching for pampered pooches for wealthy widows. Aside from a few standout sequences, and a central appearance of Eiji Okada (from Alain Resnais' *Hiroshima, Mon Amour* (1959) and a number of Hiroshi Teshigahara's films such as *Woman in the Dunes/Suna no Onna*, 1964), the results are fairly forgettable, with the addition of color coming as rather a step back from the original film's knockout visual style. The downward trend continues in the third part of the series, *The Trap*, which grants Hama some love interest in the form of a mute Catholic nursery school teacher, Yuriko (played by Yui Natsukawa of Kore-eda's *Distance*), whilst introducing an off-note psycho thriller element to the proceedings in Nagase's doppelganger role as the incestuous young sicko, Mikki.

CHAPTER 9

Shinya Tsukamoto
塚本晋也

Shinya Tsukamoto is still often referred to as "the cyberpunk director." His films are generally seen as being all about grotesque transformations in which flesh fuses with metal and human beings mutate into giant scrap heaps, cannon-firing their way through the Tokyo technopolis.

The cyberpunk influence is one that Tsukamoto himself readily acknowledges, but it's odd that his films are still most commonly referred to in this way when in fact only two of them deal with the topic. Though it's not an entirely fair representation, the predominance of this image is a testament to the impact those two early films made, an impact that was felt on an international scale.

As a Tokyo native, the experience of life in the megalopolis would come to infuse Shinya Tsukamoto's work. Born in 1960 in Shibuya Ward, young Shinya grew up on an exclusive diet of *kaijū* monster movies.

"When I was a little kid, my mother would take me to the cinema, and the monster films were the first films I saw. Seeing this big monster on a big screen really impressed me. I became really fascinated with monster movies as a result."

Inevitably, the *kaijū* films would have a strong influence on his work. This influence is seen not only in his breakthrough film ***Tetsuo: The Iron Man***, whose protagonist transforms into a sluggish heap of metal whose design replicates the burly forms of the reptilian *kaijū*, but also in the experimental shorts Tsukamoto made on 8mm as a teenager. Early trials like *Genshi-san* (1974) [trans: Mister primitive] and *Kyodai Gokiburi Monogatari* (1975) [trans: Giant cockroach story], made with the camera he had borrowed from his father, were Tsukamoto's own attempts at making monster movies. When he founded his own independent theater company as a student, he named the group Kaijū Theater and built himself a stage in the shape of a sea monster.

"Our company's style was like 1960s or 1970s underground theater. Ours weren't really stage plays; we would go outside and perform on the street. Our first play was in a small park near school. I started making 8mm films at age 14 and then I started doing theater at age 17. To me, those underground plays were like 8mm theater, but the difference is that you're not constrained to a frame. When you're a teenager you are more sensitive and you feel that theater appeals more directly to an audience than filmmaking does."

Directing, writing, and performing, Tsukamoto formed a repertory company of actors and collaborators around him, many of whom would go on to work on his films, like actress Kei Fujiwara, who would become Tsukamoto's lead actress, assistant director, and second director of photography on *Tetsuo*. Tsukamoto's collaborations with actor Tomorowo Taguchi continue even to this day.

Throughout the '70s, the budding director continued to combine 8mm filmmaking with experimental theater, in some instances making films of 90 minutes or even two hours in length. But the creative expression stopped when he graduated from art school and found a job directing television commercials. He became the employee of a company, a salaryman who took the overcrowded train to work every morning and back home again at night. When he eventually returned to independent filmmaking in the latter half of the '80s, this experience would have a profound effect on his work.

In 1986, seven years after he'd last made an 8mm film, Tsukamoto picked up his camera again and made an additional two shorts: *The Phantom of Regular Size* and, the following year, *The Adventure of Denchu Kozo*. Though still partially inspired by the *kaijū* films as the former's title witnessed, the films were closer to the realm of cyberpunk and science fiction. Having by now been exposed to Western science fiction films, with Ridley Scott's *Blade Runner* (1982) and David Cronenberg's *Videodrome* (1983) making a particularly strong impact, the focus of his work widened somewhat. Often regarded as test runs for *Tetsuo*, *The Phantom of Regular Size* concerned a man transformed into a human cannon, while *The Adventure of Denchu Kozo* featured a young man shunned by his environment on account of the electric rod growing out of his back. The premises of the two shorts would form the basis of *Tetsuo: The Iron Man*, which Tsukamoto began filming the same year as *Denchu Kozo*, but which would take him almost two years to complete.

The Phantom of Regular Size won Tsukamoto his first critical notice, while a jury that included Nagisa Ōshima awarded him the Grand Prix at the PIA Film Festival for *The Adventure of Denchu Kozo*. His confidence bolstered, the young director set out to make *Tetsuo* with the intention of getting it seen by a wider audience. With 8mm films being almost impossible to exhibit, Tsukamoto bought a secondhand 16mm camera to shoot *Tetsuo*, the story of a man who transforms into a grotesque heap of metal after a hit-and-run accident. Financed with money from his day job in advertising, *Tetsuo* was in every way a handmade film, abundantly employing such "primitive" special effects as stop motion

Filmography

1974
• *Genshi-san* [short]

1975
• *Kyodai Gokiburi Monogatari* [short]
• *Tsubasa* [short]

1976
• *Donten* [short]

1977
• *Jigokumachi Shōben Geshuku ni Te Tondayo*

1978
• *Shin Tsubasa* [short]

1979
• *Hasu no Hana Tobe*

1986
• *The Phantom of Regular Size* (*Futsū Saizu no Kaijin*) [short]

1987
• *The Adventure of Denchu Kozo* (*Denchū Kozō no Bōken*) [short]

1989
• *Tetsuo: The Iron Man* (*Tetsuo*)

1991
• *Hiruko the Goblin* (*Hiruko: Yōkai Hantā*)

1992
• *Tetsuo II: Body Hammer*

1995
• *Tokyo Fist* (*Tōkyō Fisuto*)

1998
• *Bullet Ballet* (*Baretto Barē*)

1999
• *Gemini* (*Sōseiji*)

2002
• *A Snake of June* (*Rokugatsu no Hebi*)

2004
• *Vital* (*Vitāru*)

The Adventure of Denchu Kozo

and using scotch tape to stick electronic parts from discarded TV sets to actor Tomorowo Taguchi's face. But shot in black and white and using strongly expressionistic lighting, the result was incredibly effective.

> "I didn't have any money to do it differently. I couldn't use effects like in Hollywood. If a gun grows out of someone's body, we couldn't use computer graphics, so we had to do it frame by frame with the gun appearing bit by bit from the body. But I like the 'realness' of this way of working, so even today I find it hard to let go of this handmade approach, even though I can use more advanced effects techniques now."

To complement his images of mutating metal, Tsukamoto wanted a soundtrack that would resonate with the subject and found a suitable partner in experimental noise musician Chū Ishikawa, who would go on to become Tsukamoto's regular composer.

© 1998 Kaiju Theater / Tsukamoto Shinya

Bullet Ballet

"I already had the idea of using the sound of beating iron for *Tetsuo*'s soundtrack, sampling that noise and using it as music. But I didn't know any musicians, so I asked a producer and he introduced me to several people. Ishikawa was the second person whose work I listened to. The first guy's music was too different from what I wanted, so I tried another tape and that was Ishikawa. His tape was exactly like the sound of beating iron I'd envisioned and I really liked it. So I asked him if he would be interested in doing the music for the film and told him I wanted to work with him at all cost. That's how we met. In the beginning he had no idea how to approach making music for films. So he said he would just make the music and I could use the parts of it I liked. He made several long pieces of music in different styles that I could choose from. Today we work differently. What I ask of him now is different and more complicated because the films themselves have changed over the years. He puts a lot of concentration and effort into each song, and he approaches the combination of sound and images with a lot more care.

"If I were to really make a film that is completely different from my other stuff and I think it really won't fit with his music, in that case there is the possibility that I would ask a different composer. But until now, even if the film is not related to metal, I've always thought his music would fit. So I've always asked him to do the music. Even if I'm very demanding or ask him to do something new, the results are always really satisfying. If I throw him one ball, he'll throw me back several more. Maybe it's difficult for him at times, but for me it's a great joy to work with him."

The lengthy production time of the film had left its traces on Tsukamoto. His cast and crew had quit in despair and, as the director admitted in an interview in the French film magazine *HK*, he was on the verge of burning the negative in the hope of exorcising all the bad experiences. In addition, few Japanese media were even interested in his 67-minute black-and-white film.

All this would change drastically when *Tetsuo* was invited to the Fantastic Film Festival in Rome, Italy, in late 1989. Playing without subtitles (Tsukamoto had no money for a translation) to an audience that included Chilean surrealist filmmaker Alejandro Jodorowsky, the film took the festival by storm and snatched the top prize.

> "The foreign acclaim was crucial in allowing me to continue directing because it changed how I was regarded. At the time of *Tetsuo*, nobody cared about me. Even if I did a press screening, nobody was interested in speaking to me afterward. But once I won the grand prize at the Fantastic Film Festival in Rome, distributors would come up to me with excuses, telling me that they had been thinking about buying the film all along. At that time it was very rare for a Japanese film to be shown at a foreign festival, let alone that one would win a prize. So getting that prize resulted in getting appreciation in Japan as well."

Tetsuo's international success would prove to be the breakthrough for contemporary Japanese film on the international scene. It had already been six years since the Palme d'Or in Cannes for Shōhei Imamura's *The Ballad of Narayama* (*Narayama Bushikō*), and Japanese cinema had all but disappeared from the Western radar. *Tetsuo*, which went on to play at numerous festivals garnering just as many foreign distribution deals, put Japan back on the map and paved the way for the international breakthrough of Takeshi Kitano a few years later, as well as for the numerous festival successes for Japanese films in the latter half of the '90s. With *Tetsuo*, the new generation of Japanese filmmakers arrived on the international scene.

At home too, the film did well. Although only shown at late-night screenings, the film attracted sell-out crowds as a result of the publicity devoted to its award victory. This in turn attracted the interest of the industry, landing Tsukamoto his first commission when Shochiku studios invited him to adapt the short manga story *Hiruko the Goblin*.

Tsukamoto wrote the script himself, greatly expanding the slim storyline to fit in an archaeologist character, played by singer Kenji Sawada, who faces off against the powers of hell in a school basement. Shot in color with a professional cast and crew, *Hiruko* was more conventional in style and subject than *Tetsuo*, resulting in disappointing reactions from fans of the director's breakthrough film.

Disappointments didn't last long, however. After finishing *Hiruko*, Tsukamoto launched into production of the sequel to *Tetsuo* without skipping a beat. *Tetsuo II: Body Hammer* had already been in the planning stages when the opportunity to make *Hiruko* presented itself, and backed by money from entertainment conglomerate Toshiba EMI, the film was in theaters a mere year after *Hiruko*.

Tetsuo II: Body Hammer essentially replays the basic scenario of its predecessor, with an unwitting everyman gradually transforming into a monstrous mechanical contraption. Tsukamoto had expanded the situation to include more plot and a much more deliberate, focused thematic substance. *Tetsuo* was largely a film made on instinct, with a variety of pop-cultural influences and a strong sense of eroticism weighing heavier than the actual investigation of thematic implications. *Tetsuo II* was made in a much more contemplative manner, allowing for the emergence of what would become the director's recurring thematic concerns: contemporary city life and how it has detached us from our own physical sensations. Another enormously important characteristic established by *Tetsuo II* (although already present to a lesser extent in the first film) is the central position of the family unit in the narrative. The disruption of this unit would become the premise for the plots of all his subsequent films.

These motifs and concerns were never clearer nor more succinctly explored than in his following film *Tokyo Fist* (1995), in many ways the epitome of Tsukamoto's work. Revolving around a young couple broken apart by the intrusion of an old acquaintance of the husband's, the film featured numerous bloody and intense bouts of boxing and co-starred Tsukamoto's younger brother Kōji as the interloper.

> "When Kōji was 18 he was a boxer. He had one professional fight and got damaged pretty badly, so he immediately gave it up. He was still involved with boxing as a trainer, but he didn't fight again. Then when he passed thirty he got this idea into his head that he wanted to get up into the ring again, so my mother became very worried about him. That's when I got the idea that instead of getting into the ring for real, he could get into the ring in my film. That way everybody was happy: I had a new story to tell, he could be in the ring, and my mother could be at ease."

With boxing and physical training replacing the metallic mutations of the *Tetsuo* films, *Tokyo Fist* dispensed entirely with the element of science fiction. Tsukamoto concentrated on treating his very worldly, contemporary themes in a worldly, contemporary setting, thus allowing them to come to their full maturation and significance.

> "There hasn't been a war in Japan in over fifty years, which is of course a good thing. But the result is that people have gotten used to peace and have fallen half asleep. One thing I want to achieve with my films is to wake them up. To smash them over the skull with a metal hammer. But I have to do that to myself, too. I have a tendency to take it easy in life, and it's only through making movies that I feel awake

and alive. I want to warn people that being too complacent and taking things for granted is dangerous. Of course, I'm not telling people that they should start a new war, but I want them to better appreciate the peace that they have. They should be aware of how fortunate they are and not take things for granted."

Tsukamoto's films revolve around such people who take things for granted, many of them salarymen (as in the *Tetsuo* films, *Tokyo Fist*, and *Bullet Ballet*). Living their lives on autopilot, riding the waves of duty and routine, they have become detached from their own sensations. They live in the megalopolis of Tokyo, which has banished any signs of decay from its gleaming streets. For Tsukamoto it's this decay that holds the key to life. Pain, destruction, and confrontation with death remind one of what it feels like to be alive, much more than going through the daily grind does. To this end, Tsukamoto puts his characters through the most terrible ordeals in order to remind them of how it feels to be alive. The physical transformations in the Tetsuo films find much more resonance in the insurance salesman who takes up boxing and has himself beaten to a pulp in *Tokyo Fist*, in the housewife who rediscovers her femininity and conquers disease through being the victim of sexual blackmail in *A Snake of June*, and in the upper-class doctor in *Gemini*, who is forced to spend weeks at the bottom of a dried-up well with only a few bowls of rice to eat, and who is thereby reduced to the spitting image of the dirt-covered slum dwellers he refuses to treat.

With this belief that in destruction lies rebirth and that luxury is false comfort, Tsukamoto's films are remarkably close to those of Kiyoshi Kurosawa. Remarkably, because the two filmmakers are such stylistic opposites few have ever noticed the link. Both men's work in turn was prefigured by that of Kinji Fukasaku, who also regarded the destruction of old values as a liberation and viewed the reconstruction of Japan's cities into gleaming masses of tower blocks as a lie that covered up the decaying truth.

Tokyo Fist is, as noted, perhaps the purest expression of these themes within Tsukamoto's body of work. What makes it stand out even more is that this is not all it treats. *Tokyo Fist* also sees the emergence of a strong current of feminism or female empowerment in the director's films. In its scant 87 minutes, *Tokyo Fist* focuses not only on the battle between two men, but gives equal opportunities for self-development to the female factor in the equation. The insurance salesman's wife seems to be merely the catalyst for the fight between two men, and this is certainly how the men treat her. But while the testosterone-charged boys pound each other into submission, the woman goes her own way and achieves physical and spiritual enlightenment.

> "I don't know why exactly, but when I look at my mother, who is part of a previous generation in which a woman's situation was weaker and aimed at supporting the man, I feel compassion for her and I get this urge to be supportive of women."

© 1992 Kaijyu Theater / Tsukamoto Shinya

Shinya Tsukamoto

This feminist trope would reappear in all his subsequent films. In *Bullet Ballet* a young woman joins a gang of young street punks only because it serves her own needs. In *Gemini*, which again features two men fighting over a woman, the female protagonist goes through a transformation and a self-discovery that is as profound as the men's. *A Snake of June* is perhaps the culmination, revolving as it does around one woman's complete individual liberation, even from a potentially lethal disease.

With *Tokyo Fist* also came Shinya Tsukamoto's first attempt at playing a lead role. Having played the villain in *Tetsuo* and *Tetsuo II* and appeared in films by Kaizō Hayashi and Naoto Takenaka, his acting work had always been in secondary parts. Playing *Tokyo Fist*'s insurance salesman protagonist, Tsukamoto acquitted himself well in the lead.

> "For me, acting is like very seriously engaging in a hobby. I like all aspects of filmmaking, including acting, but it goes back further. As a boy I used to be rather shy and not very good at dealing with other people. It was only when I entered a theater group and started appearing in school plays that I learned how to relate to people and be more socially adept. Another thing is that I don't have a background as an assistant director. I never saw other directors at work, so as an actor I get a chance to do that after all, which is an interesting experience. But I only act in the films of directors I like."

Tsukamoto went on to work with such directors as Shunichi Nagasaki (*Some Kinda Love/Romansu* and *Dogs*), Takashi Miike (*Dead or Alive*

2 and *Ichi the Killer/Koroshiya Ichi*), Gō Rijū (*Chloe/Kuroe*), Kaizō Hayashi (*The Most Terrible Time in My Life*), and Teruo Ishii (*Blind Beast vs. Dwarf/Mōjū Tai Issun Boshi*), and also played the lead in his next film *Bullet Ballet*, as an advertising executive who comes home to find that his longtime partner has committed suicide. The exec develops a fascination for handguns and falls in with a group of thugs who aimlessly drift around Tokyo beating up hapless salarymen.

The film, intensely shot with handheld cameras and in black and white, again took three years to reach the screen, just as it had taken Tsukamoto three years to get *Tokyo Fist* into theaters.

"Up until now I've been making my films in a very independent way. I write my own scripts, I do the production independently. Instead of one month of shooting, which is common for Japanese films, I take about four months. I also do the editing myself and take care of the distribution. All of those things combined mean I can easily spend three years on a single film. It's because I'm involved in my films from start to finish that I don't make that many of them. In the beginning when I made *Tetsuo* there simply was nobody else to do it, so I was forced to do everything myself. But while doing so, I discovered that I found all these aspects of the process very interesting. I like to draw pictures, I like to tell stories, I like to write scripts and I like to act too. I also like to make posters for the promotional campaign. I even like figuring out where in the city we should hang those posters and what effect that will have. I'm really interested in all these aspects, so I don't really want to give any of them up. In that sense I don't want to compromise."

It's a testament to Tsukamoto's fierce independence that he chose a way of working that is hardly a route to financial prosperity.

"I do voice-over work for TV commercials to make a living. Those pay really well. One job doesn't pay a huge amount of money, but it only takes a day of work at most, so the pay is relatively high given how little time it takes. In Japan, aside from a director like Takashi Miike who makes films as a professional with other people's money, filmmakers can't make a lot of money, especially directors who make independent films and who try to realize their own projects. I don't want to complain too much about the situation, because I think if you make that choice in life, it comes with the territory. But you can't make another film if you lose money, so I'm conscious of the need to make enough money off a film in order to allow myself to make the next one.

"I always borrow and gather money from friends and acquaintances. Each time I promise them that they will get back what they lent me, and I always keep that promise. Of course these are not enormous budgets, but I can gather enough money to make my films. The income from foreign sales is very important. In the beginning of my career, that was like an unexpected gift and I felt very lucky. Today I calculate the budget based on the expectancy of making foreign sales. So my budgets today are higher than in the past, meaning that I will have a problem if I don't make enough from foreign sales."

Tsukamoto does not entirely turn his back on work for hire, however. Particularly with the creative freedom afforded to filmmakers in Japan, even a commissioned work like *Gemini* allows him to write, direct, shoot, edit, invite Chū Ishikawa to provide the score, and make the film entirely according to his own tastes. This is how a costume horror film set in the Meiji period and based on a story by Edogawa Rampo can end up being an unmistakable Shinya Tsukamoto production.

Although he has long since moved away from cyber sci-fi, *Tetsuo* and its central concept still beckon. Tsukamoto brushed off several attempts from American producers to get a third episode into production, including a *Flying Tetsuo* that was to have been produced by Quentin Tarantino.

> "A *Tetsuo* film needs to be made in complete freedom, so as soon as an outside producer comes on board, it stops being interesting for me."

Nevertheless, the setting he envisions for *Tetsuo III* is that of a *Tetsuo in America*, a film that is to be an overt reflection of American cinema. Tsukamoto sees the project as "a Japanese film, shot independently in the United States." This would, however, mean quite a drastic departure from his regular themes, which after all derive strongly from the experience of life in urban Japan.

> "Probably the main subject of the *Tetsuo* films is the relationship between the human body and the city. That subject will probably change a little bit in a third episode. It would focus more on weapons of war, treating the body as such a weapon. That kind of theme would be easier to understand for foreign audiences, because it's closer to American films. The body as weapon, which is either restrained or unleashed, is not an uncommon subject in American cinema."

Shinya Tsukamoto, critical commentator of life in contemporary urban Japan, clearly doesn't hide his admiration for American science fiction. This child of cyberpunk and giant monsters harbors a secret wish to one day make his own contribution.

> "If I make *Tetsuo III* and it's received very well in the United States, after that I'd like to make *Alien 5*. And then Ridley Scott will come back and make *Alien 6* and that would be the final film in the series. That would be the ideal scenario. Maybe nobody else would think of that possibility, but I keep it in mind."

© 1989 Kaiju Theater / Tsukamoto Shinya

Tetsuo: The Iron Man

↓ Tetsuo: The Iron Man

鉄男

Tetsuo

1989. CAST: Tomorowo Taguchi, Kei Fujiwara, Nobu Kanaoka, Renji Ishibashi, Naomasa Musaka. 67 minutes. RELEASES: DVD, Tartan Video (U.S., English subtitles), Asia Extreme/Tartan Video (U.K., English subtitles), Studio Canal (France, French subtitles), Beam Entertainment (Japan, no subtitles).

Tsukamoto's signature film and international breakthrough, both for him and for contemporary Japanese cinema. A hand-crafted black-and-white nightmare of jittery metal fused with flesh that is a singular cinematic experience.

At the end of the '80s, when mainstream Japanese cinema was dead in the water and the West had all but forgotten that films were even made in the country that once gave us Kurosawa and Mizoguchi, along came a grainy, black-and-white 16mm film that wiped the floor with anything made in Japan for several years. Shinya Tsukamoto's *Tetsuo* was a relentlessly energetic film made at a time when the energy had all but disappeared from Japanese cinema. The culmination of two decades' worth of short filmmaking, *Tetsuo* had all the characteristics of unbridled zeal and amateur enthusiasm, and all the signs of true filmmaking talent.

An anonymous stranger haunts a scrap heap, puncturing his flesh with discarded metal in a mixture of pain and ecstasy. A young couple run him over with their car, discard his body when they think he is dead, and continue living their lives. Then one morning the male half of the couple finds a small metal nail protruding from his cheek. The same day he is assaulted by a woman possessed with the spirit of the hit-and-run victim, her hand a grotesque metal claw. That night, in the midst of making love to his girlfriend, the man's penis transforms into a large drill and quickly the rest of his body starts to mutate into a gigantic heap of ambulant scrap.

Tetsuo is in many ways a naïve (or perhaps instinctive is the better word) film. The themes that would come to dominate Tsukamoto's work are present in their rudimentary forms, but are nowhere near being fleshed out. The social relevance is absent; instead the film is packed with eroticism: It portrays sex as a catalyst for the mutations, jealousy as the villain's main motivation (the couple had sex in full sight of the villain after they ran him over with their car), more than a hint of masochism, and oodles of fetishism (the villain character is often, and quite appropriately, referred to in translations as "The Fetishist," although in the Japanese credits he is rather more anonymously referred to as *yatsu*: "guy").

The instinctive approach also resulted in a film that is wholly original while at the same time wearing its influences on its sleeve. The film's triumphant use of camerawork and editing are continuations of the style pioneered by Sōgo Ishii, taking both to an even higher level of intensity than that on display in Ishii's seminal **Crazy Thunder Road** and **Burst City**, while the use of stop-motion recalls the scrap animations of Jan Svankmayer, the expressionistic close-ups echo classic Japanese horror films, and at the center of it all the actors move as if they were performers in a modern dance piece, revealing the participants' origins in experimental theater. With almost no dialogue, the result is strikingly reminiscent of silent film, which is quite an achievement considering all the noise produced by Chū Ishikawa's brain-pounding score and the exaggerated sound effects.

But the most important influence on *Tetsuo* was without doubt the *kaijū* film. Young Shinya Tsukamoto was reared on the adventures of Godzilla and company, and the design of the clumsily stomping iron man clearly shows their influence. The comparison is not just a visual one, since the theme of mutation which lies at the heart of the big monster movies (particularly Ishirō Honda's first *Godzilla/Gojira*, 1954) is replayed here. To what thematic end wouldn't become clear until the follow-up four years later, but Tsukamoto's fusion of all that was dear to him did remind the world that there was such a thing as Japanese cinema and that the films it created were, on occasion, still unique indeed.

↓ Tokyo Fist

東京フィスト

Tōkyō Fisuto

1995. CAST: Kaori Fujii, Shinya Tsukamoto, Kōji Tsukamoto, Naomasa Musaka, Naoto Takenaka. 87 minutes. RELEASES: DVD, Manga Video (U.S., English subtitles), Studio Canal (France, French subtitles), Beam Entertainment (Japan, no subtitles).

Ferocious boxing film that saw Tsukamoto deviate from cyber sci-fi into more worldly realms, delivering his best work in the process. Like an uppercut to the solar plexus, but a challenge to the mind at the same time.

It's ironic that Shinya Tsukamoto would make his best film when he left his trademark mutagenic science fiction behind him. Still best known for his two *Tetsuo* films, with *Tokyo Fist* he turned over a new leaf and, despite popular misconception, he has never looked back.

The significance of *Tokyo Fist* is twofold. Not only does it represent the director's emergence from sci-fi, it also marks the start of his exploration of a much broader world view, one in which women take center stage. In *Tokyo Fist* we see two men beating each other to a pulp over a woman who regards their testosterone-driven behavior with contempt and seizes the opportunity to achieve complete social and personal liberation.

Tokyo Fist's three protagonists are insurance salesman Tsuda, his wife, Hizuru, and boxer Kojima. Tsuda (the director's first, and successful, attempt at playing a leading character role)

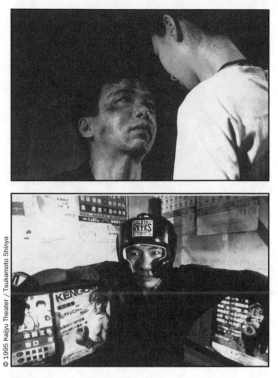

© 1995 Kaiju Theater / Tsukamoto Shinya

Tokyo Fist

is a corporate drone, sweating his way through the humid Tokyo summer in his suit and tie as he tries to sell all-risk policies door-to-door. Coming home dead tired every day, he customarily falls asleep in front of the TV with his head on Hizuru's shoulder. Like all of Tsukamoto's protagonists, Tsuda has lost touch completely with his own body, as his incessant wiping of his sweaty brow demonstrates: the only manifestation of physicality is a nuisance to him. This is emphasized all the more when Tsuda meets Kojima, a former high school classmate turned professional boxer (played by the director's younger brother Kōji). Tsuda wants nothing to do with Kojima, but when the latter turns up on his doorstep one afternoon, Hizuru lets him in, much to the dismay of Tsuda, who comes home to find the two chatting at the kitchen table. The tension mounts quickly: Kojima continues his advances toward pretty Hizuru, while Tsuda's

© 1999 Sedic International

Gemini

herself. In much the same way, the two men increasingly start feeding off each other's fury, discovering the development of their bodies and constant adrenalin levels as sources of pleasure, as ends unto themselves. Office wimp Tsuda, whose body his wife once described as being soft as a baby's, becomes as tightly wound and muscular as Kojima. The boxer in turn feeds off the rivalry with Tsuda as a way to prepare for his upcoming match, which sees him squaring off against the most feared fighter in the league.

What starts off as a love triangle becomes a story of three people reaching liberation through pain, in which the men willingly revert to knuckle-headed cavemen with bloated, bleeding faces, and the woman attains first physical and then spiritual enlightenment, literally drifting up to the light of total liberation in the final scene. And so an intense and furious film about men beating each other to a pulp becomes one of the more potent feminist statements of the 1990s.

insecurity make him increasingly jealous of the boxer's passes at his wife. Even though Hizuru refuses Kojima's attempts, Tsuda is convinced the pair is having an affair. When his jealousy reaches fever pitch, Hizuru leaves the house to shack up with Kojima and Tsuda starts taking boxing lessons at Kojima's gym.

This, however, is only the start of Tsukamoto's highly original take on the love triangle structure (he would use it again for *Gemini* and *A Snake of June*). Hizuru may be living under one roof with Kojima, but she refuses to go any further than that. She demonstratively sleeps separately from him and follows her own agenda. As the macho rivalry pushes Tsuda and Kojima to start working out harder and harder in the gym, she discovers tattooing and body piercing as a way to liberate and strengthen

↓ Gemini
双生児
Sōseiji

1999. CAST: Masahiro Motoki, Ryō, Yasutaka Tsutsui, Tadanobu Asano, Renji Ishibashi, Tomorowo Taguchi, Naoto Takenaka. 84 minutes. RELEASES: DVD, Warner Bros (Japan, English/Japanese subtitles), Filmfreak (The Netherlands, English/Dutch/French subtitles), Ocean Shores (Hong Kong, English/Chinese subtitles).

Tsukamoto's colorful adaptation of Edogawa Rampo's tale of savage sibling rivalry is in marked contrast to the stark chillers that typify late '90s Japanese horror.

On the surface of things, Dr Yukio Daitokuji (Motoki) leads a pretty enviable life, with his status at the newly inherited family practice in the Tokyo suburbs assured, thanks to his work with the war-wounded, and a beautiful wife, Rin (Ryō), to come home to in the evenings. And yet fissures are beginning to appear in the delicate fabric of his daily routine. For a start, his parents make little secret of their disapproval of his choice of new bride, an amnesiac discovered on the banks of a nearby river with absolutely no indication as to where she came from or how she got there. Furthermore, a plague is currently running rife in the nearby slums, and the time-pressed doctor finds himself rapidly becoming the subject of animosity amongst his mangy neighbors due to the higher precedence he places on treating the wealthier citizens of the area.

Not long after strange smells begin exuding from his comfortable abode, a dark figure is spotted sneaking around the house by night, and his father is soon found dead with a clod of earth in his mouth. Mother knows something she's not telling, and after alluding to potential problems with Yukio's inheritance, likewise shuffles off her mortal coil before she is given the chance to fill in the details.

After a nocturnal besiegement by the pox-ridden shanty dwellers, the righteous physician comes face to face with his doppelgänger, Sutekichi. Cast aside at birth due to a prominent snake-like scar and raised in the neighboring slums, Yukio's lost twin is understandably irked by his rather unfair share of the birthrights and promptly shoves his brother down the dried-up well at the bottom of the garden. The interloper then closes the practice to shack up with the waif-like Rin, overzealously pitching himself into Yukio's conjugal duties whilst his brother languishes in the pit. Despite having undertaken painstaking studies of his brother in order to mask his unwanted presence at the clinic, Sutekichi's appearance soon begins to stir up long forgotten memories of Rin's former life.

Taking the Edogawa Rampo short story *The Twins* as his starting point, Tsukamoto's modernist Meiji period horror represents quite a departure from his usual work. Further proof of the enduring appeal of the author's dark mystery fiction for Japanese filmmakers, this grotesque story represents the director's first foray into period costume horror and fleshes out the bare bones of Rampo's original tale of savage sibling rivalry considerably. With the addition of the character of Rin fueling the antagonism between the doctor and his dark flip side, and the added weight given to detailing Sutekichi's underclass origins, the original short story really only serves as a starting point for Tsukamoto to explore the "sins of our fathers" motif whilst vividly evoking the social conditions that were still the norm when Rampo wrote his stories in the 1920s.

Former teen heartthrob Motoki (no stranger to the world of Edogawa Rampo, having played Akechi in Shochiku's hypnotic biopic, *The Mystery of Rampo*) adapts well to his dual roles, as the sangfroid suave of Yukio is severely knocked off kilter by the appearance of his manic simulacrum in the guise of a cart-wheeling wolfman. Marked out by its bold, hyper-realistic color palate, exaggerated make up and costume design, and an absurd taste for the carnivalesque, this chilling psychological tale should prove more than a sufficient antidote to those left jaded by the restrained, by-the-numbers approach adopted by the majority of late '90s horrors that appeared in the wake of *The Ring*.

↓ A Snake of June
六月の蛇
Rokugatsu no Hebi

2002. CAST: Asuka Kurosawa, Yūji Kotari, Shinya Tsukamoto, Susumu Terajima, Tomorowo Taguchi. 77 minutes. RELEASES: DVD, Universe (Hong Kong, English/Chinese subtitles), Tartan Video (U.S./U.K., English subtitles), Happinet Pictures (Japan, English subtitles).

The story of a woman's physical and sexual reawakening, *A Snake of June* dispenses with any notion of genre and becomes perhaps the

A Snake of June

purest expression yet of Shinya Tsukamoto's thematic concerns.

Recycling the love triangle premise of his earlier films **Gemini** and **Tokyo Fist**, but dispensing with the horror/fantasy overtones of the former and the bloodspurting brutality of the latter, *A Snake of June* is the story of a couple first and foremost, not a genre film that happens to have a couple as its subject.

The couple in question are Rinko (stage actress Asuka Kurosawa) and Shigehiko (novelist Yūji Kotari), whose physical mismatch (she a lithe beauty, he an overweight, balding neurotic obsessed with cleanliness) is reflected in the complete lack of intimacy between them. They connect as human beings, but they live more like friends than as lovers and lead nearly independent lives. Both seem comfortable with this coexistence, but the desires that lurk beneath its surface are brought out with the introduction of a third element into the equation. When Rinko receives a package of candid photographs of herself masturbating and the sender (played by Shinya Tsukamoto himself) contacts her with the threat of exposing them to her husband, she submits herself to the anonymous voyeur's sexual games. In order to get hold of all the negatives and prints, the mysterious caller orders her to complete a set of assignments that are constantly on the borderline between humiliation and pleasure—the voyeur knows exactly what Rinko's personal erotic fantasies are and makes her act them out one by one.

Although the material lends itself all too easily to an exploitative approach, Tsukamoto keeps his attention rigorously focused on the characters and their emotional responses. *A Snake of June* never once feels like exploitation—or worse, pornography—and the only explicitness on offer here is in the actors' faces rather than other parts of their anatomy. The film is a character piece, one that despite its intimate point of view manages to incorporate the characters' positions in society. In order to confront her with what she's allowing herself to hide, the blackmailer forces her to play out her innermost desires in public. He coerces her into breaking a barrier, to behave in a way that requires her to violate society's rules of how she is expected to behave, because it's those rules that have allowed her to continue living in denial of her own desires, to coexist with her husband instead of sharing her life with him.

It's in this aspect that the film reveals depth in its attitude towards the female protagonist. Although the premise would suggest a very male perspective, with the woman taking the role of object of sexual gratification, the real gratification and liberation are Rinko's. Like the female protagonist of *Tokyo Fist*, she develops into a self-aware and self-confident individual in touch with her own personality, a woman who doesn't let the rules imposed on her by her environment decide how she should live her life. Without going so far as to call *A Snake of June* feminist, Tsukamoto's film displays a degree of empathy with its female protagonist that unfortunately is still all too rare in the male-dominated world of cinema, Japanese or otherwise (it won the Special Jury Prize at the Venice Film Festival 2002, where French feminist director Catherine Breillat was one of its staunchest supporters).

Despite doing away with the genre-based surface that has been the most eye-catching, and popular, element of the director's previous work, stylistically this is instantly recognizable as a Tsukamoto film. Shot in blue-tinted monochrome, the images are as beautiful and the photography and editing as intense as any of his earlier efforts. Although he places more emphasis than ever on the human form as is, untainted by mutation or mutilation, the director does occasionally add some of his beloved biomechanical imagery. Though seemingly at odds with the realistic tone of the film, these moments have a more symbolic function, serving as the visualization of the characters' emotions. These fantasy scenes, only two in number, are both experienced by Shigehiko, whose obsession allows for such delusions: His discovery of a huge glob of filth in the sink (an exaggerated, almost mutant version of what most of us hesitantly scrape from the drain on occasion) is what forms the catalyst for these nightmarish visions.

With its focus on human beings and organic life (also present in the incessant downpour that forms the backdrop to Rinko's sexual reawakening), rather than machinery and physical deformations, *A Snake of June* might well be the thematic culmination of all of Tsukamoto's past work. For the same reason it might also prove to be the most accessible point of entry for the uninitiated, illustrating that an artist doesn't necessarily have to compromise his message in order to communicate with a larger audience.

CHAPTER 10

Takeshi Kitano
北野武

During the early '90s, as far as foreign audiences were concerned, the Golden Age of Japanese cinema was well and truly over, dead and buried in a mythic past represented by names such as Ozu, Naruse, and Mizoguchi. Budgets had certainly got bigger during the bubble years of the '80s, and the films accordingly glossier, but the industry had become more and more hermetic, with internationally renowned directors such as Nagisa Ōshima, and even that living legend Akira Kurosawa, forced to look abroad for funding.

Aside from a handful of films that included Jūzō Itami's feel-good food comedy *Tampopo* (1985), Katsuhiro Ōtomo's ground-breaking animation *Akira* (1988), and the freak cult success of Shinya Tsukamoto's independently produced *Tetsuo* (1989), not much made it far from Japanese shores, the major companies focusing purely on the domestic market without seemingly giving a passing thought to foreign audiences. In fact, looking at a number of staple genres from the period—nurse dramas, salaryman comedies, and an endless parade of cute live-action children's films with animals at their center—you have to wonder what kind of audience they had in mind at all.

With the bubble slowly but surely deflating throughout the '90s, even the major studio product had lost its sheen, leaving precious little else beneath it. It's easy to forget it but, to dis-

tant observers at least, it looked like Japanese cinema barely had it in it to limp through to the next millennium. That the industry managed to survive at all in the Western perception is entirely due to one man—Takeshi Kitano. For the best part of the '90s, he was the dominating representative of Japanese cinema abroad, cutting an imposing figure as he appeared on movie posters, his gnarled visage set in an inexpressive mask, clad in shades and a black suit, smoking pistol in hand, as if cast from the same mold as one of the suave contract criminals of Quentin Tarantino's *Reservoir Dogs* (1992).

Even this widespread approbation from Westerners was fairly late in coming. Though a number of Kitano's movies had previously aired at international festivals and received theatrical or video releases outside of the United States, it was only in the wake of the surprise Golden Lion award for *Fireworks* at the 1997 Venice International Film Festival that Kitano can truly be said to have "arrived," guns blazing, on the international scene. Less savvy critics and fans thought they'd discovered the next John Woo—albeit one whose presence manifested itself in front of the camera as well as behind it—and the bloodier end of Kitano's back catalogue was once more unleashed onto the West in a hail of bullets and blood squibs: *Sonatine* was reissued on a limited theatrical run by Tarantino's Rolling Thunder Pictures (a subsidiary of Miramax) in the United States in 1998, with *Violent Cop* and *Boiling Point* following in 1999, almost ten years after their first domestic releases.

Back at home, the Japanese were confused. Heralded in the West as a cinematic auteur who cited Jean-Luc Godard as an influence and who had elevated the yakuza genre to the realms of High Art, was this really the same fast-talking Beat Takeshi who had played buffoon to Beat Kiyoshi's straight man as part of *The Two Beats* comedy double act during the '70s and early '80s? Was this the same comic persona who had dominated Japanese TV airwaves during the '80s, terrorizing the general public and subjecting them to all sorts of ignominies in shows such as *Tensai Takeshi no Genki ga Deru Terebi* [trans: Genius Takeshi's TV that makes you lively]; the smirking mastermind behind a plethora of dangerous high-profile public pranks, who broke into people's houses disguised in ninja costumes or as a giant *daikon* radish? Was this the comic lynchpin of the '80s sketch show *Oretachi Hyōkinzoku* [trans: Us jokers]; *Takechanman* the halfwit superhero who pitted his wits on a weekly basis against his evil opponent, the Black Devil? Was this the same taboo-breaking compère with the penchant for cross-dressing and the trademark obscene downward thrust of the hands inspired by the '70s Russian gymnast Nadia Comaneci, who dared to laugh at the old and fat, who exposed himself in public like a naughty schoolboy, and who peppered his peak-time performances with a colorful spray of vulgarities? Was this the same volatile hothead who burst into the offices of the tabloid magazine *Friday* with his *Gundan*, the loyal fan club of TV associates, drinking buddies, and hangers-on, in the wake of a scandal involving published pictures of an alleged mistress?

Still to this day Kitano is amongst the most familiar faces on Japanese TV, and very much a part of the media establishment. His endearing public persona as the tearaway brat that never quite grew up, like *Crayon Shin-chan* with Tourette's syndrome, has ensured that he is constantly in demand, with barely a week going by when he doesn't appear onscreen in some capacity. Along with Hayao Miyazaki of Ghibli studios, he is the one other name in this book that can be said to be a household one. He is without peer or parallel elsewhere in the world, a multipurpose entertainer, whose talent is seemingly limitless. Alongside the endless TV appearances, columns in newspapers and magazines, his fifty or so books, acting in other people's films, his paintings, and fronting the Office Kitano production company, it's amazing the man even has time to eat, yet alone make films.

And herein lies the irony of Kitano's status as industry savior. Back at home, his movies are not the high-profile blockbusters that his international reputation might lead you to believe, his filmmaking work being something he does on the side. In the eyes of local audiences, his films are seen as too violent and nihilistic for general consumption. This is undoubtedly one of the factors for his thematic about-turn into melodrama with *Dolls*, which he stated at the time of its release as aimed at a more mainstream, female-oriented market.

Filmography

1989
- *Violent Cop* (*Sono Otoko, Kyōbō ni Tsuki*)

1990
- *Boiling Point* (*3-4 X Jūgatsu*)

1991
- *A Scene at the Sea* (*Ano Natsu, Ichiban Shizukana Umi*)

1993
- *Sonatine* (*Sonachine*)

1995
- *Getting Any?* (*Minna Yatteruka!*)

1996
- *Kids Return*
- *Begin* [music video]

1997
- *Fireworks* (*Hana-Bi*)

1999
- *Kikujiro* (*Kikujirō no Natsu*)

2000
- *Brother*

2002
- *Dolls* (*Dōruzu*)

2003
- *Zatoichi* (*Zatōichi*)

Actually, even Kitano's reputation in the West during the latter half of the '90s was somewhat misleading, his tough-guy image sustained by further yakuza roles in Takashi Ishii's sleek *Gonin* (1995), Kōji Wakamatsu's Parisian-set *Erotic Liaisons* (*Erotikku na Kankei*, 1992), and cameos in the flawed Hollywood sci-fi thriller *Johnny Mnemonic* (Robert Longo, 1995) and Jean-Pierre Limosin's Japanese-French co-production *Tokyo Eyes* (1998). Those films that didn't fall comfortably into this canon representing the teleological cinematic evolution that culminated in *Fireworks*—for example, the lucidly simple *A Scene at the Sea*, or the refreshingly idiotic *Getting Any?*—were never widely distributed outside of Japan. Whilst this may be because he didn't actually star in these two particular films, his stony-faced demeanor being the most identifiable hook for international audiences, these films are nevertheless still clearly recognizable as the work of one man, a factor which fully justifies the auteur tag. Kitano doesn't just bring a new slant to tired material. He makes films that clearly look like no one else's, bringing a radically new approach to both plot and visuals.

It is undoubtedly his long and unconventional route to the director's chair that makes Kitano's work so idiosyncratic. Kitano's path to stardom has been well documented, notably by himself, in his books and in the frequent autobiographical aspects to his work. His novel, *Takeshi-kun Hai*, aimed at teenagers but with an appeal that stretched far beyond, was published in 1984, and detailed his early years. Born on January 18, 1947, Takeshi-kun was raised in the Adachi Ward of Tokyo, still lying in ruins after the war, in a cramped one-room house shared with his mother, three siblings, and lorded over by his father, Kikujirō, a stern drinking man whose influence was heavily ingrained in the later film that took his name. Kikujirō was a painter and decorator, and the house doubled as a workshop where he used to mix his paints in the front room, the outside walls shifting colors like a chameleon on an almost daily basis as he tried out the new hues.

Kids Return, which Kitano co-wrote with journalist Akira Tamura, and also made into a film, is a tale of two high school dropouts, close friends whose paths later diverge when they turn respectively to boxing and becoming a runner for the yakuza. Though it was not based directly on Kitano's own life, it takes place in a world familiar to the one in which the director grew up, and contains numerous semi-autobiographical elements, such as the fact that as a teenager Kitano was also drawn to the world of boxing.

In the latter part of the '60s, Kitano dropped out of Meiji University, where he was enrolled in a mechanical engineering course. His university years had been spent leading a bohemian lifestyle, hanging around the student haunts of Shinjuku and Ikebukuro, then a hotbed for student protests and home of a vibrant alternative culture scene. His dream, however, had always been to become a comedian and, after quitting university, he eventually found work at the France Theater in Asakusa, a kind of burlesque variety venue where he acted as both emcee and warm-up act, introducing the older starring comedians and the strippers that the male white-collar audiences had really come to see. This period of his life is detailed in his book *Asakusa Kid*, later adapted into a TV movie for the Sky Perfect cable channel by Makoto Shinozaki in 2002.

Kitano plugged away with his stage performance for the better part of the decade. During this time, he made the acquaintance of a certain Kiyoshi Kaneko, and the two decided to join forces as a double act under the name the Two Beats—Beat Takeshi and Beat Kiyoshi. Their specialist style was based on a brand of comedy known as *manzai*, a two man stand-up act where one of the comedians recounted a long humorous story and the other responded with a string of quick-witted interjections. But Kitano's stream of consciousness and obscenities were too quick for Kiyoshi, and by the time their act had reached a broader audience on the back of the huge boom in popularity of *manzai* during the latter half of the '70s, it was clear who the real star of the show was.

The pair made their first TV appearance in 1976, but despite their popularity as an alternative to the mainstream glibness of the established TV comedians of the period, the collaboration barely stretched into the next decade. Whilst the early '80s saw Kitano hosting a late-night radio show, where his crude sense of humor and quick-thinking charm won a swarm of fans amongst college kids across the land, Beat Kiyoshi soon faded from the public eye. Kitano later honored their early friendship with a small cameo in *Kikujiro*, as a man waiting at a bus stop with a chronic wind problem. Meanwhile, Kitano had become hot property on TV, and his shows dominated the airwaves the best part of the next decade.

In 1989, Kitano made his filmmaking debut with *Violent Cop*, a hard-boiled *Dirty Harry*-esque thriller in which he was slated to play the leading role. But by a coincidence, he might never have become a director at all. His chance came by accident when Kinji Fukasaku, the original director, stepped down from the project due to ill health. The end result of also putting the movie's star behind the camera might have ended up as little more than a publicity gimmick for Kazuyoshi Okuyama, the film's producer and then head of Shochiku studios production unit, but the fledgling director took to his new vocation like a duck to water.

What could the public have thought of Kitano in this new actor-director guise? Interestingly, Kitano's turn as cold, smoldering detective Azuma, a hard-drinking, gambling renegade who constantly borrows money from his co-workers, raging out of control within the rigid organization of the police force, wasn't the first time he had appeared in a serious acting role so far removed from his TV comedic persona. He'd already impressed foreign audiences with his part as Hara, the brutal sergeant in a prisoner-of-war camp who befriends Tom Conti in Nagisa Ōshima's *Merry Christmas, Mr. Lawrence*

(*Senjō no Merī Kurisumasu*, 1983). He had also railed against his popular TV persona in a series of TV dramas during the '80s. In *Ōkubo Kiyoshi no Hanzai* [trans: The crime of Kiyoshi Ōkubo], he played a brutal serial rapist who strangled his victims in a story based on a real-life case, whilst in *Iesu no Hakobune* [trans: The ark of Jesus] he was the fanatical leader of a religious cult who abducted his female followers.

In the cinema he had perfected his yakuza shtick in Yasuo Furuhata's *Demon* (*Yasha*) released in 1985, starring the iconic Ken Takakura, Toei's most popular hard man, best known abroad for his appearances in Ridley Scott's *Black Rain* (1989) and Fred Schepisi's *Mr. Baseball* (1992). Takakura plays Shūji, a gangster who moves back from Osaka to a remote coastal village to start a new life with his family, his arrival from the city coinciding with that of the beautiful bar hostess Keiko, whose new bar is soon acting as a magnet for all the local fishermen, much to the chagrin of their wives. Almost completely stealing the show from under the nose of Takakura, the real star of the piece, Kitano plays Keiko's roguish lover, Yajima, another ex-mobster who has fallen on bad times due to a vicious drug habit, and who severely rocks the boat in this close-knit fishing community when he reveals Shūji's underworld past.

So it is fair to say that by the end of the '80s, the public was in the process of getting used to seeing Kitano as a serious actor. But how did he fare behind the camera? *Violent Cop*, as its U.S. re-titling suggests (the Japanese title translates as "That Man Is Brutal"), is fairly generic material, with little in the script to inspire claims of genius. But similar to Azuma's methods of policing, Kitano's approach was maverick and dazzlingly original, and it got the job done with breathtaking efficiency.

Though in this particular film, editing duties fell to Nobutake Kamiya (it was not until *A Scene at the Sea* that Kitano took over the role), Kitano reveals an implicit understanding of montage to link cause and effect, resulting in a style that is concise and uncluttered, oblique yet robust. Ushering in "the detached style" that came to typify Japanese cinema during the '90s, his debut unfolds in a series of long takes, made up of long to mid-shots and a minimum of close-ups, and an editing rhythm that is laid back and composed, a style that almost seems to consciously hark back to the good old days of Yasujirō Ozu. Most noteworthy is his cunning way of reframing key scenes, and the unorthodox unfolding of otherwise generic plot details. The daylight escape of one criminal from an apartment building is shot as a slow motion ballet of flailing fists accompanied by a soft piano, a sequence that comes to an abrupt end with the sudden crack of a baseball bat connecting with a skull.

Though originally intended as a one-off, the critical plaudits that greeted his debut brought the director back for a second film the following year, and the first to be scripted by Kitano himself. If, by virtue of style alone, *Violent Cop* is a vital opening point in the Kitano canon, then its follow-up, *Boiling Point* would introduce a number of motifs that would come to be more readily identifiable in his later work. In it, two players on a minor baseball team, Masaki and Kazuo, get mixed up with the local yakuza, prompting them on a quest down to Okinawa to buy a gun to exact their revenge for their wounded coach. Here they run into Uehara, played by Kitano, a mobster bully with homosexual tendencies thrown out of his local gang for trying to embezzle money, and ordered by his boss to return the following day with both the missing cash and his own severed pinkie.

Boiling Point is a less cohesive work than its predecessor, unclear in its focus and lacking a strong central character. Kitano's hoodlum yakuza turns up at about midpoint in the film, and for the most part the film seems like a wild goose chase, as we follow the two ineffectual baseball rookies through a plot that occasionally seems little more than an extended series of skits. It is also lighter in tone, the banter between the various characters more or less played for laughs,

though there is also strong violence, some of a rather sadistic sexual nature, that doesn't quite seem to gel with the rest of the film.

In the role of Kazuo is Dankan, here acting under his real name of Minoru Iizuka. A regular collaborator of Kitano's stretching back to their TV comedy days together in the '80s when he was one of the leading members of the *Takeshi Gundan* (Takeshi Army), he later played the accident prone, sex-hungry dimwit at the center of *Getting Any?* His presence here, one of a pair of bumbling idiots who skirt around under the noses of a local yakuza gang against the sub-tropical backdrop of Okinawa, the archipelago that forms the most southerly point of Japan, was later echoed in Shinji Aoyama's **Two Punks** (1996). This setting, and Kitano's Hawaiian-shirt-wearing anti-hero would also crop up in **Sonatine** a few years later. Dankan was also at the heart of the first film produced by Office Kitano (the company formed by the star director to make his next film, *A Scene at the Sea*) not directed by Kitano himself. Hiroshi Shimizu's *Ikinai* (1998) was a quirky black comedy in which a busload of tourists forge their way across the islands on a one-way trip that will end in mass suicide.

Whilst perhaps one of the least accessible entry points into Kitano's oeuvre, in many ways *Boiling Point* represents a vital stepping stone for the director, and an experimental dry run for much of his later work. The action takes place beneath sunny, clear blue skies, with the film opening in the midst of a baseball game. This extended scene is focused more on the relationships among the characters, both the spectators and the players, than the outcome of the match itself, as they either squabble, pat each other on the back, or indulge in idle chit-chat. This way of bringing the key players of the drama together in one location, fleshing out characters, and establishing intra-group dynamics would prove a recurrent set piece in a number of Kitano's films, for example in *Brother*'s basketball sequence, by which Omar Epps and Susumu Terajima manage to establish a cross-linguistic rapport. The childish beach games in *Sonatine* that the yakuza use to pass the time as they await orders are also reminiscent of the comedy game shows Kitano used to host in the '80s, and are later echoed in *Kikujiro*, when the two main characters camp out with a couple of affable bikers, during which one of them seems to be permanently naked.

With the cruel black comedy of *Boiling Point* and the dour solemnity of *Violent Cop*, Kitano quickly and rather solidly established a reputation for violence. It's not an entirely fair assessment of the director's work, because if one looks at his work across the board, he has always intermingled his rougher side with softer works such as his *A Scene at the Sea*, or his later *Kikujiro*. Kitano's films can at times be incredibly shocking, but deceptively so. In keeping with his efficient editing style, very little is actually shown on-screen, either happening off the frame—as in a knife fight in *Fireworks*, portrayed like a shadow puppet theater, or the final inter-mob bloodbath at the end of *Brother*—or even between frames, as in the chopstick-up-the-nose-scene in this latter film.

Violence in Kitano's films is all the more shocking because it is so understated. There is no dramatic build-up, and unlike the hyper-kinetic ballets of action directors whose lineage can be traced from Sam Peckinpah through John Woo, it never serves as an aesthetic stimulus in its own right, one that can be enjoyed outside of its overarching narrative context. When it does occur, it is sudden, unexpected, and straight to the point—a short, sharp shock that punctuates the dominating sense of stillness, and the build-up is often more grueling than the actuality. It is significant that variations on the game of Russian roulette recur frequently in Kitano's work.

The mixture of tranquility and brutality seems to reach its apogee in Kitano's most celebrated film and one of the true modern masterpieces of Japanese cinema, *Fireworks*. The original Japanese titling sums up the Kitano method succinctly: *Hana-Bi* is a composite of the Chinese characters "flower" and "fire," and this juxtaposition of tenderness and destruction, pathos and paroxysm, and life and death, seeps into the film at every level. The film's misleading marketing in the West as a violent cop thriller distracts from the sheer poetry of this vision.

In the film, Kitano plays Nishi, a man literally staring mortality in the face. His daughter mysteriously died at the age of five, and his wife is now terminally ill with cancer. Haunted by guilt over the death of a former colleague, which may or may not have been due to his own negligence, he can't help but replay the event over and over in his mind. Whilst he is visiting his wife, another police colleague, Horibe, is wounded in the course of duty, confining him to a wheelchair for the rest of his life. Nishi's problems are compounded by an outstanding debt owed to the yakuza, who now want repayment. He is a man at the end of the line. When his wife is discharged from the hospital to live out her final days at home, Nishi resigns from the force, and then, unexpectedly and in full uniform, holds up a bank and takes both the money and his wife on a final road trip across Japan.

Fireworks balances the pessimism and sense of futility that seemed so prevalent in Japanese independent cinema at the end of the millennium (for example, Shinji Aoyama's *Eureka*) with a laid-back pictorial beauty, interspersed with dramatic flare-ups of exuberant emotion and explosive violence. It is an immensely personal film, and one which seems to be the summation of the director's creative output until this point. It also became the first Japanese film in years to play widely in South Korea, when it was released at the end of 1998 after the lifting of a long-term ban on Japanese cultural products following the Pacific War, though it fared comparatively poorly at the box office.

Perhaps Kitano's sense of his own human frailty had been triggered by a significant earth-shattering event. On August 2, 1994, Kitano suffered a serious motorbike accident that fractured his skull, causing permanent scarring and paralyzing one side of his face. Kitano spent over two months in hospital, and his condition was the subject of endless press conjecture for months. During his recovery, he spent a lot of time painting, and his work shows up at numerous points in *Fireworks*. Whilst Kitano had always been an active artist (his charming child-like illustrations had graced the pages of his autobiographical *Takeshi-kun Hai*), in this later film his work served a more vital plot purpose. Following his disability and the subsequent departure of his wife and daughter, the character of Horibe is initially filled with suicidal thoughts. In one scene we see him expressionlessly gazing at the ocean. He looks down to see the waves lapping at his feet, as he sits stranded in his wheelchair, impotent against the weight of his future. To channel his energies, Horibe takes up painting as a new hobby, and is immediately awakened to the beauty in the external world. An excursion past a local flower shop triggers a stunning series of visions, in which he sees animals with flowered heads. Inspired, he returns home to commit them to canvas. Through art, Horibe manages to transcend his physical disability, and the progression of his work (in reality, Kitano's paintings) acts as a visual counterpoint to Nishi's emotional death throes that manifest themselves through destruction.

Fireworks caused enormous critical waves internationally, ending up on numerous top ten lists and bringing Kitano's name to an entirely new arthouse audience. Now he had the world's attention, there seemed to be enormous pressure to follow it up with something that matched its poignancy. His next work, *Kikujiro*, again covered immensely personal territory, but somehow the sentiments felt a little less sincere. A lightweight and whimsical comedy road movie, in the film Kitano plays a clueless reprobate charged with the task of escorting a young boy to a far-off town to visit his estranged mother, whom he has not seen since he was a baby. Initially the surly layabout is immune to the boy's affections, remaining distant and aloof, con-

tinuously snapping at the child he labels "brat." Over the course of their journey, however, he succumbs to the boy's childish innocence, and is reminded of his lapsed relationship with his own mother, now lying aging in an old folks' home.

Reminiscent of Brazilian director Walter Salles' *Central Station* (*Central do Brasil*, 1998), which received an Oscar nomination for best foreign language picture in 1999, *Kikujiro* was intended as an ode to his distant father of the same name, who had died years before in 1979. Belying all expectations raised by his earlier work, the film at least served the purpose of introducing the charismatic performer's lighter side to the wider world. His next attempt at crossing over to a larger foreign market, however, was a very strange piece indeed.

Conceived of as an attempt at bringing the Japanese aesthetic to the United States, with shooting predominantly taking place in Los Angeles, *Brother* was actually a collaboration between Japan and the United Kingdom, produced by Office Kitano's Masayuki Mori and Englishman Jeremy Thomas, who had also produced Ōshima's *Merry Christmas, Mr. Lawrence*, the movie in which Kitano had made his feature acting debut. Whilst never falling short of entertaining, the end results of this cross-cultural miscegenation are endearingly daffy, but ultimately ill-conceived.

Brother's title hinges on the linguistic nuances of the yakuza concept of loyalty contained within the word *aniki*, and the vernacular usage of "brother" in Black street gangs. In it, Kitano returns to his stoic yakuza role as Yamamoto, who flees to L.A. after his own gang back in Tokyo has been rubbed out by rival mobsters. Upon his arrival, he traces his younger half-brother Ken, who is supposedly in America to study, but in reality has holed up with a local crew of Black drug pushers. The rest of the story details Yamamoto's attempts at transforming his brother's gang into a genuine organized crime outfit, against the backdrop of an escalating turf war between rival gangs of Hispanic, Blacks, and Japanese.

There's a definite lack of clarity of purpose about *Brother*. Kitano's static approach doesn't really lend itself to the genre expectations of Western action movie fans, and yet there doesn't seem to be any higher message to the film, either. Is Kitano trying to say anything about the Japan's relationship with the rest of the world—an unyielding, timeless institution buddying up with and eventually sacrificing itself for its younger, hipper rivals? It's difficult to say. If there is a gulf of understanding between East and West, then Kitano doesn't come close to bridging it, but he throws up some interesting questions all the same, proving that when it comes to racial stereotyping, Japan can match anything Hollywood has to offer.

His portrayal of L.A. as a multicultural melting pot is so crudely drawn it is almost quaint. Pandering to the Japanese fetish for all things Afro-American, as brother Ken, Claude Maki stomps and waves his hands about like a West Coast rude boy as he hangs out with the local posse of street corner punks, initially intimidating but good boys at heart who love their mothers. The Japanese fare little better. Within minutes of the opening, Kitano gets to reinforce lots of clichés about stiff, uncomprehending Japanese tourists lost in a foreign country where they don't speak the language, throwing money about as if it were paper, before treating us to a parade of cold-faced brutality, *hara-kiri*, pinkie chopping, and an isolated pocket of Japan Inc. on far-flung shores that seems to come straight from the pages of Michael Crichton's novel *Rising Sun*. Inscrutable, unpredictable, and fueled by a kamikaze mentality, Kitano gives us the Japanese as the Americans have seen them, and as the Japanese have seen themselves reflected in American eyes ever since Ruth Benedict's *The Chrysanthemum and the Sword: Patterns of Japanese Culture* was first published in 1946.

None of this is helped by the dialogue, which considering that half the film is in English, comes across as stilted and never more than perfunctory—"Ain't you the Jap that beat up my boss?" a representative from a rival drug cartel barks out at one point. It would be easy to blame these unconvincing performances on the non-Japanese actors in the film, with the nadir being Omar Epps' over-earnest soliloquy with which the film ends, but ultimately their lines are painfully underwritten, and the film suffers accordingly. At the end of the day, the multicultural hotchpotch of *Brother* comes across as a terrible wasted opportunity more than anything else.

A major appearance in Kinji Fukasaku's ***Battle Royale*** as the sadistic teacher, ironically named Kitano, who oversees the high school death match, was more successful at boosting Kitano's international profile (in Europe at least, though the film was never released in America), as did his prominent part in Ōshima's ***Gohatto***. Meanwhile, Kitano's global reputation had made him the subject of two European documentaries. The first was *Cinéma de notre temps: Takeshi Kitano, l'Imprévisible* [trans: Cinema of our time: Takeshi Kitano, the unpredictable], made in 1999 by Jean-Pierre Limosin, the French filmmaker who directed Kitano in *Tokyo Eyes*, with Japan's most respected film critic Shigehiko Hasumi conducting the interviews. The second was *Scenes by the Sea: Takeshi Kitano*, directed by Louis Heaton for the British company FilmFour, centering around the production of *Brother*.

Kitano retreated back behind the camera for his next work, *Dolls*, for which he turned to the traditional Japanese art form of *bunraku* doll drama. *Dolls* was a portmanteau film of three criss-crossing stories based around the theme of eternal love, all linked by the device of the play *The Courier for Hell* (*Meido no Hikyaku*), written in 1711 by Monzaemon Chikamatsu (1673–1724), the best known *bunraku* playwright. The film's minimal narrative features two star-crossed lovers roaming through a succession of picturesque seasonal landscapes, bound together by a red chord whilst an aging *oyabun* (yakuza boss) is reunited with the lost love of his youth and a pop idol disfigured in a car crash is confronted by an unhealthily devoted fan. Utilizing the services of fashion designer Yōji Yamamoto, *Dolls* sees Kitano at his most self-indulgent and his most lazy. Critics were quick to praise the film's cosmetic elements, its vivid color palate, the exquisite set design, and cinematography, though many saw these as a smokescreen to distract from the lack of any core ideas. As with *Brother*, it lacked the personal element of his more successful works, and was not well received either at home or abroad.

On the other hand, his next project was a triumphal return to form. *Zatoichi* saw Kitano bringing one of Japan's most enduring movie heroes back to the screen, the eponymous blind masseur and master swordsman that had originally been played by Shintarō Katsu in a score of titles throughout the '60s and '70s. With the director himself taking the lead role, his hair dyed peroxide blonde, Kitano's first attempt at costume drama saw him exploring his usual aesthetic concerns in his most commercial film to date, pitting himself, with the aid of two beautiful geishas seeking revenge for the murder of their parents, against a brutal samurai played by Tadanobu Asano and a gang of heavies who have overrun a quiet rural town.

For the first time Kitano made extensive use of moving cameras, as well as the services of composer Keiichi Suzuki (from the group Moonriders), whose percussive compositions give the film a compulsive rhythm that blend with the ambient sounds of driving rain, workmen's tools, and the clash of swords, before giving way to a full-blown, Stomp-inspired tap dance routine with all of the cast clad in wooden *geta* clogs assembling for a colorful, show-stopping finale. An unashamed crowd pleaser, *Zatoichi* was a rousing success at the 60th Venice Film Festival in 2003, where it won the Silver Lion award for best director (at the same festival, Asano received the best actor award for his role in *Last Life in the Universe* by Thai director

Pen-ek Ratanaruang) days before snagging the People's Choice audience award at the 28th Toronto International Film Festival.

Having lived under 24/7 media coverage in Japan for well over twenty years, and bared his soul to foreign audiences in a series of works that are both finely crafted and intensely personal, perhaps there's nothing major Kitano can do anymore to shock or surprise. Whilst his current highly respected status in the industry allows him the flexibility to make any film he wants, there also is clearly a need in Kitano to go against his lovable public image and the expectations raised by his previous work. Coupled with his continuing acting roles in other people's films, it's unlikely that he will shrink from the spotlight at any time in the near future, but will he be able to recapture the magic of his finest work? Ultimately it's not an issue: Kitano's films look like no other director's, and no Kitano film looks like another. The one certainty is that he will continue to surprise and entertain us with his originality for years to come.

↓ Violent Cop
その男、凶暴につき
Sono Otoko, Kyōbō ni Tsuki

1989. CAST: Beat Takeshi, Hakuryū, Mikiko Otonashi, Shirō Sano, Ittoku Kishibe, Sei Hiraizumi. 98 minutes. RELEASES: DVD, Fox Lorber (U.S., English subtitles), Tokyo Bullet/MIA Video (U.K., English subtitles).

Kitano's directorial debut is the tale of a policeman whose short-fuse methods create more trouble than solutions. Many of the elements that would become typical of the Kitano style find their origin here.

Takeshi Kitano's directorial debut is often compared to Don Siegel's *Dirty Harry* (1971). The reasons are obvious: Both films feature a renegade police detective who uses decidedly unorthodox methods in fighting crime. But where Eastwood's Harry Callahan was a man who, according to the tagline "doesn't crack murder cases, but smashes them," Kitano's detective Azuma creates more trouble than he solves.

The comparisons are reinforced by *Violent Cop*'s opening scene, in which Kitano calmly wanders into the home of one of the teenage vandals who moments earlier were molesting a defenseless drunk, and beats the underage rascal into submission while his mother waits downstairs. But whatever this scene says about the effectiveness of Azuma's methods is immediately undermined by the scene that follows, which sees four toddlers on a bridge pelleting the ship that passes underneath with rocks. The boys run away and cross Azuma's path, but the detective is oblivious to what the tykes have been up to and passes them calmly to continue on his way to work. Azuma is not a superman or even a supercop. He is extremely fallible.

This is the impression that remains throughout the film. Although we see him beating up, driving over, stabbing, and even executing criminals, Azuma is not the cool rogue cop who vicariously embodies the viewer's vigilante dreams. He is human and his actions have repercussions, ones that eventually spell doom for him and those around him.

Violent Cop's plot follows Azuma's investigation of a murder that leads to a hitman named Kiyohiro operating for a drug ring. While he is assigned a wide-eyed young partner named Kikuchi, Azuma goes crashing into the case, beating up suspects for confessions or information and repeatedly being summoned into the office of his superior on account of his brutal behavior. When he has finally arrested the elusive hitman, he proceeds to beat him in the police station locker room, hoping to provoke a reaction that would be enough cause for Azuma to shoot him on the spot. Instead, the criminal remains composed as other officers come running in to restrain the mad dog Azuma. This is where it all starts to go wrong for the detective, who is fired from his job while Kiyohiro kidnaps his mentally ill sister and has her raped and drugged, hoping in turn to provoke Azuma into coming for revenge.

The psychological grounding for the lead character becomes increasingly clear as the film progresses. Although Kitano plays him with the kind of straight-faced composure that would become his acting trademark, Azuma is essentially a misfit, a man who doesn't feel at home in his environment and who can't communicate with the people around him. His behavior is not a pose, it's an expression of awkwardness. It's only fitting that he wouldn't be aware of the consequences of his own actions, the extent of which is implied marvelously well in the closing moments of the film's finale, in which a character who has remained entirely inconspicuous throughout the bulk of the plot rises to the top of the hierarchy thanks to Azuma's murderous rage—and comes to finish him off.

Although he got to take his place in the director's chair by accident, *Violent Cop* proved that Kitano was a man with a perhaps instinctive grasp of cinema. In addition to the excellent characterization, the film shows a clear understanding of montage—achieving maximum effect with a minimal number of set-ups, as is very clear in the expertly mounted car chase scene—and boasts terrific shot compositions. The film contains numerous elements that would become Kitano's directorial trademarks, from the passive female character to the dryly understated way of showing violence. Many of these characteristics he would improve and fine-tune in future films, with one exception: his future protagonists would never be as human as Azuma. Although the prototype of the Kitano hard man, his stoicism is the key to a complex character, where it would later often veer dangerously close to being a gimmick.

↓ A Scene at the Sea
あの夏、いちばん静かな海
Ano Natsu, Ichiban Shizukana Umi

1991. **CAST:** Claude Maki, Hiroko Ōshima, Sabu Kawahara, Susumu Terajima. 101 minutes. **RELEASES:** DVD, Image Entertainment (U.S., English, subtitles), Bandai Visual (Japan, no subtitles).

A young deaf-mute garbage collector learns to master the waves on a discarded surfboard that he finds on his rounds. An idiosyncratic and therapeutic work standing way outside of Kitano's usual canon of gangster films.

Though it was his revolutionary, genre-bending takes on the yakuza or cop format, typified by *Sonatine* and *Fireworks*, that thrust him to the forefront of the international scene, throughout his career as a director Kitano has always managed to maintain a fine balance between the brutal, the beautiful, and the downright bizarre, shifting focus with every film. It's a factor that is often overlooked for a director known primarily for violence, but any more than a cursory glance at his oeuvre will reveal this startling diversity, with the soft visual poetry of *A Scene at the Sea* and the unrelenting slapstick mayhem of *Getting Any?* to name but two titles, throwing his body of work into an entirely different light.

Kitano's third film as a director, and the first in which he took on the role of editor, *A Scene at the Sea* is also the first time he didn't appear in front of the camera. Nevertheless, charting the trials and tribulations of a deaf-mute teenager who seeks integration with the wider world through mastery of the waves, it bears all the director's usual hallmarks. With its pared-down, visual-based approach to storytelling, its judicious use of sound and silence, and its subtle but assured pacing, it is the purest example of Kitano's style, and perhaps out of all his films, the one that most justifies critical claims of an innate cinematic talent.

Teenager Shigeru leads a life of drudgery as a refuse collector, until one summer the discovery of a broken and discarded surfboard on his rounds finds him drawn to the ocean. With his doting girlfriend, the similarly mute Takako, trailing dutifully behind him, his early faltering efforts are initially ridiculed by the local surfing clique. However, as he spends his every spare waking hour trying to master the waves, eventually his determination catches the eye of the owner of a nearby surf shop, who persuades him to enter a local contest. His first attempt at competition ends in disappointment when he fails to hear the announcement for his category. Nevertheless, his unwavering perseverance begins to impress the surfer crowd, and very soon both he and Takako are accepted as part of the group.

Kitano's trademark minimalism here results in a film that unreels like an idyllic series of snapshot reminiscences of a perfect summer: long static bands of brightly colored skies and azure waters broken up by sporadic flashes of bold color in the form of the wet-suited youths basking on the beach. This visual economy also stretches to the story. Due to the nature of its two mute protagonists, the drama unfolds virtually wordlessly against the soft susurrus of the sea breaking against the shoreline.

The drama is slight, but somehow this is irrelevant. *A Scene at the Sea* is as close to the definition of "pure cinema" as it gets, an almost transcendental appeal to the emotions where the eye is definitely fixed on nuance and observation. The looks exchanged between the young couple hold more emotional weight than a ream of spoken dialogue. As the crowd of privileged surfers initially laugh mockingly at Shigeru flailing around in the surf, Kitano cuts to Takako, who is also laughing, but her smile is affectionate, one of pleasure shared with Shigeru, tinged with admiration, and as we notice this we can't but smile ourselves.

Throughout the film, characterization is stressed purely in terms of actions rather than words. One of the surfers' girlfriends flirts with various members of the surfing in-crowd by getting them to peel oranges for her. Takako sits patiently on the beach folding her boyfriend's jeans. The repeatedly mirrored scenes in the first quarter of the young couple carrying the surfboard to and from the beach appear as bonded by Shigeru's new hobby as surely as the couple in *Dolls* are bound by fate in the symbolic form of the red rope as they roam through a series of picturesque landscapes. The antics of two buffoonish surfer neophytes foreshadow the comic attempts of a similar duo in *Kids Return* (1996).

A Scene at the Sea (the Japanese title translates as "That Summer, a Most Quiet Ocean") marked the first collaboration with Joe Hisaishi, Japan's top film composer, perhaps best known for his regular work with Studio Ghibli, and even a director in his own right with his debut *Quartet* (2001). With the exception of *Getting Any?* and *Zatoichi*, Hisaishi's music has made itself a vital part of the Kitano aesthetic on every one of his subsequent films, and his standout musical accompaniment to the long visual passages here ensures that *A Scene at the Sea* is a film that can be enjoyed purely without recourse to the spoken world, with the distracting chattering of the subsidiary characters as relevant to the plot development as it is to Shigeru's world.

Kitano has sketched a warm and unpatronizing view of nostalgia and the innocent simplicity of youth to create a film that can be watched again and again and again. Like the contented smile that breaks across Shigeru's face as he gazes out at the ocean, he shows us that the simplest pleasures are the best.

↓ Sonatine
ソナチネ
Sonachine

1993. CAST: Beat Takeshi, Aya Kokumai, Tetsu Watanabe, Masanobu Katsumura, Susumu Terajima, Ren Ōsugi, Tonbo Zushi, Kenichi Yajima, Eiji Minakata. 94 minutes. RELEASES: DVD, Tokyo Bullet/MIA Video (U.K., English subtitles), Studio Canal (France, French subtitles, as part of a boxed set with Boiling Point). VHS, Miramax (U.S., English subtitles).

World-weary gangster is dispatched for one final mission to help out in a turf war between rival gangs in Okinawa, in Kitano's visionary and revisionist take on the yakuza genre.

Surprisingly, *Sonatine* is Kitano's first real entry into the overcrowded yakuza genre. Whilst he turned in a memorable performance as the sadistic Uehara in *Boiling Point*, the film itself was centered around the antics of its two clueless junior baseball players peering wide-eyed into this dangerous world from the outside. In his fourth film, he situates himself more centrally amongst the internal power struggles and dynamics within the mob. But calling it a "proper" yakuza film would be stretching the definition of the term. Rather than the standard play-out between *giri* ("duty") and *ninjō* ("human feelings") that has formed the core of the yakuza drama since its inception, Kitano throws out everything bar the gangsters, transplanting his characters far from their urban environment to the balmy island locale of Okinawa and playing his film as if it were an existential meditation on death and violence. The results are like *Waiting for Godot* on a beach, with guns and Hawaiian shirts.

Kitano plays Murakawa, a world-weary yakuza who, having reached the pinnacle of his career in extortion and racketeering, is beginning to lose his edge. Just as he confesses to his loyal right-hand man Ken (Terajima) that he is thinking of throwing in the towel, he is ordered down to Okinawa by his boss, Kitajima. It turns out that an affiliated group, the Nakamatsu family, are having a spot of trouble with their neighboring rivals the Annan. Murakawa, with a gang of his most able-bodied killers, is requested to loan his firepower.

Upon their arrival, after finding out that no assistance is actually needed, half of Murakawa's men are mown down in the crossfire between the two gangs. The handful of survivors retreat and hide out in a small beach cabin, where they await further instructions from Kitajima back in Tokyo. As the group pass the time kidding around in a series of childish games such as sumo wrestling, digging sandpits, and fighting each other with roman candles, they are joined by a beautiful local girl named Miyuki, who becomes Murakawa's lover after he saves her from being raped by her roughneck boyfriend. But tensions mount as they camp out waiting for their next orders, and the whole mission soon begins to reek of a set up.

Sonatine hardly plays like a conventional gangster movie. With its mixture of oblique comic interludes and unflinching widescreen violence, all rendered in the usual stark Kitano style, to the casual viewer it might seem rather difficult to fathom what the film is actually about. But beneath the fun and games that mask the stifling atmosphere of anticipation in the extended mid-section, there is clearly a method to all this onscreen madness. Kitano puts us in the mind of a character emotionally drained through the exertion of maintaining his status within the dog-eat-dog world of the yakuza code, one whose only possible escape route is through the occupational hazard of death.

In an early scene back in Tokyo, as he is busy putting the frighteners on a bad debtor by suspending him head first from a crane and dunking him underwater, Murakawa is temporarily distracted by a conversation about the dubious nature of the Okinawa job. After several minutes, his attention returns to the matter at hand, but when he realizes that his victim has in fact drowned due to his negligence, he shrugs the matter off, dispassionately. Even during the scenes in the Okinawan paradise, oblivion is no more than a thought away. At one moment, as his gang members are alleviating the boredom by shooting tin cans from each other's heads, Murakawa decides to raise the stakes by talking them into a game of Russian roulette. Love also

promises a possible diversion to his malaise, but only until the past catches up with him.

Whether any of this would work without Kitano taking center stage is debatable. His role here is somewhat akin to the image he cultivated with his TV guise of Beat Takeshi. As they play in the sand, Murakawa maintains a patriarchal aloofness from his vassals in a similar manner as in the days when he acted as instigator for the often destructive pranks of the Takeshi Army in his comedy shows during the '80s and early '90s. Nevertheless, this cold-faced about-turn with his affable comic persona must have proved shocking to Japanese audiences, because beneath all the surface fun, *Sonatine*'s vision is wholeheartedly bleak.

Sonatine ended up being Kitano's last film for Shochiku. Its idiosyncratic approach turned out to be too much for the then head of the studios and later director of **The Mystery of Rampo**, Kazuyoshi Okuyama. In a very public bust-up, Kitano left the studios, mounting his next production, **Getting Any?** through his own Office Kitano, where he had earlier made the touchingly low-key **A Scene at the Sea**.

Nevertheless, *Sonatine* is a pivotal Kitano film, and one of his best loved by foreign fans. Whilst setting in motion the more personal auteurist concerns that would reach their apogee with *Fireworks*, it consolidates the stylistic tics and motifs laid down in his earlier films, surrounding himself with the usual familiar team of actors—Ōsugi, Terajima, and Watanabe—to play his gangster stalwarts, revisiting the same carefree locales of *Boiling Point*, whilst bringing to his vision the same aesthetic clarity to the editing as he did in *A Scene at the Sea*. All of this is laid down to a divine score from Joe Hisaishi, which riffs on the Boom's classic rock rendition of *Shima Uta* [trans: Island song] to bring a more local flavor to his sublime electronic melodies. *Sonatine* represents Kitano at his most quintessential.

↓ Getting Any?

みんな〜やってるか！

Minna Yatteruka!

1994. **CAST:** Dankan, Shōji Kobayashi, Susumu Terajima, Beat Takeshi, Tetsuya Yūki. 76 minutes (Japanese version: 110 minutes). **RELEASES:** DVD, Dreamquest Films (U.S., English subtitles), Artsmagic (U.K., English subtitles), Panorama (Hong Kong, English/Chinese subtitles), Beam Entertainment (Japan, no subtitles).

A bizarre, over the top, zany piece of slapstick silliness which will probably leave Western Kitano fans wondering what the hell got into their favorite director. Yet it's a crucial and revealing entry in the director's filmography, one that tells us more about 'Beat' Takeshi than most of his better-known gangster films.

For a long time, the image we Westerners had of Takeshi Kitano was that of the stoic, deadpan man of violence he portrayed in the gangster films that made it to our shores. Sure, we heard about his background as a comedian and some of the silly stuff he did on Japanese television ("eight TV guest spots a week!"), but all we ever got to see him do was semi-suicidally punch and shoot his way through criminal scum in both his own films and those of other directors.

It's one thing to hear about Kitano's comic side, but quite another to be confronted with it. Particularly if that confrontation is with *Getting Any?*, a cinematic barrage of pop culture references, social satire, movie parodies, a surprising amount of T&A, and lots of jokes involving shit. Performed by numerous faces from his "Takeshi Army," *Getting Any?* is a lewd awakening for arthouse crowds, the flip side of the Kitano coin. You don't get one without the other.

The story, if one can call it a story, concerns nerdy Asao (Dankan) whose main goal in life is, as the title suggests, to get laid. And the only way to do so, he believes, is to have a flashy sports car to pull the girls with and have sex in. After trying out several snazzy convertibles for their capacities of housing copulating couples (in his underwear and using the salesman's female assistant as a stand-in), it quickly becomes apparent Asao's limited budget will only allow him to buy the most un-appealing car in the showroom.

After a number of very unsuccessful attempts at picking up women (Asao's most sophisticated pick up line is: "Hey lady! Car sex?"), his vehicle is crushed under the wheels of a passing truck. Without car or money, he decides to sell his grandfather's internal organs in order to buy a first-class airplane ticket. First class flying means first-class service from a first-class stewardess. Obviously one with no clothes on. When the organ sale doesn't garner sufficient funds, he tries to rob a bank. This, too, fails and Asao concludes that the only thing that excites girls more than a man with a flashy car or a man flying first class is an actor. And so . . .

There is very little that is sacred in *Getting Any?* The jokes are less subtle than those in a Zucker brothers spoof, and done with not nearly as much taste. Targets range from politics to monster movies (including a dig at blind samurai hero *Zatoichi*, whom Kitano would later bring to the screen himself) and the whole thing culminates with Asao turning into a giant fly who needs to be caught using all the fecal matter in Japan.

But for all the unashamedly tasteless antics Kitano throws at us, he is by no means indulging himself. Along with the later *Kikujiro*, *Getting Any?* is without doubt his most personal film, the cinematic manifestation of all his interests and obsessions. And if the result is so audacious, that can only mean he is being admirably honest.

CHAPTER 11
Ryōsuke Hashiguchi
橋口亮輔

Ryōsuke Hashiguchi is one of several Japanese directors during the past two decades who have had an influence on the film industry and on fellow filmmakers. But in addition, his work has achieved something that very few filmmakers in any country ever do: to effect social change. Hashiguchi accomplished both of these feats with his debut film.

Born in Nagasaki in 1962, Hashiguchi's homosexuality got him into conflict with his own family during his teenage years. His father sent him into the Self Defense Forces in the hopes of turning him into "a real man," but the only thing that resulted from this was a perpetually strained relationship between father and son. Like many of his contemporaries, Hashiguchi experimented with 8mm filmmaking while in high school, and after his slipshod stint in uniform he moved, or perhaps escaped, to Osaka to study at the local Arts University. He dropped out and became a director of television programs until his short film *A Secret Evening* won the grand prize at the 1989 PIA Film Festival.

The PIA scholarship money and some additional funding from production company Pony Canyon allowed Hashiguchi to make his first feature. The money he had at his disposal was minimal and both he and his actors made the film without pay, but the reward would be quite priceless. Taking as a premise Hashiguchi's

own adolescent experiences of insecurity over his sexuality, *A Touch of Fever* (1993) portrayed two teenagers working as rent boys in a gay bar. Their confusion over their own feelings is illustrated by the fact that they each have a "regular" relationship with a girl their own age, relationships they drift through distractedly, despite the genuine affection expressed by their girlfriends. Throughout the film they are bounced back and forth between the two sides of their lives, which they inevitably find harder and harder to separate. This blurring of two worlds culminates in a ruthless confrontation with their own immaturity when a wealthy client (played by Hashiguchi himself) forces them to face up to what it means to live the life of a prostitute, which leaves them as they really are: crying, vulnerable, insecure children.

More an intimate portrayal of adolescent confusion than an exposé of headline-grabbing teenage prostitution phenomena like the later **Bounce KoGals**, **Scoutman,** and *Love & Pop*, *A Touch of Fever* would nevertheless create a small revolution at the box office, out-grossing numerous higher budgeted films from the major studios. Independent Japanese cinema had, in commercial terms, finally arrived; the success of Hashiguchi's film paved the way for the wave of independent filmmakers that would emerge in the latter half of the decade, securing them a lasting opportunity to have their films shown theatrically.

"*A Touch of Fever* was shot on 16mm with very little money and no payment for me or the actors. A homosexual character leading a normal life had never been dealt with in a Japanese film before, certainly not in a film released in general circulation. It was a very risky subject, but the film was a lot more successful than a number of commercial studio productions released that same year which were shot at many times the budget I had to work with. People in the industry were quite shocked by this, because they found out that a successful film could be made even on a small budget. So they suddenly started making films at much lower budgets, resulting in a whole series of awful, cheap studio films.

"Since that time many more filmmakers have done the same thing as I and made independent films with very small budgets and they've had the opportunity to release them theatrically. As a result of this, more money became available to independent filmmakers and the distribution channels opened up to independent films. Now there are many young filmmakers, including myself, who have the opportunity to get their work made and shown even abroad at festivals, so a lot has changed in that respect."

But the effect the film had was not limited to cinema alone. With its sincere portrayal of homosexuality and homosexual characters, the success of the film also contributed to the social acceptance and emancipation of homosexuals in Japan.

"My film introduced the word 'gay' into Japanese society. With *A Touch of Fever*, that word became a common expression, so the film also had a positive effect on gay culture in Japan."

With the film's selection for the Berlin Film Festival further raising his profile, Hashiguchi would soon be asked to speak on television talk shows, becoming one of the country's foremost spokesmen on the issue of homosexuality.

One very practical result from *A Touch of Fever*'s success was the partnership between the PIA Film Festival and major studio Toho to form Young Entertainment Square (YES), a project aimed at producing feature films by young filmmakers. Toho, with its history of Akira Kurosawa *jidai geki* and endless *Godzilla* sequels, was not exactly known for its flexible and open-minded attitude toward film production, and the move surprised Hashiguchi. It was, however, a testament to the impact his debut feature had made on the industry, and the director himself was the first to benefit from the YES project when he was invited to develop his second film.

Like Grains of Sand again took adolescent struggles with homosexuality as its premise, but Hashiguchi expanded this into a much more universal story of teenage confusion. With the film set in a high school environment, this expansion resulted in the full emergence of the main motif in Hashiguchi's work: the conflict between the individual and his environment in the former's attempt to accept himself. Built around a triangle of unrequited yearning between two boys and one girl, the film's genuine observations of characters gay and straight, and their intricate relationships as a group, signaled a big step forward in Hashiguchi's abilities as a filmmaker, as did his increased grasp of form.

Filmography

1989
- *A Secret Evening (Yūbe no Himitsu)* (a.k.a. *The Secret of Last Night*) [short]

1993
- *A Touch of Fever (Hatachi no Binetsu)*

1995
- *Like Grains of Sand (Nagisa no Shindobaddo)*

2001
- *Hush! (Hasshu!)*

As in his debut film, Hashiguchi made extensive use of the principle of one scene—one take, letting his scenes play out without edits in order to show the full extent of characters' emotions and behavior. Resulting from a desire to achieve realism and truthfulness, such scenes witness the director's ability to, as Donald Richie described it, make you cry about what you were just laughing at. And vice versa. The film's finale does exactly that, initially emphasizing the playfulness of the young characters, but then using it to deliver a climax that takes each of its three protagonists into the darkest regions of their repressed emotions. A similarly compelling scene can be found in *A Touch of Fever*, when one of its prostitute protagonists visits his girlfriend's family only to discover that her father is one of his regular clients. While the incessant chitchat of the blissfully ignorant mother and daughter dominates the soundtrack, the non-verbal behavior of the father and the boy commands our attention, taking us from the initial irony of the situation into much darker realms and back again, as the scene progresses.

Although less successful at the box office than its predecessor, *Like Grains of Sand* received almost universal acclaim from critics at home and abroad, and went on to a lengthy international festival run, starting with a Tiger Award at the Rotterdam Film Festival. In this story of a love triangle between two boys and a girl in high school, one of the film's young leads was a then unknown teenager named Ayumi Hamasaki, who a few years later would grow into the undisputed queen of Japan's pop charts.

"During the production of that film we would sometimes do karaoke together and I thought she was a really good singer. So I suggested she should try to become a singer. She was seventeen at the time and she replied that she would also like to become a singer, but she wasn't sure about taking that step."

When it came around to developing his next feature, however, the praise for his second film had a stifling effect on Hashiguchi, who retreated from filmmaking for the next six years. As other independent filmmakers started reaping the rewards of his trailblazing, Hashiguchi escaped into theater, television, and writing.

"*Like Grains of Sand* was a kind of turning point in my career. Making that film was like a state of bliss, because everything went so smoothly and the atmosphere on set was very close to how I would ideally like to see it. The great reviews the film received both at home and abroad were part of that, too. As a result I felt pressure to create something even better with my next film, but at that moment I lacked the confidence that I could pull that off immediately. I felt it would be necessary to spend some time working in other areas, away from cinema, to educate myself. I acted on stage, wrote for another director, and tried being a TV presenter, in the hope of finding enough ideas and courage to eventually return to cinema and make my next film."

One of his extracurricular activities involved a guest performance in the TV series *Tsuge Yoshiharu no Sekai* [trans: Yoshiharu Tsuge's world], directed by actor Etsushi Toyokawa, who was then at the height of his popularity thanks to hit TV series like Jōji Iida's *Night Head* and films like Junji Sakamoto's *Battered Angels* (*Kizudarake no Tenshi*, 1998).

"He approached me with this idea and at first I refused, but he insisted. Since he is a famous actor in Japan, I was very curious to see what he would be like as a director. So I agreed in the end and played a part in his television series."

Hashiguchi's exile certainly wasn't for lack of ideas. Indeed, the foundation of what would become his next film can be traced back to *Like Grains of Sand*'s international premiere at the

Rotterdam Film Festival. During his stay in Holland, Hashiguchi researched a magazine article he was asked to write about the Dutch laws concerning child adoption by gay couples. Hashiguchi interviewed several couples and had discovered a remarkable flexibility towards the definition of the term "family."

These experiences would form the basis for his third film, *Hush!*, which would receive its world premiere at the Cannes Film Festival in 2001, six years after *Like Grains of Sand* had been unveiled in Rotterdam. *Hush!* reprised the love triangle structure of the previous film, applying it to a trio of adult protagonists that aside from their age were not entirely dissimilar to the three protagonists of *Like Grains of Sand*. Featuring a homosexual couple, one of them openly gay, the other still in the closet to avoid complications at work, and the single woman who wants one of them to father her child, the structure allowed Hashiguchi a good deal of latitude to emphasize the more comic aspects of his characters' lives.

Courtesy of PIA Film Festival

Ryōsuke Hashiguchi (left) with Nagisa Ōshima

"It was not my intention from the start to make a comedy. It was, however, my intention to tell a story about people of my generation and to give a fairly realistic portrait of the lives they lead. What I discovered was that humor and laughter form inextricable parts of these people's lives. So it started out as one thing and the comedy grew out of it in quite a natural way. Aside from that, since the characters lead very lonely, somewhat depressed lives, I felt that an element of comedy would actually emphasize this loneliness and depression."

Hush! is certainly the funniest of the director's films, but it never comes at the expense of the dramatic impact. Richie's description is as valid for *Hush!* as it was for the director's previous films, as witnessed by several powerful scenes that pit the three protagonists against the incomprehension of their relatives and colleagues.

"I had the opportunity to rehearse with many of

the actors for a period of sixteen days before we started shooting, which is quite exceptional in Japanese film. The approach was largely theatrical in that sense and it's an approach that suits me well, even though it's rare in the Japanese film industry. I think this period of rehearsal gives actors the opportunity to really immerse themselves in their characters. As a result, the off-screen behavior between the actors remains the same as it is in the film, so that is reflected in the energy of such scenes."

These scenes are entirely in line with Hashiguchi's recurring theme of conflict between individual and environment, a theme that in *Hush!* is stronger than ever, since the story revolves around the protagonists' attempt to live a life that is a radical departure from traditional family structure. This was interpreted by many as a plea for a new definition of the meaning and the role of the family in society. The French distributor of the film even went so far as to give the film the tagline "*La nouvelle famille….*" The director himself, however, was rather less militant in his intentions.

"I wasn't aiming to criticize anything or to present the three characters' unusual relationship as an example of a new kind of family. I also didn't want to criticize the strongly held belief among the Japanese that blood ties are the best foundation for a family. What I was trying to do was to portray characters at that juncture in their lives, a point at which they went through bad experiences but want to overcome those difficulties. I wanted to show the flexibility and the determination these people have to not only keep moving forward, but also to hold on to the hope that they can still achieve something in their lives. The characters in the film choose to look for a solution in forming a family unit, but it might as well have been something else."

The personal aspects that had been so clearly present in his two previous films were also evident in *Hush!*, with several instances being direct reflections of elements of the director's private life. His difficult relationship with his father (also present in his second film) was reflected in the character of Asako's brief and terse meeting with her cab driver father, and the personality of Hashiguchi's mother found itself transplanted to the film in a near carbon copy.

"All characters are in a way my alter egos. Naoya's mother is quite similar to my own mother. She still doesn't understand what it means to me to be homosexual. She still thinks that I spent my nights working at a gay bar in Nichōme, even though I explained to her that I'm a film director. She also still thinks that I will grow breasts one day. That incoherent, absurd way of thinking of my mother's is directly reflected in that character."

Working with mature professional actors allowed Hashiguchi to deliver his first statement on adult life in contemporary society, resulting in a film that showed how fundamentally Japanese society is changing in comparison to fifteen or twenty years ago. But the casting of these actors caused problems that demonstrated that whatever effect *A Touch of Fever* had had on the social acceptance of homosexuality in Japan, things were still far from ideal. Both male leads

had played gay characters before, Kazuya Takahashi on stage and Seiichi Tanabe in Takashi Miike's *Blues Harp* (1998), but not everyone was as open to acting in a film about homosexuality.

"I think there are many actors who would be able to play gay roles, but decide not to do so from a strategic standpoint. Famous actors in particular feel that they would be risking their careers. The part of Katsuhiro's sister-in-law, played in the film by Yōko Akino, I first offered to an actress who is quite famous. She initially agreed, but later went back on her decision, telling me she didn't want to play in a 'homo film.'"

It's no doubt experiences like these that will continue to motivate Ryōsuke Hashiguchi to fight for equal rights and acceptance. With the beauty of his cinematic statements, this is a blessing in more ways than one.

↓ Like Grains of Sand
渚のシンドバッド
Nagisa no Shindobaddo

1995. CAST: Yoshinori Okada, Kōta Kusano, Ayumi Hamasaki, Kumi Takada, Kōji Yamaguchi. 124 minutes. RELEASES: DVD, Eklipse (France, French subtitles), Home Screen (Holland, Dutch subtitles). VHS, Dangerous to Know (U.K., English subtitles).

Burgeoning homosexuality in high school and its collisions with adolescent peer pressure. Hashiguchi's second feature is a very earnest portrayal of the difficulties of puberty, whether gay or otherwise. Personal cinema with universal resonance.

Where his debut feature *A Touch of Fever* still required Hashiguchi to see through a framework (in this case teenage prostitution) in order to get close to his characters, in *Like Grains of Sand* he dares to strip his portrayal of misfit youths of all artifice. It was the right step to take, because the director's sophomore effort is as powerful as it is sincere.

Set in that melting pot of raging hormones we know as high school, *Like Grains of Sand* depicts an impossible love triangle between two boys and one girl. As he would do in the opening scenes of the later *Hush!*, Hashiguchi establishes the personalities of his three protagonists, as well as the exact extent of the romantic complications between them, within the first few shots, using hardly a word of dialogue. We see Itō (Okada) staring at his classmate Yoshida (Kusano) as they mix chalk in the storage room of the school sports field. After the two boys emerge onto the pitch, Itō's repressed excitement and the sweltering summer heat cause him to lose consciousness. In the infirmary, their classmate Aihara (Hamasaki) stares at the unconscious Itō. The next day, she is the first to taunt him into admitting his feelings for Yoshida. Yoshida himself meanwhile distractedly dates pretty and pristine Shimizu (Takada), but yearns from a distance for the non-conformist, mysterious Aihara, whose dark past makes her shun human contact.

Ryōsuke Hashiguchi's films are never about what they seem to be about. *Like Grains of Sand* is not about homosexuality, and also not about a love triangle. The director always refuses to isolate his characters in their own microcosm, instead choosing to describe them at least partially by way of the influence their environment has on them. When Itō's father finds a letter from a 55-year old man addressed to his son, he takes him to a psychiatrist to have him cured of his homosexuality. There Itō runs into Aihara, who is also in therapy, and with the two of them no longer able to hide their biggest secrets from each other, she becomes his closest confidante despite her eccentricities. The class finds out about Itō's affection for Yoshida when Itō's friend Kanbara (Yamaguchi) mistakenly thinks Itō is after the same girl as he is, effectively forcing a confession out of him. The conflict between environment and individual that is at the heart of Hashiguchi's work is readily apparent here.

It's such intricate relationships and use of cause and effect that make *Like Grains of Sand* an infinitely more sincere portrait of the tribulations of adolescence than a film like John Hughes's *The Breakfast Club* (1985). There's no defiant fist waving at the end, no "united we stand against the obnoxious teacher" resolution. It's the lack of resolutions that makes *Like Grains of Sand* work so well, as well as the refusal to ever take the easy route and go for simplification or stereotyping. Hashiguchi depicts the same-sex affection inherent in the high school environment (a shot of mingling naked torsos opens the film, the character of Kanbara constantly hugs, grabs, and wrestles with his male classmates) as a way to show the hypocrisy of the bullying that Itō undergoes after Kanbara makes his sexuality a public secret. But instead of chastising anyone, this serves as another example of the contradictions and complexities of the characters and their relationships with each other. Despite obviously sympathizing with Itō, Hashiguchi shows that feelings of insecurity are not exclusive to his protagonist.

Like Grains of Sand is a perfect illustration of Hashiguchi's ability to give his personal cinema universal resonance. Rather than self-obsessed navel gazing, it talks about feelings we know all too well ourselves. Both naturalistic and stylized, intimate and universal, *Like Grains of Sand* is exemplary cinema.

↓ Hush!

ハッシュ！
Hasshu!

2001. **CAST:** Kazuya Takahashi, Reiko Kataoka, Seiichi Tanabe, Yōko Akino, Tsugumi. 135 minutes. **RELEASES:** DVD, Strand Releasing (U.S., English subtitles), Happynet Pictures (Japan, English subtitles), Fox Pathé (France, French subtitles).

© 2001 Siglo

Hush!

Ryōsuke Hashiguchi reprises the love triangle structure of his previous film and turns it into a more outright comedic venture. Focusing on adults this time, the comedy never compromises the film's sincerity or dramatic impact.

When we meet our three lead characters, they are all single and lonely. Naoya (Takahashi) is an otherwise carefree guy who works in a pet shop catering to rich and eccentric clientele. An avid visitor of Shinjuku's gay scene, he is open about his sexuality, which seems to be accepted by everyone but his mother, who is under the eternal impression that her son will inevitably grow breasts. Katsuhiro (Tanabe), in contrast, hides his homosexuality from his colleagues at the research plant where he works and does such a good job of it that one female colleague (Tsugumi) is hopelessly in love with him. Naoya and Katsuhiro meet one evening outside Naoya's fa-

vorite bar and are soon on their way to an actual relationship.

The third element in the equation is Asako, a young woman who has lived a life resembling self-destruction. Now in her thirties, she wishes to turn over a new leaf and wants to have a baby. After a gynecologist advises her to have a totally unnecessary hysterectomy, this wish only becomes stronger—having a child as a single mother becomes the ultimate form of rebellion. When her umbrella is stolen in a restaurant and she waits in vain for the incessant downpour to end, Katsuhiro offers her his, and from that moment Asako has found the ideal father for her child.

With the names and locations changed, the above premise might well sound like the pitch for Rupert Everett's next romantic comedy of errors. Indeed, based on the above outline it's not hard to imagine Hollywood chasing this one for the remake rights. However, it's doubtful whether that remake would ever achieve the level of subtlety, characterization, and careful observation that follow those opening twenty minutes and which so typically define a Hashiguchi film. Far from being a breezy, formulaic romantic comedy, *Hush!* is a truthful document of the lives of three human beings and the constant pressure they feel to succeed in life and face up to their environment.

No longer focusing on teenagers, the director's third film does, however, allow itself to be more light and humorous in order to reflect the lives and experiences of its three lead characters. In their early thirties and therefore older and wiser than the confused high school kids of *A Touch of Fever* and **Like Grains of Sand**, Asako, Naoya and Katsuhiro are people who can put things into perspective. As a result, the film also shows different facets. *Hush!* at times certainly resembles a comedy, especially in the crowd-pleasing scenes involving barfly Yūji, a loud, abrasive but ultimately lovable fellow patron at Naoya's favorite hangout. But it's not the laughs that make such scenes work, it's how much they feel like episodes from the character's lives. This goes equally for the film's more dramatic scenes, which never exist to wallow in misery but offer subtlety even when characters are screaming at each other.

Despite the seemingly breezy premise, Hashiguchi covers a lot of thematic ground in his script. The very fundamental motif of the individual's struggle against society in deciding his own life here results in what seems like a wish to re-address the definition of the term "family." All three characters are shown in scenes with their direct relatives: Naoya with his ignorant mother, Asako with her estranged taxi driver father, and Katsuhiro with the family of his brother. Although Hashiguchi has denied the existence of an agenda, compared to the loveless atmosphere in the arranged marriage of Katsuhiro's brother and the last remnants of family that are Naoya's and Asako's respective mother and father, the ménage-à-trois the three leads decide to undertake seems like a more than healthy alternative.

Hush! is a winning, funny, and often poignant comedy/drama, revolving around a threesome of magnificent performances. It once again bears witness to the director's extraordinary talent for portraying utterly believable human characters, whose emotions resonate whether the audience is gay or straight. Ryōsuke Hashiguchi deserves much more credit than the misguided label "gay filmmaker" allows.

CHAPTER 12
Takashi Miike
三池崇史

The meteoric rise to fame of Takashi Miike in the early days of the new millennium was all the more remarkable in that it was largely thanks to one film: *Audition*. It quickly became clear to many, however, that this director had made a lot more than one film. A whole lot more.

Miike's astounding productivity (fifty films, three TV series, two music videos, one documentary, and one commercial in eleven years) quickly became part of his legend, as did his knack for crossing accepted boundaries of excess and good taste in his work. Films like *Dead or Alive*, *Visitor Q*, and ***Ichi the Killer***, with their potentially offensive scenes and subject matter, provoked fierce discussions about the merits of his work, while the same films garnered the director an ever growing circle of fans, partly as a result of that very same willingness to cross boundaries. Meanwhile, none of this deterred Miike himself in the slightest, and he kept on churning out new films with undiminished zeal.

One of the sources for Miike's productivity lies in his background in the V-cinema industry. Even more so than Kiyoshi Kurosawa, he works as a freelance director-for-hire, one who never writes his own screenplays but who is asked by producers to direct projects that already have a script, and often also a main cast, attached.

Miike debuted as a director in 1991, after spending several years working as an assistant

director to filmmakers like Shōhei Imamura, on *Zegen* (1987) and *Black Rain* (1989, in which he can briefly be seen as an actor), Toshio Masuda, Hideo Onchi, and Kazuo Kuroki. With his debut he already set the tone for his later output by directing two films back to back: the comedy *Eyecatch Junction* and the action film *Lady Hunter*. Both films were true V-cinema productions, released straight to video without ever seeing theatrical release.

Miike continued working almost exclusively in the straight-to-video industry for the next five years, making mainly comedies and martial arts action films but gradually specializing in the genre that would come to dominate V-cinema: the yakuza film. His early gangster offerings include *Jingi naki Yabō* 1 and 2 (1996/'97), a pair of ersatz *ninkyō* films for Toei whose title obviously mimicked that of Fukasaku's ***Battles without Honor and Humanity***. His first films to see theatrical release were 1995's *Daisan no Gokudō* [trans: The third gangster] and *Shinjuku Triad Society*, although the first never made it past a single screen in Osaka and was originally intended for the video market only.

Shinjuku Triad Society is commonly seen as the starting point of Takashi Miike the artist. Although many of its themes were already present in a yakuza film he made a year earlier called *Shinjuku Outlaw*, *Shinjuku Triad Society* was a much more accomplished film in all respects. Featuring actor and later director Sabu in a supporting role, it tells the tale of a policeman of mixed Chinese-Japanese descent whose pursuit of a disturbed Taiwanese criminal through the neon-lit streets of Tokyo's Shinjuku district ultimately confronts him with his own heritage and the past that he has tried to hide in order to succeed in Japanese society.

The film contained all the themes that would come to dominate Miike's work: rootless human beings who feel detached from the culture they live in, who long for a place where they will be accepted, though at the same time knowing that such a place is merely a nostalgic fantasy. It's the characters' detachment and the sadness inherent in their predicament that often result in violence, a violence that is omnipresent in *Shinjuku Triad Society*.

The film was the first part in an unofficial trilogy, whose entries all deal very overtly with the themes of rootlessness and displacement. *Shinjuku Triad Society*, *Rainy Dog*, and **Ley Lines** form what could be regarded as the thematic backbone of Miike's body of work. Nearly every aspect of Takashi Miike's cinema can be found in these three films, although he has gone on to further explore those aspects in subsequent films.

> "These three films are about insignificant characters. If they were in another film, they would never be protagonists. They all live in a small corner of the underbelly of a big city. In that sense it's a trilogy; they're similar in that way. *The City of Lost Souls* is also similar to these films, but I think of it as a different film. In the three films, people try to escape from something or float passively, never wanting to climb up in life. I like those kinds of people, because I feel sympathy for them, I have that in common with them. This doesn't mean the characters themselves are similar to me, I just like these stories."

Rainy Dog takes a different approach to

© 1997 Kadokawa-Daiei

Rainy Dog

rootlessness by focusing on a Japanese character abroad rather than vice versa. Shō Aikawa stars as Yūji, a yakuza exiled in Taipei, who learns that his expulsion has become permanent due to the eradication of his syndicate by a rival gang. Living in a squalid house, he has a night job hauling pig carcasses to a slaughterhouse and a day job performing executions for a local crime lord. When the brother of one of his victims swears revenge, Yūji's employer unceremoniously leaves him to fend for himself. The problem is that he also has to fend for the young boy who was dropped on his doorstep by an ex-lover, and who may or may not be his son.

Understated and sober, with sparse dialogue and a powerful central performance from Aikawa, *Rainy Dog* remains, with its follow-up *Ley Lines*, one of Miike's strongest works. It unmistakably shows Miike's capacity for tenderness

© 2003 The Klockworx

Takashi Miike

that gradually gains overtones of fantasy, as the jittery salaryman loses his way and finds himself in a village where a young woman teaches the local children to fly.

The Bird People in China was something of a turning point for Miike, specifically in terms of how he was regarded within the Japanese film industry. Still seen largely as a V-cinema yakuza film director, the fact that he could take a small film crew and a low budget into the heart of China and re-emerge a few weeks later with a film of the quality and beauty of *The Bird People in China* changed the opinion of many of his peers.

and for creating emotionally harrowing films, a capacity that has gone largely unrecognized due to the overemphasis that has been put on his more excessive work.

That tenderness also shows through in a film like *The Bird People in China*, which focuses on a young, upwardly mobile Japanese salaryman who is sent to investigate a jade deposit in a remote region of China. Using a similar premise to *Rainy Dog*, Miike creates a thoughtful comedy

"They regarded me as being able to make a normal film. They also noticed that under the harsh condition of shooting a low-budget Japanese film in the heart of rural China, I was able to pick the fruits and bring them back to Japan. Normally the producer takes care of everything and the director just complains about the conditions, which is why many previous directors failed to accomplish that. I feel that

Filmography

1991
- *Eyecatch Junction* (Toppū! Minipato Tai—Aikyatchi Jankshon) [video]
- *Lady Hunter* (Redī Hantā—Koroshi no Pureryūdo) [video]

1992
- *Last Run* (Rasuto Ran—Ai to Uragiri no Hyaku-oku Yen) [TV]
- *A Human Murder Weapon* (Ningen Kyōki—Ai to Ikari no Ringu) [video]

1993
- *Bodyguard Kiba* (Bodigādo Kiba) [video]
- *Oretachi wa Tenshi Ja Nai* [video]
- *Oretachi wa Tenshi Ja Nai 2* [video]

1994
- *Bodyguard Kiba 2* (Bodigādo Kiba—Shura no Mokushiroku) [video]
- *Shinjuku Outlaw* (Shinjuku Autorō) [video]

1995
- *Bodyguard Kiba 3* (Bodigādo Kiba—Shura no Mokushiroku 2) [video]
- *Daisan no Gokudō*
- *Naniwa Yūkyōden* [video]
- *Shinjuku Triad Society* (Shinjuku Kuroshakai—China Mafia Sensō)

1996
- *Shin Daisan no Gokudō: Boppatsu Kansai Gokudō Uōzu!!* [video]
- *Shin Daisan no Gokudō 2* [video]
- *Jingi naki Yabō* [video]
- *Peanuts* (Pīnatsu—Rakkasei) (video)
- *The Way to Fight* (Kenka no Hanamichi—Ōsaka Saikyō Densetsu) [video]
- *Fudoh: The New Generation* (Gokudō Sengokushi Fudō)

1997
- *Jingi naki Yabō 2* [video]
- *Young Thugs: Innocent Blood* (Kishiwada Shōnen Gurentai—Chikemuri Junjō Hen)
- *Rainy Dog* (Gokudō Kuroshakai—Reinī Doggu)
- *Full Metal Yakuza* (Furu Metaru Gokudō) [video]

1998
- *The Bird People in China* (Chūgoku no Chōjin)
- *Andromedia* (Andoromedia)
- *Blues Harp* (Burūsu Hāpu)
- *Young Thugs: Nostalgia*
- *Zuiketsu Gensō—Tonkararin Yume Densetsu* [short]

1999
- *Tennen Shōjo Mann* [TV series, 3 episodes]

a director doesn't go there just to complain, but to shoot as much and as well as he can under those conditions."

Aside from *Rainy Dog*, only two other Miike films had received a cinema release in the two years between *Shinjuku Triad Society* and *The Bird People in China*. One of these was the larger-than-life manga adaptation *Fudoh: The New Generation*, which originally was not even intended to receive a theatrical release. It wasn't until its producer was thoroughly impressed by a rough cut that it was decided that the film would be shown in theaters instead of being launched directly through video.

It was a more than fortunate decision, since *Fudoh* would go on to be the first Takashi Miike film to play to foreign audiences. A film about a high school student who leads a gang of underage assassins in a blood feud with his own yakuza father, its gleefully exaggerated violence went down a storm at film festivals in Brussels, Montreal, and Toronto, earning *Fudoh* an American

© 1999 Kadokawa-Daiei

Miike and Riki Takeuchi on the set of *Dead or Alive*

video release and a place in *Time* magazine's list of the top ten films of the year 1997.

Violent high school students were also the subject of his other theatrically released film at the time, *Young Thugs: Innocent Blood*. A sequel to Kazuyuki Izutsu's *Boys Be Ambitious* (*Kishiwada Shōnen Gurentai*, 1996), it is for this very fact a unique film in Miike's career since he never again made a sequel to another director's film.

- Ley Lines (*Nihon Kuroshakai—Ley Lines*)
- Silver (*Shirubā*) [video]
- White-Collar Worker Kintaro (*Sararīman Kintarō*)
- Tennen Shōjo Mann Next [TV series, 2 episodes]
- Dead or Alive (*DOA Deddo Oa Araibu—Hanzaisha*)

2000
- Kikuchi-Jō Monogatari—Sakimori-Tachi no Uta [short]
- Audition
- MPD-Psycho (*Tajū Jinkaku Tantei Saiko—Amamiya Kazuhiko no Kikan*) [TV series, 6 episodes]
- The City of Lost Souls (*Hyōryūgai*)
- Dead or Alive 2 (*Deddo Oa Araibu 2—Tōbōsha*)
- The Making of Gemini (*Tsukamoto Shinya ga Rampo Suru*) [video]

2001
- Visitor Q (*Bijitā Q*)
- Family (*Famirī*)
- The Guys from Paradise (*Tengoku Kara Kita Otoko Tachi*)
- Ichi the Killer (*Koroshiya 1*)

2002
- Dead or Alive: Final
- Onna Kunishū Ikki
- The Happiness of the Katakuris (*Katakurike no Kōfuku*)
- Agitator (*Araburu Tamashii Tachi*)
- Sabu [TV]
- Graveyard of Honor (*Shin Jingi no Hakaba*)
- Go! Go! Fushimi Jet [music video]
- Shangri-La (*Kinyū Hametsu Nippon—Tōgenkyō no Hitobito*)
- Deadly Outlaw: Rekka (*Jitsuroku—Andō Noboru*

Kyōdō-Den: Rekka)
- The Gundogs [music video]
- Part Time Tantei [TV]

2003
- Koi no Jerrīfisshu [music video]
- The Man in White (*Yurusarezaru Mono*)
- Kikoku [video]
- Gozu (*Gokudō Kyōfu Daigekijō—Gozu*)
- The Negotiator (*Kōshōnin*) [TV]

2004
- One Missed Call (*Chakushin Ari*) (a.k.a. *You've Got A Call*)
- Zebraman (*Zeburaman*)
- Part Time Tantei 2 [TV]
- Izo (*Izo—Kaosu, Mata wa Fujōri no Kijin*)
- Three . . . Extremes [co-directed with Fruit Chan and Chan-Wook Park]

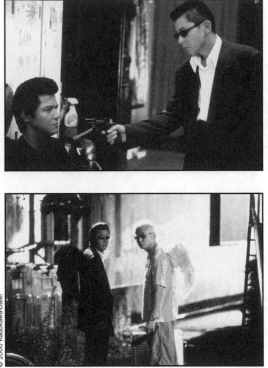

© 2000 Kadokawa-Daiei

Dead or Alive (top), and *Dead or Alive 2*

"Izutsu's original had quite a high budget and had a very wide release as a result. But for my film, the sequel, the budget was just a little but higher than for a V-cinema film. So just in that sense it's a very different film. Izutsu is a very particular director whose films I really like. Also because of that I didn't want to make something similar. At the time, the people who offered me the film already understood that if they asked me, it wouldn't just become a normal sequel."

In fact, it might as well have been a follow-up to one of Miike's own films, *The Way to Fight*, released straight to video one year earlier. Both films are set in 1970s Osaka and feature brash adolescent boys for whom fighting is the ultimate rebellion against growing up. This setting is very significant, since Miike was himself a teenager in Osaka in the '70s. Both films

exude a strong sense of nostalgia that renders their frequent violence more like joyful celebrations of youth than intentionally harmful. Their protagonists spend much of the film covered in bruises and limping, but they wouldn't have it any other way.

This nostalgia and a longing for childhood is another major motif that runs through Miike's entire body of work. As much as *Shinjuku Triad Society*, *Rainy Dog*, and *Ley Lines* can be considered the trilogy of rootlessness, so can the triptych of Osaka-set films be regarded as Miike's nostalgia cycle. This triptych is completed by its third entry, ***Young Thugs: Nostalgia*** (1998). The sequel to the previous year's sequel, it goes back to its protagonist's early youth in the late '60s. Depicting him growing up in a broken home, with a father who prefers gambling, drinking, and sleeping around with strippers to spending time with his subservient wife, Miike managed to portray childhood with a complete lack of sentimentality. Instead the film showed an astute understanding of a child's mind, as translated into comedy, a good-natured and playful depiction of violence and occasional flights of fancy. It also bore witness to its director's keen talent for directing child actors, a talent previously apparent in both *Rainy Dog* and *The Bird People in China*.

The fact that the three films in Miike's nostalgia trilogy do not have English release titles is an indication of how a large and essential part of the director's work has remained hidden to Western eyes. The unavailability of such films as *Young Thugs: Nostalgia* is a major factor affecting the way Miike is perceived as a filmmaker outside Japan, although in all fairness it must be pointed out that even in Japan few people are familiar with the full scope of his work. It's perhaps an inevitable situation, seeing how difficult it is to keep up with Miike's recent output, let alone his past films.

As if big-screen production didn't keep him busy enough already, Miike also directed three

Gozu

miniseries for Japanese television. The first aired in early 1999, entitled *Tennen Shōjo Mann* [trans: Natural girl Mann], and followed the adventures of a schoolgirl in Tokyo's Shibuya district, the leisure area of choice of the Japanese capital's teenage population. Consisting of three essentially feature-length episodes, the series played like a mixture of *Buffy the Vampire Slayer* and *West Side Story*, as gangs of schoolgirls battle each other over turf and one superpowered lass named Mann tries her best to keep her friends out of the hands of dubious model scouts. A further two episodes followed later the same year, in which much of the cast was replaced and the series became even more like *Buffy*, with Mann squaring off against a group of vampires and falling in love with one of them.

The third TV series, broadcast in 2000, was a rather more ambitious undertaking. A six-hour adaptation of Eiji Ōtsuka's graphically violent and twisty horror manga *MPD-Psycho*, Miike himself scripted the fiendishly complicated plotline and filmed it using a dazzling array of visual trickery whose style bordered on surreal.

By the time the series aired, the name Takashi Miike was rapidly gaining notoriety outside Japan. The selection of three of his films—*Dead or Alive, Ley Lines*, and *Audition*—for the Rotterdam Film Festival in The Netherlands in early 2000 had been an astonishing success. Winning two sets of critics' prizes for *Audition*, Miike saw himself launched as the next big thing in the European and American film press. *Audition* went on to wider international distribution, earning more money on its American theatrical run than it had at the box office in Japan. Helping to usher in the vogue for Japanese horror films, it nevertheless remained exempt from Hollywood remake treatment, most likely because few American producers would

Agitator

risk their money on re-enacting the film's climactic torture scene, which famously caused numerous audience members to run for the exits wherever it was shown.

Audition's finale also established Miike's reputation as a director who was more than willing to cross boundaries, an image many of the subsequent films released abroad did little to change. *Visitor Q* (2001) was an exaggerated, no-holds-barred depiction of a thoroughly dysfunctional family that featured bullying, drug abuse, murder, incest, and necrophilia. Shot on a US $70,000 budget and with digital video, its minimal production values rendered the subject matter even more confrontational, provoking hectic debate over whether the satire of Japan's nuclear family was worth all the excess. In Japan meanwhile, the film slipped quietly below everyone's radar and caused no fuss whatsoever.

The outrageously violent gangster saga *Ichi the Killer* (2001) fared rather less quietly, although not so much in terms of controversy, but rather in terms of box office success—in Japan at least, because foreign audiences greeted it with the same mixture of applause and revulsion that was by then becoming the norm for a new Miike film. In the eyes of many, *Ichi the Killer* took things just a little bit too far, and particularly the sexual violence endured by its female characters rubbed many the wrong way.

"If they criticize me because of that, there's nothing I can do about it. I don't think there is only one way to look at a film. There isn't one truth. I always try to have some kindness for the female characters, I allow them to try to realize their own desires, for example. But generally I feel no need to explain my films

© 2002 Kadokawa-Daiei

Graveyard of Honor

to an audience. If they feel differently about it than I do, then that's their right. I'm not always sure that I was able to make my feelings clear enough in a film, so if the audience misunderstands it, it's okay. I accept the misunderstandings."

With its running time of more than two hours, however, Miike's intentions for the film went a lot deeper and were a lot more thoughtful than a mere attempt to shock. For all its excessive violence, *Ichi the Killer* was ironically a rather potent meditation on the depiction of violent images and the interaction between those images and the spectator.

Controversies notwithstanding, the director continued working in a characteristically unperturbed and diverse manner in 2002, delivering the second sequel to *Dead or Alive* (*Dead or Alive:*

Final) a musical (*The Happiness of the Katakuris*), a three-and-a-half hour gangster epic (*Agitator*), a period drama for TV (*Sabu*), and a stunning remake of Kinji Fukasaku's 1975 film *Graveyard of Honor*.

Bolstered by an intense central performance by Gorō Kishitani, Miike's version of *Graveyard of Honor* updates the post-war setting of the source novel and Fukasaku's film to the 1980s and '90s, setting the blood-drenched downfall of its gangster protagonist Rikuo Ishimatsu against a background of the burst of Japan's bubble economy and the social upheaval that causes the emergence of such extremist phenomena as the Aum Shinrikyo cult. As in Fukasaku's original, Ishimatsu is not only the product of the chaos and insecurity of the society he lives in, he is the very embodiment of that chaos, the symbol of a country in turmoil. Kishitani portrays him not simply as a frighteningly cold-blooded thug, but as a man with an emotional core who lacks the ability to express his emotions in any way beside violence and (self-) abuse. He is the victim of his own underdeveloped emotional register, a "violoholic" who hides guns in every nook and cranny of his apartment instead of liquor. This makes the film as much a fascinating character study as a confronting social document.

The jury still out on the merit of his work, Miike's reputation was bolstered quite a bit when, to the surprise of many both inside and outside Japan, one of his films was selected for the Cannes Film Festival in 2003. Playing in one of the festival sidebars, *Gozu* is a surreal tale of a young, virginal yakuza whose search for his missing gang elder is a descent into the darker realms of his own psyche. Leading through numerous encounters with assorted suburban eccentrics and an attic-dwelling, cow-headed demon, the film played like a mixture of David Lynch and Monty Python. The Cannes selection was followed by an invitation to the Berlin Film Festival for *One Missed Call*. A middling horror yarn in the vein of Hideo Nakata's **The Ring**, the film slipped by almost unnoticed by the critics. Foreign buyers, however, were lining up to aquire the rights to what looked to them like the next J-horror sensation. The same year also saw Miike teaming up for the first time with Takeshi Kitano for a reworking of the Hideo Gosha/Shintarō Katsu *chanbara* film *Hitokiri* (1969), under the title *Izo*.

Tirelessly moving from project to project, Takashi Miike will no doubt continue to throw surprises at his audience. His work may provoke heated debate over its merit, but he is undeniably a unique presence, not only in Japanese cinema but in the world. Personal opinions aside, the simple fact that he still manages to surprise and shock audiences while making six films a year should be enough of a reason to appreciate Takashi Miike.

↓ Bird People in China
中国の鳥人
Chūgoku no Chōjin

1998. CAST: Masahiro Motoki, Renji Ishibashi, Mako Iwamatsu, Michiko Yoshise, Yūichi Minato, Tomohiko Okuda, Li Li Wang. 118 minutes. RELEASES: DVD, Artsmagic (USA, English subtitles), Universe (Hong Kong, English and Chinese subtitles).

Breathtaking spiritual journey to the heart of mainland China for two men from very different backgrounds.

Mention the name Miike and most people will immediately start thinking in terms of gory yakuza movies such as *Ichi the Killer* or *Dead or Alive*, a hail of raucous images drenched in blood, spit, and semen. Both revered and reviled for his onscreen excesses, there is actually another side to the director's work that often gets overlooked in favor of descriptions of the aberrant content of these and similarly excessive films such as *Fudoh* or *Visitor Q*.

Bird People in China is one such film. One of the director's first forays outside of the ghetto of V-cinema, not only is it one of his most accessible works, and one suitable for all audiences, but it is also far greater in scope and scale than anything that preceded it. An adaptation of a novel by Makoto Shiina, it is part road movie, part buddy movie, part fish-out-of-water comedy: the story of two men rediscovering themselves after being ordered, against their wishes and for very different reasons, away from the familiarity of their home turf into the depths of rural China.

Leaving the claustrophobic confines of his homeland behind him, we join Wada (Motoki), a diligent and rather bland businessman on a slow train across a timeless land. As he records his every thought in a handheld tape recorder, we learn that he has been sent by his company to replace a sick colleague who was scouting a particularly rich seam of jade deposit found in the remote Yunnan Province of southwest China. But even so far from the hectic day-to-day existence in Tokyo, portrayed in a montaged rush of fast-forwarded images of gym workouts and commuter trains, Wada finds himself unable to completely escape from his homeland, as his tranquility is shattered by two locals with a large portable stereo blaring out Japanese *enka* songs inviting him to sing along as he tries unsuccessfully, in English, to fend them off.

More sinister is the lurking presence of a man in a white suit and Hawaiian shirt who is shadowing him. Upon his arrival at the station, where Wada is greeted by his guide, a Japanese-speaking local known as Shen (Mako), the third man violently introduces himself as Ujiie (Ishibashi), a yakuza punk unwillingly sent by his boss to trail Wada across China to settle debts owed to the mob by Wada's company. He orders Wada and Shen to take him along with them.

After a few initial blows, the three characters embark on an epic journey across a breathtaking landscape, occasionally punctuated by the odd dusty village consisting of wooden huts and rife with chickens running wildly through the streets. Despite the happy-go-lucky attitude of their unflustered guide, tension between the two Japanese runs high, not helped by the constant griping of Ujiie, nor the fact that the van they are traveling in is progressively disintegrating, beginning with its door falling off, the further they get from home. Drenched by a freak storm, the voyagers are sidetracked off course, and soon find themselves irreversibly lost. When Wada's work documents end up as a goat's breakfast, and Shen's memory is lost after a blow to the head, not only does the loyal salaryman lose his initial reason for the journey, but all means of contacting his bosses for further instructions.

And then, events take a further plunge into the fantastical when they undertake the next leg of their voyage on a raft pulled by river turtles, transporting them to a remote village in Yunnan Province, secluded from the outside world by

Bird People in China

mountains. Here they make the acquaintance of Yan (Li Li Wang), a teenage Chinese girl with limpid blue eyes, who is trying to teach the local children to fly, using makeshift wings of cardboard and wood. The tailfin of an abandoned World War II fighter plane stands protruding from a nearby lake, and Yan continuously sings a strange tune to herself in broken English, which Wada eventually pieces together using his portable tape recorder and an electronic dictionary, to identify it as the old Scottish folk song *Annie Laurie*. Slowly they begin to construct the meaning behind the legend of the bird man who fell from the sky many years before.

Bird People in China is one of a sub-genre of films that feature Japanese characters transported away from the concrete jungle of Tokyo to a neighboring Asian country and the dizzy, disorienting effect of such a dramatic change in basic environment. Examples include Shūsuke Kaneko's *Trip to a Strange Kingdom* (*Sotsugyō Ryokō: Nihon Kara Kimashita*, 1992) and Yōjirō Takita's *Made in Japan* (*Bokura wa Minna Ikiteiru*, a.k.a. *We Are Not Alone*, 1993). It is a theme that Miike would later explore in a different context with *The Guys from Paradise*. Here the effect, as lensed by cinematographer Hideo Yamamoto (a regular collaborator of Miike's who worked his way up from assistant cameraman on the films of Takeshi Kitano, from *Boiling Point* on, to eventually shooting *Fireworks*) is quite intoxicating. Contrasting the bleak grays of the bracketing Tokyo scenes with rich, earthy reds, verdant greens, and sepia-toned misty mountains, the very setting of Miike's film is so breathtaking that the plot often seems secondary to it.

Whilst conjuring up some undeniably beautiful travelogue footage, like its two wide-eyed protagonists, Miike perhaps too often wanders off track gazing at scenery at the expense of any sense of urgency in the narrative. The rather languorous approach to pacing results in a film that feels composed of two very distinct halves, beginning with a journey, and stalling at the midpoint to become distracted in its rather whimsical back story. We are not sure where Miike is leading us, or how it will end, but we do get to see an awful lot of the countryside en route.

Nevertheless, Miike achieved impressive enough results, using a limited budget in a foreign environment to demonstrate a high degree of flexibility and professional ability, and as such *Bird People in China* stands as a crucial marker in the director's career: the transition point between his generic straight-to-video origins and his more major budgeted productions.

↓ Young Thugs: Nostalgia
岸和田少年愚連隊 望郷
Kishiwada Shōnen Gurentai: Bōkyō

1998. CAST: Naoto Takenaka, Saki Takaoka, Yūki Nagata, Setsuko Karasumaru, Takeshi Caesar, Riichi Nakaba. 94 minutes. RELEASES: DVD, Artsmagic (USA, English subtitles).

A nostalgic tale of growing up in 1960s Osaka, this portrait of childhood is mercifully devoid of cuteness and false retro stylistics. Funny, touching, sad, and violent all at once, this is Takashi Miike in grand form.

The *Kishiwada Shōnen Gurentai* [trans: Boy hooligans from Kishiwada] series has moved into some very diverse territory in its seven-year lifespan. Based on the fictionalized autobiography of Osaka truck driver Riichi Nakaba, the first film, made for Shochiku studios by former ATG director Kazuyuki Izutsu in 1996, depicted the life of a Nakaba-derived high school student in the mid-1970s and his numerous violent punchups with rivals from the working class Osaka neighborhood of Kishiwada. The film, which starred a pair of popular young *manzai* comedians, celebrated its protagonist's eternal dropout status and presented the violence as a kind of slapstick not played for laughs.

Takashi Miike took over the reins on part two, which he made less as a sequel to Izutsu's film than as a follow-up to his own earlier work about adolescent Osaka brawlers *Kenka no Hanamichi: Ōsaka Saikyō Densetsu* (1996). Miike chose to focus on the Riichi character's life after graduation and the inevitable need to face maturity. Although he too cast a pair of *manzai* comedians in the lead, the brothers Kōji and Yasushi Chihara, the subject matter resulted in a stronger emphasis on the dramatic aspect and a surprisingly well-balanced film.

For part three, Miike went in the opposite direction and delivered a prequel. *Bōkyō* [trans: Nostalgia] shows us Riichi Nakaba's pre-adolescent period in the late 1960s, going into a lot more detail about the boy's relationship with his good-for-nothing father, Toshio, played by Naoto Takenaka. In his numerous films to deal with the subject, Miike's portrayal of childhood and adolescence is nostalgic to the point of idyllic. The younger the children, the more capable they are of survival, happiness, and imagination. *Young Thugs: Nostalgia* gives us children who have not even reached puberty yet, and while they spend much of the film with bruised faces, no real harm is ever done. When a drunken Toshio gives his son Riichi a beating, the boy most of the time strikes back. The bond between the two actually becomes tighter after ten-year-old Riichi gives his father a sound thrashing with a baseball bat.

But violence certainly isn't all this film is about. It runs the gamut of emotions with admirable skill, with Riichi's adventures being funny, touching, sad, or exciting in turn. Mercifully, the respectful way in which the director treats his child actors and characters keeps the film free of artificial cuteness. Even though it dares to take flights of imaginative fancy, Miike never loses sight of reality, keeping his characters genuine at all times, whether they are children or adults.

Young Thugs: Nostalgia's narrative is largely episodic, playing like an extract from the life of its protagonist rather than as a plot-driven story. But the appeal is not in the plot, it's in the portrayal. With the material being so close to Miike's own life (both he and Nakaba are from working class Osaka families and were born in the early '60s), this film is perhaps the closest a Miike movie will ever come to realism. That

it also dares to be imaginative and throw that same reality into the wind only underlines the quality of the film. Full of autobiographical elements from his own life, probably the best point of reference for *Young Thugs: Nostalgia* is not one of Miike's own films, but François Truffaut's mother of all nostalgia films *The 400 Blows* (*Les 400 coups*, 1959).

With seven entries in as many years, the *Kishiwada Shōnen Gurentai* series, meanwhile, has become something of a V-cinema mainstay. With a wide variety of directors helming the various episodes (including Rokurō Mochizuki for part five) the series switched focus halfway through, evolving into a vehicle for V-cinema superstar Riki Takeuchi. Miike never returned to the series, but would continue his voyage of nostalgia with the equally impressive *Dead or Alive 2*.

↓ Ley Lines

日本黒社会 Ley Lines
Nihon Kuroshakai: Ley Lines

1999. **CAST:** Kazuki Kitamura, Tomorowo Taguchi, Dan Li, Michisuke Kashiwaya, Naoto Takenaka, Shō Aikawa. 105 minutes. **RELEASES:** DVD, Artsmagic (U.S., English subtitles), Asia Extreme/Tartan Video (U.K., English subtitles), Toshiba (Japan, no subtitles).

An elegiac account of the misadventures of a trio of young country misfits in the big city. Probably the most representative film in Takashi Miike's oeuvre, and crucial viewing for anyone with more than a passing interest in the director's work.

The third film in the director's unofficial *kuroshakai* (literally: "black society") trilogy is probably the film that best sums up the cinema of Takashi Miike. *Ley Lines* is the quintessential Miike film, the best representation one is likely

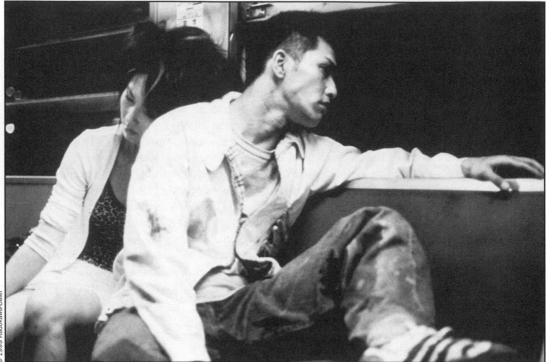

Ley Lines

to find of the director's thematic and stylistic preoccupations, with the concept of rootlessness at its very heart.

The protagonists are a trio of boys from a countryside smallville, bored with their uneventful lives. But boredom is not the only thing that drives them. A bigger factor is frustration. Children of Chinese immigrants, Ryūichi, Shunrei, and Chan are discriminated against on a regular basis. The film's opening scene sees Ryūichi denied a passport by a local bureaucrat on account of his non-Japanese origins. He vents his anger by smashing a ceramic plant pot over the bigot's head, landing him a trip to the police station, where he is again treated with racist contempt. When the boys go too far in releasing their anger one night and nearly kill the owner of a scrap yard, they take the next train for Tokyo, leaving everything but a few necessities behind.

They end up in the grimmer parts of Tokyo's Shinjuku district, which is populated with ethnic minorities, outcasts like them. But understanding and pity are the last things these people are willing to show them. Their first encounter is with the Chinese hooker Anita, who lures them to an abandoned building with the promise of sex, only to make off with their wallets. It's the classic law of dog eat dog, but Miike humanizes the situation by showing us Anita's less than glamorous life, in which she is forced to serve a wide variety of perverted or downright disgusting clients by her Chinese pimp, who often gives her a beating afterward for good measure. When she robs the boys' money she does it because it saves her having to do the dirty with another sweaty slob or fetishist salaryman.

Their money gone, the boys go looking for jobs and end up pushing makeshift drugs for a small-time dealer and his black sidekick. A chance encounter with a bruised and battered Anita on the neon-lit nighttime streets of Kabu-kichō makes the boys realize that the desperate hooker is in the same boat as them, and the trio of outcasts becomes a quartet. Learning about the riches of the local Chinese crime lord Wong from Anita, the group decides to rob Wong's restaurant and use the loot to buy fake passports and escape to Brazil, where they hope to find happiness.

All three entries in the *kuroshakai* series express a fundamental and intense sadness. Their rootless protagonists try hard to find the place or the environment that will give them happiness, but the world does not allow them to reach it. Many of Miike's films derive their true power from this sense of sadness, and *Ley Lines* is one of the best examples. If maybe it's not a surprise that these boys will never achieve their happiness, it's a testament to the director's abilities that this has no impact on our emotional involvement in their tribulations. The film's final shot is of such intense beauty because Miike dares to create hope where there should logically be only sadness, or, depending on one's point of view, dares to add a deep undertone of sadness to what seems like an unexpected ray of hope.

Featuring great camerawork by Naosuke Imaizumi and some terrific performances (including lead actor and frequent Miike collaborator Kazuki Kitamura, who would later feature in Quentin Tarantino's *Kill Bill*), *Ley Lines* has been unjustly overshadowed by Miike's more obviously audacious works like *Dead or Alive*, **Audition**, **Ichi the Killer**, or *Visitor Q*. If it lacks their attention grabbing moments, it's only because the film is evocatively inspired for every single second of its 105-minute running time.

↓ Audition
オーディション

2000. **CAST:** Ryō Ishibashi, Eihi Shiina, Renji Ishibashi, Tetsu Sawaki, Miyuki Matsuda, Jun Kunimura, Toshie Negishi, Ren Ōsugi, Ken Mitsuishi. 115 minutes. **RELEASES:** DVD, Ventura Distribution/Chimera (U.S., English subtitles), Tartan Video/Asia Extreme (U.K., English subtitles), Rapid Eye Video (Germany, German/English subtitles), Universe (Hong Kong, English/Chinese subtitles), Studio Canal (France, French subtitles), Filmfreak (Netherlands, Dutch/French subtitles).

Middle-aged widower holds a mock audition to find a new wife, and soon finds himself with more than he bargained for. A romantic drama that turns into a white-knuckle endurance test of horror in its final reel.

Few films from Japan have created such a stir overseas in recent years as *Audition* did when it first rocked the Rotterdam International Film Festival in 2000. With half the audience wondering how such a talented director had escaped the world's attention for so long and the other half charging headlong for the exit during the memorably over-the-top finale, here was a film no one was going to forget in a hurry. Miike was the talk of the town, and *Audition* went on to become the first film of the director, with already a score of works under his belt back home, to be theatrically distributed in the West.

The key-line of Miike's visceral shocker is simple. After seven years, widowed Aoyama (Ryō Ishibashi) is encouraged by both his teenage son Shigehiko and his colleagues at the film production company where he works to finally let go of the past and find a new wife. But how does a middle-aged workaholic come across someone suitable? His producer friend hits upon the idea of digging out an unmade script from a couple of years ago and holding a fake audition for the leading lady. Whilst perusing the reams of applications, a spillt coffee ring draws him towards Asami, a former ballet dancer who seems to embody all of the virtues of the traditional wife that Aoyama is looking for. After an initial face-to-face meeting with her in the awkward studio-bound context of the audition hall, he telephones her that same evening to arrange a less formal rendezvous.

It's best to go into *Audition* with a minimum of preconceptions for it to achieve its maximum power. Miike's chief weapon here is surprise. In fact, it is almost impossible to describe the film without giving away vital plot points. Suffice to say, *Audition* is not structured like a conventional horror. It is, in fact, a cunning piece of genre subversion, with the first half building up slowly, a simple and surely paced tale of boy meets girl, before the rug is pulled from under our feet and we find ourselves in far darker territory.

With the turning point left deliberately vague, much of what makes *Audition*'s tonal shift from sedate romantic drama to visceral horror all the more convincing can be attributed to the moral ambiguity of its central character, Aoyama, admirably portrayed by Ishibashi. Though his methods of finding a new bride, chosen as if she were an item on a restaurant menu, may reek of a flagrant abuse of his job position, his motivations, however misguided, at heart remain dreamily idealistic. Prompted to seek a replacement for his deceased spouse by others, in Asami he sees the very incarnation of what society would consider "a good wife" for a man of his status, as well as a suitable mother surrogate for his son.

Aoyama is chasing an impossible ideal, but still, as the idea takes firmer hold, it rapidly turns into an unwavering private obsession. Furtively waiting until his son is out of earshot before making his covert phone calls, Aoyama's secret is compounded by the all-pervasive ghost of his dead wife hanging over him. Whilst rifling through the initial applications, we see a brief, almost subliminal shot of her sitting up and glaring admonishingly at him from their matrimonial bed. These resurgent memories reach critical mass in the latter stages of the film, as Aoyama's psyche caves in on itself

under the collective weight of repressed guilt and sexual hysteria, warping into a feverish dream, tingeing reality with sickly reds, blues, and yellows.

Miike's master stroke here is in the casting of former Benetton model Eihi Shiina as Asami. Eyes permanently cast downward, her voice a barely audible mew, slim, gentle, and elegant, she is the very essence of demure compliance, a paragon of the Japanese ideal of femininity. Though, surprisingly, subsequent screen outings from this elfin beauty have been restricted to minor appearances in **Eureka** and **Harmful Insect**, it is difficult to imagine *Audition* with anyone else in the role.

Adapted by Daisuke Tengan, the son of Miike's mentor Shōhei Imamura, *Audition* is based on a novel of the same name by cult writer Ryū Murakami. Murakami is known to the West through his translated works such as *Almost Transparent Blue* (1976) and *Coin Locker Babies* (1997), which cast a cynical eye on the dark underside of contemporary Japanese life, and has also adapted a number of his own works for the screen, the best known of which is *Topāzu* (1991), released overseas as *Tokyo Decadence*, which details the increasing emotional alienation of a call girl who specializes in S/M.

Though some viewers have misread criticisms of the Japanese patriarchal order within *Audition*, Miike himself denies that any such social aspect is to be found in his work. Like Murakami, he adopts the psychological vantage point of his protagonist, forcing viewers to confront their own feelings and fears, rather than looking down at his characters from any higher moral perspective. More literal readings therefore may lay the film open to the standard accusations of Miike as a director who is all glitz and flourish and little substance, but it is this moral ambivalence that makes the wham-bam descent into nightmarish grotesquery such an undeniably potent experience. Indisputably a technical tour de force, *Audition* rises far above the slick stylistic glibness that has occasionally marred other films from the director, such as *The City of Lost Souls*, to create something truly discomforting.

↓ Ichi the Killer
殺し屋1
Koroshiya 1

2001. **CAST:** Tadanobu Asano, Nao Ōmori, Shinya Tsukamoto, Alien Sun, Sabu, Shun Sugata, Jun Kunimura, Susumu Terajima. 128 minutes. **RE-LEASES:** DVD, Media Blasters (U.S., English subtitles). World Wide Cinema (The Netherlands, English/Dutch/French subtitles), Medusa (U.K., English subtitles). Universe (Hong Kong, English/Chinese subtitles), Pioneer (Japan, no subtitles).

Possibly the most deliriously violent film ever made. Denounced by many, but in spite of its seemingly gratuitous nature, Ichi the Killer is a strongly critical examination of the relationship between violent images and the spectator, as well as an excellent character piece.

How do we explain Takashi Miike's popularity surge of the last few years? Without launching into a sociological study, a major factor is without doubt the audaciousness of his work, in particular of its violence. However, Miike had been making audaciously violent films for quite a while until *Audition* finally proved his international breakthrough. And a number of those had already played to foreign audiences. The secret lies in the fact that *Audition* had such an impact because it gave the violence a context. And context means resonance.

Miike's films, however violent they may at times be, nearly always contain such context. Not always is it as apparent to foreign eyes as in *Audition*, but rarely are his films gratuitous. *Ichi the Killer*, one of the most violent films ever made, is far from being gratuitous. It shows us people sliced in half, decapitated, mangled, raped, tortured, run through with needles, and

Ichi the Killer

Courtesy of Omega Micott

covered in boiling oil (and this is only an excerpt, some of the acts on display simply can't be summed up in a few words), but the point is not *what* it shows but *how* it shows it.

Based on the equally outrageous manga by Hideo Yamamoto (not to be confused with the film's cameraman of the same name), the film stays fairly loyal to its source. Entire scenes are transposed from page to screen and the plot is followed closely. However, when the film went into production, the serialized manga was still running, meaning Miike and screenwriter Sakichi Satō had to come up with their own ending. It's this necessity to rethink the outcome that gave the director the possibility to completely alter the meaning of the story. This resulted in a fair amount of mystification and ambivalence (the motivation of main villain Jijii, played by Shinya Tsukamoto, remains an enigma, for instance), and a complete revision of the implication of the story's violent aspects, both in terms of its meaning within the film and its effect on cinema audiences.

Despite its seemingly straightforward revenge plot (mysterious killer murders yakuza boss, the boss's right-hand man goes looking for the killer), *Ichi the Killer* is a phenomenally intricate film. The simple narrative is given extra dimension by turning it into a doomed love story, with the quest for vengeance becoming a search for the ideal partner: The only one who can fill the void in protagonist Kakihara's life is the same person who created that void, the titular Ichi the killer. The characters surrounding this would-be couple are defined in similar terms of dependency, being either predominantly masochist or sadist. Some try to deny their personalities in the hope of attracting a partner, but the truth inevitably catches up with the self-deception (as in Kakihara's brusque dismissal of the love-struck Karen when she is unable to give him the pain he so desires).

The most interesting aspect of *Ichi the Killer*, however, is its treatment of images of violence. The way it portrays the abundance of violent acts in terms of angles, framing, editing, and use of special effects is meticulously thought through, resulting in a division between almost cartoon-like exaggeration and savage realism. This division is at the heart of Miike's approach to the violence, dragging his viewers from one extreme to the other, making them laugh one moment and cringe the next in the hope of creating an awareness of why they react like they do.

There is a lot of provocation in *Ichi the Killer*'s formal approach to the portrayal of violence. Literally, since it is intended to provoke certain reactions (first) and actions (second) in the audience. The most hard-hitting scenes of violence, many of them involving violence against female characters, are edited and framed in such way that most of the actual acts are not shown. Their impact results largely from the audience filling in the blanks for themselves, thereby looking for violence within themselves. The film's finale, which, as noted, Miike and his screenwriter made up themselves, seems to promise a big showdown that it subsequently refuses to deliver. Here again we have provocation at work. If the viewer is disappointed that the showdown, a confrontation between the two most violent characters in the film, did not happen, he or she is effectively acknowledging his or her own desire to consume more violence.

Ichi the Killer is a provocative film, which is probably why reactions to it are so strong. But these reactions show that Miike's approach is successful: those who walked out of the film or fumed in outrage were those who had been most painfully confronted with their own limits in consuming violent images. By setting their boundaries, they actively and consciously reconsidered their relationships with such images.

CHAPTER 13
Makoto Shinozaki
篠崎誠

One of the most interesting Japanese filmmakers to debut in the 1990s is also one of the most overlooked. Makoto Shinozaki remains a virtual unknown on the international scene, despite having directed two of the most outstanding Japanese films in recent years. Exact reasons for Shinozaki's relative obscurity remain unclear, but one factor might perhaps be that even on his home turf he is seen as operating in the shadow of two other filmmakers, Takeshi Kitano and Kiyoshi Kurosawa.

Despite the pigeonholing, Makoto Shinozaki is a true all-round cinephile. Generally regarded as an exponent of the "intellectual stream" of 1990s filmmakers, Shinozaki is as much a fan of genre films and B-movies as he is of Abbas Kiarostami and John Cassavetes. When he bought himself a used 8mm camera at age 14, the films he made with it were horror movies.

> "I like horror and action films as genres because you see human beings at their extremes. So it's not really as different as you might imagine. There are no rolling heads or spurting blood in my films, but there is discommunication, which is in fact more frightening to me."

While studying psychology at Rikkyō University, his interest in filmmaking prompted him to join the university's now famous ciné-club, whose soon-to-be illustrious members were strongly under the influence of film theorist Shigehiko Hasumi and his protégé and Rikkyō alumnus, Kiyoshi Kurosawa.

His university years further intensifying his cinephilia, Shinozaki graduated in the latter half of the 1980s with the wish to make a living in film. With the path that led via studio apprenticeship permanently cut off, he first considered a compromise by working in IT, but renounced the job just as he was on the verge of being hired. Instead he was employed as a projectionist at the theatrical facilities of Tokyo's Athénée Français cultural center. Rather than being exclusively devoted to French culture, the place was an all-round arthouse cinema and a gathering point for the city's young film enthusiasts. Also handling other chores like selling tickets, Shinozaki found at his job an ambience not unlike that of his university ciné-club, with many of the same faces attending the screenings. In the meantime he continued making short films on 8mm and, like a number of those contemporaries, also started exercising his all-encompassing passion for cinema as a film critic.

> "Our theater was kind of like an arthouse and there was one film that I really wanted to see succeed, which was John Cassavetes' *Love Streams*. A friend of mine happened to be

editing a magazine. It wasn't a film magazine, but he said, 'Well, I can't pay you, but you can write whatever you want about movies.' So I wrote about *Love Streams,* and that was the beginning of my writing about films. When *Cahiers du Cinéma Japan* started about that time, the editors decided to include articles about Japanese directors. Takeshi Kitano had only made his first two films, *Violent Cop* and *Boiling Point*, but I wrote a long essay about Kitano for *Cahiers Japan*. And Kitano read that essay. At the same time a rather large mainstream culture magazine called *Switch* asked me if I would interview Takeshi Kitano."

With this, a tradition and a reputation were born. Starting from *A Scene at the Sea*, Shinozaki interviewing Kitano at length about his latest film would become a *Switch* tradition that lasted up through *Fireworks*. His work having received favorable reactions, he was soon asked to exercise his particular brand of lengthy, perceptive interviews on foreign filmmakers. Doubtlessly aided by his excellent command of English, Shinozaki interviewed leading international independent filmmakers like Jim Jarmusch, Alex Cox, Quentin Tarantino, and Abbas Kiarostami for various Japanese film media.

"I kept on writing scripts and making 8mm films throughout. I knew that no distributor would look at me seriously because I was completely unknown and relatively inexperienced, so I worked as a projectionist for four years and saved up enough money to make the film. Also I worked on a Kiyoshi Kurosawa film called *The Guard from Underground*. I was there to watch him work, but they had so little money and so little staff that by the time I realized it, I was already part of the crew. Watching the very talented Kurosawa-san labor under really brutal production conditions because of the lack of money, I thought: 'I can't work this way. I have to raise my own money, put my own money aside, and do it completely independent.'"

The completely independent film that resulted from Shinozaki's determination was *Okaeri*, a thoughtful portrait of a young married couple struggling with the wife's schizophrenia. Aided by his background as a psychology student and numerous conversations with the relatives of schizophrenics, the fledgling director managed to portray the issues of mental illness with a great deal of consideration, while showing remarkable skill at creating wholly believable, human characters.

"No matter how much time we spend with our family or our loved ones, ultimately we're a separate consciousness and we can't ultimately understand or know each other. And that's where misunderstandings and friction arise. Nonetheless it is for that reason that we attempt to get to know one another. It's that very process that I'm interested in. Some people assume that at the end of *Okaeri* the wife is cured and it's a happy ending. I think what I was really trying to portray was a sense of two people born from completely different backgrounds attempting to share the same time and space."

Filmography

1990
- *Nobody Home* [short]

1995
- *Okaeri*

1997
- *Buraddī Marī no Yūwaku* [TV]

1999
- *Jam Session—The Unofficial Bootleg of Kikujiro* (*Jamu Sesshon—Kikujirō no Natsu Kōshiki Kaizokuban*)

2000
- *Not Forgotten* (*Wasurerarenu Hitobito*)

2002
- *Asakusa Kid* [TV]

2003
- *Cop Festival* (*Deka Matsuri*) [co-director]

2004
- *Walking with the Dog* (*Inu to Arukeba—Chirori to Tamara*)

After meeting him numerous times on the set of Kitano's films, Shinozaki cast Susumu Terajima in a rare dramatic lead role as husband Takashi. For the role of his wife, Yuriko, Shinozaki asked the unknown and non-professional Miho Uemura, who was working as a store clerk at the time (a profession she has since returned to). In a small role, Shinozaki cast former child star of the silent era and Ozu cohort Tomio Aoki, once best known as one of the two tykes in *I Was Born, But…* (*Umareta wa Mita Keredo*, 1932), but now an affable pensioner with a knack for pulling funny faces (he would play one of the lead parts in Shinozaki's *Not Forgotten* five years later). The result was a film featuring particularly confident performances, in no small amount brought out by Shinozaki's willingness to adapt his shooting style to the needs of his players.

Courtesy of Bitter's End

Makoto Shinozaki on the set of *Not Forgotten*

"If anything, I would prefer to employ a documentary approach in fiction, rather than clear storyboarding and first shooting this and then that. Because I believe if you shoot it that way it's so predictable. The unexpected rarely happens. I'd like for it to become something I couldn't have imagined. Inevitably when you start shooting, reality intervenes and it changes things, so you really have to take a much more documentary approach to dealing with what happens."

One scene in *Okaeri* is a particularly strong example of Shinozaki's approach to adapting to the circumstances. A sequence in which Yuriko locks herself in the bathroom and Takashi tries to comfort her while he stands outside the door was shot as a continuous take with two different cameras. The director's reason for using two cameras was the result of the rehearsals, in which Uemura and Terajima improvised from the scripted scene, giving it an emotional resonance that was lacking on the printed page. In order to give them the freedom to recreate that experience on set during the actual shooting, the two cameras allowed the two actors all the leeway they needed. The result was an astonishing, strongly emotional scene that forms the beating heart of the film.

"Until that moment, the characters in the script for me had sort of remained puppets and I was the puppet master. Finally watching the actors doing that scene, they started to feel like real-life humans. They were so powerful they blew away all the anxieties I had working on my first film. Their acting felt so rich and happy in that moment, in an odd way, that I knew I could make a film. That experience gave me true confidence as a filmmaker."

The director's independent gamble paid off. *Okaeri* was screened at numerous festivals and won several prizes, most notably the award for best new director in Berlin. Along with Hashiguchi's *Like Grains of Sand* and Kore-eda's *Maborosi*, both doing the rounds the same year, it helped usher in the international breakthrough of Japanese independent film. The following year, Shinozaki was asked to direct the TV film *Buradī Marī no Yūwaku* (1997) [trans: Bloody Mary's seduction], a more thriller-oriented entry in the *Koi, Shita* [trans: Fallen, in love] series of romance-themed TV dramas. Although he never entered the V-cinema industry with its minimal budgets and tight schedules, perhaps as a result of his experiences on the set of Kiyoshi Kurosawa's *The Guard from Underground*, he would work in the slightly more affluent television market on more than one occasion.

If *Okaeri* showed that Shinozaki's approach to filmmaking is inherently documentary-like in its flexibility toward changing circumstances, he would get a chance to show his mettle with a proper documentary in 1999. The project would re-unite him with Takeshi Kitano, this time not as an interviewer, but as a director. *Jam Session: The Official Bootleg of Kikujiro* was a feature-length documentary on the making of Kitano's first film since winning the Golden Lion for *Fireworks* in Venice. With his popularity and international bankability on the rise as a result of the prize, Kitano's production company felt it was time to change the way the director was presented to the world, while at the same time seeing an opportunity to make some additional money.

"Before *Jam Session*, several 'making-ofs' of the Kitano films had been made, but usually by TV companies, as a result of Mr. Kitano's TV activities. Office Kitano decided they didn't want that anymore, they wanted something different. But because Mr. Kitano is quite shy, they didn't want to shove some different director they didn't know in his face, which is why they approached me. I didn't want to just show up with a camera one day, so I started going into production meetings and saying hello and had the crew get used to me being around. So by the time shooting started, people pretty much knew who I was."

Shot on digital video for reasons of practicality and cost efficiency, it allowed Shinozaki and his minimal crew (one or two people at most) to record the maximum amount of material for the allotted budget, but more importantly it allowed him to move freely and without being a hindrance to any of *Kikujiro*'s crew. As a result he catches a good amount of candid and intimate moments, which reveal a lot about the personality of Takeshi Kitano, though more as a film-

maker than as a human being. In some ways, the change from Shinozaki's previous interviews with Kitano isn't so dramatic, since *Jam Session* primarily comes across as one filmmaker observing another from a somewhat reverential distance. Kitano's shyness shines through on a few occasions, and those who might have confused the director's personal nature with his big-screen tough guy persona (or with his small-screen clowning) are in for a surprise, but the documentary remains above all a filmmakers' tête-à-tête.

In the meantime, Shinozaki expanded his extracurricular activities by teaching filmmaking at the newly formed Film School of Tokyo (Eiga Bigakkō), alongside Kiyoshi Kurosawa and several of his generation's brightest hopes: Hirokazu Kore-eda, Shinji Aoyama, Nobuhiro Suwa, Akihiko Shiota, and Takahisa Zeze. He also came full circle by following in the footsteps of Kurosawa and Hasumi, becoming a lecturer in film studies at Rikkyō.

His next film project saw Shinozaki working entirely with his own material again. *Not Forgotten*, the story of three veteran World War II soldiers and their encounters with the young, was at least as successful on an emotional level as *Okaeri* had been, but was more polished and more self-assured. With a large cast that included three enormously experienced studio stars from yesteryear, confident direction, and a script that tied subplots together in an admirable fashion, *Not Forgotten* certainly fulfilled the promise of *Okaeri*. Unfortunately it never made it into the major film festivals and garnered no foreign distribution as a result. It won best actor and actress prizes for its veteran leads at the Three Continents festival in Nantes, France, which rejuvenated the careers of Tatsuya Mihashi and Tomio Aoki in particular (the former was promptly cast by Takeshi Kitano in *Dolls*, the latter appeared in Seijun Suzuki's ***Pistol Opera***), but Berlin, Cannes, and Venice snubbed it. What's more, its domestic box office performance was downright poor. What should have been, and in artistic terms certainly was,

Shinozaki's definitive breakthrough turned into something of a deception instead. No doubt its focus on the elderly made it a less than obvious box office draw, but perhaps the disappointing reactions from the foreign market were the result of the film's sudden, swift burst of violence in the finale, which must have come particularly unexpected for those who had Shinozaki tagged as a demure humanist intellectual on the basis of *Okaeri*. Its merits within the context of the film aside, the scene demonstrated the way in which Shinozaki's attitude toward cinema differs from those contemporaries he is sometimes lumped together with, like Hashiguchi and Kore-eda.

"There are several filmmakers in my generation who are not so caught up with the big fiction idea, but who are staying closer to home, closer to their daily lives. But me, I guess I do need to create some kind of a fictional world that's believable. Kinji Fukasaku has said that his approach was to take a fictionalized world and try to hammer away at it. Whereas the approach of the younger generation is to not even start out with creating a fictionalized world, to start out almost with reality and build up a little bit from there. That's something I agree with, but if you stick too close to reality, the film just shrinks and shrinks. Out of a 24-hour day a film lasts at most about two hours and the size of the frame is quite small compared to what we see of the world, so in a way because it's so limited in time and space, the more you try to make it be like reality the more you realize it's not.

"People say that film is freedom and that by using computer graphics you have a limitless ability to express everything. I don't agree with that. In a way film may be the most limiting medium of all. Even when you're talking to people you're familiar with, you don't always know when you've communicated. There's a certain sense of limitations there and that's identical to the kinds of limitations you have in film. Also, there's something about film where the more you try to show, the more you lose in a way. But then if you try to limit it too much, it starts to shrink as well."

This balance between fiction and realism is particularly noticeable in his TV adaptation of Takeshi Kitano's autobiography *Asakusa Kid*. Scripted by former Kitano Army member Dankan, the story of Kitano's apprenticeship as a young comedian under the aged master of ceremonies at a *manzai*/strip club called the France Theater, Shinozaki transposed its early '70s setting to the present day. While the film contained plenty of comedy and comic stylization, the choice to set the story in the early 2000s was (though partly budgetary) an attempt on the director's part to show how little the atmosphere of Tokyo's Asakusa district has changed since Kitano's early days. Traditionally the city's entertainment district, the area lost much of its luster in the post-war years, as Shibuya and Shinjuku increasingly attracted those looking for quick pleasures, leaving Asakusa with a patronage of more advanced age.

In *Asakusa Kid*, the character of the young Kitano (played by comedian Hakase Suidōbashi, of the Asakusa Kid comedy duo) spends more practice time on his tap dance routine than on his comedy, but the atmosphere of the area and of the cramped backstage sections of Asakusa's entertainment clubs are vividly captured. Shot with TV movie production values and with minimal time for production and editing, however, its ambitions are bigger than its means, and for Shinozaki it was a case of doing the best job possible under the circumstances.

His next project tried to make a virtue of minimal means. He had already contributed to Shinobu Yaguchi's and Takuji Suzuki's *One Piece* project, a kind of playful counterpart to Lars Von Trier's Dogma manifesto, in which each director must make a digital short of several minutes' length, shot from a single, fixed camera position. In 2003 Shinozaki came up with his own variation on the challenge of cinematic self-limitation, a series of ten-minute short films shot on digital video, all featuring a detective character and containing at least one gag every minute. Shinozaki managed to drum up several of his director friends who were willing to take on the challenge, including such unlikely candidates for a short cop comedy as Kiyoshi Kurosawa, Shinji Aoyama, Ryūichi Hiroki, and Kunitoshi Manda. *Cop Festival* did surprisingly good business and before the year was even half up, it had already spawned three additional collections of shorts based on the same concept, with directors including Takahisa Zeze, Hirokazu Kore-eda, Akihiko Shiota, Kazuyoshi Kumakiri, Nobuhiro Yamashita, and V-cinema stalwart Hitoshi Ozawa. The fourth film was entirely made by actors making their directorial debuts, including Nao Ōmori (*Ichi the Killer*) and Mami Nakamura (*Tokyo Trash Baby*). Shinozaki acted as producer and supervisor throughout.

If one thing stands out about Makoto Shinozaki's filmography, it's the staggering diversity of the work. His 2004 feature *Walking with the Dog* was a gentle melodrama about the training of a "Therapy Dogs" for the infirm and terminally ill (and the final screen appearance of Tomio Aoki, who died on January 24, 2004, at the venerable age of 80). In Shinozaki's case, the consistency of his body of work is found in his approach to filmmaking, instead of in the subject matter or themes. This makes him a pure filmmaker, rather than an artist whose self-expression happens to be through the medium of film.

> "This is the best for me, being a film director. I can't sit in a room alone and try to think up things. I hate writing scripts. I always work with a writer and with the producer on scripts. And I have people who have nothing to do with the film business read my scripts. I'm interested in their opinions."

With his open-minded attitude toward the diversity of cinema, his dedication to genuine and truthful portrayal of human beings, and his very conscious, exploratory approach to the medium, Makoto Shinozaki has grown into a unique filmmaker.

> "I think if I stayed too close to myself, my work would start to shrink. Imagination is very important, but it has to feel real. I think that certainly with *Okaeri*, part of the reason why I couldn't turn it into the film I really wanted it to be was that maybe I hadn't lived enough. But I actually think there was a lot to learn from making the film itself. My cameraman was 74 and he had worked with Fukasaku-san at Toei. When you work with people so different from you, you really see the possibility for change inside yourself. So I want to continue to grow through the process of making films. I think in fact it's not so much the director who makes the film as the film that makes the director."

↓ Okaeri
おかえり

1995. CAST: Susumu Terajima, Miho Uemura, Shōichi Komatsu, Tomio Aoki. 96 minutes. RELEASE: VHS, K Films (France, French subtitles).

Powerful and earnest portrayal of a young marriage straining under the wife's mental illness. The debut feature of former film critic Shinozaki sets the tone for late-'90s independent Japanese cinema.

Takashi and Yuriko are like any other young couple. He is a high school teacher, while she takes care of the household chores and holds a job on the side transcribing audio recordings for a publishing house. Their marriage follows the traditional model: Yuriko has given up a promising career as a concert pianist in favor of family life (and still laments the decision), Takashi stays out until late every day, spending his time after work with his colleagues rather than with his wife. Though dinners regularly go cold and the look on his wife's face is far from happy, Takashi remains oblivious to the feelings of abandonment he inflicts on Yuriko.

As a result, he fails to notice the gradual changes in his wife's personality. Yuriko has regularly been leaving the house on uncharacteristic walks, claiming she must "go on patrol" to protect the neighborhood from a conspiracy by "the organization" (an idea later swiped by Kiyoshi Kurosawa for *Cure*). When he realizes his wife might suffer from mental illness, Takashi is at a loss, feeling confused and above all ashamed. He stealthily visits the psychology section of a bookstore to read up on schizophrenia and carefully hides the book he buys there from his colleagues. When on one of her patrols Yuriko steals a car and almost kills herself and her husband in the ensuing chase, he finally takes her to a hospital, where she is indeed diagnosed with schizophrenia.

Though it might be argued that the point Makoto Shinozaki tries to make is that the male-dominated society of Japan is in itself an organization intent on conspiring against women like Yuriko, the director doesn't condemn the situation. Rather, he presents it as a given, showing the consequences of it in order for the audience to draw their own conclusions (an approach also employed in his next fiction film *Not Forgotten*). Even in the portrayal of Takashi, he is surprisingly mild. Takashi is presented as a man who could perhaps be blamed for many things, but not for not loving his wife. He is just a product of the society he lives in and when circumstances call for it, he does manage to break with what is imposed on him and lets himself be guided by his love for Yuriko.

Shinozaki's debut *Okaeri* (the traditional greeting to welcome someone home) is shot in static, fixed shots. Though the director has cited the reason for this as being time and cost (he privately financed the film and shot it on leftover film stock donated by Swiss direc-

© 1995 Comteg

Okaeri

tor Daniel Schmid), this method proves to be very effective. Combining with the pale lighting and subdued color scheme, it presents an image of suburban life which is rather downbeat and cold, serving well to intensify the circumstances of Yuriko's mental deterioration.

This method of shooting also allows the actors

a lot of room for excellent, semi-improvisational performances. The sequence of Takashi trying to comfort his wife while she has locked herself in the bathroom is representative of the tone of the entire film, which treats the subject of mental illness with a rare degree of earnestness and care. Its ambivalent open ending adheres to this, refusing to give a clear-cut solution or take the easy route by presenting a false happy end.

Truthful, touching, and thoroughly well-made, *Okaeri* deservedly won a slew of prizes at film festivals around the world, launching Shinozaki into the vanguard of Japan's young filmmakers.

↓ Not Forgotten

忘れられぬ人々
Wasurerarenu Hitobito

2000. CAST: Tatsuya Mihashi, Minoru Ōki, Tomio Aoki, Keiko Utsumi, Masumi Sanada, Masashi Endō, Nao Ōmori. 120 minutes. RELEASE: DVD, Taki Corporation (Japan, no subtitles).

Shinozaki's second feature runs the gamut of emotions, while not forgetting to deliver a strong dose of social criticism at the same time. A tribute to old age in general and its three veteran lead actors in particular.

A joyful celebration of life and old age, *Not Forgotten* is a film that is by turns tender, funny, thought-provoking, and shocking. Three veterans of World War II symbolize the zest for life that contemporary society not so much lacks, but simply fails to see, caught up as it is in careers and the haste of day-to-day life.

The three veterans are Kijima (Mihashi), Itō (Aoki), and Murata (Ōki). Murata does his best to run a small restaurant while his ailing wife is in hospital. Kijima leads a quiet life, the guilt over the death of his wartime comrade Kanayama still hanging over him. He treasures the harmonica that used to belong to his fallen

friend. Itō finally has an unbeatable love for life, particularly after he falls in love with an elderly lady from his neighborhood. While his daughter and granddaughter hole themselves up inside the house watching TV, Itō is outside smelling flowers and taking strolls.

One day, Itō visits Kijima to invite him to a veterans' reunion, an event Kijima normally shuns. Hearing that Kanayama's granddaughter Yuriko, a young nurse who takes care of Murata's wife, will be at the reunion, he finally agrees. He sees it as a chance to finally hand the harmonica to its rightful heir. The reunion turns out to be a joyous night, despite the girl's refusal to accept the gesture, feeling the instrument should stay with Kijima. Aside from being a reunion, the gathering is also a celebration, since Yuriko's boyfriend, Hitoshi, has just started a new job at a corporation called Utopia and looks forward to this new phase in his life.

But we soon discover that this job trains him for deception, as the company's aim is to cheat the elderly out of their savings. Hitoshi refuses to see the evil he is being made to do and wants nothing more than to become a fully accepted member of this corporate society. Then Itō's neighbor and subsequently Murata fall victim to the scheme. When he sees his bride-to-be withering under the strain, Itō decides to take drastic action, but gets himself killed when he attacks a Utopia manager with a knife. When Yuriko comes clean about the activities of the Utopia Corporation to Kijima and Murata, the two veteran soldiers decide to fight once again and avenge their fallen comrade.

Makoto Shinozaki's choice to combine his humanistic portrait with a strongly fictional element in the guise of the morally corrupt, sect-like corporation, seems jarring at first but ends up an inspired move. Most significantly, the corporation's methods reflect those of Japan's wartime regime: reinterpreting the past to suit its own needs (the young recruits are shown endless instruction videos that hammer on about "the spirit of Japan") and subjecting its subordinates to the regimentary discipline of a military boot camp. The three veteran soldiers know the truth about Japan's past, however, as well as the destructive consequences of such leadership, whether it's by a government or corporate management. The aged are the watchdogs of history, and when the young won't (or can't) listen they need to stand up and take action themselves.

It also adds a lot of dimension to *Not Forgotten*, making it not only a film about the relationship between old and young, but also an exploration of how the old can have a function in guiding the young on the path to adulthood. In this respect, the film echoes Sam Peckinpah's *Ride the High Country* (1963), one of Shinozaki's all-time favorite films, in which a pair of retired gunfighters take on a group of younger bandits and turn the young hothead in their company into a man of courage.

Not Forgotten additionally poses questions about work ethics and the level of loyalty and allegiance corporate life demands of employees, concerns which were also present in **Okaeri**. This is particularly tangible in that the recruitment program of Utopia seems geared at teenagers who, once enrolled into the corporate structure, are deprived of the chance to discover more about life around them. They, like the elderly they are taught to deceive, are impressionable and thus weak and easy prey. It's not surprising that when the strong unite end Utopia's devious practices it crumbles to dust.

Though on the surface *Not Forgotten* may seem to be a nostalgic work, its message is definitely one of hope and progress, as witnessed by the three lead characters. Their lust for life is carried over to the younger generations to whom they are so open. Symbolic in this sense is the harmonica Kijima carries with him. It eventually serves to remind him that this life should be lived, not spent moping and pondering about the past. When he and his friend Murata go off to fight the corporation, he passes the instrument on to the (half American) little boy that often comes to

© 2001 Bitter's End

Not Forgotten

play in his garden. Their sacrifice is not only for their own comrade, but also for the sake of the generations that will outlive them.

Not Forgotten does not relate to one subject, but rather to a multitude of things we should remember to honor and appreciate. Not forgotten should be the aged, the fallen comrades, the deeds of the past, and the beauty that life continues to give us. And finally, not forgotten should be veteran actors Tatsuya Mihashi, Minoru Ōki, and Tomio Aoki, and Japan's cinematic legacy, which is sometimes overshadowed by feverish attempts to churn out new product. This film is perhaps Shinozaki's humble attempt at cherishing part of his nation's celluloid legacy and a call for others to do the same. The director's passion shines through on every level, resulting in a film full of love for its characters and the lives they lead.

CHAPTER 14

Hirokazu Kore-eda

是枝裕和

Although he is seen as the quintessential example of today's independent Japanese filmmaker, the career path of Hirokazu Kore-eda has been an entirely different one from that walked by the majority of his contemporaries. The devout cinephilia that motivated people like Makoto Shinozaki, Akihiko Shiota, and Shinji Aoyama to start experimenting with 8mm short films in college or even earlier, expressed itself in a different way with Kore-eda. Despite a voracious appetite for watching films and reading scripts, Kore-eda wouldn't touch a camera until 1991, at age 29, a mere four years before his debut feature.

His ambition as a teenager was to become a novelist and it wasn't until after entering Tokyo's Waseda University that cinema came to dominate his interests. Content simply to watch films and read scripts, Kore-eda never joined the university film club, a decision that was indicative of his later idiosyncratic career trajectory, which would be characterized by an enterprising individuality and a detached, studious approach to the art form.

In 1987, fresh out of university and with a desire to, as he told Aaron Gerow in an interview for the magazine *Documentary Box*, "work with images," Kore-eda ignored both the collapsed studio system and independent filmmaking and joined TV Man Union, a television production company known for its challenging and experimental documentary work from the 1960s. But upon his entry, he found that most of TV Man Union's production slate was taken up by run-of-the-mill programs and that the directors responsible for the experimental work Kore-eda admired had long been promoted away from the production floor.

Largely as a result of this disappointment, he reluctantly settled into a role as assistant director, a job he now admits he wasn't very good at. His disillusion with the unchallenging programs he worked on drove him to pursue his own filmmaking interests, and while pretending to be at the library for research, he sneaked off to make his own documentary—on the boss's time and entirely by himself. The result, *Lessons From a Calf* (1991), documented a class of elementary school children collectively raising a cow. Though made while sneaking off from work, the documentary made such an impression on Kore-eda's superiors at TV Man Union that they quickly promoted him to the status of director, something that was unlikely to have happened on the basis of his meager achievements as an assistant.

He was now in a position to make the kind of experimental and challenging films that he had been hoping to work on when he joined the company. His first official production for TV Man Union, that same year, saw him very conscientiously approaching the aspect of form in filmmaking. *However*...investigated the case of a high-ranking civil servant's suicide and its connections with the cover-up of a pollution scandal. The documentary featured interviews with the subject's widow, a woman who had previously been harassed by the media even during her husband's funeral. Careful to avoid sensationalising the subject or using the grieving wife as a weapon in an ideological battle, Kore-eda took great care over the editing and camerawork, painstakingly trying to prevent any misleading suggestions or insinuations that might arise from the form of the work.

In the three years that followed, Kore-eda directed five additional documentaries, with subjects ranging from the life of an AIDS patient who gives lectures as a way to support his treatment to a portrait of Taiwanese filmmakers Hou Hsiao-Hsien and Edward Yang. The TV production regime, which essentially boils down to filling time slots, allowed him to further expand his technical and formal experimentations within an environment of almost constant production, a situation that resembled that of filmmakers like Kiyoshi Kurosawa, who gained invaluable experience and opportunities to experiment while toiling away on the V-cinema production line.

© 2001 TV Man Union

Hirokazu Kore-eda

"It certainly was a time in which I matured a lot and I'm putting those experiences very much to work now. I really can't speak for other people, since I don't know about their situations, but it seems like Kiyoshi Kurosawa for instance did a lot of experimenting in his V-cine films. The documentaries I made were TV programs, so there were particular restrictions about what could and couldn't be done. In that

Filmography

1991
- *Lessons from a Calf* (*Mō Hitotsu no Kyōiku—Ina Shōgakkō Haru Gumi no Kiroku*) [TV]
- *However...* (*Shikashi... Fukushi Kirisute no Jidai ni*) [TV]

1992
- *Nihonjin ni Narita Katta* [TV]

1993
- *Shinshō Suketchi—Sorezore no Miyazawa Kenji* [TV]
- *Yottsu no Shibu Jikoku* [TV]

- *Eiga ga Jidai o Utsusu Toki—Hou Hsiao Hsien to Edward Yang* [TV]

1994
- *August without Him* (*Kare no Inai Hachigatsu Ga—Aids o Seigen Shita Hirata Yutaka Ninenkan no Seikatsu Kiroku*) [TV]

1995
- *Maborosi* (*Maboroshi no Hikari*)

1996
- *This World* (*Arawashiyo*) [co-directed with Naomi Kawase]

1997
- *Without Memory* (*Kioku ga Ushinawareta Toki*)

1998
- *After Life* (*Wandafuru Raifu*)

2001
- *Distance*

2003
- *Kaette Kita Deka Matsuri* [co-director]

2004
- *Nobody Knows* (*Dare Mo Shiranai*)

© 2001 TV Man Union

Distance

sense there probably is a time in a filmmaker's life when it's good to be making a lot under certain prescribed conditions."

In addition to his directorial chores, Kore-eda also wrote his first book, an account of the research he had done into the suicide case that formed the subject of *However*.... His involvement in the case would also have a great effect on his first fiction feature, which dealt with a woman trying to cope with the unexplained suicide of her husband. *Maborosi* (1995) was in many ways as meticulously planned on a formal level as the documentary that inspired it. In attempting to express the emotions and feelings of his protagonist Yumiko (Makiko Esumi), Kore-eda carefully used (natural) light and darkness, sound effects, and shot composition, intentionally avoiding facial expressions as a way to convey those emotions. The film was praised by many for its visual beauty and after an extended festival run it received a limited release in American cinemas, to largely rave reviews.

The festival success of his debut feature did two things for Kore-eda. Firstly, it brought him into contact with fellow filmmaker Naomi Kawase, who also had a background in documentary filmmaking, albeit of a more personal nature, making numerous short films on 8mm with her own family and environment as subjects. The

two decided to collaborate on a project that would be entitled *This World*, a series of 8mm film correspondences between the two directors intended for a film exhibition held by the Yokohama Museum of Modern Art.

"I was at the Yamagata film festival with her. One of her 8mm films was showing there and I had never made an 8mm film before. She asked me if I would like to make a movie with her, so we made a one-hour film in 1996."

Secondly, Kore-eda suddenly saw himself launched into the limelight, lumped together with a group of fellow Japanese filmmakers that included Makoto Shinozaki, Shinji Aoyama, Nobuhiro Suwa, and the aforementioned Naomi Kawase. All of them arriving with their independently made debut features in the second half of the 1990s, the media and festivals were quick to pronounce these young hopefuls a 'New Japanese New Wave,' pointing somewhat vaguely to similarities in themes, concerns and stylistic approaches in their work, and misleadingly suggesting the existence of a movement.

"I guess we come from the generation that never apprenticed at a movie studio, we're all in our late thirties, and we all started showing up at film festivals in the late '90s. So maybe it's inevitable. But we are all quite different. I think all those people would violently deny that they have anything in common with each other. When I saw Kiyoshi Kurosawa in Cannes, I asked him how he felt about being described as part of a Japanese *nouvelle* Nouvelle Vague. And he said that all of those in the French Nouvelle Vague were completely idiosyncratic individuals who didn't think of themselves as a group, but only appeared as a group to outsiders. So you might as well take advantage of the fact that somebody thinks that something big is happening."

The media attention certainly did not hurt

Kore-eda himself or his films. Festivals fell over themselves to screen the films of this supposed movement, recalling the fever for Japanese films that swept Europe's major festivals in the 1950s after the Golden Lion in Venice for Akira Kurosawa's *Rashomon*. Kore-eda's second feature *After Life* was almost naturally swept up in this craze and again went on to garner numerous international distribution deals. This time, though, the interest went a few steps further, with Hollywood studio 20th Century Fox buying the rights for an American remake and Kore-eda pocketing a good amount of the proceeds.

Set at a halfway station between the world of the living and the realm of the dead, *After Life* follows a small group of supernatural "caseworkers" whose job it is to prepare the souls of the recently deceased for their passage to the spirit world. Each deceased is asked to choose his or her fondest memory from life, a memory which is then re-enacted and recorded on film for its subject to retain and relive for eternity.

After Life is in many ways the quintessential Kore-eda film. It is infused with numerous concerns and themes that the director has dealt with in his life and career as a filmmaker, the most central being a fascination with memory, the relationship between past and present, and the documentation or recording of events on camera. Despite its extremely fictional setting (or perhaps because of it), the correlation between fact and fiction is one of the central premises of the film, both on a thematic and on a stylistic level. One of the characters in the film notes that the re-enactment of his memory is merely a surrogate that can never replace the actual event, and that the caseworkers' jobs are therefore completely futile, a statement that witnessed Kore-eda's reflective stance towards his own art form. Additionally, the film's narrative is regularly interrupted by documentary footage of people being interviewed about the memories of their own past.

"I hope that, if anything, my films can break down some of the fences that have been arti-

Maborosi

ficially created to distinguish between fiction and documentary. I hope my movies can be like fence-sitters because those fences are actually quite artificially constructed and not very stable. I think that both *After Life* and *Distance* have really explored those questions."

If its execution defied any compatibility with Hollywood filmmaking methods, *After Life*'s central premise of the dead reliving their fondest memories before moving on to the hereafter held the kind of high concept potential that goes down well with studio executives. Amy Heckerling, director of *Clueless*, *Fast Times at Ridgemont High*, and *Look Who's Talking*, was drafted to take the directorial reins and Kore-eda himself was consulted in the early stages of the project, but a result has so far failed to materialize.

"In the summer of 2000 I went to 20th Century Fox and they asked me for various opinions of what the remake should look like. Then I believe they wrote a screenplay but the director slated to direct it didn't like the screenplay, so she rewrote it herself. So then she asked me some more questions, which I answered and that's all."

Much as in the way *Maborosi* was inspired by the experience of one of his previous documentaries, the central element in *After Life* was carried over from a documentary about a man with short-term memory loss that Kore-eda had made a year earlier, entitled *Without Memory*. And in turn, *After Life* itself inspired Kore-eda's next film *Distance*, in which he blurred the lines between documentary and fiction even further. Also harking back to *Maborosi*'s investigation into surviving the loss of a loved one, *Distance* told the tale of four people with one thing in common: they all had a relative who died in a massacre perpetrated by a religious cult. In a quest to learn more about the circumstances of their deaths, and also to find solace in shared grief, the four embark on a trek into the forest that was once home to the sect. There they run into one of the cult's former members, who, like them, wishes to come to terms with his own past.

With a cast that included *After Life*'s Susumu Terajima, Arata, and Yūsuke Iseya, and *Maborosi*'s Tadanobu Asano, Kore-eda made improvisation a central part of the filmmaking process, employing the method of keeping his actors in the dark about the motivations and direction he had given to each of them. Often given conflicting information, the actors were forced to improvise when they realized their scripts weren't compatible with those of the others.

> "I started out on *Distance* with just the actors from *After Life* and no script. I would give them a situation and a kind of character background, and then the emotions, the response, and the language would emerge from the actors. So that came first. As the plot grew, I decided to make the characters surviving family members of the perpetrators of some kind of religious cult disaster. So that element definitely came later.
>
> "I wasn't specifically influenced or inspired by anything, but in general, in terms of direction I would say John Cassavetes more than anything else, that spirit of his films. I think it's wonderful the way he worked with actors to evoke different kinds of expression. I think it's fairly easy to do something like *The Blair Witch Project*, where you scare actors into screaming. I think that's pretty simple. It's much more challenging for a director to try to figure out a way to get an actor to generate natural emotions. Whether or not you use other actors to do it or whether it's just me. I think that's a separate challenge and that's what I enjoyed about it.
>
> "But I think it must be taxing for actors, since they don't have a full script. I'm sure they were nervous about doing it, but for the most part they enjoyed it. Especially Arata and Yūsuke Iseya, whose first experience of working on a film was *After Life*, where they also did a lot of improvisation. For them it was natural. The one person who had never worked with anything other than scripted dialogue was Yui Natsukawa. She needed some work in the rehearsals to get to a point where she could come up with language that wasn't scripted. It was really interesting to watch her grow and be able to express herself in non-scripted language. It was very challenging and rewarding."

With handheld cameras recording the more or less spontaneous actions of the cast, *Distance* came as close as a fiction film could to being a documentary.

> "It partly depends on what your definition of a documentary is, but if you define a documentary as a record on camera of self-generated emotions and expressions from a subject, then certainly yes, *Distance* is a documentary. But the big difference is that the premise is entirely fictional."

But as warm and genuinely entertaining as *After Life* had been, *Distance*, despite portraying an abundance of emotional crises, came across as aloof, detached, and indeed distant. The film felt like the product of a director who put experimentation first and the need to deliver a cohesive film second. Kore-eda himself, however, felt that there were points he wanted to raise to his viewers.

"I think it may be a universal modern condition, but certainly in Japan people don't believe in God. There aren't any clear values and there's a great deal of ambivalence about living modern life. I was very clear about why I made this movie. I wanted to pose a question to the people who saw the film, ask them to re-evaluate and re-investigate how to deal with that very complex challenge of living modern life. I didn't make it to entertain people, or for people to come out of the movie theater and say, 'That was fun, let's go have something to eat.'"

As he had done in the past, Kore-eda documented the experience of making his film in the form of a book. In fact, for the years that followed *Distance*, the director would concentrate on writing. Even his position as a teacher of documentary filmmaking at the Film School of Tokyo he used as a way to research a book project. For Kore-eda, who wishes to pull down what he sees as artificial boundaries between documentary and fiction, the literary form is as effective, powerful, and valid a tool as cinema in achieving his goals.

"I think that all my work is in some way deeply connected somewhere, but precisely because I don't try to rigidly define what is fiction and what is non-fiction, in writing or in images, because I leave that so loose, I have to sort of re-invent the definitions each time I take on a project. That's what makes it challenging."

↓ After Life

ワンダフルライフ

Wandafuru Raifu, a.k.a. Wonderful Life

1998. CAST: Arata, Erika Oda, Susumu Terajima, Takashi Naitō, Kyōko Kagawa, Kei Tani, Taketoshi Naitō, Tōru Yuri, Yūsuke Iseya. 118 minutes. RELEASES: DVD, New Yorker (U.S., English subtitles), Bandai Visual (Japan, English subtitles).

Set in a gloomy way station between this world and the next, a group of people are made to select their most precious memories to relive for all eternity in a heaven of their own making. A masterful dissection of emotion, memory, reality, and imagination.

A derelict school building surrounded by dead autumnal leaves with the walls crawling with dead ivy serves as a halfway house between the worlds of the living and the dead. This bureaucratic purgatory, filled with dark, musty corridors penetrated by shafts of light, is where the newly deceased are greeted every Monday morning by a staff of "counselors" consigned with the task of aiding their passing guests to find their own personal vision of heaven.

The week's intake are given their own private rooms and three days to chose their most meaningful and precious memories. This memory will then be recreated on film by the counselors to be screened in front of everyone before they are finally allowed to pass onto the other side where they will forget everything except their chosen moment, to be relived over and over again at the expense of all other memories.

With his debut *Maborosi*, Kore-eda more or less single-handedly brought about the birth of the arthouse genre in Japan in the mid-'90s. A slow-moving, meditative, and naturalistically shot piece in which the drama is secondary to the emotional impact, it is easy to forget what a landmark film *Maborosi* was, given the rash of similarly styled works from directors such as Naomi Kawase and Nobuhiro Suwa that followed it.

But whilst *Maborosi*'s tale of a young woman trying to forge a new life for herself and her young son after the mysterious suicide of her husband seems consciously modeled in the same mold as the work of internationally renowned arthouse directors like Theo Angelopoulos and Hou Hsiao-Hsien, Kore-eda's follow-up is a genuinely unique film, whose greatest asset lies in its singularly ingenious premise.

Released under the katakana-ized title

© 2001 TV Man Union

After Life

Wonderful Life in Japan, Kore-eda wisely chose to rename his film for its overseas releases in order to avoid associations with Frank Capra's *It's a Wonderful Life* (1946). With the characters of both reassessing the incidents that have made up their time on the planet from their divine vantage points within the film, the thematic similarities are obvious. But whereas Capra's film represents the archetypal life-affirming Hollywood narrative, with James Stewart coming to realize that in the turbulent tragicomedy of life, it is he who plays the leading role, Kore-eda's view is all the more humanistic and down to earth.

Firstly, with over twenty new intakes to the *After Life* way station, no single person is allowed to take center stage at the expense of others. Moreover, Kore-eda dwells on nuance and the little details rather than sweeping emotional arcs, resulting in a pathos and identification with the characters that no dramatic contrivance can emulate.

The bulk of the film is taken up by the counseling sessions, which are shot as if they were job interviews, as each of the guests delivers his or her recollections facing the camera with occasional questioning or prompting from the counselor occurring offscreen. This stark approach reminds us that Kore-eda's background lies in documentary, and that the very genesis of *After Life* came during the making of two nonfiction works touching on similar themes: *Without Memory*, about a man who due to a medical mishap is left unable to form new memories, and *August without Him*, in which a dying AIDS victim tries to assemble the most important memories from the last year and a half of his life onto a video (Naomi Kawase's *Letter from a Yellow Cherry Blossom* was similar in subject, though it took a different approach). In researching the film, Kore-eda interviewed a large number of people, and some of these non-actors appear in the film alongside the professionals, though you would be hard-pressed to tell whose memories are real and whose are not.

After Life trades on the notion that it is our memories that make us what we are, and even those living the most mundane of routines have something inside that they treasure. One woman recalls being reunited with her lover after the war. A simple meal is enough for one elderly war veteran, as he recalls stumbling across a grove of coconuts and bananas in the jungle after spending days without food and water, only to be encircled by a troop of American soldiers, all bristling with guns. Figuring he is going to die anyway, he requests a cigarette and some food and is amazed when the enemy soldiers lead him back to base camp and grant his request, feeding him a delicious meal of chicken and rice. Kore-eda humorously follows this tale with a high school girl's description of a day out at Disneyland, where, unable to afford a pancake, a friend offers her one of hers before they head off together for a ride on Splash Mountain.

Others have a hard time remembering anything salient about their lives at all. Yamamoto, an austere middle-aged man in a black suit, proclaims he only has bad memories. When pursued to choose a favorite, he regresses back to his childhood secret hiding place, a dark cupboard filled with junk.

Kore-eda shows us that our view of the past, and indeed who we are, is largely dependant on our position in time, which in this case is the point of death. A ponderous old man with a goatee and glasses, Watanabe, seems barely alive as he looks back from the point where death has caught up with him. With no children and no hobbies, after an entire life spent behind a desk at a large steel corporation since graduation, he finds himself with no memories to choose from.

In order to jog him, his counselor Mochizuki (Arata, later seen in the crowd pleasing *Ping Pong*, 2002) breaks with regulations and grants him access to a video archive of his life, with one cassette for each of his 71 years of existence. As he looks back and reassesses key moments from his own life story, his blank face is intercut with the hazy video images, viewing the material with a third-person detachment: an agitated student ranting about wanting to be remembered for doing just that one thing to change Japan rather than spending his life rotting in a company office, a stumbling candlelit dinner conversation with a beautiful woman who later becomes his wife, a touching conversation with that same spouse from the autumn of his years. Like Ernst Lubitsch's *Heaven Can Wait* (1943), these glimpses into his past life are made all the more poignant given their inevitable trajectory.

His situation is juxtaposed with that of a defiant young man named Iseya, played by Yūsuke Iseya, whose own directorial debut *Kakuto* (2003), a spirited depiction of a wild aimless night of a group of youths bombed out on drugs, was later produced by Kore-eda. Obviously annoyed at being forced in the position of having to choose the best moment of his life prematurely, he steadfastly refuses to select just one exclusive incident.

Aside from the images on Watanabe's videos, we are never shown the individual memories as they are recounted by the characters, just the expressions and responses of the interviewees as they are delivered. One old dear gazes vacantly out of the window, unresponsive to the question she is posed. One man chuckles, reminiscing over his days of whoring, but for whose benefit are these stories intended, and what basis do they have in truth? As one lady is picked up on an inconsistency in her tale by one of the counselors, we are shown that often our memories do not gel with reality, and either consciously or unconsciously, our views of our past can often amount to little more than mere personal fictional creations.

Kore-eda takes this idea one step further in the film's later stages when the counselors are shown during the stages of reconstructing these memories, discussing production details such as sounds and color balance. But how possible is it to recreate these experiences accurately in a convincing concrete, external form? The intentionally cheap-looking sound stages where the memories are to be filmed seem unlikely to convince anyone, yet alone the holders of these original experiences.

This idea of the difficulties in recreating subjective experience is but one of many aspects of Kore-eda's tantalizing work. As a new week begins and a new batch of visitors arrive, there is another way of looking at the role of the counselors, day in day out, trapped in a limbo of their own volition. Rather than take the plunge and choose their own happiness, they have opted to observe and act out other people's dreams. The cinematic metaphor is just one of the dazzling multitude of facets *After Life* reveals upon repeated viewings, making it one of the most intriguing, absorbing and humanistic works of art cinema of the decade, from any country.

CHAPTER 15

Shinji Aoyama
青山真治

Shinji Aoyama is a difficult figure to place within the context of the last decade of Japanese filmmaking. Kicking off his career with a series of films that ostensibly seem to fit snugly within their established genres, be they gangster, horror, or romance, Aoyama himself stresses that his background is firmly entrenched within commercial cinema. This is perhaps an odd comment from a man who, outside of Japan at least, is best known for *Eureka*, a film that runs over three and a half hours in length, is in black and white, and charts the slow emotional healing process of the three survivors of a random bus hijacking incident.

A trawl through Aoyama's back catalogue perhaps better reveals where he's coming from. From his "youth on the rampage" theatrical debut *Helpless* in 1996, through the noir-ish police thriller *An Obsession*, the gory B-movie horror of *Embalming*, and the romantic drama of *Shady Grove*, Aoyama's films certainly slot well into their relevant pigeon holes in terms of their commercial format. Yet, marked out by a thematic ambition that effectively twists the concept of genre inside out on itself and aspiring to so much more than safe, neatly packaged pieces of escapism tied up with a tidy self-affirming sense of narrative closure, they hardly fit into any commercial landscape of the time when they were made. Throughout his early

work, one can detect a continuous accumulation of concepts and concerns that reach critical mass in *Eureka*, his film most obviously targeted at the arthouse market.

Still, it is this commercial background, he asserts, that sets him apart from other more obvious practitioners of art cinema such as Naomi Kawase, Nobuhiro Suwa, or Hirokazu Koreeda, with whom Aoyama has often been lumped together as part of a vanguard of directors who were seen to represent a New Wave of Japanese cinema during the late '90s. If there is any perceivable common ground between these names, it is the fact that they are all roughly of the same age, all began appearing at film festivals together at around the same time, and (with the exception of Kore-eda) have all at some time or other fallen under the patronage of producer Takenori Sentō, whose company, Suncent Cinema Works, eagerly courted the foreign art cinema market and thus ensured a higher profile abroad for these names.

One other thing that links Aoyama to these directors is that they all, in their own different ways, have come to be spokespeople for their generation, a generation whose formative college years were spent during the bubble decade of the '80s only to have the rug cruelly snatched from under their feet when the bubble burst. This is a generation who can be accurately described as the last generation of idealists, and if one year can be said to mark the dividing gap, it would be 1989, the year in which, on January 7, the Shōwa Emperor Hirohito died.

As a symbolic post-war figurehead, Hirohito had led the country from the rubble of defeat, through the mass industrialization of the '60s, to being one of the world's greatest economies. Japan had changed immutably since Hirohito's accession in 1926. Leaving a huge mark on the psyches of the modern Japanese, his death was something more than just a national tragedy. It represented the collapse of an ideology—the nation as family with the Shōwa Emperor as its inscrutable patriarch. His son and heir, Akihito, has proven almost imperceptible in comparison, more low-key and down to earth, and somehow less relevant to a modern nation. His role compromised by the demands of a twenty-first century media, Akihito has retreated to the sidelines, symbolically leaving a generation adrift without a father figure.

Many have observed this subsequent void, which has run concurrently with the sharp downturn in Japan's economic fortunes. It permeates heavily throughout Aoyama's first film, *Helpless*, in which a young man is released from jail and returns to his hometown in search of his missing yakuza boss, whilst his father lies terminally ill and bedridden in hospital. Utilizing a style that is both austere and spare to invoke a powerful sensation of emptiness and thinly concealed yearning at the heart of contemporary Japan, Aoyama portrays a bleak, loveless society populated by alienated youths, listless wanderers, and outsiders unable to communicate their frustration through any other means than violence.

Too many people had been marginalized in the huge accumulation of wealth of the bubble years. The slow, steady rise of the '80s, followed by its subsequent collapse, effectively left many trapped outside the system, analogous with the pathetic figures of Michio and Yōichi, the "*Chinpira*" or ***Two Punks*** of Aoyama's film of the same name. A slightly lighter work than its predecessor, *Chinpira* is more a buddy movie than a yakuza one. Its two hapless protagonists are merely errand boys for Ryō Ishibashi's tattooed gangster boss. Unable and unwilling to commit themselves on a full-time basis, they play-act the tough guys. It's only when they attempt to cross this dividing line that they fall afoul of the mob.

Such rapid modernization had left a country all but cut off from its roots, and people began to turn to anything outside to cling to. One of the results was a growth in membership of obscure religious sects, a phenomenon that reached an illogical conclusion with the sarin gas attacks on the Tokyo subway in 1995 by the Aum cult. An errant religious group pops up in the gory

Filmography

1995
- *Kyōkasho ni Nai!* [video]

1996
- *A Cop, a Bitch and a Killer (Waga Mune ni Kyōki Ari)* [video]
- *Helpless*
- *Two Punks (Chinpira)*

1997
- *Wild Life (Wild Life: Jump into the Dark)*

1998
- *An Obsession (Tsumetai Chi)*

1999
- *June 12, 1998: The Edge of Chaos (Kaosu no Fuchi)*
- *Embalming (Embāmingu)*
- *Shady Grove*

2000
- *Eureka (Yuriika)*
- *To the Alley (Roji e: Nakagami Kenji no Nokoshita Fuirumu)*

2001
- *Desert Moon (Tsuki no Sabaku)*

2002
- *Sude ni Oita Kanojo no Subete ni Tsuite wa Kataranu Tame ni*
- *A Forest with No Name (Shiritsu Tantei Hama Maiku: Namae no Nai Mori)*

2003
- *Cop Festival (Deka Matsuri)* [co-director]
- *Ajimaa no Uta: Uehara Tomoko Tenjō no Utagoe*

2004
- *Lakeside Murder Case (Reikusaido Mādākēsu)*

Embalming, and *An Obsession* uses a similar backdrop in a film based around the same premise of Akira Kurosawa's *Stray Dog*, in this case featuring a terminally ill cult member who performs a string of random homicides using a pistol stolen from a detective, gunned down in action during the arrest of the cult's leader.

> **"*Stray Dog* might not be the greatest of Kurosawa's films, but it portrays the post-war period and the people that lived in it very vividly. It's a poignant film that isolates and portrays the atmosphere of the time strongly—the helplessness, disorientation, and loss of direction—so in that respect it is a great film. When I shot *An Obsession* I felt that the zeitgeist of Japan was very similar to this post-war period, in that we were facing a danger which we hadn't faced in ten or twenty years, which had manifested itself in the sarin gas attacks of 1995. Something very strange was happening in Japan which we couldn't quite put our fingers on. I wanted to use this raw feeling from *Stray Dog* in my film too."**

Aoyama clearly sees cinema as a medium in which to present an alternate world, one that effectively holds up a mirror to modern society. Superficially, nothing seems different, but there are occasional cracks in the surface details which hint that something is awry. The radiation-suited enforcers of a government curfew remain extraneous to the main narrative in *An Obsession*, only highlighting that this is not really modern-day Tokyo, but in all other respects, it could be. More subtle details hint at this in the romantic drama *Shady Grove*. In one scene a character dates his resignation letter in the Japanese format as Shōwa 74: the Shōwa period ended in Shōwa 64 with Hirohito's death, so 1999 would be Heisei 11.

> **"I wanted to show it is as if the Shōwa era was still going on, and again, there might be people running around in radiation suits off-screen too."**

Stylistically Aoyama's films fit into a similar terrain as that of his mentor, Kiyoshi Kurosawa. Slow, meditative, and sometimes maddeningly oblique, they effectively deny the pleasures one expects from standard genre pieces, and yet at the same time, their deviations from their template bringing to light more metaphysical notions about the nature of cinema and its relationship to reality. Continually probing the question, "What is a movie?" they work from the basis that technical and thematic concerns are ultimately inextricably linked.

Aoyama first met Kurosawa whilst he was a student at Rikkyō University in Tokyo, belonging to a cinema club whose other members included Makoto Shinozaki, Akihito Shiota, and Kunitoshi Manda. They studied under scholar and critic Shigehiko Hasumi, who was significant for spearheading a whole new approach to cinema criticism in the late '70s and early '80s, and this new way of looking at cinema and interpreting it had already had a large effect on Kurosawa. When the future director of *Cure* visited their club as a guest speaker, he immediately proved a decisive influence on the younger students.

Prompted by a friend at high school, Aoyama had been experimenting with the 8mm format prior to this meeting, and was still feeling around in the dark, discovering the various tricks, techniques, and methodologies utilized in professional filmmaking. The early '80s represented a time when the Japanese film industry seemed closed off to newcomers, and the idea of making films such as the Hollywood blockbusters on which he'd been weaned seemed like an impossible dream. After entering college, however, Aoyama first encountered the films of Jean-Luc Godard, whose punkish improvisational energy and freshness proved an inspiration. In the meantime, Sōgo Ishii had just started making a stir on the independent circuit.

> **"My feeling was that there wasn't that much of a leap from the type of films my friend was**

shooting on 8mm to Godard. *Apocalypse Now* might have been impossible for me to shoot, but this sort of thing was well within my grasp. Looking back, it was a little cocky of me, but it's what I thought at the time."

Aoyama's initial explorations in filmmaking were mainly intellectual, to satisfy his burgeoning curiosity regarding such questions as what goes on behind the scenes on a movie and how are films constructed. At the time, he never imagined himself making a career as a film director. However, his developing close friendship with Kurosawa led to assistant director work on the director's low-budget slasher movie *The Guard from Underground* (1992), the gangster comedy *Yakuza Taxi* (1993), and the first two films in the **Suit Yourself or Shoot Yourself!** series (1995). Whilst also a regular contributor of essays and reviews to the publication *Cahiers du Cinéma Japan*, Aoyama worked on the script of pink director Takahisa Zeze's ethereal *The Dream of Garuda* (*Kōkyō Sōpu Tekunikku 4 Monzetsuhigi*, 1994) and worked as an assistant director on both Gō Rijū's *Berlin* (1995) and Icelandic director Fridrik Thór Fridriksson's cult classic *Cold Fever* (1994).

This latter film also featured a small acting role by the veteran director Seijun Suzuki, whose non-conformist approach to cinema and outlandish body of work had already struck a chord with Aoyama as a young film fan. Aoyama later cast Suzuki in *Embalming* as the assistant at the EM embalming studio where the main character plies her trade.

> "When Suzuki appeared in *Embalming* he was in his seventies, but he had no problem in moving around like an actor much younger than he was. There were times when I wondered if he would be able to do what I asked of him, but I never had to even ask him. He'd just go ahead and do it. He's incredibly young. Maybe it's because he's the type of man who can make movies such as his that keeps him so young."

Kyōkasho ni Nai! [trans: Not in the textbook!] officially marked Aoyama's directorial debut, a straight-to-video high school sex comedy whose level of wit and production values are reminiscent of the U.S. TV sitcom *Saved by the Bell*. Aoyama himself barely acknowledges this long-deleted offering for the Pink Pineapple production company, claiming post-production interference, and indeed, apart from a cameo by Kiyoshi Kurosawa and appearances from Aoyama regular Yōichirō Saitō and the omnipresent Tarō Suwa, there's little to recommend here to even the most ardent of Japanese film fans.

It was *Helpless* that first put Aoyama's name on the map, when it won the Grand Prix at the 1996 Japan Film Industry Professional Awards. For this, his first mainstream feature, Aoyama returned to his birthplace of Fukuoka Prefecture on Kyushu, the southernmost of the four main islands that make up Japan and an area whose reliance on mining and heavy industry has meant it has been particularly hard hit by the nation's economic decline.

Putting a new slant on the yakuza genre, *Helpless* was a raw, cryptic and in places almost unbearably violent look at a new generation, shot with a clinical objectivity by cameraman Masaki Tamura. Tamura had started out working on Shinsuke Ogawa's hard-hitting political documentaries on the protest movements surrounding the building of Tokyo International Airport in Narita in the late '60s, beginning with *The Frontline for the Liberation of Japan* (*Nihon Kaihō Sensen*, 1968). A highly influential presence throughout three decades of filmmaking in Japan, he was later responsible for making Naomi Kawase's feature debut *Suzaku* (1997) the stunning visual treat that it was, and contributing to the raw improvisational aesthetic of Nobuhiro Suwa's *2/Duo* (1997). His later work with Aoyama led through *Shady Grove* to arguably his crowning achievement in recent years with *Eureka*.

> "I first worked with Tamura on *Helpless*, and I knew he was the only person right for this film.

It's very difficult to explain why, but maybe subconsciously he has something, a sort of profoundness, maybe his view on things—it's totally different from other Japanese. It's not something I can put into words, but I felt strongly that I could only make my movie with this man. And so I worked with him and it turned out that I was right. And again, like Seijun Suzuki, this man is incredibly young for his age."

Helpless also benefited from the dark, smoldering presence of Tadanobu Asano in an early leading feature film role, an actor who has gone on to take center stage in some of the most notable Japanese productions of recent years, in cult favorites such as Miike's *Ichi the Killer*, esoteric fare like Kore-eda's *Distance*, to more mainstream releases such as Ōshima's comeback film *Gohatto*.

"Helpless was Asano's first feature film. Before that he had played a couple of small roles, but I didn't know anything about him at the time. He was recommended to me by a member of my crew, so I met him and the moment I saw him I knew I wanted to use him for my film. He was the perfect guy for *Helpless*, so I gave him the role instantly. He had this wildness coupled with a certain naïveté. There was something animalistic about him, which isn't something you generally find in people who come from Tokyo. That's obviously the key to his popularity. At the same time, his technique as an actor was still a little raw, and he was still learning. Recently I saw a film entitled *Kaza-Hana*, and I was amazed at how much he had improved. With no disrespect to him, I never realized he had it in him to become such a wonderful actor."

Aoyama followed up *Helpless* with two films in the same year. *Two Punks* was preceded by the straight-to-video *A Cop, a Bitch and a Killer* (*Waga Mune ni Kyōki Ari*, a title which translates as There's a Weapon by My Chest), a standard genre action movie chock-full of woodland slayings, fist fights, guns, girls, and motorbike chases, set to a soundtrack of MIDI synths and electric guitar wailings. Whilst this film hardly represents a typical Aoyama movie—in this case, what you see is clearly what you get—within the confines of its market, it is a highly polished piece of action entertainment, one of the purest examples of the director's technical capabilities of the time and certainly more distinguished than his previous foray into V-cinema with *Kyōkasho ni Nai!*

This staggeringly fast turnaround of initial features, which also included *Wild Life* and *An Obsession*, began to take its toll on the director's health, stopping him from working for about six months and forcing him to slow down his output. This change in pace went hand-in-hand with a change in focus, beginning with the female-centered drama of *Shady Grove*. For this film, Aoyama took inspiration from the celebrated Meiji-period author Sōseki Natsume (1867–1916), best known for his novels *Kokoro* and *I Am a Cat*. Sōseki's story *The Poppy* (*Gubijinsō*, 1907) became the starting point for his script.

"First of all, I wanted to make a film that featured a female protagonist, so I was looking for material with which to do this, and the idea of marriage came to me. I was thinking about such things as marrying someone, divorcing someone, marital difficulties, etc. One day I just happened to be reading *Gubijinsō*, and found that this story contained all of these things surrounding marriage but set in an older time period. Sōseki said in a letter to a friend that the female character at the center of this story who kills herself at the end is not meant to be living in this particular era, and so she has to die. She is the wrong person for this age. I felt I had to depict this same woman who had to die in Sōseki's time as someone wouldn't have had to die in our time."

Shady Grove was followed by *June 12, 1998: The Edge of Chaos*, a 65-minute documentary account of a solo concert given in Tokyo by the British experimental composer and musician Chris Cutler, featuring a brief interview with the artist, but predominantly based on the performance itself.

After this, Aoyama was offered the chance to contribute to the rapidly proliferating slew of horror films that were being released at around the time of **The Ring** with *Embalming*. The end results are a rather overstated and not entirely successful tale centered on the goings-on at a mortician's studio. The McGuffin here is the stolen head of a politician's son, whose decapitated corpse is found still clothed in his school uniform. This sets in motion a chain of gruesome autopsies, religious rituals, and hammy acting, all set against a quasi-Egyptian backdrop. Constantly teetering on the verge of the parodic, *Embalming* does at least manage to be fun, evoking fond memories of H.G. Lewis's 1963 gore classic *Blood Feast*.

> "There's a fine line between horror and parody, and with *Embalming* I was trying to stick to the edge and not cross over onto either side. At the time, especially, I really would have hated to fall into this category of 'Japanese horror.' Also, Kiyoshi Kurosawa and I have always had an unspoken agreement that we don't wander into each other's territory. So this was my way of sort of just strolling past it and waving 'Hello!'"

Coming as it did right after *Embalming*, with perhaps the exception of *Shady Grove* there had been little in scale and ambition thus far in Aoyama's oeuvre to point to the stunning achievement of *Eureka*. Epic in size, scope, ambition, and length, this meditative and meandering tale follows the healing process of a trio of shell-shocked survivors after the stability of their lives is shattered in a violent bus-jacking incident. Taking its title from a solo album released in 1999 by U.S. experimental guitarist Jim O' Rourke (ironically, itself named after the

Shinji Aoyama

1983 film by British director Nicholas Roeg, after whose work O'Rourke also named his albums *Bad Timing* and *Insignificance*), *Eureka*'s influences can be traced to such disparate sources as John Ford's *The Searchers* (1956) and the films of Wim Wenders.

With already a significant body of work to his name in under five years, the epic *Eureka* saw the director coming full circle back to the starting point of his debut film, *Helpless*, returning not only to his native land of northern Kyushu, where his first film was set, but rekindling his association with that film's producer, Takenori Sentō. He also brought back cameraman Tamura, whose crisp sepia-tinged Cinemascope compositions wowed foreign critics, as, after garnering a FIPRESCI (International Federation of Film Critics) award at the 2000 Cannes film festival,

Eureka became the first film of Aoyama's to gain significant exposure in the West.

"The one thing that was interesting was that the reaction from foreign countries and Japan was totally opposite from what I expected. In Japan people took it as a pure fantasy, and said, 'This couldn't possibly happen here,' whereas I made the film thinking that such an event was a quite viable possibility. In fact, after the film a very similar event actually happened here, in which a teenager held up a bus with a gun. In France, at Cannes, a young guy I met said that it would be easy to believe such a thing really happening in his home town, so the people outside of Japan found it a lot closer to their experiences than here."

With the film having won international awards, Aoyama picked up further plaudits for *Eureka* when his own novelization received the prestigious Yukio Mishima award for new literature in Japan in 2001. He has subsequently adapted *Helpless* and his later film *Desert Moon*, though sees writing very much as a sideline, with his primary career still as a filmmaker. Meanwhile, as Aoyama occupied himself expressing his cinematic work in a more literary form, his cinematic work began to get more experimental. The 64-minute long *To the Alley* saw him further moving away from his commercial background in a mixed media semi-documentary piece based on a similar premise as *Shady Grove*—a link with the past represented by a single surviving image of a place that has been long destroyed, in this instance a fragment of 16mm film footage.

The footage in question was shot by Kenji Nakagami (1946–92), an award-winning writer whose gritty writings such as *The Cape* (*Misaki*, published in 1976 and available along with other works by the author in English translation) documented his own personal plight growing up in one of Japan's stigmatized *burakumin* communities. The *burakumin* still face a degree of discrimination today for a host of obscure quasi-

historical and religious reasons dating back to the ninth century. Their name literally translates as "village people," referring to the ghettos in which these outcasts lived. The piece of film in question was shot before Nakagami's own *buraku* settlement was destroyed in the '70s, and one of the purposes of Aoyama's film was to preserve this sole testament to the author's childhood as a historical document, while at the same time presenting it to a wider audience. The bulk of the film itself, boasting music by Ryūichi Sakamoto and new footage shot by Tamura, is composed predominantly of the filmmaker Kishū Izuchi driving around the harbor town of Shingū where the author grew up, interspersed with him reading aloud passages of his work in the various locations where they are set.

Aoyama was to adopt a similar elliptical approach in his 51-minute-long *Sude ni Oita Kanojo no Subete ni Tsuite wa Kataranu Tame ni*, but prior to this, his next feature failed to attain the same level of critical approval of the previous year's *Eureka* when it received its premiere at Cannes in 2001. With Tamura acting again in the role of cameraman, *Desert Moon*'s drama revolves around the boss of a successful IT start-up company, whose wife leaves him upon the realization that she is unable to compete with work for his affections. Aoyama uses this premise to explore the nature of reality, illusion, the dynamic shifts in values in contemporary society, and the role of the modern family and the individual within it in the broader context of such intangible constraints as interconnected communities and the new virtual economy.

"Both the producer Takenori Sentō and I expected this reaction. The main problem seems to be with the central character. He's a businessman in the IT field. The image of IT—the world of information, business, and new technology—these sorts of things are completely out of the scope of these Cannes people, which caused some problems. They were sort of wondering what the hell the main character was talking

about. This kind of new business, in Japan and every other country, is difficult for people to visualize or understand. For example, new terminology relating to technology, such as e-mail, isn't really understood by the people of this older generation, so it is omitted from their critical discourse. For this reason I felt that the Cannes reaction was fairly predictable."

The director himself sees *Desert Moon* as the strongest of his films, and the most accurate reflection of his intentions as an artist. Unfortunately, following the financial collapse of Takenori Sentō's production company, Suncent Cinema Works, in the latter half of 2001, it received only a limited release in Tokyo late in 2003, and few people outside of the festival circuit and a short run in Paris have been given the opportunity to make up their own minds whether the director has succeeded in getting his message across.

In the meantime, Aoyama has involved himself in a few more commercial projects, including *A Forest with No Name*, one of the more impressive sections of Yomiuri TV's series *Shiritsu Tantei Hama Maiku* featuring the Maiku Hama character created by Kaizō Hayashi and played by Masatoshi Nagase. Though made for TV, it was shot on film in two versions, with the feature-length version intended for theatrical release. In 2003, as well as directing a concert film for the Okinawan singer Tomoko Uehara entitled *Ajimaa no Uta: Uehara Tomoko Tenjo no Utagoe* [trans: Song of Ajimar: Uehara Tomoko, voice of heaven], Aoyama was also one of the twelve directors, alongside Kiyoshi Kurosawa and Hirohisa Sasaki, who contributed one of the ten-minute segments of Makoto Shinozaki's *Cop Festival* omnibus film.

↓ Two Punks
チンピラ
Chinpira

1996. CAST: Takao Ōsawa, Dankan, Reiko Kataoka, Ryō Ishibashi, Susumu Terajima, Ken Mitsuishi, Yōichirō Saitō. 101 minutes. RELEASE: VHS, Les Films du Paradoxe (France, French subtitles).

Two young men live their lives on the fringes of the yakuza, without ever really becoming part of it. Aoyama's look at outsiders is an unconventional and surprisingly human take on the yakuza genre, signaling his developing eye for emotional subtleties.

Though *Eureka* made his name internationally, festivalgoers might have already been familiar with Aoyama from his earlier riff on the gangster film, *Two Punks*. Its exposure was nowhere near as wide as *Eureka*'s (the only distribution deal it garnered was a French theatrical release followed by a now out-of-print video), but it nevertheless introduced Western audiences to Aoyama's particular approach to genre filmmaking.

Following on two rather more straightforward genre exercises for the straight-to-video market, *Two Punks* was adapted from a script by the late Shōji Kaneko, which had been filmed once already by Tōru Kawashima in 1984. Aoyama's version was rewritten by Toshiyuki Morioka, known for his work on unconventional gangster films like Takashi Miike's *Fudoh: The New Generation* and *Blues Harp* (1998), and Rokurō Mochizuki's *Another Lonely Hitman* (*Shin Kanashiki Hittoman*, 1995) and *Onibi, The Fire Within* (1997). The film would be the start of Aoyama's more ambitious exploration of the genre film that would continue with the likes of *An Obsession* and *Shady Grove*, and which would ironically result in the decidedly non-genre *Eureka*.

Yōichi (Ōsawa) is a Shikoku country boy freshly arrived in the big city. He finds a job sweeping floors at a nightclub, but when he violently trounces a coke-snorting punk, his bosses, the yakuza Ōtani (Ishibashi) and his right-hand man Masao (Terajima), realize he's capable of a lot more. Yōichi has no interest in joining the yakuza, however, since his headstrong and violent behavior makes him contemptuous of the organizational hierarchy. Instead he is drawn to Michio (Dankan), a fellow outsider who works with the yakuza but is not a part of them because, as he explains, "I'm not made for it."

Michio involves Yōichi in his plan to become a bookmaker and soon enough the two are making deals and collecting gambling debts. They remain allied to Ōtani, who takes a liking to the misfit couple, but tensions mount when Yōichi takes a shine to Masao's girlfriend Yōko (Kataoka). When he saves her from a beating by the yakuza lieutenant, catching a knife in the flank for his efforts, the two fall in love and an ongoing feud with Masao begins. To make matters worse, Michio goes gaga for Ōtani's girlfriend and flees with her after getting her pregnant.

Aoyama's approach to this tale closely resembles Yōichi and Michio's attitude toward the yakuza: intentional distance but emotional closeness. In many cases he chooses to shoot his scenes in long, wide takes as the action unravels before the camera. The spatial distance does not make this film aloof, however. Aoyama has an eye for the emotional subtleties of his characters, and not only those of Yōichi and Michio. Ōtani, played by the hugely talented Ishibashi, is an unconventional man with a strong emotional core, the opposite of his full-body tattoo, which consists of only an outline. Although he is capable of torturing people by pushing chopsticks into their ears, his reaction to the news that his mistress is pregnant with another man is remarkably restrained. Even Masao, who for a long time seems merely a violent hothead, is increasingly portrayed in shades of gray through his conflict with Yōichi.

It's this fine eye for human nuances that Aoyama would develop further in his subsequent work. Beneath the seemingly formalist genre explorations is where the director's true growth would take place.

↓ An Obsession

冷たい血

Tsumetai Chi

1997. CAST: Ryō Ishibashi, Kazuma Suzuki, Kyōko Tōyama, Yūrei Yanagi, Tarō Suwa, Akiko Izumi, Eiko Nagashima. 108 minutes. RELEASES: DVD, Artsmagic (U.S./U.K., English subtitles), Wishbone (Japan, English subtitles).

A workaholic cop who's lost his gun, and a serial killer with a death wish: Aoyama reworks the story of Kurosawa's *Stray Dog* into an alternate modern day Tokyo backdrop.

Within the first couple of years after hitting the public eye with his raw portrait of the estranged, directionless youths of *Helpless*, the prodigious Aoyama kept up an almost production-line rate of output, churning out a further three films over the course of the next year. Shooting from his own script, *An Obsession* (the Japanese title translates as "Cold Blood") sees the continuing development of a number of recurring themes that permeate the director's work: the outsider's struggle for identity against the backdrop of modern day urban alienation interwoven with a search for some deeper reason for existence. Yet here he switches from the gangster milieu to the format of the police thriller.

Sōsuke (Ishibashi) is a workaholic detective who would rather spend time enforcing justice than passing the hours at home with his wife. However, his assertive espousal of "individualism" to his buddy cop (Suwa) receives a severe knock-back when he is caught in the crossfire during the arrest of a religious cult leader, gunned down as he exits the building where he has been held siege. Sōsuke immediately sets off in pursuit of the killer, but is shot in the resulting chase, leaving him critically wounded.

After years of playing second fiddle to his career, Sōsuke's wife Rie (Nagashima) is loath to hang around and pick up the pieces, and promptly packs her bags and leaves. Pitched headlong into a major life crisis, Sōsuke immediately resigns from the force, but there's one problem left outstanding. Whilst unconscious after the shooting, the detective's gun was lifted from him and is now being used in a series of methodical yet seemingly motiveless homicides across the city. Plagued with guilt, Sōsuke begins his own private investigation in order to apprehend the killer and get his gun back, finally pinpointing the culprit as Shimano (Suzuki), a lank-haired youth somewhere in his twenties, terminally ill with congenital leukemia and morbidly fixated on his own death.

Those with some knowledge of Japanese cinema may recognize in the above synopsis elements of Akira Kurosawa's *Stray Dog* (*Nora Inu*, 1949), a point which Aoyama further stresses by setting his final showdown in a deserted baseball field. For his original film, Kurosawa admitted to being taken by the compelling plot-driven narratives of Belgium's most famous writer of *policier* fiction, Georges Simenon, and had earlier written a novel based on this premise of a policeman in search of his stolen weapon, though it was never actually published. *Stray Dog*'s structure allowed the director to work in his own arguments about the nature of good and evil against the backdrop of post-wartime shortages and the Allied Occupation, with its black-market operator antagonist driven to murder through economic hardship and a value system completely up-ended in the aftermath of Japan's defeat.

For Aoyama, whose film is set amongst the cold, modern face of late-'90s Tokyo, the dualistic opposition between cop and killer is not so cut and dry. U.S. Occupation forces driving around in jeeps are here replaced by mysterious figures clad in anti-radiation suits who perform random executions that pass by unremarked on the sidelines, whilst echoes of the Aum cult, whose gas attacks on commuters on the capital's subway made world news in 1995, are present in the figure of the assassinated leader of the Great Truth Cult, Kunihiro. Indeed, Aoyama's film is not so

© 1998 Taki Corporation

An Obsession

much a remake of Kurosawa's, as a reworking of its basic premise to fit his own intellectual ends.

The opening quote from F. Scott Fitzgerald, "Of course all life's a process of breaking down, but . . . " presages the conflict which forms the backbone of *An Obsession*, a collision between the dual wills of a man struggling to live, and one drawn inexorably toward the void. As with its model, Sōsuke's nemesis is kept off-screen until near the end of the film, a shadowy mysterious figure alluded to in the third person by a string of characters closely related to him, including ex-cult member Mita (Yanagi) and an ex-girlfriend, Kimiko (Tōyama) who harbors a pretty deep-rooted death wish of her own. "Your hollowness will draw him to you," an associate of Shimano warns Sōsuke early on in the proceedings.

Kurosawa was later to dismiss *Stray Dog* as having too much emphasis on technical detail and not enough on the development of its central concept, though such memorably virtuoso set pieces as the killer's night-time flight from the hotel in which he finds himself cornered by Toshirō Mifune certainly made up for any perceived dramatic shortcomings. With its austere, fixed shooting manner interspersed with poetic slow, gliding camera movements, and the periodic onscreen blackouts from its protagonist's perspective serving to break up the contiguity within scenes, *An Obsession* goes to the other extreme. Somber in its manner and spare in its details, it is a far cry from Kurosawa's cat and mouse games with the audience.

In its desire to probe the inner motivations of both investigator and killer rather than satisfy the more audience-related concerns of "whodunit," key moments in the plot progression are glossed over, with a number of major twists in the tale occurring off-screen. This apparent ambivalence to pacing and suspense may prove the make or break point with casual viewers. Taken as a thriller, Aoyama's film more often than not fails to thrill. Taken on its own merits, however, as a stepping stone in the director's increasingly sophisticated oeuvre, *An Obsession* still provides enough food for thought to be of interest, but within a rather more conventional format than some of his later work.

↓ Shady Grove

1999. CAST: Urara Awata, Tomohiro Sekiguchi, Arata, Yōichirō Saitō, Ken Mitsuishi, Rei Kurita. 99 minutes. RELEASES: DVD, Wishbone (Japan, no subtitles).

More than just a romantic weepie, as a jilted office lady seeks connection in a heartless world.

Yuppie love is ostensibly the focus of Aoyama's first departure from the world of guns and violence, in a tortured tale in which pert young twenty-something Rika (Kurita) is rather unceremoniously dumped by her boyfriend Ono (Sekiguchi) within minutes of the opening credits. One minute she is discussing the wine she was planning to buy to go with the new glasses she bought for his apartment, the next she is swigging it from the bottle to drown her sorrows in the wake of his decision, cruelly delivered by mobile phone. Rika is understandably left crumpled by this bolt from the blue, yet still futilely clings on to the hope that they'll be back together again before too long. Alone in her apartment, with no one to turn to, she takes to phoning random strangers for comfort, most of whom, understandably, give her short shrift before hanging up. One, however, doesn't, comforting her over the phone before leaving with the consolatory message, "Wait, and he'll come back."

Spurred on by this advice, Rika refuses to let go, repeatedly phoning her ex-boyfriend's apartment to leave messages on his answering machine, trawling through pop-psychology romantic self-help texts, and even going as far as to hire a private detective to find out how Ono is coping with single life. After a confrontation with another girl who answers the door of Ono's apartment, Rika threatens suicide, but is sent on her way by her unmoved ex-lover. "You never think of anyone but yourself," he rather hypocritically adds. Distraught, Rika contacts the only person she knows she can turn to, the sympathetic stranger from the previous evening who shows up to drive her back home to her apartment.

This young man, Shingo (Arata), is cur-

Shady Grove

rently having a few troubles of his own, having just dramatically resigned from his job as a graphic designer. Nonetheless, as he offers her a shoulder to cry on, he notices a blown-up photograph of a small wooded copse on the wall of her apartment, the Shady Grove of the title. When questioned about it, Rika explains that it was next to the house where she grew up. As a girl, her father always used to tell her that if she waited there long enough, her prince would arrive. Before Shingo leaves, she hands him a few more photos of this mysterious place. His imagination captured by this seemingly random meeting, and ignoring the advice that the grove has long since been swallowed up by the suburbs, he decides to go in search of the spot where the pictures were taken.

Shady Grove seems worlds apart from the violent meditations on death and existential angst that permeate Aoyama's earlier work, in its lighter moments playing like yet another ditzy chick flick before developing a more meditative aspect toward the end. Whilst on the surface this makes for one of his most accessible films, it also represents another clever case of genre subversion. Dig deeper beneath the apparent parody of romantic comedy conventions, and you'll see the same themes being developed that reach their zenith with the epic *Eureka*, with which the film shares the cameraman Masaki Tamura.

Aoyama shoots the bulk of the film using the austere digital video medium to portray the banality of modern urban existence in all its glib superficiality, only occasionally switching to 35mm film for the scenes in the wooded glade that appear first in Rika's and later in Shingo's dreams. Toying with such ideas as the search for connection and the misleading expectations people have of one another, *Shady Grove* is a keystone in the director's oeuvre in which

Shady Grove

the often oblique approach of his earlier work finally begins to attain a little more substance. As such, it arguably represents one his most satisfyingly well-rounded and mature films.

↓ Eureka
ユリイカ
Yuriika

2000. **CAST:** Kōji Yakusho, Aoi Miyazaki, Yōichirō Saitō, Masaru Miyazaki, Eihi Shiina, Ken Mitsuishi, Gō Rijū. 217 minutes. **RELEASES:** DVD, Artificial Eye (U.K., English subtitles), J-Works (Japan, English/French subtitles).

A bus driver and two children are witness to the hijack of their bus, and survive only to find that their trauma has detached them from the world at large. Nearly four hours in length, this sepia-toned drama is not the easiest film to watch, but emerges rewarding and gripping against all expectations.

When two children take their daily bus ride to school, a young businessman pulls out a gun and hijacks the bus. Three executions and one police siege later, the hijacker is dead and the two children plus bus driver Makoto (Yakusho) are the only ones to remain physically unscathed.

The trauma of the event runs deep within all three of them, having not only lived through the hijack, but also witnessed from up close the shooting and killing of the hijacker by the police. Not surprisingly, they are unable to resume their normal lives. Two years after the incident, Makoto has left his wife and is kicked out of his brother's house, while the children are left to survive on their own after their mother has run away, the death of her husband making it impossible for her to care for her troubled children. With no place to go, Makoto decides he will put some purpose into his life by moving in with the children, who are now the only inhabitants of a family home whose interiors have come to resemble a trash heap. Makoto cleans up the place and takes on the role of surrogate father and mother, the traumatized trio realizing that they only feel comfortable in each other's presence. This is the start of a slow and difficult process of healing, which leads past the arrival of the children's cousin, a murder, and a new bus trip before finally arriving at something resembling liberation.

Eureka was a breakthrough film in many ways. Firstly for Aoyama, whose previous work had been genre exercises that showed an increasing preoccupation with characters and emotions, but who here achieves the reverse, making a film about human emotions that contains occasional elements of genre. *Eureka* was also Aoyama's international breakthrough. He had had the odd film shown at foreign film festivals in the past, but now saw himself competing for the Palme d'Or in Cannes, where he garnered the international film critics' prize and numerous foreign distribution deals.

Secondly, it was a breakthrough for young actress Aoi Miyazaki. She had appeared in two films and a television series the previous year, but her almost wordless performance in *Eureka* made her a favorite choice with independent directors, making a particularly strong impression in Akihiko Shiota's ***Harmful Insect***.

Stylistically the film was also something of a breakthrough. Aoyama shot it in Cinemascope, a format that had become virtually extinct in Japanese film since the 1970s, when 16mm cameras became the medium of choice for those who had come from an independent background as well as for the V-cinema industry, for which widescreen formats were completely useless. With its sepia-toned images, *Eureka* is certainly one of the most visually overwhelming films to come

out of Japan in a long time. Shot in the northern Kyushu countryside, the impressive landscapes become all the more prominent thanks to the long takes, many of them wide shots that emphasize the relationship between the individuals and the landscape that surrounds them.

The visual splendor of the film functions in an interestingly paradoxical way, as it is both overwhelming and underwhelming. The images may be beautiful to look at, but the sepia tinting avoids the risk of burying the dramatic heart of the film under the opulence, expressing a solemnity that fits well with the less than cheerful proceedings. This paradox is an essential element of the film. While *Eureka*'s characters endure emotional crises that most of us never hope to go through, it is above all a film about reconstruction, about starting anew and finding a way of living when the old way has disappeared forever. The visual beauty, particularly that of the landscapes, works as an influence on this process of regeneration. The protagonists need to search for happiness in their surroundings, not within themselves. It's very appropriate, then, that the film's second half takes the form of a road movie.

This search for happiness and reconstruction is where *Eureka* differs from much of his earlier work. Always fascinated by outcast characters who find themselves alienated from an increasingly absurd society, Aoyama manages to take his characters in *Eureka* a step further, achieving what most of his earlier protagonists never did: the possibility of happiness, a means to live a life in one's own little niche within an insane world. For the first time, Aoyama truly mimics his mentor, Kiyoshi Kurosawa, in suggesting possibilities to start anew after destruction has wiped away all we hold dear. "A tidal wave is coming. And it will engulf everyone," Aoi Miyazaki voices in the first minutes of the film, just before embarking on the ill-fated bus trip. Engulf her it does, leaving her and her brother behind in stunned silence, a silence that lasts for most of the film's nearly four-hour running time. The aftermath of a tidal wave is always calmer than the onset.

CHAPTER 16

Naomi Kawase
河瀬直美

Perhaps more than anything else the past century of cinema has been notable for a conspicuous lack of female filmmakers. This goes for all territories, though in the traditionally male-dominated industry in Japan, the problem seems to be that much more acute, at least at first glance. Delve a little deeper, however, and you'll see that there are actually quite a few women directors working in places you might not have dreamt of looking. The first, and best known, is Kinuyo Tanaka (1910–77) who, when she wasn't busy appearing as leading lady for Kenji Mizoguchi made a number of films throughout the '50s and '60s, debuting with *Love Letter* (*Koibumi*) in 1953. Since then, in the last decade we've had two extremes of cinema represented by a new generation of women directors in works as dissimilar as Kei Fujiwara's Cronenberg-esque cyberpunk splatterfest ***Organ*** (1996) and Hisako Matsui's *Solitude Point* (*Yukie*, 1997) and *Oriume* (2003), both stories that explore the problems associated with Alzheimer's disease.

Kaze Shindō, granddaughter of the great scriptwriter/director Kaneto Shindō, gave us the lesbian drama *Love/Juice* (2000) at the tender age of 23, and then there's 28-year-old Miwa Nishikawa's first offering, *Wild Berries* (*Hebi Ichigo*, 2003), a contemporary take on the family unit. Let's also not forget that Shimako Satō's high-school horror *Wizard of Darkness*

(*Eko Eko Azaraku*, 1995) long preceded Hideo Nakata's ***The Ring*** in the revival of mainstream teen-oriented horror. Women filmmakers are even in on the act in the arena of the erotic film, with the likes of Yumi Yoshiyuki and Sachi Hamano contributing literally dozens of titles to the *pinku* genre.

Indeed, at closer inspection the problem is not so much the absence of female film directors as their invisibility, which is certainly not a problem you can accuse Naomi Kawase of. For a start, even though in Japan she remains a somewhat marginal figure (like all who work outside of the studios making independent films for the arthouse market), overseas her name is certainly better known than any of the aforementioned directors, if only due to the huge impact her feature debut ***Suzaku*** (1997) had on the festival jury at Cannes. A second factor is the intensely personal nature of her films, especially in the early 8mm documentaries with which she first began making a name for herself, *Embracing* (1992) and *Katatsumori* (1994). Whether onscreen or off, Naomi is clearly the center of her films, and even if this pigeonholing as a "woman" director is not something Kawase is entirely happy with, Naomi is still quite clearly a woman.

Basing herself in her home town of Nara in the western Kansai area of Japan, near both

Kyoto and Osaka but away from the main hub of the industry in Tokyo, Kawase's films represent a change in focus from what foreign audiences are used to seeing from Japan—the bizarre, the sexy, the violent, the proud, the historical—toward the apolitical, the habitual, and the personal. Either within the documentary format, or in the raw naturalism of her documentary-styled fiction, by presenting her footage in lengthy, unrefined chunks without the stylistic window dressing of rousing music in the background or actors emoting wildly to the camera, she holds the artificiality of the film medium at bay, often giving the viewer the impression that they are eavesdropping on other people's private lives. This is never more true than in the films she has made about herself.

Born in 1969, Kawase received her artistic training at the Osaka School of Photography (now the School of Visual Arts). Whilst there, she discovered the 8mm film format, and immediately turned the camera on herself and her immediate surroundings in a series of short works whose content is hinted at in titles such as *I Focus on That Which Interests Me*, *The Concretization of These Things Flying Around Me* and *My Solo Family*. After graduating in 1989, she stayed on to work as a lecturer at the college for the next four years. Indeed, she still lectures there when not making films. During this time, she continued to work on her own projects, the first of which to receive significant attention was *Embracing*, shot in 8mm but later blown up to 16mm for theatrical exhibition. One of the most mesmeric and emotive of her works, *Embracing* is an intimate self-portrait of the director, looking closely at her own personal environment and back to her childhood in which she was abandoned by her parents when they divorced and she was sent to live with her "granny"—actually her great-aunt and not a blood relation.

"I often think that I should only show these things to people that are close to me, to close friends and not to the entire world. But the age

© 2002 Martin Mes

Naomi Kawase

when I came into contact with film was a time when I didn't really have a way to talk about intimate things with the people around me, because there weren't any people around to share them with. I also discovered that when I used film as a medium, people were ready to listen to what I had to say very carefully, more so than when I didn't use film. So I found that it functioned as a tool of communication for me at the time. It was convenient."

Throughout the film, Naomi's monotonal, disembodied voice details the gradual journey of self-awakening that occurs during the quest to find the father she never knew, alongside a hypnotic collage of shots of flora, fauna, and various natural phenomena. In this film and in her other 8mm work, Kawase focuses heavily on textures and forms of everyday things—grass billowing in the wind, time-lapse cloud formations, a ploughed field with mosquitoes dancing in the sunlight, a kitchen full of glistening foodstuffs, a messy skyscape of roofs silhouetted across a blood-red sunset, the smudged-gradated grays that score across the sky. These strangely beautiful images betray a mastery of the medium as an art form. There's an oddly affecting sequence in which, after rifling through her childhood snapshots, each photo is held up in front of the camera against the original background where it was taken. The sparing use of sound, existing solely as an ambient accompaniment to the whirr of the camera, enhances the feeling of emotional distance. Raw and unpolished, *Embracing* evokes the excitement of early primitive cinema, or of stumbling across the real-life footage of someone else's private drama, as it ends with Naomi finally making phone contact with her father. *Embracing* won the Award For Excellence at the Image Forum Festival in 1993 and also a FIPRESCI special mention at the Yamagata International Documentary Film Festival in 1995.

> **"When I made *Embracing* about my father, the main intention was not to show it to the world afterward. It was first and foremost an exploration and a way of dealing with it for myself. It more or less just happened to develop that way, that this became my way of communicating intimately and closely. But once in a while I still have my doubts about the appropriateness of it all."**

Throughout the early '90s, the young director persistently continued working Tokyo's independent filmmaking scene, and with her work beginning to pick up critical attention at festivals both home and abroad, she formed Kumie, a group of similar-minded filmmakers dedicated to getting their work screened in as many venues as possible. Her first stab at fiction came with the fifty-five-minute *White Moon*, which she followed with another personal documentary, *Katatsumori*.

Katatsumori's title comes from a play on the words "*katatsumuri*," for snail, and "*tsumori*," meaning plan or intention, stemming from a childhood misunderstanding in which she believed that slugs were snails without shells, likening her own family situation to a slug waiting for its house. At forty minutes, it is the same length as *Embracing*, and similarly features another subject close to the heart of the director, the woman who acted as her adoptive mother as she grew up. Opening with a slow pan across a tabletop covered in scattered pieces of paper and a 10,000-yen banknote, a sound of snuf-

Filmography

1988
- *I Focus on That Which Interests Me* (*Watashi ga Tsuyoku Kyōmi o Motta Mono o Ōkiku Fix de Kiritoru*) [short]
- *The Concretization of These Things Flying around Me* (*Watashi ga Iki-Iki to Kakawatte Ikō to Suru Jibutsu no Gutaika*) [short]
- *My J-W-F* [short]
- *Papa's Ice Cream* (*Papa no Sofuto Kurīmu*) [short]

1989
- *My Solo Family* (*Tatta Hitori no Kazoku*) [short]
- *Presently* (*Ima*) [short]
- *A Small Largeness* (*Chiisana Ōkisa*) [short]

1990
- *The Girls' Daily Bread* (*Megamitachi no Pan*) [short]

1991
- *Like Happiness* (*Shiawase Modoki*) [short]

1992
- *Embracing* (*Ni Tsutsumarete*) [short]

1993
- *White Moon* (*Shiroi Tsuki*) [short]

1994
- *Katatsumori* [short]

1995
- *See the Heavens* (*Ten Mitake*) [short]
- *Memory of the Wind: At Shibuya on December 26, 1995* (*Kaze no Kioku—1995, 12, 26 Shibuya nite*) [short]

1996
- *This World* (*Arawashiyo*) [co-directed with Hirokazu Kore-eda]

- *The Setting Sun* (*Hi wa Katabuki*) [short]
- *Suzaku* (*Moe no Suzaku*)

1997
- *The Weald* (*Somaudo Monogatari*)

1999
- *Kaleidoscope* (*Mangekyō*)
- *Wandering at Home: The Third Fall Since Starting to Live Alone* (*Tayutafu ni Kokyō—Hitorigurashi o Hajimete, Sannenme no Aki ni*) [TV]

2000
- *Hotaru*

2001
- *Kya Kara Ba A* [TV]

2002
- *Letter from a Yellow Cherry Blossom* (*Tsuioku no Dansu*)

2003
- *Shara* (*Sharasōju*)

fling appears on soundtrack as "granny" is introduced. Again, the matter-of-fact naturalism is the notable aspect here, as we are treated to a multitude of shots charting a year in life within this two-person micro-family, with the adoptive mother responding to Kawase's offscreen questioning as she potters around the kitchen or the garden, planting peas, the camera occasionally fixating on some peripheral detail such as a worm squirming on the pavement, marooned from the soil. Though somewhat more conventional-looking than its predecessor, *Katatsumori* similarly demonstrates the stylistic traits in depicting textures onscreen, and the non-diegesic use of background sound, either intensified or interchanged to act as counterpoint to shots to which they obviously don't belong.

> **"I see myself as some sort of axis connecting these images and sounds. I don't record images and sounds simultaneously. There are the images and afterward there will be sound or music that is unrelated. They are combined with the function that I have within the film."**

The most fascinating part of these early films is clearly the person behind the camera. Kawase is not afraid to draw attention to the medium, either. In one shot, as the camera pans around the freshly raked soil of the garden, we see her shadow holding the camera, and when Kawase allows her granny to finally turn the camera on her, a lens flare obscures her face as the older woman shoots into the sun.

Kawase's increasing exposure on the domestic festival circuit brought her to the attention of a number of influential figures in the industry, including *After Life* director Hirokazu Kore-eda, whom she met at the Yamagata Documentary Film Festival in 1995, and more importantly, a producer by the name of Takenori Sentō. With the former, she collaborated on *This World* (1996), a series of 8mm film correspondences between the two directors intended for a film exhibition held by the Yokohama Museum of Modern Art.

The latter was to have an even more decisive impact on the young director, when he agreed to produce Kawase's first major work for the large screen, the fictional feature *Suzaku*.

Using 35mm for the first time and utilizing the talents of veteran cinematographer Masaki Tamura, later responsible for the crisp sepia panoramas of Shinji Aoyama's *Eureka* (2000), Kawase's foundations in documentary resulted in a work that blurred the divisions between fiction and reality. Using a cast largely made up of non-professionals and set in a provincial village high in the wooded mountains of Nara Prefecture where Kawase was born and raised, *Suzaku* focuses on the internal dynamics of a small rural community when the construction of a railroad tunnel is abandoned, failing to bring the local economy the much needed boost that it seeks.

Suzaku went on to play widely on the foreign festival circuit to significant acclaim, and at the tender age of 27 Kawase found herself romping home with not only a FIPRESCI award from Rotterdam, but also the prestigious Camera d'Or prize for new directors from the Cannes Film Festival, the first female Japanese director ever to gain such a high degree of international acclaim. Perhaps more surprisingly, the Japanese press back at home pricked up their ears. At a time when many saw the domestic film industry as having little to offer the rest of the world, the idea that a young girl from Nara who cut her teeth making autobiographical home movies could compete on the international circuit and win a major prize came as quite a shock. The hubbub swelled even louder when shortly afterward the marriage between Kawase and her producer for *Suzaku*, Takenori Sentō, was announced. Few in the mainstream media took time to note that Kawase was still making films.

> **"At the time this was really a big thing and I felt like a panda in a zoo. There were a lot of different kinds of offers, like, could I give a lecture**

Shara

here and there, and I couldn't concentrate on my next film for a long time because of that."

For her next work, stemming from a dissatisfaction with the way the fictional elements of *Suzaku* failed to match the harsh economic reality of the area, Kawase returned to the wooded village of Nishi Yoshino, the location of the first film, to shoot a documentary on the real-life community of foresters who work there. The end result was *The Weald*, filmed on a mixture of video, 8mm, and 16mm. Focusing on the aging members of six families still making their living from the forest, Kawase allows her subjects—introduced in monochrome photos from their younger days—to deliver their stories to the camera.

None of them are exactly in the springtime of their youth, and Kawase dwells on this physicality, their gnarled hands and leathery skin, but

somehow her subjects seem more fully rounded and alive than the fictional characters of *Suzaku*. One character bares a shattered crenellation of teeth in a smile, though another later bashfully holds up his hand in front of the camera as it focuses in on his gummy maw as he tries to eat. But the portrait is never less than an affectionate one, recording a lifestyle that is as unfamiliar to urban Japanese as it is to foreign audiences.

The subject may be different, but both the technique and the subjective focus used in *The Weald* remain similar to that of Kawase's earlier 8mm films. Complementing the tales of the woodcutters are sequences detailing the daily life of the community. An old man stokes his charcoal stove in his hut. Solitary figures trudge along forest paths, dwarfed beneath the magnificence of the wooded landscape. A communal traditional dance is shot hand-held, played back in slow motion, the figures advancing frame by frame. Between this Kawase focuses on the minutiae of nature—icicles dripping and trees rustling in the wind—and just as in her earlier films, the continuing hum of the camera shutter, the muffled sound of the wind buffeting the microphone, and the lack of music on the soundtrack remind us that all of this is real.

It is for this subjective aspect that Kawase has come in for criticism. In the face of mass depopulation for the city from the younger sectors of the community, a phenomenon that has struck the rural sectors of Japan particularly hard over the past few decades, arguably some sort of political or social context is required for these films in this age of hard-hitting, one-sided media polemic. Using the same scene shot throughout various parts of the year to show the seasons, a recurrent device throughout her work, Kawase presents the countryside with a mystical, timeless quality, seemingly isolated from outside forces. Such criticism is perhaps valid. Kawase can be accused of "prettifying" the impoverished rural areas of Japan. But at least she gives us time to contemplate the images and what they mean, whilst evoking a particularly vivid sense of an undocumented lifestyle.

Whilst Kawase's marriage to Sentō outlasted the interest from the press, the couple divorced less than two years later. During this time, she made a further two documentaries under her married name, Naomi Sentō. The first was a 45-minute special for TV Tokyo, entitled *Wandering at Home: The Third Fall Since Starting to Live Alone*, which screened in 1998, again using 8mm and video and again returning to the subject of a missing father, in this case not her own, but that of the three grown-up children of a middle-aged widow whose husband, it is revealed, had committed suicide. Then in 1999 came *Kaleidoscope*, in which she charted prize-winning photographer Shinya Arimoto as he prepared a series of portraits for two girls from radically different social backgrounds—Machiko Ono, the non-actress plucked from the village of Nishi Yoshino to star in *Suzaku*, and Mika Mifune, daughter of one of Japan's most famous actors, *Seven Samurai*'s Toshirō Mifune. Captured onscreen here is the power play between the two artistic forces behind the cameras as they vie for the attention of the two models, which soon escalates into a full-blown conflict between Kawase and Arimoto.

Following her divorce, Kawase returned to her maiden name and retreated back into fiction filmmaking in her home territory of Nara. Fortunately Sentō was still on hand to produce her next film under the J-Works banner of his Suncent Cinema Works production company. Aimed at courting a broader world audience, the films produced by J-Works were targeted squarely, and rather self-consciously, at the international arthouse market rather than mainstream domestic audiences, directed by names already well established and respected outside of Japan. Some of the films worked, such as Shinji Aoyama's *Eureka*. Others, such as Nobuhiro Suwa's *H-Story* (2001), were less well received. Probably Sentō's greatest error was in allowing the directors so much leeway in realizing their individual visions. Picking up a number of awards and critical plaudits at foreign festivals is one thing, but J-Works was not so successful in persuading people at home to watch Japanese films. In late 2001 Suncent Cinema Works folded, with Sōgo Ishii's costly production of *Gojoe* touted as the reason, leaving a large proportion of the company's back catalogue unreleased outside of the festival circuit.

Kawase's contribution to J-Works was *Hotaru*, and coming so soon after her divorce as it did, it is difficult not to read any personal feelings into this long and grueling but sensitive portrayal of the difficulties in the relationship between two emotionally scarred people in a small town in Nara. Shooting in a naturalistic cinema vérité style over the course of a year allowed Kawase, as with her documentary work, to chart the relationship through the four seasons.

"I wanted to draw out more reality by describing the seasons very much in detail, like the same

Shara

trees are wet in June, and when the summer comes they are more green and lively, so you can say it is symbolic, but it is very much connected with reality for me."

This documentary style veracity also stretches to the performances, which are almost painfully direct. In one scene, set the day after the couple make love for the first time, they meet in the street outside one of their homes. After having already shared such a great degree of physical intimacy together, they both seem very awkward with each other in terms of direct communication. In this lengthy scene the camera lingers like a bystander, keeping the viewer at a similar literal and emotional distance from the couple as they linger at opposing sides of the frame, avoiding each other's eyes.

"What I wanted to say was that people tend to

think that after getting intimate physically you can get really closer to the person. But actually I wanted to show by the positioning of the actors that you can't get so far inside of somebody so quickly or so easily. You can't find somebody really important just through sex."

With *Hotaru*, Kawase's reputation became firmly cemented in Europe, despite the film only playing in a limited number of venues in Tokyo. When the producer Luciano Rigolini from the French/German TV-channel Arte approached her with the proposition of financing a kind of sequel to *Embracing*, she accepted the offer. The second instigating factor was the death of her long-estranged father. Covering similar territory as her early films on her family situation and clocking in at little under an hour, the result was *Kya Kara Ba A*, whose title comes from a Buddhist term, a Sanskrit expression that has to do with the five elements of air, wind, fire, earth, and water.

> "When I first heard of this concept I was intrigued by it, because the philosophy behind it is that each of these elements on its own has little meaning, but when they are brought together in the right combination something gets across and things start to happen. I thought I could draw a parallel with my own life and work up 'til now. There's the relationship with my father, the relationship with other members of my family. They're elements that I had not dealt with in the right combination before. So I thought it would be appropriate to name this film after the five elements, because if I brought together all the elements that have been present in my work so far into this one film, it would be the best way to get across what I wanted to convey about life."

Kya Kara Ba A mixes the personal documentary format of her earlier films with more artificially staged sections, including a scene where Kawase receives a (fake) tattoo. The pain of the tattoo and the act of having that tattoo made, of having pain inflicted on you and in that process becoming stronger, acts as a metaphor for her childhood rite of passage. Occasionally we get to see the clapper board and the camera crew, harking back to Shōhei Imamura's groundbreaking experimental documentary *A Man Vanishes*, the director a magician-like figure capable of dictating, within the confines of this onscreen world, reality. Even if *Kya Kara Ba A* does cover familiar territory from her earlier work, these sections do prove that, at last, Kawase has come back to her starting point and is finally, in film form at least, in control of her own reality.

> "This is of course a very private film and also in my previous films I've delved into my own private life a lot. I don't think I can get any deeper than I've gotten now, so from now on I think it's important to use these experiences I've had in my life and turn them into fiction."

Whether Kawase will totally abandon her own personal experiences in her documentary work remains as yet to be seen. Her presence was inevitably felt in *Letter from a Yellow Cherry Blossom*, which covered the final 18 hours of the respected critic and photographer Kazuo Nishii as he passed away with terminal cancer, and was filmed as a two-way dialogue between the subject and his portrayer.

Still, Kawase seemed to be retreading old ground with her next fictional feature, *Shara*. Released in 2003, it covers the lives of a family living in Nara five years after the unexplained disappearance of their 12-year-old son. Kawase herself took the role of the heavily pregnant mother after the original star, Reiko Kataoka (*Hush!*) was forced to drop out due to ill health, but the end results were all too reminiscent of both *Suzaku* and *Hotaru*.

Recently, similar to Shinji Aoyama, she has been responsible for transforming her own film fiction into literary fiction with the novelizations of both *Suzaku* and *Hotaru*. In the meantime, despite retrospectives in 2000 at the Nyon Documentary Film Festival in Switzerland, and in 2002 at the Infinity Festival in Alba, Italy and the Musée du Jeu de Paume in Paris, her work still remains difficult to see, poorly circulated both in Japan and abroad. It's a crying shame. For all her critics, Kawase remains a unique voice in Japan, and one that cries out to be heard by far more people.

↓ Suzaku
萌の朱雀
Moe no Suzaku

1997. CAST: Jun Kunimura, Machiko Ono, Sachiko Izumi, Kotarō Shibata, Yasuyo Kamimura, Sayaka Yamaguchi, Kazufumi Mukōhira. 95 minutes.

RELEASES: DVD, Les Films du Paradoxe (France, French subtitles); VHS, Paradoxe (France, French subtitles); VCD, Edko Films (Hong Kong, English/Chinese subtitles).

Scenic and beautiful, Kawase's Cannes winner set amongst the rural backdrop of the village of Nishi Yoshino in Nara Prefecture may prove a little slow moving for some tastes.

The ancient Nara region, considered the spiritual nexus of Shinto in Japan, is wild, wooded, mountainous, mysterious, and, above all else, traditional. The city itself was Japan's first fixed capital between the years 710 and 784, the time known as the Nara period, and, like nearby Kyoto, every year millions of tourists arrive by the busload to visit the ancient temples, the deer park, and the famous 16-meter-tall bronze Buddha statue. Nara Prefecture is also home to one of the most intriguing directors working in Japan today, Naomi Kawase.

Kawase's first foray into fictional feature making stays within these geographical environs, but sees her entering new territory in terms of its subject matter. *Suzaku* sees her broadening the focus from her own immediate emotional world to take in the dynamics of a whole community, with a tale on three generations of the Tahara family, a household inhabiting the remote cedar logging village of Nishi Yoshino.

Suzaku is divided into two segments. A lengthy prelude set some fifteen years before portrays a community depleted by an earlier economic crisis that saw half of its inhabitants departing for the city. Those who remain await with baited breath the completion of a railroad project that will connect them to the outside world and bring much needed economic relief to the area. Flash forward fifteen years, however, and the project has been abandoned, leaving the villagers stranded from modernization and seemingly forgotten. Grandmother Tahara is sent off to an old person's home, whilst the toddler Michiru is now a high school student, ferried around the village on the back of her elder cousin Eisuke's scooter. Life goes on as usual as the family continue to eke out a living from the land, until one day the father, Kōzō, wanders off into the night. Later the family receives a phone call from the police reporting that his dead body has been found, his treasured 8mm camera lying beside it.

The urban-rural divide in Japan is a big one. Since the war, and especially during the rapid industrialization of the '60s, the countryside has faced a mass exodus as millions have headed for the cities in search of work. With film production companies now almost exclusively based in Tokyo, despite a small independent filmmaking scene in Osaka, few have remained to document the void that has been left. In *Suzaku*, Kawase attempts to show this other side of a Japan that has been all but buried in neon and ferro-concrete during the developments of the past century, and how this rapid urbanization, whilst maybe not to the same extent leaving its physical mark on the countryside, has left a hole in the lives of its inhabitants. This is symbolized by the gaping tunnel mouth of the railroad that is under construction, which in the modern sequences is shown blocked up and barricaded.

With the services of Masaki Tamura at her disposal, *Suzaku*, whose title refers to the name of a Chinese deity, certainly captures the mountainous region in all its majestic beauty. Kawase tells her tale in a series of long, unedited takes, utilizing a pseudo-documentary style that strives for veracity in its attempt to portray the habitual lives of those that inhabit this emotional heart of Japan and their place its this broader environment. Background music, as well, is kept down to the bare minimum of a simple piano refrain that periodically interrupts the soft throb of cicadas of this halcyon summer.

To further her end, all the roles in *Suzaku* are taken by non-professionals cast from the village, with the exception of Jun Kunimura, who plays the head of the family, a fairly familiar face throughout the '90s, debuting in Yōichi Sai's *All* under the Moon (*Tsuki wa Dotchi ni Deteiru*) in 1993, and going on to play in such important titles as **Gojoe**, **Audition**, and **Chaos**. Machiko Ono, who plays Michiru, won the Best Actress award at the Singapore Film Festival the same year and later became one of the focal points of Kawase's documentary, *Kaleidoscope*. However, due to the approach taken in *Suzaku*, no single character is really ever allowed to take center stage. The characters don't act, they just float around in front of the camera: digging the garden, riding up and down the street on bicycles, shuffling in and out of the house, muttering pleasantries and inconsequentialities to one another, mere figures to be shown going about their daily business against an awesome mountainous backdrop.

As a result, Kawase's faked documentary style is ultimately rather difficult to get a grip on. *Suzaku* is so subservient to portraying daily reality that it ignores the drama. The characters never make any decisions that will influence the flow of the narrative, and one knows that once the running time has expired, life will go on as usual. There's no higher message, no political agenda, no attempt at putting forward any sort of judgment on events. *Suzaku* is just there to be taken at face value.

Because of this, the viewer may feel like a distant observer watching these people's actions through a telescope. Lyrical and poetic, raw and beautiful—all of these are adjectives that can be applied to Kawase's films, but *Suzaku*'s picture postcard socio-realism lacks the intimacy that made her earlier, smaller-scaled work so powerful.

↓ Hotaru
火垂

2000. **CAST:** Yūko Nakamura, Toshiya Nagasawa, Miyako Yamaguchi, Toshiyuki Kitami, Ken Mitsuishi. 164 minutes.

Beautiful, naturalistic tale of the troubled development of a relationship between a young stripper and a potter is the crowning moment of Kawase's feature fiction.

There's a concept known as *honne-tatemae* in Japan, which governs how members of society negotiate their interactions with one another, a dichotomy between an individual's true feelings or motivation (*honne*) and the surface appearance or façade that he or she puts forward (*tatemae*). It has proven a fundamental conceptual cornerstone for numerous writers, both Japanese and foreign, to explain a whole host of aspects of Japanese society to uncomprehending outsiders: the inscrutable nature of the people and their apparent inability to express emotion, or the way that their quiet, polite, and unassuming nature masks a society where discretion goes in hand and hand with what would pass as the most flagrant of moral transgressions in other cultures. And finally there's the sleek modern image which the city of Tokyo projects, masking the fact that outside of the Kantō plains, much of Japan has been left far behind in the rural past.

In *Hotaru*, Kawase lets the mask slip on several fronts. Firstly, as with all her work, it is set in what might as well be a world away from Tokyo's urban bustle, in the earthier territories of provincial Nara. Secondly, it deals with human emotions in a way that is both raw and brutally honest. It is perhaps why her work has proven a lot more popular abroad than at home. This film picked up a FIPRESCI Award for the director at the 2000 Locarno International Festival, and yet slipped onto screens back in Japan virtually unnoticed. *Hotaru* certainly has a lot to recommend it, and can certainly be said to represent the purest summation of Kawase's approach throughout her first decade of filmmaking. In this respect, it showcases both her strengths and weaknesses as a fiction feature director.

Hotaru is centered around the character of Ayako, first seen as a teary-eyed seven-year-old in the film's early stages, after the suicide of her mother leaves her marooned in an adult world. Flash forward twenty years and she is still bearing the emotional scars, as she works during the evenings as a stripper whilst living with her elder sister, Kyōko. Daiji is a reclusive artisan, carrying on the family tradition of making pottery for the local temple and still living firmly under the shadow of the reputation of his recently deceased grandfather, whose kiln stands symbolically in the middle of the forest near his home. When the two meet, Ayako is recovering after an abusive relationship which ended with an unwanted pregnancy and an abortion. She is immediately impressed with Daiji's gruff honesty and the two begin a relationship, though one that suffers further complications when Ayako's grandmother dies and Kyōko becomes terminally ill with cancer.

The word *hotaru* means firefly, and is a commonplace motif in Japanese arts and literature. Indeed, a big-budgeted film directed by Yasuo Furuhata starring the iconic presence of Ken Takakura was released in Japan with the same title in the same year as Kawase's film. And yet, as Kawase has pointed out, in the urban areas of Japan fireflies can no longer be seen. The reason is that the elaborate mating displays with which the insects signal to each other are now literally buried in the neon glare of the city. Kawase uses this metaphor throughout the film to detail how difficult it is for two isolated people to find each other in a modern world with its myriad distractions. The shows put on by the strippers in the tawdry club where Ayako plies her trade to a horde of captivated men are an obvious parallel with the lighting displays of the fireflies.

Moreover, the *kanji* Kawase uses in the film's title is not the conventional one for the firefly, but an alternative compound word made up of the two characters meaning "falling fire"—the same used in Studio Ghibli's **Grave of the Fireflies**. Kawase makes full use of this falling fire as a further visual metaphor, filling the frame with as much natural light as possible—from the showers of embers falling from the burning brands wielded at the *hi-matsuri*, or fire festi-

val, with which the film opens, the faces of the spectators outside the temple, including a young Ayako, bathed with the glow; the dancing lights from the glitterball suspended above the stage at the strip club; the dying embers of Daiji's kiln; the fireworks display that sears the sky at the end of the film. Indeed, courtesy of camerawork by Masami Inomoto, who also shot Nobuhiro Suwa's highly acclaimed improvisational piece *M/ Other* (1999), another Takenori Sentō production, *Hotaru* is never short of stunning. Shooting over the course of a year, Kawase fills her film with such naturally beautiful images as a slow time-lapse sequence of clouds drifting across the face of the moon, and a ferry crossing the sea, against the golden light of a setting sun.

Like her previous *Suzaku*, *Hotaru* is shot in a manner which obscures the distinction between documentary and fiction, using handheld cameras and natural light. In this case however, Kawase benefits from having fewer characters to depict, and a more human hook into the drama in the form of the central romance. Whilst using a non-professional in the central role of Ayako (Nakamura, who despite a memorable enough performance, has subsequently not appeared in anything significant), Nagasawa, who plays Daiji has had roles in a number of films during the '90s, including Aoyama's *Helpless*, Kaze Shindō's *Love/Juice*, and Miike's *Family*. A more intriguing presence is Yamaguchi in the role of Kyōko, a former starlet in Nikkatsu's Roman Porno films of the '70s, including Shōgorō Nishimura's version of *Gate of Flesh* (*Nikutai no Mon*, 1977), Noboru Tanaka's contribution to the series based on Takashi Ishii's violent rape manga, *Angel Guts: Nami* (*Tenshi no Harawata: Nami*, 1979), and Kōyū Ohara's nasty nun flick, *Wet Rope Confession* (*Shūdōjo Nurenawa Zange*, 1979). She has made more recent appearances in Gō Rijū's *Chloe* (2001) and Yoshinari Nishikori's *A White Ship* (*Shiroi Fune*, 2001).

The raw improvisational approach certainly contributes to a lot of the film's power, though to some eyes may appear its biggest stumbling block. Kawase's lovers are so moody, withdrawn, and unresponsive to one another that you sometimes wonder why they got together in the first place. Ayako in particular revels in her role as the neurotic little girl who never quite grew up, desperately seeking a father figure in the form of Daiji's hairy craftsman to restrain her and shake her when she gets too hysteric.

Both characters clearly have a lot of psychological hurdles to clear before emerging reborn at the end of the film. After first spending the night together, the two sit in near silence for almost five minutes, trying to gauge each other's feelings by reading the subtle shifts in each other's expressions. Ayako confesses to Daiji that she's a stripper, and asks if it bothers him before insisting he come to watch her performance. Embarrassed, he deflects her questions with more questions, verbal brush-offs. The cut and parry is interspersed with long pregnant pauses. It's a grueling scene, not only due to its length, but also for its painfully earnest nature.

Kawase's script consists of a number of similar emotional crises steering this central relationship, giving the film an episodic feel that makes its lengthy running time felt. *Hotaru* is undoubtedly too long, a criticism which can be leveled at all of Sentō's J-Works productions and attributed to the amount of creative leeway he gave the directors working under his aegis. But this is perhaps beside the point. In a global film culture where new releases from whatever part of the world seem to invoke the same tired feelings of déjà vu, it's a marvel that a film like this can still get financed at all. Kawase is the only person doing this sort of thing, the only person with a finger on the pulse of what is going on in the less well-documented sectors of Japan. As such, *Hotaru* remains a powerful and unique invocation of both time and place, and a remarkably emotive depiction of its two central characters as they come to terms with their roles within it.

CHAPTER 17
Sabu
(Hiroyuki Tanaka)
サブ (田中博樹)

It's not uncommon to spot film directors from the Japanese independent sector popping up in roles in each other's films. Seijun Suzuki, who has developed a neat sideline in TV appearances, was a conspicuous presence in Shinji Aoyama's *Embalming*. Aoyama himself has appeared briefly in Kiyoshi Kurosawa's *License to Live* (sitting at a nightclub table alongside Akihiko Shiota) and the experimental *Barren Illusion*, and Gō Rijū's *Chloe* (*Kuroe*, 2001). Rijū turned up in a small role as the bus hijacker in **Eureka** in return and one of the few guilty pleasures of Aoyama's straight-to-video debut *Kyōkasho ni Nai!* was finding Kiyoshi Kurosawa in a cameo. Rijū also played in Yōichi Sai's debut *All under the Moon* (*Tsuki wa Dotchi ni Dete Iru*) back in 1993, and Sai had a major part in the drama of Nagisa Ōshima's **Gohatto** (1999). Takeshi Kitano, of course, turns up everywhere, and Shinya Tsukamoto, when not playing in his own work, has graced our screens in a variety of roles, from Kaizō Hayashi's **The Most Terrible Time in My Life** to a colorful appearance as a cross-dressing bottled water salesman in Ben Wada's *The Perfect Education* (*Kanzen Naru Shiiku*, 1998), and a more serious recent outing like Naoki Ichio's *A Drowning Man* (*Oboreru Hito*, 2002). None of these filmmakers, however, would count acting as their main profession.

Unusually, director Sabu, real-life name Hiroyuki Tanaka (sometimes credited as Hiroki Tanaka), has come from the opposite angle, so to speak, having started his career in the industry as an actor. Even more unusual is that the transition to film directing has been pretty much absolute. Aside from an appearance in Miike's **Ichi the Killer** and, up until **Monday**, occasional bit parts in his own work, since his debut with **Dangan Runner** in 1996 the mild-spoken director appears to have little desire to return to his days in front of the camera, opting almost exclusively to remain behind the scenes.

In doing so, over the past decade he has proven himself to be one of the most popular and dependable directors working in Japanese cinema. Both at home and, perhaps to an even greater extent, abroad, he has gained a legion of fans through his unique approach of developing and refining a trademark style of wild and free-form, quirky action-comedies populated by characters who hurtle headlong though squirming narratives steered more by the forces of incidence and coincidence than their own individual actions. Sabu's films are reckless charges to who-knows-where, in which the ride is more important than the destination.

And the ride is seldom a smooth one. The most unforeseen of factors or the simplest of misunderstandings can send the plot flying off obliquely in any number of unpredictable directions, with a surprise usually lurking around every corner. Take *Unlucky Monkey*, for instance, in which the story is launched when two bungling first-time bank robbers (played by the director himself and his favorite lead, Shinichi Tsutsumi) arrive at their target only to find that another thief, wearing an identical white ski mask, has already got there first. When this first unexpected burglar is gunned down by the bank's security guards as he runs across the road to where the two would-be thieves are standing open-mouthed, the bag of swag sails through the air into the waiting arms of Sabu, and then, after the security guards' rifles are turned on him, to Tsutsumi's character, Yamazaki. Making his escape into a maze of back streets, Yamazaki's first potential heist becomes more fraught when he spins around into the path of a young beauty wearing a walkman who fails to notice him, landing himself even further in hot water when the knife he is clutching plunges deep into her chest.

"It might appear as circumstance of course, but if you look at it more closely there's always a reason why you are somewhere in someplace at some time. Even though from the outside it looks like things happen without a reason, there's still also a kind of necessity there. When you move about or when you are confronted by a situation in which you end up by luck or whatever, it is still your reaction to it that creates something new. So it is not entirely by chance that these things happen."

Unlucky Monkey is perhaps the archetypal Sabu set-up, in every respect. Multiple subplots play side by side, diverging and converging again to combine and interfere with each other, as characters barely conscious of each other's existence come into conflict in unexpected and often quite bizarre ways. As Yamazaki in *Unlucky Monkey* is fleeing from the police, in another part of town a trio of yakuza accidentally brain their boss (Ren Ōsugi) with a bottle whilst pouring a drink for him, when another gang member, for a joke, bursts into the room wearing the same ski mask Yamazaki dropped into a dumpster earlier on, and the others spin around in panic. Later, Yamazaki finds himself seated alongside the panicked mobsters in a shop selling *ramen* noodles.

Similarly *Dangan Runner*'s trajectory is launched by a chance meeting at the local convenience store of three characters who are all having a particularly bad day, whilst the dim-witted protagonist of *Postman Blues* goes about his daily rounds blissfully unaware that he is being simultaneously pursued by both the cops and the mob. *Drive* kicks off when Asakura, a lonely office worker who parks in the same spot at the same time every day to watch the fantasy figure of Kō Shibasaki rounding the same corner and making a purchase at the local florist, one day finds his car invaded by a trio of unwanted joyriders on the lam after a major bank job. In a witty twist on the central concept of Jan de Bont's *Speed* (1994), the stressed out white-collar, first seen being diagnosed for hypertension by his doctor, refuses to break the 40kph speed limit.

It is this combination of unpredictability, apparent illogicality, slapstick, and keen-eyed observation of the more absurd details of others' external behavior that lies at the heart of the popularity of Sabu's films. They present us with a very down-to-earth form of escapism, and one that anyone can identify with. They typically

Filmography

1996
- *Dangan Runner* (*Dangan Rannā*) (a.k.a. *Non-Stop*)

1997
- *Postman Blues* (*Posutoman Burūsu*)

1998
- *Unlucky Monkey* (*Anrakkī Monkī*)

2000
- *Monday*

2002
- *A1012K* [short]
- *Drive*

2003
- *The Blessing Bell* (*Kōfuku no Kane*)
- *Hard Luck Hero*

© 1996 Nikkatsu Corporation

Sabu (right) on set

ness that surrounds them. In one part of *Unlucky Monkey*, Yamazaki attempts to avoid capture by concealing himself in a crowd of men and women ducking into a hotel, finding himself unwittingly stuck in the heart of a huge debate between a group of environmentalists and a company accused of pollution. In *The Blessing Bell*, the main character, Igarashi, stops for a drink in a tiny bar situated beneath the rail tracks, where he sits as a silent, inscrutable witness to an argument going on between the barkeep and a customer refusing to pay, followed by the emotional breakdown of a fourth party to this scene, an aging salaryman who out of the blue declares that he's dying of cancer.

"The main interest for me there is the drollness of normal people's everyday lives, how simply it can turn into something bizarre. Let's say that this helplessness sometimes shows you how funny life can be. People are supposed to be composed and know how to behave, but can suddenly deviate from what is expected as normal behavior. Those moments are very reflective on how people really are, I think."

Hiroyuki Tanaka's creative path into filmmaking is as convoluted as one of his scripts. In fact, his initial plan was to make it big in the music industry, starting out as frontman for a cover band whilst at high school in the Wakayama area where he grew up. After working on their own material, the band released one self-financed album in a limited run of 500 copies, which all ended up being given to the people who'd lent them the money to record it in the first place. High school came to an end, and the individual band members all went their separate ways to continue their studies, with Tanaka going on to spend the next two years at a design school in Osaka. Here he formed another band, but when it came to graduation, the pattern repeated itself once more and he found himself heading up to Tokyo, alone, where he moved on to his next musical project.

deal with characters that you might spot on an everyday basis going about their daily business, your average everyday Joe.

There's the salaryman of *Monday*, who wakes up in a strange hotel room, fully clothed and in a muck sweat, his memory a huge drunken void from the night before. There's the eponymous hero of *Postman Blues*, who learns to his cost what it means to read other people's letters. There's the down-trodden factory worker in **The Blessing Bell**, barely conscious of the broader world around him as his long walk to clear his head after being laid off from work eventually leads him back to his front door.

At heart, Sabu's characters are blank canvases for the audience to project upon, passive participants to the absurdities of the situations they find themselves in and silent spectators to the mad-

Tanaka's creative destiny was not to lie within this particular industry, however, and somewhere along the line he switched to acting. His first break was a minor role in *Sorobanzuku* in 1986, directed by *Family Game* director Yoshimitsu Morita, and starring a famous double act that broke through at around this time. In a story about a TV advertising agency, he played an actor for one of the commercials, cast for the ability to make a mean face.

For the next five years, he kept up acting using his real name in a series of small uncredited parts, which were, according to the director himself, "mostly gangster roles, yakuza, or '*chinpira*' " for films that did little to bring him to the attention of critics or the wider public, until a breakthrough appearance in Katsuhiro Ōtomo's *World Apartment Horror* (1993) garnered him a Best Newcomer award at the Yokohama Film Festival. The film, a rare foray into live action from the manga artist and director of *Akira* (1988), tackled the issue of racial prejudice against Southeast Asian immigrants in a high-spirited horror comic-styled rendition of a story which saw Tanaka's mean yakuza trying to evict a building-full of Asian immigrants living in Tokyo. They eventually ward him off by evoking the spirit of a toilet-dwelling demon.

"Again I played a yakuza, but this time it was a completely different experience for me: the director was a lot more demanding and I had to work a lot harder for this role, and it was very interesting to do. Since then I became a little bit spoilt and raised my level for the sort of roles I would accept, but the quality of the scripts of the work that was offered to me at that time was below this level. I kept on acting but after a while I started to think that it might be better to start writing and directing my own stories. So this is why I chose to switch to directing."

The roles didn't get much better after *World Apartment Horror*, seldom straying too far from low-budget V-cinema territory, although he did get to appear in supporting parts in Ryūichi Hiroki's critically acclaimed mainstream youth movie *800 Two Lap Runners* (*Happyaku Two Lap Runners*, 1994) and Takashi Miike's *Shinjuku Triad Society*.

"Up until *World Apartment Horror* I used my real name, but after that I played a character called Sabu. On the set it is common for the actors to call each other by their character's name, and it stuck as my nickname, so I decided to keep on using it. A lot of people asked me about it. It sounds good, it stands out, and people always remember it. When I started directing I stuck to this name."

By 1996, Tanaka, under his new moniker of Sabu, had successfully steered his career into directing. His first film, *Dangan Runner*, was for a newly revitalized Nikkatsu, which had just returned to film production, albeit in a rather slimmed-down manner. Sabu's debut work stems out of a dissatisfaction with the type of films being made in Japan at that time, and doesn't fit into any of the standard types of genre filmmaking then popular—the violent, stylized yakuza films typified by the work of Takeshi Kitano, Takashi Miike, or Takashi Ishii; the slow naturalistic arthouse pictures from directors such as Nobuhiro Suwa, Naomi Kawase, and Hirokazu Kore-eda; or the wave of pre-millennial horrors represented by *The Ring* and *Cure*.

As with the best Japanese movies of the era, *Dangan Runner* is a triumph of inventiveness in the light of harsh budgetary reality, forcing Sabu to carve out a niche with his own peculiar approach to storytelling. Though in terms of plot, it is little more than an extended on-foot chase scene between three unrelated characters—a petty thief, a convenience store clerk, and a lowly gangster—it is a model of narrative ingenuity in the way that it keeps the action jogging along for the duration of its running time, adding the weight of characterization to the

© Jonny Office Co., Ltd. / avex inc.

Hard Luck Hero

three-man tag team by means of flashbacks and their own imagined projections of the outcome of the chase, as their minds begin to wander and their bodies begin to tire.

> "In *Dangan Runner*, my first film, I made the characters run throughout the film. If I would have had to do a car chase it would have cost a lot more money, so in that way there's always a limitation when you make a film, and from that limitation, I differ from other people in that I can make a kind of shift and develop a story along lines that are unpredictable for viewers, I think. Probably that will remain my style from now on as well. I think it's proven to be successful and has achieved what I want— to entertain people and also to get them thinking about the points in the story. I am still the only person that does it this way."

A bigger budget meant that Sabu's next offering was slightly more substantial, though certainly no less inventive. *Postman Blues* features a happy-go-lucky postal worker named Sawaki who, whilst delivering a letter to Noguchi, an old school friend who is now part of the yakuza, walks off by chance with his freshly severed finger after it rolls off the table and falls into his mailbag. Not only does this land his former classmate in trouble with his mobster bosses, who need the chopped-off pinkie as proof of the young man's allegiance to the gang, but it also lands Sawaki in hot water when he is spotted by the police leaving his friend's apartment and unwittingly becomes the main suspect in a drug-trafficking case. A worthy second step to Sabu's directing career, *Postman Blues* is fast paced and funny, though the steam was somewhat knocked out of what seemed at first glance a unique premise by a further coincidence: It traveled several international film festivals together with another film revolving around the adventures of an errant postal worker, Norwegian director Pål Sletaune's *Junk Mail* (*Budbringeren*, 1997).

Like *Dangan Runner*, *Postman Blues* is structured around a multiple pursuit, a format that would be refined throughout much of Sabu's oeuvre. It also features Shinichi Tsutsumi in the lead role, an actor who has starred in all of Sabu's work up until *The Blessing Bell*, and whose work outside of Sabu's oeuvre lies predominantly on the stage. It also takes great delight in its repeated potshots at the tough guy image of the yakuza, attempting to perforate the myth put forward for years in cinema, that their lifestyle is a particularly glamorous one. Noguchi's character in *Postman Blues* is even shown visibly worshipping a poster on his wall of the iconic Ken Takakura, star of dozens of films in the genre from Toei studios. Making heavy use of such familiar regulars as Susumu Terajima and Ren Ōsugi, instead, Sabu's work has a tendency to portray the yakuza as a mixture of bumbling buffoons and craven cowards, constantly running scared or squabbling like children. In *Unlucky Monkey*, when one unfortunate trips, the gun secretly tucked into his belt goes off and blows a bloody hole in his crotch.

> "Of course this is a genre in Japan that is still treated very seriously, and there are a lot of films in which they are shown as real cool guys that the viewer either tries to emulate or feel nostalgic about. And actually the young people that go to watch these films sometimes end up going on to become yakuza themselves. I think that's not a good thing, because in the end gangsters are really not very nice people. On the other hand, because they have such a clear and dangerous image it's very easy to make fun of them.
>
> "I acted myself for a very long time and I've done a lot of yakuza roles, so I know how you are supposed to look as a gangster and

> I think to myself, it's very hard to look mean all the time. The scene in *Monday* where the boss starts complaining about how tough it is to be a yakuza, it's not completely distant from the truth, because when you start thinking about what type of life they lead, and really think seriously about it and not believe all the things they show you in normal yakuza films, you start wondering whether it's such a nice way to live after all. The thing I picked out was comedy, but there are lots of other things we can imagine about them."

Sabu's films have been ready-made hits on the underground cult circuit and have proven wildly popular when they have played on the festival circuit. *Monday* won the FIPRESCI prize at Berlin in 2000, and many of Sabu's films have been released abroad. Until recently the applause at home has been somewhat muted, with the director falling some way beneath the radar as far as the serious film critics are concerned. Nevertheless, with six features under his belt, Sabu has established himself firmly enough to find his fan base growing ever wider and his status in the industry more secure. Shortly before the release of *Drive* in 2002, he was called in to direct the 17-minute short film, *A1012K*, intended as an advertisement for a range of mobile phones. *A1012K* features a stand-off between a renegade robot and a SWAT team wielding cell phones, set in the Shibuya branch of the Tsutaya chain of video shops, who also made the film available for free rental on video as a promotion (though the film was later released on DVD).

In the meantime, whilst arguably yet to chart much in the way of new territory, his films have continued to get bigger and better, slicker and more efficient, and still as wildly entertaining as they ever were. Though recent work like *The Blessing Bell* has hinted at a change in pace and direction, it remains to be seen just how deeply the Sabu style is ingrained within his work.

At any rate, Sabu's work still manages to re-

main popular abroad. After a domestic theatrical premiere at the 2003 Tokyo International Film Festival, his *Hard Luck Hero*, a rock-about vehicle for the prefab boy band V6 set in the world of underground kickboxing, was released directly to DVD in Japan. It's a typical work for the director, but in a review for *Variety*, Derek Elley accused the filmmaker of "hasty scripting" and as "largely marking time, with only occasional flashes of real inspiration." Nevertheless, the film was selected for the Special Invitation section of the 2004 Berlin Film Festival.

↓ Dangan Runner

弾丸ランナー

Dangan Rannā, a.k.a. Bullet Runner, Non-Stop

1996. CAST: Tomorowo Taguchi, Shinichi Tsutsumi, Diamond Yukai. 82 minutes. RELEASES: DVD, Beam (Japan, no subtitles); VCD, Universe (Hong Kong, English/Chinese subtitles).

A wild rollercoaster ride or a wild goose chase? Sabu's characteristically charismatic debut is an inventive piece of narrative ingenuity, and sets the pace for an entire career.

Things aren't going well for Yasuda (*Tetsuo* star Taguchi). Shortly after his dismissal from the lowly post of kitchen porter sees him upended like a turtle on the galley floor covered in shredded cabbage, he is next seen cruelly being given his marching orders by his girlfriend, shortly before she exits stage left into the night, arm in arm with another man.

Desperate measures are called for to salvage his crumpled pride, and so he conceives a plan to hold up a local bank. Even this has its obstacles, however. The simple act of buying a face mask from a local convenience store to disguise his features is scuppered when he discovers he has left his wallet at home. In desperation he

Dangan Runner

© 1996 Nikkatsu Corporation

stuffs the mask in his pocket anyway, though he is spotted by checkout boy Aizawa, who chases him out of the shop and into the street.

Meanwhile Aizawa (Yukai), a washed-up and drug-addled rock singer, is having trouble paying for his latest fix. Obviously his menial employment in a convenience store won't support his habit, and the sight of some lowlife reprobate pilfering from the shop aisles doesn't do much to improve his humor, either. He sets off in hot pursuit, though the chase is rudely interrupted by the arrival of his local yakuza dope-peddler Takeda (Tsutsumi), out to collect payment for the fairly hefty backlog of unpaid-for drugs.

Takeda has problems of his own, however. Even whilst hot on the trail of the other two losers, he has his own reasons to run. After accidentally allowing his own boss to be rubbed out by a rival gang, he finds that the rest of his mob are rather eager to catch up with him. The three men, pursued by a carload of irate mobsters, set off on a lengthy on-foot chase through the streets of Tokyo.

Sabu's directorial debut sees the former actor asserting his unique approach to the action-comedy: a frenetic, chaotically busy style that would be refined and perfected over his successive films. The simple premise set up swiftly with the convergence of our main trio of protagonists, the film initially threatens to follow the route of the sort of extended multiple chase sketches favored by lewd British funnyman Benny Hill or the Keystone Cops. Yet Sabu's approach to such a potentially restrictive linear narrative is in no way as straightforward as the film's title—*dangan* means bullet—would suggest. Turning conventional approaches to plot structure inside out, Sabu lets the characters shape the plot rather than the plot shape the characters.

The result is wildly unpredictable and often quirkily humorous. Rather than more traditional means such as dialogue, the three runners' characters are fleshed out by use of flashbacks, daydreams, bizarre POV shots, and seemingly random thought patterns as, tired out by their exertions, their minds begin to wander. In one nicely amusing scene, while they jog along the pavement, the sight of a pretty young woman triggers off a series of sexual flights of fancy in all of the runners, as they all imagine themselves making love to her before coming around to the reality of their situation and continuing the chase.

By hardly allowing himself to draw breath in the early stages of the story set-up, Sabu has some difficulty in maintaining the same momentum throughout the rest of the film, and just like that of the three running men of the title, its pace does begin to flag towards the final quarter. However, considering the evidently low budget, *Dangan Runner* is a remarkably accomplished debut with a refreshingly different approach. A wild rollercoaster ride, or a wild goose chase, it's probably best left up to the individual viewer to decide, but it's a fast one nonetheless, and you do get to see an awful lot of scenery along the way.

↓ Monday

1999. CAST: Shinichi Tsutsumi, Ren Ōsugi, Yasuko Matsuyuki, Masanobu Andō, Susumu Terajima, Tomorowo Taguchi, Naomi Nishida. 100 minutes. RELEASE: DVD, Rapid Eye Video (Germany, German subtitles), Taki Corporation (Japan, no subtitles).

A salaryman wakes up in a hotel room with a hangover and a gaping hole in his memory. Based on objects he finds in his pockets and around his room, he manages to retrace the events of the previous night and comes to a shocking discovery. A more character-based effort for director Sabu, and quite a leap forward from his previous films.

When young salaryman Takagi wakes up one Monday morning, he finds himself in a strange hotel room, fully clothed and with a gaping hole in his memory. How did he get there and what happened to him the night before? As beads of sweat start trickling down his forehead, he fumbles through his pockets in search of a handkerchief.

Out falls a bag of purification salt, an item traditionally used at Japanese funerals to ward off evil spirits. It brings back the memory of a wake over the dead body of young Mitsuo (Masanobu Andō, the younger of the two layabout delinquents from Takeshi Kitano's *Kids Return* and also seen in **Battle Royale**), an event which quite literally ends with a bang and saves the family the cost of a cremation. From there on, the previous night's events slowly start to unfold in Takagi's mind, spurred on by small objects he finds around the room and in his own pockets—objects whose significance for Takagi's fate grows increasingly ominous.

With *Monday*, Sabu steers well clear of the frenetic, high-speed hijinks he had up until that moment been known for, going instead for calculated, cleverly constructed situational storytelling. This change of pace allows the director to show that he is not a one-trick pony working in the vacuum of his own self-created genre niche, but that he can handle characterization, can carefully build up his story, and that he actually has something to say.

In *Monday*, Sabu's trademark brand of absurdist comedy retains a strong down-to-earth quality which is very much grounded in everyday life and which makes it instantly recognizable and thus more effective. The premise of a drunken businessman, for instance, carries even more weight when one knows that every weeknight around the midnight hour, Tokyo subway trains are full of heavily intoxicated salaryman.

Monday establishes Sabu as a keen observer, not only of the society around him, but also of human nature and behavior, and, as the film's guns-versus-reason finale shows, of man's moral fiber. As a director and storyteller, he has a gift for mixing comedy and drama that is second to none. In his films, the two are mutually advantageous, with one element enhancing the weight and impact of the other. Playing a big part in this is his eye for detail, born of his observational skills, which makes small things play a major role in the unfolding of the story.

Masterfully constructed and at times achingly funny, with another rock-solid tragicomic performance by the underrated Shinichi Tsutsumi, this is one *Monday* you won't want to give a miss.

↓ The Blessing Bell

幸福の鐘

Kōfuku no Kane

2002. CAST: Susumu Terajima, Naomi Nishida, Itsuji Itao, Seijun Suzuki, Ryōko Shinohara, Tōru Masuoka. 87 minutes.

A slower-paced film for Sabu, but is this more meditative tale of a recently fired blue-collar worker embarking on a quest for meaning in his life really a change in direction?

To those taken with Sabu's approach, his films just keep getting better and better, but to his detractors there's still an anticipation that the director might someday be capable of deviating from the template to deliver something a little more substantial, and at first glance, *The Blessing Bell* would appear to be such a film. Having progressed from on-foot chases, with his 1996 debut **Dangan Runner**, through bicycle chases in *Postman Blues*, and culminating in the four-wheel pursuits of his previous film, *Drive*, as if they all represented the various rungs on the evolutionary ladder, it looked like the director's automotive obsessions had reached their pinnacle.

Given this, for those awaiting something different from the director, the opening lengthy

The Blessing Bell

static shot of a rusting, empty train track filling the frame accompanied by the strains of a howling wind seems rather encouraging. However, it soon becomes clear that Sabu's ostensible stab at an art film is not so much a departure as a change of pace.

The Blessing Bell follows the slow, head-down trudge of its blue-collar protagonist, Igarashi, through the twenty-four hours succeeding the moment he is laid off from his factory when it announces it has ceased operations. After fruitlessly scouring the local job ads, Igarashi pauses to sit and ponder his fate by the banks of a river. Here, his silent musings are interrupted by the mumbled confessions of a penitent yakuza seated a couple of meters in front of him, seemingly in the midst of a religious conversion. After finishing his speech, the gangster slumps forward and rolls down the slope, collapsing in a heap at the bottom to reveal a large knife jarred between his ribs. A passing policeman rides into the frame on his bicycle, and Igarashi is promptly ushered off to jail.

In prison, a confession from his cellmate opens up a new sense of purpose for the redundant worker. Upon his release a few hours later, his innocence proven, a visit to the Chance Bar, where the killer's deceased wife used to work as a hostess, sets in motion a chain of events that take in an encounter with a ghostly Seijun Suzuki and a lucky stumble across a winning lottery ticket.

Susumu Terajima as Igarashi, here replacing Sabu's regular leading man Shinichi Tsutsumi for the first time, makes for a wonderful audience identification figure, plodding through the film as if carrying the weight of the world on his shoulders. Bemused brow furrowed in concentration as he peers frettingly into the beyond, our hapless agent is shuffled by the caprices of fate through a series of vignettes in which he stumbles into the daily lives of a host of unrelated characters.

With no dialogue for the first twenty minutes, *The Blessing Bell* is both slower and more lyrical than Sabu's usual fare, but no less enjoyable because of it. Melding a host of subtle visual gags in an episodic structure marked by humorous about-turns in both tone and trajectory, perhaps an apt description would have the gloomy melancholy of Mike Leigh's *Naked* (1993) rubbing shoulders with an absurdly escalating chain reaction narrative akin to Kitano's ***Getting Any?***.

For all that, though, *The Blessing Bell* still ends up back exactly in the same place where it started, and those expecting any radical change of tack from the director might find themselves disappointed. At the risk of damning it with faint praise, Sabu's latest still makes for steady and compelling viewing, and even if it doesn't quite satisfy the lofty expectations it initially engenders, there's still plenty to enjoy here for both fans and casual viewers alike.

CHAPTER 18
Hideo Nakata
中田秀夫

There have been few more gripping images conjured up by turn-of-the-century fantasy cinema than that of the pallid-faced figure of Sadako, a solitary bloodshot eye peering through her lank, greasy locks, emerging jerkily from the cathode-ray tube towards the viewer. With its spare, less-is-more approach, *The Ring* launched a thousand nightmares across Asia and Europe, and spawned a Hollywood remake en route. Japan had a new king of horror, and his name was Hideo Nakata.

Nakata's strength, most efficiently showcased in *The Ring*, is an ability to evoke a brooding sense of anxiety without resorting to cheap scare tactics, short sharp shocks, or buckets of blood and offal. The chilling efficiency of his method has ensured that Nakata's name has become firmly identified with the macabre, something about which the director is not entirely happy, especially when considering that even a cursory glimpse at his track record reveals a surprising diversity of works in a number of different genres, from documentary to teen-oriented drama.

Like so many filmmakers of his generation, Nakata's passage into the industry came via erotic films, specifically those being produced en masse by Nikkatsu. Born in 1961 in Okayama Prefecture, by the time Nakata got involved with the company in the mid-'80s, shortly after graduating from the prestigious Tokyo University, the heyday of Roman Porno was limping to

an end. With the growing popularity of cheaply shot straight-to-video pornography during the '80s, the market for large-screen erotica was rapidly shrinking. Nikkatsu's production had slimmed down from the previous decade (their peak year was 1973, when they released just under 70 titles), and to counter competition from the AV market, were making their films rougher and "harder"—not to mention a good deal cheaper.

Nakata entered Nikkatsu as an assistant to the director Masaru Konuma. One of the studio's most treasured possessions, the prolific Konuma was the figure behind glossy sado-masochistic spectacles such as *Flower and Snake* (*Hana to Hebi*, 1974), and *Wife to Be Sacrificed* (*Ikenie Fujin*, 1974), both starring the statuesque figure of Japan's favorite fetish actress, Naomi Tani. During the mid-'80s, even this studio veteran was beginning to feel the pinch, and was forced to film *Woman in a Box: Virgin Sacrifice* (*Hako no Naka no Onna: Shōjo Ikenie*, 1985) on video to be released as part of their new Roman X straight-to-video hardcore series. In it, a sadistic couple kidnap a young girl and take her to their underground lair. Over an hour of rape and torture ensues, culminating in the young girl being imprisoned in a large box with her head poking out the top. Though considered a classic in some circles, *Woman in a Box*, based on a script by Kazuo Komizu under his customary pseudonym of Gaira, is pretty strong stuff, boasting an endless parade of horrific scenes of graphic violence acted out by hideous cast members and shot with the production values of an Australian soap opera. Indeed, Nakata's first job in the film industry was anything but glamorous.

> "In many people's minds Roman Porno is very artistic, but in reality, I was treated almost like a slave. We worked for very long hours with a low budget, shooting a 60–70 minute long feature film in just seven or eight days, and we often didn't sleep for 36 hours or so. It was a very hard, tough job. Sometimes we had to shoot in the crowds, so we had to hide the camera. For example, in *Woman in a Box* we shot the first scene in a car very near to Shinjuku station, so we had to put a black cloth up so that passers-by couldn't see what was going on. The camera was hidden but there was a light on the top of it, and the car wasn't moving, so the passers-by could sometimes figure out what was going on and would laugh. We had a sort of inferiority complex, which is contradictory as we were making a movie and, of course, this movie would end up being shown at film theaters, but we had to hide ourselves during the film shoot. Sometimes we had to lie to the people who owned the property. For example, we had shot lots of sexual scenes in an amusement park, so we had to pretend that it was for a TV production and carried different scripts."

And yet, Nakata still harbors a good deal of affection for these days. He went on to work with Konuma on the older director's final works in the erotic arena, the first film's glossier large screen sequel, *Woman in a Box 2* (*Hako no Naka no Onna 2*), as well as *Rinbu* (a.k.a. *La Ronde*) in 1988. After a break from filmmaking of over ten years, Konuma returned to the screens with the more mainstream offerings of the nostalgic piece of family entertainment, *Nagisa* (2000), a rite-of-passage movie about a young 13-year-old growing up in the '60s, and *Mizue* (*Onna wa Basutei de Fuku o Torikaeta*, 2002), by which time Nakata's career path had led him not only to the other side of the world and back, but also to the top of the Japanese box office. Still, he paid homage to his mentor with the documentary *Sadistic and Masochistic* in 2001, made partially for his own enjoyment and partially to introduce the name of the director whom Nakata still considers a major stylistic and technical influence on a wider number of people.

Interestingly, one of Konuma's earlier assistants from the '70s was a certain Toshiharu Ikeda, whose ultra-violent, ultra-stylized *Evil Dead Trap* (*Shiryō no Wana*, 1986), a macabre slasher film owing much to the films of Dario

Filmography

1986
- *Natsutsuki Monogatari* [short]

1992
- *Hontō ni Atta Kowai Hanashi* [TV series, 4 episodes, co-director]

1995
- *Jokyōshi Nikki: Kinjirareta Sei*

1996
- *(Ura) Tōsatsu Nanpa Dō*
- *Ghost Actress* (*Joyūrei*)

1997
- *A Town Without Pity* (*Ansatsu no Machi—Gokudō Sōsasen*) (a.k.a. *Assassin Town*)
- *Haunted School F* (*Gakkō no Kaidan F*) [TV, co-directed with Kiyoshi Kurosawa]

1998
- *The Ring* (*Ringu*)
- *Joseph Losey: The Man with Four Names* (*Joseph Losey: Yottsu no Na o Motsu Otoko*)

1999
- *Ring 2* (*Ringu 2*)

2000
- *The Sleeping Bride* (*Garasu no Nō*)
- *Jushiryō: Gaiten* [video]
- *Jushiryō: Gaiten 2* [video]
- *Chaos* (*Kaosu*)

2001
- *Sadistic and Masochistic*

2002
- *Dark Water* (*Honogurai Mizu no Soko kara*)

2003
- *Last Scene*

Argento and David Cronenberg, is to Japanese horror of the '80s what Nakata's *The Ring* is to the '90s. Graphically gruesome and played straight-faced, Ikeda's film is often seen as the apotheosis of the splatter movie, foreshadowing the genre's decline throughout most of the '90s, until Nakata's film pointed toward new and subtler directions for horror to pursue.

"**The least I can say is that I never liked splatter movies in the '80s, the Hollywood style ones. I never watched them. Perhaps people are bored with them now. I personally think there are different waves and trends in the horror genre, so maybe in five or ten years Hollywood might start producing these kinds of splatter movies again. Maybe because of the developments in computer technology in film production we can create every kind of cruel image we can imagine, so probably at the end of the '80s, we'd reached this extreme point of expressions of cruelty. So now we are aware that maybe this kind of violence and cruelty is too much for the audience: with so many serial murders happening in the real world, we regularly watch this sort of thing on the news. This is just my opinion. These days, I think that the audience would like to watch more sophisticated or subtle psychological horrors.**"

It was during these early days at Nikkatsu that Nakata made his very first film as a director, independently produced outside of the studios for his own fun, a 30-minute short called *Natsutsuki Monogatari* [trans: Summer moon story]. Shot over a course of weekends using friends from an independent theater company, the story was a straightforward drama about a film projectionist who is asked by a female elementary teacher to show Buster Keaton silent comedies at the rural school where she works. Filmed silent in 16mm monochrome, it was never intended for commercial distribution, and screened only a couple of times, with a live music accompaniment.

© 2000 Nikkatsu Corporation

Hideo Nakata

In 1992, Nakata took his first job as a director, prophetically enough, within the field of horror. *Hontō ni Atta Kowai Hanashi* [trans: Scary stories that really happened] was a series of one-hour TV shows which ran for about six months on TV Asahi, each divided into two twenty-minute episodes. Nakata directed three of these episodes; *Shiryō no Taki* [trans: The waterfall of the evil dead], *Norowareta Ningyō* [trans: Cursed doll], and *Yūrei no Sumu Ryokan* [trans: The inn where the ghost lives].

Meanwhile, at the beginning of the '90s Nikkatsu had decided to get out of the market of erotica, and after a period of over twenty years had returned to more mainstream film productions, albeit low-budget ones for TV or the straight-to-video market. It was at this time that Nakata moved to London on an artistic scholarship to study the British Free Cinema movement at the capital's National Film Archive. Coming about due to technical changes that resulted in the increased availability of lightweight 16mm camera equipment, this movement of the late '50s and early '60s has parallels with the French Nouvelle Vague. Stating in its manifesto that it believed "in the importance of people and the significance of the everyday," its foundations lay in a number of low-budget documentaries that centered around the seldom before portrayed lives of the working classes. Intended as a kickback against the more literary based classical model of British post-war cinema, the

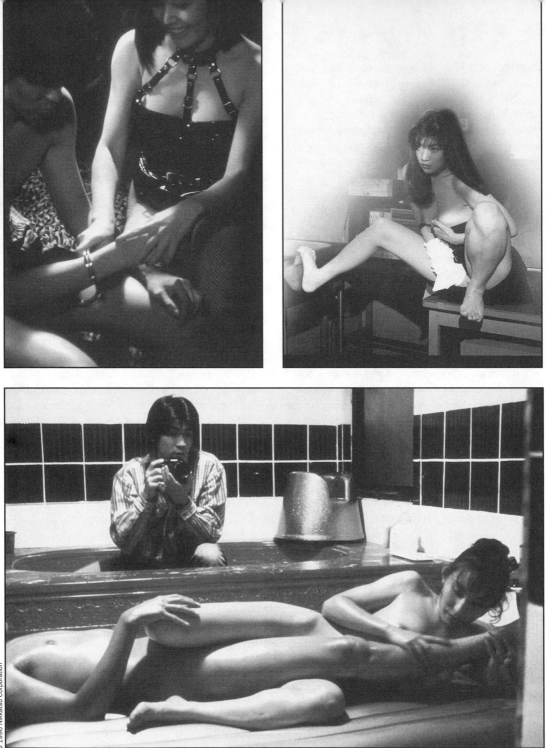

(Ura) Tōsatsu Nanpa Dō

movement's socio-realistic "kitchen sink" approach resulted in a number of works sketched out against the backdrop of a crumbling British class structure, amongst which are the films of Lindsay Anderson (*O Dreamland*, 1953; *This Sporting Life*, 1963; *If...*, 1968); Czechoslovakian-born Karel Reisz (*Saturday Night and Sunday Morning*, 1960); Tony Richardson (*A Taste of Honey*, 1961); and John Schlesinger (*Billy Liar*, 1963), as well as a new émigré to the capitol from Poland (via France), Roman Polanski (*Repulsion*, 1965; *Cul-de-Sac*, 1966).

What attracted Nakata to the movement is unclear, but at any rate, the movement had been a fairly short-lived one, and it wasn't long before he had seen all of the films he had come to watch, allowing him more time to fill in the gaps in his film knowledge by watching a lot of early Hollywood classics and to travel around mainland Europe.

> **"I also realized that film production in England and in Europe in general at that time, around 1993, was not so active. I watched a special effects shoot at Pinewood Studios for Bernardo Bertolucci's *Little Buddha*, but that was my only active experience of a film shoot in England. I traveled around continental Europe a little and then I decided I needed to do something creative."**

In 1993, whilst Nakata was still in Europe, Nikkatsu went bankrupt. With the future of the film industry in Japan looking just as shaky as it did in Europe, his own career path as a director looked uncertain. Nakata decided to stay on in England for a short while longer to make a documentary on the director Joseph Losey (1909–84). The U.S.-born filmmaker proved a fascinating subject. Having moved to Britain in the '50s as a result of the McCarthy anti-communist witch-hunts, the left-leaning Losey directed his first films there under a series of pseudonyms, first putting his name to *Time without Pity* (1956). Best known for his col-

laborations with the acerbic scriptwriter Harold Pinter, *The Servant* (1963), *The Accident* (1967), and *The Go-Between* (1970), memorable for their disturbing psychological and warts-and-all depictions of the British aristocracy and the thin divide that separates them from the masses, Losey later was responsible for a number of pan-European co-productions such as an adaptation of Norwegian playwright Henrik Ibsen's *The Doll House* (1973) and *Les Routes du Sud* (1978), about an exiled Spanish revolutionary who having forged a successful career as a screenwriter, returns years later to his homeland.

> **"He actually came to Japan to shoot parts of his second-to-last film, *La Truite (The Trout*, 1982). This French film has Japanese scenes at the beginning of the film. That was the time I was in college and went to a seminar about cinema. This seminar influenced me a lot. The professor was a big fan of Losey's works, but we couldn't see any of his American films other than *The Boy With Green Hair*, nor any of his early British films before *The Servant* and *The Criminal*."**

After completing his scholarship, Nakata came back to Japan, returning to London in 1994 to shoot the interviews for his documentary, though it was to be several years before postproduction was completed. In order to finance this pet project, Nakata luckily found several directing jobs, including an erotic feature distributed by Toei, *Jokyōshi Nikki: Kinjirareta Sei* [trans: Female teacher's diary: forbidden sex]. The Losey documentary was eventually released in 1998, between the two *Ring* films, to accompany a retrospective of the director's previously unreleased work in Japan, as *Joseph Losey: The Man with Four Names*, referring to the pseudonyms under which he had to work.

Nakata has made no secret of his disinterest in horror. *Ghost Actress* was written purely as a commercial exercise in order to gain enough money to complete his documentary on Losey, yet at the same time his first feature foray in the genre, based around a cursed film production, makes an interesting precursor to *The Ring*. Produced by wunderkind Takenori Sentō under his J-Movie Wars production house, a subsidiary of Japan's first satellite broadcasting company Wowow, the story revolves around an attempt to make a period drama set during the Second World War. Opening with a sequence of traditional Japanese dolls staged in various postures against a backdrop of translucent *shōji* paper screens, we join the story as the preliminary preparations for the shoot are underway. During the casting of the film's two main actresses, a ghostly subjective presence peers down on the crew from above the lighting rig.

Ghost Actress showcases all the stylistic devices that the director would use in his later film, *The Ring*. Perfectly crafted, and demonstrating the director's restrained, even-handed approach to pacing to create an unnerving atmosphere, it gained Nakata an award for Best New Director at the Michinoku International Mystery Film Festival in 1997. The film world setting is perhaps the greatest masterstroke, allowing for some effective film-within-a-film trickery, with the subliminal shots of a beautiful young actress as she materializes on the daily rushes preparing the ground for Sadako's cursed video in the later film. As with Italian director Michele Soavi's *Deliria* (a.k.a. *Stage Fright*, 1987), and Nakata's later non-horror offering *Last Scene*, the setting also allowed the director to get around the problem of a limited budget.

> **"When I thought of the idea for *Ghost Actress*, I understood that the budget of this project was very limited, so I thought that if I shot the film just in the studios, we could avoid the problems of location shooting: hiring cars, transportation from location to location, etc. We shot *Ghost Actress* in ten and a half days, and *Last Scene* in fifteen days. We were very budget conscious again when we shot *Last Scene*. *Ghost Actress* is of course a horror film. *Last Scene* is not such a realistic depiction of the Japanese film industry, from my point of view. But probably those two films share something that has to do with my love for filmmaking. One of my favorite films is *Day for Night* by François Truffaut. These two films don't look like this, but probably one of the reasons why I was attracted to that kind of "film production" sub-genre is because I worked as an assistant director at Nikkatsu studios for seven years, where those two films were shot. For *Last Scene*, maybe 95% of it was shot at Nikkatsu studios, and most of the scenes of *Ghost Actress* were, too."**

Shortly after its bankruptcy, Nikkatsu studios was bought up by the electronic games giant Namco, and in 1996 started production once more. One director who was to make his debut feature with the newly opened company was Sabu. He was present in *Ghost Actress* in his original capacity as an actor, playing the role of the first assistant director, and also appeared in Nakata's next work, an erotic film produced by Nikkatsu directly for the video market.

(Ura) Tōsatsu Nanpa Dō [trans: (Behind the scenes) Hidden camera pick-up technique] is about a recently graduated photographer who harbors lofty artistic intentions, but instead finds himself freelancing as an assistant cameraman for a glossy men's magazine. He soon finds he gets more than he bargains for when he becomes entangled with the secretary working in the front office of the publication. Nakata himself sees parallels with the main character of the story, and with his own path into filmmaking working for Konuma, in this amusing and well-crafted pink film. It was also one of the final roles for Sabu (who sheds his clothes at one point to join in the action) before he decided to leave the acting profession in favor of directing.

Less entertaining was Nakata's next film, *A Town without Pity*, a perfunctory thriller about a police detective who goes undercover to infiltrate a gang of local mobsters in an attempt to disclose allegations of murder and corruption by a senior colleague. Nakata handles the material in a proficient and assured enough manner, but being slow-moving and with not much in the way of action, the end results provide little in the way of a hook for the viewer.

Fortunately bigger things were round the corner. In the following year he directed the first two episodes of the three-part Kansai TV omnibus, *Haunted School F*, further strengthening his reputation as a director with the ability to handle supernatural material in a unique and chilling fashion (the third episode was directed by Nakata's main rival in the horror stakes in Japan, Kiyoshi Kurosawa). But it was his next production that would bring Nakata to the forefront of contemporary Japanese filmmaking.

Kōji Suzuki's first novel, *The Ring*, caused a huge stir when it was published in the summer of 1991, an intriguing mix of mystery, horror, and pseudo-science involving a murdered child psychic named Sadako, now expressing her rage via a telepathic curse spread like a virus by means of a video cassette. The writer followed up this roaraway success with *The Spiral (Rasen)* in 1995.

The *Ring* film project was initiated by three producers: Takenori Sentō, with whom Nakata had made *Ghost Actress*; Takashige Ichise, the young hotshot who produced Kaizō Hayashi's debut **To Sleep So As to Dream** at the tender age of 24 and later went on to produce *The Grudge (Juon)* series; and Shinya Kawai, later producer of Jōji Iida's *Another Heaven* (2000). The production had been in development for over a year before Nakata was brought on board, joining scriptwriter Hiroshi Takahashi with whom Nakata had worked already on the *Hontō ni Atta Kowai Hanashi* TV series and the films *Ghost Actress* and *A Town without Pity*.

Straight away the two got to work on a script, one which departed in several aspects from Suzuki's source material, re-treading already proven material from their previous collaborations and developing new angles to the

© 1998 Shusaku Kobo

Joseph Losey: The Man with Four Names

story to make it work better dramatically. The first major alteration was in changing the character of the novel's central investigator from a man into a young single mother. However, perhaps the most significant deviations came with the character of Sadako. A prototype of the shambling figure in a white dress, hair brushed over her face, had already appeared in the *Yūrei no Sumu Ryokan* episode from the 1992 TV series, which the two had worked on together, and was reprised in *Ghost Actress*. In Sadako it reached its most effective incarnation. Moreover, the scenes from this previous film in which the *Ghost Actress*'s blank visage appears between frames on the newly shot film footage are an obvious antecedent for Sadako's cursed video, developed further in Nakata's *Rei Bideo* [trans: Spirit video] episode from *Haunted School*. And finally, the scene in which Sadako crawls from the television screen came not from Suzuki, but was inspired by the Western horrors of David Cronenberg's *Videodrome* (1983) and Tobe Hooper's *Poltergeist* (1982).

In an unusual step for the '90s, the producers decided to release the first two Suzuki adaptations together as part of a double bill. Nakata's film opened alongside Jōji Iida's *The Spiral* on January 31, 1998, and became an instant success. Iida had already been involved in the more faithful TV movie version of the first novel, *Ringu: Kanzenban* [trans: Ring: complete edition] in a scripting capacity. His adaptation of *The Spiral* concentrated more on the scientific aspects of Suzuki's second novel, downplaying the horror and mystery in an attempt to explain, rather than mystify. Playing more along the lines of a classical horror mystery, Nakata's slow and assured pace and disturbing ambiance, in which evil lurks within every household appliance, considerably overshadowed Iida's film. *The Ring* set in vogue a horror boom which lasted several years, plugged into the end-of-millennium feeling of uncertainty and unease many were sensing, and not just in Japan.

The immense success of *The Ring* made it inevitable that a sequel would be demanded. The problem was, of course, that Suzuki's second novel, *The Spiral*, had already been adapted, and his third, *Loop*, had yet to be published (it appeared mid-1998, and as yet remains unfilmed). Nevertheless, Suzuki's publishing

company Kadokawa Shoten insisted, and a competition was announced to find a suitable script to take off from where the first film ended. About four hundred scripts were submitted, but none proved suitable, so Nakata and Takahashi sat down and came up with a story that would start off almost immediately after the ending of the first one and exist independently from the events of *The Spiral*. Branching off to follow the character of Mai (played by Miki Nakatani), the girlfriend of one of the now-deceased victims of the videotape in the first film, *Ring 2* is a complete departure from Suzuki's novels, a hospital horror that builds on the myth of Sadako whilst filling in parts of the back story.

> "*The Spiral* and *Ring 2* have a sort of parallel world. I understand it's a bit confusing. When we made *Ring 2* we were thinking of John Boorman's *Exorcist 2*. That's a very peculiar horror movie. I shared his desire to make a very strange horror film: scientific, sad, and lots of elegance in one film. His intention is what inspired us. There are a few similar scenes."

Ring 2 came out at the beginning of 1999 on a double bill with Shunichi Nagasaki's *Shikoku*, a ghostly tale not related to Suzuki's novels. As is usually the case with sequels, despite similarities in style with its predecessor, as a standalone film it rarely reached the same terrifying heights, and Nakata sensibly decided to opt out of the third *Ring* film, *Ring 0: Birthday*.

The Sleeping Bride, Nakata's next feature project, was a complete about turn into romantic fantasy, an adaptation of the manga *Garasu no Nō* [trans: The glass brain] by *Astroboy* creator Osamu Tezuka, based loosely on the fairytale *Sleeping Beauty*. This gentle film, an oft-overlooked and underrated part of Nakata's oeuvre, was not a commercial success, however. Released in the same year was **Chaos**, a taut and intricately plotted kidnapping movie, but nevertheless, Nakata's attempts at spreading his wings into other genres seemed hindered. With horror still a marketable genre to be tapped into, 2000 saw the resurrection of Nakata and Takahashi's three original *Hontō ni Atta Kowai Hanashi* episodes on a video omnibus entitled, *Jushiryō: Gaiten* [trans: Cursed ghost: supplementary story].

> **"Honestly speaking, I don't like horror films, as a person or as an audience member. But critics and reporters look upon me as a horror film director, so it's almost inescapable for me now. People in Hollywood now also look upon me in the same way, so now, maybe, it's become my fate. But I'd like to produce different kinds of movies."**

Given their immensely successful track record, Nakata and Takahashi seemed the obvious choice to adapt Suzuki's 1997 horror novel *Honogurai Mizu no Soko kara* [trans: From the bottom of the murky water]. *Dark Water* fits comfortably within the genre of Old Dark House chillers with obvious precedents in Nicholas Roeg's *Don't Look Now* (1973) and Stanley Kubrick's *The Shining* (1980), featuring an emotionally unstable single mother trapped in the midst of a complicated custody battle with an abusive ex-husband for their five-year-old daughter. Moving to a dilapidated old tenement block on the outskirts of town, both mother and daughter are subjected to increasingly frequent visions of a young girl in a yellow raincoat. Meanwhile, the dripping taps, leaking roofs, and overrunning gutters are welling up at an alarmingly steady rate, eventually threatening to saturate the entire building. Though not causing quite the same ripples as *The Ring*, *Dark Water* did little to harm Nakata's reputation as a sturdy and efficient crafter of scary supernatural stories. It received a relatively widespread release around the globe for a Japanese horror film, and joined *Chaos* to become the third of Nakata's films to be bought up for Hollywood treatment.

In the meantime, shortly after the Hollywood remake of *The Ring* arrived in the States in October 2002, his next film premiered in Berlin. *Last Scene* told the tale of a rather self-inflated '60s movie idol left in a commercial wilderness after his onscreen partner quits to get married and his wife dies in a car accident. Thirty-seven years later he arrives, as an old man, to work as an extra on a rather banal production financed by a TV company. Here he forges a friendship with a cynical prop girl who, like him, has become disillusioned about the state of the industry. However, as the production progresses, through their relationship they both rediscover the joy of movie making.

> **"*Last Scene* is a straightforward melodrama. The main idea is to make the audience cry. Melodrama is my favorite genre, but I cannot survive just making melodramas, as they don't make so much money."**

The story is based on an original idea by the film's producer, Takashige Ichise, who also produced the first two *Ring* films. Beginning with a film-within-film sequence, it uses the 1965 prologue to contrast the difference in Japanese production methods over the past thirty years. According to Nakata, the main character is loosely based on Chishu Ryū, a star actor from the '50s and '60s who appeared in a number of Ozu's better-known movies such as *Tokyo Story*, and who died in 1993. Though some reviewers in Japan saw the film as an implicit criticism of the new industry structure, Nakata himself stressed that the film was not meant to be anything more than a nostalgic melodrama, realistic in neither its portrayal of the industry working methods nor its central narrative arc. Unfortunately the South Korean company that produced it went bankrupt shortly after its completion, meaning that this further attempt by the director to escape the horror genre into more personally favorable territory was, disappointingly, not widely distributed theatrically in Japan, surfacing on video a few months later.

With *The Ring* standing amongst of the most prominent Japanese films known abroad at the tail end of the millenium, there has been significant foreign interest in its director, who had a number of discussions with Hollywood studios. Nakata himself is eager to go wherever the work takes him, be it Hollywood, Europe, or continuing to make films within his home country, though he harbors a desire not to be typecast. The question that is on everybody's lips at this early stage in his career is whether he will be able to shake off Sadako's curse. Having already covered such diverse ground in such a short time, this seems a very likely possibility.

↓ The Ring

リング

Ringu

1998. CAST: Nanako Matsushima, Hiroyuki Sanada, Miki Nakatani, Rikiya Ōtaka, Yūko Takeuchi, Hitomi Satō. 95 minutes. RELEASES: DVD, Universal (U.S., English subtitles), Tartan (U.K., English subtitles), Spectrum DVD (Korea, English/Korean subtitles).

"The key line is very simple. There is a cursed video which can kill very quickly, in seven days exactly, and the three main characters watch the video. How can they get away from the curse? That kind of very simple and strong story, it might not be very realistic, but, well, VCRs and TVs have become so common in our daily lives, in Japan and in other Asian countries, as well as in Europe and America. And of course, Kōji Suzuki's ideas are very suitable for popular horror movies, especially for teenagers."—Hideo Nakata

The mysterious death of her teenage niece, Tomoko, and the seemingly unconnected demise of three of her friends at exactly the same time leads TV journalist and single mother Reiko

Asakawa into an investigation as to the cause. There seems to be some link with a news report she is working on regarding urban myths, specifically one regarding a video cassette that kills anyone who watches it, with the only way to remove the curse being to show it to someone else within the space of a week. Reiko follows the trail of corpses down the Izu peninsula to a rented holiday cabin where Tomoko had been holidaying with her deceased companions. Here she discovers an unmarked video tape, which she puts into the machine. The tape contains a sequence that shows a young girl brushing her hair in a mirror, overlaid with the Chinese characters that spell the name "Sadako," followed by a grainy sequence of a girl crawling from a well and towards the viewer.

Realizing the link, and haunted with the premonition of her own demise, Reiko turns for help to her ex-husband Ryūji (played by former action idol and protégé of Sonny Chiba, Hiroyuki "Henry" Sanada—star of Norifumi Suzuki's messy 1982 actioner *Roaring Fire/Hoero Tekken*, who much later took center stage in Yōji Yamada's *Twilight Samurai/Tasogare Seibei*, 2002, and had a sizeable part in the U.S. production *The Last Samurai*, 2003).

Following a series of clues in a race against time to save her life, the two eventually pinpoint the source of the curse on the island of Ōshima, just south of the Izu peninsula. Here they uncover the legend of Sadako Yamamura, a child psychic pitched down a well thirty years prior, and now somehow manifesting herself by means of the video.

Kōji Suzuki's novel *The Ring* was first published in 1991. Its simple plotline of a cryptic message encoded onto a videocassette that kills anyone who watches it proved familiar and simple enough to grasp the public's imagination firmly in its steely grip, finding such analogies in the real world as chain letters, computer viruses, and bootleg videos. Its popularity way exceeded the author's expectations, leading to a new interest in horror in Japan and prompting the publication of *The Spiral* in 1995 and *Loop* in 1998 to form an ad hoc trilogy that appears to have evolved rather than being constructed to any set plan.

First transferring from the page to the screen by way of a plodding TV adaptation, *Ringu: Kanzenban* (directed by Chisui Takigawa), Nakata's theatrical representation is where the curse of Sadako found its ideal host. It radically reshaped the source material, assimilating aspects of Nakata's own film oeuvre into the substance to dress up the original pseudo-scientific horrors in the guise of a traditional mystery chiller, with its precedents in the *onryō*, or vengeful ghost, scenario deeply ingrained in Japanese folklore. Released on a double bill with Jōji Iida's adaptation of Suzuki's follow-up novel *The Spiral*, the first split occurred when both films spawned their own parallel TV series, both diverging wildly from their respective literary sources: *Rasen: The Series*, delivered in an ominous thirteen episodes, and the twelve episodes of *Ringu: Saishūshō* [trans: Ring: the final chapter].

Nakata's adaptation rapidly became the top-grossing horror film of all time at the domestic box office, and set in motion a torrent of terrors that included *Uzumaki* and the *Tomie* series (*Tomie* directed by Ataru Oikawa in 1998; *Tomie Replay* directed by Fujirō Mitsuishi in 2000; *Tomie Rebirth* from *The Grudge* director Takashi Shimizu in 2001; and *Tomie Final Chapter Forbidden Fruit/Tomie Saishūshō Kindan no Kajitsu* directed by Shun Nakahara).

Taking off like a storm across Southeast Asia, spawning a Korean remake along the way (Kim Dong-bin's *The Ring: Virus* in 1999), the story modeled the very method by which Sadako's curse transmitted itself. *The Ring*'s reputation spread across the world by means of video dupes, Hong Kong VCDs and word of mouth, with well-received festival screenings followed by more widespread theatrical distribution throughout much of Western Europe.

Meanwhile, with *The Spiral* already adapted,

Ring 2 branched off from the original concept in a well-constructed but uncalled-for sequel that continued right where the original left off, before Nakata stepped out of the franchise to make way for Norio Tsuruta, later director of the disappointing adaptation of Junji Itō's manga about a rural town besieged by killer scarecrows, *Kakashi* (2001). The final theatrical release of this series was the "prequel" film *Ring 0: Birthday* (*Ringu 0: Bāsudē*), based on one of a compendium of short stories that made up *Birthday*, Suzuki's fourth book in the series. Its disappointing box office result when it was released on the same double bill as Toshiyuki Mizutani's *Isola* (*Tajū Jinkaku Shōjo Isola*) in 2000 put pay to any further sequels in Japan, but by this time the accountants in Los Angeles had already got a whiff of *The Ring*'s box office success.

DreamWorks rapidly snatched up the remake rights, along with a host of other Asian films unknown to the broader film-going populace, with Sadako mutating to Samara in the process. The U.S. version of *The Ring*, directed by Gore Verbinski, of *Mouse Hunt* (1997) and *The Mexican* (2001) fame, and penned by *Scream 3* screenwriter Ehren Kruger, was released in 2002, and preceded the U.S. DVD release of the Japanese original (released under its romanized Japanese katakana title *Ringu* to avoid confusion) by about six months. The box office receipts were good enough to warrant a sequel, which, in a further deviation, was not only based on an original script unrelated to its Japanese models but also marked Nakata's long-awaited debut as a Hollywood director.

Looking back on Nakata's version, as so many attracted by the U.S. remake have done, it might seem difficult to see what the original fuss was about. After all, *The Ring*'s central premise, high on concept and low on plot logic, is only one short step away from such silly films as Wes Craven's *Shocker* (1989) that had seen the slasher genre falling on its feet just ten years before.

After a wane in popularity during the first half of the decade, Craven had rekindled the horror genre himself in the West with the *Scream* series (1996), a tongue-in-cheek spin on the films with which the director had made his name. However, the postmodernist conceit central to *Scream* and the mini-wave of films that followed it, of ironically distancing themselves from the full force of their violent fantasies by not taking themselves as anything more serious than mere entertainment, "a laugh and a scream," was already beginning to lose its novelty by the tail end of the millennium. With horror re-established as a marketable genre worldwide, the ground was prepared for a more back-to-basics approach.

Outside of such obviously U.S.-modeled slasher offerings as Toshiharu Ikeda's *Evil Dead Trap* or Kiyoshi Kurosawa's *The Guard from Underground*, Japanese horrors had previously either been grounded in folklore and legend, in ghost stories such as Masaki Kobayashi's portmanteau of Lafcadio Hearn short stories, *Kwaidan* (1964) or Satsuo Yamamoto's *The Bride from Hell* (*Kaidan Botandōrō*, 1968), or merely Asian riffs on transplanted Western gothic staples, such as Michio Yamamoto's *Lake of Dracula* (*Chi o Suu Me*, 1971) or Hajime Satō's *The Ghost of the Hunchback* (*Kaidan Semushi Otoko*, 1965).

Where *The Ring* succeeded was in marrying the vengeful ghost scenario with the sanitized teen-pitched genre revival of Craven's films. In doing so, it got back to the very basis of what made the horror genre work in the first place—the mystery element, the feeling that there is something inexplicable lurking just beneath the surface of normal everyday living. In its modern-day setting, Nakata realizes that the strongest light creates the darkest shadows, allowing him to play his horrors entirely straight-faced.

The Ring's urban mythological basis struck a chord with a general public who had flocked in droves to see Daniel Myrick's and Eduardo Sánchez's then popular *The Blair Witch Project* (1999). The parallel is all the more seductive thanks to the similarity in style between that film's hand-held VHS cinema-verité and Nakata's creepy handling of the flickering found footage of Sadako's video (the contents of which were never described in the original novel), full of grainy, drenched-out colors periodically interrupted by bursts of static.

But perhaps the most notable aspect is the restrained handling of the material. *The Ring* has nothing in the way of gore or nudity. There are no loud shocks or screams or bangs and bumps. Using an unobtrusively even style of long takes and mid to long shots, Nakata adopts a somber and narrative-driven approach to evoke the innate uncanniness of its central premise, conjuring up an all-pervading aura of anxiety and unease that lingers long after the film has finished. Plugging into the pre-millennial zeitgeist of its time of release, *The Ring* sports some incredibly effective moments, all laid down to an electronic soundtrack of onomatopoeic groans and whirs. You can feel the goosebumps during Sadako's manifestation through the TV screen.

This first film, however, leaves the whys and wherefores of its plot to its successors. It is undoubtedly why some find the very vagueness of the story so unsatisfying, as Hiroshi Takahashi's script provides very little in the way of explanation and many plot strands are left untied at the end. Intriguingly, Iida's *The Spiral* suffers from the reverse, explaining too much in its attempt to get beneath the surface of Sadako's character.

Kōji Suzuki has subsequently moved away from horror writing. Nakata, despite misgivings about being typecast in the genre with which he made his name, after two further films returned with the haunted house thriller *Dark Water* in 2001. With the character of Sadako now co-opted in the U.S. as Samara for any number of potential remakes, the producers of the original have literally given up the ghost. On Sunday, August 11, 2002, during the Japanese public holiday of O-Bon, the Festival of the Dead, a symbolic funeral for Sadako was held in Tokyo's Harajuku area.

↓ The Sleeping Bride

ガラスの脳

Garasu no Nō

2000. **CAST:** Yūki Kohara, Risa Gotō, Kōmei Eno-
moto, Tomoka Hayashi, Michiko Kawai, Yūko Na-
tori. 100 minutes. **RELEASES:** DVD, Winson (Hong
Kong, English/Chinese subtitles).

**A young girl awakes from her coma when she
is kissed by the boy who grew up with her in
the private sanatorium where she has lived
since her birth, but for how long will she remain awake? Teen-oriented romantic drama
based on a manga by Osamu Tezuka.**

In 1954, a plane crashes in the environs of
Mount Fuji. The sole survivor is a heavily pregnant woman named Masako, carrying a baby girl
inside of her, but she dies several weeks later.
Before doing so, however, she gives birth. Flaw-
less in every other way, the child, named Yumi,
is born in a coma and refuses to wake up. Years
later, housed in a private sanatorium paid for by
her father, Yumi is tended to by Dr. Hikawa and
a host of surrounding nurses as they search for a
possible cure to her strange condition.

Several years later, a fellow patient at this
private clinic, a six-year-old named Yūichi being
treated for asthma, stumbles into Yumi's private
room to discover her asleep in her bed. After
being warned to keep away from this private
space by one of the nurses, he chances upon an
illustrated children's book in the nursery containing the story *Sleeping Beauty*. Inspired by the
tale, he rushes to her bedside every day, muttering the words "Wake up. I'm a prince" as he
kisses her, a habit which continues, fair weather
or foul, long after he has been discharged from
the hospital. In 1972, a TV news bulletin on the
still sleeping Yumi stirs up distant memories in
the now 17-year-old Yūichi, drawing him to
her bedside to plant a kiss on the lips of his own
sleeping beauty just one more time. This time,
however, she wakes up.

© 2000 Nikkatsu Corporation

The Sleeping Bride

As with the two works that bracket it, ***The
Ring*** and ***Chaos***, it's difficult to know how much
to give away in terms of a synopsis for *Sleeping
Bride*. The story has the clarity of a fable, un-
ravelling slowly and evenly in a linear fashion,
with no sudden twists or great fanfares to signify
crucial turning points, and every scene taking us
in new and unexpected directions. Because of
this, the film remains a joy to watch from start
to finish.

It's a testament to the strength of the material Nakata has to work with. *Sleeping Bride* is based on the manga *Garasu no Nō* [trans: The glass brain] by Osamu Tezuka (1928–89). Often referred to as the "The God of Manga," Tezuka is a household name in Japan. His first work, the revolutionary 200-page *Shintakarajima* [trans: New treasure island] published in 1947, pioneered the format of the graphic novel, setting in motion Japan's multi-million-yen comic industry. Tezuka's comics introduced close-ups, different frame sizes, *katakana* sound effects, and lengthy action sequences sometimes spread across a number of pages, and over the next 40 years the prolific artist went on to create a plethora of well-known works in the same style, including *Mighty Atom* (*Tetsuwan Atomu*), *Black Jack* (*Burakku Jakku*) and *Princess Knight* (*Ribon no Kishi*). A number of these have been published in English language versions. Setting up his own production house named Mushi Productions in 1962, he also developed a healthy sideline in animation, adapting a number of his works for both the small and large screen, including the seminal TV series of *Mighty Atom* (1963), better known under the international title of *Astro Boy*, and *Kimba the White Lion* (*Janguru Taitei*, 1965).

Though a good proportion of Tezuka's work has been adapted to the screen as animation, *Sleeping Bride* is one of the few attempts to realize the artist's vision as a live-action film. Nakata himself speaks disparagingly about his first major turn away from the horror genre, claiming that Tezuka's world is too pure for a successful live-action treatment. The film was not a great commercial success, labeled at the time of its release as an "idol movie," whose sole purpose was to showcase its two unfeasibly beautiful teenage leads (neither of whom have achieved any subsequent level of success within the film industry). Whilst perversely one can't help thinking that the material might be better suited to the cartoon format, the lucidity of Tezuka's core idea is well served here by Nakata's no-frills approach to storytelling, and the charming end results certainly have a lot to recommend.

↓ Chaos
カオス
Kaosu

2000. CAST: Masato Hagiwara, Miki Nakatani, Ken Mitsuishi, Tarō Suwa. 104 minutes. RELEASES: DVD, Kino International (U.S., English subtitles), Taki Corporation (Japan, English subtitles), Tartan (U.K., English subtitles), Spectrum DVD (Korea, English/Korean subtitles).

Tricky but meticulously structured mystery thriller unfolding around a kidnapping and an alluring femme fatale, handled with the same assured pacing that makes Nakata's horror so effective.

In an expensive French restaurant, a wealthy-looking older man, Komiyama, is having lunch with a beautiful woman. After getting up to leave, the elegantly dressed younger lady slips out of the restaurant whilst her partner is paying the bill. Initially unconcerned by her disappearance, he returns to work assuming she has gone back home. Shortly after getting back to his office, he receives a phone call from a desperate-sounding voice informing him that his young wife, Saori, has been kidnapped, and telling him to dump off a taped-up plastic bag containing 30 million yen in a rest area by a suburban road junction. Komiyama immediately gets the police involved, but to no avail, and the kidnapper manages to disappear into thin air with both his money and his wife.

The story now shifts to a different viewpoint, in which the man we have already seen as the kidnapper is approached in his house by a young lady dressed in shabby-looking clothes. After removing her hat and glasses, we recognize her as the beautiful young diner from the first scene, now willingly offering herself up for capture in order to dupe 30 million yen from her wealthy spouse. Saori has been left the keys of an apartment belonging to a friend of hers, so that she can feed her friend's pet fish while she is out of town for a couple of months, providing a convenient place to hide out for a few days. In order to stage a more convincing kidnapping, her abductor lays down a series of rules during her stay there, which include not feeding the fish, not touching anything, and to await the three rings on the telephone to signal her to unlock the apartment door to let him in when he returns. He then binds her up and leaves to pick up the money. However, when he gets back, he finds the fish alive in the tank, and Saori dead on the floor. He is then startled by a phone call, through which a muffled voice delivers his next set of instructions, ones that will implicate him even deeper in this dangerous triangle of deception.

Following the fairytale simplicity of **The Sleeping Bride**, Nakata's *Chaos* surely lives up to its name as one of the most complex and torturously plotted thrillers released in recent years. Based on the mystery novel *Sarawaretai Onna* by Shōgo Utano and adapted for the sceen by Hisashi Saitō, a sometime director who in that same year made *Sunday Drive* from his own script, it is a meticulously crafted kidnapping movie revolving around a series of body doubles, double crossings, and double bluffs, adroitly plotted and unfolding its mystery at a slow and steady pace. Saitō's script certainly

proves dense and satisfying enough to reward repeated viewings, with every five minutes delivering an abrupt about-turn in our handle of what is going on.

Chaos also proves that Nakata's assured pacing is just as well suited to the mystery thriller as it is to horror, using a trademark visual economy to create a slow-burning aura of tension and mystery. This is further fueled by the underlying sexual frisson between abductor and abducted, the latter played by a stunning-looking Miki Nakatani, the actress who had bridged the gap between Nakata's **The Ring**, *Ring 2*, and Iida's *The Spiral* in the role of Mai.

Nevertheless, Nakata's restrained handling of the material, whilst bringing a subtle moral ambivalence to the characters, upon a single viewing also occasionally threatens to obscure crucial plot turning points, something exacerbated by Nakata's technique of keeping the camera predominantly at mid shot, rarely allowing us a full view of the characters' faces.

Chaos is a film that requires a lot of attention by the viewer. Constantly twisting between events and perspectives and with only the occasional visual cue to aid the viewer in positioning each scene on the narrative timeline—the pounding shot of rain with which the film begins, for example—it will prove anything but an easy ride for people who like every plot point spelled out in bold capitals. Still, those that can follow its torturous path will find themselves gripped from start to finish.

mal relationship with a normal man. But she is with a masochistic man and actually she becomes a sadist herself. Even if she didn't think of herself as being a sadist, she changes little by little. Then there's this kind of explosion when she says, 'Why, if I'm normal, do I have to be with a man like you?'"

This acute grasp of children's psychology has become the main characteristic of Shiota's work. His next film, *Don't Look Back*, released in Japan the same year as *Moonlight Whispers*, focused on the friendship between two ten-year-old boys and the onset of adolescence and maturity that slowly begins to cloud over their camaraderie. Partially set to the theme of *The Longest Day* (as played by three little girls on portable keyboards), the boys fall out with each other, make new friends, discover girls, and try to cope with loss and tragedy.

It sounds like a meandering plotline, but for Shiota it's a tool to have the children express a wealth of often confused emotions. Stripping his work even further of excess baggage, there is not even the slightest hint of anything potentially lurid. What we are left with is a very pure and genuine look at children and their behavior.

It's tempting and easy to refer to any film about childhood as nostalgic. However, as the title indicates, there is no nostalgia as such in *Don't Look Back*. This is not an adult's teary-eyed retrospective of the innocent days of childhood, in which all is harmless mischief caught in golden hues. There is no sun to cast those golden hues, as the film seems almost perpetually caught in twilight, expressing these children's state of being in between childhood's daylight and maturity's darkness. The former is lost, the latter is inevitable but, as is better indicated by the film's Japanese title, which translates roughly as "Let's go as far as we can," that darkness needn't be a bad thing. With Shiota frequently shooting his young actors from the back, the message is clear from the film's style alone.

As the boys seek ways to deal with the onset of maturity, one of their methods lies in disobedience. Delinquency is a way to achieve freedom, to grow up but not conform. The gap between individuality and conformity, illustrated by way of delinquent behavior, is a theme the director would explore in more (and more painful) detail in *Harmful Insect* two years later.

"I wanted to portray this gap. It's a gap between the ones who can fit in with the rules of society and the ones who choose to stay outside these social rules. For example, a child can go to school and learn all kinds of things, but he has no alternatives in life. He has no other choices besides going to school. This causes a double identity in young people, especially at thirteen, fourteen years old. On the outside they look satisfied with their lives and the way things are going, because everything has been organized in every detail, but in their inner personality they can have some very violent aspects. There is an ambivalence between the two."

Don't Look Back was co-produced by Eiga Bigakkō, the Film School of Tokyo, a privately run film school founded by producer/exhibitor Eurospace and Tokyo's cinephilic Athénée Français cultural center. Shiota, who by that time had also garnered a reputation as a film critic for the now defunct Japanese edition of *Cahiers du Cinéma*, is one of the filmmakers employed as a teacher. The school not only co-produced the film, but sent many of its students to work on the crew (Kiyoshi Kurosawa's *Barren Illusion* and Jōji Matsuoka's *Acacia Walk/Akashia no Michi* (2001) were two other such experiments). Shiota used his school ties well, since his next two films, *Gips* and *Harmful Insect*, were both co-scripted by students.

Gips (2001) was an entry into the Love Cinema project, a series of six low-budget features shot on digital video by some of the country's foremost young directors, chiefly among them

Ryūichi Hiroki's ***Tokyo Trash Baby*** (2000), Isao Yukisada's *Enclosed Pain* (*Tojiru Hi*, 2000), and Takashi Miike's *Visitor Q* (2001). Named after the Japanese word for plaster of paris, the film dealt again with the awakening of desire and obsession in female characters. With additional hints at lesbianism and murder, the story concerned a young woman's fetish for wearing a cast around her leg, a fixation that found its source in an incident during puberty in which she broke her leg and subsequently found herself the center of amorous attention from a teacher. She befriends a girl who helps her when she clumsily fiddles around with her shoe, and the discovery that the two are the same age is only the beginning of the newcomer's increasing identification with the fake invalid, which reaches its completion when she tries on the cast herself.

Shiota lets the intriguing plot unravel at a sure but steady pace, and the drama is compelling and entertaining. But while the film is technically proficient enough, the director does little to fully exploit the advantages of the digital medium, sticking with a limited number of locations, minimal set dressing, and a visual style predominantly composed of static long shots. With the medium imposed upon him by the producers and the minimal budget, Shiota himself recognizes the film's shortcomings.

> "***Gips*** was composed mainly of still shots, because the film dealt with a certain psychological matter. So in this case, digital video was not the best medium to use. But I do have great interest in digital video, and in the future I'd like to make a movie about teenagers using digital video. It could be a very good way to express the vitality of young people."

Gips turned out to be only a temporary sidestep away from the subject of children and adolescents. The theme continued to fascinate him and he returned to his trusted territory with 2001's *Harmful Insect*. Shiota has a simple explanation for his preoccupation with the subject of

Falala

childhood, one that also displays his preferences for staying close to reality:

> "If you want to describe the problems of Japanese society today, teenagers are a fitting symbol. It's always they who are confronted with and related to those problems."

The story of a young girl growing up in a broken home, *Harmful Insect* returned to a number of the themes present in *Don't Look Back*, most notably the advent of maturity in children. Here, Shiota intensifies the situation by presenting a character who is outwardly still a child, but whose home life forces her to grow up at an almost unnaturally fast pace. With a single mother who fails to juggle her job and the care for her daughter, *Harmful Insect*'s protagonist, Sachiko, is left to her own devices and finds herself alienated first from her friends and classmates, then gradually from society as a whole.

> "She is a very sad young girl, and this sadness lies in the fact that she is forced to become an adult. Maybe when you see her in this film, you think she is very strong and she is very close to being an adult. She's becoming an adult, so she certainly has a kind of strength that's unusual in people who are so young. But I think that she is actually a very weak young girl who is hiding all her weak points. She tries

not to show them to others. Also, she doesn't speak so much because words always come from feelings. If she speaks only one phrase, her feelings come out and she wouldn't be able to stop that feeling which she has kept hidden deep inside her."

The character of Sachiko is played by the young actress Aoi Miyazaki, who first came to prominence in Shinji Aoyama's *Eureka* in a role that showed off her ability to act with little or no dialogue. Like her work in Aoyama's film, in *Harmful Insect* her almost wordless performance communicates a wealth of emotions and confusion.

"I think she's the best actress I could ever hope to find. Maybe from now on, I won't be able to find another actress who is that good. She has great intuition, so even if this character can't be explained with dialogue, she understood well what it was she had to express by using her face and posture. From the beginning I only thought of Aoi for this role because I had seen *Eureka* and thought she was wonderful in that film. I got to meet her soon after that and found that she was also a wonderful person in real life, as well as being very charming."

Although his career so far has been characterized by sensitive portrayals of children, Akihiko Shiota has said that he wants to branch out and treat other subjects as well. His passion for genre cinema, nurtured during his days at Rikkyō, has never left him. After toying with the idea of making a musical about female assassins, which he quickly abandoned after Seijun Suzuki's **Pistol Opera**, he took on his first big-budget commercial assignment. *Resurrection*, produced by Toho studios, was set up as a romantic drama about the deceased returning to their loved ones from the beyond, but was given a shot in the arm by Shiota's unsentimental treatment of the subject matter. He focused on the confusion and insecurity the reappearances cause to surviving

relatives and lovers, many of whom have moved on and started new lives. Saddled with relatively lightweight leads, Shiota populated the supporting roles with experienced and talented actors like Kunie Tanaka, Shō Aikawa, and Yūsuke Iseya, and maintained the solemn tone of the film admirably, until a finale somewhat convolutedly revolving around a rock concert turned it into a promo for the singing career of actress Kō Shibasaki.

Resurrection was a welcome change of pace for Shiota, showing that the director has more aces up his sleeve, which he will no doubt continue to play in the years to come.

↓ Moonlight Whispers
月光の囁き

Gekkō no Sasayaki, a.k.a. *Sasayaki*

1999. CAST: Kenji Mizuhashi, Tsugumi, Kōta Kusano, Harumi Inoue. 96 minutes. RELEASE: DVD, Kino on Video (U.S., English subtitles).

A teenager falls in love with his glamorous classmate, but he expresses his affection through masochistic behavior. Confronted with this, the girl gradually discovers her own latent sadistic tendencies. Shiota films this potentially racy storyline with the emphasis on psychological depth rather than titillation.

Released in theaters in Japan on the same day as *Don't Look Back*, *Moonlight Whispers* marks the beginning of Akihiko Shiota's exploration of the theme that has continued to fascinate him in his subsequent productions: the emerging maturity in adolescents. Based on a manga by Masahiko Kikuni, *Moonlight Whispers* is a tale of the awakening sexuality in two high school students that emerges as a poignant, emotional, and touching drama.

Takuya (Mizuhashi) appears to be a student like any other. Somewhat withdrawn, he admires his beautiful classmate Satsuki (Tsugumi), with whom he shares a long friendship and a talent for the sport of kendo. In the opening scene, we see the two practicing this sword fighting form, in which they are the bright young hopes of their school. In an empty sports hall, Takuya lets himself be beaten by Satsuki. Though she blames it on his lack of concentration, the truth behind his intentional defeat becomes clear as the story starts to develop: Takuya's burgeoning sexuality manifests itself in masochistic behavior.

Since his urges initially only manifest themselves in very subtle ways, Satsuki remains blissfully unaware of Takuya's dark side and the relationship between the two grows stronger, blossoming into a typical teenage love affair. The happiness is violently interrupted when Satsuki discovers that Takuya has not only been collecting her soiled underwear, but that he has also been recording her on the toilet with a hidden tape recorder and taking pictures of her in secret. When she tells him in no uncertain terms that their relationship is over, Takuya begs her to stay, pledging total obedience and pronouncing himself her "dog." Although she wishes to have nothing more to do with this *hentai* (pervert) and subsequently avoids him completely, when she takes up with another classmate in order to hurt him, she doesn't realize that she is in fact giving in to Takuya's urges. But the boy's insistence leads her to discover that she too has a hidden side to her sexuality, and she soon starts to enjoy inflicting mental and physical pain on Takuya, ironically bringing the two of them closer in the process.

In the reviews that accompanied this film's limited U.S. theatrical release in late 2000 (where it played under the title *Sasayaki*), the word "disturbing" was used more than once to describe *Moonlight Whispers*. But despite the potentially provocative—or to some perhaps even offensive—subject matter, this film is anything but disturbing. With two characters whose actions ring true in every scene and an admirably restrained handling of the film's sexual compo-

© 1999 Nikkatsu Corporation

Moonlight Whispers

nents, *Moonlight Whispers* becomes an unexpectedly touching film. It portrays two young people struggling against themselves and against their environment, revealing along the way just how much, in the course of growing up, the self is shaped by the environment. Shiota arrives at the conclusion that stepping outside society is the only road open to his characters if they wish to be truthful to themselves as individuals. It's a conclusion that continues to infuse the films in his still short career, in particular *Don't Look Back* and *Harmful Insect*.

But for all of a director's intentions, the ability to express them still hinges on the talents of his lead actors. Thankfully, in *Moonlight Whispers*, as in Shiota's later films, the young leads show an uncanny ability to express the innermost feelings of their characters by way of their actions and expressions. Kenji Mizuhashi in particular succeeds in bringing across the ambivalence in Takuya admirably. The implication of maturity in his masochism and in his sad countenance contrasts strongly with his childlike appearance: the school uniform he wears and the bicycle he holds in his hands. The fact that he was much older than the character he portrays (he was 24 when the film was made) is impossible to guess from his appearance, but must have been a major factor in the strength of his performance. Mizuhashi finds a good match in Tsugumi, who veers from lovestruck teen via broken blossom to fledgling sadist in a way that is always believable, all along managing to give Satsuki the aura of distant desirability that drives Takuya's actions. She would a few years later play Seiichi Tanabe's stalking colleague in Ryōsuke Hashiguchi's **Hush!**

With his two leads, Shiota creates a tale that refreshingly ignores its own potential for provocation. Instead he delves deeper and dares to be much more profound, portraying the ambivalence in two young people whose choice is between forever denying what they are or going through misery in order to accept themselves.

↓ Harmful Insect
害虫
Gaichū

2001. CAST: Aoi Miyazaki, Ryō, Seiichi Tanabe, Yūsuke Iseya, Eihi Shiina, Yūsaku Suzuki, Tetsu Sawaki. 92 minutes. RELEASE: DVD, Beam Entertainment (Japan, no subtitles).

A sometimes difficult but ultimately poignant and truthful portrait of a young girl lost in the big, bad world. Akihiko Shiota's ultimate expression of childhood isolation.

With the exception of the sidestep into the digital realm with *Gips*, the films of director Akihiko Shiota have shown a strong affinity and concern for the world of teenagers. But rather than making bittersweet and predictable coming-of-age dramas, the director has consistently explored the deeper motivations and the psychology of adolescents on the brink of physical and mental maturity.

Harmful Insect is no exception, and in some ways it is perhaps even his ultimate statement on the subject. As with his earlier films, Shiota pays particular attention to the maturity of his lead character, the 13-year-old Sachiko. The girl has come out of a failed love affair with her high school math teacher, an affair whose implications are intentionally kept vague but which resulted in the teacher leaving school for a remote region of the country, where he now works at a nuclear power plant. The two still correspond, but their letters, shown in captions throughout the film, never arrive in neat order and follow a criss-cross pattern making proper communication virtually impossible. It's emblematic for the lack of communication Sachiko feels with most of the people around her.

Sachiko's single mother (Ryō) is unable to juggle motherhood and the need to make a living, and after her failed suicide attempt Sachiko drops out of school. Secretive, quiet, and hiding her emotional problems from the world, Sachiko seems unable to communicate with her mother or her school friends and soon takes up with a young loner (Tetsu Sawaki), who comes to her aid when the girl is stalked at night by a lusty salaryman.

The young man lives with his retarded uncle in a scrap yard as an outcast from society. Sachiko seems to find something to relate to in the lives of these two outsiders, who are as misunderstood by people around them as she is, but any illusion of happiness is quickly dispelled when the boy becomes the target of a violent gang of juvenile delinquents and Sachiko finds herself once again the victim of sexual aggression, this time from her mother's new live-in boyfriend.

As witnessed from the synopsis, *Harmful Insect* certainly doesn't handle its protagonists with kid gloves. Sachiko suffers through a series of tragedies that push her toward an early, disillusioned maturity. At times when her classmates are going though all the rituals of early adolescence, she retreats further and further into her shell where confusion reigns. A brief return to school at the insistence of her best friend only confronts her with the fact that she no longer feels any mental connection with children her own age, and results in more hurt for both her and her friends. But contrary to a film like Lars Von Trier's *Dancer in the Dark*, the tragedy that befalls the lead character is not a tool for the director to manipulate his audience into shedding tears. *Harmful Insect* attempts to signal social ills and translates them into one of the people who suffers from them the most: a confused and vulnerable girl confronted with the violence of society at too early an age.

Generally, non-Japanese still tend to hold the belief that Japan is a very safe society. Perhaps when compared to many other countries it relatively is, but the way Shiota portrays it creates a very different impression. It's this belief (or misconception) that could be *Harmful Insect*'s greatest stumbling block in communicating with a foreign audience. There is no window for us as foreign viewers through which to view the tragedies that befall Sachiko, no immediately recognizable framework to aid us in sympathizing with the filmmaker's good intentions—like the indictment of child prostitution in Swedish director Lukas Moodysson's similarly themed *Lilya 4-Ever* (2002).

As a result, *Harmful Insect* is not an easy film to take in, and the persistent images of a

© 2001 Nikkatsu Corporation

Harmful Insect

13-year-old girl being harassed and bothered by adult males might well rub some the wrong way (as they did at the film's world premiere at the 2001 Venice Film Festival, where angered booing could be heard when the credits rolled). The implication that Sachiko was involved in a possibly sexual, and thus pedophilic, relationship with her math teacher does nothing to soften the impact, even though it is never stated that the meeting between them ever went to such extremes.

Thankfully, Shiota avoids the pitfalls of exploitation and dares to put himself in a vulnerable position. By focusing so strongly on Sachiko's psychology he is being very honest, but it's an honesty not many people will easily sympathize with, since it touches on something many of us prefer to deny. The ambivalence between child and adult that forms the core of Sachiko's character (as it did with the characters in *Moonlight Whispers*) is a much more truthful representation of child psychology than syrupy sweet depictions of childhood as a period of untainted innocence and bliss. It may be hard to swallow for some, but it does confront us with how we have distorted the memories of our own childhood to fit a socially accepted ideal of what growing up should be like. The seeds of maturity are present in children and young adolescents, and these include the seeds of violence and sexuality. Shiota doesn't exploit these aspects, but shows the process of those seeds coming into bloom, and how that developing maturity is in contrast (or perhaps even in conflict) with the child who carries it. In this very contrast lies the confusion that is such a major factor of our adolescence, a confusion whose implications are much greater than the inoffensively awkward fiddlings with tampons and pimples that pass for portraits of puberty in the average John Hughes comedy. *Harmful Insect* is brave enough to confront us with what we prefer to deny—an essential function of art if ever there was one.

CHAPTER 20

The Other Players

↓ The Man Who Stole the Sun
太陽を盗んだ男

Taiyō o Nusunda Otoko

1979. **DIRECTOR:** Kazuhiko Hasegawa, 長谷川和彦. **CAST:** Kenji Sawada, Bunta Sugawara, Kimiko Ikegami, Yutaka Mizutani, Toshiyuki Nishida, Kazuo Kitamura. 141 minutes. **RELEASES:** DVD, Amuse Pictures (Japan, English subtitles). Mei Ah (Hong Kong, English/Chinese subtitles).

A young high school science teacher builds his own atomic bomb and drives the police mad with a set of outrageous demands. This critical look at the nuclear arms race and the hedonism of the bubble economy is an overlooked gem badly in need of rediscovery.

Though largely unknown outside its home country, *The Man Who Stole the Sun* is one of the pivotal films in Japanese film history. Almost a final twitch of the old studio system, it was half a studio film and half independent: On the one hand it had two major stars in the lead and was distributed nationwide by Toho; on the other it was produced by an independent company and had a crew consisting of some of the more important names in early '80s independent film. Director Kazuhiko Hasegawa co-wrote the script with American writer Leonard Schrader, brother of *Mishima* director Paul and a Japanophile who had previously written the novel from which Sidney Pollack's *The Yakuza* (1975, starring Robert Mitchum and Ken Takakura) had been adapted, as well as having scripted an entry in the long-running *Otoko wa Tsurai yo/Tora-san* series with Yōji Yamada.

Kenji Sawada plays long-haired, bubble-gum-chewing high school chemistry teacher Makoto Kidō, an unwilling slave to the daily grind of packed commuter trains, teaching to students whose only interest is passing their exams so they can forget what he taught them as quickly as possible. While returning from a field trip with his class, his school bus is hijacked by a stressed-out salaryman who threatens to blow up the bus and himself and the children with it. The police intervene, and it's thanks to Makoto and the detective Yamashita (Bunta Sugawara) that the hijacker is apprehended.

Despite his seeming heroics, Makoto nurtures some odd tendencies of his own. After experimenting with an anesthetic spray on his cat and on the beat cop at the local *kōban*, he executes a carefully planned break-in into a power station, where he steals an amount of plutonium. With instruments taken from his school, he proceeds to build his own football-sized atomic bomb, all the while chewing gum, singing the theme song to *Astroboy*, or watching TV. Although he has taken safety precautions, his distractions make him screw up badly, causing an element to explode inside his oven while he is too busy watching TV to pay attention to what he's doing. He manages to build the bomb despite the setback, but the accident has released some radiation.

The bomb finished and working, Makoto swiftly proceeds to the next step: urban terrorism. He threatens to blow up the capital if his demands are not met. His first: no interruption of the live broadcast of the baseball game by the nine o'clock news. The police, led by the same detective Yamashita of the bus hijack, have to move heaven and earth to meet the demand, even calling for the prime minister to intervene. Watching on his TV set how the game continues at nine that evening, Makoto concocts a new ransom demand: allow The Rolling Stones into the country to play a concert in Tokyo (they had been banned from entering Japan for drug use). But just as it looks like this plan too will be a success, Makoto notices his hair is starting to fall out and that some of his teeth are coming loose.

The Man Who Stole the Sun is undeniably dated, both in its message and in its style. However, in many ways it is also more modern than the vast majority of films made in Japan around that time. Not many mainstream films were tackling contemporary issues and setting them to Bob Marley music. It's in the fact that *The Man Who Stole the Sun* is so very much of its time that the film finds a lot of its validity. Despite the plot, this is not a hijack thriller in the mold of John Frankenheimer's *Black Sunday* (1977) or John McTiernan's *Die Hard* (1987). While it certainly doesn't lack for tension and excitement, there are real-life concerns at play here. The film's opening shot is of the mushroom cloud, with the national symbol of the rising sun superimposed over it. Makoto's ransom demands can be read as a metaphor for the lie that harnessed atomic power is a benign force that will bring happiness and progress, except that the young man's hair is falling out and his gums are starting to bleed.

The film's finale pits Makoto and Yamashita against each other, like two superpowers fighting over the ultimate prize: the nuclear bomb. Although one of them emerges victorious from the battle, in the end it's the bomb itself that will win, as the ominous freeze frame of the ticking contraption expresses.

The Man Who Stole the Sun also comments on the darker consequences of the bubble economy: the stuffed commuter trains, the disaffected students, the suicides and freak-outs among stressed salaryman. Hasegawa suggests that there lurks a Makoto in every single participant in that rat race, that anyone can snap and do unpredictable things. Hasegawa's portrayal of these problems is not one-sided, however. One effect of the bubble he emphasizes in particular is hedonism, illustrated by Makoto's carelessness as he goes about building his homemade bomb and the absurdity of his ransom demands. Makoto may be the victim of a sick society, but he makes little constructive effort to escape from it. This is where the film differs from other treatises on contemporary urban frustration, in particular the rather self-righteous Michael Douglas vehicle *Falling Down* (Joel Schumacher, 1993).

For a film so rich and significant, it's a mystery this never saw wider exposure. Its themes are anything but culturally specific and Hasegawa's abilities as a filmmaker are evident throughout, including some very perceptive and subtle use of flashbacks in exploring the relationship between his two main characters. Western reappraisals are definitely in order for both the film and director Kazuhiko Hasegawa, who started out in the late '60s as an assistant director to Shōhei Imamura on **The Profound Desire of the Gods** and *A History of Post-War Japan as Told by a Bar Hostess*. Hasegawa went on to work at Nikkatsu under Roman Porno directors Tatsumi Kumashiro and Toshiya Fujita and wrote the scripts for Kumashiro's *Bitterness of Youth* (*Seishun no Satetsu*) and *Yoimachigusa* (both 1974) before making his own directorial debut in 1976 with *Young Murderer* (*Seishun no*

Satsujinsha). The film, co-produced by Imamura Productions and New Wave luminaries ATG, was invited to the Cannes Film Festival the following year.

Despite the considerable popularity of *The Man Who Stole the Sun*, Hasegawa went into early retirement as a director after his second film, as if consciously making way for a new generation of filmmakers like Sōgo Ishii and Kiyoshi Kurosawa, both of whom he took under his wing as participants in the newly founded Director's Company (Kurosawa worked as assistant director on the film). Both through his work and his founding of the Director's Company, Hasegawa became the bridge between the studio system and the independent scene of the 1980s, a position he shares with indie pioneer Shinji Sōmai.

Hasegawa is still highly regarded in Japan. Both his films were the subject of high-profile special edition DVD reissues, and many a film buff harbors the wish to one day see him return to the director's chair. Although he didn't entirely become a hermit—his macho nightlife antics still garner publicity—aside from an acting appearance in Seijun Suzuki's *Yumeji* (1991) he hasn't been very involved with cinema. He long nurtured a project about the 1972 Red Army hostage situation at Asama Sansō, but took so long to bring it to the screen that two other directors beat him to it: Masato Harada's de-politicized *The Choice of Hercules* (*Totsunyū Seyo! Asama Sansō Jiken*, 2002) and *Rain of Light* (*Hikari no Ame*, 2002), directed by Hasegawa's own former Director's Company protégé Banmei Takahashi.

↓ Family Game
家族ゲーム
Kazoku Gēmu

1983. **DIRECTOR:** Yoshimitsu Morita. 森田芳光. **CAST:** Yūsaku Matsuda, Jūzō Itami, Ichirōta Miyakawa, Saori Yuki, Junichi Tsujita, Yōko Aki. 106 minutes. **RELEASES:** DVD, Pioneer (Japan, no subtitles).

Seminal satire on the workings of the family unit. Unconventional comedy by former 8mm experimentalist Yoshimitsu Morita became a box office hit, partially thanks to the involvement of star actor Yūsaku Matsuda.

Living in an apartment on the outskirts of Tokyo, the Numatas seem like the model Japanese nuclear family. The father (Itami) leaves for work early and comes back late, usually drunk from after-work social gatherings. Mother (Yuki) seems competent only in the kitchen and subsequently spends most of her time there. Elder son Shinichi (Tsujita) is in a top high school and cruises through without much effort. Younger son Shigeyuki (Miyakawa), however, is the black sheep: He is unmotivated by schoolwork, his grades are a disaster, and he regularly skips classes by feigning sickness in front of his over-caring mother. The only classmate that has worse grades is Hamamoto, the class's "stupid and ugly" girl, as Shigeyuki calls her. His grades, though, aren't that much better than hers.

A parade of private tutors has already visited the Numata household, most of them giving up on the boy's unwillingness to perform. But Mom and Dad are dead set on seeing Shigeyuki follow in his brother's footsteps and go to a top high school and from there to a top university, the only chance of getting a good job later in life. And so another teacher is drafted in, but this particular gentleman, a university student named Yoshimoto (Matsuda), uses rather different methods from his predecessors.

Yoshimoto is himself only an average student from an average university, but where the long line of previous tutors failed, it's exactly his lack of academic prowess that makes him connect with Shigeyuki. Yoshimoto's solution is not to make the boy conform, but to boost his confidence, to render him a strong individual rather than another brick in the wall. Tactically influencing the various family members with his non-conformist behavior, he brings the absurdity of their loveless and uncommunicative lives to the surface, culminating in a chaotic family dinner in which all illusions are shattered and the education of Shigeyuki is completed.

Although based on a novel by Yōhei Honma, *Family Game*'s structure is similar to the one used by Pier Paolo Pasolini on *Theorem* (*Teorema*, 1968), with the entry of a young stranger into the family unit resulting in the exposure of hypocrisy and the destruction of norms. Here, the conclusion is that the way to escape the social conveyor belt of school, exams, university, and lifetime employment is through individualism. The message is deftly translated by director Morita into the style of the film, which consistently emphasizes the absurdity of the middle class ideal. The apartment building looks out over an industrial no man's land, while the Numata residence itself is so cramped that no privacy is possible. Shinichi can only get to his room through Shigeyuki's, and he is able to hear every word exchanged between his little brother and the tutor. When Mom and Dad want to talk in private, they do it in their car outside. Morita uses no music in the film but amplifies sound effects instead, particularly the sounds produced during meals, underlining the intrusive nature of the environment. At the same time, even though the family members are always confronted with each other, real communication never takes place. At the dinner table, they sit side by side instead of facing one another, and the climactic "last supper," which sees the entire family plus Yoshimoto all squeezed in on the same side of the table, is an unforgettably glorious mess.

Another master stroke on the part of the director was the casting of Yūsaku Matsuda in the role of Yoshimoto. For Matsuda, the role was a radical break with his image. One of the biggest stars of the 1970s, on both TV and silver screen, Matsuda came to prominence as an action hero in the purest sense of the term. Best known abroad as the villain who taunts Michael Douglas in Ridley Scott's *Black Rain* (1989), Matsuda was in some ways the Japanese equiva-lent of Steve McQueen. First making a splash as the rookie detective in the cop series *Taiyō ni Hoero* [trans: Howl at the sun] he moved on to co-star in several films, including the Kadokawa production *Proof of the Man* (*Ningen no Shōmei*, 1978). His first true starring vehicle was *Mottomo Kiken na Yūgi* [trans: The most dangerous game] in 1978, in which he played a professional assassin. The popularity of the film led to two sequels, after which he took on the role for which he is still best remembered, that of the dandy private eye hero in the TV series *Tantei Monogatari* [trans: Detective story].

At the height of his popularity he sought to diversify and started accepting more challenging roles, playing the gaunt psychopath in *Yajū Shisubeshi* [trans: The beast must die] (1980, for which the already wiry actor lost 10 lbs. and allegedly even had some of his teeth removed), the bearded playwright in Seijun Suzuki's *Mirage Theater* (*Kagerō-Za*, 1981), and the dorky Yoshimoto in *Family Game*. He also directed and starred in *A Homansu* (1985, the title is an untranslatable play on words, a combination of 'idiot' and 'performance'), a hyper-stylized manga adaptation that saw Matsuda both playing up to and making fun of his own macho image. After starring in Kinji Fukasaku's *The Rage of Love*, Matsuda was diagnosed with cancer of the bladder, but he decided to postpone medical treatment to appear in *Black Rain*, realizing his dream of being in a Hollywood film. It would be his last work. He died in November 1989, leaving behind his actress wife Miyuki (from Takashi Miike's **Audition**) and three children, including his son Ryūhei (**Gohatto**, **Blue Spring**), as well as an enduring fan following (more than a decade after his death, his likeness was used in the Capcom video game *Onimusha 2*).

The commercial success of *Family Game* certainly helped in establishing Matsuda as a proper actor, rather than as merely an action star. It also meant a great change for director Yoshimitsu Morita, who today is pegged as a mainstream director and potential hit maker, but who started out on a much more modest level. Debuting with the 8mm feature *Raibu: Chigasaki* in 1978, he became part of the Nikkatsu Roman Porno treadmill, directing *The Stripper* (*Maruhon Uwasa no Sutorippā*, 1982) and *Pink Salon* (*Pinku Katto: Futoku Aishite Fukaku Aishite*, 1983) before moving to ATG for *Family Game*. The success of the film made him a sought-after director, resulting in a career that would see him work in a variety of genres. Morita was quickly adopted into the entourage of producer Haruki Kadokawa, as ever shrewdly in tune with any chance to make big bucks, for whom he made *Main Theme* (*Mein Tēma*, 1984). He then re-teamed with Yūsaku Matsuda for the romantic drama *And Then* (*Sorekara*, 1985) and a year later directed *Sorobanzuku*, a satire set in the world of advertising that is now a footnote in the annals of Japanese cinema history for being the acting debut of Sabu (then billed as Hiroki Tanaka). In 1989 Morita signed the first big-screen adaptation of Banana Yoshimoto's novel *Kitchen* (the second was made eight years later by Hong Kong director Yim Ho), which featured former Bond girl Mie Hama.

Surviving admirably through the barren landscape of the '80s, Morita kept up the pace and the promise the following decade, delivering one of the box office smashes of the watershed year 1997 with the steamy romance *Lost Paradise* (*Shitsurakuen*), one of several films that year that would launch Kōji Yakusho to screen stardom. Yakusho plays floppy-haired, 50-year-old book editor Shōichirō, who falls in love with 37-year-old calligraphy teacher Rinko (played by Hitomi Kuroki). Both are married, and when the affair is discovered, the obsessive couple lose their jobs and respective spouses. With nothing left in the world but each other, they retire to a hut on the slopes of snow-covered Mount Fuji to die together locked in a mortal embrace, ingesting poisoned wine before engaging in their final coupling. Admirably, Morita refused to play it safe after the success of *Lost Paradise*, and went off into a completely different direction, delivering three dark thrillers in a row: *Keiho* (*39 Keihō Dai Sanjūkyū Jō*, 1999), *The Black House* (*Kuroi Ie*, also '99) and *Copycat Killer* (*Mohōhan*, 2002).

His versatility notwithstanding, *Family Game* remains as perhaps the defining Yoshimitsu Morita film. Powerful enough to become a hit with both audiences and critics and to inspire no less than two reactions/remakes: Sōgo Ishii's *Crazy Family* (*Gyakufunsha Kazoku*, 1984) and Takashi Miike's *Visitor Q* (2001), the latter a kind of *Family Game* in reverse that takes the chaos at the end of Morita's film as its starting point and shows how a family is reconstructed rather than deconstructed. Quite rightly, *Family Game* is still regarded as one of the standout Japanese films of the '80s.

↓ Fire Festival
火まつり
Hi-Matsuri

1985. DIRECTOR: Mitsuo Yanagimachi, 柳町光男. CAST: Kinya Kitaōji, Kiwako Taichi, Ryōta Nakamoto, Norihei Miki, Rikiya Yasuoka, Junko Miyashita, Kin Sugai, Sachiko Matsushita. 123 minutes. RELEASES: DVD, Kine Jumpōsha (Japan, no subtitles).

Man at the mercy of the environment, in this vivid and mystical celebration of nature's primal forces set against a backdrop of small-town gossip and longstanding feuds.

Situated between the mountains of Kumano and the deep blue sea, the fishing town of Nigishima has a population that is neatly divided into one of three categories: mountain people, sea people, and outsiders. Tatsuo is of the first group, a rough and boorish lumberjack who not only depends on the wooded forests above the town for his economic survival, but also takes an almost primal delight in hunting, setting snares for wild animals and standing naked in the rain communing with the ancient goddess of the mountain.

Plans for the development of a new marine park, whilst broadening the economic base of a community that has hitherto been dependant on logging and fishing for its survival, threaten to disturb the region's natural equilibrium. Still, this new economic incursion is strongly welcomed by the town's fishermen, not to mention such operators as sleazy land broker Yamakawa, who sees a unique business opportunity in the new tourism trade that the development will bring to area (a neighboring town, Yamakawa notes, has even been graced with a nuclear power station).

Tatsuo's refusal to sign away his house to the developers, effectively blocking the project, strains his relationship with the local community, and when an oil slick leaves a wake of dead fish floating belly-up in their nursery pool, the fingers of accusation point to him for sabotaging the project. After he believes he has been spoken to directly by the Shinto gods of the forest, Tatsuo violently interrupts the town's annual purification rites, the *hi-matsuri* (the fire festival of the film's title) before returning to his home to slay his family and turn the shotgun on himself.

One of the more salient films from the by and large otherwise barren cinematic landscape of the '80s, *Fire Festival* is generally considered to be the crowning achievement of the period's foremost independent director Yanagimachi, who set up his own production company Gunrō Films in 1974 in order to make his legendarily titled 16mm documentary on Tokyo's *bōsōzoku* biker gangs, *Godspeed You! Black Emperor* (*Goddo Supīdo Yū! Black Emperor*, 1976). After two forays into independent feature making, *A 19 Year Old's Map* (*Jūkyūsai no Chizu*, 1979) and *Farewell to the Land* (*Saraba Itoshiki Daichi*, 1982), Yanagimachi found financing for his next film from the Seibu chain of department stores, then looking to expand its interests into the realm of the arts. Based on a script by Kenji Nakagami, the writer whose life and work formed the basis of Shinji Aoyama's *To the Alley*, and who was born in the Kumano region where the film is set, *Fire Festival* became the first of the director's films to be released in the United States, premiering at the 23rd New York Film Festival and also picking up a Silver Leopard Award at Locarno in Switzerland.

Set amongst the scenic natural beauty of the Kumano area just south of Osaka, considered to be a traditional stronghold for Japan's indigenous Shinto religion, it is inspired by a real-life case in which a local man murdered his family before killing himself. In a rousing and mystical celebration of nature's primal forces set against a backdrop of small-town gossip and longstanding feuds, Yanagimachi carefully balances environmental concerns with the sociological, adopting an objective, non-judgmental, and almost documentary-styled approach, majestically depicted by cinematographer Masaki Tamura in a manner not dissimilar to his work on Naomi Kawase's *Suzaku*.

Much of the film's apparent ambivalence lies in its complex yet unsympathetic central character. A coarse bully who cheats on his wife (played by Junko Miyashita, the Nikkatsu starlet of such '70s Roman Porno classics as Noboru Tanaka's *Watcher in the Attic/Edogawa Rampo Ryōkikan Yaneura no Sanposha*, 1976, and Tatsumi Kumashiro's *The Woman with Red Hair/Akai Kami no Onna*, 1979) and two young children when his old girlfriend Kimiko returns to the area, Tatsuo's love of the outdoors seemingly has little to do with environmental protection. In an early scene we see him training his hunting dogs to attack a wild boar kept in a pen in his garden, cruelly reveling in the bloodshed.

His arrogant adoption of the role of elected spokesman to the ancient Shinto deities is similarly compromised as he swims in sacred waters and hunts for the protected monkeys that inhabit the forest. When his naïve protégé, Ryōta, mistakenly uses a piece of wood from a sacred tree to catch a pigeon in a snare, Tatsuo orders him to drop his pants and expose himself to the mountain goddess for this mistake, bullishly claiming he himself has made love to the goddess. A pigheaded reactionary, he is unable to articulate exactly why he is against the development other than a Luddite's unwillingness to change.

With the subsequent killing spree invoked by Tatsuo's tree-hugging communion with the gods in the final reel, stunningly rendered against a windswept backdrop of rustling trees and driving rain, Yanagimachi seems to be suggesting that man is more shaped by his environment than vice versa. Intrusions of modernity, most obviously manifested in the recurrent motif of a truck that drives around the area pathetically blaring out tinny radio jingles over a loudspeaker, are pointedly overwhelmed by the sweeping natural settings, with their unrelenting aural soundscape of wind howling through towering forest canopies, vast billowing expanses of foliage, and the slow susurrus of the sea.

Fire Festival is evenly paced, meditative and thought-provoking, providing little in the way of explanation or resolution to the events that unfold on its broad canvas, instead placing that responsibility firmly within the hands of the viewer. It's a challenging approach but a potentially rewarding one. Either way, *Fire Festival* is a remarkable achievement.

↓ Tampopo

タンポポ

Tanpopo

1985. **DIRECTOR:** Jūzō Itami, 伊丹十三. **CAST:** Nobuko Miyamoto, Tsutomu Yamazaki, Ken Watanabe, Rikiya Yasuoka, Kōji Yakusho. 115 minutes. **RELEASES:** DVD, Fox Lorber (U.S., English subtitles).

Longish but charming hit comedy about the search for the perfect noodle soup, this established the Jūzō Itami style and virtually defined Japanese cinema for Western audiences in the 1980s.

Built around the framework of a female noodle shop owner's quest for the perfect *ramen*, *Tampopo* is an episodic trip through mankind's obsession with food. The eponymous heroine (Miyamoto, whose character's name is the Japanese word for dandelion) is not altogether successful at preparing a good bowl of noodle soup, something a couple of macho truck drivers (Yamazaki and Watanabe) are quick to point out. Experts on the subject thanks to the countless breaks spent in roadside noodle bars, the two men decide to tutor Tampopo in the art of *ramen*, taking her on spying trips to competing restaurants and putting her through her paces with a series of kitchen drills.

This main story of *Tampopo* is interspersed with comic skits featuring characters from various layers of Japanese society and their relationships with food. In one of these, a group of senior corporate managers and their junior colleague have dinner at a French gourmet restaurant, where the respectable superiors all order the same course because of their inability to read the French-language menu. The bumbling junior exec, however, speaks the language fluently and effortlessly orders himself a sumptuous meal where his superiors are all stuck with soup and fish. This scene is representative of the tone of these sketches, all of which show that whatever status we prefer to see ourselves in and however we wish to distance ourselves from our fellow man, in the end all human beings are united in their dependence on, and love for, food.

Featuring an early co-starring role by Kōji Yakusho as a suave gangster who uses food as part of the erotic interplay with his pretty mistress, *Tampopo* is a likable comedy. Although many of the jokes develop along predictable lines, the film's jabs at society are nicely observed, nearly always sympathizing with the downtrodden and the underdogs, while Miyamoto (Itami's wife and frequent lead actress) forms a charismatic lead.

Tampopo established Itami's name on an international level, where his work became all the more appreciated as a result of the dearth of decent films that made it out of Japan at the time. Subsequently, Itami became firmly associated with directing satiric comedies, but his presence within the Japanese film industry stretches back a lot further than his directorial work of the 1980s. Real name Yoshihiro Ikeuchi, he is the son of pre-war *jidai-geki* director Mansaku Itami (Yoshitoyo Ikeuchi). Keeping his father's *nom de plume*, though initially with the first name Ichizō, he made his debut as an actor in the early 1960s, playing mainly supporting parts for the next three deacades, including turns in Asian-flavored Hollywood epics like Nicholas Ray's *55 Days at Peking* (1963) and Richard Brooks' *Lord Jim* (1965). He was also seen in Kon Ichikawa's adaptation of Sōseki Natsume's novel *I Am a Cat* (*Wagahai wa Neko de Aru*, 1975) and opposite Meiko Kaji and a young Yoshio Harada in the second installment of the *Lady Snowblood* series (*Shurayukihime: Urami Renka*, 1974, directed by Toshiya Fujita).

After playing the salaryman father in Yoshimitsu Morita's wildly successful **Family Game**, Itami set up his own production company, Itami Productions and moved behind the camera to direct *The Funeral* (*Osōshiki*) in 1984. Well received both at home and abroad (it won an award at the Taormina Film Festival in Italy), the film was a forerunner to *Tampopo* in its episodic structure and in its gently satirical look at the clashes between various social groups, as well in the casting of Nobuko Miyamoto and Tsutomu Yamazaki in the lead roles.

Itami continued in comedy for the next few years, his wife taking the lead roles in *A Taxing Woman* (*Marusa no Onna*, 1987) and its sequel *A Taxing Woman Returns* (*Marusa no Onna 2*, 1988), about a tax inspector who falls in love with the embezzler she is supposed to be investigating. Miyamoto also took the lead in the comedies *Tales of a Golden Geisha* (*Ageman*, 1990) and *Minbo, or the Gentle Art of Japanese Extortion* (*Minbō no Onna*, 1992), the latter a veritable encyclopedia of the extortion practices of the yakuza that landed its director in hospital, after an attempt on his life by what were allegedly gangsters unhappy with the frankness of his film. Itami used his own hospital experiences as the basis for *The Last Dance* (*Daibyōnin*, 1993), a satire of the medical world about a film director trying to finish his final film while suffering from terminal cancer. His adaptation of Nobel Prize winner Kenzaburō Ōe's novel *A Quiet Life* (*Shizukana Seikatsu*, 1995) was a major departure from Itami's normal formula, its source material based on the birth of the novelist's brain-damaged son. Itami swiftly returned to familiar ground, however, with retreads of the *Tampopo* formula in *Supermarket Woman* (*Sūpā no Onna*, 1996) and *Marutai no Onna* (1997) [trans: Woman under police protection], once again starring Miyamoto.

In late 1997, with *Marutai no Onna* showing in theaters, Itami committed suicide by jumping off a seven-story building in Tokyo, allegedly over the impending tabloid revelation of an affair with a 26-year-old office lady, although some people speculated over links between his death and his earlier troubles with the mob.

↓ The Mystery of Rampo
Rampo

1994. **DIRECTORS**: Rintarō Mayuzumi/Kazuyoshi Okuyama, 黛りんたろう / 奥山和由. **CAST**: Masahiro Motoki, Naoto Takenaka, Michiko Hada, Teruyuki Kagawa, Mikijirō Hira. 93/97/100 minutes. **RELEASES**: VHS, Bandai Visual (Japan, no subtitles, Okuyama version). Collection Auteurs (France, French subtitles, international version).

It's wild, but it works. Shochiku's centenary bash attempts to plumb the minds of one of Japan's most celebrated pulp writers in a bizarre mishmash of animation, smoldering period drama, obscure psycho-sexual imagery, and state of the art special effects.

Sexy, fantastic, vivid, subversive—for over 50 years the collected works of the writer Edogawa

Rampo (1894–1965), Japan's celebrated master of mystery fiction, have enjoyed a persistent run of success in Japan, in print, on screen, and even on stage, as in Yukio Mishima's 1956 adaptation of **Black Lizard**, later filmed by Kinji Fukasaku in 1968.

Born Tarō Hirai, the son of a merchant-lawyer, Rampo spent the best part of his youth avidly feeding his fertile imagination with the newly translated writings of such notable Western practitioners of the detective story as Sir Arthur Conan Doyle and Maurice Leblanc, which had begun making their way into the country at the turn of the twentieth century. When it finally came to putting the fruits of his own fervent imagination down in print with the 1923 short story *Ni-sen Dōka* [trans: The two sen copper coin], he settled for the phonemic approximation of the name of one of his literary heroes, Edgar Allan Poe (e-do-ga-wa-ran-po), as his *nom de plume*. This name is somewhat of a double pun, as the Chinese characters used by Hirai translate into "walking in disarray by the Edo River."

Rampo's acclaim in the English language lies pretty much exclusively with *Japanese Tales of Mystery and Imagination*, an anthology of short horror stories first translated in 1956 by the Charles Tuttle publishing house. The limited number of film adaptations of his writing released outside of Japan have similarly been oriented around his more horrifically perverse works—*Blind Beast* (*Mōjū*, Yasuzō Masumura, 1969); *Horror of the Malformed Men* (*Kyōfu Kikai Ningen*, Teruo Ishii, 1968), and Shinya Tsukamoto's **Gemini**.

However, peeping toms, sightless psychopathic sculptors, and deadly doppelgängers actually make up a rather small part of Rampo's fiction, and in his homeland he is remembered more for his detective stories, predominantly featuring the dashing master of logic and disguise, detective Kogorō Akechi, and his later Boys Detective Gang series of children's books, about an agency of amateur juvenile detectives who featured in a number of films for Toei during the '50s and a long running TV series

during the '60s. In the summer of 2002, TBS Television screened a one-off special directed by Seita Yamamoto, which saw Masakazu Tamura as Akechi pitted against "Beat" Takeshi in the oft-filmed *Kogoro Akechi vs. the Fiend with Twenty Faces* (*Akechi Kogorō Tai Kaijin Nijū Mensō*).

The year 1994 saw the hundredth anniversary of Rampo's birth, and was marked with a number of film adaptations of his work. Akio Jissōji made *The Watcher in the Attic* (*Yaneura no Sanposha*)—a work which had already been adapted for Nikkatsu by Noboru Tanaka in 1976, and is considered one of the high points of the studio's Roman Porno output—and Tōru Kawashima directed *Oshie to Tabi Suru Otoko* [trans: The traveling man with the pressed picture]. The year also marked the centenary of the Shochiku Corporation film company. Top producer Kazuyoshi Okuyama, son of Shochiku's then president Tōru Okuyama, decided to celebrate both events in epic style with a film based on the writer's life.

Rintarō Mayuzumi, a TV director from NHK, was drafted to direct, and two of the nation's most recognizable faces took the leading roles. Rampo himself was played by the pug-faced Naoto Takenaka, a popular comedian with a film career stretching back to the mid-'80s. He has also played in harder, more straight-faced fare such as a number of films for *Gonin* director Takashi Ishii, and is himself an occasional director with films like *Nowhere Man* (*Munō no Hito*, 1991) and *Tōkyō Biyori* (1997). The part of Rampo's charming literary hero, detective Akechi, was filled by the suave Masahiro Motoki, a former teen model and pinup poster boy from the boy band Shibugakitai ("The Cool Kid Trio") from 1982 to 1988. After a string of roles in TV dramas, Motoki's first major film role came in Masayuki Suō's *Fancy Dance* in 1989, after which he bared his body to the world in a nude photo book published in 1991 entitled "White Room." *Rampo* marked the first of three consecutive films in which Motoki appeared alongside Takenaka, the following two being **Gonin** and **Shall We Dance?**.

Taking Rampo's unpublished novella *Osei Tōjō* [trans: The appearance of Osei] as its starting point, *Rampo* is not so exactly a cinematic reconstruction of the author's life, though by using a number of props such as a hat and a box of matches that actually belonged to the author, it certainly makes bold claims to period detail. Nor is it a straightforward adaptation of Rampo's banned source novel. Instead it takes upon its shoulders the rather ambitious task or putting the author's work into a historical context in order to portray the conditions which gave rise to his uniquely flamboyant output. It is also an attempt to delve into the very soul of the author to get to the heart of what exactly it was that made his work so enduringly resonant with the general public.

The fact is, in his day Rampo was really not well regarded by the literary establishment, who looked upon his work as mere pulp fodder for the masses. The increasingly militarist government regime at the beginning of the Shōwa period wasn't too keen on it either, objecting to the "aberrant moral content" found in such spine-chilling short stories as *The Caterpillar* (*Imomushi*) and *The Red Chamber* (*Akai Heya*). With the opening up to the rest of the world in the latter half of the nineteenth century after almost 300 years of self-imposed isolation, the subsequent period had seen a vast influx of cultural and artistic values pouring into Japan. Foppish men sashayed down the streets in frock jackets. Jazz music blared into the streets from European-styled cafés. The *moga* (modern girl) wore her hair in a short bobbed cut, shedding the traditional kimono in favor of the flapper dress. Artists in every field began assimilating such alien ideas as Romanticism, Surrealism, Futurism, and abstraction into their work, and intellectuals flirted with political ideals like Communism and freedom of speech.

By the mid-1920s the pendulum had swung too far. The Peace Preservation Law of 1925 is often considered the turning point, severely curtailing the powers of those political groups who advocated changes in the national constitution. The accession of the Shōwa Emperor Hirohito in 1926 marked a time when the increasingly nationalistic political tide was being officially weighted toward a return to traditional Japanese values and culture. Rampo's books, with their appeal to the masses, lack of any higher message, and such an obviously decadent and "foreign" source of inspiration, were obvious targets. A number of them were banned outright by the state censors, including *Osei Tōjō*, leading Rampo to withdraw from creative writing for a couple of years. During this time he began work on his autobiography, in which he expressed his own disillusionment with the increasingly oppressive nature of early Shōwa Japan. History, of course, would bear him out over the next couple of decades.

"Rampo was a man who felt at odds with the times and departed from it by creating his own world," Okuyama stated in the press notes at the time of the film's release. *Rampo* takes a speculative peak inside the writer's mind during this time when his work was increasingly falling foul of the censors. After an animated rendition of *Osei Tōjō*'s basic setup—that of a mysterious woman who locks her husband in her *nagamochi* (the antique chest in which a bride stores her trousseau, the possessions she takes with her when she moves to the household of her new husband), and leaves him to suffocate—we see a rather sullen-looking Rampo being hauled up in front of a government representative who orders his latest work to be destroyed. Rampo mopes back home and puts a match to the only existing copy of the offending manuscript, but shortly afterward his editor shows him a newspaper clipping detailing a woman convicted of exactly the same offense.

Rampo is drawn into his own investigation, and tracks down the beautiful widow, Shizuko, (played by Japanese supermodel Michiko Hada in her big screen debut) in the antiques shop that she ran with her deceased husband. Unable to reconcile the startling link between his unpublished novel and this eerie real-life crime, he invokes his alter ego, handsome detective Akechi, in an attempt at bringing a fictional conclusion to these strange events. From this moment on we're immersed in a world of fantasy, where Shizuko is now playing mistress to the twisted Marquis Ogawara, a sadistic old pervert who seeks gratification by dressing up as his dead mother.

Biopics about writers are notoriously difficult to pull off. When Mayuzumi turned in his version, producer Okuyama—a man seemingly dedicated to rubbing up his directors the wrong way, having already had a major bust-up with Kitano over *Sonatine*—thought the piece lacked a little oomph for such a high-profile cinematic event, and promptly re-shot over half of it. As a result, *Rampo* surfaced theatrically in two versions in Japan, released simultaneously: Mayuzumi's original weighs in at 93 minutes, whilst the Okuyama version is 97 minutes. To further complicate matters, an extra three minutes made it onto the latter when it was released worldwide as *The Mystery of Rampo* in an "International Version," which was curiously also made available on video in Japan.

Despite taking the magnanimous step of releasing both versions of the film at the same time to allow audiences to decide which was the better, Mayuzumi's version barely stood a chance against Okuyama's media-courting showmanship that accompanied the new edit. The new animated opening sequence (Mayuzumi begins straight in the banning scene) and scenes such as an opulent party to which Rampo gives an address to a number of prominent Japanese celebrities (look carefully for Kinji Fukasaku and Kōji Wakamatsu) highlight the "big is better" approach that is adopted throughout the entire exercise. Okuyama's film was more than just an homage to Rampo. It was a calculated cinematic event.

Okuyama makes ostentatious use of the full complement of state-of-the-art cinema techniques available to him at the time, including complicated optical effects and innovative CGI technology. Despite such technology being then fairly much in its infancy and without the resources available to Hollywood filmmakers, this imagery not only integrates smoothly within the film's ambitious narrative, but also manages to bring a slick veneer to the look of the film without drawing attention to itself. A scene in which the Marquis projects pornographic film footage onto the naked body of his captive mistress, overlaying it with more and more erotic imagery to invoke the spiraling sense of delirium that lies at the heart of Rampo's potent prose, suits perfectly the central conceit of using cinema as a means of investigating the various layers that exist between reality and fantasy. One of the most sensational set pieces of Japanese cinema of the decade, its explicitness also managed to whip up further press coverage.

This daring collage of film styles and media (which also includes archival footage of Meiji-period Japan and clips taken from Susumu Yugei's 1954 three-part serialization of Shochiku's early version of *The Fiend with Twenty Faces*) fits in with the fragmentary approach to the narrative, though perhaps the sum of the parts add up to rather less than their whole in their attempt to invoke the full force of Rampo's wildly fantastical imagination, especially when laid aside the subtle poetry of Mayuzumi's more cohesive narrative. Nevertheless, Okuyama just about pulls it off. *Rampo* is indeed an unrestrained visual extravaganza that is difficult to ignore, looking a great deal slicker and more adventurous than anything else released from Japan in the '90s. It was also the highest-grossing domestic release of its year, and successfully played overseas in a number of territories where it was greeted by audiences with a mixture of admiration and slack-jawed incomprehension.

Mayuzumi returned to TV production, later bringing to the big screen *Suzuran Shōjo Moe no Monogatari* [trans: Lily of the valley: the story of young girl Moe], a Shochiku production of an NHK drama about a twelve-year-old girl growing up in Hokkaido. Aside from the 1996 *Daitōryō no Kurisumasu Tsurī* [trans: The president's Christmas tree], an unashamed tearjerker set in New York, Okuyama kept away from direction until the 2003 documentary about Formula One racing, *Crash* (*Kurasshu*). His next few stints at production for Shochiku include the Tarantino-esque action movie *Score* (Atsushi Muroga, 1995), *Gonin*, Shōhei Imamura's **The Eel**, and the feature-length anime based on Osamu Tezuka's classic manga, *Black Jack* (Osamu Dezaki, 1996), though his subsequent attempts at creating the same stir overseas as *Rampo* with Masato Harada's *Rowing Through*, a U.S.-based movie about a rowing team, met a marked box office failure. After a series of expensive failures, he was later ousted from his role as one of the top figures at Shochiku on January 19, 1998, in a much publicized boardroom coup, going on to form the Team Okuyama production company responsible for, amongst other films, *Dora Heita* (2000), Kon Ichikawa's period action comedy based on a script co-written with Akira Kurosawa, Keisuke Kinoshita, and Masaki Kobayashi almost thirty years before.

↓ Gonin

1995. **DIRECTOR:** Takashi Ishii, 石井隆. **CAST:** Naoto Takenaka, Kōichi Satō, Takeshi Kitano, Masahiro Motoki, Kazuya Kimura, Kippei Shiina, Jinpachi Nezu. 109 minutes. **RELEASES:** DVD, Leo Films (U.S., English subtitles), Tokyo Bullet/MIA Video (U.K., English subtitles), Ocean Shores (Hong Kong, English/Chinese subtitles).

Stylish and moody action thriller in which five washed-up everymen take on the yakuza in a suicidal smash-and-grab. A grim account of Japan's rapid economic and moral decline, and one of the most significant films by genre stylist Takashi Ishii.

One of the major Japanese films of the '90s, *Gonin* is a grim, violent, but also gorgeously stylized reflection of a country's rapid social decline. Remorselessly tapping into the zeitgeist and laying his findings bare for all to see, director Takashi Ishii goes one better than his normal portrayal of human beings under duress and finds a way to express his favorite theme with social relevance.

Five men represent the rupture in the social fabric caused by the burst of Japan's bubble economy: Ogiwara (Takenaka) is a salaryman who after 20 years of loyal service is fired from his company. Venting his frustrations at a rooftop batting cage, he encounters Bandai (Satō), a club owner deep in debt with the yakuza. Mitsuya (Motoki) is a flamboyant gay misfit who lives off blackmailing his rich partners, including Bandai. Hizu (Nezu) is a washed-up ex-cop and ex-con who now works as a bouncer at a hostess club, using an eagerness for violence as a way to hide his self-loathing. Jimmy (Shiina), finally, is the boyfriend of Thai hooker Nami, whom he tries to buy off the same yakuza group that is tightening the screws on Bandai.

All of them men who either have nothing left to lose or carry a grudge against the gangsters, the five are united by the club owner's daring plan to raid the yakuza headquarters and steal all their cash. The desperate Ogiwara handed his résumé to Bandai for a job, Mitsuya refuses to leave his side before seeing the money, Hizu is an old acquaintance, and Jimmy is someone Bandai saw at the yakuza offices and recognized as a fellow victim. The group is formed and the plan carried out, chaotically and not without bloodshed on account of Ogiwara's increasing psychosis, but the men manage to snag the loot and get away.

Bandai immediately becomes the main suspect, but the gang quickly figures out who else were behind the heist when they first realize Nami's passport has been lifted from their safe and then find Ogiwara's CV in Bandai's office. A pair of hitmen (Kitano and Kimura) is drummed up to find and punish the culprits, but in their search a lot of dark secrets about the five men, as well as the killers themselves, are revealed.

Director Takashi Ishii is known for his love of genre, and most of his work consists of variations on some of the staples of the crime genre: the film noir redux of *Original Sin* (*Shinde mo Ii*, 1992), *A Night in the Nude* (*Nūdo no Yoru*, 1993), and *Tenshi no Harawata: Akai Senkō* (1994); the rape-revenge film with *Freeze Me* (2000); and the hitman dramas *Black Angel Vol. 1* and *Vol. 2* (*Kuro no Tenshi*, 1998/99). The basic plot of *Gonin* is the most classic form of heist movie: An assorted group of individuals pull off a seemingly impossible robbery, but find themselves hunted by their own targets. While Ishii nearly always approaches the basic genres of his films with a sense of personalized innovation, with *Gonin* he takes a step further and has it reflect and comment on the social climate in his country.

One of the first Japanese films to do so, preceding a wave of socially committed independent films from the second half of the '90s, it's also one of the most pessimistic. Made during the fact, rather than after it, the film reflects the uncertainty and the feeling of hopelessness of seeing 50 years of unbridled prosperity and security crumble to dust. The basic foundations of contemporary life receive crippling blows in *Gonin*: Job opportunities are non-existent, one of the good guys butchers his own wife and child, suicide is a realistic option, violence is ubiquitous, and to top it all off Ishii kills off the audience identification figure twenty minutes before the end of the film, brutally depriving both his viewers and his protagonists of their final strands of hope.

If any further proof were needed of *Gonin*'s depth and relevance, it was Ishii himself who delivered it with the sequel *Gonin 2* the following year. In it he revisited the same plot structure, but this time it was devoid of any deeper meaning or allusion. In a flatly directed and written film, which lacked even its predecessor's carefully constructed narrative and beautiful cinematography, an uninspired Ishii relied entirely on the central gimmick of having five women as protagonists instead of five men. Even his recurring motif, that of the human body and mind under extreme duress, lacked resonance on account of several underwritten characters.

Ishii's films replay the motif of humans under pressure with admirable consistency. This makes them something of an acquired taste, since the director's preferred method of inflicting pain and stress on his (mostly female) characters is through rape. This approach goes all the way back to Ishii's origins as a manga artist, finding fame through the *Angel Guts* series. The series was brought to the screen as Nikkatsu Roman Porno in the late 1970s, directed by such studio veterans Chūsei Sone and Noboru Tanaka. Ishii himself wrote the screenplays, which would become his main activity in the following decade when he also penned films like Toshiharu Ikeda's stylish slasher *Evil Dead Trap* (*Shiryō no Wana*, 1987). He made his own directorial debut with *Angel Guts: Red Vertigo* (*Tenshi no Harawata: Akai Memai*) in 1988, which set the pattern for his later films by featuring a woman named Nami (the name shared by most of his suffering heroines) who is first raped and subsequently almost run over by a car. The driver thinks she is dead and takes her body along, after which the story takes several unexpected turns that confront its protagonist with additional threats.

Ishii has been making variations on this basic scenario ever since, always featuring a woman in extreme peril who often ends up fighting her way out and conquering her subjugation. Although not all his films offer satisfactory context and motivation for their portrayal of rape, Ishii's main interest lies in how the body and mind can cope with such conditions, which he translates formally through the use of wide-angle lenses that distort and thereby emphasize the human body and its movements, by shooting scenes of violence in long single takes, as well as by capturing his characters within cramped and restricted spaces. Despite being the only all-male entry in his filmography, *Gonin* essentially explored the same subject matter.

Ishii's approach reached its apex with *Freeze Me*, the story of a young woman who is left by her boyfriend after she is raped, and who is revisited by the three men who violated her after she has started to build a new life for herself. Reminiscent of Meir Zarchi's notorious *I Spit on Your Grave* (1978), *Freeze Me* took Ishii's main motif about as far as it could go. Perhaps this was the reason why, after directing a one-hour straight-to-video vehicle for a group of Japanese rappers called *Tokyo GP*, he seemingly disappeared off the face of the earth for the following four years. He re-emerged in 2004, and was back to his old tricks with an adaptation of S/M expert Oniroku Dan's novel *Flower and Snake* (*Hana to Hebi*), previously filmed by Roman Porno stalwart Masaru Konuma.

↓ Love Letter
a.k.a. *When I Close My Eyes*

1995. **DIRECTOR:** Shunji Iwai. 岩井俊二. **CAST:** Miho Nakayama, Etsushi Toyokawa, Bunjaku Han, Katsuyuki Shinohara, Miki Sakai, Takashi Kashiwabara, Mariko Kaga, Keiichi Suzuki, Ken Mitsuishi, Tomorowo Taguchi. 117 minutes. **RELEASES:** DVD, King (Japan, English subtitles), Dawoori (Korea, English/Japanese/Korean subtitles).

Iwai's romantic debut is a slick treatise on time and memory, centered around a case of mistaken identity and the impossibility of really knowing someone.

After the anniversary of the death of her fiancé, Itsuki Fuji, in a mountaineering accident, Hiroko Watanabe chances upon an old junior high school yearbook at his mother's house in Kobe. It lists their old family address in the town of Otaru, Hokkaido. Though Itsuki's mother assures her that the old house has long since been demolished, Hiroko is seized by the romantic notion of writing a brief letter to her dead lover at his childhood home inquiring after his well-being. After dispatching it in a gesture intended to lay his memory to rest, she embarks on a romantic affair with Itsuki's former best friend, a local glassblower named Shigeru.

She is astonished when a few days later a reply comes back, from someone signed Itsuki, stating briefly and succinctly that aside from a bad cold that won't shift, its sender is alive and well. Initially she dismisses it as a cruel joke, until Shigeru points out that if the house was indeed lying beneath a recently constructed highway, as Itsuki's mother told her, then the letter would never have been delivered. Intrigued, Hiroko finds herself unable to resist writing back.

Meanwhile in Otaru, there's clearly been a case of mistaken identity, as a young single woman named Itsuki Fuji finds herself receiving a string of strange letters from the lady in Kobe. Humoring Hiroko, she replies to them, before coming clean and revealing that the bane of her junior high school years was a young boy in the same class who coincidentally shared exactly the same name as her. For several long and hard years, the two endured the taunts and teasings of their classmates, finding themselves unable to break from each other's company due to their neighboring position on the school register, as they shared such duties as working after class in the school library together.

Shigeru suggests that both Hiroko and he make a pilgrimage to Otaru to meet this common link with her past face to face, though by a twist of fate they never actually cross paths with her new correspondent. By this time, however, it seems that Itsuki shares even more in common with Hiroko than the name of her dead classmate.

Shunji Iwai sits rather distinctly from the other directors who made their names in the '90s, in that rather than working his way up the hierarchy within the major studios or working on the production of pink films, he cut his teeth on music video production and work for cable TV. Prior to *Love Letter*, he directed a number of TV dramas running just short of an hour, including *Ghost Soup* (1992), a twee comedy in which a man finds that the apartment he has moved into is haunted by some exceedingly irritating ghosts, and *Fried Dragon Fish: Thomas Earwing's Arowana* (1993), featuring an early role for Tadanobu Asano as a fanatical fish collector embroiled in smuggling the valuable Arowana dragon fish.

Both of these TV works laid out the stylistic agenda for the director's later film work: the gliding cameras and the super-saturated colors of *Fried Dragon Fish*, the lengthy sequence as the cast of *Ghost Soup* perform a dance number clearly modeled on Michael Jackson's *Thriller*. Iwai effectively brought in a new visual aesthetic sense adopted from the pop promo world, filling his work with musical interludes set to contemporary music and a host of visual tricks culled from the video mixing desk.

But these two works really only laid the groundwork for Iwai's later experimentations. Though both were made more widely available on video and DVD following the success of *Love Letter* and his next feature, *Swallowtail Butterfly* (*Suwarōteiru*, 1996), perhaps they are better suited for TV, diverting enough but ultimately fairly vacuous. Nevertheless, even in his TV work Iwai soon managed to strike a more satisfying balance between the cosmetic and the dramatic. His 52-minute drama *Fireworks, Should We See It From the Side or the Bottom?* (*Uchiage Hana Bi. Shita Kara Miruka? Yoko Kara Miruka?*, 1993) earned him the Best Newcomer award from the Japanese Directors' Association in 1993. An innocent tale of young love as two elementary school boys, Norimichi and Yūsuke, vie for the attention of classmate Nazuna. What they don't realize is that Nazuna's parents are on the verge of divorcing, with Nazuna following her mother. One day Nazuna packs her bags to run away from home, but she is not going alone.

Undo (1994) was a slightly more adult-oriented tale, about a young cohabiting couple whose relationship difficulties have driven the woman to the brink of mental collapse. Madness was again the theme of *Picnic* (1994), featuring three mental patients who escape from their asylum, and then rather perversely decide that rather than jump over the wall, they should walk along it.

With the success of *Love Letter* and the popularity of his TV work, unusual for a Japanese film director, Iwai achieved a legendary status akin to a rock star. With his shoulder-length hair he even looked like one. By waving aside any distinction between cinema, music video, and TV drama, he appealed to an audience that had previously been uncatered to, keeping his finger firmly on the pulse of contemporary youth culture by cannily associating himself with some of the most popular musical talents of the day. *Love Letter*'s central star, Miho Nakayama, had conducted a successful singing career ever since 1986, and another popular songstress in the form of Chara starred in *Picnic* (alongside Asano, whom she later married).

But it was his second feature, *Swallowtail Butterfly*, again starring Chara, that came to define an entire generation. Set amongst the denizens of Yen Town, a community of Asian immigrants who speak in a mixture of broken English, Mandarin, and Japanese, drawn to Japan believing in the power of the "Yen." This they find in the form of a cassette of Frank Sinatra's *My Way*, discovered in the stomach of a dead gangster, which strangely holds the key, in the form of a cryptic magnetic code, to a money-printing scam that seems the answer to all their dreams.

Both critics and audiences were firmly divided, mainly down age lines, as to the merits of *Swallowtail*. Clocking in at 147 minutes it is undoubtedly overlong, but more than that, its story, couched within the template of a simple morality tale, seems merely an excuse to showcase Iwai's aesthetic sensibilities. Undeniably well-crafted, still there's something vaguely patronizing about its portrayal of Asians in Japan, living on the perimeters of Tokyo eking out their survival by drug dealing, prostitution, and scavenging around in scrap metal tips, with the modern-day Tokyo of the real world barely alluded to. Rather than any convincing portrayal, the ersatz shanty town of *Swallowtail* seems little more than a soundstage for Iwai to stage his gaudy musical numbers (the soundtrack, sung by the band in the film led by Chara, became a top-seller), his images buried in a technical virtuosity verging on glibness, and the outlaw glamor of its inhabitants catering squarely to the youth market. A few years later, it already looked passé.

Iwai's films don't lend themselves particularly well to analysis. From the self-conscious mugging of *Ghost Soup* and *Fried Dragon Fish* to the overblown street-savvy hipness of *Swallowtail*, they are all firmly rooted in the era in which they are made. But in the case of *Love Letter*, produced by Fuji Television as with all of his previous works, he seems to have pitched the level just right. Rather than dating his work by orchestrating it to a soundtrack of contemporary music, the score, by Remedios, here consists of a number of sweeping classically influenced motifs. Quirky characters whose presence grated in his earlier dramas seem less crudely drawn here, such as the twitching schoolgirl who elicits the female Itsuki's help in approaching her namesake, and the cast (including Toyokawa, fresh from Iwai's previous *Undo*, and his role as one of the brooding psychokinetic brothers from Jōji Iida's popular TV series and theatrical spin-off *Night Head* in 1994) all do their job admirably.

Whilst the plot, which is no less contrived than his other works, feels hot from the squeaky-clean pages of a *shōjo manga* (girls comic), its simplicity works in its favor. It also touches on deeper themes than Iwai's other films, even going as far as to checklist *À la recherche du temps perdu* (*Remembrance of Things Past*) by Marcel Proust

(1871–1922) in its meditation on time, identity, and reconstructed memory, as Itsuki recounts how her namesake used to sign his names on slips inside all the books on the library shelves to make it look like he had read them all.

By the time their correspondence reveals a hitherto hidden side to Itsuki's former fiancé's personality, it becomes clear that Iwai's film is more about surface appearances than straightforward nostalgia, fitting for a director whose work has often been criticized as mere window-dressing. In this instance, the polished veneer of the image complements rather than detracts from the central premise. From the opening snowbound moments, *Love Letter* is a very polished work indeed, a faultlessly paced flow of beautifully controlled widescreen images. Taking his lead from his work in music video, Iwai carefully storyboarded the entire film before shooting, and these animated storyboards are included on the DVD releases to be played alongside the original soundtrack.

Iwai only really recaptured the buoyant simplicity of his polished debut with *April Story* (*Shigatsu Monogatari*, 1998), a slight story about the experiences of girl from Hokkaido embarking on a co-ed college career in Tokyo. During a lull in his filmmaking output of several years, he continued to explore new technology and the means of visual expression it provided by developing his story for *All About Lily Chou-Chou* (*Ririi Shushu no Subete*) as an "interactive novel" made available over the Internet. The resulting film version, released theatrically in 2001, saw the director moving into darker territory. It tells the story of an ostracized 14-year-old's obsession with the fictional pop idol of the film's title, escaping into a virtual community of the singer's fans by means of a chat room that he has set up. This was followed by *Arita*, one of the seven shorts included in the compendium *Jam Films* (2002), alongside works by Jōji Iida (*Another Heaven*), Ryūhei Kitamura (*Versus*), Rokurō Mochizuki (*Onibi*), and Iwai's assistant director on *Love Letter*, Isao Yukisada (*GO*).

↓ MARKS
マークスの山
Mākusu no Yama

1995. **DIRECTOR:** Yōichi Sai, 崔洋一. **CAST:** Kiichi Nakai, Ittoku Kishibe, Masato Furuoya, Masato Hagiwara, Ren Ōsugi, Nenji Kobayashi, Susumu Terajima. 138 minutes. **RELEASES:** VCD, Asia Video Publishing (Hong Kong, English/Chinese subtitles).

A young former asylum resident might hold the key to a seemingly unrelated spate of murders sweeping Tokyo, in Sai's dark and slow-moving existential thriller.

When the appearance of the corpse of a former mobster in a classy residential district of Tokyo is followed a few days later by the murder of a Ministry of Justice official, there's seemingly nothing to link the two victims except the modus operandi: a gory seven-inch-long wound penetrating through the victims' left eyes and exiting through the top of their heads.

Workmanlike detective Aida (Nakai) is assigned to the first case, but his obstinate methods are soon putting noses out of joint, especially when a rival homicide division is assigned to the case of the second murder. Meanwhile Hiroyuki (Hagiwara), a disturbed young man tormented by long-suppressed memories of his parents' suicide beneath a windswept mountain, is released from his mental asylum and finds shelter and a warm bosom to lay his head on with his former nurse. But what is the significance of the acronym MARKS scribbled into the private diary of the troubled twenty-seven-year-old, and what is his link to the members of a university mountaineering club and a murder committed by a group of student radicals before he was even born?

Based on a novel by Kaoru Takamura, this haunting mystery thriller is an opaque and perplexing piece. Director Sai establishes from the very offset that he is concerned more with mood and character than with providing a convoluted "logical" solution to what might otherwise be a straightforward murder mystery. Despite apparently masquerading as a conventional police procedural, *MARKS* soon adopts a more fragmentary approach to the narrative in a collage of seemingly unrelated plot strands that never quite tie up.

In attempting to find the murderer purely by inference from the limited clues provided, the steadfast Aida finds himself so far off the mark that it is only by a lucky coincidence that the case is finally tied up at the film's conclusion (albeit rather messily). Though the plot reveals information unavailable to the inspector, it is presented in such a scattershot fashion that whether the viewer will be able to forge the connections to come out any less confused at the end than its protagonist is debatable.

In this way Sai is justified in depicting his search against the squabbling and infighting of the raincoated ranks of the Seventh Homicide Section, who by opting to do their detective work without leaving the office, barely scrape the surface of the impenetrable mystery. Comprising a host of familiar faces such as Susumu Terajima and Ren Ōsugi, these scenes provide some of the film's most intriguing and amusing moments.

Sai has to be admired for the way in which he conjures up a hauntingly austere atmosphere to suggest the existential void that lies at the heart of any obsessive quest for truth or self-knowledge. Hiroyuki's desire to return to the slopes of Mount Kitadake after years of being cooped away in a mental institution is paralleled with Aida's frustrated attempts to find the link between the double murder, prompting the detective's oft-repeated line, "It's one helluva job being a cop."

For all its cool visual detachment, though, Sai's approach to the original source comes across as remarkably deferential. The pace is languorous and literal, denying the viewer the pleasure of a single audience focus, and peppered as it is with such unpalatable moments as the opening buggery scene and an unflinching depiction of an attempt to stall a corpse's potential dental identification by means of a climbing pick, *MARKS*'s bleak vision is not going to appeal to all tastes.

Born in Nagano in 1949, a second-generation Korean, Sai started working in film in 1975, in the capacity of assistant director on Yoshihiko Okamoto's documentary *Kokuhatsu: Zainichi Kankokujin Seijihan Repōto* [trans: Indictment: Crimes against Japanese-born Koreans report], and acted as producer on Tetsurō Nunokawa's *Bastard on the Border* (*Maboroshi no Konminzoku Kyōwakoku* [trans: The illusion of a mixed-race republic]). His first work in commercial filmmaking came as an assistant director on Nagisa Ōshima's *In the Realm of the Senses*. He much later appeared in front of the camera in the same director's **Gohatto**.

After serving his dues as an assistant director, he made his debut in 1983 with *Jukkai no Mosukito* [trans: The mosquito on the 10th floor], starring the flamboyant rocker Yūya Uchida, who made a controversial bid for governor of Tokyo in the early '90s. This was followed swiftly by an erotic thriller for Nikkatsu, *Seiteki Hanzai* [trans: Sexual crime] in the same year. Throughout the '80s he worked on a number of hard-boiled crime dramas such as *Tomo yo, Shizuka ni Nemure* [trans: Sleep quietly, friend] for Kadokawa in 1985.

But Sai's major contribution to Japanese cinema in the '90s was his depiction of the discrimination faced by a Korean cab driver and his Filipino barmaid girlfriend in the acclaimed comedy drama *All under the Moon* (*Tsuki wa Dotchi ni Deteiru*, 1993). Since then, Sai has tended toward mainstream productions such as *Tokyo Deluxe* (*Heisei Musekinin Ikka Tokyo Derakkusu*, 1995), a black comedy about a family of conmen; the comic Japanese-cop-vs.-Korean-gangster antics of *Dog Race* (*Inu Hashiru*, 1998); the Okinawan-set *The Pig's Retribution* (*Buta no Mukui*, 1999); the prison reform drama *Doing Time* (*Keimusho no Naka*, 2002); and *Quill* (*Kuīru*, 2004), a drama about a guide dog, and the most successful of the wave of canine dramas that proved so popular in Japan around the year of its release.

↓ Memories

Memories Episode 1: Magnetic Rose
彼女の想いで
Kanojo no Omoide

DIRECTOR: Kōji Morimoto, 森本晃司.

Memories Episode 2: Stink Bomb
最臭兵器
Saishū Heiki

DIRECTOR: Tensai Okamura, 岡村天斎.

Memories Episode 3: Cannon Fodder
大砲の街
Taihō no Machi

DIRECTOR: Katsuhiro Ōtomo, 大友克洋. 1996. **VOICE CAST:** Tsutomu Isobe, Gara Takashima, Kōichi Yamadera, Shōzō Iizuka, Shigeru Chiba, Hideyuki Hori, Isamu Hayashi. 113 minutes. **RELEASES:** DVD, Emotion (Japan, English/Japanese subtitles), Mac (Hong Kong, English/Chinese subtitles).

Portmanteau film based on three original stories by manga maestro Ōtomo is a perfect entry point into the world of Japanese animation.

Akira (1988) is widely credited as the first full-length animated feature to play widely in cinemas outside of Japan, opening the eyes of foreign audiences to the joys of what is sometimes referred to as "Japanimation." A dazzling tale of a young teenager with psychic powers run amok in a Tokyo of the future who unearths a government-sponsored terrorist conspiracy, this cyberpunk classic almost single-handedly set in motion the *otaku* (fanboy) craze in the West in the early '90s. The name of its director, Katsuhiro Ōtomo, rapidly became almost synonymous with Japanese animation, though surprisingly his work in the field has actually proven rather sparse.

One of the reasons for this may be that Ōtomo's background lies not within the film world, but in the field of manga comics. Nevertheless, thanks to his numerous collaborations with other respected practitioners in the animation field, he has come to be seen as the figurehead of a school of thought whose members include Satoshi Kon (**Perfect Blue**, 1998), Yoshiaki Kawajiri (*Ninja Scroll*, 1993), and Rintarō (*Metropolis*, 2001). All of these directors share the same vision of utilizing a hyper-realistic style, its basis firmly within cinematic technique, to create intelligent and well-wrought stories within richly rendered worlds. The three-part omnibus film, *Memories*, is a testament to the talents of several of Ōtomo's contemporaries and makes for a perfect introduction to this domain.

Born in 1954 in Miyagi, Ōtomo began his career as an illustrator in the early '70s, before his first manga story *Gun Report* (*Jūsei*), a loose adaptation of Prosper Mérimée's short story *Mateo Falcone* was published in 1973. For the rest of the '70s he contributed numerous short works to the comic magazine *Action*, including some adaptations of Western writers, before beginning work in 1979 on his first longer serialized story, *Fireball*. It was his first major work in the field of science fiction, revolving around the theme of humans pitted against a large omnipotent computer, though the serial was never in fact completed.

Fireball was followed by Ōtomo's breakthrough manga *Domu: A Child's Dream*, which, like *Akira*, featured protagonists with psychic powers, this time battling it out against the background of crumbling tenement blocks in a decaying future. The serialization, which began in 1980, was compiled into a single volume and released in 1983 when it bore the distinction of becoming the first graphic novel to win the Science Fiction Grand Prix in Japan, an award previously only applicable to literary fiction.

This was swiftly succeeded by the sweeping vision of *Akira*, an epic 2,000-page manga that ran from 1982 to 1990, set in the metropolis of Neo Tokyo in 2019, thirty-one years after World War III. This long-running series cemented Ōtomo's name in Japan as a pioneer of the manga form, and overseas too, when the translated version was released as a series of volumes that first saw publication in the United States in 1988, coinciding with the release of the film. Ōtomo's increasing involvement with animation was to drag him away from the printed page, his last major work being *The Legend of Mother Sarah* in 1990.

During the eight years he worked on the manga of *Akira*, Ōtomo began to make increasingly frequent forays into the world of film. In 1982 he took time out to make his 16mm debut, a 60-minute self-produced experimental live-action work about a group of gun crazy teenagers, *Jiyū o Warera ni* [trans: Give us freedom, the title contains a pun with the similarity between the words for freedom (*jiyū*) and gun (*jū*)], but his first real work in anime came when he contributed character designs to Rintarō's *Harmagedon* (*Genma Taisen*, 1983).

Ōtomo made his official directorial debut in animation with one of the three parts of the anime compendium *Manie Manie Meikyū Monogatari* in 1987, known as *Labyrinth Story* but also released abroad as *Neo Tokyo*. Alongside episodes by Rintarō and Yoshiaki Kawajiri, his *Kōji Chūshi Meirei* [trans: Order to stop construction] was a riff on the "machines gone mad" idea, with a group of mechanized workers deep in the heart of the Amazon rain forest refusing to terminate their program, even after the contract with the Japanese construction company that owns them is canceled by the country's corrupt government. The next year he contributed two segments to another omnibus film, *Robot Carnival* (1988), alongside some of what would become the major names of Japanese animation over the coming years, before he was put at the helm of the animated version of *Akira*.

Considering the scale of the success of *Akira*, it seems a little strange that for his next film Ōtomo would turn to live-action. *World Apartment Horror* (1991) centered around a building full of Asians living in Tokyo harassed by an ineffectual yakuza eager to evict them (played by Hiroyuki Tanaka, who would later move on to feature directing himself under the pseudonym Sabu). *Perfect Blue* director Satoshi Kon was responsible for drawing the manga adaptation. Kon also worked designing the backgrounds for Hiroyuki Kitakubo's *Rōjin Z* (1991), which was scripted by the *Akira* director. Its highly original story featured residents of a geriatric community used as guinea pigs for a new military machine disguised as a hospital bed that tends to the every need of its patient.

But though Ōtomo managed to maintain his profile in the anime world on the back of the lofty reputation of *Akira*, his only real significant work during the '90s was *Memories*. The film was a portmanteau of three films based on previously written short manga stories by Ōtomo. For the film, he took the role of project planner, scripted two of the parts, and also directed the film's third and final one.

Memories' first segment, *Magnetic Rose*, is perhaps the most substantial and impressive of the three, and the only one not scripted by Ōtomo. Instead, Satoshi Kon's screenplay, directed by Kōji Morimoto, in many ways foreshadows the approach he utilized for *Perfect Blue*, playing with the same themes of memory, fantasy, and phantasm, and prompting the eternal question, "What is reality?" A ragtag team of deep space salvage operators stray into the Sargasso Zone and are drawn toward a huge rose-shaped hunk of matter floating through the ether. Entering, they find themselves in a baroque opera house dominated by a huge chandelier and flanked by marble pillars. This setting turns out to be the floating tomb of a long dead female opera singer

named Eva, whose presence soon manifests itself by means of an array of projections and holographic images. The unwanted visitors soon find themselves overwhelmed by the singer's memories, active participants in a drama where the ghosts of Eva's past, including her deceased lover, act out their roles within this illusionary stage. The Japanese title of this segment, and the original story on which it is based, is *Kanojo no Omoide*, which translates as *Her Memories*.

Okamura's second part, *Stink Bomb*, takes itself slightly less seriously. It features a laboratory researcher for a pharmaceutical company who finds himself pursued by the entire Japanese Self Defense Forces and the American army after unwittingly ingesting a substance he believes to be a cure for the cold. The substance, in fact developed for biochemical warfare, makes him exude foul odorous clouds of gas, which cause everyone around him to pass out as he heads toward his company head office in Tokyo.

Ōtomo's intriguing and technically innovative *Cannon Fodder*, at fifteen minutes, is the shortest of the three stories. Set in a dystopian no-man's-land of the future, a young boy dreams of taking his father's role as one of the legions of operators of the huge cannons that encase the city walls firing shells off at a distant, unnamed foe. Stylistically poles apart from the other segments, it is memorable for the opening sequence consisting of a lengthy unbroken take, and its flat blocky visuals and muted color palate, reminiscent of animation from the Soviet Republic and Eastern Bloc countries during the communist period.

For a long time, *Memories* remained undistributed outside of Japan, only available on imported DVD or laserdisc, which is a shame, because there is something for everyone in it. The three stories are radically different in terms of their tone, style, and execution, a testimony to the diversity of Japanese animation during the '90s, and all feature top-notch production values.

In the meantime, aside from scripting Rintarō's *Metropolis* (2001), based on a Tezuka manga from 1949, and contributing to Hirotsugu Kawasaki's *Spriggan* (1998), Ōtomo spent nine years overseeing the troubled development of his pet project, *Steam Boy*, which was finally released in July 2004.

↓ **Organ**
オルガン
Orugan

1996. **DIRECTOR:** Kei Fujiwara, 藤原京. **CAST:** Kimihiko Hasegawa, Kenjin Nasa, Kei Fujiwara, Ryū Ōkubo, Shun Sugata, Reona Hirota. 110 minutes (Japanese theatrical release: 102 minutes). **RELEASE:** DVD, Synapse Films (U.S., English subtitles).

Violent, chaotic, and gory tale about underground organ trade, performed by the members of an experimental theater group. A suitably sickly atmosphere pervades the proceedings, but the film's images of decay allude to post-bubble social collapse as much as to unabashed splatter.

The directorial debut of Shinya Tsukamoto's former collaborator is notorious for its over-the-top gore. But although it has been called everything from fetid to mean-spirited, the film has more going for it than festering boils and bleeding stumps. Admittedly, much of the film's visuals contain just such gory, freak-out nastiness. It certainly doesn't shy away from showing or occasionally reveling in it.

Cops Numata and Tosaka manage to infiltrate the gang of organ traders they have been shadowing for ages, but the pair are unmasked in the middle of surgery on a corpse than turns out to still be alive. After a messy battle, Numata is given an injection of an unknown barbiturate, while Tosaka is kidnapped by the gang. Numata goes walkabout in a stupor and is fired from the force. His colleagues, headed by Tosaka's identical twin, go searching for the missing policeman, who is now a human vegetable in the makeshift lab of Junichi Saeki, half of the

brother-sister pair that runs the organ gang. Junichi's day job is as a biology teacher at a girls' high school, where he uses the virgin blood of his students to keep the limbless Tosaka alive. Junichi's one-eyed sister, Yūko (director Fujiwara), meanwhile tries to fend off the police investigation as well as their yakuza masters, who are eager to eliminate her and her brother for attracting the cops with the mess they made.

If there is one positive thing to be said about *Organ*'s all-pervasive images of decay, it's that they are admirably consistent. From the film's plot to its grotesque make-up effects and its locations, putrefaction is the constant defining factor. People rat each other out, cops rape the wife of one of their own colleagues, men are beaten within an inch of their lives and left to die in the gutter, Junichi keeps his diseased liver in check with experimental drugs that spawn a festering growth on his torso. All of this unravels amid run-down structures and squalid buildings.

The world of *Organ* is a world gone mad. But it's a world that is built on true foundations; the film's relentless pessimism has its roots in daily life. As one character explains when the cops investigate the dilapidated, rickety shed where the organ gang performed an operation the previous night, "Before the bubble burst, this used to be a thriving business." *Organ* is a reflection of post-bubble Japan, a society in chaos where old values have died, where what was once prosperous is now in a state of squalor. With business in disarray, money is made by slicing people open. To emphasize this chaotic, amoral confusion, Fujiwara edited the film in a non-continuous manner, jump-cutting within scenes and ignoring smooth transitions between sequences. *Organ*'s chaos is all-encompassing, in form as well as content.

That the director/actress would so fortuitously tap into the post-bubble vibe can be traced back to her pre-cinema days. The child of a poor country family with a history of mental illness, Fujiwara moved to Tokyo and spent years heading her own underground theater companies. Perhaps partially by choice, the country's prosperity was never hers to share in. She collaborated with Shinya Tsukamoto on his plays and early 8mm films, culminating in roles both in front of and behind the camera on *Tetsuo: The Iron Man*. But when Tsukamoto went off to make *Hiruko the Goblin* for major studio Shochiku, Fujiwara went back to street theater. She formed the Organ Vital company, with whom she eventually mounted and performed *Organ*, first as a play and subsequently as a film. Released in Japan with eight minutes of cuts ordered by censorship body Eirin, the film was sold to several foreign distributors in its full 110-minute "director's cut" version. Fujiwara has long planned to make *Organ 2*, but while she shot some footage for it, the film itself never materialized. Perhaps she realized that her own debut film is one tough act to follow.

↓ Shall We Dance?

Shall We ダンス?

Shall We Dansu?

1996. **DIRECTOR:** Masayuki Suō, 周防正行. **CAST:** Kōji Yakusho, Tamiyo Kusakari, Naoto Takenaka, Eriko Watanabe, Masahiro Motoki. 136 minutes (international version 118 minutes). **RELEASES:** VHS, Miramax (U.S., English subtitles); VCD, Edko (Hong Kong, English/Chinese subtitles).

Time-serving office drone finds himself a valued member of a ballroom dancing club in one of the top-grossing foreign film releases of its time in the United States.

The average man in the street feeling increasingly alienated from his daily life reintegrated into the fold and, in the process, stumbling across his own unique way of expressing his identity in a celebration of song and dance—the cross-cultural appeal of *Shall We Dance?* is not so surprising. The story bears all the hallmarks of the classical dramatic model of comedy. The themes are universal and the emotional scale is large. It's perhaps small wonder that, with its advertising campaign that downplayed the film's Asian aspects in a poster featuring merely a pair of male and female legs, Masayuki Suō's film had audiences flocking into U.S. cinemas in droves.

Released by Miramax in a slimmed-down 118-minute edit, *Shall We Dance?* is a far warmer film than most Japanese works showcased abroad and went on to become one of the highest-earning foreign language titles of all time, grossing $9.7 million in America, though due to Academy rules was deprived of a Best Foreign Language Academy Award nomination in 1997 because it had already been shown on television in Japan the previous year.

Kōji Yakusho, one of the top box office draws in the late '90s through his roles in *Cure* and *Lost Paradise*, plays Sugiyama, the ultimate time-serving, clock-watching employee. Married with a teenage daughter, mortgaged up to his eyeballs, and financially trapped in an insipid career in accountancy outside of which he has no interests nor any time or energy for them, he is but one of the millions of faceless salarymen that rise before daybreak, trudge dutifully into the office to stare out of the window all day, and shamble home twelve hours later on their long commute back to the suburbs. The only glimmer of excitement in his monotonous lifestyle is the beautiful young woman (Kusakari) whom he spots from the train home every evening, gazing wistfully from the window of a nearby dance school. Against his better judgment, he secretly enrolls and is soon drawn into the surreptitious world of private lessons and weekend socials.

However, the girl, whose name is Mai, has no time for the amorous advances of the hordes of lonely men who stumble through the door of the dance school every night. She has her own psychological cross to bear in the form of a tumble taken during the final rounds of the international championships years before at that Mecca of ballroom dancing, Blackpool, England. Meanwhile, as Sugiyama overcomes his initial awkwardness on the dance floor, along with the others in his beginners' class he soon finds himself loving dance as an end in itself. His wife, suspicious of his recent spate of exuberance and the lingering scent of perfume on his shirts, hires a private detective to find out what exactly is going on.

Director Masayuki Suō warrants a mention in any serious look at Japanese film, if only for his irreverent debut, a soft-porn pastiche of the films of one of the national cinema's most treasured possessions, Yasujirō Ozu, with *Abnormal Family* (*Hentai Kazoku Aniki no Yome-San*, 1984). Made for the prolific skin-flick producers Kokuei and distributed by Shintoho, in a year in which Japanese cinema had seemingly reached its furthest point from the Golden Age of the '50s, this sixty-two-minute pink film was shot in the same long static takes that Ozu was famed for, the camera position low on the ground and perpendicular to the action, with allusions to a number of the master's films, including *Tokyo Story* (*Tōkyō Monogatari*, 1953) and his final work, *An Autumn Afternoon* (*Sanma no Aji*, 1963). Here the nuclear family unit of Ozu's films has transformed to meet the requirements of the genre. The youngest son peeps on as elder brother indulges his voracious sexual appetite with the buxom young bride who has just moved in under the family roof. The daughter has secretly left her job as an office lady for a more lucrative role working in a sex sauna, where her first customer turns out to be her elder brother. Father's serenely contented grins are this time induced by saké rather than any innate feelings of Zen, as he dreams of the girl working at the local bar whom he fantasizes as looking like his deceased wife. A hilarious collection of film buff in-jokes ladled out with liberal doses of eroticism, *Abnormal Family* went far beyond the requirements of the sex film genre to achieve cult status in its own country.

Suō's first mainstream feature, *Fancy Dance*, not only brought young teen idol Masahiro Motoki his first large-screen success, but also established the template for the director's two subsequent comedies—a group of men forced together by circumstance in a colorful milieu far removed from their usual element. In this first film, the location was a Buddhist monastery, in which Motoki's singer in a ska band decides to hide out from his fans for a year. Whilst there, he finds himself amongst a motley assortment of shaven-headed characters who have similarly opted for the ascetic life, humorously detailing the grudging acolyte's nocturnal secret feasts with sneaked-in buckets of KFC and the harsh administrations by a long wooden stick for breaking the strict monastic code.

Sumo Do, Sumo Don't (*Shiko Funjatta*, 1992) saw Motoki's return in the lead role, this time as a student about to flunk his graduation unless he redeems himself by entering the college's sumo wrestling club. In both of these films, Suō makes use of a comic troupe who would join him for *Shall We Dance?*, including the smiling, corpulent Hiromasa Taguchi and the scrawny Naoto Takenaka, in the second film making for an unlikely figure to carry on the college sumo tradition. Returning under the same character name of Aoki, Takenaka's performance in *Shall We Dance?* as the systems analyst at Sugiyama's company is a master stroke. By day the butt of office ridicule, at night transformed *Flashdance*-style into a testosterone-dripping King of the Pasadoble, he almost completely steals the show in one of the finest comic turns of the past few years. Unfortunately, overexposure and a predilection for sticking with the same type of part in numerous films including Shinobu Yaguchi's *Waterboys* (2001) and Fumihiko "Sori" Masuri's *Ping Pong* (2002) has rendered Takenaka's comic schtick somewhat less effective, a sort of Japanese equivalent of Robin Williams.

If Suō's previous two films worked by pitching their modern-day protagonists into more traditionally Japanese milieus, perhaps the reason for the wider international success of *Shall We Dance?* lies in making a film for an audience that remains largely uncatered to—the middle-aged professional. Its characters are reserved and self-conscious males who have willingly thrown themselves into a world where women predominate, overcoming their initial inhibitions to guiltily indulge in their harmless pleasures to the full. All of those enrolled in the dance course are there for reasons that they'd rather not have to explain. "Yeah, they all say that!" counters one character when Sugiyama explains that he took up ballroom dancing after he heard it was a good form of exercise. "People will think I'm only here for the girls," says another.

It is the dancers' discovery of a mutual bond via this secret life that ultimately proves so heartwarming, with perhaps the most exhilarating aspect being that they all look as if they're enjoying themselves so much. The vivacious dance sequences are packed full of visual detail, taking in each of the characters and their individual dancing styles as they all maintain a degree of buoyant absurdity all the more endearing for the fact that they are expressed in terms of their physicality rather than language. From his first awkward steps onto the dance floor, stuttering Sugiyama's emotional journey from respected but unfulfilled office drudge to an assured and valued member of the dance school is uplifting in the extreme. *Shall We Dance?* is colorful, moving, and inspiring, and still, after the initial critical clamoring has subsided, its simple-minded escapism is just as hard to resist as ever.

Picking up an impressive thirteen Japanese Academy Awards upon its release in its home country in 1996, the U.S. success ensured that the remake rights were immediately snapped up. The original package, with Tom Hanks tipped to star and John Turteltaub (guiding hand behind *Cool Runnings*, *Phenomenon*, and *Instinct*) to direct, was never actually green-lighted, but years later the project was once more given the go-ahead, this time with Richard Gere and Jennifer Lopez in the central roles, and Peter Chelsom helming the production.

In the meantime, one of Japan's most undervalued directors has been left on the sidelines.

Despite preliminary discussions with Miramax for the remake project, which he detailed in the book *'Shall We Dansu?' Amerika o Iku* [trans: 'Shall we dance?' Going to America], he has not directed anything subsequently. He did, however, get to marry the film's lead actress, the beautiful Tamiyo Kusakari, whose ethereal presence first lured Yakusho from his commuter train.

↓ Kichiku
鬼畜大宴会
Kichiku Dai Enkai

1997. DIRECTOR: Kazuyoshi Kumakiri, 熊切和嘉. CAST: Sumiko Mikami, Shunsuke Sawada, Shigeru Bokuda, Toshiyuki Sugihara, Kentarō Ogiso. 103 minutes. RELEASES: DVD, Japan Shock Entertainment (The Netherlands, English/Dutch/German subtitles), Artsmagic (U.S., English subtitles).

With its leader in jail, the radical idealism of a small group of student activists quickly makes way for abuse of power, culminating in a countryside bloodbath. Low-budget, experimental debut that turned heads (and stomachs) and made its student director the darling of the most prestigious film festivals.

While studying at the Osaka Arts University, Kazuyoshi Kumakiri allegedly found several rolls of archival footage of student riots from the 1970s in a closet. Kumakiri had previously attempted unsuccessfully to make several Monty Python-esque black comedy shorts, and was planning to make a feature as his graduation project. The found footage provided the spark for what would become *Kichiku*, the portrait of a group of out-of-control student radicals.

Sometime during the 1970s Aizawa, the leader of a left-wing student group, is locked up in a jail cell. When his cellmate Fujiwara is released, Aizawa asks him to look up and join his group, which he left in the care of girlfriend Masami.

Arriving at their hideaway, Fujiwara quickly learns that radical ideas are few and far between and that the political cause has become merely an excuse to hang out and party together, and for a few hangers-on to find some sense of their own identity. Masami switches sexual partners just about every night, taking her pick from the all-male membership. Aizawa's imminent release and Masami's temporary, status quo leadership create a sense of security and comfort.

When news reaches them that Aizawa has committed suicide in his jail cell, mere days before he is to be set free, the bubble bursts. Uncertainty over the future of the group and questions of loyalty surface. Soon, the merest of doubts is enough to awake paranoia in Masami, her sexual experiences with the young men becoming a major factor in deciding who stays and who goes. When Yamane, the most openly critical member, attempts to leave the group and start a more politically active cell of his own, he is taken into the woods and brutally beaten. Then Masami has Kumagaya, the only one of the group to have rebuffed her sexual advances, undergo the same treatment. The beatings soon turn to torture, the torture to maiming, and the maiming to murder. In a true descent into hell, the others are dragged along with Masami's manipulative madness, and the members of the group turn on one another.

"In university just before making *Kichiku*, I made a ten-minute short with a few other students. I directed it, because I noticed most of the others didn't think about directing seriously. To me it was very serious, so there was a clear difference in our states of mind. They didn't work very seriously, and that annoyed me. So sometimes I felt like I wanted to kill the other students, especially when I was all alone doing the editing. The premise of *Kichiku* really reflected this. In a way it's a very personal film. I liberated my own desires for violence and tried to open the inside of my mind to let out all the poison. And it's all there in the film. It made me feel ashamed of myself, like I was the worst person in the world to be able to think of those things."—Kazuyoshi Kumakiri

Kichiku certainly is violent. It takes a sharp turn into gross-out territory in its second half, with a lingering close-up of Yamane's half-exploded head as its gory highlight. The change is sudden, too sudden some critics have noted, and the low budget renders the effects more silly than shocking.

However, delivering shocks does not seem to be the main motivating factor. What matters more is the absurdity of what goes on, and in this sense the exaggeration certainly has a function. Kumakiri's targets are the enforced hierarchy of the group unit and the abuse of power this can all too easily provoke. The student group forms a miniature society that degenerates beneath the surface, a degeneration that had already started before Aizawa's suicide, which was merely the catalyst that brought it out into the open. Masami's sexual games and the hanger-on mentality of most of the members, who try desperately to find a group to belong to and from which to derive their identity, form a dangerous mixture, the extent of which goes unnoticed by everyone until it's too late. It is a very real danger for any society that has turned hierarchy and the group unit into an ideal.

Kumakiri, who was twenty-three when he made *Kichiku*, handles the group dynamics well. The sudden change in the film is less apparent in the story, which builds up to the eruption of violence through the aforementioned degeneration, than in the form: The location changes from the claustrophobic apartment to a wooded hillside, where the tensions are at last released. The director also adds a subtle supernatural spin to his tale in the person of Fujiwara. Remaining a sidelined observer throughout, he becomes the avenging spirit of his friend Aizawa, who has come to judge his former disciples for betraying the group's ideological principles. *Katana* in hand, he stands and watches until even the most passive member has turned into a homicidal loony before meting out his swift judgment.

It took the young director four years to come up with his sophomore effort *Hole in the Sky* (*Sora no Ana*), a slower-paced drama that nevertheless dealt with a similar theme to *Kichiku*: that of the effects of isolation on human relationships. Yakuza movie stalwart Susumu Terajima played the owner of a roadside restaurant in Hokkaido, a man with a mother complex who falls in love with a young woman dumped on the doorstep by her boyfriend in the middle of a holiday trip. The film received good critical notices and played some festivals, but didn't do much to set the world on fire. Kumakiri's third film, *Antenna*, however, saw him elevated back to the highest platform, receiving its world premiere at the 2003 Venice Film Festival.

Kumakiri was only the first of a number of graduates of the Osaka Arts University (Ōsaka Geidai) to make an impact on the Japanese film scene at the change of the millennium. Several of his fellow alumni came out with their first independent features as *Kichiku* made its round of the international festivals: Nobuhiro Yamashita, whose dry-witted slacker comedy *Hazy Life* (*Donten Seikatsu*, 1999) swiftly gained him enough critical favor, and comparisons with Jim Jarmusch, to mount his follow-ups in rapid succession. *No One's Ark* (*Baka no Hakobune*, 2002) was both touching and absurd in its portrayal of an underachieving couple trying to make a fortune in post-bubble Japan by selling an undrinkable health beverage. Receiving its world premiere in Toronto a year later, *Ramblers* (*Riarizumu no Yado*, 2003) sees Yamashita continuing his amiably meandering portraits of youth in search of a set of values.

Slightly less observant is the wildly tongue-in-cheek work of Ryūichi Honda, director of the ultra-campy declaration of love to '60s pop cinema *Tokyo Shameless Paradise* (*Tōkyō Harenchi Tengoku Sayonara no Blues*, 2001), while Takashi Ujita has a sensibility closer to Kumakiri's, his

Ryuko, in the Unfaithful Evening (*Kanashiku Naruhodo Fujitsu na Yozora Ni*, 2000) portraying an unhinged family that stemmed in a direct lineage from Yoshimitsu Morita's *Family Game* and that would find resonance in Kumakiri's *Antenna*. United in the Planet Studyo +1 production company, these Osaka-based filmmakers set up an alternative to the filmmaking monolith of Tokyo, producing, distributing, and handling the international sales of their own works. With the first festival retrospective already devoted to them at the 2002 Hong Kong Film Festival and the swift acceptance of their work by Japanese critics and fellow filmmakers (Kumakiri, Yamashita, and Honda all contributed to Makoto Shinozaki's *Cop Festival* project), it looks as if they are succeeding in carving out their own permanent niche within the Japanese cinema landscape.

↓ Onibi: The Fire Within
鬼火
Onibi

1997. **DIRECTOR:** Rokurō Mochizuki, 望月六郎. **CAST:** Yoshio Harada, Reiko Kataoka, Shō Aikawa, Eiji Okuda, Kazuki Kitamura. 101 minutes. **RELEASES:** DVD, Gaga Communications (Japan, no subtitles), Artsmagic (U.S./U.K., English subtitles); VHS, Les Films du Paradoxe (France, French subtitles).

A middle-aged ex-con and former yakuza hit man tries to lead a quiet life, but is pulled back into violence by a young woman trying desperately to bury her seedy past. Japan's most overlooked yakuza film director takes a tired plot and injects it with so much pathos that he delivers his masterpiece in the process.

Genre films can be much more effective vehicles for the portrayal of human emotions than straightforward dramas. This goes for gangster films in particular, with their portraits of human beings leading short but intense lives and the central role played by the extreme contrast between life and death. It's a genre that exaggerates human life, that enlarges and intensifies the individual's emotions, thereby creating the possibility of delivering profoundly affecting statements. There are few better examples of this in contemporary cinema than Rokurō Mochizuki's *Onibi: The Fire Within*.

Kunihiro (Harada), once nicknamed "Fireball'" for his intense, sure-fire methods, is a former mob killer recently released from his second stretch in prison. Knowing full well that a third conviction will automatically mean a life sentence, he is determined to stay on the straight and narrow. Renting a room in the house of a former fellow inmate, he is more than willing to spend the rest of his life doing odd jobs to get by, but his extremely reverent and extremely persistent former underling Tanizawa (Aikawa) keeps trying to persuade him to return to yakuza life. "Today's yakuza are all about money," he explains his determination to a colleague, "but they're wrong. Being a yakuza is all about violence. And if you have a killer like Kunihiro on your side, you need nothing else."

Kunihiro resists, no longer feeling allegiance to his old gang, which has been absorbed by their former rivals while he was in jail. Tanizawa offers an envelope of money as a gift, but the middle-aged killer asks to have his photo camera instead. Then when the offer comes to be a driver for the gang's boss Myōjin (Okuda), he feels it sufficiently risk-free and legal enough and takes it. While the boss apologizes for the drop in rank, Kunihiro is more than happy to spend his time behind the wheel, filling in the long stretches of inactivity with reading, sleeping, and listening to classical music.

When Myōjin asks him to help out two of his men in a scuffle with a rival gang who owe them money, Kunihiro not only saves the bumbling pair, he also comes back with all the money the other gang owes the Myōjin group. The boss treats him to drinks at a hostess club and a night with the club's pretty pianist Yōko (Kataoka), and the old fox quickly finds himself falling for this young woman who can play his favorite classical pieces. But Yōko has a dark past she is eager to erase and she asks Kunihiro to teach her how to kill the man she feels is responsible for her sorrow.

Onibi's plot is a mixture of two of the genre's most enduring and well-traveled narratives: the gangster who returns from jail to find his world completely changed, and the killer who takes on one last job to help the woman he loves. But the resulting film is anything but a tired retread. With a career-best performance from Yoshio Harada, whose macho swagger took him to great heights of popularity in the '80s but who here is all calmness and restraint, *Onibi* is one of the most emotionally involving and moving Japanese gangster films in many years. We love Kunihiro from the first moment we see him burning incense at his old boss's grave. When we get to know about his past, we love him even more for making the choice he's made. But then we are slowly tortured by seeing him slip back into a life of violence, especially because he remains so likable throughout.

To this end, Mochizuki uses the inherent exaggeration of the gangster genre well, getting us to care deeply for his protagonist through the extreme situation that forces him to make his moral choices. The director manages to sustain this all the way through the very end of the film, with a payoff that comes after the end credits are over.

In addition to its portrait of the emotional consequences of one man's moral choices, *Onibi* is also an exploration of images as an affirmation of existence. Initially by way of the snapshots Kunihiro takes with Tanizawa's camera, but gradually the affirmation of the negative aspects are brought into play through the photographs from Yōko's past she is so eager to wipe out of existence. This exploration of the relationship between recorded images and life also played a part in a previous Mochizuki film, *Another Lonely Hitman* (*Shin Kanashiki Hittoman*, 1995), and hints at his very conscious approach to cinema, which goes all the way back to his days as a film student.

After a failed stint in university studying literature, Mochizuki joined the film classes of Image Forum, Tokyo's bastion of experimental cinema. He was invited to work on a film by one of his teachers, but the project was canceled soon thereafter. He joined Nikkatsu studios, but did so right when the studio was shutting down its Roman Porno production line. Before he'd properly entered, he was already on his way out, along with most of the studio's other contract staff. He joined Nikkatsu director Genji Nakamura's independent *pinku eiga* production company, first as a scriptwriter, later also as a director. When the porn market made its switch to video in the mid-'80s, Mochizuki left Nakamura's circle and founded his own company, E-Staff Union, churning out an astonishing volume of porn videos (the number ranges from 120 to 300, depending on whom you believe), with titles like *Onanie Musume: Midarana Shiseikatsu* [trans: Masturbation girl: my lewd private life]. He poured his feelings about this period into his autobiographical debut feature *Skinless Night* (1990), about a porn director who is reminded of his original artistic ambitions after stumbling upon the film he made as a student. The conclusion Mochizuki reached in the film, that pragmatism will always conquer idealism, would become illustrative for his own career. Because even though he was gradually able to leave the porn industry behind him, he's had to compromise in order to find freedom of creative expression.

Like many of his contemporaries, Mochizuki made a name for himself directing yakuza films. He has professed to hate the yakuza in real life, and this stance is reflected in his films, which shun macho heroism and favor the doomed outsider. After definitely establishing himself with *The Wicked Reporter* (*Gokudō Kisha*, 1994) and its two sequels, he went on to make the elegiac gangster films *Another Lonely Hitman*, *A Yakuza in Love* (*Koi Gokudō*, 1997) and *Mobster's Confessions* (*Gokudō Zangeroku*, 1998). On occasion he

had the chance to show his non-conformist side with *Apron Stage* (*Debeso*, 1996), about the trials and tribulations of a traveling vaudeville troupe, and *The Outer Way* (*Gedō*, 1998), an absurdist tale of a humiliated cop who helps clean up the scum in a small town but who proves to be lacking in moral fiber himself.

Less audacious than Takashi Miike and less arty than Kiyoshi Kurosawa, and therefore less obvious to be singled out for foreign exposure, Mochizuki has largely been shorn of the recognition he deserves. He seemed to be on the verge of an international breakthrough in 1998, when the Rotterdam Film Festival showed a retrospective of ten of his films and *Onibi* was released theatrically in France. However, any follow-up has been curiously lacking. Two films did the rounds of the occasional festival: *Minazuki* (1999), the tale of a middle-aged salaryman's search for his missing wife, and *Coward* (*Chinpira*, 2000) a film about a misfit young gangster and his involvement with three women, not to be confused with Shinji Aoyama's *Chinpira*, a.k.a. **Two Punks**.

Suffering business setbacks at the start of the new millennium (the bankruptcy of his production company and the cancelation of two film projects), Mochizuki is now mainly active, and quite prolifically so, in the straight-to-video arena, whereas internationally recognized filmmakers like Takashi Miike, Kiyoshi Kurosawa, and Shinji Aoyama have managed increasingly to move away from it, finding critical acclaim in the process.

It certainly is not his own lack of devotion that is to blame for the situation. Still fiercely original, in 2002 he made *Kamachi*, based on the life of precocious poet and painter Kamachi Yamada, who electrocuted himself on his electric guitar at age 17, leaving behind a legacy of work dealing with the pressures of conformity. Rokurō Mochizuki will no doubt continue to turn out idiosyncratic films, within genre restrictions and without them. Whether the rest of the world will ever sit up and take proper notice is something we can only guess. And hope.

↓ **Raigyo**
黒い下着の女—雷魚
Kuroi Shitagi no Onna: Raigyo

1997. **DIRECTOR:** Takahisa Zeze, 瀬々敬久. **CAST:** Moe Sakura, Takeshi Itō, Takuji Suzuki, Sumiko Nogi. 75 minutes. **RELEASES:** DVD, Salvation (U.K., English subtitles), Kokuei (Japan, no subtitles).

A bleak tale of murder and revenge, Zeze's atmospheric erotic thriller balances beauty and brutality, playing more like an arthouse pic than a grindhouse flick.

Erotic cinema is alive and well in Japan. A distinct entity from the ever-burgeoning cheaply produced hardcore Adult Video (AV) market, a large number of softcore *pinku eiga* (pink films) are still made for the big screen every year. Shot on film, they enjoy theatrical runs in the small number of specialist cinemas that cater to them, before circulating more widely on video and cable TV. With most countries' domestic industries almost entirely eschewing celluloid in favor of videotape, the niche market of the Japanese sex film represents an almost unique phenomenon in contemporary cinema.

Not only does *pinku eiga* embody a significant sector of independent film production, but during the '80s and early '90s, it also represented a major training ground for new directors to hone their craft before moving on to more ambitious mainstream productions. To name but two directors not mentioned elsewhere in this book, Yōjirō Takita went from steering such titles as *Renzoku Bōkan* [trans: Serial rape, 1983] and a number of films in the long-running *Chikan Densha* [trans: Train pervert] series during the '80s, to the sumptuous period studio spectacles of *The Yin Yang Master* (*Onmyōji*, 2001) and *When the Last Sword Is Drawn* (*Mibugishiden*, 2003). Banmei Takashi cut his teeth on the likes of *Nihon no Gōmon* [trans: Japanese torture, 1978] and *Kinbaku Nawa no Seifuku* [trans: Tightly bound rope uniform, 1982], before mas-

terminding, amongst other works, *Rain of Light* (*Hikari no Ame*, 2001), a filmic recreation of the United Red Army Incident in 1972, in which two revolutionary groups, the Revolutionary Front and the Red Color Partisans, holed themselves up in a remote mountain camp in Nagano in order to conduct training in preparation for an armed insurgency, resulting in the unexplained deaths of fourteen of their members.

If Nikkatsu had led the way with their long-running Roman Porno series during the '70s and '80s, then the true inheritor of the tradition has to be the prolific Kokuei, founded in the '60s and one of the first pink production companies. This company produced many of the works of the four directors who came to dominate the sex film during the '90s: Hisayasu Satō, Toshiki Satō, Kazuhiro Sano, and Takahisa Zeze. Often gracing their films with outrageous titles, which considerably up-played the sleaze quotient for obvious marketing reasons, Kokuei provided an arena for their directors to experiment within the feature format. Unlike AV productions, which often consist of endless sequences of unsimulated sexual activity, the simple specifications were to deliver a set number of nude or softcore sex scenes (with both male and female genitalia buried beneath digital mosaics) within a running time of little over an hour: the rest was almost entirely up to the director's discretion.

> "I do feel that in my case, it was a kind of training ground, a space for experimentation. Maybe other directors feel differently, but for me that was certainly true. But even though we're talking about training or experimenting, it's not like going to school where you learn and prepare for the real thing that follows after. I made independent films that were shown in cinemas, so it was not just training and learning. The fact that I was actually already making films was always on my mind."—Takahisa Zeze

Using this medium to slip in their own philosophical, political, or dramatic ideas, each of the four directors brought his own individual approach, going far beyond the simple requirements of the skin-flick. Hisayasu Satō's films, typified by *The Bedroom* (*Shisenjō no Aria*, 1992) and the straight-to-video production of *Naked Blood* (*Megyaku: Naked Blood*, 1996), used an experimental array of visual media, from 8mm, videotape, and computer graphics to a hallucinatory and often very violent effect. Toshiki Satō invoked the hollowness and lack of real connection at the heart of modern living, shoe-horning social critique into the format of the sex film potboiler in films such as *Abnormal Ecstasy* (*Abunōmaru Ekusutashī*, 1991) and *Atashi wa Jūsu* [trans: Me Juice, 1996], along the way directing two mainstream films, *Lunatic* (1996) and a live-action version of the novel that formed the basis of the animation **Perfect Blue**. Kazuhiro Sano's primary profession was as an actor who, when he wasn't appearing in both pink or non-pink films (he played in Sōgo Ishii's **Burst City**), made films such as *Shūdan Chikan Hitozuma Nozoki* [trans: Mass pervert peeping at married woman, 1991], *Furin Haha Musume* [trans: Mother daughter adultery, 1993], and *Don't Let it Bring you Down* (*Hentai Terefon Onanie*, 1993).

A graduate of the respected Kyoto University, Takahisa Zeze's initial motivation for embarking on a career within this déclassé industry was simple: the path from assistant to director was that much quicker. He began as an assistant director to Hisayasu Satō, who had already been making films since the late '70s, before making his debut in 1989 with *Good Luck Japan*. Released originally under the title of *Kagai Jugyō Bōkō* [trans: Extracurricular lesson assault] but also known under the director's title of *Haneda ni Ittemiro Soko ni wa Kaizoku ni Natta Gakidomo ga Imaya to Shuppatsu o Matteiru* [trans: Go to Haneda and you will see kids who have become pirates waiting to depart], the film centered around a gang of Taiwanese mafia living around Haneda Airport, and the *Japa-yuki* girls who come to Japan from countries such as the Philippines or Taiwan to work as prostitutes.

> **"Hisayasu Satō had been working in pink for a while, but we other three started working later, and all made our debuts around 1989. This year was not a particularly good time for the pink film, because AV had so much power, and were using lots of cutesy "idol"-style actresses, so for the films we made from '86 to '89 we had lots of requests to use these type of actresses. This year we felt that the pink film was very much in danger of extinction, so that was what made me think, if they're disappearing anyway, then we can do what we want with them."**

Sharing a similar theoretical perspective to cinema as film critic Shigehiko Hasumi and the directors Kiyoshi Kurosawa and Shinji Aoyama (who scripted his *The Dream of Garuda*, 1994), Zeze's subsequent pink films became even more bold and experimental. *No Man's Land* (*Waisetsu Bōsō Shūdan Kedamono*, 1991) dwelt on modern-day loneliness and urban alienation, all set against the backdrop of the Gulf War. The four main characters never form more than superficial acquaintances. Despite living together or sleeping together, they are never able to establish a bond, either amongst each other or with the world that passes around them. Meanwhile, in every room we see television sets tuned to pictures of smart bombings and allied press conferences. The war functions as the ultimate symbol of alienation from reality: a conflict over oil resulting in the deaths of 200,000 people, served up as easy-to-digest infotainment, complete with its own logos, its own faces, its own vocabulary and commercial breaks. Zeze's influences in this piece of guerrilla filmmaking, Godard and Jim Jarmusch, are spelt out by the bogus director credit at the end titles of the film: Jean-Luc Zezemusch!

The foregrounding of political and social concerns by Zeze and his three associates failed to amuse the owners of the sex cinemas that screened their works, as well as their regular patrons. But it did attract the interest of the critics, who in the early '90s labeled them the *Shi-Tennō* (Four Devils) of pink cinema. These four angry young men soon became an established part of the independent filmmaking scene, pushing their work to be screened alongside other arthouse productions at venues such as the Athenée Français in Tokyo. They also became the focus of two retrospectives in Europe: one in Rotterdam in 1997, the other at the Far East Film Festival in Udine in 2002, with a number of their films receiving video releases.

> "It's true that in the early '90s I and other directors making pink films tried to sell our films as art films, because the genre in itself was something nobody cared about. So we tried to have our films shown in small theaters at special screenings, to bring them to people as a new type of arthouse film.
>
> "We didn't intend to make 'art films,' but we were talking about heading in that direction. One thing for sure was that we were a group of people, so we were creating a movement. It's similar to Jean-Luc Godard and the directors of the French New Wave, or Masao Adachi and Kōji Wakamatsu with Wakamatsu Productions. We knew that we needed a few of us to make a movement."

Zeze bears the distinction of being the only director out of the *Shi-Tennō* who has managed to use pink film as a springboard to launch a successful career in mainstream filmmaking. His first non-erotic work was *Kokkuri* (1997), a supernatural horror produced by Nikkatsu about a group of high school girls and a *kokkuri-san*, or Ouija board. This was followed by such films as the criminal lovers-on-the lam saga *Hysteric* (2000); the action comedy *Rush* (2001), starring Shō Aikawa; the romantic fantasy *Dog Star* (2002), in which a Seeing Eye dog finds himself in human form after his master is run

over; and the low-budget sci-fi comedy *SF Whip Cream* (*SF Huippu Kurīmu*, 2002), which like his first film, *Good Luck Japan*, deals with the subject of discrimination against illegal aliens in Japan, though this time they all had pointy ears. His most successful production to date has been Shochiku's box office bonanza *Moon Child* (2003), a camp futuristic action movie featuring rock stars HYDE and Gackt set in the fictional pan-Asian melting pot of the city of Maleppa.

Zeze's transition from erotic cinema has not been total, and during this period he continued to make the occasional erotic film, including *Anarchy in Japan* (*Anākī in Nippon Japansuke: Mirarete Iku Onna*, 1999) and *Tokyo X Erotica* (*Tōkyō X Erotika: Shibireru Kairaku*, 2001), which was the first ever pink film in Japan to be shot and projected digitally. But the two films of his that most successfully transcended the genre are *Raigyo* and *Dirty Maria* (*Kegarete Maria: Hiatoku no Nibi*, 1998), a tale of adultery and murder set against a snowy backdrop.

> "It's not really one particular type of film I'm making. What I like to do is something I haven't done before, both inside and outside of the pink genre, mainstream or whatever. Some of my mainstream films look like my pink films and some of my pink films seem more mainstream than others. I tend to shoot pink and mainstream alternately, so when they are lined up together, my body of work seems to have a slightly confused look, or a strange alignment with one another."

Despite being produced by Kokuei, *Raigyo* is not a conventional pink film. Not only does it feature fewer sex scenes than the typical product, but it is also marked out by stunning cinematography and a tone that takes the film into arthouse territory. A bleak portrayal of the dark side of human nature in the vein of Roman Polanski's *Repulsion* (1965), the film centers around a disturbed woman seen initially creeping out of a hospital where she is being treated for a chronic pancreatic condition. After a series of phone calls she eventually hooks up in a Love Hotel with a man she has contacted via a *tel-club* dating service, and in a brutally shocking sequence, murders him.

Raigyo takes its title from a swamp-dwelling fish imported from Taiwan known as the snake-head mullet, which not only can exist for three days out of water, but is famed for its peculiar flesh-eating habits during the spawning season, when the male stays to protect the eggs, savagely attacking anything that comes near. This fish is a recurrent motif throughout the film, first seen hauled from a canal in the polluted marshland surrounding an industrial plant, writhing as it is doused in petrol and set on fire.

An immensely powerful work, *Raigyo* will disappoint those drawn to it for the sexual content, and its cold, detached air punctuated with moments of unflinching savagery will undoubtedly turn off most viewers. But the film is filled with hauntingly beautiful passages, such as the mesmeric, sepia-toned shots of the deserted wasteland in which the story unfolds, interpolated with the vicious reds of the scenes in the motel.

Raigyo's leading lady, Moe Sakura, also moved into erotic film direction, with films that include *Ijimeru Jukujo-tachi Inran Chōkyō* [trans: Bullying mature women debauchery training, 2002]. As the legions of pink directors become swelled with an increasing number of female directors and women in Japanese society become more open about sex, pink film appears to be moving away from more male-oriented fantasies and also retreating further from politics into the realm of the interpersonal, where women are often seen as the stronger partner. In 1999, male director Yūji Tajiri's *Rustling in Bed* (*OL no Rabu Jūsu* a.k.a. *OL's Love Juice*) depicted the relationship between a career woman, just dumped by her long-term boyfriend, and a young man she meets one night after he falls asleep on her shoulder on the train, missing his stop.

Whether viewed artistically, commercially, or as a mirror to the society in which it is made, with its position now firmly established on video, *pinku eiga* currently represents an aspect of contemporary Japanese cinema that is here to stay.

↓ Perfect Blue

1998. **DIRECTOR:** Satoshi Kon, 今敏. **VOICE CAST:** Junko Iwao, Rika Matsumoto, Shinpachi Tsuji, Masaaki Ōkura. 82 minutes. **RELEASES:** DVD, Manga Entertainment (U.S./U.K., English subtitles, Japanese/English dialogue).

Unforgettable animated psycho-horror thriller detailing a teen singing idol's spiraling descent into insanity.

When Mima Kirigoe announces her ambition to leave the pre-fabricated all-girl pop trio Cham to embark on an acting career, she has little inkling of the effect it might have on some of her fans. "The idol image is suffocating me," she later coos over the phone to her mother, slipping back into her natural country hick girl accent with one of the few people in front of whom she doesn't need to act.

But Mima's new career is not moving with quite the speed she'd hoped. Her initial role of a one-line part in a psychological TV drama called *Double Bind* is unpromising—that is, until she is pressured by the ambitious manager of her talent agency, Tadokoro, alongside the show's producer Tejima and scriptwriter Shibuya, to move further away from her original squeaky-clean image by agreeing to play a salacious rape scene. It's a decision she's not entirely happy with, and following the shoot she destroys her room and collapses into tears.

Nevertheless, as the remaining two members of Cham move on to greater things without her, Mima is egged on by Tadokoro to maintain her media profile and is soon modeling in steamy nude photo shoots. What's more, someone is charting her inner thoughts in diary form on the *Mima's Room* Internet fan site with an unerring degree of accuracy. Initially concerned with documenting such obsessive details as her favorite brand of milk and which foot she puts down first after alighting from the subway train, this first-person written account soon begins to stray from Mima's own take on daily events.

Shadowed by the lank-haired, pock-marked presence of an obsessive fan who calls himself Mi-Maniac, and with only her chaperone Rumi to turn to as she feels her grip on reality beginning to slip through her fingers, Mima is soon questioning just to what extent she is the master of her own self-image or merely an extension of her *otaku* fan-base's fantasies. As the divisions between her personal, public, and imaginary identity become ever more blurred, she begins to find herself repeatedly subjected to the taunts of the delusionary manifestation of her former pop persona, a hallucinatory sprite kitted out in the full mini-skirted Cham regalia. And that's when the murders start.

An absolutely dazzling debut from former manga artist Satoshi Kon, *Perfect Blue* isn't quite what you would expect from an animated feature. Firstly, it features some comparatively strong adult content, with scenes of titillatory nudity running hand in hand with a string of gruesome murders set up with a verve to match the gorier work of Dario Argento or Brian De-Palma. Secondly, its complex narrative structure, a labyrinthine series of flashbacks, dreams, and film-within-film sequences, will leave the viewer as disoriented and in the dark as our beleaguered protagonist until the final reel.

This latter aspect is perhaps what marks out *Perfect Blue*, and more specifically its director Kon and scriptwriter Sadayuki Murai, for more singular attention, as although based on a novel, by all accounts the finished work bears only the scantest of similarities to its original source. Yoshikazu Takeuchi's first published work, *Pāfeku-to Burū: Kanzen Hentai* [trans: Perfect blue: total pervert] came out in 1991 and was rewritten and republished in 1995 as *Yume Nara Samete* [trans:

If it's a dream, wake up]. The author himself describes both these books as source material for the film, with the earlier publication containing a lot more "splatter." Neither has been translated into English. However, though the film project, intended originally as live action, was initiated by Takeuchi and the first book was later re-issued to coincide with the release of the animation, many of the film's more memorable elements—the innovative plotting, the *Mima's Room* internet site, the *Double Bind* film-within-film sequences, even the actual murder scenes—are not present in the book, which Kon claims he never read.

> **"I never read the novel, but I didn't find his script very interesting at all. So I said: 'If you want to stick with this screenplay, I don't want to direct this film. But if you accept my making changes to it, I will do it.' They were okay with that, so I accepted. They wanted to keep three elements of the story: 'idol,' 'horror,' and 'stalker.' Aside from that I could make any changes I wanted, so we changed many things, even the plot."—Satoshi Kon**

Takeuchi was later the driving force behind a more faithful live-action adaptation of the second novel, *Perfect Blue: Yume Nara Samete* released in 2002 and directed by Toshiki Satō, a major practitioner of erotic "pink" cinema during the late '80s and '90s with such films as *Danchi Tsuma Hakuchū no Furin* [trans: Apartment complex wife midday adultery, 1997]. Satō's version is sufficiently different from the animation to highlight the radical deviations from the source material made by Murai with Kon's (uncredited) input. Whilst retaining Takeuchi's basic premise, the finished animation is actually far closer in theme—the subjectivity of memory and the blurred divisions between memory, fantasy, and reality—to Kon's first major work, scripting the *Magnetic Rose* segment of the 1995 animated omnibus feature, ***Memories***.

A savvy dissection of media manipulation or

a stunning technical tour de force, by the very nature of its "idol" subject matter—and one which it shares with Hiroaki Satō's 1994 animated video series, *Key: The Metal Idol*, to which Mima's voice actress Junko Iwao also lent her vocal chords—*Perfect Blue* certainly raises many questions regarding the peddling of female youth fantasies and the psychological effect on the "product" in question, with Mima very much the young victim at the mercy of the machiavellian media executives steering her career path. With such fresh-faced youths as a school uniform-clad Britney Spears and lollipop-sucking Spice Girl Emma Bunton permeating the global pop-consciousness over the past years, obviously this is not a phenomenon exclusively reserved to Japan, but still, a cursory glance over the past decade of *tarento* culture would suggest that the Japanese do generally like their idols both younger and cuter.

> "No, the film is not based on any criticism. If the audience get the impression from watching the film that the idol system in Japan is like that, I'm embarrassed. Of course I did research before making the film and I visited a number of these idol events, but I didn't see the kind of example that is used in the film. Also, to reveal behind-the-scenes secrets about the entertainment world was never my intention. I simply wanted to show the process of a young girl maturing, becoming confused because her old set of values gets shattered, but who is reborn as a mature being as a result of that. That's what I wanted to describe. But because I had to stick with the idea of an idol, the film came to talk about that particular world."

One's enjoyment of the film may hinge on this acceptance of whether a film can raise questions without providing tidy answers to all of them, or whether it is possible to just take Mima's predicament at face value. Ultimately, attempts to read too much into the film detract from what Kon has achieved. *Perfect Blue* is first and foremost a thriller, a shock vehicle and a damn effective one at that. More than that, it is also a very canny exercise in storytelling, and prepares the ground for Kon's next work *Millennium Actress* (*Sennen Joyū*), with the director elevated alongside Sadayuki Murai to the status of co-scripter this time. A romantic mystery drama detailing the life of a retired actress against the backdrop of 50 years of Japan's cinematic history, *Millennium Actress* uses its elliptical approach to a lighter yet nonetheless involving effect this time around, whilst toying with the same concepts of subjectivity and spectatorship as its precursor.

> "*Perfect Blue* and *Millennium Actress* are two sides of the same coin, I think. When I was making *Perfect Blue* I thought it would be a positive film, but little by little it became negative, darker. That exhausted me in a way. When I started working on *Millennium Actress* with the producer, based on the premise I mentioned before, I had the intention of making the two films like sisters, through the depiction of the relationship between admirer and idol. So in adapting that relationship I wanted to make *Millennium Actress* in completely opposite, more positive images. In this way, these two films are very important for me, because they show the dark side and the light side of the same relationship."

Kon was to take yet another abrupt thematic about-turn with the 2003 release of *Tokyo Godfathers* (*Tōkyō Goddofāzās*), in which three homeless people living in the streets of Shinjuku discover an abandoned baby lying in the trash over Christmas. With his first three features, Kon has pushed anime in some fascinating new directions, and it remains to be seen just where he can take it next.

↓ Gamera 3: Revenge of Iris
ガメラ3 邪神（イリス）覚醒

Gamera 3: Jashin (Irisu) Kakusei
a.k.a. *Gamera 3: Awakening of Iris*

1999. **DIRECTOR:** Shūsuke Kaneko, 金子修介. **CAST:** Shinobu Nakayama, Ai Maeda, Ayako Fujitani, Senri Yamasaki. 108 minutes. **RELEASES:** DVD. ADV Films (U.S., English subtitles). Daiei Video (Japan, no subtitles).

The third episode in the resurrection of giant monster Gamera is a hugely dynamic, enormously enjoyable piece of monster mayhem. Never were those city stomping monster movies as effective as they are here.

When Toho studios launched the *Godzilla/Gojira* series in the 1960s (the first two installments were made in the mid '50s, but the series didn't kick off until 1962's *King Kong Vs. Godzilla/Kingu Kongu Tai Gojira*) and hit box office pay dirt as a result, rival Daiei was quick to cash in by introducing its own monster: Gamera the giant turtle, who made his debut in 1965.

A villainous city stomper in his first (black and white) outing, Gamera quickly developed into a good guy and "friend of all children" (resulting in more and more kids running around to get in the flying turtle's way as the series progressed). Seven episodes were made in as many years, until Daiei went bankrupt in 1971. An impoverished attempt at reviving both the studio and the series with the extremely belated *Gamera: Super Monster* (*Uchū Kaijū Gamera*) in 1980 failed miserably, due in no small part to all the Gamera action being stock footage from earlier films.

Fourteen years later, Daiei was resurrected as part of the Tokuma publishing empire and the series, too, was dusted off. Thankfully, the studio was serious about making a fresh start this time, and invited versatile director Shūsuke Kaneko to breathe life into the flying turtle with what would become a trilogy of brand-new Gamera films: *Gamera: Guardian of the Universe* (*Gamera: Daikaijū Kūchū Kessen*, 1995), *Gamera 2: Advent of Legion* (*Gamera 2: Legion Shūrai*, 1996), and this one. Kaneko, previously best

known in the West for co-directing the H. P. Lovecraft anthology *Necronomicon* with Brian Yuzna and *Brotherhood of the Wolf*'s Christophe Gans, started out as an anime scriptwriter and Nikkatsu Roman Porno director in the mid-'80s. He directed films like *Princess Eve* (*Ibu-Chan no Hime*, 1984) and *I'm All Yours* (*Minna Agechau*, 1985) before moving on to comedies and the occasional horror film (*My Soul Is Slashed/Kamitsukitai*, 1991, starring Ken Ogata).

Despite their millions of adoring fans, the appreciation for the classic *kaijū eiga* is strongly colored by oceans of nostalgia. Watching the *Godzilla* movies of the '60s and '70s, for example, is on the whole a rather dull experience. *Destroy All Monsters!* (*Kaijū Sōshingeki*, 1969), a film so fondly remembered for featuring all the Toho monsters in a big end battle, is a film that plods along at a leaden pace before finally arriving at the last fifteen minutes of mayhem. In a nutshell, the *kaijū* movies left a fair bit to be desired.

This was exactly the feeling that motivated Shūsuke Kaneko when he went about revamping Gamera: to make a monster movie the way monster movies should have been made in the first place. This resulted in a series that put Toho's neverending efforts to keep Godzilla alive with much-hyped rehashes of the same old thing to shame (until they invited Kaneko to direct *Godzilla, Mothra, King Ghidorah: Giant Monsters All-Out Attack* in 2001, that is). No *kaijū* movie had ever been as dynamic, action-packed, and alive as Kaneko's reborn *Gamera*.

Because a rebirth it is. This, the best of the new Gameras and after the original *Godzilla* the best *kaijū* film ever made, delivers everything a movie about huge, fighting, city-stomping monsters should have: excitement, slam-bang action sequences, beautifully designed creatures, and, yes, even stunning special effects. The days of the noticeable man-in-a-rubber-suit stomping on lifeless cardboard houses are definitely over. Suit work and computer graphics are seamlessly blended to mutual benefit, cinematographer Junichi Tozawa makes the giant monsters look truly giant, and Kazunori Itō's script actually gives us some genuine human beings to care about.

Gamera 3's dynamics rival the best anime out there and beat anything Hollywood high-concept sci-fi has thrown at us in a long time, including the American version of *Godzilla*. Of course, in the end it's still a film about a big turtle stomping on Tokyo and your appreciation depends on your willingness to accept that premise, but if there has ever been the slightest fondness in your heart for giant monsters, this dynamic piece of high-class pulp will knock you out of your seat.

↓ Gohatto
御法度
a.k.a. *Taboo*

1999. **DIRECTOR:** Nagisa Ōshima, 大島渚. **CAST:** 'Beat' Takeshi Kitano, Ryūhei Matsuda, Shinji Takeda, Tadanobu Asano, Yōichi Sai, Tomorowo Taguchi, Susumu Terajima. 100 minutes. **RE-LEASES:** New Yorker (U.S., English subtitles), Momentum (U.K., English subtitles), Ocean Shores (Hong Kong, English /Chinese subtitles), Shochiku (Japan, English subtitles).

Homosexual lust, infighting, murder and betrayal within the barracks of the Shinsengumi, in Ōshima's take on events leading up to the fall of the shogunate.

In 1865, during the last turbulent years leading up to the end of Tokugawa period, the imperial capital of Kyoto is under the fearsome reign of terror of the Shinsengumi. An extremist "peace-keeping" force of around 300 strong, loyal to the Bakufu shogunate, their aim is to maintain the status quo and quash any insurrectionary activity in the area, especially that of the breakaway forces of the Tosa, Satsuma, and Chōshū clans.

After a demonstration of their kendo sword-fighting talents in front of Shinsengumi captain Isami Kondō (Sai) and his vice captain Toshizō Hijikata (Takeshi), the fresh-faced Sōzaburō Kanō (Matsuda) and Hyōzō Tashiro (Asano) are drafted into the ranks. Kanō's arrival causes quite a stir in the testosterone-heavy atmosphere of the troop house, and when his boyish good looks find favor with Kondō and he is chosen as the captain's page, Tashiro finds himself beset by the flames of jealousy, none the least because he himself also has his eyes set on Kanō. But military life within the Shinsengumi is heavily codified, and any violation of these rules results in nothing short of decapitation. However, there seems to be no shortage of contenders ready to lose their heads over this *bishōnen* (pretty young boy).

The name of Nagisa Ōshima should need little introduction to those with more than a passing interest in Japanese cinema. He is the foremost independent director of his generation, beginning his career at Shochiku studios as an assistant director, before the company decided to capitalize on the "Sun Tribe" (*taiyōzoku*) youth films popular at the time by affording several of their younger employees the opportunity to make their debuts whilst still under the age of thirty. Ōshima was the first of three directors, which included Masahiro Shinoda and Yoshishige Yoshida, to get a film released. His *A Town of Love and Hope* (*Ai to Kibō no Machi*, 1959) came out in 1959, swiftly followed by *The Sun's Burial* (*Taiyō no Hakaba*, 1959), and *Cruel Story of Youth* (*Seishun Zankoku Monogatari*, 1960).

Paralleling both developments in the French Nouvelle Vague led by Jean-Luc Godard and the British Free Cinema movement of the late '50s, Ōshima and his contemporaries came to spearhead what is known as the Japanese New Wave. Their stories centered around disaffected youths from working class backgrounds, with more than a hint of political dimension and a strong focus on the individual, echoing the protagonists of popular American films like Elia Kazan's *On the Waterfront* (1954) and Nicholas Ray's *Rebel Without a Cause* (1955) and fore-grounding their dramas by such cinematic digressions from the in-house style as the use of handheld cameras and on-location shooting.

When his most overtly political film, *Night and Fog in Japan* (*Nihon no Yoru to Kiri*, 1960), was pulled from Japanese cinemas after a tiny four-day run for its explicit critique of the renewal of the Security Pact that allowed the U.S. military to retain its presence on Japanese soil, Ōshima left Shochiku to form his own independent production company. Throughout the '60s, he kept up a steady output of politically motivated works that included *Pleasures of the Flesh* (*Etsuraku*, 1965), *Violence at Noon* (*Hakuchū no Tōrima*, 1966), the animation *Manual of the Ninja Arts* (*Ninja Bugeichō*, 1967), *Death by Hanging* (*Kōshikei*, 1968), and *Diary of a Shinjuku Thief* (*Shinjuku Dorobō Nikki*, 1969).

In the West, however, he is probably best known for a film that, despite for many years playing prominently on the arthouse circuit in Europe, wasn't even released in Japan until twenty-five years after it was made: *In the Realm of the Senses* (*Ai no Korīda*, 1975). The film was based on the famous Sada Abe incident of 1936, in which a courtesan was found wandering around the streets of Kyoto with a knife, a rope, and a severed penis in her hands. The latter turned out to belong to her rich patron and lover, Kichi. The two had just spent a month together locked in a violent and passionate amour fou, barely emerging from their room. As Sada's love became more obsessive, she began to take to throttling him to maintain his passion, eventually seeking to possess him entirely.

The same story had already been recounted within the format of a Nikkatsu Roman Porno film the previous year as *A Woman Called Abe Sada* (*Jitsuroku Abe Sada*, Noboru Tanaka, 1975), starring Junko Miyashita. Ōshima's version, however, adds a political element, contextualizing it within the same year in which the attempted military coup known as the *Ni Ni Roku* incident took place (cf. Seijun Suzuki's **Elegy To Violence**). As soldiers patrol the surrounding streets, Sada and Kichi's exhaustive lovemak-

ing is seen as a complete voluntary removal not only from the social constraints that would keep them apart, but also from the political domain, into "the realm of the senses," in which in this case the woman is the empowered member—a parallel reaction to the blinkered fanaticism of the military right-wingers who would later lead the country into war.

The film's co-production with Anatole Dauman's Argos Pictures in France also circumvented the strict rules imposed by the Japanese censorship board Eirin, which ensured that the "decency" of the Japanese film industry was maintained by the banning of any onscreen portrayal of male or female genitalia. In this way, Ōshima's extremely sexually explicit film is a critique of Nikkatsu's version, which whilst crafted artfully enough in its own right, carried its own cultural conservatism by adhering to these censorship norms, whilst at the same pandering to the standard pornographic cliché of the woman as submissive but sexually voracious. Ōshima would end up in court a few years later when a book containing pictures from the production was prosecuted for obscenity.

In many ways, *Gohatto* shares commonalities with *In the Realm of the Senses*, in that it analyzes the events of a crucial historical point in time within the director's favored intellectual framework of the connection between fervid sexual desire, politics, and death, recurrent themes throughout his work. Its mise-en-scène is a microcosm of society, its characters too absorbed with their immediate passions to fully notice that they are being overtaken by sweeping historical forces beyond their control.

Unlike the underlying homoerotic tensions of one of Ōshima's finest films, the Anglo-Japanese production of *Merry Christmas, Mr. Lawrence* (*Senjō no Merī Kurisumasu*, 1983), based on a story by Laurens Van Der Post and set within a Japanese POW camp where women are forbidden, in *Gohatto* Kanō's desires are allowed to go unchecked. In this respect, the title has a slightly ironic air to it. Though its meaning is closer to "Prohibited" than the film's foreign release title of "Taboo," contrary to expectations, Kanō's flagrant homosexuality is not discouraged within the Shinsengumi, but used tactically by both Kondō and Hijikata (along with Takeda's character of the handsome young captain, Sōji Okita, real-life historical figures within the Shinsengumi) to control their ranks.

Whilst as a modern social phenomenon the subject is only rarely alluded to seriously by contemporary media (a "taboo" in its own right), historically homosexuality in Japan has never been considered a crime, a sin against religion or, by extension, the State. It is tacitly acknowledged that same-sex love was fairly widespread within the ranks of the Shogun's army, though this is an aspect that sits at odds with the cruelly detached and bloodily efficient warrior image of the samurai and unsurprisingly, has not found its way into other takes on the subject.

Other films based on the Shinsengumi include animation, such as Hiromi Noda and Takenori Kawata's irreverent *Shinsengumi Farce* (*Shōgeki Shinsengumi*, 1989) or veteran director Kon Ichikawa's puppet animation *Shinsengumi* (2000), and live action films such as *Cruel Story of the Shogunate's Downfall* (*Bakumatsu Zankoku Monogatari*, Tai Katō, 1964) or *Shinsengumi Keppūroku Kondō Isami* (Shigehiro Ozawa, 1963). This latter film by Ozawa was based on a story within a series of books known as *Shinsengumi Keppūroku* [trans: Shinsengumi bloody chronicles] by the celebrated writer of factually based Tokugawa-period fiction, Ryōtarō Shiba (1923–96). *Gohatto* was based on two novellas from Shiba's series—*Maegami no Sōzaburō* [trans: Sōzaburō's forelock] and *Sanjōgawara Ranjin* [trans: The Sanjō riverbank rebels].

Expectations for an adaptation of Japan's foremost historical writer from one of Japan's most important directors of his generation were therefore very high, especially as it remains Ōshima's only major work of the '90s. After *Merry Christmas, Mr. Lawrence*, he had decided to divorce himself one step further from Japanese culture with *Max, Mon Amour* (1986), made in France, in which Charlotte Rampling falls in love with a large ape. Since this, aside from two documentaries for British television—*Kyoto: My Mother's Place* (1991) and *100 Years of Japanese Cinema* (1995)—Ōshima spent much of the '90s struggling to get further projects off the ground, until a stroke in 1995 looked set to put an end to his directorial career.

Returning to Shochiku for the first time since *Night and Fog in Japan*, and directed at their studios from a wheelchair, the then 68-year-old director's first Tokugawa period *jidai-geki* certainly looks magnificent. The lavish costumes were provided by Emi Wada, who previously worked on Peter Greenaway's *Prospero's Books* (1991) and Akira Kurosawa's *Ran* (1985) and *Dreams* (*Yume*, 1990). The dark, brooding undercurrent of decaying sexuality and imminent death is heightened by a haunting score from Ryūichi Sakamoto, whose most famous collaboration with the director was with *Merry Christmas, Mr. Lawrence*, in which he also acted. The actors are some of the finest in Japan: "Beat" Takeshi Kitano, who played his first major acting role alongside David Bowie and Tom Conti in *Merry Christmas, Mr. Lawrence*; the pivotal presence of the androgynous Matsuda (**Blue Spring**) in his first film role; arthouse stalwart Asano; and director Sai (**MARKS**), stepping before the camera as the authoritarian Kondō.

Certainly an amount of background knowledge will be required to understand the context of the era, but still, dramatically the over-talky *Gohatto*, despite an invitation to the Palme d'Or competition at Cannes in 2000, remains one of the least successful of Ōshima's works. Like the *chanbara* films which it references, the film is filled with a highly stylized non-naturalistic beauty—the set-bound final showdown on the wooden bridge, swirling with dry ice, swords flashing in the moonlight; the spectral presence of the courtesan to whom Kanō is led in order to introduce him to the joys of women. But if such deliberately theatrical sequences fit within the genre, they perhaps act as a cosmetic smokescreen to what the film is actually about.

In his work in the '60s, Ōshima often made use of Brechtian distancing devices of laying the bare bones of filmmaking visible to the viewer in order to mediate between story and storyteller, message and medium. Here, however, the recurrent use of text intertitles, the omnipresent voice of the narrator and the use of other cinematic devices such as screen wipes come across more like manifestations of post-production salvage work.

Gohatto is an undeniably beautiful-looking film, well-crafted, rich in content, and atmospheric, but it only touches on themes better explored elsewhere in the director's oeuvre. As a self-contained work in its own right, its lack of focus denies the dramatic flair that made his early work so acerbic and so essential to its day.

↓ The New God
新しい神様
Atarashii Kamisama

2000. **DIRECTOR:** Yutaka Tsuchiya, 土屋豊. **CAST:** Yutaka Tsuchiya, Karin Amamiya, Hidehito Itō, Umitarō Tanaka, Takaya Shiomi. 99 minutes. **RELEASES:** DVD, Uplink (Japan, English subtitles).

> "Well, for example someone might hear about those right-wing trucks blasting through the city and think that everybody just passively sits by and watches it happen, but I think *The New God* shows that there's more going on than just that. There's a lot happening behind the scenes. Actually I think Japan needs to stand up and tell other countries that there's more happening here, that it's not nearly such a cut and dried issue. Japan doesn't seem to, how should I say it, analyze its own situation as much as it should. The Japanese mass media do a lot of stereotyping too."—Yutaka Tsuchiya

> "It's been a long time since I started hearing that Japan's becoming more right-wing. When I was right-wing I really thought so, but after I got away from that I realized it's not true at all. There's a huge difference between what we hear and what happens in people's day-to-day lives. But when *The New God* was released, a rightist told us that there's no way this film would have been accepted 10 years ago. Maybe the right wing is more accepted than it was 10 years ago; maybe it's gained regular 'civil rights.' I think that's because there are more right-leaning figures in the cultural arena now."—Karin Amamiya

"Tora, Tora, Tora! Pearl Harbor was our only choice. Our race was corrupted from the day we lost the war . . ." Karin Amamiya, lead singer of ultra-nationalist hardcore punk band Ishinseki-seijuku (a.k.a. The Revolutionary Truth), looms large center stage, barking out aggressively heartfelt anti-American sentiments to a notably sparse and dwindling audience.

Troubled music for troubled times, one might think, though on the surface at least, there seems to be little of immediate worry for the citizens of modern-day Japan, currently one of the safest and most stable places on the planet. However, many visitors have found it difficult to ignore the worm in the apple, manifesting itself in the form of the black trucks named *gaisensha*, emblazoned with the *hinomaru* (Japanese flag) motif on their sides and blaring out militant anthems. In recent times, and especially since the death of Emperor Hirohito marked the end of the Shōwa period in 1989, the Heisei period has seen a notable revival in the nationalist movement, small, but vocal enough to prove difficult to ignore.

Nationalism, with its indelible associations of racism and the military right wing, is a fairly dirty word to most people, and a subject which most would prefer to waft aside without giving a second thought. But for documentary maker Tsuchiya, who stands amongst the cowed observers at the gig with which the film opens, viewing the proceedings firmly from the other

Courtesy of Yutaka Tsuchiya

The New God

side of the political fence, there's something more heartfelt about Amamiya's plea. "I shivered. I don't know why. I felt her pain, somehow, like a reflected light beam stabbing the heart."

Besides working actively in film criticism in Japan, Yutaka Tsuchiya is also one of the leading lights of the underground video documentary group Video Act. The group meets every couple of months to screen a selection of politically motivated video shorts covering a multitude of contemporary issues. Maintaining close connections with similarly minded video activist groups around the world, such as the Amsterdam-based Next Five Minutes and Paper Tiger Television in the United States, Tsuchiya is positive that organizations such as Video Act, by distributing its work either on videotape or via the Internet, still have the ability to democratize the filmmaking and distribution process and share a plurality of political viewpoints and ideas distinct from the unilateral voice of a more dominant mass media.

In his first feature-length film, Tsuchiya attempts to delve beyond the political rhetoric and intimidating façade of the fascinatingly complex figures of Amamiya and guitarist/bandleader Hidehito Itō of the Revolutionary Truth. Tsuchiya initially met the two musicians in 1998 whilst interviewing a number of young people about a controversial manga entitled *Sensōron* [trans: On war] written by a man named Yoshinori Kobayashi. The manga, which proved immensely popular at the time, selling 500,000 copies shortly after its release, was a revisionist look at Japanese war history, which amongst other things denied events such as the Nanking Massacre or the existence of comfort women. It sold very well among young people.

"Some people protested against the book, tell-

ing people not to read it and so on. At the time I understood how they felt, but I also thought that they wouldn't be able to change the feelings of the young readers just by protesting like that. Why were they reading it? Why did they think Kobayashi's comic was so cool? As long as they weren't asking questions like that I was sure the book would keep selling. I wanted to think about that, and I wanted to hear what younger people had to say about the comic, so that's when I met Amamiya and Itō from the band the Revolutionary Truth."—Yutaka Tsuchiya

The focus of *The New God* is quite clearly singer Amamiya. Handing her a video camera with which to film herself in a series of talking head shots over the course of little over a month, and through the course of numerous drunken political discussions with her and bandleader Itō, Tsuchiya soon manages to get a whole lot more than he initially bargained for, in the process discovering that all three of them have a lot more in common than their seemingly diametrically opposed standpoints first led him to believe.

At the beginning of the film, Amamiya is beginning to question her own nationalistic beliefs after a trip to North Korea to see the effect of Communism on the daily lives of its citizens. At the invitation of a radical left-winger and former head of the Japanese Red Army, Takaya Shiomi, Amamiya first arrives in Pyongyang, where she is welcomed with open arms by her compatriots, Red Army exiles from Japan in the wake of a famous hijacking incident, who are seemingly unconcerned by their opposing political beliefs. As someone points out: "Left or right is just a label for someone caring about their race. Anti-imperial America is what we agree on." However, once the drinking stops and the politicizing begins, she confides to the camera in the privacy of her hotel room that her own views might be causing some problems with the older activists. Nevertheless, she is markedly struck by the way the North Koreans are bound together by a common value system: "Words such as solidarity touched my heart as a nationalist." In contrast, she sees the only shared values the Japanese possess is via consumerism and value systems imposed from outside. "The Japanese can't make friends. Only cut their wrists and call sex lines."

It is statements such as these that throw light on where Amamiya is coming from in her politics. At numerous points in the film she confesses that a troubled upbringing left her feeling an outsider. Nationalism provided a channel for her feelings of ostracism and self-loathing. Similarly, in an unguarded moment, Itō confesses he embraced nationalism to stop being a nerd. "When did you force these two ideas, 'to stop being a nerd,' and 'anti-America' together?" asks Tsuchiya. "Well, after joining the Nationalists, actually," Itō admits.

"Many people just act like they're thinking about those issues, but some are just doing it because they're bored. They feel a sense of solidarity by creating enemies, talking crap about America, China, or Korea. In one sense those groups are like clubs for strange people who just have nothing better to do. People do it just to kill time."—Karin Amamiya

With such moments of honesty, both Amamiya and Itō cease to become threatening political extremists and start really developing as fully rounded and sympathetic characters, plagued by self-doubt and fully aware of their irreconcilable idealism. It's an angle which Tsuchiya pursues admirably as he becomes closer to the two band members, turning the film into a three-way dialogue between the filmmaker and his subjects. "I know what she means. Something has created an emptiness covering Japan. To her it's America, to me it's the Emperor system," he muses between scenes.

Both Itō's and Amamiya's viewpoint is that the modern Japanese, dulled by the "suffocating peace" of the Heisei period (literally meaning "attainment of peace") have forgotten their

Courtesy of Yutaka Tsuchiya

The New God

roots and are content to remain as "America's fat dog," and that as a result, without even its own self-written constitution, the nation has lost any significance in global affairs. They argue that the deaths of Japanese soldiers during the Pacific War should not be forgotten, as they were acting in the interests of the Emperor at a time when every man and woman gave his or her life for the country, and that to deny one's nation's history is to deny one's national identity.

Whilst Itō and Amimaya's desire for a return to the "Nation as Family" as opposed to American-styled "individualism" might merely be seen as nostalgia, the underlying desire for a shared value system and common identity is perhaps not so outrageous: "The Emperor is the ideal, not the system," as Itō says. Translating their wishes into a political agenda, however, is slightly more problematic. As Tsuchiya points out, his problem with nationalist politics is that

it excludes minorities, a factor which Amamiya admits had always bothered her about the right-wing Nationalist Party of which the two musicians are active members.

It is after her return from North Korea that Amamiya's disillusionment with hard-line politics really begins to grow, sparked by the lackluster reception of her talk on her pilgrimage at a meeting of Red Army members, who'd rather revel in drunken rhetoric to feel their camaraderie than reach out to the broader general public. Itō's street-level activism, yelling, "You fuckers are all just livestock!" down a megaphone to indifferent passers-by, doesn't seem to be much more effective, either.

In true *Spinal Tap* form, the presence of the Svengali-like Tsuchiya is soon acting as a catalyst for problems already latent within the band, and so a new "liberal" guitarist is drafted in to ease the tension. Umitarō Tanaka plays the "Lukewarm Water" role between Amamiya's "Fire" and Itō's "Ice." "Singing the national anthem before the gig just isn't my thing," he mumbles during a band practice session. After they meet with hostile receptions from audiences and are kicked out of a series of venues, one begins to wonder whether it is perhaps the medium rather than the message that is the problem.

Of course, it is Amamiya that fuels the whole endeavor, invoking a fair degree of sexual tension between the two males as we see her being drawn away from Itō's radical polemic to the filmmaker's more liberal suave. We see Itō yawning and nodding off when excluded from a heated drunken political discussion between Amamiya and her new hero figure in a bar. Later Amamiya bounces up and down gushing appreciatively as Tsuchiya nonchalantly sums up his political stance: "All I know is that my work says it all." When Itō tries to get in on the act shouting, "Yes, it's great to be creative, isn't it!" he is silenced by a condescending "Go and bake a cake, then!" from Amamiya.

> "The band's break-up didn't have anything to do with the movie, but the film did have an influence on us in ways. It made me realize how dependent I was on right-wing ideology, and as I started to realize that I had become unable to continue that sort of activity."—Karin Amamiya

Both entertaining and thought-provoking, not to mention often very funny, the transformation of The Revolutionary Truth's stance via its rejection of both hard-line right-wing and left-wing politics to a more comfortable form of nationalism is absolutely riveting from start to finish. Painting a complex yet colorful picture of the current state of the question of national identity in Japan, it is a work which never feels the need to resort to shock tactics or heavy-handed proselytizing to get its point across, throwing out an open challenge to the viewer to go away and think about the issues it raises. At a time when the old political arguments are ceasing to have any relevance, Tsuchiya introduces us to two absolutely remarkable characters whom we might otherwise dismiss completely out of hand, as he reminds us that, whether left or right, at the end of the day politics is about people.

↓ Scoutman

ペイン

a.k.a. *Pain*

2000. **DIRECTOR:** Masato Ishioka, 石岡正人. **CAST:** Miku Matsumoto, Hideo Nakaizumi, Yuka Fujimoto, Akihito Yoshiie, Yuri Komuro, Shirō Shimomoto. 114 minutes. **RELEASES:** VCD, Winson (Hong Kong, English Subtitles).

Gritty documentary-styled drama set in the seamy streets of Ikebukuro, a rich recruiting ground for the sleazy scoutmen of the Adult Video industry.

Walk around the streets of any large city in Japan and you will soon come across the sight of young girls darting for cover after being approached by solitary men in cheap suits. It's the method of choice used by these *chinpira*, runners for illicit sex industry operations, in order to recruit new fresh meat for pornographic live shows, magazines, or videos, and oddly enough, it seems to work. In other countries such behavior would immediately lead to arrest on sexual harassment charges, but in Japan it's a common enough sight.

Whatever else you might have to say about it, the sex industry in Japan is certainly not a small one. At its peak at the tail end of the '70s, it accounted for over a third of the nation's cinematic output. With the introduction of the VCR, from the early '80s onward the production of what is euphemistically termed "Adult Entertainment" really snowballed, as an increasing number of viewers opted to take their viewing pleasures

© 2000 Goldview

Scoutman

solitarily in the privacy of their own bedrooms rather than share their appreciation in a crowded theater. The AV video market in Japan is second only to that of the United States.

Against this background comes *Scoutman*, a grimy portrayal of the pony-tailed hustlers, per-oxide-headed pimps, and sleazy moustachioed casting directors who ferret the streets of Tokyo's Ikebukuro district in search of the latest *tantai* (star quality) AV actresses with which to provoke frenetic bouts of one-handed adulation from their cloistered male admirers. Any single young girl is fair game, as prospective starlets are harangued on the street with such blunt catcalls as: "You've passed! I'll get you the nicest job you've ever had. You can earn extra money with your tits."

Into this urban jungle wanders 20-year-old Atsushi (Nakaizumi), with his lame girlfriend Mari (Matsumoto) hobbling in tow, both freshly arrived from the provinces in search of a bright golden future in the big city. However, with no place to stay, it's not long before young ideal-ism gives way to empty stomachs, and unbe-knownst to his partner, Atsushi is soon taking cash scouring the streets for suitable actresses in the employment of an AV production company managed by the weasely Sugishita (Shimomoto), learning the tricks of the trade from veteran tal-ent scout Yoshiya (Yoshiie): "What are you talk-ing to them about music for? You're not trying to pick them up!"—All of this, at the same time as recklessly dabbling with fading *tantai* Miki, whose own onscreen career has so far evaded the notice of her husband.

Meanwhile Mari's own job-hunting pros-pects take a different turn after she is offered a stick of chewing gum by a leggy, mini-skirted bottle-blonde introducing herself as Kana (Fu-jimoto), who only five minutes later asks for the semi-chewed lump back before selling it on to a lecherous creep hiding in a nearby phonebox. Initially disgusted, Mari is soon lured away by her new friend for a makeover and drafted into selling tickets for swingers parties.

Scoutman was one of several films released at the turn of the millennium centered around the Japanese sex industry, though after doing the rounds on the international festival circuit it received only a limited release back in Japan under the title of *Pain*. Unlike Harada's more commercially pitched **Bounce KoGals**, Ishioka's shockingly frank take on the AV world doesn't see Japanese society's rampant preoccupation with sex so much as a problem as another facet of modern urban existence.

With its predominance of handheld location shots, a cast including a number of industry professionals, and a sparing use of background music, Ishioka's raw-edged approach is more concerned with documentation than attribution. Whereas Harada wags his finger censoriously, Ishioka shoots strictly from street level, counterpointing the banality behind the alluring façade of hardcore video production with Mari's spiraling descent from handing out flyers for organized orgies into pimping out high school girls to desperate salarymen for a quick fondle in a quiet, secluded alleyway.

Like the world they inhabit, Ishioka's characters aren't particularly likable, but they are recognizable in their warts-and-all portrayal and it's obvious that the director knows his subject well. After all, it's where he came from, cutting his directorial teeth in the sleazy world of Adult Entertainment with a string of porno quickies such as *Chikanhakusho 1: The Statement of Pervert* (1995).

It's a perspective that lends *Scoutman* some of its most convincing scenes. As Atsushi is promoted to the role of Miki's personal manager, we are invited behind the scenes to a video shoot taking place in a house in the suburbs. Here, whilst preparing for her first onscreen appearance, one of Atsushi's recent recruits receives a phone call from an anxious boyfriend, whose mind is seemingly put at rest after confirmation from the makeup artist that her first shoot is girl-on-girl. All smiles and forced playfulness,

the new girl immediately breaks down into tears as the camera starts to roll.

Scoutman's view is that pornography is neither glamorous nor seductively dangerous, but ultimately nothing less than trite and debasing for both practitioners and consumers alike. A number of the girls lured into this false paradise by the smooth-talking scouts are soon making rapid beelines for the exit after their first "interview" on the rancid Sugishita's casting couch, whereas the demand from the shop front suppliers to go further than the last time eventually leads to his being busted for child pornography. The best Ishioka's starlets can hope for after being pushed to greater excesses by the increasing demands of a jaded market is being farmed out to a *fūzoku* "soapland" where they can make more intimate acquaintance with their desperate clients while being pawed over in private booths, rather than go the whole hog down the SM video route.

With its twin narratives diverging from the opening moments as it charts the lives of its two young protagonists (both played by first-time actors), *Scoutman* cracks off at quite a pace, leaving no stone unturned as it exhaustively charts its sordid milieu. Whilst it's definitely not a place you'll want to linger too long, it is the most honest and realistic of all of the films about the sex industry that came out around the same time. Simultaneously grueling and compelling, rather than begging for more, *Scoutman* instead leaves you feeling in need of a good hose-down.

↓ Tokyo Trash Baby

東京ゴミ女
Tōkyō Gomi Onna
a.k.a. *Tokyo Garbage Girl*

2000. **DIRECTOR:** Ryūichi Hiroki, 廣木隆一. **CAST:** Mami Nakamura, Kazuma Suzuki, Tomorowo Taguchi, Kō Shibasaki. 88 minutes. **RELEASES:** DVD. Pony Canyon (Japan, no subtitles).

Breezy, digitally shot romantic drama pointing out the pitfalls of modern life in a consumer culture whose foundations are set in polystyrene. A change of pace for former pink film director Ryūichi Hiroki.

Empty plastic drinks bottles, crushed styrofoam cups, used *bentō* lunch boxes and splintered wooden chopsticks, newspapers, magazines, polyethylene bags, soiled tissues, and paper towels: discarded ornaments of an obsessive consumer culture, all bagged, bundled, and sorted into the relevant categories of burnable, non-burnable, recyclable, and hazardous waste to be left for the garbage men daily. If such a rapid turnaround in production, consumption, and excretion is considered the benchmark of modern economic development, then it's no small wonder that Japan, a country which has dragged itself up from post-war ruin to being the world's second-largest economy within the space of just fifty years, has created such a hell of a mess along the way.

In the Kantō area, which has had to bear the main brunt of the nation's unwavering pursuit of a high GNP, the continuing mass influx of citizens to the capital and its environs that has accompanied this modernization has been equally matched by a concurrent reduction in the number of places to dispose of their daily by-products. The ingenious solution to the problem has been to dump it all into giant landfill sites that pockmark Tokyo Bay, and which have subsequently been remolded as the glitzy new industrial zone of Odaiba. In a nutshell, Tokyo is not only an environmental mess, a large part of it is quite literally built upon garbage.

A gentle critique of this consumer culture, Ryūchi Hiroki's cannily conceived, DV-shot slice-of-life drama equates this rapid development with the gaping emotional voids that fill the lives of its modern-day citizens, as the first generation to be weaned on the spoils of such rampant consumerism come of age. Embodying this is Miyuki (Nakamura), a teenage waitress in a Tokyo café who develops an obsessive crush on grimy aspiring young rock musician Yoshinori (Suzuki) living in the upstairs apartment in her block. She takes to bringing in his garbage bags and rifling through his refuse. Collecting his empty cigarette packets and hoarding the smoked cigarette ends in a jar, cutting out pictures from discarded magazines, and wearing his shredded denim jacket, the ultimate trophy, in the privacy of her own room, she begins to identify with him through the by-products of his day-to-day existence.

When she unravels a screwed-up tissue paper to discover a soiled condom wrapped inside, she realizes that she has competition for his affections. Regardless, she approaches Yoshinori as he practices his guitar in a deserted club, and after humming along a melody found on a torn up pencil-sketched score she had pieced together to his accompaniment, she allows herself to become the next in a string of his sexual conquests. The following morning he confesses that he knew she had been sifting through his trash, and she flees from his apartment, another one of his castaways. She then makes the long journey across Tokyo to finally lay his memory to rest by burying his rubbish on a large island of refuse.

Tokyo Trash Baby is a sympathetic look at the dilemma faced by a generation who have opted out of college and the stifled ranks of the office workplace in favor of minimum wage, *furītā* (part-time "free arbeiter") employment. Eschewing the rigid social structures and dominant work ethic of their parents' generation, they are desperately seeking to replace it with something else. What, who knows, but as Miyuki soon finds out, it takes more than using the same shampoo, eating the same breakfast cereal, and smoking the same strength Marlboros as Yoshinori to find anything more than the most transient emotional fulfillment with him.

Tightly scripted and acted with a touching humanism throughout, Hiroki's film is nicely carried along by a strong central performance from Mami Nakamura, an actress best known

© 2000 Goldview

Tokyo Trash Baby

for her leading role in the adaptation of Junji Itō's horror manga *Tomie* (Ataru Oikawa, 1998). She later went on to play in Yoshinari Nishiko-ri's *A White Ship* (*Shiroi Fune*, 2001) and Masaru Konuma's *Mizue* (*Onna wa Basutei de Fuku o Tori-kaeta*, 2002).

Miyuki's role is underscored by the host of subsidiary characters that inhabit the café where she works. Her fellow waitress and confidante, Kyōko, keeps her up to date with her own frequent and fleeting sexual liaisons. An older customer exaggerates wildly how it was he who worked on the construction of the *Shinkansen* Bullet Train and Tokyo Tower and oversaw the first landfills that gave rise to the futuristic development of Tokyo Bay. "Being a coffee shop owner is all right," he tells Miyuki's employer, "but a man is judged by what he has done." It was, after all, his generation, he boasts with pride, that was responsible for everything that

symbolizes modern Japan, whilst the new generation seems content to drip around and do nothing. Miyuki rebuffs the continuing advances of lonely young salaryman Kawashima, whose blind obedience and lack of imagination seem both bland and pathetic. Apparently the best he has to offer her against Yoshinori's seductively dangerous rock 'n' roll ambivalence is a night in the batting cage practicing baseball swings.

Tokyo Trash Baby was the first, and one of the strongest, of the six films comprising the Love Cinema series produced by CineRocket, all focusing on young, contemporary female protagonists and shot on digital video. The films in the series were originally intended as straight-to-video releases, though all enjoyed a limited run in the Cinema Shimokitazawa in Tokyo. The rest of the series consists of Mitsuhiro Miura's *Amen, Somen and Rugger Men!* (*Eri ni Kubittake*), Isao Yukisada's *Enclosed Pain* (*Tojiru Hi*), Tetsuo

Shinohara's *Stake Out* (*Harikomi*), Akihiko Shiota's *Gips* and Takashi Miike's *Visitor Q*.

Hiroki's addition to the series was released in Tokyo on the same weekend as his higher-budgeted *I Am an SM Writer* (*Futei no Kisetsu*), a tongue-in-cheek sex drama based on a book by Japan's most notorious purveyor of rope-and-flesh erotic fantasies, Oniroku Dan. Ren Ōsugi plays the eponymous narrator in this piece, a successful SM novelist who recounts the details of why his wife left him some 20 years before due to his preoccupation with the more intellectual side of the sexual act as opposed to the physical. Immersed in his own fantasies, he feverishly documents staged sexual scenarios acted out in his living room by his assistant, and fails to notice the inevitable consequences of his wife's increasingly frequent dalliances with her English teacher, a brash young American hunk played by Brian William Churchill. His reaction, after the initial rage, is to scribble down the details of their imagined liaison.

Though it is difficult to imagine two more diverse pieces of filmmaking, like so many of his contemporaries, director Hiroki is no stranger to such extremes of eroticism, having begun his career as an assistant director to the prolific director Genji Nakamura, one of the foremost practitioners of pink cinema in the '70s. His own debut came in 1982 with *Seigyaku! Onna o Abaku* [trans: Sexual abuse! exposed woman], before turning to a triptych of *Barazoku* (or Rose Tribe films, a variant on the pink film aimed at gay audiences) beginning with *Bokura no Jidai* [trans: Our generation, 1983] and continuing with *Bokura no Kisetsu* [trans: Our season, 1983] and *Bokura no Shunkan* [trans: Our moment, 1984]. In 1984 both he and Nakamura made several works for Nikkatsu, whose Roman Porno line of sex films were increasing their sadistic component, creating such memorable titles as *Sensei, Watashi no Karada ni Hi o Tsukenaide* [trans: Teacher, don't turn me on, 1984] and *Chikan to Sukāto* [trans: Pervert and skirt, 1984] along the way. *I Am an SM Writer* was scripted by Hitoshi

Ishikawa, a former collaborator of Hiroki's with whom, alongside Genji Nakamura, he had hid behind the collective pseudonym Gō Ijuin for a series of SM-heavy productions in the mid-'80s.

After a brief spell working in television during the early '90s, Hiroki's first real stab at a non-sex film came with the V-cinema production, *Sadistic City* (*Maōgai*, 1993) and the athletic youth movie, *800 Two Lap Runners* (*Happyaku Two Lap Runners*, 1994), which was voted seventh-best film in the year of its release by the *Kinema Jumpo* critics. In 1996 he directed the steamy coming-of-age drama *Midori*. After making *Barber's Sorrow* (*Rihatsuten Aruji no Kanashimi*, 2002), a film about shoe fetishism, the boldly experimental drama *Vibrator* (2003) saw Hiroki not only returning to the digital video format, but also continuing his look at the problems facing contemporary Japanese women in this tale based on a popular novel by Mari Akasaka. Rei Hayakawa (Shinobu Terashima) is a freelance journalist whose basic desires have been cowed into submission by a deafening interior monologue culled from the voices of her friends and family, advertisements, gossip columns, and the front cover headlines of women's magazines—"be thin, be beautiful, the perfect man is just around the corner." Unable to express her true emotions, she retreats into a world of insecurity, insomnia, alcohol abuse, and eating disorders, the only external sensation being the surrogate heartbeat of her vibrating mobile phone in her breast pocket—the vibrator of the film's title. Then one night, as she browses aimlessly around the all-night convenience store supposedly in search of a bottle of wine, she makes eye contact with another customer, a truck driver named Okabe (*Ichi the Killer*'s Nao Ōmori). On the spur of the moment, she decides to follow him from the store and into his truck cab. With seemingly nothing better to do, she persuades him to let her accompany him on his long haul along the highways of Japan, escaping far away from the societal pressures of home.

Vibrator unfolds as a serious two person

chamber piece set for the most part within the warmly lit, womb-like confines of the truck cab, the rhythms and cadences of the dialogue taking place against the muffled throb of the engine. As well as utilizing all the advantages of the lightweight digital format to the full, it sees Hiroki's oeuvre continuing to evolve in ever more tantalizing and provocative directions.

↓ Uzumaki
うずまき
a.k.a. *Spiral, Vortex*

2000. **DIRECTOR:** Higuchinsky (a.k.a. Akihiro Higuchi), ヒグチンスキー. **CAST:** Eriko Hatsune, Fhi Fan, Hinako Saeki, Shin Eun Kyung, Keiko Takahashi, Ren Ōsugi. 91 minutes. **RELEASES:** DVD, Eastern Cult Cinema (U.K., English subtitles), Elite Entertainment (U.S., English subtitles), Universe (Hong Kong, English/Chinese subtitles), Toei Video (Japan, no subtitles).

Left stone cold by the deadpan minimalism of Hideo Nakata's ghostly *Ring*? Baffled by the cold metaphysics of Kiyoshi Kurosawa's *Cure*? Turned off by *Tomie*? Were you perhaps amongst the droves stampeding from the auditorium during the grisly resolution of *Audition*? Well, why don't you give *Uzumaki* a whirl, by far one of the most deliriously entertaining horrors to emerge from Japan at the tail end of the millennium.

High school student Kirie's first glimpse that something is awry in Kurouzu comes when she discovers the father of her nerdy best friend Shūichi filming a snail, or more precisely the corkscrew pattern of its shell. He is in the process of making a video scrapbook composed of images of vortexes and spiral-like phenomena, and his bizarre obsession is soon threatening to spin dangerously out of control. One evening at the dinner table he flies off the handle when he runs out of *naruto* roll (a Japanese fish sausage

colored pink and white with a spiral motif running through it), frantically creating whirlpools in his miso soup whilst proclaiming that a vortex is the highest form of art. He eventually comes a cropper when he crawls in for a point-of-view shot from the inside of a spin drier.

It's not long before the whole town is beset by all manner of otherworldly whirly weirdery. Kirie's high school is populated by a host of grotesques—twitching teachers, preening pretty girls, and slimy student Katayama, who walks at a snail's pace and only comes to school when it rains. Soon a number of her schoolmates are sprouting shells and crawling up the school walls. It's a game of spot the spiral as digital vortexes crawl across the floor and materialize in cloudy skies. Shūichi's mother, hospitalized after the death of her husband, cuts off her fingertips to remove the whorl-like patterns on them and eventually succumbs to the power of the vortex after a millipede crawls into her ear and takes up residence in her cochlea. And just what is the secret behind arch-bitch Sekino's unfeasibly curly locks?

The debut feature of Ukrainian-born director Higuchinsky (who previously helmed episodes of the *Eko Eko Azarak/Misa the Dark Angel* TV series in 1997) deals with the helical horrors that occur when a small town is besieged by spirals. Not to be confused with Jōji Iida's *The Spiral (Rasen)*, which supported Nakata's *The Ring* during its initial theatrical run, *Uzumaki*, meaning "Vortex" or "Whirlpool," was originally paired on a double bill with *Tomie Replay* (Fujirō Mitsuishi, 2000). Like the *Tomie* series, it is based on a manga series by the cult artist Junji Itō, whose work (some of which has been published in English translations) also formed the basis of *Kakashi* (2001), a perfunctory but lackluster tale of ghostly scarecrows directed by Norio Tsuruta.

Combining the Lynchian concerns of the unseen horrors that lurk behind the superficial normality of small town existence with the same intense psychotropic visuals that glossed the surface of Darren Aronofsky's 1998 stunner *Pi*, *Uzumaki* is not a case of style over substance. Here, the style is the substance. The camera twists and spins, as bodies are twisted and characters are menaced by hallucinatory swirls and pop promo director Higuchinsky, who later gave us *Tokyo 10 + 01* (2002), empties out his entire technical bag of tricks, making full use of a whole gamut of split-screens, subliminal vortex animations, playful shot transitions, and razor-sharp editing to deliciously skittish effect.

Couple this with a parade of quirkily exaggerated performances and you have a particularly loony film, irrational, totally without cinematic precedent, and wholly in keeping with its manga origins. A dazzling plunge into the abstract in which the threat is illusory, not physical. A spiral isn't a material thing, it is a state of mind, and Higuchinsky takes us there.

↓ Avalon
アヴァロン
Avalon

2001. **DIRECTOR:** Mamoru Oshii, 押井守. **CAST:** Malgorzata Foremniak, Wladyslaw Kowalski, Jerzy Gudejko, Dariusz Biskupski, Bartek Swiderski, Michal Breitenwald. 106 minutes. **RELEASES:** DVD, Buena Vista Home Video (U.S., English subtitles), Emotion (Japan, Japanese/English subtitles), C2 Communications (Korea, English/Japanese/Korean subtitles), Studio Canal (France, French subtitles).

Disillusioned members of a crumbling futuristic society seek escapism from their existence by means of an illegal interactive war game, in this bleak fusion of live action and CGI technology, shot in Poland by acclaimed anime director Oshii.

Avalon is the legendary island of Arthurian mythology where departed heroes come to rest, placing the Crown of Oblivion on their heads that enables them to forget their homeland. It is also the name of the illegal computer game that forms the stage for Mamoru Oshii's stunning peeling back of the layers of illusion, an addictive virtual reality battlefield simulation in which the disenchanted inhabitants of a decaying futuristic society seek escape from reality, and in which the most adept players are able to win enough money to further fuel their addiction.

Ash (Foremniak), a single thirty-something, is one such player. A previous member of the notorious Wizard team, she is legendary in the world of Avalon, though with her old team disbanded due to her maverick approach to team play, she has built up a bit of a reputation as a lone wolf and is now operating solo as a character of Warrior class.

Rumors abound of a secret level to the game, Class Special A. The gateway into this higher domain can only be accessed through a strange glitch in the program, with the appearance of a silent, sad-eyed young girl, said to be a bug placed by the Nine Sisters, the game's original programmers. Class Special A is the Holy Grail of Avalon, a level in which the player cannot be "reset" (i.e. killed) and returned to the real world.

When Ash learns from former teammate Stunner (Swiderski) that the last person to attempt to reach this higher level was the Wizard's former leader Murphy (Gudejko), whose current status as "unreturned" has left him comatose in a hospital bed in the real world, her desire to seek out the truth behind Avalon becomes overwhelming, but to do so she must reassemble a new team to assist her.

In recent years, the word anime has become increasingly divorced from its original meaning in the minds of most people, that of the straightforward Japanese word for "animation," to represent a distinct self-contained genre all of its own. With its associated elements of realistic character designs, rich background detail, and furious action sequences, it provides the perfect arena to pose probing philosophical questions within sweeping hi-tech environments. Its thematic concerns touch upon such issues as conspiracy theories, the blurring of the distinctions between different levels of reality, and mankind's vulnerability within the world(s) that it has created.

This generic reframing of the label no doubt rests on the limited sample of films from the higher end of the market best known outside of Japan—films such as Katsuhiro Ōtomo's *Akira* (1988) and Rintarō's *Metropolis* (2001)—rather than the broader world of Japanese animation inhabited by the likes of *Pikachu*, *Doraemon*, and giggling schoolgirl *Chibi Maruko-chan*. Oshii's previous work in animation—from his first theatrical film *Urusei Yatsura: Beautiful Dreamer* (1984), through *Angel's Egg* (*Tenshi no Tamago*, 1985), the *Patlabor* video series (*Kidō Keisatsu Patorebā*, 1988–90) and its theatrical spin-off *Patlabor: The Movie* (1990), to his script for Hiroyuki Okiura's *The Wolf Brigade* (*Jin-Roh*, 1999)—certainly fits snugly within this preconceived niche. He was, after all, one of the key figures in elevating the worldwide status of Japanese animation to the level it enjoys today.

Around the turn of the millennium it became increasingly common for Hollywood directors to checklist the "anime style" as a source of inspiration. Upon the release of *The Matrix Reloaded* (Larry and Andy Wachowski, 2003), as an acknowledgement of this influence, a compendium of nine short films was produced in conjunction with a number of Japan's top animation houses and computer game developers, and released onto video under the title *The Animatrix*, explaining various facets of the back story of *The Matrix* (1999).

Furthermore, the Wachowski brothers explicitly cited director Oshii's *Ghost in the Shell* (*Kōkaku Kidōtai*, 1995), made prior to the live-action *Avalon*, as a film which helped shape their vision for *The Matrix Reloaded*. A touchstone of techno-animation, it posits a future society reliant upon computer networks for all its economic transactions, enslaved by the caprices of a rebellious consciousness that has evolved from a rogue computer virus.

Increases in CGI technology have meant that the possibilities for complete artistic control over how the film looks need not be the reserve of the animator. Having already directed *Akai Megane* [trans: Crimson glasses, 1987], *Keruberosu, Jigoku no Banken* [trans: Cerberus, watchdog of hell, 1991] and *Talking Head* (*Tōkingu Heddo*, 1992), *Avalon* is not Oshii's first live-action movie, but it does represent the first time that the director has had the ability to provide an adequately scaled stage on which to present his ideas within this format.

On a basic level, *The Matrix* and *Avalon* appear to explore similar concerns readily identifiable from Oshii's previous body of work. *The Matrix* does so within the tightly crafted framework of the Hollywood action movie, as Keanu Reeves' character awakens to the fact that the world he took for granted is in the hands of a higher power. With *Avalon*'s central axis Ash drawn voluntarily into this pixelated simulacrum of reality, Oshii's vision is less apocalyptic, but nonetheless wholeheartedly pessimistic, almost disdainfully so, a highly feasible extrapolation based on modern trends in technology and its application.

Embellishing the live-action footage with computer-generated imagery to create the epic self-contained universe in which the film unfolds and in which the elaborate, high-precision, video game-inspired action sequences are staged, *The Matrix* celebrates the power of technology in a liberating, explosive fashion. *Avalon* laments it, adopting techniques of digital manipulation to investigate Ash's various levels of reality by selectively stripping away the colors from the image. Shot in Poland, *Avalon* plays like an Eastern European art movie, its look often reminiscent of Andrei Tarkovsky's *Stalker* (1979). The majority of the "reality" scenes are shot in sepia-toned monochrome, with more color filtering through to the image the further Ash is from the coldly inhuman shades of Avalon's false paradise: for example, the warm tungsten glow coming from the windows of the tram that Ash rides home in through the austere urban landscape, its sky scoured with telephone cables.

After a violent "reset," our heroine returns to her bare apartment to prepare herself a meal, the cabbage a lush field of green against a monochrome background as she slices into it to serve alongside a luridly bloody hunk of red meat. In another scene, Stunner wolfs down a plate of eggs and bacon, his chin becoming smeared with vibrant hues of the egg yolk. Compare this to the colorless, tasteless slop that gets served up at the end of the food queue in the Avalon canteen. Ash's later emergence into Class Real is almost overwhelming.

Given this use of Polish locations, oppressive and nightmarishly shot by local cinematographer Grzegorz Kedzierski, it's no surprise that Oshii has declared his admiration for post-war Eastern bloc cinema, particularly the work of Andrzej Wajda, director of such films as *Generation* (*Pokolenie*, 1954), *Kanal* (1957), and *Ashes and Diamonds* (*Popiol I Diament*, 1958), from whose title Ash takes her name. Rather than a gleaming mirage of utopia, the future face of the city in *Avalon* is a purely functional one, bleak and rundown, where those constructions that have served their purpose are left to decay and those who have fallen through the gaps in the social fabric seek escapism from their humdrum everyday existence through ultra-violent interactive computer gaming, their behavior goal-directed toward the entirely abstract—winning is all that matters. If this is reality, then one can understand the desire to transcend it, but the virtual world of Avalon hardly seems more palatable: a terrifying war zone in which death lies around every corner.

The sequences within the game of Avalon itself are almost intentionally non-dramatic, like fragments of a forgotten dream that break up Ash's waking life. Nevertheless, Oshii's onscreen rendition of the advanced gameworld is nothing short of stunning. Tanks roll across open plains as the players hide out in towering fortresses, assailed by helicopters and heavy duty artillery fire. When hit, bodies flatten into two-dimensional planar projections before shattering into a myriad of triangular shards. One of the reasons given for basing the film in Poland was that the cost of utilizing the Polish army made these large-scale battle scenes an affordable option. But it also serves a double purpose, that of the distancing effect that the impenetrably alien-sounding language of Polish has. *Avalon*'s characters are addicts, and as such barely in control of their own destiny. They are not conventional dramatic hooks.

With Oshii keeping his characters at a deliberate arm's length, the stylishly austere visuals and rousing operatic score (courtesy of Kenji Kawai, composer for *Ghost in the Shell* and the first two *Ring* films) impress rather than involve. However, the sophisticated Russian doll-like plotting of scriptwriter Kazunori Itō, who along with Oshii's previous film also put his name to **Gamera 3** and **Pistol Opera**, reveals a plethora of new levels on subsequent viewings. A testament to Oshii's pioneering vision, *Avalon* is a technically stunning achievement, offering a myriad of new avenues to be explored for both viewers and future filmmakers alike.

↓ Bad Company
まぶだち
Mabudachi

2001. Tomoyuki Furumaya, 古厩智之. CAST: Yamato Okitsu, Ryōsuke Takahashi, Yūta Nakajima, Ken Mitsuishi. 98 minutes. RELEASES: VHS, Tiger Releases (Holland, Dutch subtitles).

A junior high school student rebels against the stifling school climate, where discipline is all and the individual means nothing. An unsentimental look back at growing up in the '80s, sometimes disturbing, but often poignant.

Largely autobiographical, *Bad Company* is the tale of junior high school rebel Sadatomo and his clashes with teachers, authorities, and parents. A layabout, Sadatomo takes his two closest friends (both impressionable lads, as boys in their early teens tend to be) on extended sessions of school-skipping, shoplifting, and vandalism. Their transgressions usually amount to little more than mischief and none of them truly has the making of a criminal, but for Sadatomo this mischief is a method of rebellion against the heavily regimented school climate—a climate which not so much exists to teach children knowledge, but rather to program them for their inevitable role in adult society.

In fact, throughout the film the children are taught virtually nothing in the way of factual knowledge. Their teacher, Mr. Kobayashi, gives lessons in discipline and obedience instead of math or literature. Though he often raises valid points, his methods are Spartan, even abusive. Since the children are obliged to go to school, there is no escaping his often humiliating and sometimes downright degrading psychological approach, which includes categorizing his young pupils in a "humanity index" with the levels "delinquents," "scum," and "people." The end result may make them obedient citizens ready to do their part for the greater good of society, but it comes at the price of their individual free wills.

> "My junior high school years were probably the hardest time I've had. Even if I had a time machine, I would never want to go back to that period. What's shown in the film is pretty much what I've lived through. *Bad Company* was the result of reflections about my junior high period and how I could have lived a more joyful high school life. What was lacking? The film came out of those reflections."—Tomoyuki Furumaya

Refreshingly free of sentimentality and rose-tinted nostalgia, *Bad Company*'s autobiographical look at childhood is one of nuance and truthfulness. The character of Mr. Kobayashi is portrayed as an authoritarian and patriarchal figure, but also a human one. He is a man who believes he is doing the right thing and he is capable of giving his pupils genuine encouragement, even if those moments are few and far between. Likewise, the children themselves are three-dimensional characters, whose often conflicting actions show the confusion they must be feeling in their situations. Furumaya's view of growing up is the point of view of an adult who realizes that if he wishes to come to terms with his past, he can't escape the need for honesty.

> "I like Stephen King's *Stand By Me* a lot, the novel rather than the film. The ending is similar to that of *Bad Company*, except that all the characters die, aside from the protagonist. They went on an adventure to search for a dead body, and by going through that adventure they became adults. But once they were adults, they died. To me, it seems that the author says that it isn't so easy to become an adult—to become an adult simply by passing an initiation no longer holds true. To think so is fruitless. If you manage to escape from that way of thinking, then you are free to tell your own stories."

As with Akihiko Shiota's *Don't Look Back*, which it in some ways resembles, *Bad Company* is a universal story transposed to the world of children. Story-wise it is modeled on a pair of Stanley Kubrick films; the teacher's relentless hammering on discipline, obedience, and rules echoes R. Lee Ermey's memorable performance as the drill sergeant in *Full Metal Jacket*, while the behavior of Sadatomo and his two friends and the development they go through in the course of the film is remarkably similar to that of Alex DeLarge and his droogs in *A Clockwork Orange*. In fact, the story structure of *Bad Company* and Kubrick's 1971 masterpiece are virtually identical, with the main character going through a process that takes him from delinquency to punishment to submission and back to delinquency again. And like Kubrick's film, *Bad Company* contrasts conformity with free individual thought in a manner that is challenging and thought provoking. By having delinquency represent free thought, Furumaya makes the moral choice more difficult for the audience, testing their tolerance and forcing them to question their own value system. How much of our individual freedom are we willing to give up to stamp out those we label delinquents (or criminals, or terrorists)? It's an effect similar to that achieved by Kinji Fukasaku's *Battle Royale*, to which this is an excellent companion piece.

> "I haven't seen *Battle Royale*. There's only one death in *Bad Company*. If it's true that fifty people die in *Battle Royale*, and I managed to say the same things with only one character dying, then I think I did pretty well."

Bad Company was only director Furumaya's second film. It was made after a six-year hiatus from directing that followed his debut film *This Window Is Yours* (*Kono Mado wa Kimi no Mono*, 1996). Despite the good reception for his first film, Furumaya disappeared from the filmmaking scene, only re-emerging five years later to work as an assistant director on Shinji Aoyama's *Eureka*. That film's producer, Takenori Sentō, was also the man who had produced Furumaya's debut film, and the one responsible for dragging the young director back into filmmaking.

> "Making a movie is a lot of hard work and generally a big bother. So I think I was escaping from that burden during those seven years. I just spent my time doing a part-time job in construction. If I would escape from making films, I would escape from life. I wanted to make films, but I didn't do it because I was afraid of the effort it requires. In that situation you develop real self-loathing. But the producer Mr. Sentō pushed me to make another film, so finally I started again. Then once I'd started I noticed that it was much more comfortable

than being in my previous situation. Before, I was constantly dealing with wishing that I could do what I wanted to do, which is to make films, and with not being able to do it because I was afraid of the hard work that comes along with it. Maybe I'm just a sissy."

Sissy or not, *Bad Company* showed that the hard work paid off. The film had its world premiere at the 2001 Rotterdam Film Festival in Holland, long a hotbed for emerging young Japanese filmmakers, where it scooped both the jury prize and the international critics' prize. Although the film and its festival success went largely unnoticed by Japanese audiences, the industry certainly sat up to take notice. Furumaya's next film would be the major studio production *Robocon* (2003).

↓ Final Fantasy: The Spirits Within
ファイナルファンタジー
Fainaru Fantajī

2001. DIRECTOR: Hironobu Sakaguchi, 坂口博信. VOICE CAST: Ming-Na, Alec Baldwin, Ving Rhames, Steve Buscemi, Peri Gilpin, Donald Sutherland. 106 minutes. RELEASES: DVD, Columbia Tri-Star (U.S., English/French subtitles), Columbia Tri-Star (U.K., English subtitles), Amuse (Japan, English/Japanese subtitles).

Landmark piece of CGI animation is unfortunately flawed by a leaden script about an alien invasion of Earth, in this costly U.S.-Japanese co-production.

The year 2001 was notable for the film industry. In a summer which counted *Tomb Raider* (Simon West), *The Mummy Returns* (Stephen Sommers), and *Cats and Dogs* (Lawrence Guterman) among its list of blockbusters, throughout the big screens of the world the usual established Hollywood stars were conspicuous by their absence. Instead, the real box office draws were for the most part artificially rendered, touched up or embellished, as advances in Computer Generated Imagery (CGI) were pushed to the fore, pointing to new possible directions that the leaps in this still relatively new technology provided.

By the end of the summer audiences must have become rather blasé about all this new hi-tech razzle-dazzle, if the disappointing box office performance of *Final Fantasy: The Spirits Within* is anything to go by. Different in the scope of its ambitions from the other films of the year, rather than use CGI as a cosmetic addition to the real-life action, the goals of this U.S.-Japanese co-production based on the long running video game franchise were nothing less than the complete rendering of an artificial world so convincing that it was indistinguishable from the real thing. Rather than the cartoonish creations of such other wholly computer-modeled worlds as the same year's *Shrek*, with every skin blemish and strand of hair modeled to perfection, at times *Final Fantasy*'s avatars seemed more human than human.

But even as pundits within the industry were busy predicting a more or less total convergence of interactive gaming and large-screen entertainment, audiences were voting with their feet. Four years and an estimated $140 million in the making, *Final Fantasy* sank like a stone at the box office, a virtually forgotten memory to be consigned to the bottom of bargain DVD racks.

The costly flop of *Final Fantasy*, which led to the demise of its production company Square Pictures, rather belittles the achievements of what represented, and to some extent still does, the state of the art of 3D computer animation. The virtues of this groundbreaking technical exercise are so self-evident that they draw attention to what the film lacks. *Final Fantasy* remains a fascinating case study in that, although visually nothing short of stunning, in many ways it perhaps represents an evolutionary dead end.

With an international staff overseen by animation director Andy Jones and produced by Square Pictures, a new production company based in Honolulu overseen by Jun Aida and former head of Columbia/Tri-Star Chris Lee, and a subsidiary of one of Japan's largest games developers, Square, *Final Fantasy* might not be a Japanese film in the strictest sense of the word. But based on a series of computer games of the same name created by Hironobu Sakamoto that began in 1987, its pedigree lies firmly in the East.

Whilst its crossover appeal was undoubtedly hampered by the low expectations raised by previous cinematic tie-ins with the game world, which include the *Super Mario Brothers* (Annabel Jankel, Rocky Morton, 1993), the Jean-Claude Van Damme vehicle *Street Fighter* (Steven E. de Souza, 1994), and *Mortal Kombat* (Paul Anderson, 1995), its title notwithstanding, *The Spirits Within* is only tenuously linked to the original *Final Fantasy* video game series. The first of these, *Final Fantasy: Mystic Quest* (1987), was a two-dimensional scrolling fantasy adventure for the Nintendo Famicom with the action viewed from above, though as the series progressed through to the first for the Playstation 2 console, *Final Fantasy X*, released in the same year as the movie, the action moved toward a more three-dimensional realism.

Interestingly, there had already been an animated spin-off from the game series in 1993, *Final Fantasy: Legend of the Crystals*, directed by Rintarō, an original video series of four episodes more firmly grounded in the original material. Sakaguchi's story for *The Spirits Within*, however, divorces itself from the mystical fantasy world created in the games, into thematic and stylistic territory bearing more semblance to Japanese anime such as Mamoru Oshii's *Ghost in the Shell* (1995), though unfortunately without quite the same level of intellectual rigor.

Scripted by Al Reinart and Jeff Vintar from Sakaguchi's original idea, straightaway it becomes evident that the greatest weakness lies in a leaden script that takes itself far too seriously, a half-baked mishmash of sci-fi clichés, hackneyed dialogue, and some potentially interesting but ultimately undeveloped core ideas. It is almost ironic that, given the huge number of man-hours invested in the project, the end results should be hampered by something so fundamental.

Set on Earth in the year 2065, for the past 34 years mankind has been waging a losing war against the Phantoms, pulsating translucent beings transported to the planet on the back of a giant meteor. As the team of assorted militarists, technicians, and scientists convene for a meeting to discuss the future of their planet, with conventional weapons proving useless, Dr. Aki Ross and her mentor, Dr. Sid, stress the belief that the threat can be overcome by creating an opposing anti-energy wave to cancel out the life force of the invaders. Their research is based on James Lovelock's Gaia hypothesis, which views the Earth as a global ecosystem that sustains and regulates itself like a living organism and whose inhabitants all possess a "spirit" that endures after death. Their plan is violently dismissed out of hand by General Hein as New Age phooey. Hein himself wishes to unleash the devastating fury of the Zeus Cannon and nothing is going to stop him.

In 1995, Disney's and Pixar's *Toy Story* (directed by John Lasseter) had become the first feature film fully animated by computer to be released into theaters worldwide. There was a brief delay before Disney's main rival in the field, DreamWorks SKG, got in on the act with *Antz* (1998), its release coming almost hand in hand with the first company's *A Bug's Life* the same year, but arguably the DreamWorks film suffered for the very reason Disney's one worked. With notably more detail to the images, it was too busy trying to showcase the technical advances its makers had made in the medium than tell a good and simple story, which was one of *Toy Story*'s greatest assets.

Square's stated goal with *Final Fantasy* was to lend its world the illusion of complete photo-realism, achieving a level of detail and control that would be impossible in either conventional animation or live-action. On a frame-by-frame basis, they certainly achieve this, making full use of the ability to capture the minutiae that the camera might miss: the veins throbbing on the backs of the characters' hands, the tears forming in their eyes, every piece of grit lying on the floor, the action reflected in every sleek metallic contour of this future world.

In the opening moments of *Final Fantasy* we see our heroine, Aki, gazing over the surface of a gnarled rocky planet, hair billowing in the wind and the moon mirrored in her eye, eclipsing the iris. It is the first of many such overwhelmingly lucid images that permeate this work. But interestingly, such a strict adherence to reality is by point of reference to a familiar cinematic rendering, via such artificially introduced flaws such as focus pulls, lens flares, and camera wobbles.

Using sophisticated motion capture techniques, when seen in long shot, the characters move with such kinesthetic precision that, throughout, the eye is often fooled into believing that we are indeed watching real-life actors performing within the confines of an epic-budget science fiction action movie. Only when seen close up do the characters reveal their shortcomings. *Final Fantasy*'s synthespians look like humans, and move like humans, but are they convincing as characters?

Aki makes for an undeniably stunning creation of supermodel perfection, and in terms of the Hollywood action hero archetype her lover Captain Gray Edwards is no less charismatic than Ben Affleck, with whom he bears a certain physical resemblance. With his eyebrows arched over a broad, flattened forehead, Hein is little more than a one-dimensional caricature of militarism in the vein of Steven Seagal. But the best of Hollywood's character actors owe more than looks to their success. Tics such as the downward twitch of the mouth of Hugh Grant, the doe-eyed pout of Meg Ryan, the much emulated seditious smirk of Jack Nicholson; love them or hate them, it is these little human details that make their characters so resonant with audiences around the world. Their artificiality exacerbated by the crude dialogue, *Final Fantasy*'s characters never advance beyond the level of automatons. It will be interesting to see whether future creations within the medium will ever be able to invoke as much in the way of pathos or anxiety as their human counterparts.

Somehow, though, such lacunae in the characters lend the end results a rather dreamlike quality. In all other details, this could so easily be the real world. There are other giveaways too: A kinetic jeep ride through a desolate city lacks the inertia of a live-action chase, the vehicle looking for all the world like a scaled down toy. But these are just isolated factors, the distancing device of spectacle for the sake of spectacle drawing attention to the hallucinogenic usage of lighting, color, and form. What the film lacks in dramatic tension it more than makes up for in such extraordinary sequences as Aki's recurrent dreams of an arid planet swarming with scuttling armored killers.

Final Fantasy is undoubtedly the apogee of realistic 3D animation, and it has yet to be superseded within the full-length feature format, though prior to the plug being pulled on Square Pictures, animation director Andy Jones took the helm for *Final Flight of the Osiris*, the first and only CGI section of *The Animatrix*, the animated video compendium to the Wachowski brothers' *The Matrix* series. Using techniques developed for the *Final Fantasy* project, it was, if anything, an even more remarkable technical accomplishment. In Japan, there had already been several attempts at pursuing the cinematic hyper-realistic ends pioneered by *Final Fantasy*, albeit of a more modest nature, including the straight-to-video releases of *Malice@Doll* (Keitarō Motonaga, 2000) and *Blue Remains* (Toshifumi Takizawa, 2000), though both lack the same sense of scale and detail.

Whilst CGI technology is endless in its possibilities to control every dimension of its onscreen world, it is also a time-consuming and expensive business. Whilst *Final Fantasy*

undoubtedly raises the stakes in the field, ultimately it lacks a heart beating beneath its surface. Mainstream audiences require more than mere technical innovation, and without their support, at present such projects represent a huge commercial risk. For the field to develop further beyond the mere slavish emulation of live-action cinema into an art form in its own right, however, the risk-taking must come at a more conceptual level. Until then, it's clear that the medium is far better served by Disney's more humanistic approach of simplification and anthropomorphism.

↓ Firefly Dreams
いちばん美しい夏
Ichiban Utsukushii Natsu

2001. **DIRECTOR:** John Williams, ジョン・ウィリアムズ. **CAST:** Maho Ukai, Yoshie Minami, Tsutomu Niwa, Etsuko Kimata, Chie Miyajima, Atsushi Ono, Sadayasu Yamakawa, Kyōko Kanemoto. 104 minutes. **RELEASES:** DVD, Groove Pictures (Japan, English subtitles).

Touching tale of cross-generational friendship between a tearaway seventeen-year-old girl and a carefree octogenarian is one of the most picturesque and refreshing films made in Japan in recent years, and the director isn't even Japanese.

Kitano might have headed West to make *Brother*, and the influence of John Woo and the Hong Kong style on mainstream Hollywood cinema in the late '90s is incontestable, but there's been precious little traffic in the opposite direction. British director John Williams is an exception. Growing up in Wales, he made his first film at the age of fourteen on a secondhand 16mm Bolex camera. After studying at Cambridge University, he spent two years working as a French teacher in North London before the travel bug bit and he relocated to Nagoya in 1988.

© 2001 100 Meter Films

Firefly Dreams

Williams' first feature, the slow but assured *Firefly Dreams*, a touching story of a cross-generational friendship between a teenage tearaway and a carefree octogenarian, is the first fruit of this unique cultural background, yet you'd be hard pressed to tell it wasn't made by a local. Aside from a couple of English names on the credits list (including the composer of the bouncy musical score, Paul Rowe), *Firefly Dreams* is to all intents and purposes a Japanese film, using an all-Japanese cast and targeted at a Japanese audience. It admirably avoids projecting a foreigner's perspective on the proceedings and digs deep beneath the surface superficialities to touch on something far more universally resonant.

"Many of the reactions to the film have centered around the apparent strangeness of a 'Japanese' film made by a non-Japanese director. In some ways this is very flattering and in other senses it is somewhat disappointing. I didn't set out consciously to make a 'Japanese' film. I'm not sure what one of those is."

Seventeen-year-old Naomi could be any one of a million aimless youths in Japan: a Shibuya girl wannabe, bottle blonde and face plastered in orange foundation, mobile phone permanently grafted to her head, and her pink lipsticked pout puffing petulantly at a cigarette as her mother gives her a dressing down for skipping school and staying out all night. Problems at home could be to blame for her moody and uncooperative behavior, with Naomi making no secret of her distaste for her mother's new boyfriend. The most obvious immediate solution seems to be to ship the bolshie city brat off away from the bad influence of her friends in Nagoya to spend the summer in the country working at a rural inn owned by her father's sister and her family.

At first the change of environment seems to be doing little for the restless young girl, her brow knitted in a barely disguised scowl as she waits on tables of drunken old men at the hotel and gripes at the incessant nattering of her retarded cousin, Yumi. Seeing that things are not working out, her aunt instead suggests that she look after an aging relative, Koide-san, who lives alone on a small farm where Naomi used to play as a small child. Koide-san, however, is slowly losing her faculties to Alzheimer's and at first, much to Naomi's chagrin, doesn't even remember her as a small girl.

Initially the two respectfully keep their distance from one another, with Naomi being of little assistance in the farmyard chores as, rather than chipping her nail varnish, she leaves the resilient but dignified older woman to get on with such day-to-day duties as beheading chickens for the local inn. However, as she spends more time at the farm the ice begins to melt, and she soon comes to realize that the "daft old cow" once had a pretty adventurous life of her own, working in a munitions factory in Tokyo during the war and even appearing in a film called "Among the Fireflies." As the summer progresses, the two women find that beyond the age gap, they have considerably more in common than they first thought.

Japanese cinema at the turn of the millennium saw quite a run of dramas featuring rebellious, directionless teenage girls. These ran from Masato Harada's ***Bounce KoGals***, to Ryūichi Hiroki's ***Tokyo Trash Baby*** and Kaze Shindō's *Love/Juice* (2000). Though *Firefly Dreams*, (whose Japanese title translates as "A Most Beautiful Summer") is more obviously situated within the rite of passage genre, it makes an ideal companion piece to Makoto Shinozaki's ***Not Forgotten***. Both films are subtle reminders of just how far the offspring of Japan's bubble years, one which has had more or less everything handed to them on a plate, have grown away from the one that lived through war, defeat, and occupation. *Fire-fly Dreams*' implicit message here is that Naomi and Koide-san are essentially the same character, just at completely different stages in their lives having lived through different circumstances. In fact, Naomi's life is actually incredibly boring in comparison to that lived by the older woman.

> **"Although the members of the younger generation have so many choices in terms of what they can buy, I really wonder how many choices they actually have in terms of how they can live. Of course, the women of Koide's generation were much less free, but the women who did challenge the status quo in the pre- and post-war years were very inspiring."**

Naomi and Koide-san's cross-generational friendship is embellished by the touching interplay between newcomer Maho Ukai and 85-year-old Yoshie Minami, a veteran of the stage who started acting in the all-female Takarazuka revue troupe prior to the war. With the majority of her work spent in theater, she had a small part in Akira Kurosawa's *Ikiru* (1952), and is now a familiar face thanks to her lovable grandmother roles on television.

Similarly noteworthy is Yoshinobu Hayano's beautiful photography of the Hōraichō region in Aichi prefecture in central Japan, bringing a seductive calmness to the screen as it evokes its rural idyll against the soporific throb of cicadas. Shots such as one in which the two women walk across a grassy meadow in their kimonos beneath the shade of a parasol invoke memories of painters such as Monet or Renoir, bringing an Impressionist's attention to light and color. Curiously it remains his only film credit, for he contributes an atmosphere to the film that will linger long past its running time.

↓ GO

2001. **DIRECTOR:** Isao Yukisada, 行定勲. **CAST:** Yō-suke Kubozuka, Kō Shibasaki, Shinobu Ōtake,

© 2001 Toei Company, Ltd.

GO

Tsutomu Yamazaki, Takahito Hosoyamada, Hirofumi Arai. 122 minutes. **RELEASES:** DVD, Toei Video (Japan, no subtitles), IVL (Hong Kong, English/Chinese subtitles).

Yukisada's adaptation of Kazuki Kaneshiro's novel detailing the trials of a high school "zainichi," or North Korean foreign resident, may seem occasionally overstated, but makes for powerful, touching viewing.

Remember that old philosophical brain-teaser that states that if you have a boat, and over a period of time you replace each piece of wood bit by bit as it begins to rot, once you have replaced every last plank is it the same boat as when you started? A similar conundrum can be readily applied to the question of national identity. Perhaps more than most countries, on a purely superficial level modern Japan bears little resem-

blance to the country it was a hundred years ago. Within the cultural, political, and economic domains Japan has certainly absorbed much more from abroad than it has given in return. The only level in which pure "Japanese-ness" remains unsullied is ethnicity. You may speak Japanese, you may look Japanese, you may have been born in Japan, but unless you can trace your lineage back to the Tokugawa period, to the indigenous inhabitants you'll always be an outsider.

Hair trendily spiked, and a defiant swagger in his walk, Sugihara could be any other rebel-without-a-clue Japanese high school student, were it not for the fact that he's not just the kid from the wrong side of the tracks; he's from the wrong side of the Japan Sea, a second-generation North Korean permanent resident, or *zainichi*. However, such definitions sit badly with him. "If I'm a Japanese resident Korean, that means I'm going back." Fat chance, having already been thrown out of the austere cloistered corridors of his North Korean school for swearing at the teacher in Japanese. His decision to move to a Japanese school wins him a certain degree of respect from his former *zainichi* fellow students, but it opens him up to a stream of violence from his new classmates. Fortunately, his greatest form of defense comes from the boxing lessons he has received from his father (Yamazaki) since childhood. His second is that, like most Koreans, to the outside eye he is indistinguishable to the Japanese, a factor that seems the most likely passport into full integration with his adopted homeland in the pristine form of high school princess Sakurai (Shibasaki). However, for all their shared love of non-Japanese rap music and Bruce Lee movies, the question lingers as to whether Sakurai is still prepared to accept Sugihara once she learns about his true origins.

Foreign critics have been quick to point out Japan's strained relationship with its neighboring Asian countries and the prejudice faced by ethnic Asians living in Japan. Some have stated that the issue is completely brushed under the carpet, but the truth is *GO*, which received a simultaneous theatrical release in Japan and South Korea, is not the first film treatment of Japanese discrimination directly against Koreans. It is, however, one of the first major films to challenge existing preconceptions about Japanese identity within such a commercial format. That it does so in such a moving and high-spirited fashion makes it even more worthy of note.

It's not just the issue of prejudice, reflected in the unconscious racism of Sakurai, that is tackled, but that of racial identity in general. In the early scenes Sugihara's father cashes in his North Korean passport for a South Korean one, ostensibly so that he can take his wife (Ōtake) on holiday to Hawaii, much to the disgust of his son. One of Sugihara's former classmates from his North Korean junior high school berates him for such capitalistic acts of betrayal as wearing jeans and listening to Mariah Carey (admittedly, a heinous crime whatever part of the globe you stem from).

Sugihara's desire to break through the boundaries is shared by his best friend, nerdy brainbox Jong-Il (Hosoyamada), who sees the insularity imposed upon them through the exclusively Korean-speaking *minzoku* schools, in which they are drilled with the communist spirit, as equally unhealthy. He is instrumental in pointing to a broader world outside of both Japan and Korea when he lends Sugihara a translated copy of Shakespeare's *Romeo and Juliet*, from which the film's opening quote, "What's in a name? That which we call a rose, by any other name would smell so sweet?" is taken, a reminder that, as our hero tells us on several occasions, this is after all a love story.

Adapted from the novel of the same name by Kazuki Kaneshiro, himself a *zainichi*, from the opening scenes where our beleaguered protagonist receives a pasting on the basketball court (from his own team no less), *GO* sets forth its agenda in a vital, spirited fashion. Along with its semi-comedic asides, surrealistic touches, and a style marked out by a use of such modernist techniques as freeze frames and jump cuts, all

laid down to a compulsive pounding soundtrack and a continuous voiceover from its sage-like hero, it is deeply reminiscent of Danny Boyle's *Trainspotting* (1996) in its raw energy. This factor combined with its focus on Asian ethnics living in Japan is likely to draw attention away from director Yukisada's previous work—which includes *Sunflower* (*Himawari*, 2000) and *Luxurious Bone* (*Zeitaku na Hone*, 2001)—to his role as assistant director on Shunji Iwai's *Swallowtail Butterfly* (1996), another slick tale of Asians living in Japan.

Yukisada worked on a number of films by Iwai aside from *Swallowtail Butterfly*, including **Love Letter** (1995) and *April Story* (*Shigatsu Monogatari*, 1998), and has certainly absorbed some of his mentor's style. His next work after *GO*, the following year's *Rock 'n' Roll Mishin* (*Rokkunrōru Mishin*), was centered around a group of young friends setting up a new designer clothing brand. This was followed by a video-only release of the glossy forty-minute long promo *Tsuki ni Shizumu* [trans: Sinking into the moon] for top pop idol Ayumi Hamasaki's single *Voyage*, released at the tail end of 2002.

The year 2003 saw the long-belated release of Yukisada's debut film, *Open House*, the story of a young woman coping with loneliness in the aftermath of a divorce. An adaptation of the novel of the same name by Jinsei Tsuji, *Open House* was made in 1998 but shelved for six years due to the internal coup within its distributor Shochiku that saw the dismissal of company president Tōru Okuyama and his son, executive director Kazuyoshi Okuyama. The year 2003 also saw the premiere at the 16th Tokyo International Film Festival of *A Day on the Planet* (*Kyō no Dekigoto*), a tale of seven college students meeting for a drunken house party in Kyoto whilst news breaks over the TV about a man stuck between two buildings and a whale stranded on a local beach. Yukisada intended the film to celebrate the fleeting, inconsequential moments of our lives that go on as major climactic events rock the worlds of those around us, but with overly "cute" performances from the principal cast and a distinct lack of focus, the results are rather slight.

Whilst *GO* has far stronger source material to work with, through the in-your-face violence and dazzling virtuosity of its approach it often comes dangerously close to overstating its case in a manner that is more cinematic flourish than verisimilitude. In this respect it is easy to criticize *GO*'s exaggerated focus on the individual racism that its protagonist suffers over the deeply ingrained institutionalized racism, which ensures that even after several generations, many resident Koreans are still refused Japanese passports.

Nevertheless, Kubozuka, a top teen heart-throb in Japanese cinema in the early 2000s after his roles in Fujirō Mitsuishi's *Tomie Replay* (2000), Junichi Mori's *Laundry* (*Randorī*, 2002), Fumi-hiko "Sori" Masuri's *Ping Pong* (*Pin Pon*, 2002), and Kenji Sonoda's *Madness in Bloom* (*Kyōki no Sakura*, 2002), fills his role as Sugihara with an affable punkish charm that is hard to resist, and the film picked up a number of awards at the 2001 Japan Academy Awards, including one for Best Director. *GO*'s dramatic trajectory may be a fairly well-traveled one, but in its stronger moments, such as the romantic interplay between Kubozuka and Shibasaki, it's undeniably affecting, and as such it is one of the most compelling and thought-provoking films of its year.

↓ Kaza-Hana
風花

2001. **DIRECTOR:** Shinji Sōmai, 相米慎二. **CAST:** Tadanobu Asano, Kyōko Koizumi, Kumiko Asō. 116 minutes. **RELEASES:** DVD, Taki (Japan, English subtitles).

This tragicomedy road movie of two lost souls drifting across Hokkaido is the final offering from one of the most respected directors in Japan of the past two decades.

The year 1993 saw *Kanzen Jisatsu Manyuaru* [trans: The complete manual of suicide] riding high in the best-seller book charts in Japan, giving guidelines as to a number of the most efficient ways to kill yourself. Apparently the most painless and foolproof method is to down a bottle of saké, fall asleep in a big pile of snow, and freeze to death. This seems to be the favored approach of the two self-destructive characters of *Kaza-Hana*, as they blaze a one-way trail across the frozen expanses of Hokkaido, the northernmost of the four main islands that make up Japan. A barren, snowy wilderness settled only 120 years ago, it has long been seen as the wild frontier of the Japanese popular imagination.

Privileged Ministry of Education employee Renji's life is in a shambles. Since his mother died the previous year, his drinking habits have sent him on a downward spiral culminating in the humiliating spectacle of hitting the newspaper headlines after being caught pilfering a fish sausage from a convenience store. When the bitter aftermath of a fling with an office lady associate sees her pressing charges of sexual misconduct against him, he decides to put as much distance between himself and Tokyo as possible until things cool down. Waking up drunk in Hokkaido Airport, he bumps into Yuriko, a single young woman who tries to wave him aside. There's a vague glimmer of recollection in his eyes, but as Yuriko counters, "You'll forget me again when you're sober." Nevertheless, she agrees to let Renji tag along with her on her own particular mission. The longer the two spend in each other's company, the more he remembers of their initial meeting in a hostess bar back in the big city.

Yuriko has a rather stronger sense of purpose for being in Hokkaido as she returns to her home town to retrieve her abandoned daughter Kaori, after the five years since her husband's death in a car crash forced her down to Tokyo where she has since been working as a sex club hostess. During her absence her mother has been looking after the child, but when Yuriko returns expecting to be reintegrated into the family unit, mother seems unwilling to allow her daughter a second chance. Just as Yuriko is dismissed from the house where she was raised, Renji is dispatched from his office by a curt mobile phone call from his superior. Both now freed from any sense of responsibility, the two drift on through the expansive beauty of Hokkaido towards an uncertain future, and one in which love seems to be the last thing on either of their minds.

The title of Shinji Sōmai's film is a Japanese word used to describe soft flurries of snow carried in the wind. It is composed of the two kanji characters for "wind" and "flower," which capture the complementary natures of Asano's sullen salaryman, an obnoxious bore when he's sober but a nice guy, albeit a little wayward, when he's drunk, and Koizumi's emotionally overwrought bar hostess with the heart of gold. Pitched halfway between road movie and romantic tragicomedy, *Kaza-Hana* plays like a cross between Rob Reiner's *The Sure Thing* (1985) and Mike Figgis's *Leaving Las Vegas* (1995), downplaying the slapstick of the former and the relentless somberness of the latter to focus squarely on the burgeoning relationship between its two central characters in their mutual search for redemption.

To this end, it benefits from two outstandingly mature central performances. Asano, as the guarded yet erratic Renji, all incoherently mumbled apologies, unable to articulate that his life is falling apart around him, is leagues away from his regular roles as brooding tough guy loners. He is ably supported by Koizumi (former real-life spouse of actor Masatoshi Nagase) as Yuriko, an apparent failure in her duty as both mother and daughter and frustrated by her inability to keep Renji on track. In the pure terms of its drama, *Kaza-Hana* is near faultless, a sturdy, emotive slow-burner equally matched by its technical virtues and high production values. It's a film whose subdued humanism insinuates slowly rather than bowls over in its individual moments.

Kaza-Hana was the final film of Shinji Sōmai, who died of lung cancer on September 9, 2001, at the tragically young age of 53, after a long and fruitful career in which the distinguished film magazine *Kinema Jumpo* voted him the top Japanese director of the '80s. Starting off as an assistant director for Nikkatsu studios in the 1970s, shortly after going freelance in 1975 Sōmai became established as one of the foremost directors of strong mainstream dramas, his one-take, character-oriented approach wringing out exacting performances from his actors, especially children, in films such as his debut *Dreamy Fifteen* (*Tonda Kappuru*, 1980), *The Catch* (*Gyoei no Mure*, 1983), *Typhoon Club* (*Taifū Kurabu*, 1986), *Moving* (*Ohikkoshi*, 1993), *The Friends* (*Natsu no Niwa*, 1994), and *Wait and See* (*Aa, Haru*, 1999). That none of these ever made it far from Japanese shores and that Sōmai's work remains virtually unknown outside of his own country remains one of the greatest oversights in the West's appreciation of Asian cinema.

↓ A Tender Place
柔らかな頬
Yawaraka na Hoo

2001. **DIRECTOR:** Shunichi Nagasaki, 長崎俊一. **CAST:** Yuki Amami, Shunsuke Matsuoka, Tomokazu Miura, Kumi Nakamura, Minori Terada, Hideo Murota, Tarō Suwa. 201 minutes. **RELEASES:** DVD, Pioneer LDC (Japan, no subtitles).

Epically realized, richly detailed and absorbing character study centered around a terminally ill police detective and a young mother in search of her missing daughter across the barren wilderness of Hokkaido.

Released into the world clinging onto the coattails of Hideo Nakata's *The Ring*, Nagasaki's chilling ghost story *Shikoku* (1999) took us way off the beaten track by setting its horrors on the

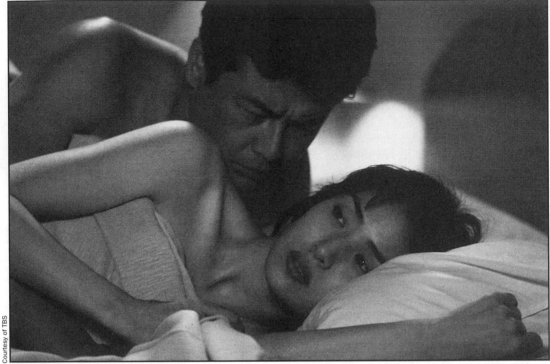

Courtesy of TBS

A Tender Place

wooded rural province of the film's name. For *A Tender Place*, the director transports us to the remote barren wilderness of Hokkaido, the most northerly of the four main islands that make up Japan, in a powerful and compelling tale shot using Hi-Vision DV equipment, and based on an original novel by Natsuo Kirino that ostensibly deals with the search of a young mother for her missing five-year-old daughter.

Kasumi originally left her isolated Hokkaido village home of Kirai at the age of fourteen, severing all ties with her parents as she moved to Tokyo to realize her dream of becoming a designer. Eighteen years on she is married to her employer, with whom she has two young children, Lisa and Yuka. When the couple decide to return to the region of her birth, vacationing in a holiday house rented by her husband, they are joined by a client of his, Ishiyama (Miura), his wife Noriko, and their children. Unbeknownst

to their respective spouses, Kasumi and Ishiyami have been conducting an affair for the past two years, and under the cover of night the pair creep down to one of the house's unused storerooms to be together. The following morning, Kasumi's husband leaves early to take the children on a walk, but when he returns to the house, their older daughter, Yuka, is not with him.

Yuka's disappearance leaves its devastating mark on both the local Hokkaido community and all those immediately involved. Four years after the fact, with the case firmly closed as far as the local police are concerned, Kasumi still clings on to the hope that her daughter is alive, the couple making an annual visit to Hokkaido to continue the search every year on October 9, the anniversary of the disappearance. With their marriage strained to the breaking point, her husband refuses to return for another year, urging Kasumi to let go of the past and accept what has happened, if not for him then for the sake of their younger daughter, Lisa. Noriko, meanwhile, refuses to return Kasumi's monthly calls and, having suspected the affair with her husband, has long since divorced Ishiyama, who, after being sent into bankruptcy by his latest business venture, has also disappeared without a trace.

After the couple make one last desperate appeal on national television, they are contacted by a woman who claims to have seen a scruffy homeless-looking man with a young girl wandering around the streets of Otaru in Hokkaido. With Kasumi's husband unwilling to spend any more time or money on their fruitless search, Kasumi returns to the area alone, where she is approached by a retired thirty-one-year-old police detective, Utsumi (Matsuoka). His offer of help is initially rebuffed by Kasumi, suspicious of further police involvement. Terminally ill with stomach cancer, his own motivations of helping with the case as a "hobby" seem obscure, but having been involved in the initial investigation, he refuses to be waved aside. Unlike Kasumi, Utsumi has nothing to gain in finding out what happened to Yuka, but with only months to live he might still have a lot to learn about himself.

Born in 1956, Shunichi Nagasaki first began make 8mm films whilst at art school. One of the pioneers of the underground 8mm scene of the late '70s, Nagasaki quickly found a kindred soul in Sōgo Ishii and the two directors resolved to collectively exhibit their work outside of the traditional theatrical circuit. He steadily earned himself an impressive reputation on the independent filmmaking circuit thanks to such films as *The Summer Yuki Threw Away Rock Music* (*Yuki ga Rokku o Suteta Natsu*, 1978), *The Back Side of Happy Street* (*Happī Sutorīto Ura*, 1979), *The Lonely Hearts Club Band in September* (*Kugatsu no Jōdan Kurabubando*, 1982), and his entry into Takenori Sentō's TV anthology series *J-Movie Wars*, entitled *Wild Side*.

Nagasaki's reputation was consolidated with a prize at the 1989 Tokyo International Film Festival for *The Enchantment* (*Yūwakusha*), a thriller about a psychotherapist who falls in love with a potentially murderous patient he is treating for multiple personality disorder. In the '90s he interspersed more commercial undertakings like the hospital drama *Nurse Call* (*Nāsu Kōru*, 1993) with films that showcase more personal concerns like *Some Kinda Love* (*Romansu*, 1996), a tale of a love triangle amongst thirty-somethings, and *Dogs* (*Doggusu*, 1998), a monochrome drama shot on video about a policewoman who, lying about a murder she has witnessed, finds herself emotionally implicated with the perpetrator.

If there is one thing that unites these films, it's Nagasaki's deft portrayal of female protagonists, also much in evidence in *A Tender Place* and in the director's most widely known work outside of film buff circles, *Shikoku*. A contract job capitalizing on the success of the late-'90s boom in supernatural horror co-written with Takenori Sentō, one of the original producers of Nakata's ***The Ring***, the film circulated on the lower half of a double bill with *Ring 2*. Taking its name from the fourth and smallest of the main islands that make up Japan, a mountainous rural province famed for its 1,400 km long pilgrimage along the eighty-eight temples established by the Buddhist saint Kōbō Daishi (774–835), and a hotbed for the country's indigenous Shinto religion, the title means quite literally, Four (*shi*) Kingdoms (*koku*), after the four original provinces of which it is made up. Four is considered an unlucky number throughout much of East and Southeast Asia for the very reason that *shi* is also the pronunciation of the Chinese character meaning "death." This alternate rendering of the first kanji of the film's title is the central conceit of Nagasaki's film, whose starting point is a children's story by Masako Bandō, a writer who grew up in the island's Kōchi Prefecture. Another one of her works, *Inugami*, was also adapted for the screen the following year by the same production group, directed by Masato Harada.

Shikoku is a fairly pedestrian addition to the genre, owing much to its predecessors in both style and formula. At the core there's the same

Courtesy of TBS

A Tender Place

male-female investigative pairing pitting their wits against a central ghostly figure of a young girl in a white dress (introducing the young Chiaki Kuriyama as the ghostly Sayori, later to appear in **Battle Royale** and Quentin Tarantino's *Kill Bill*), and an approach to the material that favors sedate and somber scares over breakneck pacing and buckets of blood and grue. Nagasaki's greatest asset is perhaps the locale of Shikoku itself, shot in bleached, hazy hues and long twilight shadows in the external scenes, and drenched out in the interiors by shafts of natural sunlight that stream through the windows of the deserted property where much of the more spine-tingling events occur.

Similar to Nagasaki's earlier film *Shikoku, A Tender Place* focuses on a modern Tokyo career woman (here superbly played by Yuki Amami, a former star of the Takarazuka revue troupe, perhaps best known in the movies for her roles in

Kenki Saegusa's glossy *Rashomon* remake *MISTY* in 1997, Takashi Ishii's *Black Angel 2* in 1998, and Masato Harada's *Inugami*) returning to the provincial region of her childhood only to be confronted by the ghosts of her past. The main difference is that Kasumi's estrangement from the bleak environment where she was brought up was her own choice, rather than Hinako's sudden uprooting from Shikoku's childhood idyll by her parents' move to the big city, and that the ensuing barriers that greet the heroine upon the return journey are manifested as psychological rather than supernatural ones.

Nagasaki adopts a similar approach in *A Tender Place* to that of Dutch director George Sluizer in *The Vanishing* (*Spoorloos*, 1988) in which a young teacher searches for his missing girlfriend abducted whilst on a holiday in France, using the compulsive drive of the classic detective story, as leads are followed desperately to their logical end points and the narrative is liberally scattered with red herrings and investigative dead ends: the mysterious disappearance of Ishiyama; the subsequent shotgun suicide of the owner of the vacation house, Izumi, apparently in the face of accumulated debt; and the alleged pedophilic activities of its caretaker, Mizushima (Suwa), now shacked up with Izumi's widow. The absence of any concrete evidence and the faltering subjective memory of all those who may or may not hold the key to the mystery lead the two investigators, and the viewer, to a multitude of differing conclusions.

> **"The author originally set out with a particular culprit in mind, but I learned later that while she was writing the novel she gave up on that idea. When I heard about that, I thought that maybe it would be better to keep this kind of ambiguity in the film as well. As I was shooting the film, I myself definitely had a guilty party in mind. But what I was interested in showing was the dark part in everybody, not just in the heroine, but also in the other characters. They all have their dark side, within the scope of this crime as well. That's what really appealed to me in the story."—Shunichi Nagasaki**

Both Kasumi and Utsumi conduct their investigation less in the hope of finding out what exactly happened, or why it happened, but as an end in itself, a continuing search for their own individual senses of identity and purpose. Deep in her heart, Kasumi knows her quest is a hopeless one, yet seems destined to remain in a permanent state of limbo until she can come to terms with her own feelings of guilt, hopelessness, and recrimination. Perhaps only then can she hope to fill the void left by Yuka and find her own tender place, whether in the almost futile hope of being reunited with her daughter, back amongst the familiar day-to-day normality of her Tokyo life, or by reconciliation with her own family, whom she left without warning so many years ago.

Originally intended as a feature length adaptation for the satellite TV channel BS-i by its producers Office Shirous, Nagasaki found his ambitiously detailed script, which uses Kirino's novel only as a starting point, soon growing rapidly in both scope and length. It was eventually screened in two parts on TV, and later theatrically in the Higashi Nakano Box cinema in Tokyo as part of a program to showcase a number of films shot in the Hi-Vision DV format. It also played at a number of international festivals which included Vancouver, London, and Rotterdam. Arguably, the story would have benefited from being shot on film to capture more fully the uncompromising savage beauty of his chosen locale. Nagasaki nevertheless handles the medium in a mature and assured manner that seldom draws attention to itself without resorting to showy technique or the standard practice of a musical accompaniment on the soundtrack to build both mood and character. That he manages to keep us riveted throughout the lengthy three-hours-plus running time is a testimony to his actors and his own skills as a filmmaker. A substantial and absorbing mood piece, rich in detail, raw in emotional charge, thought provoking, gripping, and poignant, *A Tender Place* is nothing short of a masterpiece.

↓ Blue Spring
青い春
Aoi Haru

2002. **DIRECTOR:** Toshiaki Toyoda, 豊田利晃. **CAST:** Ryūhei Matsuda, Hirofumi Arai, Sōsuke Takaoka, Yūta Yamazaki, Kee, Onimaru. 83 minutes. **RELEASES:** DVD, Artsmagic (USA, English subtitles), Winson (Hong Kong, English and Chinese subtitles).

Often violent antics at a high school where anarchy reigns. Teachers are dangled from the windows while the students have installed their own

Courtesy of There's Enterprise

Blue Spring

hierarchy. But beneath the sometimes blood-red exterior lies a thought-provoking look at a possible future for our own society.

Based on a manga by Taiyō Matsumoto, the artist also responsible for *Ping Pong*, Toshiaki Toyoda's *Blue Spring* is a story about high school anarchy in the long, bruised-and-battered tradition that stretches back at least as far as Seijun Suzuki's **Elegy to Violence**. In a school surrounded by misleadingly picturesque cherry trees in full bloom, it's the students who set the rules while uncooperative teachers are dangled from windows.

In this power structure, the leader is decided by a peculiar game of dare: Several boys hang from the rooftop fence, and he who can clap his hands the highest number of times without plummeting to his death is king. Assaults on the throne are punished with a severe bruising or, in worse cases, with a kitchen knife in the gut. The desolate concrete hallways of the building are covered floor to ceiling in black graffiti, which acquires a new coat each time another student comes to power. The hierarchy, the violent power games and the general lazing about seem to be these kids' only raisons d'être. Family life is never seen; education and career prospects are non-existent.

The only option in the world outside seems to be joining the yakuza. Gangsters regularly patrol the streets around the school grounds in their white limos, looking for new recruits to adopt into a system of hierarchy the kids know all too well. Just when we think the school seems like a training ground for organized crime and the film has little to say beyond its fights, we realize how many similarities there are between gang life, school life, and corporate life. With that, it becomes clear that Toyoda aims less to comment on a failed educational system or lawless youth than to show the universal nature of our need to rule and regulate. By using children as his subjects, it becomes poignantly clear that

Courtesy of There's Enterprise

Blue Spring

hierarchies, violence, and a craving for power are intrinsically human traits that are not specific to any single isolated part of society. Toyoda's story takes a step beyond the depictions of violent, disaffected youth seen in so many Japanese films of the late '90s and early 2000s (Fukasaku's ***Battle Royale***, Shiota's ***Harmful Insect***, Takahisa Zeze's *Hysteric* and Toyoda's own *Pornostar* to name but a few), and shows that if the young were to indeed seize power, the result may look like anarchy but in fact would be a society with the same structures as the one they have just overthrown.

Born in Osaka, director Toshiaki Toyoda is a former *shōgi* (Japanese chess) prodigy, a sport that commanded most of his childhood years. In his late teens, realizing he lacked the determination to make it as a professional, he turned his back on the sport entirely and went though a period of adolescent rebellion. After seeing Junji Sakamoto's film *Knock Out* (*Dotsuitarunen*, 1989), he realized cinema was his calling and

moved from Osaka to Tokyo with two guitars and 20,000 yen he had borrowed from his parents. In 1991 he made his debut as a scriptwriter and assistant director with *Checkmate* (*Ōte*) for that same Junji Sakamoto, an event that occurred after Toyoda sent the director a letter asking if he could work on Sakamoto's films. Toyoda made his directorial debut with 1998's *Pornostar*, a portrait of youth on a rampage in Tokyo's Shibuya district that took less after real life than after Sergio Leone westerns, with the poncho-wearing Man With No Name, whose guns speak louder than his words, replaced by a catatonic, knife-wielding, disaffected kid in an anorak. Toyoda followed it up with the feature-length documentary *Unchain*, about a boxer who has never won a bout in his entire career.

As noted, *Blue Spring* is in some ways a follow-up to his debut film. Whereas *Pornostar* was criticized for relying too much on posture and coolness, *Blue Spring* adds more dimension to its portrayal of a generation of don't-fuck-with-me kids, both in terms of surface style and characterization. There is posturing here, certainly, but this film has real attitude. Toyoda uses familiar methods like slow motion and a blazing rock score to reinforce the nature of his characters, yet *Blue Spring*'s style is not the artificially imposed wannabe toughness of a hip-hop video, nor does it depend on the manga excess of a film like *Fudoh: The New Generation* (Takashi Miike, 1996). Toyoda understands that he is using tools, means to get to an end. In *Blue Spring*'s guitar-driven slow motion sequences, stories are told, characters are established, and relationships are made clear. This certainly isn't a case of style over substance, it's a case of a filmmaker knowing his craft.

Whether or not those methods will be successful in the final results does, however, depend on one crucial thing: the cast. In a film like *Blue Spring*, if the actors lack the ability and the presence to portray the no-holds-barred roughness of the characters (plus their humanity, to make it just that little bit more difficult), all the director's trickeries won't save it from coming across as a film that tries too hard to be tough. But despite their young age, these kids are completely convincing, with Ryūhei Matsuda's magnetic central performance in front. The son of the late great Yūsaku Matsuda shows a tremendous growth from his eye-catching breakthrough role in Nagisa Ōshima's **Gohatto**, both as an actor and as a man. In the two years that separate both films, he has become less the androgynous curiosity piece and has instead gained a boyish masculinity, as well as a seeming boost of confidence. By sheer charisma and presence, and without showing the slightest effort, he commands every shot he's in. Even with the excellent Hirofumi Arai as his sidekick and would-be rival, Matsuda is the undisputed star of this show, and his performance in *Blue Spring* was the start of a very prosperous career as a leading man.

Although *Blue Spring* is filled with fights, deaths, and murder, Toyoda keeps the violence subtly but resolutely off-screen, proving quite succinctly that less is more. If the film feels like a barrage of blood-drenched confrontations, it's because the director does such a good job at implying them. *Blue Spring* is not a violent film for the sake of being a violent film; its characters are too well rounded, its touches of dreamlike beauty too poetic for it to be dismissed as such. And its director is far too good a filmmaker to be suckered into making a pretentious bloodbath. Toyoda certainly made good on this promise when he followed up *Blue Spring* with the subtle, multi-vignetted character piece *9 Souls* in 2003.

↓ Bokunchi: My House

ぼくんち
Bokunchi

2002. DIRECTOR: Junji Sakamoto, 阪本順治. CAST: Alisa Mizuki, Yūki Tanaka, Yūma Yamoto, Claude Maki, Ran Ōtori, Masaru Shiga, Ittoku Kishibe. 116 minutes.

Peculiarly stylized drama of small-town eccentrics based on a manga, featuring utterly winning performances. The confirmation of the versatility of director Junji Sakamoto, a former specialist in more macho subjects.

Set in a rundown little harbor town on an unnamed island, *Bokunchi* is the story of seven-year-old Nita (Tanaka), who lives with his older brother Itta (Yamoto) and their mother. Mom has been away on a trip for the past six months, leaving the two boys to fend for themselves. Since the entire population of the island is chronically short of cash, the boys' own lack of funds is hardly an obstacle in their daily lives. Nita spends much of his time with Scrap Gramps (Shiga), a middle-aged man who lives a sheltered life in a shack on the edge of town. Despite his hermit status, Scrap Gramps's eccentricities are hardly exceptional compared to those of the townsfolk, which include an old lady tending to dozens of cats, a noodle restaurant run by the world's worst cook, and a young delinquent named Kōichi (Maki) who fancies himself a yakuza, but whose misdeeds remain limited to an occasional act of solitary vandalism and a big mouth.

The two little boys are so used to taking care of themselves that when their mother finally returns home, they simply ignore her presence and continue about their business. However, one thing certainly arouses their curiosity: the young woman accompanying their mother. Introduced to the boys as their half-sister Kanoko, she soon takes over the household and becomes more of a mother to them than their actual mother ever was, particularly when the latter leaves on another of her mysterious trips, taking the deed to the house with her. But where Nita warms to Kanoko, Itta rejects her and starts spending more and more time with Kōichi, the solitary delinquent.

Though essentially a coming-of-age tale, *Bokunchi* is refreshingly short on sentimentality. Adapting Ricko Saibara's manga, Sakamoto shows life in the rundown town with the necessary rough and tumble, and doesn't spare his two young leads from receiving their dose of knocks. His portrayal of growing up in the sticks is comparable to Takashi Miike's **Young Thugs: Nostalgia**, not flinching from showing the rougher aspects but at the same time with a good deal of stylization. There is quirkiness and humor, but the characters use these as a means of survival, a way to deal with their deprived existence.

With the film having no real-life social or historical context, Sakamoto is free to apply stylization. There is no need to remain true to fact, which gives the director a lot of leeway, which he in turn uses sensibly. The undertone to the comedy remains consistently tragic. The lesson Scrap Gramps teaches Nita, to always grin in the face of adversity, results in affectionate mugging from the little boy (endearingly played by the young Tanaka), but always points to the presence of that same adversity.

In the end, it all serves to show how poverty causes two little boys to mature before their age, which points exactly to how much director Junji Sakamoto has developed as a filmmaker. Once known as the director of boxing movies like his debut feature *Knock Out* (*Dotsuitarunen*, 1989), *Metallic Boxer* (*Tekken*, 1990), and *Boxer Joe* (1995), and macho fare like the kidnapping drama *Tokarev* (*Tokarefu*, 1994) and the two *Battered Angels* (*Kizudarake no Tenshi*, 1997/98) buddy movies, Sakamoto's career underwent a major change in 1999 when he directed *Face* (*Kao*), a tragicomedy about the friendship between two women on the run, which snapped up most of Japan's film prizes.

Osaka-born Sakamoto started out as an editor and assistant director to Sōgo Ishii (he is one of the three editors credited for the astonishing **Burst City**), and also worked under Kazuyuki Izutsu and Tōru Kawashima in the first half of the '80s. He shot a twenty-five-minute film entitled *Kiss* in 1986 before debuting properly with *Knock Out*, the story of a boxer making his comeback even though he knows that stepping back into the ring could kill him.

Long unknown outside Japan, *Face* turned Sakamoto's fortunes around in this respect too, turning him into a regular at the Berlin film festival, which invited both *Bokunchi* and the highly charged true-life political drama *KT* (2001). With these films, as well as with *Out of This World* (*Kono Yo no Soto e: Kurabu Shinchū-gun*, 2004), which deals with the friendships between American GIs and young jazz musicians in post-war Japan, Sakamoto increasingly found a purpose and a context for his male-centered universe, as well as showing an increasing socio-political awareness. His recent films have explored some touchy subjects, particularly the relationship between Japan and Korea. With *Out of This World* starring Scottish actor/director Peter Mullan (*Trainspotting*, *My Name Is Joe*, and *The Magdalene Sisters*), we can only hope that Sakamoto's work will finally break through to wider international audiences.

BIBLIOGRAPHY
Recommended Reading

Bornoff, Nicholas. *Pink Samurai: The Pursuit and Politics of Sex in Japan*. London: Grafton Books, 1991.
ISBN: 0246134534

Clements, Jonathan and McCarthy, Helen. *The Anime Encyclopedia*. Berkeley: Stone Bridge Press, 2001.
ISBN: 1880656647

Desser, David. *Eros Plus Massacre: An Introduction to the Japanese New Wave Cinema*. Indianapolis: Indiana University Press, 1988.
ISBN: 0253319617

Novielli, Maria Roberta. *Storia del cinema giapponese*. Venice: Marsilio, 2001.
ISBN: 8831777548

Richie, Donald. *Japanese Cinema: An Introduction*. Oxford: Oxford University Press, 1989.
ISBN: 0195849507

Richie, Donald. *A Hundred Years of Japanese Film*. Tokyo: Kodansha International, 2002.
ISBN: 477002682X

Schilling, Mark. *Contemporary Japanese Film*. New York: Weatherhill, 1999.
ISBN: 0834804158

Schilling, Mark. *The Yakuza Movie Book: A Guide to Japanese Gangster Films*. Berkeley: Stone Bridge Press, 2003.
ISBN: 1880656760

Van Haute, Luk. *Revival van de Japanse Film*. Amsterdam: Salomé/Amsterdam University Press, 2002.
ISBN: 9053565922

Chapter 1: Seijun Suzuki

Style To Kill Visual Directory
殺しの烙印 VISUAL DIRECTORY
Tokyo: Petit Grand Publishing, Inc, 2000.
ISBN: 4939102211

Suzuki Seijun: De Woestijn Onder De Kersebloesem/The Desert Under the Cherry Blossoms, De Tijgerreeks 5. Rotterdam: Intermational Film Festival Rotterdam, 1991.
ISBN: 9068250906

Ueno, Kōshi (ed.). *Suzuki Seijun, Zen Eiga*
鈴木清順全映画
Tokyo: Rippū Shobō, 1986.
ISBN: 4651780202

Chapter 2: Shōhei Imamura

MacDonald, Kevin and Cousins, Mark (eds.). *Imagining Reality: The Faber Book of Documentary*, London: Faber & Faber, 1996.
ISBN: 0571192025

Kawashima Yūzō and Mori Issei: Japanse Meesters Van De B-Film/Japanese Kings of the Bs, De Tijgerreeks 5. Rotterdam: International Film

Festival Rotterdam, 1991.
ISBN: 9068250892

Quandt, James (ed.). *Shohei Imamura*. Ontario: Cinematheque Ontario, 1997.
ISBN: 0968296904

Chapter 3: Kinji Fukasaku

Möller, Olaf. *Industrielandschaft mit Wölfen: Fukasaku Kinji eine Retrospektive*. Cologne: Japanisches Kulturinstitut (The Japan Foundation), 2000.

Gerow, Aaron. "*Fukasaku Kinji, Underworld Historiographer.*" *New Cinema From Japan News*, Vol. 2 (Tokyo), January 2000.
Also available at: http://www.asianfilms.org/japan/gerow4.html

Yamane, Sadao. "*The Struggle against Postwar Japan: Fukasaku Kinji.*" *International Film Festival Rotterdam Catalogue 2000*. Rotterdam: International Film Festival Rotterdam, 2000.

Yamane, Sadao. "*Fukasaku Kinji: radicale antiestheet.*" *Skrien*, Vol. 240 (Amsterdam), January 2000.

Chapter 5: Masato Harada

Gatto, Robin. "*Masato Harada.*" http://www.midnighteye.com/interviews/masato_harada.shtml

Chapter 6: Kiyoshi Kurosawa

Möller, Olaf. *Der Ort, der uns verheissen ward*. Cologne: Japanisches Kulturinstitut (The Japan Foundation), 2000.

Stephens, Chuck. "*Another Green World.*" *Film Comment* (New York), September/October 2001.

Pieri, Jean-Etienne. "*L'étrange inquiétude, le cinéma de Kiyoshi Kurosawa.*" *L'art d'aimer* 1 (Paris), January 2000.

Okubo, Ken. "*Aan de conventies ontstegen.*" *Skrien*, Vol. 240 (Amsterdam), January 2000.

Mes, Tom. "*Kiyoshi Kurosawa.*" http://www.projecta.net/kurosawa.html

Chapter 7: Studio Ghibli

McCarthy, Helen. *Hayao Miyazaki: Master of Japanese Animation*. Berkeley: Stone Bridge Press, 1999.
ISBN: 1880656418

Drazen, Patrick. *Anime Explosion: The What? Why? and Wow! of Japanese Animation*. Berkeley: Stone Bridge Press, 2003.
ISBN: 1880656728

Anime-Land: Le Premier Magazine De l'Animation Et Du Manga, Hors-serie #3 (Paris), January 2000.
ISSN: 12836338

http://www.nausicaa.net

Chapter 9: Shinya Tsukamoto

HK: Extreme Orient Cinema, Vol. 13 (Paris), January 2000.

Chapter 10: Takeshi Kitano

Jacobs, Brian (ed.). *'Beat' Takeshi Kitano*. Edgware: Tadao Press/RM Europe, 1999.
ISBN: 0952795116

Chapter 12: Takashi Miike

Mes, Tom. *Agitator: The Cinema of Takashi Miike*. Godalming: FAB Press, 2003.
ISBN: 1903254213

Gerow, Aaron. "*The Sadness of the Impossible Dream: Lack and Excess in the Transnational Cinema of Miike Takashi.*" *Noir In Festival*, Marina Fabri (ed.). Rome: Edizione Fahrenheit 451, 1999.
Also available at: http://www.asianfilms.org/japan/gerow3.html

Rayns, Tony. "*This Gun for Hire.*" *Sight and Sound* 5 (London), May 2000.

Chapter 14: Hirokazu Kore-eda

Gerow, Aaron and Tanaka, Junko. "*Documentarists of Japan, #12: Koreeda Hirokazu.*" *Documentary Box* 13 (Yamagata), August 1999. Also available at: http://www.city.yamagata.yamagata.jp/yidff/docbox/13/box13-1-e.html

Chapter 16: Naomi Kawase

Novielli, Maria Roberta (ed.). *Kawase Naomi i film il cinema*. Turin: Effatà Editrice, 2002. ISBN: 8874020120

Gerow, Aaron. "*Documentarists of Japan, #14: Kawase Naomi.*" *Documentary Box* 16 (Yamagata), December 2000. Also available at: http://www.city.yamagata.yamagata.jp/yidff/docbox/16/box16-1-1-e.html

INDEX

Alphabetization is by the "word-by-word" method, so that "Kyō, Machiko" appears before *Kyō no Dekigoto*. Films with titles beginning with numerals are listed twice in this index, at the beginning in numerical order and within the alphabetical entries according to spelling based on their pronunciation: e.g., the film *1/2 Mench* appears at the beginning of the listings as well as under the reasonably assumed pronunciation/spelling *Half Mench*.

349

STONE
BRIDGE
PRESS

Other Titles of Interest from Stone Bridge Press

The Yakuza Movie Book: A Guide to Japanese Gangster Films
by Mark Schilling
ISBN 1-880656-76-0

Hayao Miyazaki: Master of Japanese Animation
by Helen McCarthy
ISBN 1-880656-41-8

Anime Explosion! The What? Why? and Wow! of Japanese Animation
by Patrick Drazen
ISBN 1-880656-72-8

Tokyo Story: The Ozu/Noda Screenplay
by Yasujiro Ozu and Kogo Noda; trans. Donald Richie and Eric Klestadt
ISBN 1-880656-80-9

Watching Anime, Reading Manga: 25 Years of Essays and Reviews
by Fred Patten
ISBN 1-880656-92-2

The Dorama Encyclopedia: A Guide to Japanese TV Drama Since 1953
by Jonathan Clements and Motoko Tamamuro
ISBN 1-880656-81-7

The Japan Journals: 1947–2004
by Donald Richie; ed. Leza Lowitz
ISBN 1-880656-91-4

Available at bookstores worldwide and online